TELECOMMUNICATIONS

Fourth Edition

Warren Hioki
Community College of Southern Nevada

Prentice
Hall

Upper Saddle River, New Jersey
Columbus, Ohio

Library of Congress Cataloging in Publication Data
Hioki, Warren.
    Telecommunications / Warren Hioki.--4th ed.
      p. cm.
    Includes bibliographical references and index.
    ISBN 0-13-020031-X
    1. Telecommunication.   I. Title.

TK5101.H49 2001
621.382--dc21   00-035952

Vice President and Publisher: Dave Garza
Editor in Chief: Stephen Helba
Assistant Vice President and Publisher: Charles E. Stewart, Jr.
Production Editor: Alexandrina Benedicto Wolf
Production Coordination: York Production Services
Design Coordinator: Robin G. Chukes
Cover Designer: Tanya Burgess
Cover Image: FPG International
Production Manager: Matthew Ottenweller
Marketing Manager: Barbara Rose

This book was set in Times Roman by York Graphic Services, Inc. It was printed and bound by Courier Kendallville, Inc. The cover was printed by Phoenix Color Corp.

10   9   8   7   6   5   4   3   2   1
ISBN 0 – 13 – 020031-X

*In loving memory
of my dad,
Ernest E. Hioki*

CONTENTS

17 ERROR DETECTION, CORRECTION, AND CONTROL   519

18 FIBER OPTICS   539

PREFACE

Telecommunications, Fourth Edition, has been upgraded to include more example problems, figures, tables, and a margin glossary, and covers the latest standards and emerging technologies developed in recent years. This book is intended to provide the reader with the technical aspects and background material on telecommunications, which is still one of the fastest-growing industries in the world. A broad range of topics is covered without the intricate details of mathematical derivations and proofs. Instead, fundamental principles are emphasized in a simplified yet comprehensive and practical manner. To achieve this, numerous sketches with detailed explanations are included throughout, all aimed at providing the reader with the practical knowledge needed by today's telecommunications engineer and technician.

INTENDED AUDIENCE

This book is intended primarily for use as a college text in data communications or telecommunications. A fundamental background in mathematics, electronics, and digital circuits is a helpful requirement to using the text. This text is of great value to undergraduates and graduates seeking to extend or renew their discipline. Furthermore, the myriad tables, figures, example problems, and telecommunication standards make it an excellent reference for faculty, students, and practitioners. Instructors will find the material clear, concise, and written with sufficient depth. Experiments can be easily implemented to reinforce example problems presented in the text. This book also serves as an excellent reference guide for those in the industry who want to keep abreast with the subject matter. For those interested in achieving some degree of computer literacy, a wealth of technical terms and acronyms are defined and discussed throughout. They are also included in an extensive glossary at the end of the book.

ORGANIZATION OF THE TEXT

The chapters in this text are arranged in an order that has been successfully presented in a series of telecommunications and data communications courses over the years. It is by no means the suggested order in which the material should be taught; some chapters may be covered independently of each other. For example, some instructors may choose to cover Chapter 13, Modems, prior to Chapter 12, The Telephone Network. The same may be true of Chapter 18, Fiber Optics, which, like many chapters, is a subject in itself. Chapters are organized as follows:

Chapter 1, Introduction: An overview of telecommunications is presented in this chapter. Distinctions between analog and digital signals as well as data communications versus telecommunications are made. The 1996 Telecommunications Reform Act is also covered.

Chapter 2, Noise: Noise is an inherent problem in any communication system. This chapter introduces the various types of noise, their characteristics, and their effects on the telecommunication system. Signal-to-noise ratio, noise figure, noise factor, relative versus absolute power gain, and decibel are also introduced. Several example problems are given.

Chapter 3, Amplitude Modulation: The theory of AM is presented in this chapter. The frequency components of the AM waveform and their respective amplitudes, along with the single-sideband (SSB) and its derivation from the AM wave, are examined. Modulation index, power, and signal generation are also discussed.

Chapter 4, Frequency Modulation: The theory of FM is presented in this chapter. Bessel functions are defined and examined in terms of the frequency and amplitude components of the FM waveform. Modulation index, noise, and other important parameters associated with FM are also discussed.

Chapter 5, Pulse Modulation: Pulse modulation is used in most telecommunication systems. This chapter presents an introductory analysis and comparison of PAM, PCM, PWM, PPM, and Delta modulation. The Phase-Locked Loop (PLL) technology and encoding techniques, such as Miller, Manchester, Differential Manchester, NRZI, NRA, B8ZS, and more, are introduced.

Chapter 6, Transmission Codes and Encoding Techniques: Several codes commonly used in communication systems are examined in this chapter. Binary, octal, decimal, and hexadecimal number systems have been added to this chapter. An introduction to bar code technology is also given with emphasis on UPC, Code 39, and POSTNET.

Chapter 7, Terminals: In this chapter, various types of terminals and their features are discussed, with emphasis on the ASCII terminal. Examples of escape sequences and use of control characters, as well as the network computer (NC) terminal, are presented. Coverage of the PC Card (PCM/CIA) and the Small Computer Systems Interface (SCSI) has been added.

Chapter 8, Serial Interfaces: This chapter begins by distinguishing between synchronous and asynchronous serial transmission. Serial interfaces, RS-232 and RS-449, and its supporting standards—RS-422-A, RS-423-A, RS-485, V.35, and V.530—are examined in depth.

Chapter 9, The UART: An extensive study of the UART is given in this chapter. Transmitted and received serial characters are examined. The conversion process of these characters from serial to parallel form and vice versa are examined.

Chapter 10, The UART Interface: This chapter is devoted to interfacing the 8085A microprocessor to the 8251A USART. An asynchronous 4800-baud program is discussed, along with an interface schematic diagram. An introduction to the high-speed 16550 UART is also presented.

Chapter 11, The Telephone Set and Subscriber Loop Interface: This chapter provides a detailed look at touch-tone and rotary dial telephones and their specifications along with the tip and ring subscriber loop interface specifications. New in this chapter is the wire color coding used to identify subscriber loop wire pairs.

Chapter 12, The Telephone Network: This chapter examines the telephone network's history and how it has evolved into the world's most sophisticated network of computers. The central office and its numerous functions, characteristics, and system components are discussed. The T-carrier signaling format and multiplexing techniques used in the telephone network are also covered.

Chapter 13, Modems: The Bell family of modems and their characteristics, as well as the latest ITU-TS (formerly CCITT) modem recommendations, are discussed. Features such as data compression, scrambling and descrambling, loopback tests, and various modulation techniques are presented. An introduction to ADSL and cable modem is also presented.

Chapter 14, Protocols: Synchronous serial link protocols are discussed in this chapter. These include BISYNC, SDLC, and HDLC. In addition, various standards organizations that have given rise to the development of the ISO/OSI seven-layer model are described.

Chapter 15, Local Area Networks: Common LAN topologies, access control methods, and internetworking devices such as hubs, bridges, switches, and routers are introduced in this chapter. Emphasis is placed on the Ethernet and Token Ring protocols. A detailed presentation of LAN cabling and connector media for the 10BaseT, 10Base2, 10Base5, 100baseT, and 100BaseFL specifications are also discussed.

Chapter 16, The Internet and Emerging Technologies: An overview of the Internet and the World Wide Web is presented, along with TCP/IP (the Internet protocol suite). A detailed look at the ISDN, ATM, and SONET standards is given. New in this chapter is an introduction to the XDSL family.

Chapter 17, Error Detection, Correction, and Control: This chapter presents an in-depth look at some of the common error-detection and error-correction mechanisms used in telecommunication systems. Examples of computing the CRC block check character are given. A Hamming code is developed and used to correct single-bit errors.

Chapter 18, Fiber Optics: Fiber optics has become an integral segment of the telecommunications industry. This chapter provides a detailed look at the various grades of fiber and their respective characteristics. The theory of light, including Snell's law and the concept of total internal reflection, is examined. Multiplexing techniques of WDM and DWDM are introduced.

Chapter 19, Wireless Communications: This chapter presents an overview of the wireless industry, starting from the first-generation analog mobile and cellular telephone systems to the latest generation of digital cellular telephones, cordless telephones, wireless LANs, and personal communication services (PCS).

SUPPLEMENTARY AIDS FOR THE INSTRUCTOR

This textbook is supplemented with the revised *Laboratory Manual for Telecommunications,* Fourth Edition, which includes 38 hands-on experiments designed to reinforce the *Telecommunications* textbook.

Also available for the instructor is the *Instructor's Manual,* which provides the following:

- Over 200 Powerpoint masters of figures from the textbook (available on CD ROM).
- Solutions to all end-of-chapter problems presented in the main text.
- Solutions to questions presented in the *Laboratory Manual for Telecommunications,* Fourth Edition.

ACKNOWLEDGMENTS

This textbook could not have been written without the numerous contributions and hard work of many individuals. I wish to express my sincere gratitude to those who have made this possible.

Beverly Bellows, *Digital Equipment Corporation*
Gregg Castro, *Pacific Bell*
Michael Cole, *University of Nevada Las Vegas, System Computing Services*
Fred Dane, *San Jose City College*
Mike Goodman, *Sprint of Nevada*
Roy Goody, *Mission College*
Erich Herda, *Motorola Pager Products Group*
Andra Hioki, *Agilent Technologies*
Sheldon Hochheiser, *AT&T Bell Laboratories*
Dick Jamison, *Hewlett-Packard Optical Communication Division*
Carl Jensen, Jr., *DeVry Institute of Technology*
Ahmed S. Khan, *DeVry Institute of Technology*
Jim Lane, *Telco Systems, Inc.*
Clay Laster, *San Antonio College*
Ruth Lombardi, *AT&T Bell Laboratories*
Ken Miller, *Concord Data Systems*
Christine Mulch, *Anixter, Inc.*
Benjamin Nelson, *Markem Corporation*
Tom Novicki, *Racal-Vadic*
Joy Parillo, *AT&T Archives*
Roy Patrick, *Sprint of Nevada*
Greg Pearson, *Microcom Inc.*
Bill Peat, *Sprint of Nevada*
Preston Peek, *Northern Telecom, Inc.*
John Quick, *DeVry Institute of Technology*

Jeffrey L. Rankinen, *Pennsylvania College of Technology*
Ronald Rowe, *Adaptive Computer Technology*
Stephen Statz, *Wyse Technology*
John Uffenbeck, *Wisconsin Indianhead Technical Institute*
Michael Walt, *Alltel Communications*
Janet Wells, *AT&T Bell Laboratories*
Chuck Wojslaw, *San Jose State University*
Jerome Zornesky, *Technical Careers Institute (TCI)*

I would also like to thank the following reviewers for their valuable suggestions:

Aram Agajanian, DeVry Institute of Technology; Raj Desai, North Carolina A & T
State University; Robert Diffenderfer, DeVry Institute of Technology; Steve Kuchler,
Ivy Tech State College; Robert Morris, DeVry Institute of Technology; Jeffrey L.
Rankinen, Pennsylvania College of Technology; and Lowell D. Tawney, DeVry
Insitute of Technology.

A special thanks to Jim Lane of Telco Systems, Inc., for providing his expertise on
ATM technology; Benjamin Nelson of Markem Corp. for the wealth of information
and expertise on bar code theory; Gregg Castro of Pacific Bell for his expertise on
the PSTN and the numerous tours of Pacific Bell's switching facilities; Charles Stewart
of Prentice-Hall for his tremendous support, encouragement, and patience; Kirsten
Kauffman of York Production Services for her professionalism and absolute dedica-
tion in her job of coordinating the organization of this textbook; and Wesley Morrison
for his diligent task of editing the manuscript and aiding in the development of the
margin glossary—you were a tremendous joy to work with. This would not have been
possible without you.

The author welcomes your comments and suggestions. He can be reached by
e-mail: warren_hioki@ccsn.nevada.edu

Warren Hioki

1

INTRODUCTION TO TELECOMMUNICATIONS

We live in an era that is often referred to as the *Information Age.* An age in which the furor of the *Internet* and the emergence of the *World Wide Web (WWW),* the most interactive and fastest-growing segment of the Internet, has spawned enormous growth in technologies, standards, and products beyond anyone's imagination. Internet addresses have become as common as telephone numbers, appearing on everything from business cards and magazines to automobiles, buses, and television shows. Information has never been easier to access. With the click of a mouse, virtually every subject imaginable from anywhere in the world becomes available to us in our homes, workplaces, educational institutes, and even the most remote locations on the face of the Earth.

The era in which we live has rapidly transformed the office and factory worker into an analyzer, manipulator, gatherer, and distributor of information. This information comes in a variety of forms, all representing some meaningful arrangement of the human thought process. In this chapter, an introduction to telecommunications, one of the most explosive technological fields of our time is presented. There is a growing need to consider the importance of this highly dynamic field, which has brought millions of computers together to share their endless capabilities for providing information. Our educational system, jobs, businesses, entertainment, and very often, our everyday tasks necessitate skill in the use of information systems.

> **Internet**
> A wide area network of thousands of linked computer networks spanning the globe, making it possible for millions of users to communicate. The *Internet* is used synonymously with the *World Wide Web (WWW),* or simply the *Web.*

> **World Wide Web (WWW)**
> A global information system combining text, graphics, and sound on a series of computer-displayed documents. Simply referred to as the *Web,* it is a user-friendly network where information from many sources can be accessed from anywhere in the world with one universal program.

1.1 ROLE OF THE COMMUNICATION SYSTEM

The distribution of information from one location to another is the role of the communication system. Figure 1-1 illustrates the essential components of the communication system. Although this may seem simplified, the process of sending and receiving information in an orderly and successful manner can be extremely complex for today's modern communication system. Consider some of the factors involved:

- Nature of the information
- Format of the information
- Transmission speed
- Transmission medium
- Transmission distance
- Modulation technique
- Error control

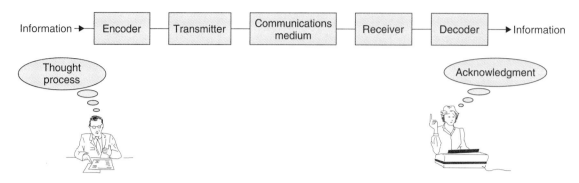

FIGURE 1-1
Basic components of a communication system.

1.2 WHAT IS TELECOMMUNICATIONS?

Telecommunications
Long-distance commu-
nications via a con-
glomeration of informa-
tion sharing networks.
These include the public
switched telephone net-
work (PSTN), data com-
munications networks,
wireless networks, the
Internet, and the World
Wide Web.

The process of distributing information can be divided into several categories. *Telecommunications* is perhaps the most extensive of these. What is telecommunications? Many definitions of this process have been given over the years, all of which are accurate to some degree, depending on the nature of the technology at that time. To begin with, the prefix *tele-* is derived from the Greek meaning for "at a distance." Historically, telecommunications encompassed the telegraph system, invented by Samuel Morse in 1854. Information was transmitted (and still is) as a series of electrical impulses generated by depressing a hand key. To communicate over such long distances through the use of the telegraph system was, at the time, a scientific marvel.

The invention of the telephone by Alexander Graham Bell in 1876 led to the growth of the telephone system, which further extended our ability to communicate "at a distance." Many milestones were yet to follow, each contributing to our ability to communicate over long distances. Telephone networks began to expand nationwide. Television and radio broadcasts spanning the globe via satellite communications added to the steady growth of an industry: the telecommunications industry, one of the largest and fastest-growing industries in our history. Thus, telecommunications has come to be regarded as *long-distance* communications via a conglomeration of information-sharing networks all tied together. These include the *public switched telephone network (PSTN)*, data communications networks, radio and television networks, and most important, the fiber that is destined to link virtually all communication systems together: the Internet and the World Wide Web. Figure 1-2 illustrates the magnitude of the telecommunication system.

**Public Switched
Telephone Network
(PSTN)**
The dial-up telephone
network, also referred
to as Telco short for
telephone company.

1.3 THE DATA COMMUNICATION SYSTEM

Analog Signal
A signal with a continu-
ous range of values as
a function of time.
Examples include sine
wave, sawtooth wave,
triangle wave, or DC
voltage or current.

In the past, most telecommunication systems transmitted voice information in *analog* form. An *analog signal* is one that has a continuous range of values as a function of time. Figure 1-3 illustrates the analog waveform. The PSTN, for example, was designed to accommodate voice transmission in analog form. Due to the enormous capabilities of the computer, however, the trend in telecommunications has been a gradual conversion from analog to digital transmission.

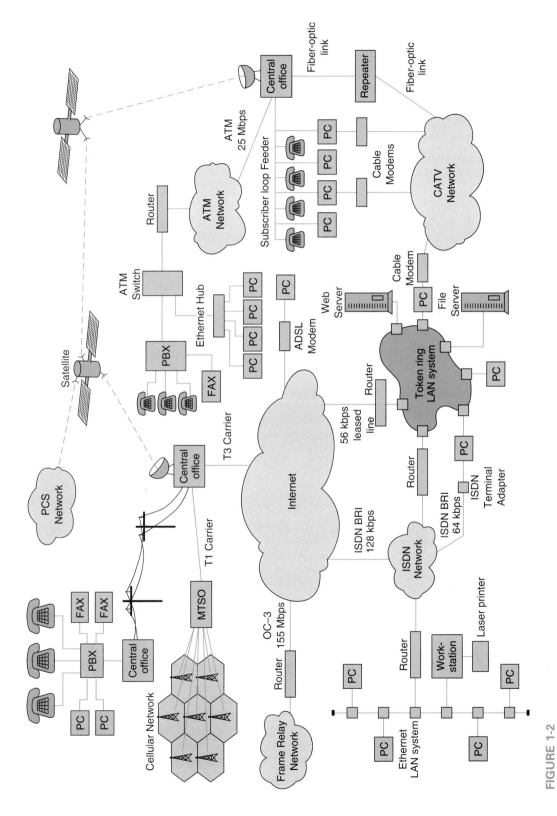

FIGURE 1-2
Telecommunication system.

3

(a)

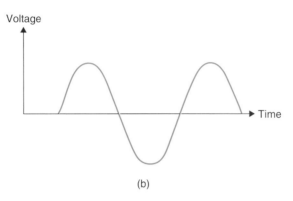

(b)

FIGURE 1-3

Analog waveforms: (a) analog voice signal; (b) sine wave.

Digital Signal
A signal characterized by two discrete binary values as a function of time. These two values are a logic 1 and a logic 0. A digital pulse stream is an example. A digital signal can also be an analog waveform with two discrete values, such as two frequencies shifting between each other.

Data Communications
The transmission and reception of digital signals from one location to another.

Local Area Network (LAN)
Typically, a privately owned network of interconnecting data communications devices that share resources, software included, within a limited physical area, such as a room, building, or cluster of buildings.

A digital transmission system transmits signals that are in *digital* form. The digital signal has discrete sets of values as a function of time, such as a binary 1 or 0. When we think of a digital waveform, we think of a pulse stream comprised of two discrete voltage levels: one for a logic high, and one for a logic low. The *digital signal* can also be an analog waveform representing two discrete values. For example, a logic 1 can be represented by a 1200-Hz tone, and a logic 0 can be represented by a 2200-Hz tone. The two discrete analog waveforms are frequency shifted from one to the other in accordance with the binary bit stream. The digital signal can also be phase shifted or amplitude shifted in the same manner. Figure 1-4 illustrates variations of the digital signal.

Data communications involves the transmission and reception of digital signals from one location to another. The digital signals typically represent information that is alphabetical, numerical, or symbolic in nature. The organization of this information is referred to as *data*. Virtually every human thought process can be represented as data and can therefore be transmitted by the data communication system. The characters that you read here are considered to be data. They can be transmitted by the data communication system to a printer, a disk drive, or even a remotely located terminal or computer that is a part of a *local area network (LAN)* in another city. The data communication system is actually a part of the telecommunication system that links together the capabilities of the computer.

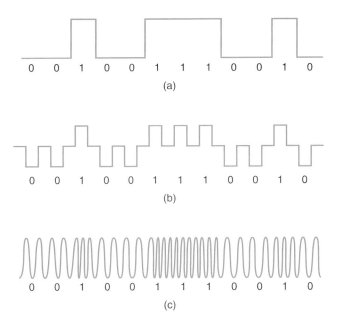

FIGURE 1-4
Variations of the digital signal: (a) digital pulse stream; (b) bipolar return-to-zero (RZ); (c) frequency shift keying (FSK).

1.4 FUTURE TRENDS IN TELECOMMUNICATIONS

Imagine living in a house where you can have access to all the recorded music and video programs in the world without a single cassette tape or disc on the premises. Imagine a 6-foot flat-screen, high-definition television set (HDTV) with which you can talk to and interact with various people around the world. Only a few years ago, this seemed far-fetched, but the future of telecommunications is headed this way. Equipment manufacturers and service providers alike have recognized this extraordinary communications era in which we live as an opportunity for technological growth. The heated competition will continually provide new products, new jobs, and new solutions to our ever-increasing demands.

Technological advancements in the telecommunications industry will continue to escalate in an exponential fashion. The LAN system and its dramatic growth in recent years is perhaps the most profound and visible example of this. Expansion of LAN-based systems in the workforce and into remote locations has created *metropolitan area networks (MANs)* and *wide area networks (WANs)* that span the globe. The interconnection of these networks via the PSTN has created a new generation of switching technologies, each of which promises to provide improved services to the home and workplace. Some of these technologies, such as *Asynchronous Transfer Mode (ATM)*, have risen from virtual obscurity to global competition for the marketplace. Others, such as *Integrated Services Digital Network (ISDN), Frame Relay, Switched Multimegabit Data Service (SMDS), Synchronous Optical Network (SONET), Fiber Distributed Data Interface (FDDI), Digital Subscriber Line (DSL),* and more, have made considerable progress with standards organizations. These combined technologies are now capable of

Metropolitan Area Network (MAN)
A collection of local area networks (LANs) covering a metropolitan area.

Wide Area Network (WAN)
A network that covers a very large geographical area and typically uses long-haul circuits provided by the public switched telephone network (PSTN) to link local (LANs) and metropolitan area networks (MANs).

delivering integrated multimedia voice, data, text, and full-motion video to virtually any terminal throughout the world.

The socioeconomic impact resulting from the telecommunications era we are transpiring into has caused an increase in worldwide productivity through the automation of engineering, manufacturing, and office activities. The effects on modern society are more apparent than ever before. If ever there has been a time when people must be able to function and succeed in a "high-tech" world, it is now. Clearly, the advances in telecommunications during the years to come will warrant considerable effort on the part of the technologist to keep abreast of the enormous number of changes that will take place. In this book, we evaluate the technical aspects of telecommunications that are so vital to our educational growth and understanding.

1.4.1 The 1996 Telecommunications Reform Act

In 1996, the U.S. government passed the *Telecommunications Act of 1996*. The goal of this new law is to eliminate the distinctions between local phone companies, also known as *local exchange carriers (LECs),* long-distance phone companies, also known as interexchange carriers (IXCs); and cable TV, cellular, broadcast, and on-line service providers. This paves the way for long-distance phone companies to get into local markets, including cable TV. Local telephone and cable TV providers can do

---

TABLE 1-1

Telecommunications Reform Act of 1996 Simplified

Long Distance Services	RBOCs (Pacific Telesis, US West, Ameritech, NYNEX, Bell Atlantic, Southwestern Bell, Bell South) can enter the long-distance market after proving they have opened local markets to competition.
Local Services	Local markets will be opened to new competitors like AT&T, MCI, Sprint, as well as cable TV companies. Appropriate access charges to be paid to local phone companies for linking to their networks must be determined.
Broadcast Services	Allows a single owner to control TV stations reaching 35% of the population (up from 25%). TV sets must be equipped with a device to block violent or sexual programming.
Cable Services	Lifts all rate regulations on big cable providers in 3 years. Rate regulations immediately eliminated for providers with less than 1% of U.S. subscribers.
Video Services	Allows phone companies to sell TV services via phone lines, satellite, or other distribution systems.
Cross-ownership	Lifts the ban on cross-ownership between cable TV companies and phone companies in small communities.
Internet Services	On-line computer services or users must restrict minors' access to "indecent" material.
Universal Phone Services	Continues to guarantee phone service everywhere (including remote rural areas). States and the FCC still must decide how to pay for these services.
Wireless Services	TV stations to get new broadcast spectrum for advanced TV services (still under discussion).

Source: Audry Daum, "U.S. Deregulation, Beyond the Letter of the Law." *Data Communications,* September 21, 1996, p. 62. Reprinted with permission from *Data Communications.*

the opposite. The law itself stretches to 110 pages and is arranged in 710 sections.* The FCC's *Rules of Engagement,* which details how the act will be put into action, add another 70 pages, and 650 pages of responses have been filed by interested parties. The details of this new legislation, guidelines, and filings can be accessed at **http://www.fcc.gov/telecom.html.** Table 1-1 provides a simplified summary of the law.

PROBLEMS

1. Explain why it is vitally important for us to learn about telecommunications.
2. Name at least five factors that must be accounted for by today's modern communication systems.
3. Define *telecommunications.*
4. Define *data communications.*
5. Draw an example of an analog signal in the time domain.
6. Describe the difference between an *analog* signal and a *digital* signal.
7. Draw an example of a digital signal in the time domain using FSK as a modulation technique.
8. What does *ATM* stand for?
9. What do *LAN, MAN,* and *WAN* stand for?
10. What do *ISDN, SMDS, SONET,* and *FDDI* stand for?
11. Use Table 1-1 to summarize how the *1996 Telecommunications Reform Act* affects **Internet Services.**
12. What does *LEC* stand for?

*Audrie Daum, *Data Communications,* September 21, 1996, p. 59.

2

NOISE

Any electrical signal transmitted from one point to another can ultimately be classified as having two parts: one that represents the original intelligence, the desirable part; and the undesirable part, which we call *noise*. In virtually all telecommunication systems, the effects of noise superimposed on the original intelligence is of major concern. The magnitude of this noise is directly related to our ability to recover the intelligence without error. In this chapter, we study the effects of noise, its various types, and the techniques used for evaluating system performance under the influence of noise.

> **Noise**
> In a telecommunication or data communication system, noise is the undesirable portion of an electrical signal that interferes with the intelligence.

2.1 EFFECTS OF NOISE

Electrical noise is inherent in all transmitted and received signals. Its effects can severely limit system performance. Today's telecommunication systems are especially vulnerable due to several factors:

- Increased volumes of traffic through central office switching centers
- Enormous channel capacities of trunk circuits
- Trend toward high speed digital and data transmission

One unfortunate circumstance of noise is that it inevitably corrupts the signal, as shown in Figure 2-1. Great measures are taken to minimize its effects. The communication system typically employs special encoding and decoding techniques to optimize the recovery of the signal. Extensive conditioning of the signal is performed through the use of filters and amplifiers. Careful attention is given to the transmission medium, its type, and how the signal is routed to its destination. Elaborate error detection and correction mechanisms in both hardware and software are built into the telecommunication system to identify and, often, correct for errors caused by noise.

2.2 NOISE MEASUREMENTS

Several mathematical tools have been developed to evaluate the effects of noise based on its magnitude relative to a given signal. The theory behind this highly complex subject is beyond the scope of this book. Several books are available on the subject, however, and the reader is encouraged to pursue his or her needs. What we are

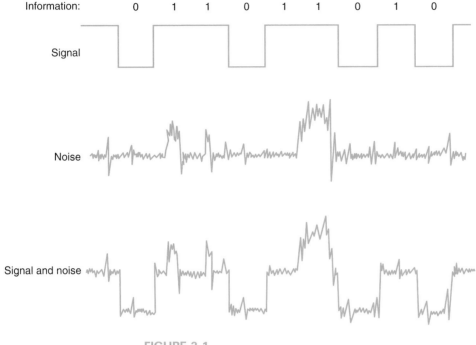

FIGURE 2-1
Effects of noise on a signal.

concerned about is the practical aspects of noise measurements commonly encountered by the communications technologist.

2.2.1   The Decibel

Historically, most communication systems have received signals that were converted to sound. It was useful to appraise the signal strength of the received signal in terms of relative loudness as registered by the human ear. A peculiarity of the ear is that an increase or decrease in loudness is related to the *ratio* of the amounts of power being delivered to the output of a speaker. Ironically, to estimate that an audible signal has increased to a level that sounds twice as loud as before, the power delivered to the speaker would have to increase by a factor, or *ratio,* of 4:1 and not 2:1. For example, a 4-W signal delivered to an ideal speaker would sound twice as loud as a 1-W signal. That is, the human audible response is logarithmic in nature.

Signal and noise levels associated with a telecommunication system, whether they are received, transmitted, or signals being processed by each, are often expressed in *decibels.* To understand signal and noise measurements, the technologist must have a basic mathematical understanding of the unit of the decibel.

A decibel is a unit that is one-tenth of a *bel,* named in honor of Alexander Graham Bell. Both the bel and the decibel (dB) were originally used to express sound levels. The unit of the *bel* is seldom used, because its original size was too large. The decibel is commonly used. A change of 1 dB is equivalent to an audible change in level, either louder or softer, that is just barely noticeable by the ear. Therefore, the decibel has been widely used as the basis for expressing relative power ratios for both audible and inaudible signal levels.

Decibel (dB)
One tenth of a *bel.* Originally a unit of sound, the decibel now is commonly used to represent relative voltage or power gain.

Bel
A unit of sound named in honor of Alexander Graham Bell.

2.2.1.1 Relative Power Gain Strictly speaking, the logarithmic unit of the decibel is defined for power ratios. However, it has become common to express voltage and current ratios in decibels as well. The *relative power gain* of a device such as an amplifier or filter, A_P, is given by

$$A_P = \frac{P_o}{P_i} \tag{2-1}$$

where P_o and P_i are the output and input power levels of the device specified in watts. As its name implies, *relative* means relative to each other. That is, the gain can be the same for different values of P_o and P_i. The relative power gain of a device specified in decibels is given by

$$A_{P(dB)} = 10 \log A_P \tag{2-2}*$$

$$= 10 \log \frac{P_o}{P_i} \tag{2-3}$$

Given an amplifier with an output power of 2.75 W and an input power of 48 mW, compute the following:
(a) The relative power gain as a ratio, A_P.
(b) The relative power gain in decibels, $A_{P(db)}$.

Solution:
(a) Using equation (2-1), we have

$$A_P = \frac{P_o}{P_i}$$

$$= \frac{2.75 \text{ W}}{48 \text{ mW}} = 57.3$$

(b) Using equation (2-2), we have

$$A_{P(dB)} = 10 \log A_P$$
$$= 10 \log 57.3 = 17.6 \text{ dB}$$

EXAMPLE
2.1

In equations (2-1) and (2-3), the values for the output and input power levels, P_o and P_i, can be substituted with the final and initial values of power levels, P_{fin} and P_{init}, respectively, of some power source.

The initial power level, P_{init}, of an amplifier is measured to be 680 mW. If the power level were to increase to a final level, P_{fin}, of 1.2 W, compute the change in decibels.

Solution:

$$A_{P(dB)} = 10 \log \frac{P_{fin}}{P_{init}} = 10 \log \frac{1.2 \text{ W}}{680 \text{ mW}} = 2.47 \text{ dB}$$

EXAMPLE
2.2

---

*In equation (2-2), the factor of 10 shown on the right side transforms the unit of the bel to decibel. Common logs (base 10) are used here; the logarithmic equations follow.

From equation (2-2), we can work backward and solve for the power gain as a ratio or the input and output power level given a power gain in decibels. Dividing both sides of equation (2-2) by 10, we have

$$\frac{A_{P(\text{dB})}}{10} = \log A_P$$

and taking the antilog of the equation gives us

$$A_P = 10^{\frac{A_{P(\text{dB})}}{10}} = \frac{P_o}{P_i} \qquad (2\text{-}4)$$

EXAMPLE 2.3

An amplifier has a power gain of 28 dB. Compute the following:
(a) The gain as a ratio, A_P.
(b) The output power, P_o, for an input power, P_i, of 80 μW.

Solution:
(a) Using equation (2-4), we have

$$A_p = 10^{\frac{A_{P(\text{dB})}}{10}} = 10^{\frac{28\text{dB}}{10}} = 631$$

(b) Rearranging equation (2-1), we can solve for the output power, P_o:

$$P_o = A_p P_i$$
$$P_o = 631 \times 80 \ \mu\text{W} = 50.48 \ \text{mW}$$

EXAMPLE 2.4

The power gain of a filter at a certain frequency is -14 dB. Compute the following:
(a) The gain as a ratio, A_P.
(b) The input power, P_i, delivered to the filter if the output power, P_o, was 550 mW.

Solution:
(a) Using equation (2-4), we have

$$A_P = 10^{\frac{A_{P(\text{dB})}}{10}} = 10^{\frac{-14\text{dB}}{10}} = 3.98 \times 10^{-2}$$

(b) Rearranging equation (2-1), we can solve for the input power, P_i.

$$P_i = \frac{P_o}{A_P} = \frac{550 \ \text{mW}}{3.98 \times 10^2} = 13.8 \ \text{W}$$

2.2.1.2 Relative Voltage Gain In many cases, it is desirable to analyze a circuit or system in terms of voltages or currents. Ohm's Law can be used to transform our power equations to voltage or current. Because we know that

$$P_o = \frac{V_o^2}{R_o}$$

and

$$P_i = \frac{V_i^2}{R_i^2}$$

where P_o and P_i are the output and input power levels of a device, respectively; V_o and V_i are the output and input voltage levels, respectively; and R_o and R_i are the output and input impedances, respectively, then substituting this into equation (2-3) gives us

$$A_{P(dB)} = 10 \log \frac{\left(\dfrac{V_o^2}{R_o}\right)}{\left(\dfrac{V_i^2}{R_i}\right)} = 10 \log \frac{\left(\dfrac{V_o}{V_i}\right)^2}{\dfrac{R_o}{R_i}}$$

If the input and output impedances are equal, that is, $R_o = R_i$, then the two cancel. The exponent of 2 can be brought down to multiply with 10, leaving us with the voltage gain equation

$$A_{V(dB)} = 20 \log A_V \tag{2-5}$$

where

$$A_V = \frac{V_o}{V_i} \tag{2-6}$$

As with our power equations, the output and input voltages, V_o and V_i, can be substituted with final and initial voltage levels, V_{fin} and V_{init}, respectively.

An effective output voltage of a telecommunications repeater is measured to be 2 V_{rms} for an input of 195 mV_{rms}. Compute the following:
(a)   The gain of the telecommunications repeater, A_V.
(b)   The gain in decibels of the repeater, $A_{V(dB)}$.

Solution:

(a)
$$A_V = \frac{V_o}{V_i} = \frac{2\ V_{\text{rms}}}{195\ \text{mV}_{\text{rms}}} = 10.26$$

where rms is the root mean square.

(b)
$$A_{V(dB)} = 20 \log A_V = 20 \log 10.26 = 20.2 \text{ dB}$$

From equation (2-5), we can work backward as we did before in our power equations, and we can solve for the voltage gain or the input or output voltage level given a voltage gain in decibels. Dividing both sides of equation (2-5) by 20, we have

$$\frac{A_{V(dB)}}{20} = \log A_V$$

and taking the antilog of the equation gives us

$$A_V = 10^{\frac{A_{V(dB)}}{20}} = \frac{V_o}{V_i} \tag{2-7}$$

The final amplifier in a wireless LAN transmitter has a voltage gain of 52 dB. Compute the following:

EXAMPLE
2.5

EXAMPLE
2.6

(a) The voltage gain of the amplifier as a ratio, A_V.
(b) The output voltage, V_o, of the amplifier given an input voltage, V_i, of 35 mV.
(c) How many decibels the signal has dropped if the input voltage decreases from 35 to 5 mV.

Solution:

(a) Using equation (2-7), we have

$$A_V = \frac{V_o}{V_i} = 10^{\frac{A_{V(dB)}}{20}} = 10^{\frac{52dB}{20}} = 398$$

(b) $V_o = A_V V_i = 398 \times 35 \text{ mV} = 13.9 \text{ V}$

(c) $A_{V(dB)} = 20 \log \frac{V_{\text{fin}}}{V_{\text{init}}} = 20 \log \frac{5 \text{ mV}}{35 \text{ mV}} = -16.9 \text{ dB}$

2.2.1.3 The dBm and Absolute Power Gain

The voltage and power gains discussed so far are *relative* gains. That is, a device having a power gain, A_P, of 10 tells us nothing specific about the input or output power level of that device other than that it has a gain of 10. There are an infinite number of ratios within the linear operating region of the amplifier that will give us a gain of 10 between its input and output. Therefore, it is often convenient to specify an "absolute" signal level at the input or output of a device, or at any given point in the telecommunication system, with reference to some standardized level. The reference level most often used is 1 mW into an impedance of 50 Ω, 600 Ω, or 900 Ω depending on the impedance of the equipment or transmission media. The unit used to specify this level is the *dBm*, which stands for decibels referenced to 1 mW. The absolute power gain, $A_{P(dBm)}$, is defined as

$$A_{P(dBm)} = 10 \log \frac{P}{1 \text{ mW}}, \text{ dBm} \qquad \textbf{(2-8)}$$

> **dBm**
> A unit of gain or loss expressed as an absolute value, because it is referenced to 1 mW or some known standard value.

where $A_{P(dBm)}$ is the power gain referenced to 1 mW, which becomes the signal level, and P is the power level at the input or output of some device or at any point in the telecommunication system.

Note that the absolute power gain in equation (2-8) specifies a power level in dBm, because it is referenced to 1 mW. Using antilogs as before, it can be shown that the power level, P, associated with the absolute power gain in equation (2-8) is given by

$$P = 1 \text{ mW} \left(10^{\frac{A_{P(dBm)}}{10}} \right) \qquad \textbf{(2-9)}$$

EXAMPLE
2.7

Compute the absolute power gain, $A_{P(dBm)}$, associated with a 2.5 W signal.

Solution:

Using equation (2-8), we have

$$A_{P(dBm)} = 10 \log \frac{P}{1 \text{ mW}} = 10 \log \frac{2.5 \text{ W}}{1 \text{ mW}} = 33.98 \text{ dBm}$$

EXAMPLE
2.8

The signal level of a 10-MHz test tone measures -15 dBm on a spectrum analyzer. Compute the power level of signal.

Solution:
Using equation (2-9), we have

$$P = 1 \text{ mW}\left(10^{\frac{A_{P(\text{dBm})}}{10}}\right) = 1 \text{ mW}\left(10^{\frac{-15\text{dBm}}{10}}\right) = 31.6 \ \mu\text{W}$$

In many cases, it is necessary to convert dBm to a respective voltage. By substituting $P = V_{\text{rms}}^2/R$ into equation (2-8), we can factor out the voltage as follows

$$A_{P(\text{dBm})} = 10 \log \frac{P}{1 \text{ mW}} = 10 \log \frac{\left(\dfrac{V_{\text{rms}}^2}{R}\right)}{1 \text{ mW}}$$

$$\left(\frac{V_{\text{rms}}^2}{R}\right) = 1 \text{ mW}\left(10^{\frac{A_{P(\text{dBm})}}{10}}\right)$$

$$V_{\text{rms}} = \sqrt{1 \text{ mW}\left(10^{\frac{A_{P(\text{dBm})}}{10}}\right)R} \qquad \qquad \textbf{(2-10)}$$

The value of R in equation (2-10) is typically standardized among equipment manufacturers. For example, most radio frequency (rf) systems, including test equipment, use 50 Ω. Typical examples include inputs to rf spectrum analyzers, outputs of signal generators, and impedances of coaxial cables. Telecommunications systems and test equipment use 600 and 900 Ω to match the impedances of telephone lines.

EXAMPLE
2.9

An rf sine-wave generator whose output impedance is 50 Ω is connected to a 50-Ω load using 50-Ω coaxial cable. The generator's output amplitude level is set to $+3$ dBm. An rms voltmeter is used to measure the effective voltage, and an oscilloscope is used to display the sine wave. Compute the following:
(a) The rms voltage measured by the rms voltmeter.
(b) The peak voltage, V_p, of the sine wave that should be displayed on the oscilloscope.
(c) The peak-to-peak voltage, $V_{p\text{-}p}$, of the sine wave that should be displayed on the oscilloscope.

Solution:
(a) Using equation (2-10) we have

$$V_{\text{rms}} = \sqrt{1 \text{ mW}\left(10^{\frac{A_{P(\text{dBm})}}{10}}\right)R}$$

$$= \sqrt{1 \text{ mW}\left(10^{\frac{3\text{dBm}}{10}}\right)50 \ \Omega}$$

$$= 316 \text{ mV}$$

(b) $$V_p = 1.414 \times V_{\text{rms}} = 1.414 \times 316 \text{ mV} = 447 \text{ mV}$$

(c) $$V_{p\text{-}p} = 2 \times V_p = 2 \times 447 \text{ mV} = 894 \text{ mV}$$

2.2.2 Signal-to-Noise Ratio

One of the most useful measures of noise from a deterministic point of view is *signal-to-noise ratio* (*SNR* or S/N). It is the ratio of signal power to noise power. SNR is of prime importance to us because it allows us to evaluate and anticipate the extraneous effects of noise. It is typically measured at the receiving end of the communication system before the detection of the signal. Mathematically, SNR is expressed in decibels by the following equation:

$$\text{SNR} = 10 \log \frac{\text{signal power}}{\text{noise power}} \text{ dB} \qquad (2\text{-}11)$$

> **Signal-to-Noise Ratio (SNR)**
> The ratio of signal power to noise power at some point in a telecommunication system expressed in decibels (dB).

If we assume that the composite signal (signal and noise) is measured across the same resistance ($R_1 = R_2$), then SNR can also be expressed by the ratio of signal voltage to noise voltage. In decibels, this is computed as

$$\text{SNR} = 10 \log \frac{S}{N}$$

$$= 10 \log \frac{(V_S)^2/R_1}{(V_N)^2/R_2}$$

$$= 10 \log \left(\frac{V_S}{V_N}\right)^2$$

and, therefore,

$$\text{SNR} = 20 \log \left(\frac{V_S}{V_N}\right) = 20 \log \frac{\text{signal voltage}}{\text{noise voltage}} \text{ dB} \qquad (2\text{-}12)$$

EXAMPLE 2.10

A 1-kHz sinusoid test tone is measured with an oscilloscope at the input of a receiver's FM detector stage. Its peak-to-peak amplitude is 3 V. With the test tone at the transmitter turned off, the noise at the same test point is measured with an rms voltmeter. Its value is 640 mV. Compute the SNR in decibels.

Solution:

$$V_S = 0.707 \, V_P = 0.707 \left(\frac{3 \, V_{p\text{-}p}}{2}\right) = 1.06 \text{ V}$$

$$V_N = 640 \text{ mV}$$

$$\text{SNR} = 20 \log \frac{V_S}{V_N} = 20 \log \frac{1.06 \text{ V}}{640 \text{ mV}} = 4.39 \text{ dB}$$

The average SNR can be measured for any composite signal with an rms voltmeter or power meter. One needs only to have control over turning the transmitted signal on and off. The resulting deflection produced on the meter's decibel scale is a direct measure of the SNR.

2.2.3 Noise Factor and Noise Figure

The SNR is useful in applications where the noise content of the signal is desired at a specific point in the communication system. It does not, however, characterize the amount of additional noise introduced by the various components in the overall communication system. A key parameter used for this purpose is *noise factor*. Noise factor is a measure of how noisy a device is. It is the ratio of signal-to-noise (S_i/N_i) power at the input of a device to the signal-to-noise (S_o/N_o) power at its output. Expressed in decibels, noise factor is called *noise figure*. All amplifiers, for example, contribute some degree of noise to the signal. If an amplifier generated no noise of its own, its input and output SNR would be equal. The noise factor would be 1 in this ideal case, which is equivalent to a noise figure of 0 dB. Noise factor and noise figure are governed by the following equations:

> **Noise Factor**
> A measure of how noisy a device is, or the ratio of a device's input signal-to-noise ratio (SNR) to its output SNR.

$$\text{noise factor} = F = \frac{S_i/N_i}{S_o/N_o} \qquad \textbf{(2-13)}$$

Noise figure (NF) is related to noise factor by the expression

> **Noise Figure**
> The same as *noise factor*, but expressed in decibels (dB).

$$\text{NF} = 10 \log F = 10 \log \frac{S_i/N_i}{S_o/N_o} \text{ dB} \qquad \textbf{(2-14)}$$

If the input and output of the device under consideration share the same impedance, NF can also be expressed in terms of voltage:

$$\text{NF} = 20 \log \frac{V_{Si}/V_{Ni}}{V_{So}/V_{No}} \text{ dB} \qquad \textbf{(2-15)}$$

EXAMPLE
2.11

The input signal to a telecommunications receiver consists of 100 μW of signal power and 1 μW of noise power. The receiver contributes an additional 80 μW of noise, N_R, and has a power gain of 20 dB. Compute the input SNR, the output SNR, and the receiver's noise figure.

Solution:

$$\frac{S_i}{N_i} = \frac{100 \ \mu\text{W}}{1 \ \mu\text{W}} = 100$$

As stated, 20 dB equal a power gain, A_p, of 100. Therefore, the signal out is

$$S_o = S_i A_p = 100 \ \mu\text{W} \times 100 = 10 \text{ mW}$$

The output noise is

$$N_o = N_i A_p + N_R = 1 \ \mu\text{W} \times 100 + 80 \ \mu\text{W} = 180 \ \mu\text{W}$$

The output SNR is

$$\frac{S_o}{N_o} = \frac{10 \text{ mW}}{180 \ \mu\text{W}} = 55.6$$

The noise factor is

$$F = \frac{S_i/N_i}{S_o/N_o} = \frac{100}{55.6} = 1.80$$

The noise figure is

$$\begin{aligned}
\text{NF} &= 10 \log F \\
&= 10 \log 1.80 \\
&= 2.55 \text{ dB}
\end{aligned}$$

EXAMPLE
2.12

A log amplifier is specified as having a noise figure of 3.9 dB. For an input signal of 65 μW, the amplifier produces an output power of 20 mW. If the noise out of the amplifier is measured to be 1 mW, compute the following:
(a) The power gain, A_P.
(b) The power gain in decibels, $A_{P(dB)}$.
(c) The noise factor, F.
(d) The input noise to the log amplifier, N_i.
(e) The noise contributed by the log amplifier, N_A.

Solution:

(a)
$$A_P = \frac{S_o}{S_i} = \frac{20 \ m\text{W}}{65 \ \mu\text{W}} = 307.69$$

(b)
$$A_P \ (\text{dB}) = 10 \log 307.69 = 24.88 \ \text{dB}$$

(c) Because
$$\text{NF} = 3.9 \ \text{dB} = 10 \log F,$$

then
$$F = 10^{\frac{3.9}{10}} = 2.4547$$

(d) Because
$$F = \frac{S_i/N_i}{S_o/N_o},$$

then
$$N_i = \frac{S_i}{(S_o/N_o)F} = \frac{65 \ \mu\text{W}}{(20 \ \text{mW}/1 \ \text{mW})(2.4547)} = 1.324 \ \mu\text{W}$$

(e) The noise output,
$$N_o = N_i \cdot A_P + N_A$$

therefore
$$N_A = N_o - N_i A_P$$
$$= 1 \ \text{mW} - (1.324 \ \mu\text{W})(307.69)$$
$$= 592.6 \ \mu\text{W}$$

2.2.4 Bit Error Rate

Another significant measure of system performance in terms of noise is *bit error rate* (BER), which specifies the number of bits that are corrupted or destroyed as data are transmitted from their source to their destination. A BER of 10^{-6}, for example, means that one bit out of every million is destroyed during transmission. Several factors contribute to BER:

- Bandwidth
- SNR
- Transmission speed
- Transmission medium
- Environment
- Transmission distance
- Transmitter and receiver performance

A BER of 10^{-5} over switched voice-grade lines is typical. For a good digital communication system, BERs of less than a few bits per million are not uncommon.

2.2.5 Channel Capacity

If the SNR for a digital communication system is large enough, it is possible to overcome any extraneous effects of noise entirely. In practice, however, this is seldom the case. Mathematical guidelines have been established to determine the maximum theoretical data transfer rate over a channel based on the channel's bandwidth and SNR. This is known as the *channel capacity*. One of the most fundamental laws used in telecommunications is *Shannon's law*. Governed by equation (2-6), Shannon's law allows us to compute channel capacity (in bps). Shannon's equation is based on a signal under the influence of Gaussian type noise, which will be explained later in this chapter.

$$C = \text{BW} \log_2\left(1 + \frac{S}{N}\right) \text{ bps} \qquad \textbf{(2-16)}$$

> **Channel Capacity**
> The maximum theoretical data transfer rate over a transmission medium based on bandwidth and signal-to-noise ratio. *Shannon's Law* is used to compute channel capacity.

> **Shannon's Law**
> A fundamental law used in telecommunications to compute *channel capacity*.

where   BW = bandwidth (Hz),
S/N = signal power to Gaussian noise power within the given BW
C = channel capacity (bps)

The standard 3002 voice-grade lines have a nominal SNR of 25 dB and a bandwidth ranging from 300 to 3400 Hz. Compute the channel capacity using equation (2-6).

Solution:

$$C = \text{BW} \log_2\left(1 + \frac{S}{N}\right)$$
$$= 3100 \log_2 (1 + 316) \text{ (a power gain of 25 dB} = 316)$$
$$= 3100 \log_2 317$$
$$= 25{,}755 \text{ bps}$$

EXAMPLE 2.13

2.3 NOISE TYPES

We have all experienced the undesirable effects of noise on our television sets, radios, and telephones. This crackling and hissing, humming and fading, severely limits the performance of any communication system. It is necessary in our studies to consider some of its sources and types.

2.3.1 Atmospheric and Extraterrestrial Noise

A significant contributor to noise in a communication system stems from natural occurrences in our atmosphere.

2.3.1.1 Lightning
Lightning is a major source of noise and is caused by the static discharge of thunderclouds. Several million volts, with currents in excess of 20,000 A, are not uncommon for lightning discharges. A wide band of frequencies is generated

during a discharge. The amplitudes of these frequency components are inversely proportional to their frequency, thus affecting mostly the low- and high-frequency bands up to 30 MHz.

2.3.1.2 Solar Noise Ionized gases of the sun produce a broad range of frequencies that penetrate the Earth's atmosphere at frequencies used by communication systems. The upper portion of our atmosphere, known as the ionosphere, is directly influenced by ultraviolet radiation of the sun. Random molecular activity in the ionosphere causes several electrical disturbances in the high-frequency region. These disturbances are especially intense when sunspot activity peaks approximately every 11 years.

2.3.1.3 Cosmic Noise Distant stars in our universe, like the sun, also radiate intense levels of noise at frequencies that penetrate Earth's atmosphere. Those frequencies affecting the communication system range from 8 MHz to as high as 2 GHz.

2.3.2 Gaussian Noise

> **Gaussian Noise**
> The cumulative effect of all random noise averaged over a period of time and generated both internal and external to a telecommunication system.

The cumulative effect of all random noise generated both external and internal to the telecommunication system, averaged over a period of time, is referred to as *Gaussian noise.* Gaussian noise includes all frequencies, similar to the manner in which white light includes all visible wavelengths of color. The distribution of Gaussian noise power for a given bandwidth forms a uniform bell curve if viewed on a spectrum analyzer. This is shown in Figure 2-2.

> **Thermal Noise**
> Generated by the random motion of free electrons and molecular vibrations in resistive components. The power associated with thermal noise is proportional to both temperature and bandwidth. Also referred to as *Johnson noise* or *white noise.*

2.3.2.1 Thermal Noise For electronic circuits, Gaussian noise is more specifically referred to as *white noise, Johnson noise,* or *thermal noise.* The three names are used interchangeably to represent noise generated by the *random* motion of free electrons and molecular vibrations exhibited by all electronic components, including conductors. This random motion results in frequency components that are evenly distributed over the entire radio frequency spectrum; thus, the noise is said to be white. If one were to tune to a frequency in the commercial FM broadcast band where there is no station and turn the volume control up, the hiss heard in the background is an example of this type of noise.

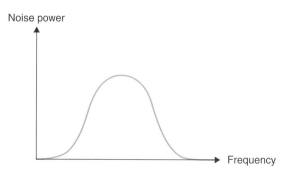

FIGURE 2-2
Gaussian noise distribution producing a uniform bell curve.

All resistive components are constant noise generators due to the thermal inter-action of atomic and subatomic particles that make up the resistive component, hence the name thermal noise. Because particles such as free electrons are in movement, they possess kinetic energy that is directly related to the temperature of the resistive body. This includes the resistive component of an impedance across which the ther-mal agitation is produced. At absolute zero (Kelvin), all motion ceases, the kinetic energy of all charged particles becomes zero, and no thermal noise is generated. At temperatures above absolute zero, the charged particles begin to move. This motion constitutes an electrical current. Although at any instant in time the number of charged particles flowing in one direction may exceed those flowing in the opposite direction, the net potential created over a period of time is equal to zero. In other words, no DC current flows. An rms value does, however, exist, which can be measured with an rms voltmeter. Typical values may be on the order of a few microvolts. Although this may not seem significant, this can be overwhelming for most high-gain receivers when compared to signal amplitudes received at the antenna input.

In 1928, J. B. Johnson, a U.S. physicist, demonstrated that resistive components generate noise power in proportion to both temperature and bandwidth. Johnson's re-search cannot be overemphasized, because it allows us to compute the *rms* noise power associated with a resistive component. Furthermore, it allows us to tailor our receiver designs accordingly. The following equation shows the mathematical relationship that Johnson developed:

$$P_n = K \cdot T \cdot \text{BW} \tag{2-17}$$

where $K =$ Boltzmann's constant of 1.38×10^{-23} J/K
$T =$ absolute temperature of the device (°K)
BW $=$ circuit bandwidth
$P_n =$ noise power output of the resistor

> **Root Mean Square (rms)**
> For the sine wave, the rms value is equal to 0.707 times the peak value of the sine wave. This is the equivalent DC value of the sine wave. The rms value is also referred to as the *effective value.*

An equivalent noise voltage, V_n, generated by the resistor, R, can be computed based on the maximum power transfer into an equivalent load resistor, R_L. The load resistance is assumed to be noiseless.*

Rewriting equation (2-17) in terms of an equivalent noise voltage, V_n, is per-formed in the following manner:

$$P_n = K \cdot T \cdot \text{BW} = \frac{V^2}{R} = \frac{V^2}{R_L}$$

For maximum power transfer into an equivalent load resistor, the voltage across the load, R_L, is one half the voltage across the noise-generating resistance, R, which yields

$$\frac{V^2}{R} = \frac{(V_n/2)^2}{R} = \frac{V_n^2}{4R}$$

and therefore

$$V_n = \sqrt{4K \cdot T \cdot \text{BW} \cdot R} \tag{2-18}$$

---

*George Kennedy, *Electronic Communication Systems,* 3rd ed. (New York, McGraw-Hill, 1985), p. 13.

EXAMPLE 2.14

An amplifier used to process an FDM channel group (12 voice channels) operates over a frequency range from 60 to 108 kHz. The input impedance has a resistive component of 10 kΩ. Compute the equivalent noise voltage at the input of the amplifier at an operating temperature of 24°C.

Solution:

$$°K = 273 + °C$$
$$= 273 + 24$$
$$= 297$$

$$BW = 108 \text{ kHz} - 60 \text{ kHz} = 48 \text{ kHz}$$

$$V_n = \sqrt{4K \cdot T \cdot BW \cdot R}$$
$$= \sqrt{4 \times 1.38 \times 10^{-23} \times 297 \times 48 \times 10^3 \times 10 \times 10^3}$$
$$= 2.81 \ \mu V$$

Shot Noise
Results from the random arrival rate of discrete current carriers (holes and electrons) at the output electrodes of semiconductor and vacuum-tube devices.

2.3.2.2 Shot Noise Another significant contributor to the distribution of Gaussian noise is *shot noise*. The name originates from the sound that it produces at the audio output of a receiver. The sound is similar to that of lead shot falling on top of a tin roof. This type of noise is generated by the random arrival rate of discrete current carriers (holes and electrons) at the output electrodes of semiconductor and vacuum-tube devices. Although the bias currents for these devices flow at a uniform rate over a period of time, at any instant in time there is a nondeterministic number of charge carriers at their outputs. This randomness generates the noise currents associated with shot noise. For semiconductor devices, this current is equal to

$$i_n = \sqrt{2qIf} \qquad (2\text{-}19)$$

where i_n = shot noise current in rms
   q = charge of an electron, 1.6×10^{-19} coulomb
   I = DC current flowing through the device (A)
   f = system bandwidth (Hz)

2.3.3 Crosstalk

Crosstalk
Electrical noise or interference caused by inductive and capacitive coupling of signals from adjacent channels.

Many of us have experienced listening to other telephone conversations taking place in the background of our own. These signals are not only annoying, they can also interfere with the transmission of data. This type of noise, called *crosstalk*, occurs as a result of inductive and capacitive coupling from adjacent channels that are in proximity to each other. Subscriber loops and trunk circuits commonly multiplexed together to form bundled cables often have severe crosstalk, particularly in long lengths of cable.

In LANs, crosstalk noise has the greater effect on system performance than all other types of noise. The problem is minimized in LANs, however, by use of unshielded twisted-pair (UTP) wire and shielded twisted-pair (STP) wire. By twisting cable pairs together, their electromagnetic fields surrounding the wires cancel out each other, leaving virtually no external field to couple into adjacent cables.

Figure 2-3 illustrates how crosstalk occurs between two adjacent channels. At high frequencies, the capacitance between conductors has a low-enough reactance to

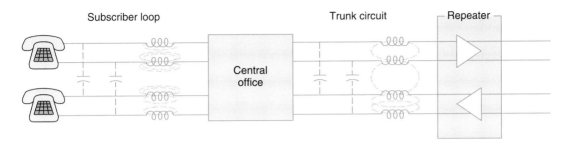

FIGURE 2-3
Crosstalk can result from capacitive and inductive coupling between adjacent channels in proximity to each other.

cause serious coupling between channels. Digital signals are especially prone to crosstalk due to the high-frequency components in the signal.

Inductive coupling between wires is based on the same principle as a transformer. If conductors are close enough to each other, the electromagnetic field generated by signals transmitted in one line will induce crosstalk currents into the others.

In telecommunication systems, crosstalk is often classified as *near end* or *far end*. As shown in Figure 2-4, near-end crosstalk occurs at the transmitting station or repeater. Strong signals radiated from the transmitter pairs are coupled into the relatively weak signals traveling in the opposite direction of the receiver pairs. Far-end crosstalk occurs at the far-end receiver due to adjacent-channel signals traveling in the same direction.

Several measures are taken to minimize crosstalk in the telecommunication system. Consider the following:

- Adjacent wire pairs are twisted at different pitches to reduce the amount of crosstalk.
- Shielding is used to prevent signals from radiating into adjacent conductors.
- Transmitted and received signals over long distances are physically separated and shielded to prevent near- and far-end crosstalk.
- Differential amplifiers and receivers are used to reject common-mode signals.

Near-End Crosstalk
Near-end crosstalk occurs at the transmitting station or repeater when strong signals radiating from the transmitting pair of wires are coupled into the adjacent, relatively weak, received signals traveling in the opposite direction.

Far-End Crosstalk
Far-end crosstalk occurs at the far-end receiver as a result of adjacent channel signals traveling in the same direction.

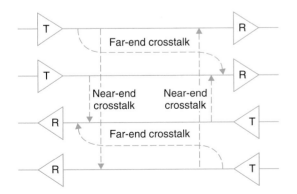

FIGURE 2-4
Near-end and far-end crosstalk.

- Balanced transformers are often used with twisted-pair media to cancel crosstalk signals coupled equally into both lines.
- Limits are set on the maximum number of channels that can be used within a cable.
- Because excessive signal amplitudes and frequencies due to overmodulation are major contributors to crosstalk, stringent regulation is placed on these parameters for digital and analog carriers.

2.3.4 Impulse Noise

Impulse Noise
Noise consisting of sudden bursts of irregularly shaped pulses and lasting for a few microseconds to several hundred milliseconds.

Impulse noise, as its name implies, consists of sudden bursts of irregularly shaped pulses. They may last for a few microseconds to several hundreds of milliseconds depending on their amplitude and origin. Common sources of impulse noise include transients induced from electromechanical switching relays at the central office, electric motors and appliances, ignition systems, poor solder joints, and lightning. Impulse noise is the familiar cracking and popping noise. It can be heard at a telephone set's receiver or the speaker output of a communications receiver. Its effect on voice is not nearly as damaging as it is on data. If a burst of noise, for example, were large enough, data could be completely blotted out for the entire duration of the impulse. For example, if a 56 kbps modem were transmitting data over the telephone lines and a 10-ms noise burst were to saturate the channel, more than 500 bits of data would be corrupted. Suppose this data corresponded to a banking transaction. Without error detection and correction, this could be catastrophic!

PROBLEMS

1. Given an amplifier with an output power of 1.5 W and an input power of 75 mW, compute the following:
   a. The relative power gain as a ratio, A_P.
   b. The relative power gain in decibels, $A_{P(dB)}$.
2. An amplifier is redesigned so that its maximum output power has increased from 0.25 W to 5 W. Compute the following:
   a. The relative power gain as a ratio, A_P.
   b. The relative power gain in decibels, $A_{P(dB)}$.
3. The power gain of an amplifier is given as 20 dB. Compute the input power, P_i, if the output power of the amplifier is 550 mW.
4. Compute the output power of the amplifier in problem 3 if the input power is set to 1 W.
5. The preamplifier in a wireless LAN transmitter has a voltage gain of 28 dB. Compute the following:
   a. The voltage gain of the amplifier as a ratio, A_V.
   b. The output voltage, V_o, of the amplifier given an input voltage, V_i, of 15 μV.
   a. If the input voltage were to decrease from 15 to 5 μV, how many decibels has the signal dropped?
6. An intermediate frequency (IF) amplifier stage has a voltage gain of 90 dB. Compute the following:
   a. The voltage gain of the IF stage as a ratio, A_V.
   b. The output voltage, V_o, of the IF stage given an input voltage, V_i, of 35 μV.
   c. If the input voltage were to decrease from 35 to 5 μV, how many decibels has the signal dropped?
7. The signal level of a 30-MHz test tone measures -30 dBm on a spectrum analyzer. Compute the power level, P, of signal.

8. The carrier frequency of an AM broadcast station measures -65 dBm on a spectrum analyzer. Compute the power level, P, of the signal.

9. An rf sine-wave generator whose output impedance is 50 Ω is connected to a 50-Ω load using 50-Ω coaxial cable. The generator's output amplitude level is set to -12 dBm. An rms voltmeter is used to measure the effective voltage, and an oscilloscope is used to display the sine wave. Compute the following:
   a. The rms voltage measured by the rms voltmeter.
   b. The peak voltage, V_p, of the sine wave that should be displayed on the oscilloscope.
   c. The peak-to-peak voltage, V_{p-p}, of the sine wave that should be displayed on the oscilloscope.

10. An audio signal generator with an output impedance of 600 Ω is directly connected to a 600 Ω voltmeter and an oscilloscope. The generator's amplitude is set to $+5$ dBm. Compute the following:
   a. The rms voltage measured by the rms voltmeter.
   b. The peak voltage, V_p, of the sine wave that should be displayed on the oscilloscope.
   c. The peak-to-peak voltage, V_{p-p}, of the sine wave that should be displayed on the oscilloscope.

11. The noise power at the output of a receiver's IF stage is measured at 45 μW. With the receiver tuned to a test signal, the output power increases to 3.58 mW. Compute the SNR.

12. An amplifier with a power gain of 40 dB produces a noise output power of 180 μW with an input noise power of 7 nW. The input signal power is 1 μW. Compute the noise factor, F, the noise figure, NF, and the noise power contributed by the amplifier.

13. The input signal to a repeater is made up of 150 μW of signal power and 1.2 μW of noise power. The repeater contributes an additional 48 μW of noise and has a power gain of 20 dB. Compute the following:
   a. Input SNR.
   b. Output SNR.
   c. Noise factor, F.
   d. Noise figure, NF.

14. What does *BER* stand for?

15. Compute the BER for a system that has a history of 25 bit errors out of every 2 million bits that are transmitted.

16. The telephone lines for a PBX system have a bandwidth ranging from 280 Hz to 5.1 kHz. The SNR is nominally 22 dB. Compute the channel capacity of the line using Shannon's law.

17. A telephone channel has a bandwidth of 3 kHz and an SNR of 1023. Compute the channel capacity.

18. Explain whether the noise produced by lightning can be considered Gaussian.

19. An amplifier operates over a bandwidth of 750 kHz and has an input resistance of 20 kΩ. Compute the thermal noise power, P_n, and noise voltage, V_n, generated at its input at an ambient temperature of 25°C.

20. Given a bandwidth of 10 kHz and an operating temperature of 27°C, compute the thermal noise voltage, V_n, generated by the following resistors:
   a. 1 kΩ.
   b. 20 kΩ.
   c. 100 kΩ.
   d. 1 MΩ.

21. A semiconductor diode operates in a circuit having a bandwidth of 2 MHz. Its bias current is 7.5 mA. Compute the rms shot-noise current.

22. Explain the difference between near-end and far-end crosstalk.

23. A 4800-bps synchronous modem, transmitting data over the switched lines, is hit with 2.5 ms of impulse noise from a lightning strike. The noise saturates the channel. Compute the number of bits that would be destroyed in this case.

3

AMPLITUDE MODULATION

One of the most fundamental forms of modulation used in telecommunications is *amplitude modulation (AM)*. The transmission of music and speech in the commercial AM broadcast band is an example of the widespread use of AM. More recently, *quadrature amplitude modulation (QAM)* and other, more sophisticated variations of AM have become important in high-speed communication systems.

In this chapter, we study the components of the AM waveform in the time and frequency domains, and we consider its power dissipation. The degree of modulation, or the modulation index, *m,* is considered in relation to the intelligence and carrier frequency component. Once we have a basic understanding of the AM wave, we look at other forms of AM, such as double-sideband suppressed carrier (DSBSC), single-sideband suppressed carrier (SSBSC), and vestigial sideband (VSB).

3.1 DEFINING AM

Amplitude modulation is defined as a *carrier* frequency whose amplitude is varied in proportion to the instantaneous amplitude of a *modulating* voltage. The modulating voltage is referred to as the *intelligence*. The carrier frequency, or carrier of the modulating voltage, is typically much higher than that of the modulating voltage. It is usually a radio frequency (RF) signal in the mid-frequency (MF) range of 300 kHz to 3 MHz or higher. In contrast, the frequency of the modulating voltage is typically an audio frequency (AF) signal in the range of 20 Hz to 20 kHz. For simplicity, we limit our discussion to sine-wave modulation.

3.2 GENERATING THE AM WAVEFORM

If a 1-kHz tone is transmitted at 1 MHZ, it is convenient to simply sum the two electrical signals to produce an RF signal that could be transmitted into free space. Figure 3-1 illustrates a plausible circuit. An op-amp summing amplifier is used to electrically sum the two sinusoids together; unfortunately, the resulting waveform is not the ubiquitous AM wave that is normally associated with sine-wave modulation. From the frequency spectrum shown, the two signals clearly remain independent of each other in terms of frequency. An attempt to transmit the composite signal would only result in the carrier frequency radiating, because it is high enough to be transmitted effectively as a radio wave. The modulating 1-kHz tone is not.

Amplitude Modulation (AM)
A fundamental modulation technique in which a carrier frequency's amplitude is varied in proportion to the instantaneous amplitude of a modulating voltage.

Quadrature Amplitude Modulation (QAM)
A modulation technique employed in high-speed modems. A combination of amplitude shift keying and differential phase shift keying is used to encode 4 bits into 16 signaling state changes.

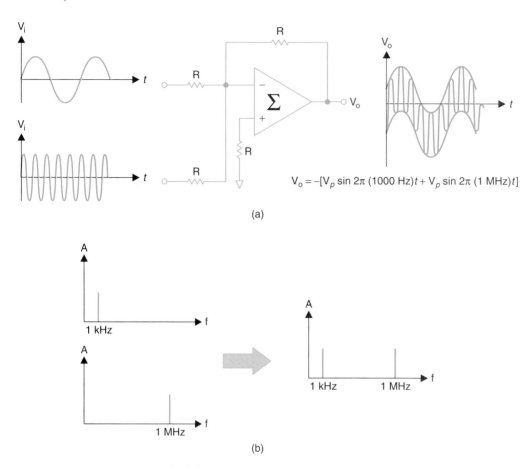

$$V_o = -[V_p \sin 2\pi\,(1000\ \text{Hz})t + V_p \sin 2\pi\,(1\ \text{MHz})t]$$

(a)

(b)

FIGURE 3-1

Electrically summing a 1-kHz tone with a 1-MHz carrier frequency does not produce an AM wave: (a) op-amp summing circuit with resulting waveform; (b) frequency spectrum of resulting wave shows the two sine waves remain independent.

Modulator

A *nonlinear* device or circuit capable of producing the sum and difference products of two signals; the carrier frequency, and the modulating frequency.

Nonlinear Device

A circuit or device capable of producing a mixing action, thus resulting in the sum and difference products. Transistors and diodes are examples of nonlinear devices.

To produce an AM wave requires a device called a *modulator*. An AM modulator produces the sum and difference products of the carrier and the modulation frequencies. Unlike the circuit in Figure 3-1, the AM modulator up-converts the intelligence to the RF carrier frequency so that it may be transmitted.

Many different types of modulator circuits are used to produce AM. Common to each of these circuits is a *nonlinear device* such as a diode or a transistor biased in its nonlinear region. Nonlinear devices produce output signals that are not in proportion to their input. Combining two frequencies through a nonlinear device produces a mixing action, resulting in harmonics as well as sum and difference frequencies of the original signals.

Figure 3-2 illustrates a simple AM modular circuit. Our summing amplifier is used again to electrically sum the modulation and carrier frequencies in Figure 3-2(a). The diode, acting as our nonlinear device, and the resistor are used to "clip" the negative half of the composite signal, thus producing a pulsating DC signal that is rich in harmonic content.

When a single pulse is fed to a tank circuit, as shown in Figure 3-2(b), it causes a *damped* oscillation to occur at the natural resonant frequency of the tank. A damped oscillation is a sinusoid function with an exponentially decaying envelope. The de-

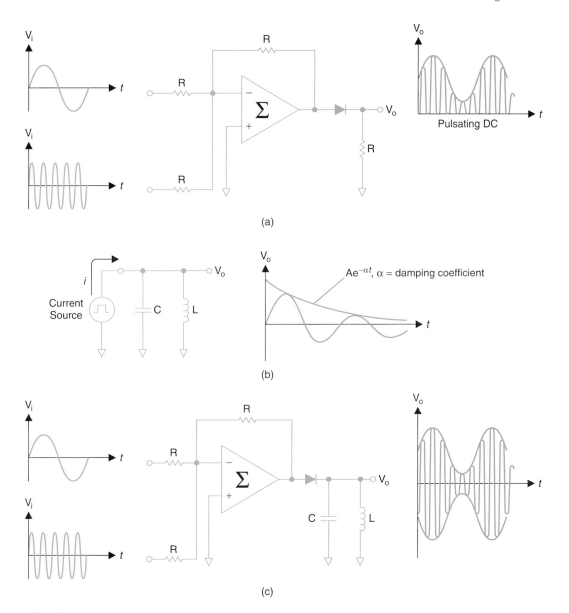

FIGURE 3-2
Diode AM modulator circuit: (a) summing amplifier and nonlinear diode circuit used to produce a pulsating DC signal rich in harmonics; (b) damping effect on the oscillatory output of a resonant tank circuit; (c) parallel resonant circuit used to produce the AM wave.

caying (or damping) envelope of the sinusoid is caused over time by resistive losses in the tank, which are not shown. If a tank circuit is attached to the output of the diode, as shown in Figure 3-2(c), the pulsating DC signal will sustain the oscillatory effect, thereby producing complete sinusoids whose amplitudes are proportional to the amplitude of each pulse. This is known as the *flywheel effect* of a tank circuit.* The resulting AM wave is effectively produced. The resonant tank circuit filters out

Flywheel Effect
An oscillatory effect sustained by applying a pulsating DC signal to a resonant tank circuit.

*George Kennedy, *Electronic Communication Systems,* 3rd ed. (New York, McGraw-Hill, 1985), p. 36.

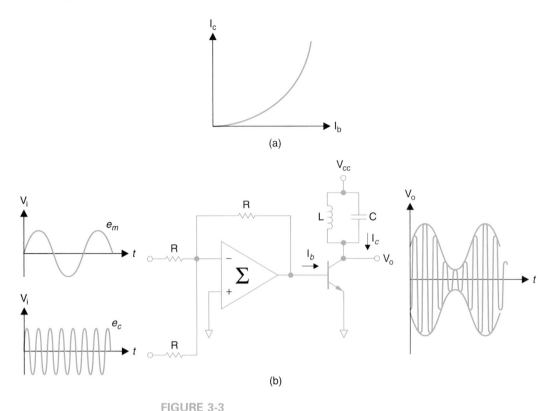

FIGURE 3-3

Transistor AM modulator circuit: (a) nonlinear characteristic curve; (b) summing amplifier used to drive the transistor modulator circuit in its nonlinear region of operation during positive peaks of the cycles, thereby producing the output AM wave.

the undesirable harmonics, and it preserves the AM frequency components, which we discuss later.

Because the diode in Figure 3-2 is a passive device, it offers no gain to the AM wave. The transistor AM modulator circuit in Figure 3-3 adds the element of gain to the signal. Its principle of operation is similar to our diode clipping circuit of Figure 3-2. The amplitudes of e_m and e_c are adjusted to turn on the transistor in its nonlinear region during the positive peaks of the cycle. During the negative peaks of the cycle, the transistor turns off, thus producing the pulsating DC signal at the tank circuit. The AM wave is produced at the collector output of the transistor.

3.3 ANALYSIS OF THE AM WAVE

Figure 3-4 illustrates the AM waveform and its components. A carrier frequency, ω_c, has been amplitude modulated with a sine wave, ω_m.* The resulting AM waveform is illustrated in the time domain. The instantaneous voltage, e_m, of the sine wave used

---

*Although ω_c and ω_m are angular velocities ($2\pi f$ radians per second), it is common practice in mathematical presentations to refer to them as *frequencies*.

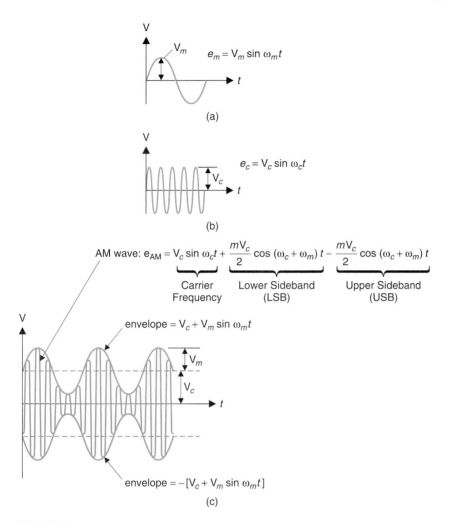

FIGURE 3-4
The AM waveform with sine wave modulation shown in the time domain: (a) modulating voltage; (b) carrier frequency; (c) resulting AM waveform.

to modulate the carrier frequency is given by

$$e_m = V_m \sin \omega_m t \qquad (3\text{-}1)$$

where ω_m is $2\pi f_m$, and V_m is the peak amplitude of the modulating signal.

The instantaneous voltage, e_c, of the carrier frequency is given by

$$e_c = V_c \sin \omega_c t \qquad (3\text{-}2)$$

where ω_c is $2\pi f_c$, and V_c is the peak amplitude of the carrier signal.

3.3.1 Modulation Index

The degree of modulation is an important parameter and is known as the *modulation index*. It is the ratio of the peak amplitude of the modulation voltage, V_m, to the peak amplitude of the carrier voltage, V_c. The modulation index, m, is also referred to as

Modulation Index
A measure of the degree of modulation. In AM, the ratio of the peak amplitude of the modulation voltage, V_m, to the peak amplitude of the carrier voltage, V_c. In FM, the ratio of the maximum frequency deviation to the modulation signal's frequency. Also referred to as *percent modulation, modulation factor,* and *depth of modulation.*

the *percent modulation, modulation factor,* and *depth of modulation.* It is a number lying between 0 and 1 and is typically expressed as a percentage. For the AM waveform in Figure 3-4, *m* is given as

$$m = \frac{V_m}{V_c} \tag{3-3}$$

Expressed as a percentage, the percent modulation index, M, is given as

$$M = \frac{V_m}{V_c} \times 100 \tag{3-4}$$

To measure the modulation index with an oscilloscope in the time domain, it is convenient to express the modulation index in terms of peak or peak-to-peak values for a sine wave. Refer to Figure 3-5. Expanding on equation (3-3), we have

$$m = \frac{V_m}{V_c}$$

$$= \frac{V_{max} - V_c}{V_c}$$

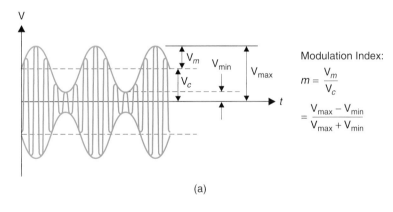

(a)

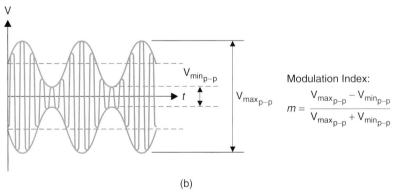

(b)

FIGURE 3-5
Measuring the modulation index, *m*, using: (a) peak values; (b) peak-to-peak values.

and because the modulation is symmetrical about the carrier frequency,

$$V_{max} - V_c = V_c - V_{min}$$

$$V_m = \frac{V_{max} - V_{min}}{2} \qquad \textbf{(3-5)}$$

$$V_c = \frac{V_{max} + V_{min}}{2} \qquad \textbf{(3-6)}$$

we can divide equation (3-5) by equation (3-6) to show that

$$m = \frac{V_{max} - V_{min}}{V_{max} + V_{min}} \qquad \textbf{(3-7)}$$

or, by using peak-to-peak (*p-p*) values, that

$$m = \frac{V_{max_{p\text{-}p}} - V_{min_{p\text{-}p}}}{V_{max_{p\text{-}p}} + V_{min_{p\text{-}p}}} \qquad \textbf{(3-8)}$$

3.3.2 Envelope of the AM Waveform

We now establish an equation representing the amplitude of the AM waveform. This is also known as the *envelope* of the AM waveform (e_{ENV}). The envelope is an imaginary line drawn between the peak values of each cycle, thus creating a shape equivalent to that of the modulating voltage. In Figures 3-4 and 3-5, the envelope outlines the peaks and troughs of the waveform. Because they are inverted from each other, e_{ENV} can be a positive or a negative signed value. For sine-wave modulation,

> **Envelope**
> In an AM waveform, the envelope is an imaginary line drawn between the peak (or trough) values of each cycle. The resulting shape is equivalent to that of the modulation voltage.

$$e_{ENV} = V_c + e_m$$
$$= V_c + V_m \sin \omega_m t \qquad \textbf{(3-9)}$$

Rearranging equation (3-3), we have

$$V_m = mV_c$$

and substituting this into equation (3-9) gives us

$$e_{ENV} = V_c + mV_c \sin \omega_m t$$
$$= V_c(1 + m \sin \omega_m t) = \text{positive envelope} \qquad \textbf{(3-10)}$$
$$= -V_c(1 + m \sin \omega_m t) = \text{negative envelope} \qquad \textbf{(3-11)}$$

Equations (3-10) and (3-11) allow us to compute the instantaneous amplitude (or envelope) of the AM waveform based on the modulation index. Adding a negative sign to equation (3-10) produces equation (3-11), which allows the negative envelope of the waveform to be computed.

A carrier signal with a peak voltage of 2.0 V is amplitude modulated with a 10-kHz sine wave. The modulation voltage has an effective value of 750 mV. Compute the following:
(a) The percent modulation index, M.
(b) The instantaneous voltage of the positive and negative envelope when the 10-kHz sine wave has completed 68 μs of its cycle.
(c) Illustrate the resulting AM waveform.

EXAMPLE 3.1

Solution:

(a) Using equation (3-4), we have

$$M = \frac{V_m}{V_c} \times 100\% = \frac{1.414 \times 750 \text{ mV}}{2.0 \text{ V}} \times 100\% = 53.04\%$$

(b) The instantaneous voltage of the positive and negative envelope can be computed with equations (3-10) and (3-11) respectively.

$$
\begin{aligned}
e_{\text{ENV}} &= V_c(1 + m \sin \omega_m t) \\
&= 2.0 \text{ V}(1 + 0.5304 \sin 2\pi \cdot 10 \text{ kHz} \cdot 68 \text{ } \mu s) \\
&= 2.0 \text{ V}(1 + 0.5304 \sin 244.8°) \\
&= 1.04 \text{ V}
\end{aligned}
$$

Therefore the negative envelope is −1.04 V.

(c)

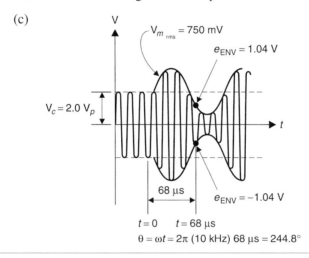

$V_{m \text{ rms}}$ = 750 mV

e_{ENV} = 1.04 V

V_c = 2.0 V_p

t

68 μs

e_{ENV} = −1.04 V

t = 0   *t* = 68 μs

θ = ω*t* = 2π (10 kHz) 68 μs = 244.8°

3.4 FREQUENCY SPECTRUM OF THE AM WAVE

Because e_{ENV} in equation (3-10) represents the peak envelope of the AM waveform at any instant in time, *t*, we can use it to prefix the carrier frequency, ω_c, as a peak value in establishing an equation representing the AM waveform in its entirety. This equation reveals the frequency components of the AM wave:

$$e_{\text{AM}} = e_{\text{ENV}} \sin \theta = e_{\text{ENV}} \sin \omega_c t \qquad \textbf{(3-12)}$$

Substituting equation (3-10) for e_{ENV}, we have

$$
\begin{aligned}
e_{\text{AM}} &= V_c(1 + m \sin \omega_m t)\sin \omega_c t \\
&= V_c \sin \omega_c t + mV_c \sin \omega_c t \sin \omega_m t \qquad \textbf{(3-13)}
\end{aligned}
$$

Applying the trigonometric identity $\sin \alpha \sin \beta = \frac{1}{2}[\cos(\alpha - \beta) - \cos(\alpha + \beta)]$ to equation (3-13) gives us our final equation representing the AM waveform in its entirety:

$$e_{\text{AM}} = V_c \sin \omega_c t + m \frac{V_c}{2} \cos(\omega_c - \omega_m)t - m \frac{V_c}{2} \cos(\omega_c + \omega_m)t \qquad \textbf{(3-14)}$$

Carrier frequency	Lower sideband (LSB)	Upper Sideband (USB)
f_c	$f_c - f_m$	$f_c + f_m$

Three very important terms in equation (3-14) are of interest to us. The first term represents the carrier frequency. The second and third terms represent the *lower sideband (LSB)* and *upper sideband (USB)*, respectively. The LSB is the mathematical difference between the carrier frequency and the modulation frequency ($f_c - f_m$), and the USB is the mathematical sum of the carrier frequency and the modulation frequency ($f_c + f_m$). Because the total composite AM signal is comprised of two sidebands and a carrier frequency, it is often referred to as *double-sideband full-carrier,* or simply *DSBFC.*

Note that the peak value terms, $\frac{mV_c}{2}$, of the LSB and USB are equal. If we call these peak values V_{LSB} and V_{USB}, respectively, then

$$\frac{mV_c}{2} = V_{LSB} = V_{USB} \qquad \textbf{(3-15)}$$

When all three frequency components are in phase, they add together linearly and form the maximum signal amplitude, V_{max}. That is,

$$V_{max} = V_c + V_{LSB} + V_{USB} \qquad \textbf{(3-16)}$$

Because V_{max} is also equal to the sum of V_c and V_m, that is,

$$V_{max} = V_c + V_m \qquad \textbf{(3-17)}$$

then from equations (3-16) and (3-17), we can say that

$$V_m = V_{LSB} + V_{USB} \qquad \textbf{(3-18)}$$

Similarly, we can also say that because the peak sideband voltages are equal,

$$V_m = 2 \times V_{LSB} \text{ or } V_m = 2 \times V_{USB} \qquad \textbf{(3-19)}$$

Figure 3-6 illustrates the AM waveform in the time and frequency domains.

> **Lower Sideband (LSB)**
> In AM, the mathematical difference between the carrier frequency, f_c, and the modulation frequency, f_m: $f_c - f_m$.

> **Upper Sideband (USB)**
> In AM, the mathematical sum of the carrier frequency, f_c, and the modulation frequency, f_m: $f_c + f_m$.

An AM broadcast station's peak carrier voltage of 2 kV has been amplitude modulated to an index of 75% with a 2-kHz test tone. The station's broadcast frequency is 810 kHz. Compute the following:
(a) The lower- and upper-sideband frequencies, LSB and USB.
(b) The peak modulation voltage, V_m.
(c) The peak lower- and upper-sideband voltages, V_{LSB} and V_{USB}.
(d) The maximum signal amplitude, V_{max}.

EXAMPLE 3.2

Solution:
(a)
$$LSB = f_c - f_m = 810 \text{ kHz} - 2 \text{ kHz} = 808 \text{ kHz}$$
$$USB = f_c + f_m = 810 \text{ kHz} + 2 \text{ kHz} = 812 \text{ kHz}$$

(b) Rearranging equation (3-3), we have
$$V_m = mV_c = 0.75 \times 2000 \text{ V} = 1500 \text{ V}$$

(c) From equations (3-18) and (3-19), we see that the peak upper- and lower-sideband voltages are equal to half the level of the modulation voltage. Therefore,

$$V_{LSB} = V_{USB} = \frac{1}{2} V_m = \frac{1}{2} \times 1500 \text{ V} = 750 \text{ V}$$

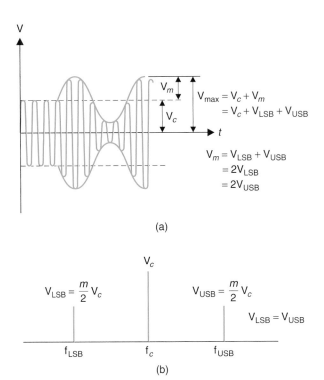

FIGURE 3-6
The AM waveform: (a) time domain; (b) frequency domain.

(d) Using equation (3-16), we have

$$V_{max} = V_c + V_{LSB} + V_{USB} = 2000 \text{ V} + 2 \times 750 \text{ V} = 3500 \text{ V}$$

3.5 POWER DISTRIBUTION IN THE AM WAVEFORM

The total effective (rms) power, P_T, in the AM wave is the sum of the effective carrier power level, P_C, and the effective sideband power levels, P_{LSB} and P_{USB}. That is,

$$P_T = P_C + P_{LSB} + P_{USB} \tag{3-20}$$

$$= \frac{V_{c_{rms}}^2}{R} + \frac{V_{LSB_{rms}}^2}{R} + \frac{V_{USB_{rms}}^2}{R} \tag{3-21}$$

$$= \frac{(0.707 \, V_c)^2}{R} + \frac{(0.707 \, V_{LSB})^2}{R} + \frac{(0.707 \, V_{USB})^2}{R} \tag{3-22}$$

$$= \frac{V_c^2}{2R} + \frac{V_{LSB}^2}{2R} + \frac{V_{USB}^2}{2R} \tag{3-23}$$

Because the power in the upper and lower sidebands is equal, the second and third terms of equation (3-22) are equal. Substituting equation (3-15) into either of these terms gives us

$$P_{LSB} = P_{USB} = \frac{\left[0.707 \left(\frac{mV_c}{2} \right) \right]^2}{R}$$

$$= \frac{m^2 V_c^2}{8R} \tag{3-24}$$

and because the total power in the carrier, P_C, is $\frac{V_c^2}{2R}$, we have

$$P_{LSB} = P_{USB} = \frac{m^2 V_c^2}{8R}$$

$$= \frac{m^2 P_C}{4} \tag{3-25}$$

A spectrum analyzer with an input impedance of 50 Ω is used to measure the power spectrum of an AM signal at the output of a preamplifier circuit. The AM signal has been modulated with a sine wave. The effective carrier power, P_C, is 750 mW, and each sideband, P_{USB} and P_{LSB}, is 120 mW. Compute the following:

EXAMPLE
3.3

(a) The total effective power, P_T.
(b) The peak carrier voltage, V_c.
(c) The modulation index, m, and the percent modulation index, M.
(d) The modulation voltage, V_m.
(e) The lower- and upper-sideband voltages, V_{LSB} and V_{USB}.
(f) Sketch the waveform that you would see with an oscilloscope if it were placed in parallel with the spectrum analyzer.

Solution:
(a) Using equation (3-20), we have

$$P_T = P_C + P_{USB} + P_{LSB}$$
$$= 750 \text{ mW} + 120 \text{ mW} + 120 \text{ mW} = 990 \text{ mW}$$

(b) From the first term in equation (3-21), we have

$$P_C = \frac{V_{c_{rms}}^2}{R}$$

and, therefore,

$$V_{c_{rms}} = \sqrt{P_C \times R} = \sqrt{750 \text{ mW} \times 50 \text{ } \Omega} = 6.124 \text{ V}$$
$$V_c = 1.414 \times 6.124 \text{ V} = 8.66 \text{ V}$$

(c) Rearranging equation (3-24), we have

$$m = \sqrt{P_{LSB} \times \frac{8R}{V_c^2}} = \sqrt{P_{USB} \times \frac{8R}{V_c^2}}$$

$$= \sqrt{120 \text{ mW} \times \frac{8(50 \text{ } \Omega)}{(8.66 \text{ V})^2}}$$

$$= 0.800 \text{ (or 80\%)}$$

(d) Rearranging equation (3-3), we have

$$V_m = mV_c = 0.8 \times 8.66 \text{ V} = 6.93 \text{ V}$$

(e)
$$P_{USB} = P_{LSB} = \frac{V^2_{USB_{rms}}}{R} = \frac{V^2_{LSB_{rms}}}{R}$$

and, therefore,

$$V_{USB_{rms}} = V_{LSB_{rms}} = \sqrt{P_{USB} \times R} = \sqrt{P_{LSB} \times R}$$
$$= \sqrt{120 \text{ mW} \times 50 \text{ }\Omega}$$
$$= 2.449 \text{ V}$$
$$V_{USB} = V_{LSB} = 1.414 \times 2.449 \text{ V} = 3.46 \text{ V}$$

(f)

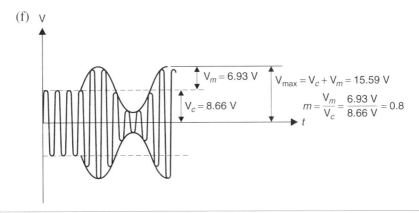

We now establish another valuable relationship in computing the total effective power, P_T. By substituting equation (3-25) into equation (3-20), we have

$$P_T = P_C + P_{LSB} + P_{USB}$$
$$= P_C + \frac{m^2 P_C}{4} + \frac{m^2 P_C}{4} \qquad \textbf{(3-26)}$$

$$= P_C + \frac{m^2 P_C}{2} \qquad \textbf{(3-27)}$$

$$= P_C\left(1 + \frac{m^2}{2}\right) \qquad \textbf{(3-28)}$$

Equations (3-26), (3-27), and (3-28) allow us to compute the total effective power of the AM waveform by knowing only the value of the carrier power and the modulation index. Figure 3-7 shows the power distribution for the AM wave in the frequency domain.

From Equation (3-28), we can solve for the modulation index, *m*, in terms of the total effective power, P_T and P_C, we have

$$m = \sqrt{\left(\frac{P_T}{P_C} - 1\right)^2}$$

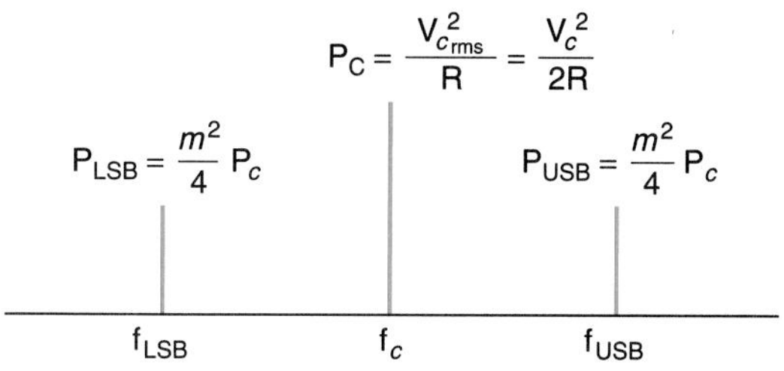

FIGURE 3-7
Power distribution for the AM wave with sine-wave modulation.

3.5.1   Power Distribution in the AM Wave for 100% Modulation

It is often necessary to consider the AM waveform in terms of power efficiency. Typically, the condition when 100% modulation is used, $m = 1$, sets the condition for maximum power utilization in the sidebands. For 100% modulation, equation (3-26) becomes

$$P_T = P_C + \frac{P_C}{4} + \frac{P_C}{4} \tag{3-29}$$

It is apparent that the power in each sideband is one-fourth the power in the carrier, P_C, for 100% modulation. Furthermore, because the total power in the sidebands is simply the sum of the P_{USB} and P_{LSB}, for $m = 1$, we can also say that

$$P_T = P_C + \frac{P_C}{2} \tag{3-30}$$

$$= 1.5\, P_C \tag{3-31}$$

Equation (3-30) states that the total effective power in the sidebands of the AM waveform for 100% modulation is half the carrier power (1/4 P_C for each sideband). Another way of stating this is through equation (3-31). For 100% modulation, two-thirds of the total power is dissipated by the carrier frequency ($P_C = P_T/1.5$). This is demonstrated in Example 3-4, and the AM waveform in the time and frequency domains for a sine wave with 100% modulation is illustrated in Figure 3-8.

An AM transmitter has an effective carrier power level of 50 kW. If the carrier is modulated with a sine wave, compute the following:
(a) The total effective transmitted power for a percent modulation index of 50%.
(b) The effective power in each sideband for a modulation index of 50%.
(c) The total effective transmitted power for 100% modulation.
(d) The effective power in each sideband for 100% modulation.

EXAMPLE 3.4

Solution:
(a) Using equation (3-28),

$$P_T = P_C\left(1 + \frac{m^2}{2}\right) = 50 \text{ kW}\left[1 + \frac{(0.5)^2}{2}\right] = 56.25 \text{ kW}$$

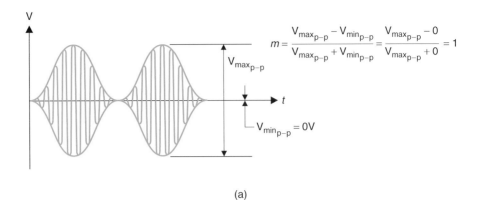

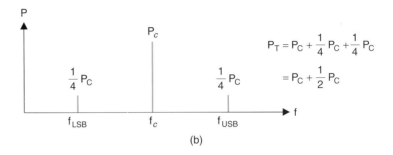

(b)

FIGURE 3-8
The AM waveform with 100% modulation ($m = 1$): (a) time domain; (b) frequency domain.

(b) Rearranging equation (3-20), we have

$$P_{USB} + P_{LSB} = P_T - P_C = 56.25 \text{ kW} - 50 \text{ kW} = 6.25 \text{ kW}$$

Because $P_{USB} = P_{LSB}$, each sideband power level must be half of 6.25 kW, or

$$P_{USB} = P_{LSB} = \frac{1}{2}(P_T - P_C) = \frac{1}{2}(6.25 \text{ kW}) = 3.125 \text{ kW}$$

(c)
$$P_T = P_C\left(1 + \frac{m^2}{2}\right) = 50 \text{ kW}\left[1 + \frac{(1)^2}{2}\right] = 75 \text{ kW}$$

(d) Using the same procedure as in step (b),

$$P_{USB} = P_{LSB} = \frac{1}{2}(P_T - P_C) = \frac{1}{2}(75 \text{ kW} - 50 \text{ kW}) = 12.5 \text{ kW}$$

Note that the power in each sideband is one-fourth the power in the carrier for 100% modulation.

3.6 AMPLITUDE MODULATION WITH SIGNALS OTHER THAN A SINE WAVE

When signals other than a sine wave are used to amplitude modulate the carrier frequency, the envelope still reflects the original shape of the modulating waveform. In addition, the spectral (frequency) content of the modulation wave is preserved in the LSB and USB. Figure 3-9 depicts various AM waveforms and their respective modulation voltages.

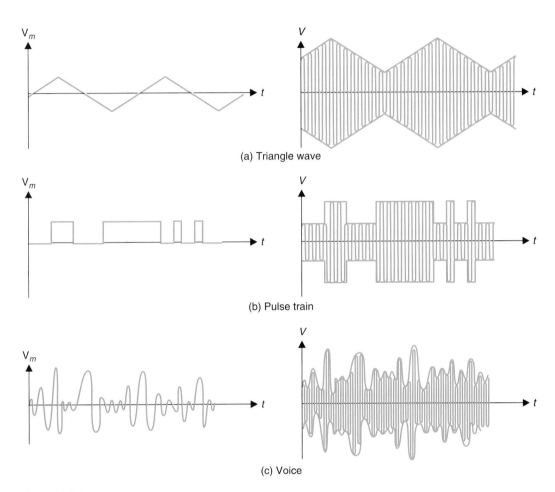

(a) Triangle wave

(b) Pulse train

(c) Voice

FIGURE 3-9
The resulting AM waveforms for various modulating voltages: (a) triangle wave;
(b) pulse train; (c) voice.

3.7 SINGLE SIDEBAND

An inherent problem with AM or, more specifically, double-sideband full carrier (DSBFC) is the enormous amount of power contained in the carrier frequency. As shown, modulating the carrier frequency with intelligence, or modulating voltage, does not alter the amplitude or the frequency of the carrier component itself. It remains independent of the modulating voltage. It is the sidebands that change in proportion to the modulating voltage and the depth of modulation. In other words, the intelligence resides entirely in the sidebands.

Aside from providing a receiver system with an easy mechanism for turning and detecting the intelligence, the power transmitted in the AM carrier frequency is essentially wasted. As discussed earlier, at 100% modulation, two-thirds of the total power in the AM wave is in the carrier. For modulation indices less than 100%, even more power is wasted by the carrier component.

The USB and LSB components in the AM signal are essentially "mirror images" or "inverted" from each other. They contain the same information, have identical power levels, and are displaced from the carrier by the same frequency. The transmission of both sidebands, like the carrier frequency, is redundant. By further suppressing one of the sidebands, an additional 50% of the power is saved. Thus, for 100% modulation, an overall power savings of at least 83.33% is realized: two-thirds for the carrier, and half of one-third for one of the sidebands. Suppressing the carrier frequency and one of the sidebands is referred to as *single-sideband suppressed carrier (SSBSC)*, or simply *SSB*. Before we discuss SSB, however, we look at how the carrier component of the AM wave is suppressed.

3.7.1 Double-Sideband Suppressed Carrier

Suppressing the carrier component of the AM signal so that the transmitted wave only consists of the upper and lower sidebands is called *double-sideband suppressed carrier (DSBSC)*. Figure 3-10 shows the time- and frequency-domain representations of a DSBSC signal with sine-wave modulation.

3.7.2 The Balanced Modulator

To produce a DSBSC signal, the carrier frequency of the AM wave must be eliminated or suppressed. A device called a *balanced modulator* is used to perform this task, and Figure 3-11 shows a block diagram of this device. There are two inputs: the carrier-frequency input, and the modulation-frequency input. A mathematical analy-

---

Single-Sideband Suppressed Carrier (SSBSC)
A modulation technique that employs suppression of the carrier frequency and one sideband to realize an overall power savings of at least 83.33% for 100% modulation. Also referred to as *SSB* or *single sideband*.

Double-Sideband Suppressed Carrier (DSBSC)
A modulation technique that employs suppression of the carrier component of the AM signal so that the transmitted wave consists of only the upper and lower sidebands.

Balanced Modulator
A device used to eliminate or suppress the carrier frequency to produce the DSBSC signal. Multiplication of two inputs, the carrier frequency input and the modulation frequency input, is performed, resulting in the sum and difference products.

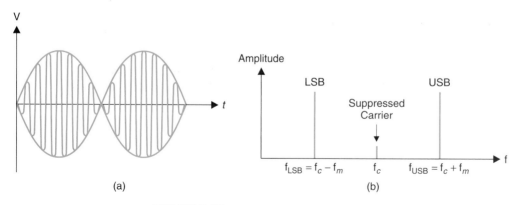

(a)   (b)

FIGURE 3-10
Double-sideband suppressed carrier (DSBSC) with sine-wave modulation: (a) time domain; (b) frequency domain.

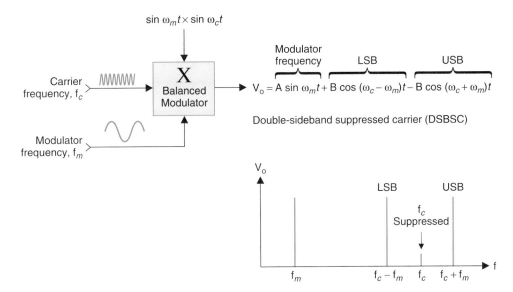

FIGURE 3-11
Block diagram of a balanced modulator.

sis of the output-frequency spectrum reveals that the balanced modulator performs a multiplication of these two input signals, thereby resulting in the sum and difference products.

The balanced modulator lends itself to a myriad of communications applications beyond generation of a DSBSC signal. It is also used extensively in communications receivers and transmitters, television sets, and high-speed modems.

3.7.2.1 Balanced Ring Modulator
Figure 3-12(a) illustrates a circuit that is commonly used as a balanced modulator; it is called a *balanced ring modulator* or a *diode ring modulator*. Semiconductor diodes are used as nonlinear devices, which are necessary to perform the *mixing* action of the carrier and the modulating frequencies. For optimum performance, the diodes and transformers should be closely matched and the amplitude of the carrier several times larger than the modulating amplitude. Operation of the balanced ring modulator circuit is as follows:

Diodes D1 through D4 in Figure 3-12(a) act as paired switches that are turned on and off during the positive and negative halves of the carrier frequency cycle. During the positive half, diodes D1 and D4 turn on, resulting in the condition shown in Figure 3-12(b), and the modulating signal is transferred from T1 to T2 with no phase change. Conversely, during the negative half, diodes D2 and D3 turn on, as shown in Figure 3-12(c). The modulating signal undergoes a 180° phase reversal from T1 to T2. The "chopped" modulation signal contains the LSB and USB frequency components, which are filtered at the output of transformer T2, thereby producing the DSBSC signal.

Suppression of the carrier frequency component occurs when the currents produced by the carrier signal split at the center taps of T1 and T2 and flow in opposite directions. This results in magnetic fields of equal magnitude and opposite phase in the upper and lower halves of transformers T1 and T2. Cancellation occurs, and the carrier frequency component is effectively suppressed. Figure 3-13 illustrates the bal-

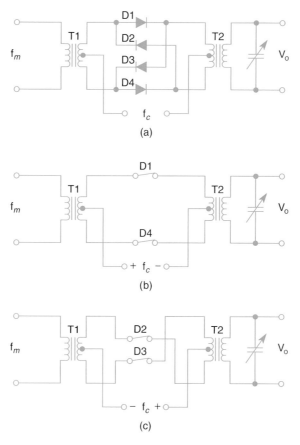

FIGURE 3-12

Balanced ring modulator circuit and its operation: (a) circuit diagram; (b) positive half of cycle D1 and D4 ON, D2 and D3 OFF; (c) negative half of cycle D2 and D3 ON, D1 and D4 OFF.

anced ring modulator's DSBSC waveform and its components. If the transformers and diodes are properly matched, the carrier component can be suppressed by as much as 60 dB.

3.7.2.2 Other Balanced Modulator Circuits

Two other common balanced modulator circuits are shown in Figure 3-14. The *dual-gate field-effect transistor (FET) balanced modulator* circuit in Figure 3-14(a) uses a standard push-pull amplifier configuration modified to include two inputs: one for the carrier frequency, and one for the modulating frequency. Like the balanced ring modulator circuit discussed earlier, a mixing action of the two signals results in the sum and difference products at the output of the circuit to the nonlinear characteristics of the FET.

The modulating frequency applied to transformer T1 is coupled to the gates of Q1 and Q2 180° out of phase from each other. A push-pull effect occurs between the two transistors. In other words, on the positive half of the modulation cycle, Q1's drain increases whereas Q2's drain current decreases, and vice versa on the negative half of the cycle. The carrier frequency signal is applied to transformer T3 and is coupled to the gates of Q1 and Q2 in phase. The drain currents produced are driven pos-

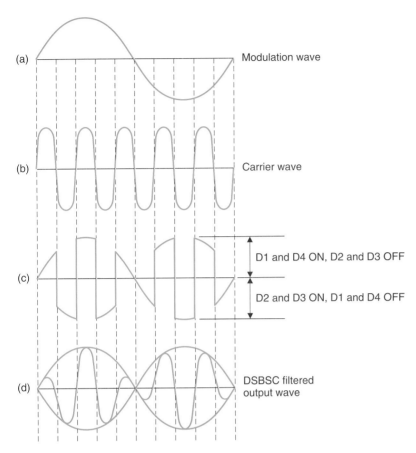

(a) Modulation wave

(b) Carrier wave

D1 and D4 ON, D2 and D3 OFF

(c)

D2 and D3 ON, D1 and D4 OFF

(d) DSBSC filtered output wave

FIGURE 3-13
The balanced ring modulator's DSBSC waveform and its components: (a) modulation wave; (b) carrier wave; (c) diode circuit output; (d) DSBSC filtered output.

itive and negative at the same time, resulting in their cancellation at transformer T2. The two signals combine with the quiescent currents from the supply to produce the sum and difference products, which must be filtered out at the output of T2.

Several integrated circuit (IC) manufacturers offer the popular 1496/1596 balanced modulator-demodulator IC. National Semiconductor's LM1496/1596 IC is shown in Figure 3-14(b). The LM1496 is specified for operation over the commercial-grade temperature range of 0°C to +70°C, whereas the LM1596 operates over the military-grade temperature range of −55°C to +125°C. The 1496/1596 offers 65-dB carrier suppression and can be used in several other applications, such as frequency doubling, SSB detection, AM generation, and more. Data sheets and application notes can be found in corresponding linear data manuals.

3.7.3 SSB Generation

We now examine how the LSB or USB from the DSBSC signal is selected to produce the SSB signal. Figure 3-15 illustrates this concept. It is apparent that SSB requires only half the bandwidth of the AM signal. Thus, SSB is not only power efficient, it is also bandwidth efficient.

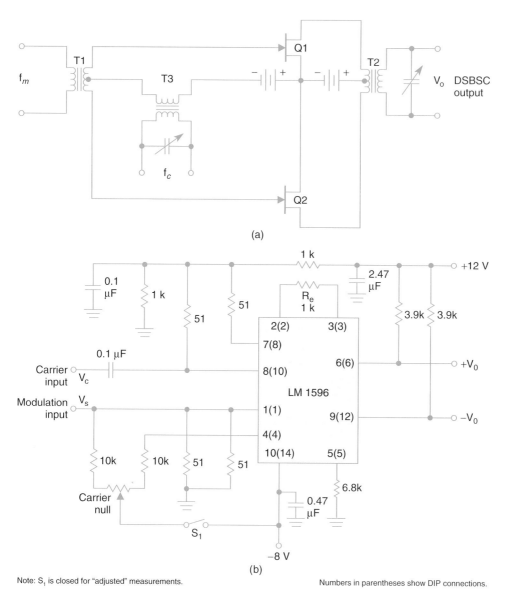

FIGURE 3-14

(a) Dual-gate field-effect transistor (FET) balanced modulator; (b) National Semiconductor's LM1496/1596 balanced modulator/demodulator integrated circuit (IC). (Courtesy of National Semiconductor Corp., *Linear Databook 3,* 1988, pp. 5–92 to 5–96.)

3.7.3.1 Filtering the SSB LSB or USB Selection of the LSB or USB for transmission in a SSB system requires high-Q (Q = resonant frequency/bandwidth) filters with steep attenuation characteristics. For example, a SSB transceiver operating in the 40-m amateur radio band may have a carrier frequency in the 7-MHz region. If the carrier frequency is modulated with a low-frequency tone of 100 Hz, then the USB and LSB are separated by only 200 Hz. Selecting the USB for transmission would require the filter to pass the USB frequency of 7.0001 MHz (f_c + 100 Hz) and totally reject 6.9999 MHz (f_c − 100 Hz). This type of selectivity over a range of 200 Hz would require a filter with a Q of 35,000 (7 MHz/200 Hz). For higher carrier fre-

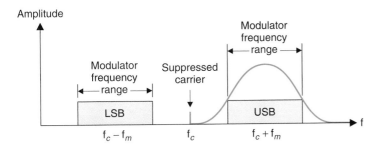

FIGURE 3-15
In a SSBSC or SSB system, the LSB or USB is selected for transmission. Here, the USB is selected.

quencies, even higher Qs would be necessary. This is highly impractical. Multistage LC filters with Qs beyond 200 are difficult and impractical to design. Furthermore, the ceramic, mechanical, and crystal filters used in SSB have Qs in the order of 2000, 10,000, and 50,000, respectively. If we lowered the carrier frequency in our example to, say, 100 khz, the Q would be significantly reduced to 500 (100 kHz/200Hz).

The USB can be selected and up-converted to the transmitting frequency. This is referred to as *dual-conversion*. The block diagram of a SSB dual-conversion filtering system is shown in Figure 3-16. The modulation frequency, f_m, is mixed with low carrier frequency, f_{c1}. The LSB and USB signals at the output of Balanced Modulator 1 are at a frequency better suited for SSB filtering. The USB is filtered out and mixed again with a higher carrier frequency, f_{c2}. The output of Balanced Modulator 2 now contains sideband frequencies that are separated by a frequency range compatible with SSB filters. (Chapter 12 shows how SSB is used with frequency division multiplexing [FDM] in the telephone system to combine thousands of voice channels onto a single coaxial cable or microwave link.)

> **Dual Conversion**
> In single-sideband generation, dual conversion refers to the process of up-converting the modulating frequency twice and selecting the upper or lower sideband for transmission.

3.8 VESTIGIAL SIDEBAND

As shown with SSB, filtering of one sideband leads to a reduction in bandwidth and transmitted power. Completely filtering out one of the sidebands requires special filtering and conversion techniques. An intermediate AM technique between SSB and DSBFC is called *vestigial sideband (VSB)*, which is used in the commercial television industry for the transmission and reception of television video signals. In VSB, a portion (or vestige) of the lower sideband is transmitted along with the full carrier power and upper-sideband content. This ensures that the USB, including the video carrier, is transmitted in its entirety. Some savings in power and bandwidth are realized over DSBFC as well.

The FCC has designated a total of 82 television channels in which the VSB video and FM sound signals are transmitted and received. Table 3-1 details these standard channels and their respective frequency bands. Each channel occupies a bandwidth of 6 MHz. There are 12 VHF channels (2 through 13) and 70 UHF channels (14 through 83). Figure 3-17(a) illustrates the format of these channels for monochrome (black and white) and color television picture and sound transmission. As an example, Figure 13-17(b) shows the frequency assignment for channel 2.

From Figure 3-17, it can be seen that the lower video sideband, or VSB, occupies the first 1.25 MHz of the 6-MHz bandwidth allocation per channel. Transmitting this portion of the lower sideband ensures that a flat response exits at the picture

> **Vestigial Sideband (VSB)**
> An intermediate AM technique between SSB and DSBFC in which a portion of the lower sideband is transmitted along with the full carrier power and upper-sideband content, ensuring that the USB, including the video carrier, is transmitted in its entirety. Used in the commercial TV industry for transmission and reception of television video signals.

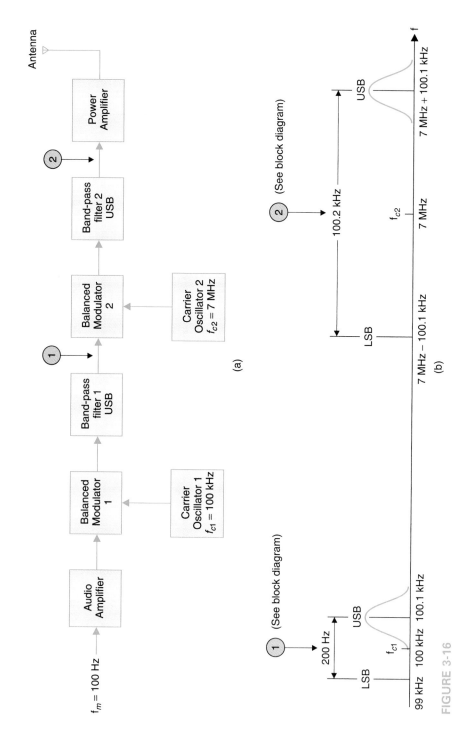

FIGURE 3-16

(a) Block diagram of a SSB dual-conversion filter system; (b) frequency response depicting the increased frequency separation between the LSB and USB because of dual conversion.

TABLE 3-1
VHF and UHF Television Channel Allocation in the United States

VHF Channels

Channel	Frequency Band, MHz
2	54–60
3	60–66
4	66–72
5	76–82
6	82–88
7	174–180
8	180–186
9	186–192
10	192–198
11	198–204
12	204–210
13	210–216

UHF Channels

Channel	Frequency Band, MHz	Channel	Frequency Band, MHz	Channel	Frequency Band, MHz	Channel	Frequency Band, MHz
14	470–476	28	554–560	42	638–644	56	722–728
15	476–482	29	560–566	43	644–650	57	728–734
16	482–488	30	566–572	44	650–656	58	734–740
17	488–494	31	572–578	45	656–662	59	740–746
18	494–500	32	578–584	46	662–668	60	746–752
19	500–506	33	584–590	47	668–674	61	752–758
20	506–512	34	590–596	48	674–680	62	758–764
21	512–518	35	596–602	49	680–686	63	764–770
22	518–524	36	602–608	50	686–692	64	770–776
23	524–530	37	608–614	51	692–698	65	776–782
24	530–536	38	614–620	52	698–704	66	782–788
25	536–542	39	620–626	53	704–710	67	788–794
26	542–548	40	626–632	54	710–716	68	794–800
27	548–554	41	632–638	55	716–722	69	800–806

Channel	Frequency Band, MHz
70	806–812
71	812–818
72	818–824
73	824–830
74	830–836
75	836–842
76	842–848
77	848–854
78	854–860
79	860–866
80	866–872
81	872–878
82	878–884
83	884–890

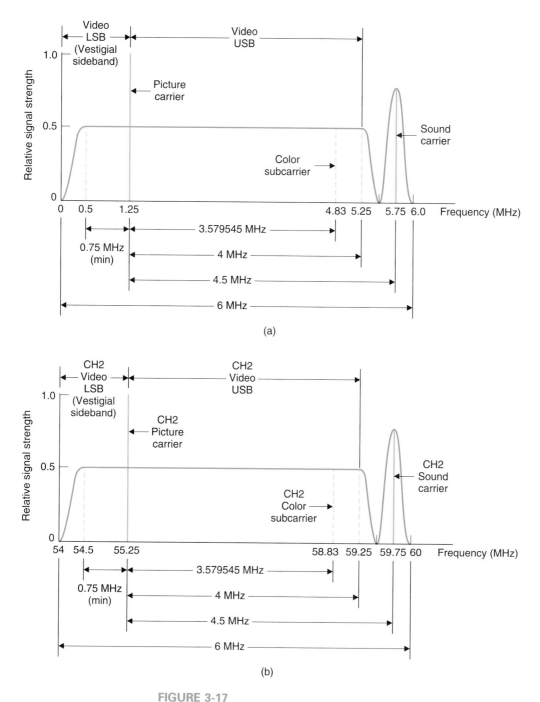

FIGURE 3-17

(a) Standard FCC channel format for monochrome and color picture transmissions in the United States; (b) channel 2 frequency assignment.

carrier frequency and video signal above it; that is, no attenuation or phase distortion of the upper sideband or picture carrier occurs. In essence, the VSB acts as a guard-band. The video signal is 4.0-MHz wide and occupies the frequency range just above the picture carrier frequency. A minimum of 0.75 MHz just below the picture carrier is flat before the frequency response rapidly falls off for the next 0.5 MHz. Because the picture carrier is preserved in a VSB, the receiver does not have the task of rein-serting it for demodulation, as in an SSB. Furthermore, tuning of the signal at the re-ceiver is simplified due to the added power of transmitting the picture carrier and the VSB.

    The sound carrier is located 4.5 MHz above the picture carrier and occupies a bandwidth of 50 kHz. Unlike the amplitude-modulated video signal, the audio signal is stereo FM (frequency modulation). The audio frequency range designated by the FCC is 50 to 15 kHz, with a maximum deviation of 25 kHz for 100% modulation.

PROBLEMS

1. Explain why the op-amp summing device shown in Figure 3.1 does not produce an AM wave.
2. What type of device is used to produce an AM wave?
3. Write the equation for the instantaneous voltage of a sine wave, e_m, used to modulate a carrier frequency given a modulation frequency, f_m, equal to 1 kHz.
4. Write the equation for the instantaneous voltage of a carrier wave, e_c, used for an AM sig-nal given a carrier frequency, f_c, equal to 625 kHz.
5. An AM wave has a peak modulation voltage, V_m, of 1.5 V and a peak carrier voltage, V_c, of 4.0 V. Compute the modulation index, m, and percent modulation index, M.
6. Compute the modulation index for the waveform:

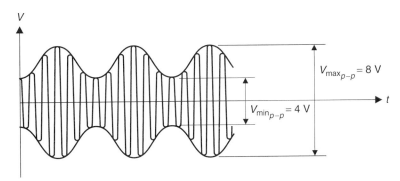

7. Compute the modulation index for the waveform:

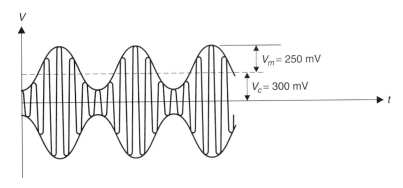

8. A carrier signal with a peak voltage of 50 V is amplitude modulated with a 1-kHz test tone. The modulation voltage has an effective value of 5 V. Compute the following:
   a. The percent modulation index, M.
   b. The instantaneous voltage of the positive and negative envelope when the 1-kHz sine wave has completed 810 μs of its cycle.
   c. Illustrate the waveform showing voltage levels and times.
9. Repeat problem 8 using a 2-kHz test tone.
10. What frequency components make up an AM wave with sine-wave modulation?
11. Write the equation for an AM waveform (sine-wave modulation) in its entirety, and identify the upper- and lower-sideband and carrier frequency components.
12. An AM broadcast station's peak carrier voltage of 1.5 kV has been amplitude modulated to a depth of 35% with a 10-kHz sine wave. The station's broadcast frequency is 1500 kHz. Compute the following:
    a. The upper- and lower-sideband frequencies, USB and LSB.
    b. The peak modulation voltage, V_m.
    c. The peak upper- and lower-sideband voltages, V_{USB} and V_{LSB}.
    d. The maximum signal amplitude.
13. An AM signal with a peak carrier voltage of 12 V has been amplitude modulated to a depth of 58% with a 5-kHz sine wave. The station's broadcast frequency is 1 MHz. Compute the following:
    a. The upper- and lower-sideband frequencies, USB and LSB.
    b. The peak modulation voltage, V_m.
    c. The peak upper- and lower-sideband voltages, V_{USB} and V_{LSB}.
    d. The maximum signal amplitude.
14. A spectrum analyzer with an input impedance of 50 Ω is used to measure the power spectrum of an AM signal at the output of an automatic gain control circuit. Sine-wave modulation is used. The effective carrier power, P_C, is 1 W, and the upper- and lower-sideband power components are 130 mW. Compute the following:
    a. The total effective power of the AM wave, P_T.
    b. The peak carrier voltage, V_c.
    c. The percent modulation index, M.
    d. The modulation voltage, V_m.
    e. The upper- and lower-sideband voltages, V_{USB} and V_{LSB}.
15. Repeat problem 14 for an effective carrier power of 3 W and the same upper- and lower-sideband power components.
16. An AM transmitter has an effective carrier power of 15 kW. If the carrier is modulated with a sine wave, compute the following:
    a. The total effective transmitted power with a 50% modulation index.
    b. The total effective power in each sideband with a 100% modulation index.
17. An AM transmitter has an effective carrier power of 25 kW. If the carrier is modulated with a sine wave, compute the following:
    a. The total effective transmitted power with a 25% modulation index.
    b. The total effective power in each sideband with a 100% modulation index.
18. Explain the function of a balanced modulator in terms of AM generation.
19. In the balanced ring modulator shown in Figure 3-12, which diodes are on during the negative halves of the carrier cycle?
20. Define *vestigial sideband.*
21. What television frequency band has the FCC allocated for channel 5?

FREQUENCY MODULATION

An inherent problem with AM is its susceptibility to noise superimposed on the modulated carrier signal. If this noise falls within the passband of the receiving system and its amplitude is large enough, it will interfere with the detected intelligence. To improve on this shortcoming, Major Edwin E. Armstrong has been credited with developing in 1936 the first *frequency modulation (FM)* radio communication system, a system that is much more immune to noise than its AM counterpart.

Since its inception, FM has remained one of the most prevalent modulation techniques in the telecommunications industry, being used in applications such as cellular and cordless telephony, paging systems, modem technology, television, commercial FM broadcast, amateur radio, and more. It is the best choice for fidelity and offers a much higher SNR than its AM counterpart.

In this chapter, the principles of FM are examined. We do not present an entire analysis of an FM transmitter and receiver; it would take several chapters to do justice to that lengthy subject. A brief comparison of phase modulation (PM) is presented, however, so the student understands that both FM and PM are regarded as *angle modulation.* Unlike amplitude modulation, FM is difficult to treat mathematically due to the complexity of the sideband behavior resulting from the modulation process. For this reason, mathematical presentations are limited to the conventional treatment, using both charts and table derivations.

> **Angle Modulation**
> A modulation technique in which the intelligence of the modulating signal is conveyed by means of varying (modulating) the frequency or phase of the carrier signal.

4.1 ANGLE MODULATION

In AM, the amplitude of the carrier signal varies as a function of the amplitude of the modulating signal. The intelligence of the modulating signal can be conveyed by varying the frequency or phase of the carrier signal. When this is the case, we have *angle modulation,* which can be subdivided into two categories: *frequency modulation (FM),* and *phase modulation (PM).* Figure 4-1 illustrates the FM and PM waveforms for sine-wave modulation. They are defined as follows:

Frequency Modulation. *The carrier's instantaneous frequency deviation from its unmodulated value varies in proportion to the instantaneous amplitude of the modulating signal.*

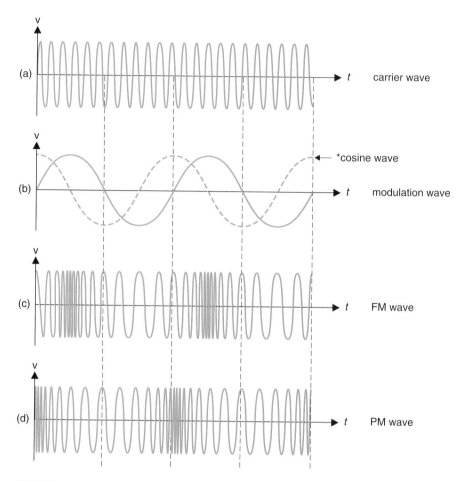

FIGURE 4-1

The FM and PM waveforms for sine-wave modulation: (a) carrier wave; (b) modulation wave; (c) FM wave; (d) PM wave. (*Note:* The derivative of the modulating sine wave is the cosine wave shown by the dotted lines. The PM wave appears to be frequency modulated by the cosine wave.)

Phase Modulation. *The carrier's instantaneous phase deviation from its unmodulated value varies as a function of the instantaneous amplitude of the modulating signal; in other words, the carrier deviation is proportional to the rate of change of the modulating signal. In calculus, this is the derivative of the modulating signal.*

The mathematical derivations for the equations representing the FM and PM waveforms are best explained through use of integral calculus. We will spare the reader from the complexity of these derivations, however, and present only their solutions.* Thus, for FM, the instantaneous voltage for the waveform with sine-wave modulation is

$$e_{\text{FM}} = A_c \sin(\omega_c t + m_f \sin \omega_m t) \tag{4-1}$$

---

*The mathematical derivations for equations (4-1) and (4-2) can be found in most electronic communications texts written for engineering students.

and, for PM,

$$e_{PM} = A_c \sin(\omega_c t + \phi_m \sin \omega_m t) \qquad \textbf{(4-2)}$$

where e_{FM} = instantaneous voltage of the FM wave
   e_{PM} = instantaneous voltage of the PM wave
   A_c = peak amplitude of the carrier
   ω_c = angular velocity of the carrier
   ω_m = angular velocity of the modulating signal
   $\omega_c t$ = carrier phase in radians
   $\omega_m t$ = modulation phase in radians
   m_f = FM modulation index
   ϕ_m = maximum phase deviation in radians caused by the modulating signal
   (also regarded as the *PM modulation index*)

4.2   MODULATION INDEX

From the waveforms and equations for FM and PM, it is apparent that an immediate distinction cannot be made between the two. It is necessary to know the modulation function.* That is, the waveform alone cannot be used to distinguish between FM and PM. It is their modulation indices, m_f and ϕ_m that differ.

The modulation index for an FM signal is defined as the ratio of the maximum *frequency deviation* to the modulating signal's frequency. It is given by

$$m_f = \frac{\delta}{f_m} \qquad \textbf{(4-3)}$$

> **Frequency Deviation**
> In an FM signal, frequency deviation, δ, is the maximum frequency deviation of the carrier frequency caused by the amplitude of the modulating signal.

where m_f = modulation index for FM
   δ = maximum frequency deviation of the carrier caused by the amplitude of the modulating signal
   f_m = frequency of the modulating signal

Note that the modulation index, m_f, for FM is *proportional* to the amplitude of the modulating signal through δ and *inversely proportional* to the frequency of the modulating signal. Herein lies the subtle difference between FM and PM. Although the modulation index, ϕ_m, for a PM signal is proportional to the amplitude of the modulating signal, in contrast to FM it is also *dependent* on the modulation frequency whereas FM is not. Figure 4-2 illustrates these subtle differences between FM and PM.

4.3   FREQUENCY ANALYSIS OF THE FM WAVE

Recall that in AM, the frequency components consist of a fixed carrier frequency with upper and lower sidebands equally displaced above and below the carrier frequency. The frequency components of the upper and lower sidebands are mirror images of each other and identical to that of the modulating signal, except that they translate up to the carrier frequency. The frequency spectrum of the FM wave is much more complex, however. In equation (4-1), a single sinusoid used to modulate the FM carrier

---

Transmission Systems for Communications, 4th ed. (Bell Laboratories, 1971), pp. 111–112.

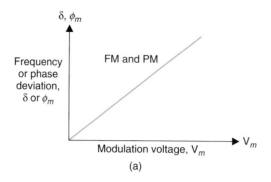

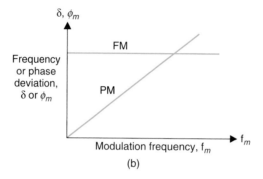

FIGURE 4-2

Comparison of FM and PM. Frequency or phase deviation versus: (a) modulation voltage; (b) modulation frequency.

produces an infinite number of sidebands. Furthermore, the complexity of the sideband activity increases with the frequency complexity in the modulating signal.

Analysis of the frequency components and their respective amplitudes in the FM wave requires use of a complex mathematical integral known as the *Bessel function of the first kind of the nth order.*[*] Evaluating this integral for sine-wave modulation yields

Bessel Function
A complex mathematical integral used in analyzing the frequency components and their respective amplitudes in the FM wave. Bessel functions are represented by each set of upper and lower sidebands displaced from the carrier frequency by an integral multiple of the modulation frequency.

$$
\begin{aligned}
e_{FM} = \; & A_c J_0 \, (m_f) \, \sin \omega_c t \\
& + A_c \, \{J_1 \, (m_f) \, [\sin(\omega_c + \omega_m)t - \sin(\omega_c - \omega_m)t]\} \\
& + A_c \, \{J_2 \, (m_f) \, [\sin(\omega_c + 2\omega_m)t - \sin(\omega_c - 2\omega_m)t]\} \\
& + A_c \, \{J_3 \, (m_f) \, [\sin(\omega_c + 3\omega_m)t - \sin(\omega_c - 3\omega_m)t]\} \\
& + A_c \, \{J_4 \, (m_f) \, [\sin(\omega_c + 4\omega_m)t - \sin(\omega_c - 4\omega_m)t]\} \\
& + \dots, \text{etc.}
\end{aligned}
\tag{4-4}
$$

where e_{FM} = the instantaneous amplitude of the modulated FM wave
  A_c = the peak amplitude of the carrier
  J_n = solution to the nth order Bessel function for a modulation index m_f.
  m_f = FM modulation index

---

[*]Leon W. Couch II, *Digital and Analog Communication Systems,* 2nd ed. (New York: MacMillan, 1987), p. 280.

and

$A_c J_0 \, (m_f) \sin \omega_c t =$ the carrier frequency component

$A_c \{ J_1 \, (m_f) \, [\sin(\omega_c + \omega_m)t - \sin(\omega_c - \omega_m)t] \} =$ the first-order sideband

$A_c \{ J_2 \, (m_f) \, [\sin(\omega_c + 2\omega_m)t - \sin(\omega_c - 2\omega_m)t] \} =$ the second-order sideband

$A_c \{ J_3 \, (m_f) \, [\sin(\omega_c + 3\omega_m)t - \sin(\omega_c - 3\omega_m)t] \} =$ the third-order sideband

$A_c \{ J_n \, (m_f) \, [\sin(\omega_c + n\omega_m)t - \sin(\omega_c - n\omega_m)t] \} =$ the nth-order sideband

It is apparent from equation (4-4) that the FM wave contains an infinite number of sideband components whose individual amplitudes are preceded by $J_n(m_f)$ coefficients. Each set of upper and lower sidebands is displaced from the carrier frequency by an integral multiple of the modulation frequency. These are the Bessel functions; tabulated Bessel functions to the sixteenth order for modulation indices ranging from 0 to 15 are listed in Table 4-1. The successive sets of sidebands are referred to as *first-order sidebands, second-order sidebands,* and so on. A plot of the Bessel functions, as shown in Figure 4-3, illustrates the relationship between the carrier and sideband amplitudes for sine-wave modulation as a function of modulation index, *m*. From the curves or the table, we can obtain the amplitudes of the carrier and sideband components in relation to the unmodulated carrier.

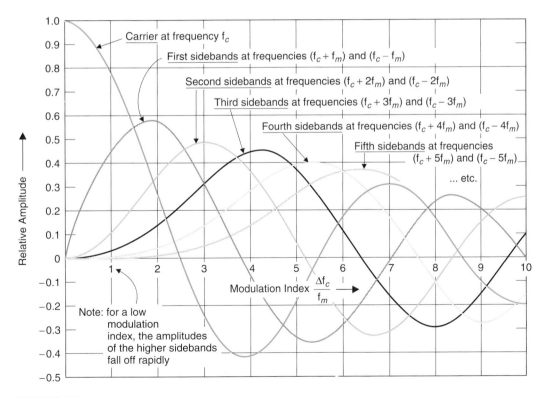

FIGURE 4-3

Spectral components of a carrier of frequency, f_c, frequency modulated by a sine wave with frequency f_m. (*Source:* James Martin, *Telecommunications and the Computer,* 2nd ed. [Englewood Cliffs, N.J.: Prentice-Hall, 1976], p. 218. Reprinted with permission from the publisher.)

TABLE 4-1
Bessel Functions of the First Kind

Modulation Index (m_f)	J_0	J_1	J_2	J_3	J_4	J_5	J_6	J_7	J_8	J_9	J_{10}	J_{11}	J_{12}	J_{13}	J_{14}	J_{15}	J_{16}
0.00	1.00	—	—	—	—	—	—	—	—	—	—	—	—	—	—	—	—
0.25	0.98	0.12	—	—	—	—	—	—	—	—	—	—	—	—	—	—	—
0.5	0.94	0.24	0.03	—	—	—	—	—	—	—	—	—	—	—	—	—	—
1.0	0.77	0.44	0.11	0.02	—	—	—	—	—	—	—	—	—	—	—	—	—
1.5	0.51	0.56	0.23	0.06	0.01	—	—	—	—	—	—	—	—	—	—	—	—
2.0	0.22	0.58	0.35	0.13	0.03	—	—	—	—	—	—	—	—	—	—	—	—
2.5	−0.05	0.50	0.45	0.22	0.07	0.02	—	—	—	—	—	—	—	—	—	—	—
3.0	−0.26	0.34	0.49	0.31	0.13	0.04	0.01	—	—	—	—	—	—	—	—	—	—
4.0	−0.40	−0.07	0.36	0.43	0.28	0.13	0.05	0.02	—	—	—	—	—	—	—	—	—
5.0	−0.18	−0.33	0.05	0.36	0.39	0.26	0.13	0.05	0.02	—	—	—	—	—	—	—	—
6.0	0.15	−0.28	−0.24	0.11	0.36	0.36	0.25	0.13	0.06	0.02	—	—	—	—	—	—	—
7.0	0.30	0.00	−0.30	−0.17	0.16	0.35	0.34	0.23	0.13	0.06	0.02	—	—	—	—	—	—
8.0	0.17	0.23	−0.11	−0.29	−0.10	0.19	0.34	0.32	0.22	0.13	0.06	0.03	—	—	—	—	—
9.0	−0.09	0.24	0.14	−0.18	−0.27	−0.06	0.20	0.33	0.30	0.21	0.12	0.06	0.03	0.01	—	—	—
10.0	−0.25	0.04	0.25	0.06	−0.22	−0.23	−0.01	0.22	0.31	0.29	0.20	0.12	0.06	0.03	0.01	—	—
12.0	0.05	−0.22	−0.08	0.20	0.18	−0.07	−0.24	−0.17	0.05	0.23	0.30	0.27	0.20	0.12	0.07	0.03	0.01
15.0	−0.01	0.21	0.04	−0.19	−0.12	0.13	0.21	0.03	−0.17	−0.22	−0.09	0.10	0.24	0.28	0.25	0.18	0.12

n or Order of Sidebands

Carrier Frequency

Source: E. Cambi, *Bessel Functions* (New York: Dover Publications, 1948). Courtesy of the publisher.

Find the carrier and sideband amplitudes to the fourth-order sideband for a modulation index of $m_f = 3$. The peak amplitude of the carrier, A_c, from equation (4-4), is 10 V.

EXAMPLE
4.1

Solution:
From Table 4-1 or Figure 4-3, we have

$$J_0(m3) = -0.26$$
$$J_1(m3) = 0.34$$
$$J_2(m3) = 0.49$$
$$J_n(m3) = 0.31$$
$$J_4(m3) = 0.13$$

and, therefore,

$$J_0 = -0.26 \times 10 \text{ V} = -2.6 \text{ V}$$
$$J_1 = 0.34 \times 10 \text{ V} = 3.4 \text{ V}$$
$$J_2 = 0.49 \times 10 \text{ V} = 4.9 \text{ V}$$
$$J_3 = 0.31 \times 10 \text{ V} = 3.1 \text{ V}$$
$$J_4 = 0.13 \times 10 \text{ V} = 1.3 \text{ V}$$

From Table 4-1 and Figure 4-3, the FM signal is characterized as follows:

- The FM wave is comprised of an infinite number of sideband components whose individual amplitudes are preceded by $J_n(m_f)$ coefficients.
- Each set of upper and lower sidebands are displaced from the carrier frequency by an integral multiple of the modulation frequency.
- As the modulation index increases from $m_f = 0$, the spectral energy shifts from the carrier frequency to an increasing number of significant sidebands. This suggests that a wider bandwidth is necessary to recover the FM signal.
- The magnitudes of the sideband amplitudes, $J_n(m_f)$ coefficients, decrease in value with increasing order, n.
- For higher-order sidebands, the magnitudes of the sideband amplitudes, $J_n(m_f)$ coefficients, increase in value with increasing modulation index, m_f.
- Sideband amplitudes with negative $J_n(m_f)$ coefficients imply a 180° phase inversion. Because a spectrum analyzer displays only absolute amplitudes, the negative signs have no significance.
- The carrier component, J_0, and various sidebands, J_n, go to zero amplitude at specific values of modulation index, m_f.

4.3.1   Carrier Frequency Eigenvalues

As stated earlier, in some cases the carrier frequency component, J_0, and the various sidebands, J_n, go to zero amplitudes at specific values of m. These values are called *eigenvalues*. Table 4-2 lists the values of the modulation index for which the carrier amplitude goes to zero, and this implies that one can easily estimate the modulation index for an FM signal with sine-wave modulation by use of a spectrum analyzer. The displayed number of sidebands and their respective amplitudes are simply noted and used in conjunction with Figure 4-3, Table 4-1, and Table 4-2 to determine the modulation index.

> **Eigenvalues**
> In an FM signal, the values of the modulation index for which the carrier amplitude or the sideband components go to zero amplitude.

TABLE 4-2
Modulation Index Values for which the Carrier Amplitude Is Zero

Order of Carrier Frequency Eigenvalues	Modulation Index, m_f
1	2.40
2	5.52
3	8.65
4	11.79
5	14.93
6	18.07
$n(n > 6)$	$18.07 + \pi(n - 6)$

Source: Spectrum Analysis Amplitude and Frequency Modulation, Hewlett-Packard Application Note 150-1, November 1971, pp. 9–11.

EXAMPLE 4.2

A spectrum analyzer is used to verify an FM signal with a carrier frequency of 100.3 MHz, a modulation frequency of 15 kHz, and a modulation index of $m_f = 2.4$.
(a) Determine the number of significant sideband pairs.
(b) Predict the spectrum-analyzer display for the signal, and show the relative amplitudes of each sideband pair.
(c) Compute the frequency deviation, δ.

Solution:

(a) The number of significant sideband pairs can be found from the Bessel functions listed in Table 4-1. For a modulation index of 2.4, we can estimate (using $m_f = 2.5$ from the table) that the number of significant sideband pairs is 5: J_1 through J_5.
(b) From Table 4-2, a modulation index of 2.4 corresponds to the first carrier frequency null or eigenvalue. We know that the carrier frequency component is zero, and the relative amplitudes of the sidebands can be determined from Table 4-1 and Figure 4-3. Figure 4-4 illustrates the frequency spectrum for the FM signal.

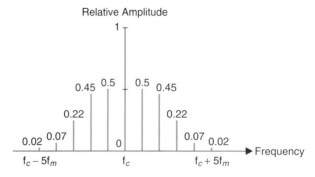

FIGURE 4-4
Frequency spectrum of an FM signal with a modulation index, m_f, of 2.4 (first carrier null or eigenvalue). Note that the carrier amplitude goes to zero. Relative amplitudes are approximated from Table 4-1 using $m_f = 2.5$.

The five sidebands on either side of the carrier frequency, f_c, and their relative amplitudes correspond to a modulation index of $m_f = 2.5$, which is a close approximation.

(c) From equation (4-3),

$$m_f = \frac{\delta}{f_m}$$

and, therefore,

$$\delta = m_f \cdot f_m = 2.4 \times 15 \text{ kHz} = 36 \text{ kHz}$$

4.3.2 Bandwidth Requirements for FM

In theory, the FM wave contains an infinite number of sidebands, thus suggesting an infinite bandwidth requirement for transmission or reception. In practice, however, the sideband amplitudes become negligible beyond a certain frequency range from the carrier. This range is a function of modulation index, m_f, that is, the ratio of carrier frequency deviation to modulating frequency (equation [4-3]). The higher the modulation index, the greater the required system bandwidth. This was shown earlier in the listing of Bessel functions (Table 4-1). Figure 4-5 is a more graphical illustration of how the FM system's bandwidth requirements grow with an increasing modulation index. Here, the modulation frequency, f_m, is held constant, whereas the carrier frequency deviation, δ, is increased (and, consequently, m_f as well) in proportion to the amplitude of the modulation signal.

Based on the Bessel functions listed in Table 4-1, Table 4-3 lists the number of significant sideband components corresponding to various modulation indices. By "significant," we usually mean all of those sidebands having a voltage of at least 1%, or -40 dB ($20 \log \frac{1}{100}$), of the voltage of the unmodulated carrier. The bandwidth requirements for an FM signal can be computed by

$$BW = 2 \, (n \cdot f_m) \tag{4-5}$$

where n is the highest number of significant sideband components and f_m is the highest modulation frequency.

4.3.2.1 Carson's Rule
From our previous discussion, it is evident that the bandwidth of an FM signal must be wider than that of an AM signal. In establishing the quality of transmission and reception desired, a limitation must be placed on the number of *significant* sidebands that the FM system must pass. In 1938, J. R. Carson first stated in an unpublished memorandum that the minimum bandwidth required for the transmission of an angle modulated wave is equal to two times the sum of the peak frequency deviation, δ, plus the highest modulating frequency, f_m, to be transmitted.* This rule is known as *Carson's Rule:*

$$BW = 2 \, (\delta + f_m) \tag{4-6}$$

> **Carson's Rule**
> For transmission of an angle-modulated wave, the minimum bandwidth required is equal to two times the sum of the peak frequency deviation, δ, plus the highest modulation frequency, f_m: BW = 2.

Transmission Systems for Communications, 4th ed. (Bell Laboratories, 1971), p. 115.

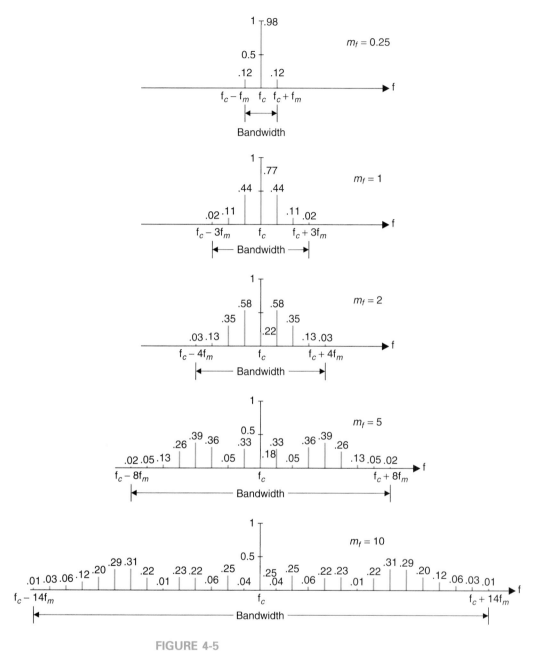

FIGURE 4-5

Amplitude versus frequency spectrum for various modulation indices (f_m fixed, δ varying): (a) $m_f = 0.25$; (b) $m_f = 1$; (c) $m_f = 2$; (d) $m_f = 5$; (e) $m_f = 10$.

EXAMPLE 4.3

The FCC permits commercial FM broadcast stations to transmit audio signals up to 15 kHz, with a maximum permissible deviation of 75 kHz. Compute the following:

(a) the modulation index, m_f.

(b) the BW of the FM signal using equation (4-5) and Table 4-3.

(c) the BW of the FM signal using Carson's Rule.

TABLE 4-3
Modulation Index versus the Number of Significant Sidebands

Modulation index, m_f	Significant sidebands, n
0.00	0
0.25	1
0.50	2
1.00	3
2.00	4
3.00	6
4.00	7
5.00	8
7.00	10
10.00	14
15.00	16

Solution:

(a) Using equation (4-3), we have

$$m_f = \frac{\delta}{f_m} = \frac{75 \text{ kHz}}{15 \text{ kHz}} = 5$$

(b) Using equation (4-5) and Table 4-3, we have

$$BW = 2(n \cdot f_m) = 2 \, (8 \cdot 15 \text{ kHz}) = 240 \text{ kHz}$$

(c) Using Carson's Rule and equation (4-6), we have

$$BW = 2 \, (\delta + f_m) = 2 \, (75 \text{ kHz} + 15 \text{ kHz}) = 180 \text{ kHz}$$

Carson's Rule gives results that agree with the bandwidths used in the telecommunications industry. It should be noted, however, that this is only an approximation used to limit the number of significant sidebands for minimal distortion.

4.3.2.2 Broadcast FM The commercial FM broadcast band, as shown in Figure 4-6, extends from 88 to 108 MHz and is divided into 100 channels. The FCC has allocated a bandwidth of 200 kHz and designated a numerical value, N, for each channel. Channels range from 88.1 MHz, where $N = 201$, to 107.9 MHz, where $N = 300$. Thus, FM broadcast stations can only be tuned at *odd* intervals of 200 kHz (e.g., 100.1 MHz, 100.3 MHz, and so on). The channel number, N, or its corresponding broadcast frequency can be computed as

> **Broadcast FM**
> Also known as *commercial FM,* the FM broadcast band extends from 88 to 108 MHz and includes 100 FM stations separated by 200 kHz.

$$N = 5(f - 47.9)$$

or

$$f = \frac{N}{5} + 47.9 \qquad \textbf{(4-7)}$$

where $N =$ the FM broadcast channel number
$f =$ the frequency in MHz

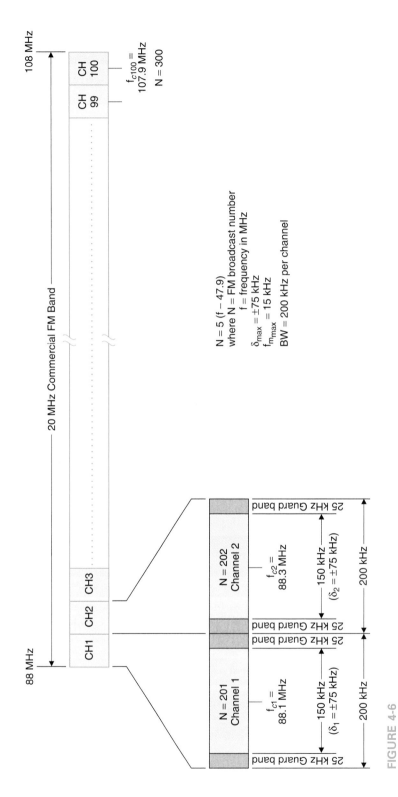

FIGURE 4-6
Commercial FM broadcast band.

$N = 5 (f - 47.9)$
where N = FM broadcast number
f = frequency in MHz
$\delta_{max} = \pm75$ kHz
$f_{m_{max}} = 15$ kHz
$BW = 200$ kHz per channel

20 MHz Commercial FM Band

108 MHz

CH 100
CH 99

$f_{c100} = 107.9$ MHz
$N = 300$

88 MHz

CH1   CH2   CH3

$N = 201$
Channel 1

$f_{c1} = 88.1$ MHz

150 kHz
$(\delta_1 = \pm75$ kHz)

200 kHz

25 kHz Guard band

$N = 202$
Channel 2

$f_{c2} = 88.3$ MHz

150 kHz
$(\delta_2 = \pm75$ kHz)

200 kHz

25 kHz Guard band

The maximum permissible carrier deviation, δ, is ± 75 kHz. The transmitter is permitted to modulate its carrier frequency with a band of frequencies ranging from 50 Hz to 15 kHz. Thus, the modulation index can range from as low as 5 for $f_m = 15$ kHz (75 kHz/15 kHz) to as high as 1500 for $f_m = 50$ Hz (75 kHz/50 Hz). The ± 75-kHz carrier deviation results in an FM bandwidth requirement of 150 kHz for the receiver. A 25-kHz *guard band* above and below the upper and lower FM sidebands makes up the remaining 50 kHz of the 200-kHz channel and prevents the sidebands from interfering with adjacent channels.

> **Guard Band**
> A range of frequencies separating transmitted channels in which no signals should be transmitted.

4.3.2.3   Narrowband FM   In contrast to the relatively wide bandwidth of broadcast FM, *narrowband FM* refers to FM systems in which the FCC has allocated bandwidths ranging from 10 to 30 kHz. The demand for use of the spectrum has led to the popularity of narrowband FM. Modulation indices are generally kept near unity so that the FM bandwidth can be computed in the same manner as the AM bandwidth. In other words, BW is simply $2 \times f_m$. Examples of narrowband FM include mobile radio systems for police, fire, and taxi services; cellular telephony; amateur radio; and so on.

4.4   POWER IN THE FM WAVE

The total power in an FM wave is distributed in the carrier and the sideband components. If we sum the power in the carrier and all the sidebands for any given modulation index, it will equal the total power of the unmodulated carrier. Thus, it can be shown that for an unmodulated carrier ($m_f = 0$),

$$P_T = \frac{V_{crms}^2}{R} \tag{4-8}$$

where P_T = the total rms power of the unmodulated wave
V_{crms} = the rms voltage of the carrier signal
R = resistance of the load

For a modulated carrier,

$$P_T = P_{J_0} + P_{J_1} + P_{J_2} + P_{J_3} + ... + P_{J_n} \tag{4-9}$$

$$= \frac{V_{J_0}^2}{R} + \frac{2(V_{J_1})^2}{R} + \frac{2(V_{J_2})^2}{R} + \frac{2(V_{J_3})^2}{R} + ... + \frac{2(V_{J_n})^2}{R} \tag{4-10}$$

where

P_T = the total rms power of the FM wave
P_{J_0} = rms power in the carrier
P_{J_1} = rms power in the first set of sidebands
P_{J_2} = rms power in the second set of sidebands
P_{J_3} = rms power in the third set of sidebands
P_{J_n} = rms power in the nth set of sidebands
V_{J_0} through V_{J_n} = the rms voltage of the carrier through the nth sideband, respectively.

EXAMPLE 4.4

In Example 4.1, the carrier and sideband amplitudes to the fourth order were solved for a modulation index of 3 and a peak carrier amplitude of 10 V. Use the solutions from Example 4.1 to prove that the total power in an unmodulated FM wave equals the total power in the modulated FM wave. Assume that the modulated and unmodulated wave is delivered to a 50-Ω load.

Solution:

We need to prove that equation (4-8) equals equation (4-9). Using equation (4-8), we have

$$P_T = \frac{V^2_{crms}}{R} = \frac{(0.707 \times 10 \text{ V})^2}{50 \ \Omega} = 1.00 \text{ W}$$

From Example 4.1 the peak carrier and sideband amplitudes can be converted to their rms values:

$$J_0 = 0.707 \times -2.6 \text{ V} = -1.838 \text{ V}$$
$$J_1 = 0.707 \times 3.4 \text{ V} = 2.404 \text{ V}$$
$$J_2 = 0.707 \times 4.9 \text{ V} = 3.464 \text{ V}$$
$$J_n = 0.707 \times 3.1 \text{ V} = 2.192 \text{ V}$$
$$J_4 = 0.707 \times 1.3 \text{ V} = 0.919 \text{ V}$$

Using these values with equations (4-9) and (4-10), we have

$$
\begin{aligned}
P_T &= P_{J_0} + P_{J_1} + P_{J_2} + P_{J_3} + P_{J_4} \\
&= \frac{V_{J_0}{}^2}{R} + \frac{2(V_{J_1})^2}{R} + \frac{2(V_{J_2})^2}{R} + \frac{2(V_{J_3})^2}{R} + \frac{2(V_{J_4})^2}{R} \\
&= \frac{(-1.838 \text{ V})^2}{50 \ \Omega} + \frac{2(2.404)^2}{50 \ \Omega} + \frac{2(3.464)^2}{50 \ \Omega} + \frac{2(2.192)^2}{50 \ \Omega} + \frac{2(0.919)^2}{50 \ \Omega} \\
&= 0.0676 + 0.2312 + 0.4800 + 0.1922 + 0.0338 \\
&= 1.005 \text{ W}
\end{aligned}
$$

The solution to equation (4-8) is 1.00 W; the solution to equation (4-9) is 1.005 W. These results are slightly different because the sideband amplitudes, originally taken from the Bessel function table, are rounded values. We have proved that the total power in an unmodulated FM carrier wave is the same as it is when it is modulated. The power is simply distributed in the carrier and sidebands when modulation occurs and is independent of the modulation index. The student is encouraged to prove this using other modulation indices.

4.5 FM NOISE

Noise affects the performance of any communications system, and it must be treated meaningfully. In Chapter 2, we learned that there are many sources of noise, and that its frequency, amplitude, and occurrence in time can be random or predictable. If the noise falls within the passband of the receiver, it can mix and add with the incoming signal, causing the original intelligence to become distorted.

The increased bandwidth of an FM system over an AM system may be used to enhance the *signal-to-noise ratio (SNR)* performance of the receiver system. This is one of the primary advantages of FM over AM. Recovering the modulation signal has an inherent noise suppression capability that AM does not; however, to take advantage of this, it is necessary to use large indices of modulation, in which case higher-order sidebands become increasingly important. Thus, a wider bandwidth is required for the transmission and reception of an FM signal.

> **Signal-to-Noise Ratio (SNR)**
> The ratio of signal power to noise power at some point in the telecommunications system. SRN is expressed in decibels (dB).

4.5.1   Phasor Analysis of FM Noise

In FM, noise added to the carrier signal causes a shift in frequency and phase from its normal state. The potential effect of the noise can be explained through use of phasor diagrams.

Recall that a phasor is essentially a vector that portrays both magnitude and direction for vector quantities. In Figure 4-7, V_c is a phasor representing the magnitude and direction of an FM signal's carrier rotating at a frequency ω_c. For simplicity, we will consider a single noise component represented by the phasor V_N, whose rotating frequency is ω_N. Ideally, only the modulating voltage phasor would be superimposed on the carrier's phasor.

From Figure 4-7, it can be seen that the phasor sum of V_c and V_N at any instant in time is represented by a resultant phasor R. It is this resultant phasor that the FM receiver processes. The magnitude of R is its length from tail to head, which can lie anywhere on the circumference of the circle outlined by rotating phasor V_N. The resultant phasor's amplitude, R, and phase deviation, α, continuously change with respect to time. The new signal is, therefore, amplitude, phase, and frequency modulated by the noise.

The FM receiver is insensitive to the amplitude variations caused by noise, whereas the AM receiver is not. A circuit in the FM receiver, called a *limiter*, removes any variations in signal amplitude before detection or demodulation of the signal. The noise is essentially "clipped off" by the limiter. The culprit is not the amplitude variations; the phase variation, α, produced by the noise voltage generates the undesirable frequency variation.

> **Limiter**
> In FM receivers, a circuit that maintains the FM signal at a constant amplitude.

The angle, α, established between the carrier and resultant phasor represents the maximum phase deviation caused by the noise. The AM receiver will not be affected by the phase changes for voice communications, whereas the FM receiver will not be affected by the amplitude changes caused by the noise. It is the phase deviation, α,

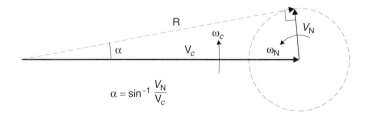

FIGURE 4-7
Phasor addition of noise on an FM signal's carrier frequency causes a phase shift, whose maximum value is α.

that distorts the FM signal. The maximum phase deviation occurs when R and V_N are at right angles to each other and can be computed by

$$\alpha = \sin^{-1} \frac{V_N}{V_c} \qquad \text{(4-11)}$$

where α = the maximum phase deviation of the carrier frequency caused by the noise
V_N = noise voltage
V_c = carrier voltage

The ratio of carrier voltage to noise voltage, $\frac{V_c}{V_N}$, is the SNR:

$$SNR = \frac{V_c}{V_N} \qquad \text{(4-12)}$$

and, therefore, equation (4-11) can also be written as

$$\alpha = \sin^{-1} \frac{1}{SNR} \qquad \text{(4-13)}$$

EXAMPLE 4.5

The input signal to an FM receiver has noise voltage of 25 μV superimposed on its carrier frequency, whose amplitude is 100 μV. Compute the following:
(a) phase deviation, α, caused by the noise.
(b) SNR.

Solution:

(a) $\alpha = \sin^{-1} \frac{V_N}{V_c} = \sin^{-1} \frac{25\ \mu V}{100\ \mu V} = 14.48° = 0.253$ radians

(b) $SNR = \frac{V_c}{V_N} = \frac{100\ \mu V}{25\ \mu V} = 4$ (or 4:1)

Because the modulation index for FM is defined as the ratio of the carrier's peak frequency deviation to the modulation frequency, α represents the equivalent modulation index produced by the noise. Using the following equation, we can compute the peak frequency deviation, δ_N, produced by the noise if we are given a modulation frequency, f_m:

$$\delta_N = \alpha \cdot f_m \qquad \text{(4-14)}$$

where δ_N = peak carrier frequency deviation produced by the noise voltage, V_N
α = maximum phase deviation of the carrier frequency expressed in radians
f_m = modulation frequency

Note the similarity between equations (4-14) and (4-3), which states that $m_f = \delta/f_m$. For commercial FM broadcast stations, the maximum modulation frequency is 15 kHz. Therefore, the peak carrier frequency deviation caused by the noise in Example 4.5 can be computed as

$$\delta_N = \alpha \cdot f_m = 0.253 \times 15 \text{ kHz} = 3.795 \text{ kHz}$$

This degree of frequency deviation, which ideally should be zero under the condition of no noise ($V_N = 0$), may or may not be significant. Equation (4-14) shows that the higher the modulation frequency, f_m, the worse the deviation becomes. Also, because f_m is directly related to the modulation index ($m_f = \delta/f_m$), we can also say that for low modulation indices (resulting from increasing f_m), the worse the deviation becomes. What must be considered is the relative deviation caused by the noise in comparison to the maximum allowed deviation, δ, of the FM system. For example, because the maximum δ for an FM broadcast system is 75 kHz, then 3.795 kHz is only a 5% shift in frequency.

It is also possible to compute the overall SNR improvement resulting from the FM process alone. The maximum allowed frequency deviation, δ, is caused by the maximum modulation amplitude, and the maximum frequency deviation caused by the noise amplitude is δ_N. Therefore, the ratio of the two represents the overall FM SNR:

$$SNR_{FM} = \frac{\delta}{\delta_N} \qquad (4\text{-}15)$$

In Example 4.5, the input signal had SNR of 4:1. Applying equation (4-14), we found that the noise produced a peak carrier deviation of 3.795 kHz for a modulation frequency of 15 kHz. Using 75 kHz as the maximum deviation for the FM signal, that is, $m_f = 5$, the resulting SNR is

$$SNR_{FM} = \frac{\delta}{\delta_N} = \frac{75 \text{ kHz}}{3.795 \text{ kHz}} = 19.8 \text{ (or 19.8:1)}$$

This is an overall improvement of 13.9 dB from the original 4:1 SNR ($20 \cdot \log 19.8 - 20 \cdot \log 4$). Of course, this assumes the FM receiver's internal noise contribution is negligible. In an AM receiver, a 4:1 SNR at the input would result in the same ratio at the output.

The input SNR to a narrowband FM receiver is 3:1. The maximum modulation frequency, f_m, is 3 kHz, with a maximum deviation, δ, of 10 kHz. Compute the modulation index, m_f, and the overall SNR improvement from input to output. Assume there is no other noise contribution to the system.

EXAMPLE
4.6

Solution:
The modulation index is computed using equation (4-3):

$$m_f = \frac{\delta}{f_m} = \frac{10 \text{ kHz}}{3 \text{ kHz}} = 3.33$$

Using equation (4-13), the maximum phase deviation of the carrier frequency caused by the noise is

$$\alpha = \sin^{-1} \frac{1}{SNR} = \sin^{-1}\left(\frac{1}{3}\right) = 19.47° = 0.3398 \text{ radians}$$

The maximum frequency deviation caused by the noise is computed using equation (4-14):

$$\delta_N = \alpha \cdot f_m = 0.3398 \times 3 \text{ kHz} = 1.019 \text{ kHz}$$

Using equation (4-14), we have

$$\text{SNR}_{\text{FM}} = \frac{\delta}{\delta_N} = \frac{10 \text{ kHz}}{1.019 \text{ kHz}} = 9.81 \text{ (or 9.81:1)}$$

The SNR improvement from input to output went from 3:1 to 9.81:1. This increase can be computed in decibels as follows:

$$\text{SNR} = 3 = 20 \cdot \log 3 = 9.54 \text{ dB}$$
$$\text{SNR} = 9.81 = 20 \cdot \log 9.81 = 19.83 \text{ dB}$$

Thus, the overall improvement in SNR is

$$19.83 \text{ dB} - 9.54 \text{ dB} = 10.3 \text{ dB}$$

Note that the SNR improvement in Example 4.6 is not as great as that in Example 5, in which a δ of 75 kHz and f_m of 15 kHz were used. The SNR was nearly 20:1 for

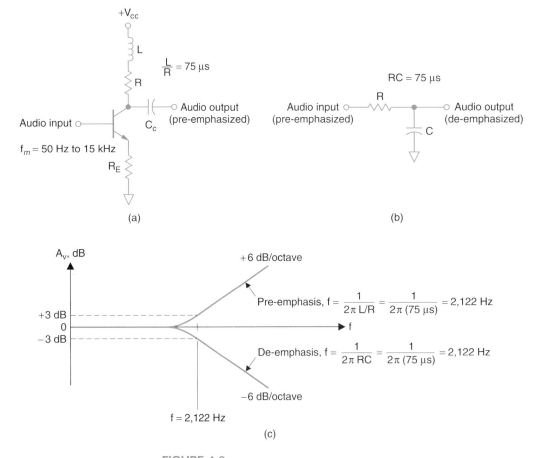

FIGURE 4-8
(a) Pre-emphasis circuit in FM transmitter with 75-μs time constant; (b) de-emphasis circuit in FM receiver with 75-μs time constant; (c) combined frequency response.

a modulation index of 5. This shows that the greater the modulation index or lower the modulation frequency, the greater the improvement in SNR.

4.5.2 Pre-emphasis and De-emphasis

As discussed, the effect of noise on an FM carrier signal is directly proportional to the modulation frequency. Increasing the modulation frequency, f_m, degrades the SNR. Unfortunately, in most cases, the modulation frequency is not fixed, as in the previous examples; instead, the modulation frequency is continually changing, depending on the nature of the intelligence. For example, voice, data, and music contain many frequencies, which are distributed throughout the given modulation passband. Therefore, the SNR is not uniform throughout.

To circumvent this, FM transmitters must boost the signal levels of the higher-modulating frequencies before the modulation process. This is to maintain a uniform SNR for the higher modulation frequencies and is called *pre-emphasis.* Because the original intelligence representing the higher frequencies has been artificially boosted in amplitude to a higher level, they no longer represent their original amplitudes. The FM receiver must de-emphasize these signals to the same extent, which is called *de-emphasis* and takes place after the FM signal has been demodulated. A simple high-pass filter is used for pre-emphasis of the signal and a low-pass filter for de-emphasis of the signal.

The FCC requires commercial FM broadcast stations to include in their transmitters an inductance-resistance (L/R) pre-emphasis network with a time constant of 75 μs. This implies that the receiver must include a de-emphasis network with the same time constant; an L/R time constant corresponds to a break frequency of 2122 Hz [$1/(2\pi L/R)$]. Figure 4-8 illustrates a pre-emphasis and a de-emphasis circuit. Note that the sum of their frequency response curves is unity gain.

4.6 FM GENERATION

There are two basic methods of generating the FM signal: *direct FM,* and *indirect FM.* The direct method occurs when the modulation signal (or intelligence) is used to directly change the carrier signal's frequency or phase. The indirect method uses the modulation signal to change the phase of the carrier signal, which indirectly changes its frequency. Indirect FM is often referred to as the *Armstrong method of FM generation,* which is named after its inventor, Major Edwin E. Armstrong. There are many types of direct and indirect FM generating circuits, but we limit our discussion to a few that are commonly used.

4.6.1 Varactor-Tuned Modulators

Varactor-tuned modulators utilize *varactor diodes* (also known as *varicaps*) in tank circuits for generating the direct FM signal. A varactor diode is a semiconductor diode that has been specifically manufactured to have its depletion region optimized for variable capacitance effect under the reverse-bias condition. Figure 4-9 shows the varactor diode symbol, its equivalent circuit, and its characteristic curve. Although all P-N junctions exhibit some degree of capacitance, what is unique about the varactor diode is its large *tuning ratio*. A varactor diode's tuning ratio is defined as the ratio of its junction capacitance, C_T, measured at a reverse-bias potential of 4 VDC, divided by

---

Pre-emphasis
The process by which FM transmitters boost the signal levels of the higher modulating frequencies before the modulation process to maintain a uniform SNR for the higher modulation frequencies.

De-emphasis
The process by which an FM receiver brings back pre-emphasized signals to their original amplitudes. De-emphasis occurs after the FM signal has been demodulated.

Direct FM
One of two basic methods of FM generation. In direct FM generation, the modulation signal is used to directly change the carrier signal's frequency or phase.

Indirect FM
In indirect FM, the modulation signal is used to change the phase of the carrier signal, which indirectly changes its frequency. The *Armstrong* method of FM generation is an example.

Varactor Diode
A semiconductor diode manufactured to have its depletion region optimized to act as a variable capacitor under the reverse-biased condition. Also known as a *varicap.*

Tuning Ratio
A varactor diode's tuning ratio is the ratio of its reverse-bias junction capacitance measured at a reverse-bias potential of 4 VDC to its junction capacitance measured at a reverse-bias potential of 60 VDC. Typical tuning ratios range from 3:1 to as high as 5:1.

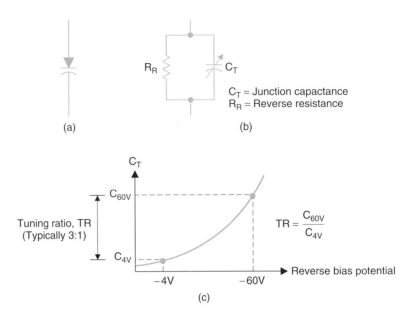

FIGURE 4-9
Varactor diode: (a) electrical symbol; (b) equivalent circuit; (c) characteristic curve.

its junction capacitance, measured at a reverse-bias potential of 60 VDC. Typical tuning ratios are 3:1 but can be as high as 5:1.

> **Colpitts Oscillator**
> A tuned oscillator circuit that uses capacitive feedback to sustain oscillations.

Two varactor-tuned modulator circuits are shown in Figure 4-10. A *Colpitts oscillator* configuration is shown in Figure 4-10(a). The varactor diode, V_{R1}, is reverse-biased through the DC supply potential, V_{CC}, and transistor Q_1's emitter potential, V_E. Feedback to sustain oscillations is tapped off of the tank circuit and fed to the emitter of Q_1. The audio input signal modulates the varactor diode's junction capacitance, hence the resonant frequency of the tank circuit changes with the instantaneous voltage of the modulating signal. The FM signal is produced at the output.

Figure 4-10(b) illustrates a *Pierce oscillator.* In this configuration, feedback to sustain oscillation is provided by the series resonant crystal, $XTAL_1$. Unlike the Colpitts oscillator, whose resonant frequency is a function of the tuned tank circuit, the Pierce oscillator has been configured for crystal control. There is no resonant tank circuit; instead, the frequency of the crystal holds the resonant frequency to a high degree of accuracy. The audio input signal modulates the capacitance of the varactor diode, V_{R1}, which in turn is said to "pull" the crystal frequency above and below its natural resonant frequency. The resulting FM signal is generated at the output of transistor Q_1. Use of a crystal provides a high degree of frequency accuracy. Pulling its frequency is limited, however, so large frequency deviations are difficult to achieve. It also should be noted that there are several variations of the Colpitts and Pierce oscillator configurations as presented here.

> **Reactance Modulator**
> A *direct FM* method of generation using inductance or capacitance that is made to vary across an oscillator's tank circuit. The inductance or capacitance is made to vary as a function of the modulating voltage.

4.6.2 Reactance Modulator

A *reactance modulator* is another popular method of direct FM generation. A reactance modulator is the equivalent of a variable inductor or capacitor. The circuit is placed across the tank circuit of the carrier frequency oscillator, and the reactance is made to vary as a function of the modulating signal.

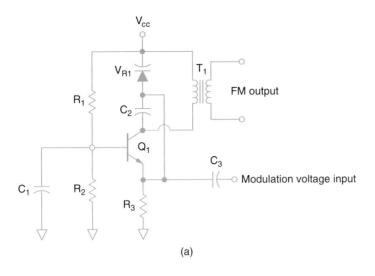

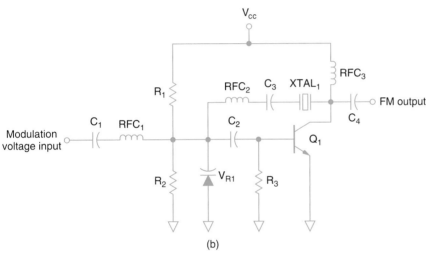

FIGURE 4-10
Varactor-tuned FM modulator circuits: (a) Colpitts oscillator; (b) Pierce oscillator.

Figure 4-11 shows the circuit diagram of a *junction field-effect transistor* (*JFET*) reactance modulator. This particular circuit is designed to look capacitive across the AB terminals. A small-signal analysis of the circuit results in the equivalent capacitance:

$$C_{eq} = g_m \ RC \qquad \textbf{(4-16)}$$
$$R << X_C \text{ at } f_c$$

where C_{eq} = the equivalent capacitance across terminals AB
g_m = the transconductance of the JFET in Siemens
R = the value of resistance in Ohms
C = the value of capacitance in Farads

The modulation voltage is applied across the gate-to-source terminals of the JFET. As the modulation voltage changes, the transconductance, g_m, and, hence, the

> **Junction Field-Effect Transistor (JFET)**
> A transistor consisting of a P-N junction and three leads: a gate, a drain, and a source.

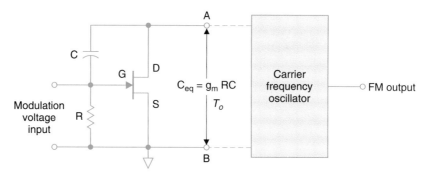

FIGURE 4-11
Reactance modulator.

equivalent capacitance, C_{eq}, changes in accordance with equation (4-16). For equation (4-16) to be accurate, however, the value of R must be much less than the capacitive reactance of C at the resonant frequency, f_c, of the carrier signal.

4.6.3   Indirect FM Using the Armstrong Method

Carrier frequency stability is an absolute requirement for many communication systems. For example, commercial FM broadcast stations must transmit their carrier frequencies in the 88- to 108-MHz band within an allowable tolerance of 2000 Hz. For an FM station transmitting in the center of this band, this is approximately 20 parts per million in terms of frequency accuracy. An inherent problem with the conventional LC oscillator, however, is its tendency to drift in frequency far beyond 20 parts per million. This degree of accuracy requires the frequency stability of a crystal.

> **Armstrong Modulator**
> An FM generator that uses *indirect FM* generation. Named after its inventor, Major Edwin E. Armstrong.

The *Armstrong modulator,* named after its inventor, Major Edwin E. Armstrong, is one of the oldest and most reliable FM modulators in use. It is considered indirect FM because it uses the modulation signal to indirectly deviate the phase of a crystal oscillator, which indirectly causes its frequency to change. Because of its relative complexity, a block diagram with corresponding phasor diagrams are illustrated in Figure 4-12.

The Armstrong modulator derives its frequency stability from the RF crystal oscillator, which is shown in the block diagram. Its frequency is shifted by $-90°$ and mixed with the conditioned modulation voltage. The purpose of the $-90°$ phase-shifting circuit is to ensure that the phasor sum of the upper- and lower-sideband components out of the balanced modulator remains in quadrature (90° out of phase) with the carrier frequency component that is summed together with it at the summing amplifier. Phase modulation (PM) is produced.

The mixing is accomplished with a balanced modulator. Recall from Chapter 3 that the balanced modulator produces sum and difference products and suppresses the carrier signal (double-sideband suppressed carrier, or DSBSC). In Figure 4-12(b), the phasor diagram representing the output of the balanced modulator, point A, is shown. Note that the phasor sum of the upper and lower sidebands, V_{USB} and V_{LSB}, results in the modulation voltage, V_m. As stated earlier, the modulation voltage is always in quadrature to the carrier frequency, ω_m, generated by the crystal oscillator. The phasor diagram for the carrier signal is shown at point B, and the summation of these two signals by the summing amplifier results in the phasor diagram shown at point

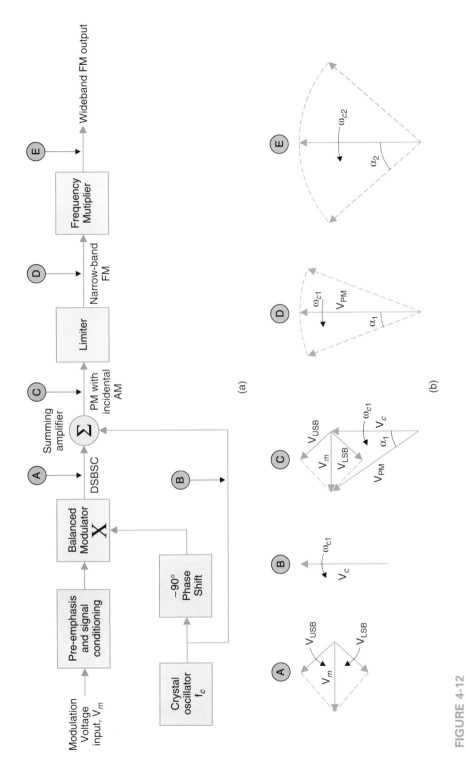

FIGURE 4-12

Armstrong FM modulator: (a) block diagram; (b) phasor diagrams depicting the various outputs of each stage of the block diagram.

C. Here, the resultant modulation voltage, V_m, can be seen phase modulating the carrier frequency, ω_m, as it shifts at a right angle to it. Unfortunately, the resulting PM signal, V_{PM}, at point C also generates an incidental AM signal as V_m changes in amplitude. The limiter's function is to eliminate this incidental AM signal, thus producing the resultant PM signal at point D. Finally, the purpose of the frequency multiplier is to increase the phase deviation from α_1 to α_2 and the carrier frequency from ω_{C1} (narrowband FM) to ω_{C2} (wideband FM), thereby producing the given FM output signal.

PROBLEMS

1. Define FM.
2. Define PM.
3. Write the equation representing the instantaneous voltage for an FM wave, and identify the carrier frequency component, the modulation frequency component, and the modulation index in that equation.
4. Write the equation representing the instantaneous voltage for a PM wave, and identify the carrier frequency component, the modulation frequency component, and the modulation index in that equation.
5. Given an FM wave with a frequency deviation, δ, of 10 kHz and a modulation frequency, f_m, of 2.5 kHz, compute the modulation index, m_f.
6. Compute the modulation frequency, f_m, for an FM wave with a modulation index, m_f, of 0.25 and a frequency deviation, δ, of 10 kHz.
7. Using Table 4-1 or Figure 4-3, find the carrier and sideband amplitudes for an FM wave with a modulation index, m_f, of 4. Assume sine-wave modulation and a peak carrier amplitude, A_C, of 5 V.
8. Using Table 4-1 or Figure 4-3, find the carrier and sideband amplitudes for an FM wave with a modulation index, m_f, of 2.5. Assume sine-wave modulation and a peak carrier amplitude, A_C, of 3 V.
9. Define *eigenvalue*.
10. What is the modulation index corresponding to the second order of the carrier frequency eigenvalue?
11. A spectrum analyzer is used to verify an FM signal with a carrier frequency of 106.5 MHz, a modulation frequency of 7.5 kHz, and a modulation index of 3.0.
    a. Determine the number of significant sideband pairs.
    b. Predict the spectrum-analyzer display for the signal, and show the relative amplitudes of each sideband pair.
    c. Compute the frequency deviation, δ.
12. Repeat problem 11 for a modulation frequency of 10 kHz and a modulation index of 2.0.
13. Given a modulation frequency of 3 kHz and a frequency deviation of 30 kHz, compute the following:
    a. The modulation index, m_f.
    b. The bandwidth of the FM signal using equation (4-5) and Table 4-3.
    c. The bandwidth of the FM signal using Carson's Rule.
14. Repeat problem 13 for a modulation frequency of 15 kHz and a frequency deviation of 60 kHz.
15. Compute the total power in the FM wave of problem 7. Assume a 50-Ω load.
16. Compute the total power in the FM wave of problem 8. Assume a 50-Ω load.
17. The input signal to an FM receiver has a noise voltage of 10 μV superimposed on its carrier frequency, whose amplitude is 150 μV. Compute the following:
    a. The phase deviation, α, caused by the noise.
    b. The signal-to-noise ratio, SNR.

18. Repeat problem 17 for a noise voltage of 50 μV superimposed on the same carrier amplitude.
19. The input SNR to a narrowband FM receiver is 5:1. For a modulation frequency of 15 kHz and a maximum frequency deviation of 75 kHz, compute the modulation index and the overall SNR improvement from input to output. Assume no other noise is contributed to the system.
20. What is the purpose of pre-emphasis and de-emphasis in FM?
21. Define a varactor diode's *tuning ratio*.

5

PULSE MODULATION AND ENCODING TECHNIQUES

In the previous chapters on AM and FM theory, we saw that a carrier signal's amplitude, frequency, or phase varied in proportion to the intelligence. In *pulse modulation* systems, a series of regularly recurring pulses is made to vary in amplitude, duration, shape, or time as a function of the modulating signal. Examples include *pulse-amplitude modulation (PAM), delta modulation (DM), pulse-width modulation (PWM), pulse-code modulation (PCM),* and *pulse-position modulation (PPM).* These techniques, along with the special encoding techniques discussed in this chapter, have long been used in commercial and military applications. In the last half century, they have dominated the telecommunications industry and, in many cases, have replaced the conventional analog system.

    Pulse modulation is used to transmit both analog and digital information, such as voice and data. An analog signal is sampled, digitized, and encoded into a digital pulse stream often referred to as a *baseband signal.* If the original signal is already in digital form, it may be encoded into a digital pulse stream. In either case, the serial pulse stream is typically transmitted onto a coaxial cable, twisted-pair wire, fiber, or even a radio frequency (RF) carrier or wireless microwave or infrared link.

    This chapter introduces the student to the pulse modulation techniques mentioned earlier, with an emphasis on PCM. A discussion of the importance of special encoding techniques used to enhance the transmission and reception of the pulse modulated signal is also presented.

> **Pulse Modulation**
> A technique whereby pulses are made to vary in amplitude, width, or period as a function of the modulation signal.

> **Baseband Signal**
> An encoded analog or digital signal transmitted directly onto a channel without modulating a carrier frequency.

5.1 ADVANTAGES AND DISADVANTAGES OF PULSE MODULATION

Pulse modulation techniques are continually replacing analog systems, primarily due to the many advantages they offer:

- Noise immunity
- Inexpensive digital circuitry
- Time-division multiplexing with other pulse modulated signals
- Increased transmission distance through the use of regenerative repeaters

- Storage of digital pulse streams
- Easily implemented error detection and correction

Although the advantages far outweigh the disadvantages, the pulse modulated signal does require a much greater bandwidth to transmit and receive than its analog counterpart. Bandwidth can be costly and, in most cases, is limited, and special encoding and decoding techniques may be necessary to increase transmission rates, thus making the pulse stream more difficult to recover. Once the pulse stream is recovered, the intelligence must be converted back to its original form. This may require precise synchronization of clocks between the transmitting and the receiving stations; in many cases, *phase-locked loop* technology, which we discuss later, is necessary.

5.2 PULSE-CODE MODULATION

Pulse-Code Modulation (PCM)
A pulse-modulation technique whereby an analog signal is sampled and converted to a digitally encoded signal.

By far, the most widely used pulse modulation technique in the telecommunications industry is *pulse-code modulation (PCM),* which was developed in 1937 at the Paris Laboratories of AT&T. Alex H. Reeves has been credited with its invention. Reeves conducted several successful transmission experiments across the English Channel using various modulation techniques, including PWM, PAM, and PPM. At the time, the circuitry involved was enormously complex and expensive. Although the significance of Reeves' experiments was acknowledged by Bell Laboratories, it was not until the semiconductor industry evolved in the 1960s that PCM became more prevalent. Currently, in the United States and the United Kingdom, PCM is the preferred method of transmission within the public switched telephone network (PSTN).

Quantized
When an analog or digital signal is divided into discrete numeric levels and represented by a binary word.

PCM is a method of serially transmitting an approximate representation of an analog signal. The PCM signal itself is a succession of discrete, numerically encoded binary values derived from digitizing the analog signal. The maximum expected amplitude of the analog signal is first *quantized;* that is, it is divided into discrete numerical levels. The number of discrete levels depends on the resolution (number of bits) of the A/D converter used to digitize the signal. If an eight-bit A/D converter is used, the analog signal range is quantized into 256 (2^8) discrete levels. The quantizing range is governed by the equation

Quantizing Range
The maximum number of discrete binary levels in which a signal can be divided.

$$quantizing\ range = 2^{(\text{no. of A/D converter bits})}$$ (5-1)

EXAMPLE 5.1

Given a 12-bit A/D converter, compute the quantizing range (number of discrete levels that a signal can be divided into).

Solution:

Quantizing range = 2^{12} = 4096 discrete levels.

Figure 5-1 illustrates the quantization of a sine wave. For simplicity, a 4-bit A/D converter is used. At any instant in time, the sine wave can be approximated to the closest quantized level from 0 to 15 ($2^4 = 16$). This assumes that the signal does not exceed the dynamic range of the A/D converter. If an A/D converter with a dynamic range of 0 to +10 V is used, the input signal shall not exceed this range.

If the resolution of the A/D converter is increased, a closer approximation of the signal can be attained, because there would be a greater number of quantized lev-

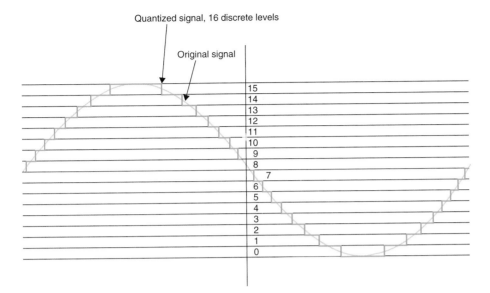

FIGURE 5-1
Quantization of an analog signal into 16 discrete levels.

els. However, the quantized value would require a larger encoded binary value. A larger bandwidth would be required to transmit the signal, as we shall see.

5.2.1 Pulse-Amplitude Modulation

Once the quantization range of an A/D converter has been established, the analog signal is *sampled* at equally spaced intervals in time. Sampling is the process of determining the instantaneous voltage at these given intervals in time. A technique called *pulse-amplitude modulation (PAM)* is used to produce a pulse when the signal is sampled. As shown in Figure 5-2, the pulse's amplitude is equal to the level at the time in which the analog signal was sampled. The amplitude of the pulses in a PAM signal contains the intelligence or modulating voltage. Each pulse of the resulting PAM signal is digitized by an A/D converter to the closest quantized value at the time of the sample. PAM serves as a preliminary step toward generating the PCM signal.

Because the A/D converter takes a finite amount of time to complete its conversion process, it is necessary to *hold* the sampled amplitude while the conversion process occurs (hence the reason for the pulse width in PAM). A *sample-and-hold (S/H) amplifier* is used to perform this task. If the analog voltage at the input to the A/D converter were allowed to change during this time, an erroneous digital word would be produced.

The encoded binary value produced by the A/D converter represents an *approximation* of the amplitude at the time of the sample. It is an approximation, because the instantaneous amplitude at the sampling interval can lie anywhere within the quantized level. The binary value representing the amplitude is then serialized to form the PCM signal and transmitted onto the communications channel. A block diagram of a PCM system is shown in Figure 5-3.

Pulse-Amplitude Modulation (PAM)
A pulse modulation technique that produces a series of pulses whose amplitudes are proportional to the modulating voltage at the time of the sample.

Sample-and-Hold (S/H) Amplifier
Samples and holds an incoming signal so it may be converted to a digital word.

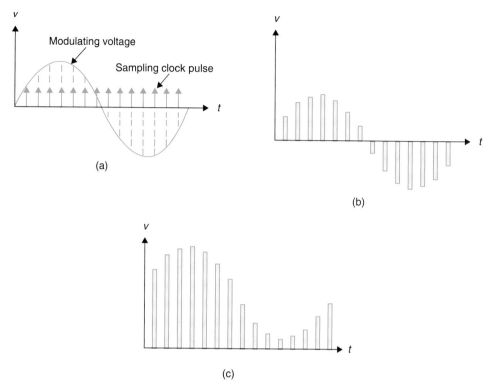

FIGURE 5-2

Phase-amplitude modulation (PAM): (a) original signal; (b) double-polarity PAM; (c) single-polarity PAM.

At the receiving end of the communications channel, the reverse process is performed. The PCM signal is received, decoded, and reconstructed by a D/A converter. The resulting signal is an approximation of the original signal.

Figure 5-4 depicts the recovered signal for various sampling rates. The higher the sampling rate, the closer the recovered signal approaches the original signal. Ideally, an infinite sampling rate would be desirable in terms of reproducing the original signal. This is not practical, however, due to the bandwidth limitation on the large amounts of data that would need to be transmitted.

In telephony, voice signals are sampled at 8 kHz. The 8-kHz sampling rate is based on the *Nyquist sampling rate theorem:*

Nyquist Sampling Theorem. *If a signal is sampled at a rate that is at least twice the highest frequency that it contains, the original signal can be completely reconstructed.*

A signal containing frequency components up to 4 kHz therefore can be recovered with minimal distortion. Because the bandwidth of the telephone lines is 300 to 3400 Hz, 8 kHz is easily more than twice the highest frequency component within this range.

5.2.2 Regenerative Repeater

The advantage of PCM lies chiefly in that it is a digital process. Digital signals have a high noise immunity. That is, it is much easier for a receiver to distinguish between

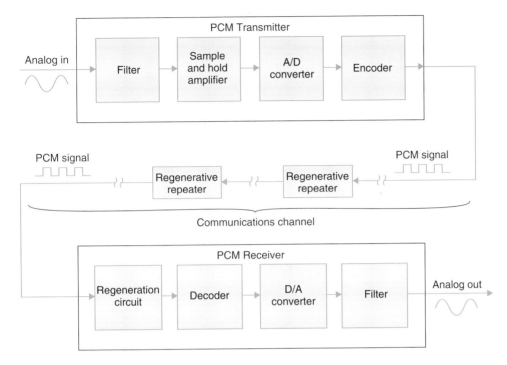

FIGURE 5-3
Block diagram of a PCM system.

a 1 and a 0 than to reproduce faithfully a continuous wave signal (or a composite of several continuous waves) when both are subjected to the same noise environment. The effect of noise on a PCM signal can be removed entirely through the use of *regenerative repeaters.* Transmission media carrying PCM signals employ regenerative repeaters that are spaced sufficiently close to each other (approximately 1 mile) to prevent any ambiguity in the recognition of the binary PCM pulses. Figure 5-3 depicts how the regenerative repeater fits into the PCM system.

When pulses arrive at the repeater, they are attenuated and distorted. The regenerative repeater conditions the received pulses through preamplifiers and equalizer circuits. The signal is then compared against a voltage *threshold,* using a *threshold detector,* as shown in Figure 5-5. Above the threshold is a logic 1, and below the threshold is a logic 0. The resulting signal is said to be *threshold detected.*

Timing circuits within the regenerative repeater are synchronized to the bit rate of the incoming signal. The threshold detected signal is sampled (see arrows in Figure 5-5) at the optimum time to determine the logic level of the signal. The resulting code is used to regenerate and retransmit the new equivalent signal. Threshold detection is an art in itself; entire books have been written on the subject.

> **Regenerative Repeater**
> A repeater that uses *threshold detection* to recover, reconstruct, and retransmit a PCM signal.

> **Threshold Detector**
> A circuit that detects when a signal is above or below a specific value.

5.2.3 Distortion in a PCM Signal

Distortion in a PCM signal lies principally in the encoded signal itself. When an analog signal is quantized, the encoded value is approximated within the limitations of the A/D converter. This quantizing error results in the signal distortion shown in Figure 5-4. The quantizing error can be as much as half a quantizing level. An 8-bit A/D

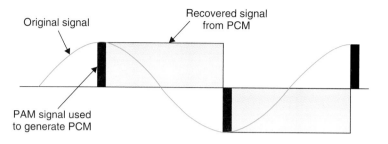

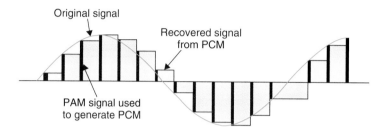

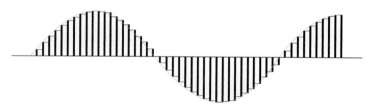

FIGURE 5-4
Recovered signals for various sampling rates.

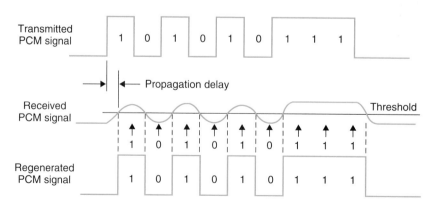

FIGURE 5-5
Regeneration of a PCM signal with a regenerative repeater.

converter, for example, can have a maximum quantizing error of $\frac{1}{512}$th of the signal ($\frac{1}{2}$ of $\frac{1}{256}$); that is, the instantaneous voltage at the time of the sample lies precisely at midpoint between quantized levels. The least significant bit of the A/D converter in this case can be either a 1 or a 0. The noise resulting from this distortion is referred to as *quantization noise*. Figure 5-6 illustrates the transfer function for a linear quantizer. The quantized signal is a staircase. Subtracting the quantizing error from the quantized staircase signal results in the original signal. The error can be reduced by increasing the number of quantized levels, consequently decreasing the quantization noise.

> **Quantization Noise**
> The noise resulting from a reconstructed signal that was quantized before transmission.

The magnitude of quantization noise power is directly related to the number of quantization levels and, therefore, is related to the number of binary bits used to represent a quantized level. To give an indication of this magnitude, for a sinusoid whose peak-to-peak amplitude utilizes the full dynamic range of the A/D converter, the rms signal-to-quantization noise ratio is given by

$$\text{SNR} = 1.8 + 6n \qquad \text{(dB)} \tag{5-2}$$

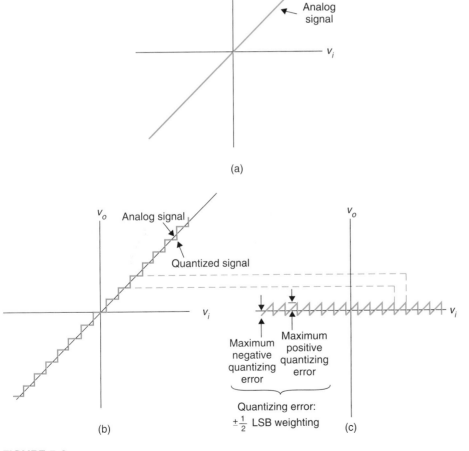

FIGURE 5-6

(a) Linear transfer function; (b) quantization of analog signal; (c) quantizing error.

TABLE 5-1
Signal-to-Quantizing Noise Ratio Versus Number of Binary Bits Used to Represent a Quantized Level

Number of Binary Bits, n	Number of Quantization Levels, 2^n	Signal-to-Quantizing Noise Ratio (dB)
4	16	25.8
5	32	31.8
6	64	37.8
7	128	43.8
8	256	49.8

where n equals the number of binary bits used to represent the quantized level. Table 5-1 shows how the signal-to-quantizing noise ratio increases with increasing quantization bits. Eight-bit quantizing (256 levels) is most commonly used in today's PCM systems to represent voice. This satisfies the trade-offs between signal resolution and transmission time.

5.2.4   Voice Compression in a PCM System

The discussion of quantization has been simplified through the use of a sine wave. In the examples given earlier, the sine wave utilized the full dynamic range of the A/D converter. The signal-to-quantizing noise ratio is optimum in this case. Voice, however, does not utilize the entire range of the A/D converter in a uniform manner as the sine wave presented earlier does. Instead, voice variations are sporadic. They contain low- to high-amplitude variations throughout the quantizing range. The ratio of this variation, or, more properly stated, the *dynamic range* of voice can be as high as 60 dB. An inherent problem exists here when attempting to use the common 8-bit A/D converter for quantization. Only 256 quantized levels are possible. This is suitable for a signal with a dynamic range of 48 dB ($20 \times \log 256$). For voice, however, much of its characteristics can be lost within quantized levels. Figure 5-7 depicts this anomaly and how it is resolved in part by *compression* of the signal.

The voice pattern shown in Figure 5-7 has been quantized and reconstructed through the PCM process. For simplicity, a 4-bit A/D converter is used again. Figure 5-7(a) depicts the reconstructed signal without compression, and Figure 5-7(b) shows the effect of compression on the same voice pattern. Note in Figure 5-7(a) that the dynamic range of the voice pattern exceeds that of the A/D converter used for quantization. Low and high amplitudes are not resolved due to the lack of quantization levels; as a result, characterization of the voice pattern through the PCM process is poor. In Figure 5-7(b), the dynamic range of the signal has been compressed to within the quantizing range of the A/D converter. Low-amplitude variations of the signal are amplified to a greater extent than higher-amplitude variations. The compressed voice pattern is a much closer representation of the original signal. The recovered signal can now be *expanded* to its original level. The PCM system shown earlier in Figure 5-3 can be improved by the addition of compandors placed before and after the A/D and D/A conversion process. Chapter 12 shows how compounding greatly improves SNR and reduces the possibility of distortion in the transmitted signal.

> **Dynamic Range**
> The functional operating range over which a device or signal operates.

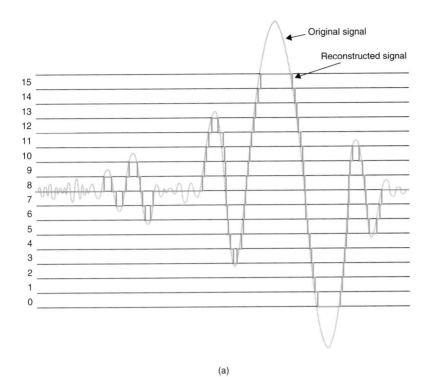

(a)

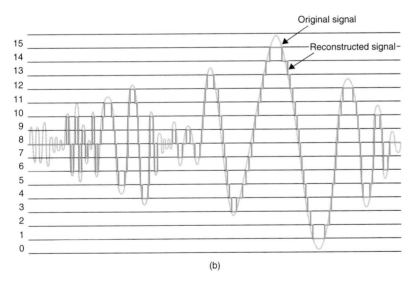

(b)

FIGURE 5-7

(a) Reconstructed voice pattern without compression; (b) reconstructed voice pattern with compression, which is much closer to the original signal.

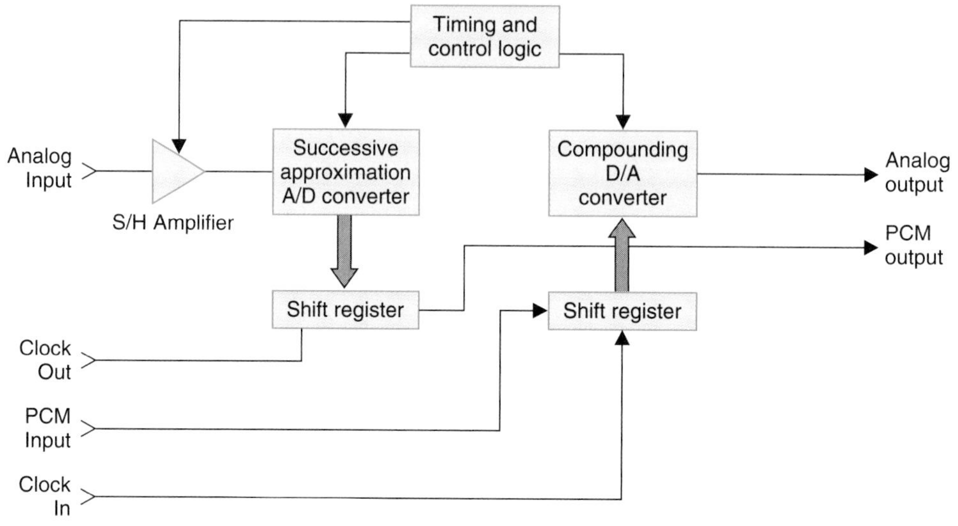

FIGURE 5-8
Simplified block diagram of a codec.

5.2.5 The Codec

Codec
A contraction of the words *coder* and *decoder*. It is a device that takes an analog signal and converts it to a digital word, and vice versa. The codec also performs *companding* of the signal.

In the telephone system, generation and reception of a PCM signal is greatly simplified by the use of an integrated circuit (IC) chip called a *codec*. The word "codec" is a contraction of the words "*co*der-*dec*oder." This device takes an analog signal, such as voice, and converts it to a binary serial bit stream (PCM signal) through the use of an interval A/D converter. It also performs the reverse process of converting a binary serial bit stream back into its original analog form. An internal D/A converter performs this task.

An additional function that the codec IC performs is companding. The degree of companding is based on the μ-*Law* standard, which is used by telephone companies in the United States. Codec ICs are also available with companding based on the *A-law* standard, which is the international standard. Both the μ-Law and A-Law standards are discussed in Chapter 12. A simplified block diagram of a codec is shown in Figure 5-8.

μ-Law
Companding law used in the United States.

A-Law
Companding law used in Europe.

5.3 PULSE-WIDTH MODULATION

Pulse-Width Modulation (PWM)
A pulse modulation technique whereby the width of a pulse carrier signal is made to vary with the modulation voltage. Also known as *pulse duration modulation (PDM)*.

Pulse-width modulation (PWM), which is also known as *pulse-duration modulation (PDM),* is a form of modulation in which the *width* of a pulse carrier is made to vary in accordance with the modulation voltage. The leading edge of the carrier pulse remains fixed, but the occurrence of the trailing edge of the pulse varies, as shown in Figure 5-9. Figure 5-10 shows how a simple 555 timer circuit can be configured as a monostable multivibrator and used to generate the PWM signal. The continuous pulse train is applied to pin 2, the trigger input, and the modulation input is applied to pin 5, the control voltage input. The PWM signal is generated at pin 3, the output of the timer.

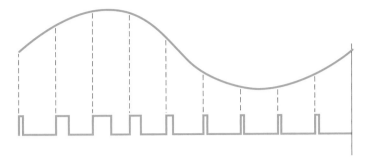

FIGURE 5-9
The PWM signal.

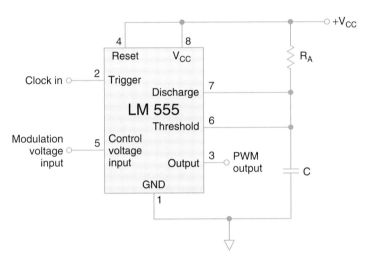

FIGURE 5-10
A 555 timer circuit configures as a PWM generator. (Courtesy of National Semiconductor.)

5.4 PULSE-POSITION MODULATION

As the instantaneous value of the modulating signal increases in PWM, wider pulses are generated, thereby expending more power. Thus, the power dissipated in the PWM signal varies with the modulation amplitude. It is possible to eliminate this power variance by preserving only the pulse transitions of the PWM signal, and this effectively creates another type of pulse modulation, called *pulse-position modulation (PPM)*. The power saved is one of the advantages of PPM over PWM.

PPM differs from PWM in that the position of a pulse relative to its unmodulated time of occurrence is made to vary in accordance with the modulation voltage. The simple circuit in Figure 5-11(a) illustrates how the PPM signal can be derived from the PWM signal. By differentiating the PWM signal with a high-pass filter and clipping off the positive pulses, the PPM signal remains. The negative-going PPM signal is inverted and used to trigger a one-shot circuit to shape the pulse width of the PPM signal. Figure 5-12 illustrates an even simpler PPM circuit, in which the 555

> **Pulse-Position Modulation (PPM)**
> A pulse modulation technique whereby the position of a pulse relative to its unmodulated time of occurrence is made to vary in accordance with the modulation voltage.

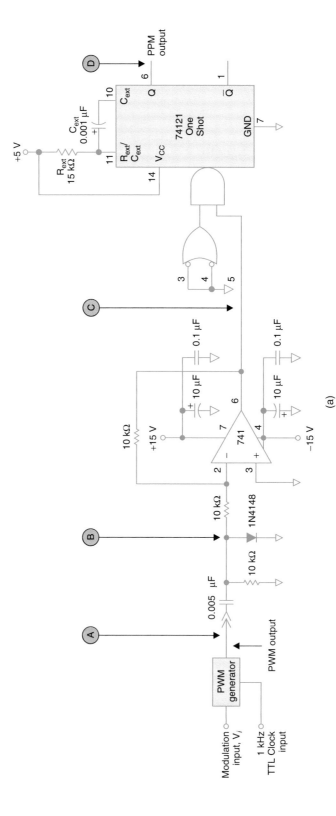

74121 One Shot output pulse width, $t_w = 0.693\ R_{ext}\ C_{ext}$
$= 0.693\ (15\ \text{k}\Omega)\ (0.001\ \mu\text{F})$
$= 10.4\ \mu\text{s}$

(a)

FIGURE 5.11

A PPM signal can be generated from a PWM signal by differentiating the PWM signal and clipping off its positive pulses: (a) PPM circuit;

(continues on next page)

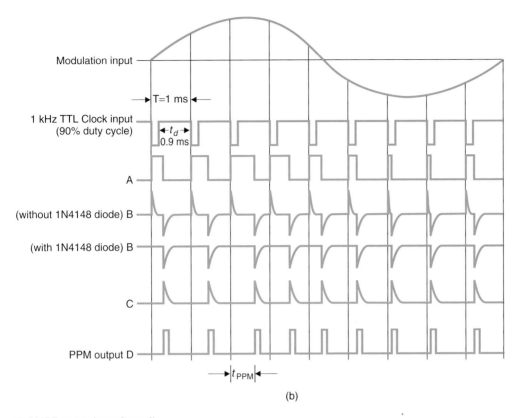

Modulation input

T=1 ms

1 kHz TTL Clock input
(90% duty cycle)

t_d
0.9 ms

A

(without 1N4148 diode) B

(with 1N4148 diode) B

C

PPM output D

t_{PPM}

(b)

FIGURE 5-11 *(continued)*
(b) waveforms at various sections of the PPM circuit.

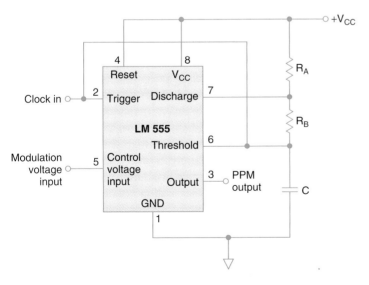

FIGURE 5-12
A 555 timer circuit configured as a PPM generator. (Courtesy of National Semiconductor.)

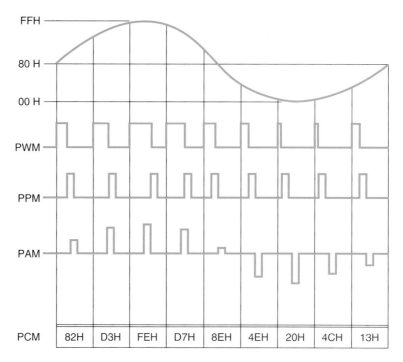

FIGURE 5-13
Comparison of PWM, PPM, PAM, and PCM.

timer can also be configured for astable operation and used as a PPM generator. Figure 5-13 illustrates a comparison of the pulse modulation techniques discussed so far.

5.5 DELTA MODULATION

Delta Modulation (DM)
A special form of PCM whereby the analog input signal is converted to a 1-bit continuous serial data stream of 1s and 0s at a rate determined by a sampling clock.

Delta modulation (DM) is a special form of *differential pulse-code modulation (DPCM)*, whereby the analog input signal is converted to a continuous serial data stream of 1s and 0s at a rate determined by a sampling clock. The delta modulator is essentially a 1-bit A/D converter. If its output is a logic 1, then the current sample of the analog input signal is greater than the previous sample. If the output is a logic 0, then the current sample is less than the value of the previous sample.

A block diagram illustrating the principle of delta modulation is shown in Figure 5-14. The analog input signal is fed to an S/H amplifier, where it is sampled, held, and applied to the noninverting input of a voltage comparator. It is compared against the output of a *digital-to-analog converter (DAC),* which is applied to the inverting input of the comparator. The output of the DAC is an analog voltage corresponding to a binary count representing the analog input value of the previous count.

Note that the up-down counter is clocked at the same rate as the S/H amplifier. As long as the input signal remains higher than the output of the DAC, the counter will continually count up with each sample. This would imply that the analog input signal is continually increasing in value. Conversely, if the input signal drops relative to its previous value, the output of the DAC would be greater than the input signal, thereby causing the up-down counter to count down a single bit with each sample. Thus, the DAC-counter combination acts as a memory device that holds a voltage

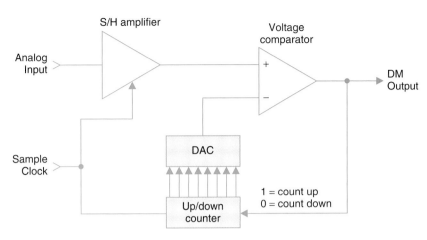

FIGURE 5-14
Block diagram of a delta modulator.

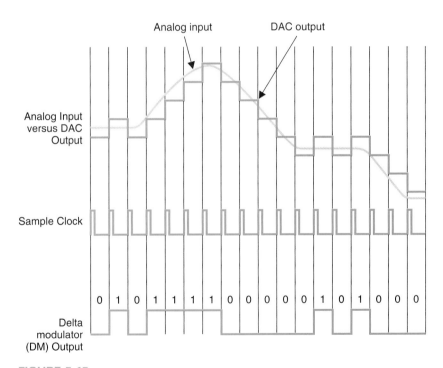

FIGURE 5-15
Waveforms generated by the delta modulator.

representing the previous sample of the analog input. Figure 5-15 illustrates the output of the DAC and resulting DM signal for the given analog input.

The DM system greatly simplifies the pulse modulation transmission and receiving system. A little thought, however, will reveal that rapidly changing signals with high slew rates (volts per microsecond) are difficult to track without increasing the sampling rates. Increased sampling rates mean an increased transmission rate for the DM signal, thereby requiring a greater bandwidth. Also, for analog input signals that do not change, quantization errors occur in the form of a square wave. This generates what is referred to as a *granular noise,* which is analogous to the *quantization noise* generated by A/D converters.

5.6 ENCODING TECHNIQUES

Whenever a serial binary bit stream is transmitted, it must be *encoded* into a sequence representing 1s and 0s. It could be as simplistic as punched paper tape where a binary 1 is represented by a perforation or hole and a binary 0 is represented by the absence of a hole. The absence or presence of light, an audible tone, or an electrical impulse are other examples of how binary data can be transmitted from one location to another to convey intelligence.

Today's high-speed data communication and telecommunication systems employ a variety of encoding techniques that have become signalling standards. They are widely used in communication links ranging from LANs and modems to telephone trunk circuits and satellite transmission links. Figure 5-16 illustrates some of the more popular encoding techniques used today.

Whereas one encoding technique may be best suited for a given application, it may not meet the requirements of another. When choosing an encoding technique, some important factors must be considered:

Channel Bandwidth The transmission medium must have a bandwidth wide enough to pass the spectral content of the encoded signal.

Self-clocking Serially transmitted data require a mechanism for synchronization to the individual bit times of the received data. If a separate clock is not provided with the signal, the encoding technique must incorporate a self-clocking mechanism so that a series of 1s or 0s does not conflict with recovery of the data.

Bit Error Rate The probability of bit errors can be minimized in noisy environments by selecting an appropriate encoding technique.

Data Transparency In some transmission protocols, the format of the data controls the operation of the receiver. Raw data must incorporate special encoding techniques into the code so that data are not mistaken for control characters.

5.6.1 Unipolar Versus Bipolar Encoding

Conceptually, the simplest transmission code is the *unipolar* format. A unipolar signal has the format of one polarity. A *transistor-transistor logic (TTL)* signal, for example, is considered a unipolar signal, because a logic 1 is represented with a positive voltage and a logic zero is represented with zero volts. Only one polarity exists. An inherent problem with unipolar codes, however, is that long strings of 1s or 0s result in reduced spectral energy for data recovery. In addition, the DC component in the pulse stream varies considerably, making recovery difficult in noisy environments.

If the polarity of a bit stream takes on positive and negative values, it is considered to be *bipolar.* Bipolar transmission has an advantage over unipolar transmission in that its DC component does not fluctuate as much as the polar signal. Furthermore, its voltage differential can be twice that of the unipolar signal.

Granular Noise
Noise generated from quantization errors occurring in the form of a square wave for analog input signals that do not change. Granular noise is analogous to *quantization noise* generated by A/D converters.

Channel Bandwidth
A transmission medium's *bandwidth* in terms of frequency or transmission speed.

Self-Clocking Signals
Serial transmitted signals encoded in such a way that an external clock is not necessary to synchronize with the data. Instead, the clock is encoded into the signal.

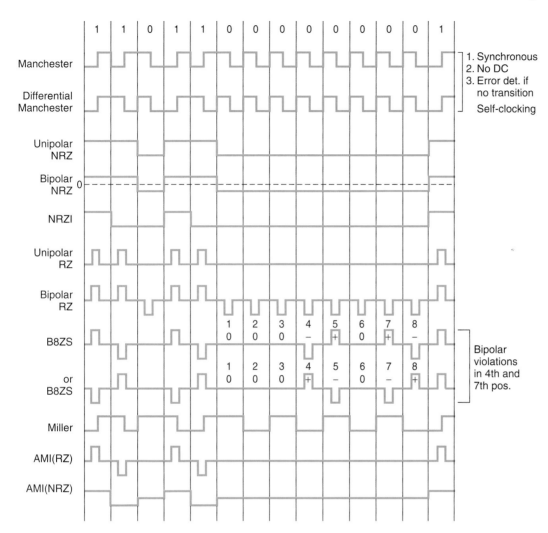

Manchester: transition at center of each cell. 1 = + trans. 0 = – trans.
Differential Manchester: transition at center of each cell. 1 = no trans. at beginning of cell. 0 = trans. at beginning of cell.
Unipolar NRZ: stays + and does not return to 0 during binary 1 cell.
Bipolar NRZ: + and – levels and does not return to 0 in cell.
NRZI: Change in signal level at beginning of bit = 1 and vice versa.
Unipolar RZ: goes + and returns to 0 from 1 during cell time.
Bipolar RZ: 2 non-zero voltage levels. 1 = +, 0 = – . (See chapter 12.)
Miller: transition at center of cell for 1s only. No transition for a 0 unless it is followed by another 0, in which case
        the transition is placed at the end of the cell for the first 0.
AMI: (Alternate Mark Inversion) A bipolar RZ signal. Pulse density at least 12.5%.

FIGURE 5-16
Standard encoding techniques.

5.6.2   Nonreturn-to-Zero

Nonreturn-to-zero (NRZ) encoding uses two discrete voltage levels to represent a
binary 1 and 0. It can be two positive voltage levels, as with unipolar NRZ, or two
discrete negative levels. This type of signal requires time coordination or synchro-

nization, because there may not be a signal change during each bit time. For example, in a long string of 0s or 1s, there are no level changes.

5.6.3   Nonreturn-to-Zero Invert

Nonreturn-to-zero invert (NRZI) is a variation of NRZ encoding and is considered to be a differential encoding technique, because its level is a function of the transition at the beginning of the signal element. If the signal element is a logic 1, there is a transition to the opposite logic level at the beginning of the cell. If the signal element is a logic 0, then no transition occurs at the beginning of the cell or throughout the cell. NRZI signals are reliably detected in the presence of noise. They are not polarity sensitive and require little power to transmit. However, a long string of 0s is a problem to detect without synchronization.

5.6.4   Return-to-Zero

Return-to-zero (RZ) encoding can be further classified into two categories: *unipolar RZ*, and *bipolar RZ*. In unipolar RZ encoding, a binary 1 is represented with a high level for half the bit time and returns to zero for the other half. Conversely, in bipolar RZ encoding, two non-zero voltages are used; a logic 1 and 0 alternate in polarities, each taking half the bit time before returning to zero. Bipolar RZ is considered to be a self-clocking code.

5.6.5   Self-Clocking Codes

Self-Clocking Codes
Encoding techniques, performed by phase-locked loop (PLL) technology, used to ensure that each bit time associated with the binary serial bit stream contains at least one level transition (1 to 0 or 0 to 1).

Self-clocking codes are encoding techniques used to ensure that each bit time associated with the binary serial bit stream contains at least one level transition (1 to 0, or 0 to 1). Sufficient spectral energy is generated at the clock frequency so that the receiver can recover the data, even when long periods of 1s or 0s occur. Phase-locked loop (PLL) technology is used to perform this task and is discussed in the next section. Examples of self-clocking codes include *bipolar RZ, Manchester* and *differential Manchester,* and *Miller.* Telephone trunk circuits use a self-clocking RZ encoding technique called *bipolar with 8 zero substitution (B8ZS),* which is also known as *alternate mark inversion (AMI).* B8ZS encoding is discussed further in Chapter 12. Before B8ZS encoding, AMI was used extensively in first-generation PCM systems. AMI can be a bipolar RZ or NRZ signal.

5.6.5.1   Manchester Encoding   In Manchester encoding, a logic 1 is represented with a low-to-high transition in the center (or beginning) of the cell, and a logic 0 is represented with a high-to-low transition in the center (or beginning) of the cell. Ethernet LAN systems employ Manchester encoding in their signalling standard.

5.6.5.2   Differential Manchester Encoding   In differential Manchester encoding, a transition from high to low or from low to high occurs at the center of each cell, which provides for the self-clocking mechanism. A logic 1 and 0 are determined by the logic level of the previous cell. If the previous cell is a logic 1, there is no transition at the beginning of the current cell. Conversely, if the previous cell is a logic 0, then a transition occurs at the beginning of the current cell. Differential Manchester encoding is the signalling standard used in Token Ring LAN systems.

5.6.5.3 Miller Encoding *Miller encoding* is a self-clocking technique in which a transition occurs at the center of each cell for logic 1s only. No transition is used for a logic 0 unless it is followed by another 0, in which case the transition is placed at the *end* of the cell for the first 0. As with Manchester and differential Manchester encoding, a string of 0s or 1s produces a square wave. Its frequency, however, is only half that of Manchester encoding and, therefore, requires only half the bandwidth. Miller encoding is commonly used in digital magnetic recording.

5.7 THE PHASE-LOCKED LOOP

Phase-locked loop (PLL) technology has been widely used in the communications industry since its first introduction in the 1920s. It is employed in satellite tracking systems, radio telemetry, signal processing, frequency synthesis, AM and FM receiver and transmitter circuits, modem technology, and a variety of other data communications and telecommunications applications. Its importance to the telecommunications technologist must not be overlooked.

> **Phase-Locked Loop (PLL)**
> A feedback circuit designed to maintain phase lock to an incoming signal.

5.7.1 PLL Theory of Operation

A block diagram representing the PLL is shown in Figure 5-17. Note that the PLL is a feedback-controlled electronic system consisting of a phase detector, a low-pass filter/amplifier combination, and a voltage-controlled oscillator (VCO). Combining these functions in a closed loop permits an input signal to be tracked in frequency and phase. When this occurs, the output of the VCO is said to be *phase-locked* to the input signal.

The VCO produces a periodic waveform whose frequency can be varied about some *free-running frequency*. This is the VCO's frequency when the PLL is not in lock or when the loop is opened. The VCO is designed so that its output frequency range is greater than the required output range of the PLL. The frequency of the VCO is controlled by the value of its input control voltage, V_c.

> **Free-Running Frequency**
> The frequency of a controlled oscillator without any control applied to it (e.g., a *PLL's* oscillator when its loop is open).

When an input signal, v_i, at a frequency, f_i, is applied to the phase detector, its frequency is compared with the output frequency, f_o, of the VCO. The phase detector generates an output error voltage, v_e, that represents the phase difference between the input frequency, f_i, and the VCO's frequency, f_o. The error voltage is filtered and amplified to produce the VCO's control voltage, V_c, which corrects the VCO's frequency so that it maintains phase lock with the input signal.

The phase detector is essentially a mixer that produces the sum and difference products of the input and the output signals. If we considered the instantaneous voltage of the input signal, v_i, and the VCO's output signal, v_o, we have

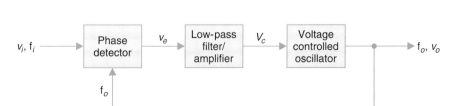

FIGURE 5-17
Block diagram of the PLL.

$$v_i = V_{ip} \sin \omega_i t \qquad \text{(5-3)}$$

$$v_o = V_{op} \sin \omega_o t \qquad \text{(5-4)}$$

where
v_i = instantaneous value of the input voltage
V_{ip} = peak value of input voltage
ω_i = input frequency in radians per second
v_o = instantaneous value of the VCO's output voltage
V_{op} = peak value of the output voltage
ω_i = VCO frequency in radians per second

The instantaneous error voltage at the output of the phase detector is

$$v_e = v_i \cdot v_o = V_{ip} \sin \omega_i t \cdot V_{op} \sin \omega_o t \qquad \text{(5-5)}$$

Applying the trigonometric identity $\sin \alpha \sin \beta = \frac{1}{2} [\cos (\alpha - \beta) - \cos (\alpha + \beta)]$ to equation (5-5) gives

$$v_e = \frac{1}{2} V_{ip} V_{op} [\cos (\omega_i - \omega_o)t - \cos(\omega_i + \omega_o)t]$$

$$= \underbrace{\frac{1}{2} V_{ip} V_{op} \cos (\omega_i - \omega_o)t}_{\text{difference term}} - \underbrace{\frac{1}{2} V_{ip} V_{op} \cos (\omega_i + \omega_o) t}_{\text{sum term}} \qquad \text{(5-6)}$$

Filtering out the sum term and amplifying the difference term in equation (5-6) leaves us with the VCO control voltage:

$$V_c = \frac{1}{2} A_v V_{ip} V_{op} \cos(\omega_i - \omega_o)t \qquad \text{(5-7)}$$

where A_v is the voltage gain of the low-pass filter/amplifier section of the PLL.

From equation (5-7), it is apparent that when the PLL is in lock ($f_i = f_o$), $\omega_i - \omega_o$ is equal to zero and the control voltage, V_c, becomes a fixed DC value. This is the voltage level necessary for the PLL to maintain lock with the input signal. If the frequency of the input signal, ω_i, were to change, the control voltage would also change and cause the VCO's output frequency to change as well. The loop essentially corrects itself and maintains phase lock with the input signal. Two of the most important PLL parameters in terms of phase lock are:

| Lock Range |
The range of frequencies over which a *PLL* stays locked.

Lock Range   When the PLL is in lock with the input signal, it can only maintain phase lock over a finite range of frequencies, which is called the *lock range*. Outside this range, the PLL is not in lock with the input signal and f_i does not equal f_o. Normally, the lock range is centered about the free-running frequency of the VCO, which is the frequency of the VCO when the loop is opened up or the PLL is not in lock. The lock range primarily depends on the overall DC gain of the loop, which includes the low-pass filter/amplifier gain.

| Capture Range |
The range of frequencies over which the PLL can acquire lock from an unlocked condition.

Capture Range   The *capture range* of a PLL is the range of frequencies over which the PLL can acquire lock from an unlocked condition. The capture range is also referred to as the *pull-in range* and primarily depends on the low-pass filter characteristics. It can be shown mathematically that the capture range will never exceed the lock range. The capture range is also centered about the free-running frequency of the VCO.

5.7.1.1 A PLL Mechanical Analogy
A mechanical analogy of the PLL can enhance one's understanding of this technology. Just as electronic circuits and devices

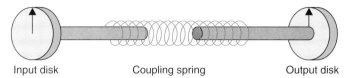

Input disk   Coupling spring   Output disk

FIGURE 5-18
Mechanical analogy of a PLL.

are used to model the behavior of a mechanical device, it is entirely possible for a mechanical device to model an electronic device.* Figure 5-18 illustrates the mechanical equivalent of a PLL. The setup consists of two heavy metal disks and a spring that is firmly attached to each disk's center shaft. The two shafts are physically separate and held together by the adjoining spring. This allows each disk to rotate clockwise or counterclockwise when some external torsional force is applied. To model the operation of a PLL, the two disks have been labeled the *input disk* and the *output disk,* which are analogous to the input and output frequencies of the PLL. The disks have been marked with reference markers.

Consider the case in Figure 5-19(a). Initially, both disks are stationary. The input disk is slowly rotated in a clockwise direction, and the massive output disk does not move at first. As the torque in the spring increases, however, the output disk begins to move and track the input disk. At any instant in time, there is a phase error between the two disks, which is determined by the equation

$$\theta_e = \theta_i - \theta_o \qquad (5\text{-}8)$$

This is analogous to the phase error between the input and the output frequencies of a PLL. From equation (5-7), this is

$$\theta_e = (\omega_i - \omega_o)t \qquad (5\text{-}9)$$

Figure 5-19(b) illustrates the effect of instantaneously rotating the input disk 180° and then stopping. Because of its enormous mass, the output disk cannot respond to the sudden torsional force in the spring. Eventually, however, the output disk begins to accelerate toward the position of the input disk, but because of its inertia, it rotates beyond the position of the input disk and, eventually, causes a torsional force in the spring in the opposite direction. The output disk then begins to rotate in the opposite direction, oscillating back and forth until the phase error between the two disks diminishes to zero.

This behavior is analogous to the *step input* in phase or frequency in a PLL circuit. If one were to monitor the control voltage, V_c, to the input of a PLL's frequency synthesizer as a function of time, it would appear the same as the phase error created in our mechanical examples. Figure 5-20 illustrates the phase error resulting from a step-input response.

The oscillatory effect in our mechanical system is a dual function of the mass of the disks and of spring characteristics such as tension, spacing, length, and so forth. In a PLL circuit, the duality is the loop filter and its gain. The important parameter representing these characteristics is called the *dampening factor,* δ. Various dampening factors are shown in Figure 5-20 as well.

> **Dampening Factor**
> A parameter related to the degree of the oscillatory effect of electrical and mechanical devices such as *PLL* circuits or mechanical springs.

Signetics Linear Data Manual Volume 1 (Signetics, 1987), p. 4-236.

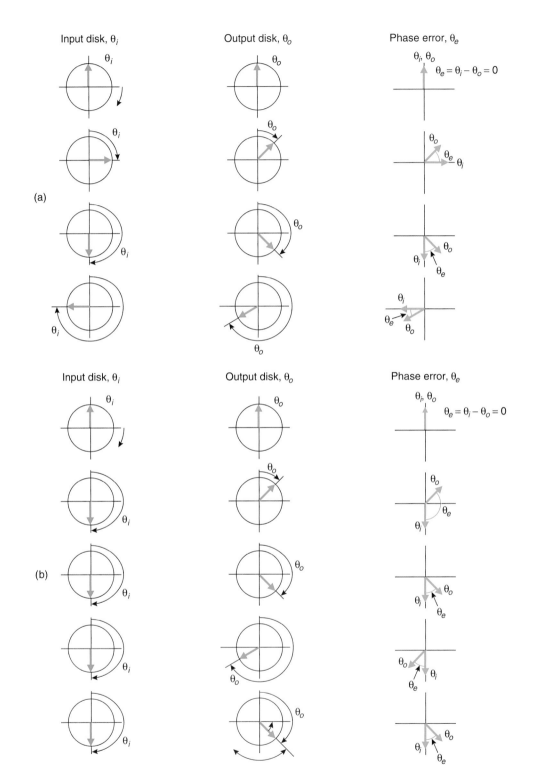

FIGURE 5-19

Disk sequence and phase error: (a) the input disk is slowly rotated clockwise while the output disk slowly tracks it; (b) the input disk instantaneously steps 180°, causing the output disk to oscillate and eventually settle.

Phase error, $\theta_e = \theta_i - \theta_o = (\omega_i - \omega_o)t$

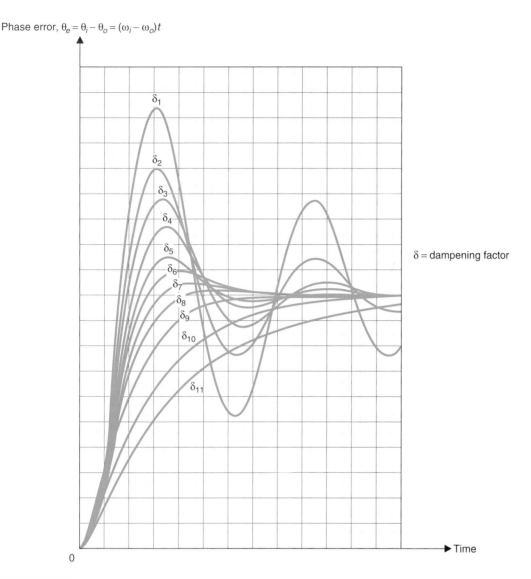

$\delta =$ dampening factor

FIGURE 5-20
The step input response for a PLL circuit is the same as in our mechanical analogy.
Note the various dampening factors.

5.7.2 Frequency Synthesizer

One of the most widely used applications of the PLL is frequency synthesis. Virtually all radio and television systems today employ frequency synthesizers as their local oscillators (LOs). The advantage of the *frequency synthesizer* is its high degree of accuracy and digital tuning capability, which makes it ideal for microprocessors and digital interfaces.

Figure 5-21 illustrates the block diagrams of several configurations for frequency synthesizers. In each case, the input frequency serves as a highly accurate reference source from which the output frequency is derived. A crystal oscillator is typically used as a reference frequency, and the output frequency is some multiple of the input frequency.

Frequency Synthesizer
A *PLL* application whereby a range of frequencies are generated or synthesized by the PLL based on a control word typically sent by a microprocessor.

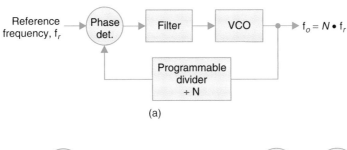

(a)

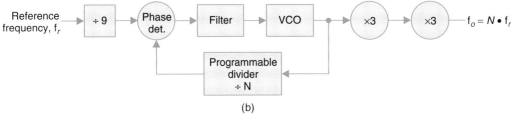

(b)

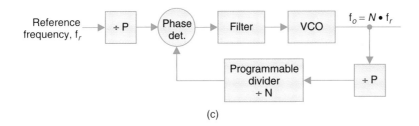

(c)

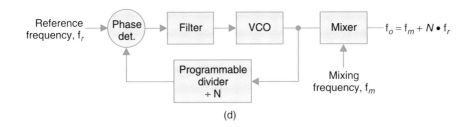

(d)

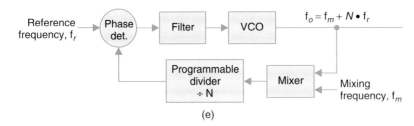

(e)

FIGURE 5-21
Various frequency synthesizer configurations: (1) frequency synthesis using a basic PLL; (b) frequency synthesis using a PLL and output multipliers; (c) frequency synthesis by prescaling in the PLL; (d) PLL frequency synthesis by mixing up; (e) PLL frequency synthesis by mixing down.

PROBLEMS

1. Name three advantages of pulse modulation over analog modulation.
2. Define *PCM*.
3. Compute the quantization range for a 10-bit A/D converter.
4. Compute the quantization range for a 16-bit A/D converter.
5. The upper cutoff frequency of a telephone line is 3400 Hz. Based on Nyquist's Sampling Theorem, what is the minimum sampling rate necessary to fully recover the highest frequency component that would pass through the line?
6. Based on Nyquist's Sampling Theorem, if a signal is sampled at a rate of 8 kHz, what would be the highest frequency component that could be recovered?
7. What is a *regenerative repeater?*
8. Given a sine wave whose peak-to-peak amplitude utilizes the full range of a 12-bit A/D converter, compute the signal-to-quantization noise ratio, SNR.
9. Explain how a *codec* works.
10. Explain the difference between pulse-width modulation and pulse-position modulation.
11. Draw the resulting output waveform, V_o, generated by a delta modulator for the sine wave shown below:

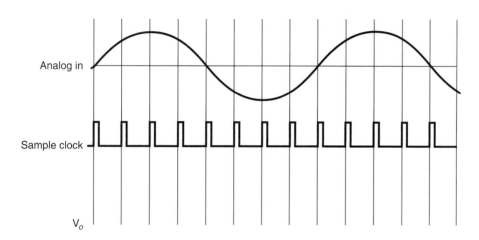

12. What are the basic functional components of a delta modulator?
13. Given the bit pattern 110100110001, draw the resulting waveforms produced by the following encoding techniques:
    a. Manchester
    b. Differential Manchester
    c. Unipolar NRZ
    d. NRZI
    e. AMI (NRZ)
14. Given the bit pattern 100101100111, draw the resulting waveforms produced by the following encoding techniques:
    a. Unipolar RZ
    b. Bipolar RZ
    c. B8ZS
    d. Miller
    e. AMI (RZ)
15. Define the *capture range* of a PLL.
16. Define the *lock range* of a PLL.

6

TRANSMISSION CODES

Transmitted data are typically prearranged in accordance with various codes developed over the years. Many of these codes are universally recognized and have become standards, whereas others are highly cryptic and applicable only to unique and limited situations. Transmission codes, such as the International Morse Code and Baudot, were developed more than a century ago. They are still used in the field of digital communications. ASCII and EBCDIC are more recent codes that have gained popularity with the advent of the computer. Codes normally overlooked in the realm of data communications are those encompassed by bar code technology, which has substantially improved productivity and materials management in the workforce. In each case, the intent of the code is to provide an alternative method of representing numbers, letters, and symbols.

It is often desirable to have codes readily available for development and troubleshooting purposes. Often, these codes are provided on reference cards or manuals. This chapter presents those codes that are most widely used in today's communication systems and serves as a reference guide for future use.

6.1 COMPUTER NUMBER SYSTEMS

The systematic and structured way of counting is seldom discussed and often taken for granted. In our discussion of transmission codes, it becomes necessary to understand the fundamental structure of our existing *decimal* (base 10) number system and apply it to computer number systems and their structure.

What are computer number systems? Computer number systems include *binary* (base 2), *octal* (base 8), and *hexadecimal* (base 16). They are rudimentary to understanding the communication system and should be mastered as well as continually reviewed through practice. Furthermore, desktop computers, laptops, peripheral devices, and virtually all digital electronic devices are said to operate using "binary" voltages or current levels. That is, the combination of 1s and 0s representing the two distinct binary states of the voltage or current are encoded and decoded into the information we utilize.

What about the octal and hexadecimal number systems, however, and their relationship to computers? These two number systems are used primarily as a form of shorthand to represent groups of binary bits or large strings of binary numbers. In addition, the architectural design of computers as well as their address and data bus

TABLE 6-1
Computer Numbers Systems

Decimal (Base 10)	Binary (Base 2)	Octal (Base 8)	Hexadecimal (Base 16)
0	0000	0	0
1	0001	1	1
2	0010	2	2
3	0011	3	3
4	0100	4	4
5	0101	5	5
6	0110	6	6
7	0111	7	7
8	1000	10	8
9	1001	11	9
10	1010	12	A
11	1011	13	B
12	1100	14	C
13	1101	15	D
14	1110	16	E
15	1111	17	F

structures, internal registers, memory, and instruction formats are ideally for use of octal and hexadecimal number systems. Table 6-1 compares these number systems to our decimal number system.

6.1.1 The Decimal Number System

> **Decimal Number System**
> The base 10 numbering system with which we are most familiar. There are 10 valid digits in base 10 (0 through 9).

The *decimal number system* is the numbering system with which we are all familiar. It uses a *base* of 10. In simple terms, the base of a numbering system is the numeric value that is raised to an exponent or power to equal another number. For example, $10^3 = 10 \cdot 10 \cdot 10$. As we shall see, raising any number-system base to an incrementing exponent gives us the weightings of the significant digits of which a number is comprised.

The base of any number system also tells us the maximum number of valid characters that can be used to represent any number within that system. Because the decimal system has a base of 10, there are 10 valid characters: 0 through 9. In contrast, the binary number system has a base of 2; the valid two characters are 0 and 1. The octal number system has a base of 8. Its valid eight characters are 0 through 7. Lastly, the hexadecimal number system has a base of 16 and, therefore, has 16 valid characters: 0 through 9 and A through F. Let us now demonstrate how the structure of a number depends on its base.

There are 365_{10} days in a year. The subscript of 10 is normally not shown and taken for granted. It becomes necessary to apply the subscript, however, so that the given number can be distinguished between that in other numbering systems. Starting from the least significant digit (LSD) of 5 and preceding to the left, each decimal character has a *weighting* of the base raised to an incrementing exponent: 10^0, which equals 1; which equals 10; 10^2, which equals 100; 10^3, which equals

1000; and so forth. This is also true if the number continued to the right of the implied decimal point, only then the exponent would be negative. That is, if there were 365.25 days in a year, the number 2 to the right of the decimal point would have a weighting of 10^{-1} and the 5 to the right of the decimal point would have a weighting of 10^{-2}.

$$
\begin{array}{ccc}
100 & 10 & 1 \\
10^2 & 10^1 & 10^0 \\
3 & 6 & 5
\end{array}
$$

100   10   1 $\longleftarrow$ Weighting of each digit

10^2 10^1 10^0 $\longleftarrow$ Base raised to incrementing exponent

3   6   5

Most significant digit (MSD)   Least significant digit (LSD)

Therefore,

$$
\begin{aligned}
365_{10} &= (3 \times 10^2) + (6 \times 10^1) + (5 \times 10^0) \\
&= (3 \times 100) + (6 \times 10) + (5 \times 1) \\
&= 300 + 60 + 5
\end{aligned}
$$

6.1.2 The Binary Number System

The importance of mastering the *binary number system* cannot be overemphasized. Our computers, radios, television sets, cell phones, pagers, test equipment, and virtually all telecommunication systems incorporate high-speed digital electronics devices that operate on binary electrical impulses. These impulses can take on one of two states: a logic 0, or a logic 1. For example, 0 V is referred to as a logic 0 and +5 V as a logic 1. The logical value of each character or digit, whether it is a 1 or 0, is called a *bit*. Eight bits is equal to a *byte*. The combination of bits and bytes makes our digital electronic devices operate properly.

> **Binary Number System**
> The base 2 system is widely used to represent digital logic circuits in computers and electronics involving signaling with two states. There are two valid digits in binary (0 and 1).

6.1.2.1 Binary-to-Decimal Conversion

A binary number can be analyzed using the same mathematical rules outlined earlier for a decimal number. Because binary has a base of 2, there are two valid characters or digits: 0, and 1. Starting from the *least significant bit (LSB)* and preceding to the *most significant bit (MSB)*, each bit has a *weighting* of the base raised to an incrementing exponent: 2^0, which equals 1; 2^1, which equals 2; 2^2, which equals 4; 2^3, which equals 8; and so forth. The binary number 110110_2 can be converted to a decimal number as follows:

> **Least Significant Bit (LSB)**
> The binary bit with the least significant weighting in a binary number.

> **Most Significant Bit (MSB)**
> The binary bit with the most significant weighting in a binary number.

32   16   8   4   2   1 $\longleftarrow$ Weighting of each bit

2^5 2^4 2^3 2^2 2^1 2^0 $\longleftarrow$ Base raised to incrementing exponent

1   1   0   1   1   0 $\longleftarrow$ Binary number

Most significant bit (MSB)   Least significant bit (LSB)

Therefore,

$$
\begin{aligned}
110110_2 &= (1 \times 2^5) + (1 \times 2^4) + (0 \times 2^3) + (1 \times 2^2) + (1 \times 2^1) + (0 \times 2^0) \\
&= (1 \times 32) + (1 \times 16) + (0 \times 8) + (1 \times 4) + (1 \times 2) + (0 \times 1) \\
&= 32 + 16 + 0 + 4 + 2 + 0 \\
&= 54_{10}
\end{aligned}
$$

TABLE 6-2
Binary Weightings to 10 bits

Exponents	2^9	2^8	2^7	2^6	2^5	2^4	2^3	2^2	2^1	2^0
Binary weightings	512	256	128	64	32	16	8	4	2	1

In decimal, the weighting of each digit went up by a factor of the base: 1, 10, 100, 1000, 10000, and so on. A binary number also goes up by a factor of the base: 1, 2, 4, 8, and so on. In fact, because the base is 2, the weighting simply "doubles" or "halves" between significant digits. We could use this observation in simplifying the conversion from binary to decimal or from decimal to binary. The conversion process is a simple matter of addition. Each bit in a binary number has only two possible states (1 or 0). Therefore, a 1 can imply a YES, or add the weighting, and a 0 can imply NO, or do not add the weighting. Students should become familiar with the binary weightings at least 10 bits (2^0 through 2^9), which are shown in Table 6-2. For conversions involving numbers larger than 10 bits, the weightings continue to double up to 2^n, where n is an exponent that is one less than the total number of bits in the binary word.

EXAMPLE
6.1

Convert the following binary numbers to decimal numbers.
(a) 1001_2.
(b) 11110010_2.
(c) 1010110010_2.

Solution:

To convert from binary to decimal, simply write down the binary weightings starting from the LSB, a weighting of 1, and ending with the weighting of the MSB of the given binary number. There is no need to write down the equivalent exponent value. A 1 in the given binary number implies YES, or add the weighting; a 0 implies NO, or do not add the corresponding weighting.

(a)

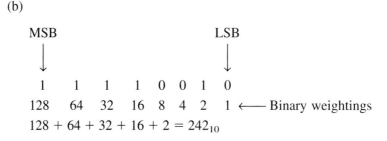

(b)

MSB   LSB

1   1   1   1   0   0   1   0
128 64 32 16 8   4   2   1   ⟵ Binary weightings
128 + 64 + 32 + 16 + 2 = 242_{10}

(c)

MSB   LSB

1	0	1	0	1	1	0	0	1	0
512	256	128	64	32	16	8	4	2	1

$512 + 128 + 32 + 16 + 2 = 690_{10}$

6.1.2.2 Decimal-to-Binary Conversion   There are basically two methods of converting a decimal number to a binary number. One is to successively divide the decimal number by two, the binary base, until the quotient is zero and then use the remainders of each division as the answer. Because binary numbers tend to be very long, however, this is not an efficient method. Thus, we reserve this method for decimal-to-octal and decimal-to-hexadecimal conversions.

The more efficient method is to use simple addition of the binary weightings listed in Table 6-2. To convert from decimal to binary, write down the binary weightings, starting from the MSB and working to the LSB, by placing a binary 1 under the appropriate weighting to total the given decimal number. Any weightings not used are bits that are equal to 0.

Convert the following decimal numbers to binary numbers:
(a) 13_{10}.   (b) 89_{10}.   (c) 337_{10}.

Solution:
(a) Because 13_{10} is less than the weighting of 16, only the weightings of 8, 4, 2, 1 should be written down:

8	4	2	1
1	1	0	1

$13_{10} = 8 + 4 + 2 = 1101_2$

(b) Because 89_{10} is less than the weighting of 128, we begin with a weight of 64:

64	32	16	8	4	2	1
1	0	1	1	0	0	1

$89_{10} = 64 + 16 + 8 + 1 = 1011001_2$

(c) Because 337_{10} is less than the weighting of 512, we begin with a weighting of 256:

256	128	64	32	16	8	4	2	1
1	0	1	0	1	0	0	0	1

$337_{10} = 256 + 64 + 16 + 1 = 101010001_2$

EXAMPLE
6.2

6.1.3   The Octal Number System

The *octal number system* is used in conjunction with some microprocessors, computers, and their respective assembly language instruction sets. This is because their internal architectural design is conveniently described in groups of three binary bits.

TABLE 6-3
The Octal Number System

Octal	Binary
0	000
1	001
2	010
3	011
4	100
5	101
6	110
7	111

> **Octal Number System**
> A computer numbering system widely used as shorthand to represent groups of 3 bits (1 octal digit). There are 8 valid digits in this number system (0 through 7).

A 16-bit register, for example, may be divided into five groups of 3 bits (15 bits), with 1 remaining bit.

Why 3 bits? Octal is a numbering system that uses base 8; therefore, there are eight valid characters; 0 through 7. With 3 bits, as shown in Table 6-3, eight combinations ($2^3 = 8$) of binary words are possible.* Each octal character can be represented with a 3-bit binary word. Conversely, 3 binary bits can be grouped together to form one octal character.

6.1.3.1 Octal-to-Decimal Conversion An octal number can be analyzed using the same mathematical rules outlined earlier for a binary or a decimal number. Starting from the LSD and preceding to the MSD, each digit has a weighting of the base raised to an incrementing exponent 8^0, which equals 1; 8^1, which equals 8; 8^2, which equals 64; 8^3, which equals 512; and so forth. The octal number 376_8 can be converted to a decimal number as follows:

$$\begin{array}{ccc} 64 & 8 & 1 \quad \longleftarrow \text{ Weighting of each digit} \\ 8^2 & 8^1 & 8^0 \quad \longleftarrow \text{ Base raised to incrementing exponent} \\ 3 & 7 & 6 \quad \longleftarrow \text{ Octal number} \end{array}$$

$$\text{MSD} \qquad\qquad \text{LSD}$$

Therefore,

$$376_8 = (3 \times 8^2) + (7 \times 8^1) + (6 \times 8^0)$$
$$= (3 \times 64) + (7 \times 8) + (6 \times 1)$$
$$= 254_{10}$$

EXAMPLE 6.3

Convert the following octal numbers to decimal numbers:
(a) 52_8.   (b) 839_8.   (c) 6145_8.

---

*The number of possible binary combinations of words is equal to 2^n, where n is equal to the number of bits in the given binary word.

Solution:
To convert from octal to decimal, write down the octal weightings starting from the LSD, a weighting of 1, and ending with the weighting of the MSD of the given octal number.

(a) 8   1 $\longleftarrow$ Weighting of each digit
    8^1 8^0 $\longleftarrow$ Base raised to incrementing exponent
    5   2 $\longleftarrow$ Octal number
    $52_8 = (5 \times 8) + (2 \times 1) = 42_{10}$

(b) Because the characters 8 and 9 do not exist in the octal number system, 839_8 is not a valid octal number. This problem is not solvable and is intended to show students that any number system has a valid set of characters that can be used.

(c) 512 64 8   1 $\longleftarrow$ Weighting of each digit
    8^3 8^2 8^1 8^0 $\longleftarrow$ Base raised to incrementing exponent
    6   1   4   5 $\longleftarrow$ Octal number
    $6145_8 = (6 \times 512) + (1 \times 64) + (4 \times 8) + (5 \times 1)$
    $= 3{,}072 + 64 + 32 + 5$
    $= 3{,}173_{10}$

6.1.3.2 Decimal-to-Octal Conversion Converting from decimal to octal can be done by systematically dividing the given decimal number by eight and then taking the remainder as an answer.

EXAMPLE
6.4

Convert the following decimal numbers to octal numbers:
(a) 42_{10}.
(b) 298_{10}.
(c) 613_{10}.

Solution:
(a) $42 \div 8 = 5$ with a remainder of 2
    $5 \div 8 = 0$ with a remainder of 5

therefore,

$42_{10} = 52_8$
Check: $52_8 = (5 \times 8) + (2 \times 1) = 42_{10}$

(b) $298 \div 8 = 37$ with a remainder of 2
    $37 \div 8 = 4$ with a remainder of 5
    $4 \div 8 = 0$ with a remainder of 4

therefore,

$298_{10} = 452_8$
Check: $451_8 = (4 \times 64) + (5 \times 8) + (2 \times 1) = 298_{10}$

(c) $613 \div 8 = 76$ with a remainder of 5

$76 \div 8 = 9$ with a remainder of 4

$9 \div 8 = 1$ with a remainder of 1

$1 \div 8 = 0$ with a remainder of 1

therefore,

$613_8 = 1145_8$

Check: $1145_8 = (1 \times 512) + (1 \times 64) + (4 \times 8) + (5 \times 1) = 613_{10}$

Grouping
The grouping of binary bits to represent other characters in other number systems. For example, 3 bits equals one octal character, and 4 bits equals one hexadecimal character.

6.1.3.3 Binary-to-Octal Conversion Binary-to-octal conversion can be performed in several ways. One method is to convert the binary number to a decimal number and then convert the decimal number to an octal number using the division process outlined earlier. The easiest way to convert from binary to octal is by *grouping* of binary bits. Referring to Table 6-2, there are 3 bits ($2^3 = 8$) used to represent one octal character. The given binary word is easily converted to an octal word by partitioning the word in groups of 3 bits, starting from the LSB.

EXAMPLE 6.5

Convert the following binary numbers to octal numbers:
(a) 1000101011_2.
(b) 111101011000001_2.
(c) 1101110000010100_2.

Solution:
Starting from the LSB of each binary word, apply a partition to each group of 3 bits. The last group to the left, or the most significant group, may end up with 1 to 3 bits. Convert each group to its equivalent decimal number using the weightings of 4 (2^2), 2 (2^1), and 1 (2^0) for each group of 3 bits. Note that octal is a subset of decimal. Because there are only 3 bits per group, the maximum value can be 7, which is a valid octal number. Table 6-2 can also be used.

(a) 1 | 0 0 0 | 1 0 1 | 0 1 1
   1   0   5   3

therefore,

$1000101011_2 = 1053_8$

(b) 1 1 | 1 1 0 | 1 0 1 | 1 0 0 | 0 0 1
  3   6   5   4   1

therefore,

$111101011000001_2 = 36541_8$

(c) 1 | 1 0 1 | 1 1 0 | 0 0 0 | 0 1 0 | 1 0 0
  1   5   6   0   2   4

therefore,

$1101110000010100_2 = 156024_8$

6.1.3.4   Octal-to-Binary Conversion   Octal-to-binary conversion is relatively straightforward, because we know there are 3 bits per octal character. Although the grouping partition is not necessary, it is shown here for learning purposes.

Convert the following octal numbers to binary numbers:

(a) 74_8.   (b) 253_8.   (c) 1260_8.

EXAMPLE
6.6

Solution:

(a)   7   4

   1 1 1 | 1 0 0

   $74_8 = 111100_2$

(b)   2   5   3

   0 1 0 | 1 0 1 | 0 1 1

   $253_8 = 10101011_2$

Note that the leading 0 for 2 is dropped.

(c)   1   2   6   0

   0 0 1 | 0 1 0 | 1 1 0 | 0 0 0

   $1260_8 = 1010110000_2$

Note that the leading two 0s in the MSD of 1 have been dropped.

6.1.4   The Hexadecimal Number System

The *hexadecimal number system,* which often is referred to as "hex," is unique in that it is the only number system discussed thus far that includes alphabetical characters. Like its counterpart, octal, hex is conducive to grouping of binary bits as a form of shorthand, particularly when describing large binary numbers such as address and data buses. Hex is also widely used in assembly and machine language programming as well as in code representation.

> **Hexadecimal Number System**
> A computer numbering system widely used as shorthand to represent groups of 4 bits (1 hexadecimal character). There are 16 valid characters in this number system (0 through 9 and A through F).

Hex uses base 16; therefore, there are 16 valid characters: 0 through 9 and A through F. Hex characters are listed in Table 6-4 along with their corresponding decimal numbers and 4-bit binary words. Note that all the number systems discussed so far—binary, octal, and decimal—include characters that are a subset of hex.

6.1.4.1   Hexadecimal-to-Decimal Conversion   A hexadecimal number can be analyzed using the same mathematical rules outlined earlier for a binary, octal, or decimal number. Once again, starting from the LSD and proceeding to the MSD, each digit has a weighting of the base raised to an incrementing exponent 16^0, which equals 1; 16^1, which equals 16; 16^2, which equals 256; and so forth. The hex number $8CD_{16}$ can be converted to a decimal number as follows:

$$256 \quad 16 \quad 1 \quad \longleftarrow \text{ Weighting of each digit}$$
$$16^2 \quad 16^1 \quad 16^0 \quad \longleftarrow \text{ Base raised to incrementing exponent}$$
$$8 \quad \text{C} \quad \text{E} \quad \longleftarrow \text{ Hex number}$$

MSD   LSD

TABLE 6-4
The Hexadecimal Number System with Equivalent Decimal Numbers
and 4-Bit Binary Words

Hex	Decimal	Binary
0	0	0000
1	1	0001
2	2	0010
3	3	0011
4	4	0100
5	5	0101
6	6	0110
7	7	0111
8	8	1000
9	9	1001
A	10	1010
B	11	1011
C	12	1100
D	13	1101
E	14	1110
E	15	1111

Therefore,

$$8CE_{16} = (8 \times 16^2) + (C \times 16^1) + (E \times 8^0)$$
$$= (8 \times 256) + (12 \times 16) + (14 \times 1)$$
$$= 2254_{10}$$

Note that $C_{16} = 12_{10}$ and $E_{16} = 14_{10}$ (see Table 6-4).

EXAMPLE 6.7

Convert the following hex numbers to decimal numbers:
(a) DA_{16}.
(b) $29B_{16}$.
(c) $3DF5_{16}$.

Solution:
To convert from hex to decimal, write down the hex weightings starting from the LSD, a weighting of 1, and ending with the weighting of the MSD of the given hex number.

(a)   16   1 $\longleftarrow$ Weighting of each digit

     16^1 16^0 $\longleftarrow$ Base raised to incrementing exponent

     D   A $\longleftarrow$ Hex number

$$DA_{16} = (D \times 16) + (A \times 1)$$
$$= (13 \times 16) + (10 \times 1)$$
$$= 208 + 10$$
$$= 218_{10}$$

(b) 256   16   1   ⟵── Weighting of each digit

16^2 16^1 16^0 ⟵── Base raised to incrementing exponent

2   9   B   ⟵── Hex number

$$29B_{16} = (2 \times 256) + (9 \times 16) + (B \times 1)$$
$$= 512 + 144 + 11$$
$$= 667_{10}$$

(c) 4096   256   16   1   ⟵── Weighting of each digit

16^3 16^2 16^1 16^0 ⟵── Base raised to incrementing exponent

3   D   F   5   ⟵── Hex number

$$3DF5_{16} = (3 \times 4096) + (D \times 256) + (F \times 16) + (5 \times 1)$$
$$= 12{,}288 + (13 \times 256) + (15 \times 16) + 5$$
$$= 12{,}288 + 3328 + 240 + 5$$
$$= 15{,}861_{10}$$

6.1.4.2   Decimal-to-Hexadecimal Conversion   Converting from decimal to hex can be done by systematically dividing the given decimal number by 16 and then taking the remainder as an answer.

Convert the following decimal numbers to hex numbers:
(a) 37_{10}.   (b) 246_{10}.   (c) 2636_{10}.

EXAMPLE
6.8

Solution:
(a) $37 \div 16 = 2$ with a remainder of 5

   $2 \div 16 = 0$ with a remainder of 2

therefore,

$$37_{10} = 25_{16}$$

Check: $25_{16} = (2 \times 16) + (5 \times 1) = 37_{10}$

(b) $246 \div 16 = 15$ with a remainder of 6

   $15 \div 16 = \ 0$ with a remainder of 15, which equals F_{16}

therefore,

$$246_{10} = F6_{16}$$

Check: $F6_{16} = (15 \times 16) + (6 \times 1) = 246_{10}$

(c) $2636 \div 16 = 164$ with a remainder of 12, which equals C_{16}

   $164 \div 16 = \ 10$ with a remainder of 4

   $10 \div 16 = \ \ 0$ with a remainder of 10, which equals A_{10}

therefore,

$$2636_{10} = A4C_{16}$$

Check: $A4C_{16} = (A \times 256) + (4 \times 16) + C$
$$= (10 \times 256) + 64 + 12$$
$$= 2636_{10}$$

6.1.4.3 Binary-to-Hexadecimal Conversion The easiest way to convert from binary to hex is by grouping of binary bits as we did for the octal system. Referring to Table 6-4, there are 4 bits ($2^4 = 16$) used to represent one hex character. The given binary word is easily converted to a hex word by partitioning the word in groups of 4 bits, starting from the LSB.

EXAMPLE 6.9

Convert the following binary numbers to hex numbers:
(a) 101000101011_2.
(b) 111110101100001_2.
(c) $10011111010011100000101001101111_2$.

Solution:

Starting from the LSB of each binary word, apply a partition to each group of 4 bits. The last group to the left, or the most significant group, may end up with 1 to 4 bits. Convert each group to its equivalent hex number using the weightings of 8 (2^3), 4 (2^2), 2 (2^1), and 1 (2^0) for each group of 4 bits. Note that each group of 4 bits can have a maximum value of F (1111). Use Table 6-4 as an aid if needed; Table 6-2 can also be used.

(a) 1 0 1 0 | 0 0 1 0 | 1 0 1 1
         A   2   B

therefore,

$$101000101011_2 = A2B_{16}$$

(b) 1 1 1 | 1 1 0 1 | 0 1 1 0 | 0 0 0 1
       7   D   6   1

therefore,

$$111110101100001_2 = 7D61_{16}$$

(c) 1 0 0 1 | 1 1 1 1 | 0 1 0 0 | 1 1 1 0 | 0 0 0 0 | 1 0 1 0 | 0 1 1 0 | 1 1 1 1
         9   F   4   E   0   A   6   F

therefore,

$$10011111010011100000101001101111_2 = 9F4E0A6F_{16}$$

Note that in Example 6.9(c), a 32-bit binary word can be reduced to 8 hex digits. Clearly, hexadecimal grouping is a form of shorthand for specifying long binary words.

6.1.4.4 Hexadecimal-to-Binary Conversion Hex-to-binary conversion is relatively straightforward, because there are 4 bits per hex character. Although the grouping partition is not necessary, it is shown here again for learning purposes.

EXAMPLE 6.10

Convert the following hex numbers to binary numbers:
(a) $D7_{16}$.   (b) $4B3F_{16}$.   (c) $912AE_{16}$.

Solution:

(a)   D   7

   1 1 0 1 | 0 1 1 1

   $D7_{16} = 11010111_2$

(b)   4   B   3   F

   0 1 0 0 | 1 0 1 1 | 0 0 1 1 | 1 1 1 1

   $4B3F_{16} = 100101100111111_2$

Note that the leading 0 for 4 is dropped.

(c)   9   1   2   A   E

   1 0 0 1 | 0 0 0 1 | 0 0 1 0 | 1 0 1 0 | 1 1 1 0

   $912AE_{16} = 10010001001010101110_2$

6.2 BINARY-CODED DECIMAL

Because computers function on binary information, binary bits are often grouped or encoded into a value representing a decimal character. One way to express a decimal character is through the use of *binary-coded decimal (BCD)*. In BCD, 4 bits are used to encode one decimal character. As we know, 4 bits can give us a possibility of 16 binary combinations. Because there are 10 decimal characters, 0 through 9, only 10 of the 16 possible combinations are necessary for encoding in BCD. The remaining six combinations are said to be *invalid numbers*.

There are several BCD codes. When a decimal character is represented with straight binary bits, the BCD code is referred to more specifically as *8421 code*. As its name implies, the weighting of the 4 binary bits representing the decimal character are in the order of 8421. Because the 8421 code is the most widely used of the BCD codes, it is generally referred to as *BCD*. Table 6-5 depicts the BCD code.

> **Binary-Coded Decimal (BCD)**
> A binary code used to express a decimal number with 4 binary bits. BCD is also referred to as *8-4-2-1 code* due to the binary weighting of each of the 4 bits.

TABLE 6-5
Binary-Coded Decimals

Decimal	BCD		
0	0000		
1	0001		
2	0010		
3	0011		
4	0100	1010	
5	0101	1011	Not
6	0110	1100	valid in
7	0111	1101	BCD
8	1000	1110	
9	1001	1111	

EXAMPLE 6.11

Convert 367_{10} to BCD.

Solution:

$$367_{10} = 0011\ 0110\ 0111$$

EXAMPLE 6.12

Convert 1249_{10} to BCD.

Solution:

$$1249_{10} = 0001\ 0010\ 0100\ 1001$$

EXAMPLE 6.13

Convert 58_{10} to BCD.

Solution:

$$58_{10} = 0101\ 1000$$

6.2.1 BCD Addition

The addition of BCD numbers can be performed using straight binary addition as long as the result does not exceed a decimal value of 9.

EXAMPLE 6.14

Add the decimal numbers 3 and 4 in BCD.

Solution:

$$
\begin{array}{rr}
3 & 0011 \\
+4 & +0100 \\
\hline
7 & 0111
\end{array}
$$

EXAMPLE 6.15

Add the decimal numbers 63 and 24 in BCD.

Solution:

$$
\begin{array}{rr}
63 & 0110\ 0011 \\
+24 & +0010\ 0100 \\
\hline
87 & 1000\ 0111
\end{array}
$$

When the sum of two numbers exceeds 9, an invalid BCD number is produced. As shown in Examples 6.16 and 6.17, the invalid number is made valid by adding 0110 (6).

Add the decimal numbers 9 and 6 in BCD.

EXAMPLE
6.16

Solution:

$$
\begin{array}{r}
9 \\
+6 \\
\hline
15
\end{array}
\qquad
\begin{array}{l}
1001 \\
+0110 \\
\hline
1111 \quad \text{Not a valid BCD number} \\
+0110 \quad \text{Add 6 for correction} \\
\hline
0001\ 0101 \quad \text{Correct BCD number}
\end{array}
$$

Add the decimal numbers 46 and 79 in BCD.

EXAMPLE
6.17

Solution:

$$
\begin{array}{r}
46 \\
+79 \\
\hline
125
\end{array}
\qquad
\begin{array}{ll}
0100 & 0110 \\
+0111 & 1001 \\
\hline
1011 & 1111 \quad \text{Not valid BCD numbers} \\
0110 & 0110 \quad \text{Add 6 for correction} \\
\hline
0001 \quad 0010 & 0101 \\
1 \quad\quad 2 & 5
\end{array}
$$

6.3 EXCESS-3 CODE

Another BCD code used to represent decimal numbers is the *excess-3 code*, which is very similar to 8421 BCD code. The only difference is that 3 is added to the decimal character before it is encoded into a 4-bit word. Table 6-6 depicts the excess-3 code. A comparison is made with BCD. Note that the excess-3 code also has six invalid characters.

Excess-3 Code
A BCD code similar to 8-4-2-1 code, except that 3 is added to the decimal number before it is encoded into a 4-bit word.

TABLE 6-6
Excess-3 Code

Decimal	BCD	Excess-3		
0	0000	0011		
1	0001	0100		
2	0010	0101		
3	0011	0110		
4	0100	0111	0000	
5	0101	1000	0001	
6	0110	1001	0010	Not
7	0111	1010	1101	valid in
8	1000	1011	1110	excess-3
9	1001	1100	1111	

The excess-3 code is useful in some mathematical operations where 8421 BCD is too cumbersome. For example, where it is desirable to perform an addition of two 8421 BCD numbers whose sum exceeds a decimal 9, excess-3 BCD code eliminates the necessity of adding a correction of 6 to the result. Example 6.18 illustrates this; note that the sum of the two excess-3 numbers results in an answer in 8421 BCD code. This occurs due to the excess value of 3 originally encoded into each number; that is, the correction of 6 (3 in each number) is already accounted for. Another advantage of the excess-3 code is that at least one 1-bit is present in all states, thus providing an error-detection advantage.

EXAMPLE 6.18

Add the decimal numbers 9 and 7 in excess-3.

Solution:

$$
\begin{array}{r@{\qquad}l}
9 & 1100 \\
+7 & 1010 \\
\hline
16 & 1\ 0110 \\
\end{array}
$$

6.4 GRAY CODE

> **Gray Code**
> An unweighted code that provides a single bit change between successive counts. Gray code reduces switching noise and bit errors.

A disadvantage with the codes discussed thus far is that several bits can change state simultaneously between adjacent counts. The *Gray code* is unique in that successive counts result in only a single bit change. For example, when changing from a count of 7 (0111) to 8 (1000) in BCD, all 4 bits change state. The switching noise generated by the associated circuits may be intolerable in some environments. The same change with Gray code undergoes only a single bit change (0100 to 1100); consequently, less noise is generated. Shaft encoders used for receiver tuning dials often use Gray code for encoding the position of the rotary shaft. Gray code is also less likely to bring about errors or erroneous results due to settling times and propagation delays associated with the given hardware. Table 6-7 lists the Gray code for the decimal numbers 0 through 15.

> **Unweighted Code**
> Any code whose bits do not have numeric weighting.

From Table 6-7, it can be seen that Gray code is an *unweighted code*. The bits associated with each 4-bit word do not have any numeric weighting as does the binary code shown. Gray code is, therefore, not suitable for arithmetic operations. There is, however, a relationship between the binary code shown and Gray code. For any given binary number, the equivalent Gray code can be established by the process described here:

Binary-to-Gray Conversion

> **Exclusive-OR**
> A logic function that compares two binary bits and is true when the two bits do not equal each other (1 and 0 or 0 and 1) and false when they do (0 and 0 or 1 and 1).

1. The *first* bit, starting from the MSB of the given binary code, becomes the leftmost bit of the Gray code.
2. *EXCLUSIVE-OR*ing the *first* and *second* bits of the given binary code yields the second bit of the Gray code.
3. The third bit of the Gray code is found by EXCLUSIVE-ORing the *second* and *third* bits of the given binary code.
4. The process continues until the last 2 bits of the binary code have been EXCLUSIVE-ORed together to produce the last bit of the equivalent Gray code.

TABLE 6-7
Gray Code

Decimal	Binary	Gray code[a]
0	0000	0000
1	0001	0001
2	0010	0011
3	0011	0010
4	0100	0110
5	0101	0111
6	0110	0101
7	0111	0100
8	1000	1100
9	1001	1101
10	1010	1111
11	1011	1110
12	1100	1010
13	1101	1011
14	1110	1001
15	1111	1000

[a]Gray code is not restricted to 4 bits.

Compute the Gray code for the binary number 11010.

EXAMPLE 6.19

Solution:

Binary code: 1   1   0   1   0

Gray code: 1   0   1   1   1

Compute the Gray code for the binary number 10001101.

EXAMPLE 6.20

Solution:

Binary code: 1   0   0   0   1   1   0   1

Gray code: 1   1   0   0   1   0   1   1

Converting from Gray code to binary is performed by the procedure described here:

Gray-to-Binary Conversion

1. The *first* bit, starting with the *leftmost* bit of the given Gray code, becomes the MSB of the binary code.
2. EXCLUSIVE-ORing the *second* Gray code bit with the MSB of the binary code yields the second binary bit.

3. EXCLUSIVE-ORing the *third* Gray code bit with the *second* binary bit yields the third binary bit.

4. EXCLUSIVE-ORing the *fourth* Gray code with the *third* binary bit yields the fourth binary bit, and so forth.

EXAMPLE 6.21

Compute the binary code for the Gray code 101101.

Solution:

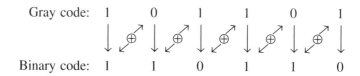

EXAMPLE 6.22

Compute the binary code for the Gray code 11011101.

Solution:

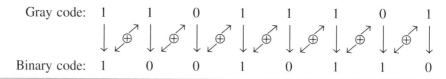

6.5 MORSE CODE

Morse Code
A digital code made of a series of dots and dashes used to represent alphanumeric characters, punctuation, and control.

One of the oldest electrical transmission codes still in use was developed and patented in 1840 by Samuel F. B. Morse. First used with the telegraph system, it was soon revised and has become known as *International Morse Code*. International Morse Code is used primarily in amateur radio. The digital code system is made up of a series of *dots* and *dashes* representing the alphabet and decimal number system. Punctuation is included in the code set. A dash is three times the duration of a dot. The relative duration of a dot and dash are dependent on sending speed, typically expressed in words per minute. The higher the sending speed, the shorter the dot and dash lengths. Sending speeds vary depending on the code proficiency of the amateur radio operator. Some amateur radio operators, often referred to as *hams,* can send and receive up to 45 words per minute.

Ham
An amateur radio operator.

Characters in Morse code are spaced for a duration equal to that of a dash, and words are spaced approximately the duration of two dashes. Table 6-8 lists the International Morse Code set.

6.6 BAUDOT

Baudot
A 5-bit alphanumeric code used in telegraphy and radio teletype (RTTY).

In 1874, Emile Baudot, a French engineer, developed the alphanumeric code known as *Baudot*. The Baudot code is used in the field of telegraphy and RTTY (radio teletype). CCITT (Consultative Committee for International Telephony and Telegraphy) has standardized the Baudot code into a version that has become known as *CCITT Alphabet No. 2*. The code is used worldwide within the international *Telex* network, which is a network of teletypes interconnected by the *public-*

TABLE 6-8
International Morse Code

A	. _	N	_ .	1	. _ _ _ _	
B	_ . . .	O	_ _ _	2	. . _ _ _	
C	_ . _ .	P	. _ _ .	3	. . . _ _	
D	_ . .	Q	_ _ . _	4	. . . . _	
E	.	R	. _ .	5	. . . .	
F	. . _ .	S	. . .	6	_	
G	_ _ .	T	_	7	_ _ . . .	
H	. . . .	U	. . _	8	_ _ _ . .	
I	. .	V	. . . _	9	_ _ _ _ .	
J	. _ _ _	W	. _ _	0	_ _ _ _ _	
K	_ . _	X	_ . . _			
L	. _ . .	Y	_ . _ _			
M	_ _	Z	_ _ . .			

Period	. _ . _ . _	Fraction bar (slash)	_ . . _ .
Comma	_ _ . . _ _	Wait	. _ . . .
Question mark	. . _ _ . .	End of message	. _ . _ .
Error	. . . .	Invitation to transmit	_ . _
Colon	_ _ _ . . .		
Semicolon	_ . _ . _ .	End of transmission	. . . _ . _
Parenthesis	_ . _ _ . _	Double dash (break)	_ . . . _

International distress (SOS) . . . _ _ _ . . . (*Save Our Ship*)

---

switched telephone network (PSTN). Over a million teletype systems are still in operation throughout the world despite its slow operating speeds of 50, 75, and 110 *baud* (bits per second).

Baudot (Table 6-9) is a 5-bit alphanumeric code. This allows the possibility of 32 (2^5) combinations of characters. Because there are more than 32 alphabetical and numerical characters, two of the 32 binary combinations are used for extending the character set. These two characters are the *letters shift (LS)* and *figures shift (FS)* characters. The letters shift character is a binary 11111. It is represented graphically by the upward arrow symbol (↑). When a Baudot receiver receives the letters shift character, subsequent characters are interpreted as those listed in the letters characters column of Table 6-9. The figures shift character is a binary 11011. It is represented by the downward arrow symbol (↓). On receiving this character, the Baudot receiver interprets characters thereafter as those listed in the figures characters column in Table 6-9. Both of these characters are nonprintable.

Baudot characters are transmitted as a series of electrical impulses, as shown in Figure 6-1. There are two possible states: a *mark,* equal to a logic 1; and a *space,* equal to a logic 0. Each character is framed by a *start bit* and *stop bit.* A mark is usually represented by a negative voltage and a space by a positive voltage. Current pulses of 20 mA are also used, whereby 20 mA is a mark and 0 mA is a space. Note that the LSB is transmitted first.

Teletype machines are often equipped with a *reperforator,* a device used to punch tape with the Baudot code (Figure 6-2). The black dots represent a perforation, or mark. The absence of a perforation is a space. A complete message can be typed out

Baud Rate
The rate at which a signal is changed or modulated. Baud rate is directly related to the number of bits transmitted per second.

Mark
A logic 1.

Space
A logic 0.

Start Bit
The first bit used to frame an asynchronously transmitted character. The start bit is always a logic 0 or Space.

Stop Bit
The last bit used to frame an asynchronously transmitted character. The stop bit is always a logic 1 or Mark.

TABLE 6-9
Baudot Code

Binary Bit Pattern 54321	Letters Characters, LS (↑)	Figures Characters, FS (↓)
00011	A	—
11001	B	?
01110	C	:
01001	D	$
00001	E	3
01101	F	!
11010	G	&
10100	H	#
00110	I	8
01011	J	Bell
01111	K	(
10010	L	)
11100	M	.
01100	N	,
11000	O	9
10110	P	0
10111	Q	1
01010	R	4
00101	S	'
10000	T	5
00111	U	7
11110	V	;
10011	W	2
11101	X	/
10101	Y	6
10001	Z	"
00100	Space (SP)	
01000	Carriage return	
00010	Line feed	
00000	Blank	
11111	Letters shift (↑)	
11011	Figure shift (↓)	

in advance and sent at a later time. A special tape reader, called a *transmitter–distributor,* is used for this process. In the past, tapes were often gummed on the reverse side to allow for cutting and pasting onto a sheet of paper for documentation purposes.

Baudot code has several deficiencies compared to modern codes. The 5-bit code does not allow for an error-detection mechanism such as *parity* (the parity bit will be defined later). Lower-case letters are not available, nor are the control functions offered by today's communications equipment. Another serious shortcoming of Baudot code is the time required to generate LS and FS to shift back and forth between letter and figure characters. Also, if a false detection of either of these characters is received, subsequent characters will be misinterpreted. These deficiencies have prevented the code from remaining popular in data and telecommunication systems.

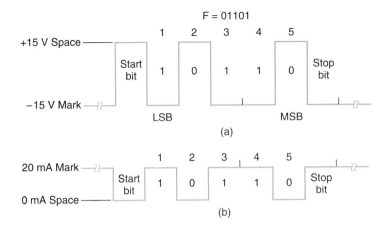

FIGURE 6-1
Electrical impulses for the Baudot character F, transmitted by a Teletype terminal: (a) voltage impulses; (b) current impulses.

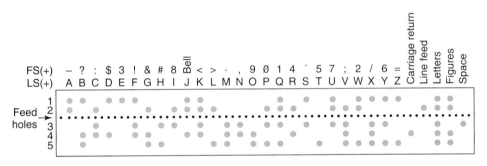

FIGURE 6-2
Paper tape perforated with Baudot characters.

6.7 EBCDIC

In 1962, IBM Corporation developed an 8-bit code called *Extended Binary-Coded Decimal Interchange Code (EBCDIC)*. EBCDIC, often pronounced "EB-SA-DIC," is used extensively in IBM's large-scale computers and peripheral equipment. The code offers a considerable improvement over the old electromagnetic teletype code, Baudot. Lower-case alphabetical characters and control functions are included. The code (Table 6-10) is a matrix that has been designed to group characters by function. Each row and column has been identified by a hexadecimal character. The most significant hexadecimal character represents the upper 4 bits of the intersecting EBCDIC character. The least significant hexadecimal character represents the lower 4 bits of the character. Each EBCDIC character is represented by a corresponding two-character hexadecimal quantity.

The first four rows of the matrix (0 through 3) contain *control characters,* which are used to control the format and transmission of data. A description of these control characters has been provided with Table 6-10. They are listed in alphabetical order along with their corresponding hexadecimal code. Many of these control characters are used in the ASCII code described in the next section. Rows 4 through 7

Extended Binary-Coded Decimal Interchange Code (EBCDIC)
An 8-bit alphanumeric code (no parity) developed by IBM for synchronous communications with mainframe computers and peripheral devices.

Control Characters
Characters used to control the format and transmission flow of data over a telecommunications channel.

TABLE 6-10

EBCDIC

Most Significant Hex Digit	Least Significant (Hex) Digit															
	0	1	2	3	4	5	6	7	8	9	A	B	C	D	E	F
0	NUL	SOH	STX	ETX	PF	HT	LC	DEL			SMM	VT	FF	CR	SO	SI
1	DLE	DC1	DC2	DC3	RES	NL	BS	IL	CAN	EM	CC		IFS	IGS	IRS	IUS
2	DS	SOS	FS		BYP	LF	EOB	PRE			SM				ENQ	ACK	BEL
3			SYN		PN	RS	UC	EOT					DC4	NAK		SUB
4	SP										¢	.	<	(	+	|
5	&										!	$	*	)	;	¬
6	-	/										,	%	−	>	?
7											:	#	@	'	=	"
8		a	b	c	d	e	f	g	h	i						
9		j	k	l	m	n	o	p	q	r						
A			s	t	u	v	w	x	y	z						
B																
C		A	B	C	D	E	F	G	H	I						
D		J	K	L	M	N	O	P	Q	R						
E			S	T	U	V	W	X	Y	Z						
F	0	1	2	3	4	5	6	7	8	9						

2E	ACK	Acknowledge		1E	IRS	Interchange record separator
2F	BEL	Bell		1F	IUS	Interchange unit separator
16	BS	Backspaced		06	LC	Lower case
24	BYP	Bypass		25	LF	Line feed
18	CAN	Cancel		3D	NAK	Negative acknowledge
1A	CC	Unit backspace		15	NL	New line (LF and CR)
0D	CR	Carriage return		00	NUL	Null (all zeros)
11	DC1	Device control 1		04	PF	Punch off
12	DC2	Device control 2		34	PN	Punch on
13	DC3	Device control 3		27	PRE	Prefix
3C	DC4	Device control 4		14	RES	Restore
07	DEL	Delete		35	RS	Record separator
10	DLE	Data link escape		0F	SI	Shift in
20	DS	Digit select		2A	SM	Start message
19	EM	End of medium		0A	SMM	Repeat
2D	ENQ	Enquiry		0E	SO	Shift out
26	EOB	End of block		01	SOH	Start of header
37	EOT	End of transmission		21	SOS	Start of significance
03	ETX	End of text		40	SP	Space
0C	FF	Form Feed		02	STX	Start of text
22	FS	File separator		3F	SUB	Substitute
05	HT	Horizontal tab		32	SYN	Synchronous idle
1C	IFS	Interchange file separator		36	UC	Upper case
1D	IGS	Interchange group separator		0B	VT	Vertical tab
17	IL	Idle				

contain punctuation characters, and rows 8 through F include upper- and lower-case alphabetical characters and decimal numbers.

The logical placement of characters within the matrix has been designed to offer programming as well as hardware development and test advantages. The decimal digits 0 through 9, for example, are represented by F0H through F9H, respectively. The lower 4 bits of the code, or least significant hexadecimal characters, equal the decimal number. Upper- and lower-case letters have a difference of 40H; that is, only one bit, bit 6, distinguishes between the two cases (a = 81H, A = C1H).

A close look at the matrix will reveal that there are 117 blank spaces. This means that almost half the matrix is not being used, or only 139 (256 − 117 = 139) of the possible 256 binary combinations are used. Because parity is not included as part of the 8-bit code, one might consider eliminating 11 of the 139 characters, thus making a total of 128 EBCDIC characters. The code could then be reduced to 7 bits instead of 8 ($2^7 = 128$). This would result in a reduction in transmission time of over 12%. The matrix, however, is designed to accommodate additional characters for more recently developed equipment.

6.8 ASCII

The *American Standard Code for Information Interchange (ASCII)* is the most widely used alphanumeric code for data transmission and data processing. ASCII was developed in 1962 specifically for computer communications systems. The code was updated by American manufacturers and published in 1967.

ASCII, pronounced "ASK-EE," is a 7-bit code that can be represented by two hexadecimal characters for simplicity. The most significant hexadecimal character in this case never exceeds 7. The ASCII code is shown in Table 6-11. Note there are no empty spaces. The placement of characters within the matrix, like EBCDIC, offers many of the same development and test advantages. The decimal digits 0 through 9, for example, are represented in the last significant digit of the hexadecimal characters 30H through 39H. Control characters have a value of less than 20H. They are grouped in the first two columns, 0 and 1, and are defined in numeric order next to Table 6-11. Columns 2 and 3 include punctuation and decimal numbers. The upper-case alphabet is contained in columns 4 and 5, and the lower-case alphabet is contained in columns 6 and 7. Upper- and lower-case alphabetical characters can be distinguished by a difference of 20H. An upper-case A, for example, is 41H, whereas a lower-case a is 61H. Various other nonalphabetical characters are distributed throughout columns 4 through 7.

A *parity* bit is generally provided with the 7-bit ASCII character, thus making the overall character length equal to a byte. The parity bit is an optional bit that takes the position of the MSB of the byte. Parity is used for error-detection purposes. When parity is not used, the MSB position of the byte representing the ASCII character is normally set to a logic 0. Some terminals and computers have the feature of disabling parity and maintaining a set or reset condition of this bit position.

> **American Standard Code for Informational Interchange (ASCII)**
> A 7-bit alphanumeric code used extensively in data communications. A parity bit is often added to the 7-bit code for error detection.

6.8.1 ASCII Control Characters

ASCII has a total of 32 control characters (00H to 1FH), most of which are included in the EBCDIC character set. As stated earlier, control characters are used to control

TABLE 6-11
ASCII

Least Significant (Hex) Digit	Most Significant (Hex) Digit										
	0	1	2	3	4	5	6	7	00	NUL	Null
									01	SOH	Start of header
0	NUL	DLE	SP	0	@	P	`	p	02	STX	Start of text
1	SOH	DC1	!	1	A	Q	a	q	03	ETX	End of text
2	STX	DC2	"	2	B	R	b	r	04	EOT	End of transmission
									05	ENQ	Enquiry
3	ETX	DC3	#	3	C	S	c	s	06	ACK	Acknowledge
4	EOT	DC4	$	4	D	T	d	t	07	BEL	Bell
5	ENQ	NAK	%	5	E	U	e	u	08	BS	Backspace
6	ACK	SYN	&	6	F	V	f	v	09	HT	Horizontal tab
									0A	LF	Line feed
7	BEL	ETB	'	7	G	W	g	w	0B	VT	Vertical tab
8	BS	CAN	(	8	H	X	h	x	0C	FF	Form feed
9	HT	EM	)	9	I	Y	i	y	0D	CR	Carriage return
									0E	SO	Shift out
A	LF	SUB	*	:	J	Z	j	z	0F	SI	Shift in
B	VT	ESC	+	;	K	[	k	{	10	DLE	Data link escape
C	FF	FS	,	<	L	\	l	|	11	DC1	Device control 1
D	CR	GS	-	=	M	]	m	}	12	DC2	Device control 2
									13	DC3	Device control 3
E	SO	RS	.	>	N	^	n	~	14	DC4	Device control 4
F	SI	US	/	?	O	—	o	DEL	15	NAK	Negative acknowledge
									16	SYN	Synchronous idle
									17	ETB	End of transmission block
									18	CAN	Cancel
									19	EM	End of medium
									1A	SUB	Substitute
									1B	ESC	Escape
									1C	FS	File separator
									1D	GS	Group separator
									1E	RS	Record separator
									1F	US	Unit separator
									7F	DEL	Delete

the format and transmission of data. Most control characters are classified into one of four categories:

1. Device control
2. Format effectors
3. Information separators
4. Transmission control

6.8.1.1 Device Control The ASCII code includes four *device control* characters: DC1, DC2, DC3, and DC4. There are no specific functions for these characters. The original intent, however, was to accommodate the control of computers and related equipment.

The control characters DC1 (XON) and DC3 (XOFF) have become a de facto standard for use in what is referred to as *flow control,* which is the process of regulating the flow of data from one point to another. Consider a computer sending a long text file to a printer. Because the printer operates at a relatively slow speed in comparison to the transmission rate of the computer, a buffer is used within the printer to temporarily store characters as they are being printed. To prevent the buffer from eventually overflowing, device control characters DC1 and DC3 are typically used by the printer to turn the transmitting source, in this case the computer, on and off. This type of flow control process is commonly referred to as XON–XOFF, whereby

DC1 = XON (transmit on)

DC3 = XOFF (transmit off)

6.8.1.2   Format Effectors   *Format effectors* are used to control a video display terminal (VDT) cursor movement or the positioning of a printing head on a printer. This allows an operator to control the physical layout of printed material. There are six ASCII format effectors, most of which can be found on an ordinary typewriter. Their values in hexadecimal range from 08H to 0DH. These format effectors are:

08	BS	Backspace
09	HT	Horizontal tabulation
0A	LF	Line feed
0B	VT	Vertical tabulation
0C	FF	Form feed
0D	CR	Carriage return

6.8.1.3   Information Separators   Five *information separators* are listed in Table 6-11. These are:

1C	FS	File separator
1D	GS	Group separator
1E	RS	Record separator
1F	US	Unit separator
19	EM	End of medium

Information separators are used as delimiters in the organization of file transfers. A hierarchy can be formed in the order listed earlier. The *unit separator,* US, delimits the smallest unit of information within the file. The *record separator,* RS, delimits a record of information that contains so many units. The *group separator,* GS, delimits a number of records contained in the group, and the *file separator,* FS, contains the groups of data. *End of medium,* EM, is used to indicate the end of a file transfer when different storage mediums are used.

6.8.1.4   Transmission Control   The 10 *transmission control* characters listed here are used for flow control and framing blocks of data:

01	SOH	Start of header
02	STX	Start of text
03	ETX	End of text
04	EOT	End of transmission
05	ENQ	Enquiry
06	ACK	Acknowledge

10	DLE	Data link escape
15	NAK	Negative acknowledge
16	SYN	Synchronous idle
17	ETB	End of transmission block

Chapter 14 considers the use of these characters for synchronous serial transmission.

6.8.1.5 Other ASCII Control Characters

There are seven remaining ASCII control characters:

00	NUL	Null
07	BEL	Bell
0E	SO	Shift out
0F	SI	Shift in
18	CAN	Cancel
1A	SUB	Substitute
1B	ESC	Escape

NUL: The null byte is a string of zeros that is used as a programming and test aid. It is often used to identify the end of a string of text. It is also used as a redundant byte to fill memory.

BEL: When the BEL character is received by a terminal or computer, an audible response is given. Its purpose is to gain the attention of the operator.

SO: Shift out is used to shift out of the normal ASCII character set and into an extended character set. The extended character set may include graphic symbols, mathematical symbols, and so on.

SI: Shift in is used to return to the normal ASCII character set.

CAN: Cancel is used to suspend or terminate an escape or control sequence. An error character is typically displayed on the screen.

SUB: Substitute is interpreted the same as CAN.

ESC: Escape is an ASCII character used for sending special command and control functions. ESC, followed by a single character or string of characters, is called an *escape sequence.* Escape sequences are used to perform special functions, such as cursor positioning, clearing the screen, and editing of text. Various commands can be sent with escape sequences. A modem or terminal, for example, can be commanded to initiate a self-test.

6.9 BAR CODES

> **Bar Code**
> A series of consistently sized white and black bars on items for identification. The black and white bars, and their widths in some codes, represent binary 1s and 0s.

Those ubiquitous black-and-white stripes that we regularly encounter in our supermarkets are called *bar codes.* They are marked on everything from boxes of cereal and cartons of milk to cans of shaving cream and bottles of aspirin. Most of us have observed how our grocery items are pulled across a viewing window at the cashier's checkout stand. Through this viewing window, a laser beam scans the bar code to identify the item being purchased and its corresponding price. The key to this automated system is the bar code, a data communications technology that applies many of the latest digital signal-processing techniques and optoelectronic devices toward the identification of commercial, industrial, and consumer products.

6.9.1 What Is Bar Code?

The bar code (Figure 6-3) is a series of consistently sized white and black bars that are wide and narrow in width. The white bars, separating the black bars, are referred to as *spaces*. Wide and narrow bars and spaces are used because they ultimately find themselves being deciphered by a digital computer; therefore, their widths and reflective abilities represent binary 1s and 0s. Bar codes are typically painted on, pasted on, or burned into the item that is being tracked—a container or box, an automobile engine, a library book, and so on.

Bar codes have been around since the early 1970s. The technology has advanced into a multibillion-dollar industry that has automated the keyboard entry task

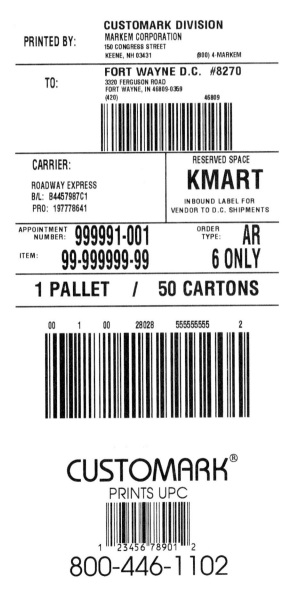

FIGURE 6-3

Typical bar code labels. (Courtesy of Benjamin Nelson, Markem Corp., Keene, N.H.)

TABLE 6-12
Advantages and Disadvantages of Bar Code

Advantages	Disadvantages
High throughput	Extra equipment required
Increased productivity	Computer system and special application software may be required
Low cost	
Little operator training	Primary use is for fixed, repetitive data input, not for variable data input
High data accuracy	
Readable by contact and noncontact scanners	

far beyond the local grocery store. More and more applications requiring an accurate, easy, and inexpensive method of data storage and data entry for computerized information management systems are utilizing bar code technology. Table 6-12 lists the advantages and disadvantages of bar code. Now consider some of the most common applications of bar code technology today:

- Inventory management and control
- Security access
- Shipping and receiving
- Production counting
- Document and order processing
- Rental car check-in and billing
- Work progress management
- Postal zip codes
- Functional programming
- Data entry
- Automatic billing
- Warranty and service tracking

The basic bar code structure is shown in Figure 6-4, and a block diagram illustrating the key elements of the bar code system is shown in Figure 6-5. The *data characters* field of the bar code represents a character corresponding to the bar code symbology or format used. Serial data stored in the data characters field are extracted from this field with an optical scanner. The optical scanner develops a logic signal corresponding to the difference in reflectivity of the printed bars and underlying spaces (white bars). Scanning over the printed bars and spaces with a smooth, continuous motion is required to retrieve data correctly. This motion can be provided by an operator in basically one of three ways: moving a handheld wand, by a rotating mirror moving a collimated beam of light, or by an operator or conveyor system moving the symbol past a fixed beam of light. The scanner is typically a laser, light-emitting diode (LED), or incandescent light bulb. A photodetector is used by the scanner to sense the reflected light and convert it to electrical signals for coding.

| Start margin | Start character | Data characters | Check character(s) | Stop character | Stop margin |

(may be optional)

FIGURE 6-4
Basic bar code structure.

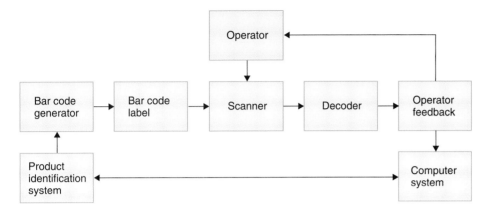

FIGURE 6-5
Block diagram of a bar code system.

6.9.2 Bar Code Formats

Several standard bar code formats are used in industry. Which format is best suited for a given application depends on what type of data are being stored, how data are being stored, system performance, and what is currently being used by the majority of similar businesses in which one is engaged. Bar codes can be classified as being either a *discrete code, continuous code,* or *2D code:*

Discrete Code A bar with intercharacter spaces or gaps between characters. Consequently, each character within the bar code symbol is independent of every other character. An example would be Code 39. (See Figure 6-6[c] for an illustration of intercharacter space.)

Continuous Code A bar code that does not have intercharacter spaces as part of its structure. An example would be Universal Product Code (UPC).

2D Code A two-dimensional bar code capable of storing over 1 kilobyte of data per symbol. Data is stored in two dimensions instead of in conventional linear bar codes that store data along one axis.

Table 6-13 lists the most common industrial codes used today and the type of industry in which they are being used. The type of code and year of inception are also listed. Although each of these codes has advantages and disadvantages over the others, we limit our discussion to two bar code formats: Code 39, and UPC.

6.9.3 Code 39

The most popular alphanumeric bar code is *Code 39,* also known as *Code 3 of 9* or *3 of 9 Code.** The code consists of 36 defined numeric and upper-case alphabetic characters, seven special characters, and a special start/stop character decoded as an

> **Code 39**
> An alphanumeric *bar code* consisting of 43 characters: the 26 alphabetical characters, 10 numeric characters, and 7 special characters.

---

*Code 39 is a registered trademark of Interface Mechanisms Inc. (now Intermec). The symbology is public domain.

TABLE 6-13
Common Industrial Bar Codes

Code	Type of Code	Industry Used In
Interleaved 2 of 5	Numeric, continuous	Industrial shipping and warehouse, retail
Codabar	Numeric, discrete	Blood banks, libraries, postal services
UPC	Numeric, continuous	Food and general retail, magazines and books
Code 39	Alphanumeric, discrete	Military, industrial, health care, automotive
EAN	Numeric, continuous	Food retail, product marketing
Code 11	Numeric, discrete	Telecom equipment tracking
Code 128	Full ASCII, continuous	Industrial shipping, retail case codes
Code 93	Full ASCII, continuous	Industrial
POSTNET	Numeric, continuous	Postal service zip codes
PDF417	2D (two-dimensional)	Printed circuit boards, pharmaceutical packaging, automotive

asterisk. The Code 39 character set along with its structure and label density is shown in Figure 6-6.

Code 39 characters can be deciphered by noting that each character is comprised of nine vertical *elements*, which are defined as bars and spaces (a space is a white bar). Each element is "width modulated" to encode the logic value of the 9 binary bits of data. Elements can be either a logic 1 or 0. A wide element, bar or space, is encoded as a logic 1, and a narrow element, bar or space, is encoded as a logic 0. A 3:1 ratio in widths is used to distinguish between a logic 1 and a logic 0 (i.e., a bar or space representing a logic 1 is three times the width of a bar or space representing a logic 0). For higher resolutions or greater information density, a 2.2:1 ratio is used.

Three of the nine elements in Code 39 are always a logic 1, and the remaining six are always a logic 0, hence the name Code 3 of 9. This can be seen in the Code 39 character set shown in Figure 6-6(a). Furthermore, of the three wide elements, two are bars and one is a space. Each Code 39 character begins and ends with a bar (black) with alternating spaces (white) in between. Individual characters within the label are separated by an *intercharacter space (CS),* which classifies Code 39 as a *discrete code.* Discrete codes are codes whose characters are separated by gaps. The CS, or "gap" between characters, is nominally one element (wide or narrow) in width.

6.9.4 Universal Product Code

Universal Product Code (UPC) was developed by the grocery industry in the early 1970s for product identification. It was officially adopted in 1974 by the National Association of Food Chains. A UPC bar code label can be found on your can of soup or box of cereal or crackers. There are three versions: A, D, and E. Version A, the regular version, is used for encoding a 12-digit number. Version E (zero-suppressed version) is used for encoding 12 digits into 6; it is used primarily for labeling small packages. Version D is a variable-length version limited to special applications such

ASCII Character	Binary Word	Bars	Spaces	Check Character Value
0	000110100	00110	0100	0
1	100100001	10001	0100	1
2	001100001	01001	0100	2
3	101100000	11000	0100	3
4	000110001	00101	0100	4
5	100110000	10100	0100	5
6	001110000	01100	0100	6
7	000100101	00011	0100	7
8	100100100	10010	0100	8
9	001100100	01010	0100	9
A	100001001	10001	0010	10
B	001001001	01001	0010	11
C	101001000	11000	0010	12
D	000011001	00101	0010	13
E	100011000	10100	0010	14
F	001011000	01100	0010	15
G	000001101	00011	0010	16
H	100001100	10010	0010	17
I	001001100	01010	0010	18
J	000011100	00110	0010	19
K	100000011	10001	0001	20
L	001000011	01001	0001	21
M	101000010	11000	0001	22
N	000010011	00101	0001	23
O	100010010	10100	0001	24
P	001010010	01100	0001	25
Q	000000111	00011	0001	26
R	100000110	10010	0001	27
S	001000110	01010	0001	28
T	000010110	00110	0001	29
U	110000001	10001	1000	30
V	011000001	01001	1000	31
W	111000000	11000	1000	32
X	010010001	00101	1000	33
Y	110010000	10100	1000	34
Z	011010000	01100	1000	35
–	010000101	00011	1000	36
.	110000100	10010	1000	37
SPACE	011000100	01010	1000	38
*	010010100	00110	1000	–
$	010101000	00000	1110	39
/	010100010	00000	1101	40
+	010001010	00000	1011	41
%	000101010	00000	0111	42

Check character example:

Message: CODE 39

Characters:	C	O	D	E		3	9
Value:	12	24	13	14	38	3	9

Sum of character values: 113

$$113 \div 43 = 2 \text{ remainder } 27$$
$$27 = \text{R check character}$$

Final message: CODE 39R

FIGURE 6-6(a)
Code 39 character set.

CODE CONFIGURATION

CODE 39 derives its name from its structure which is 3 out of 9. Each character is represented by 9 elements (5 bars and 4 spaces between the bars): 3 of the 9 elements are wide (binary value 1) and 6 elements are narrow (binary value 0). Spaces between characters have no code value. The specific structure of each character is given in the table below.

At the standard printing density of 9.4 characters per inch, the narrow bars and spaces are .0075 inches in width and the wide bars and spaces are .0168 inch. In other printing densities, the nominal ratio of wide to narrow elements should exceed 2.2:1 but be no greater than 3:1. Figure 6-6(c) shows dimensions (enlarged) for standard 9.4 character-per-inch bar code.

The start/stop (*) code precedes and follows all encoded data, defining the beginning and end of the code. These symbols typically are not transmitted by the bar code scanner.

A white margin must be present at both ends of the printed code. The minimum white margin is one-half of a nominal character. If practical, the margin should exceed 1/4 inch so that an operator can easily begin scanning in the margin.

CODE 39 Code Configuration

CHAR.	PATTERN	BARS	SPACES	CHAR.	PATTERN	BARS	SPACES
1		10001	0100	M		11000	0001
2		01001	0100	N		00101	0001
3		11000	0100	O		10100	0001
4		00101	0100	P		01100	0001
5		10100	0100	Q		00011	0001
6		01100	0100	R		10010	0001
7		00011	0100	S		01010	0001
8		10010	0100	T		00110	0001
9		01010	0100	U		10001	1000
0		00110	0100	V		01001	1000
A		10001	0010	W		11000	1000
B		01001	0010	X		00101	1000
C		11000	0010	Y		10100	1000
D		00101	0010	Z		01100	1000
E		10100	0010	-		00011	1000
F		01100	0010	.		10010	1000
G		00011	0010	SPACE		01010	1000
H		10010	0010	*		00110	1000
I		01010	0010	$		00000	1110
J		00110	0010	/		00000	1101
K		10001	0001	+		00000	1011
L		01001	0001	%		00000	0111

* Denotes a start/stop code which must precede and follow every bar code message.

Note that * is used only for the start/stop code.

FIGURE 6-6(b)
Code 39 code configuration. (Courtesy of Benjamin Nelson, Markem Corp., Keene, N.H.)

CS = intercharacter space

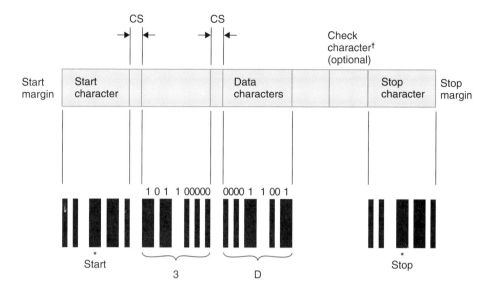

†An optional checksum character may be added at the end of a Code 39 message. This character is used to check that the correct number and type of data is present, thus providing data security.

FIGURE 6-6(c)
Code 39 label structure. (Courtesy of Hewlett-Packard Co.)

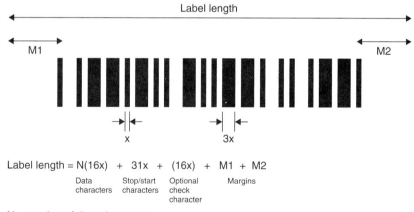

Label length = N(16x) + 31x + (16x) + M1 + M2

| Data characters | Stop/start characters | Optional check character | Margins |

N = number of data characters
x = narrow element width
Wide-to-narrow ratio = 3:1

FIGURE 6-6(d)
Code 39 label density. (Courtesy of Hewlett-Packard Co.)

Start Guard Pattern
Marks the beginning of a 12-digit *UPC bar code.* The two long black bars separated by a white bar (logic 101) on a UPC label can readily be identified at the beginning of the bar code.

Stop Guard Pattern
Marks the end of a 12-digit *UPC bar code.* The two long black bars separated by a white bar (logic 101) on a UPC label can readily be identified at the end of the bar code.

UPC Number System Character
The first of 12 digits on a *UPC bar code* that identifies how the UPC symbol is used (e.g., a coupon, regular sales item).

Check Character
In a *UPC Bar Code,* the last or 12th digit used for error detection when the bar code is scanned.

as credit cards. International interest in UPC led to the adoption of JAN (Japanese Article Numbering) and EAN (European Article Numbering). Both JAN and EAN codes have several features in common with UPC. Our discussion is limited to UPC, Version A.

The character set, label structure, and label density of UPC, Version A, are shown in Figure 6-7. A 12-digit number is encoded within each label. The two long bars on the outermost left- and right-hand sides of the label are called the *start guard pattern* and *stop guard pattern,* respectively. They form a binary pattern of 101 (bar space bar) and are used to frame the 12-digit number. Six of the 12 numbers (five data characters and one number system character) are encoded on the left half of the label. These digits are called the *left-hand characters.* The remaining six numbers (five data characters and one check character) are encoded on the right-hand side of the label. These are called the *right-hand characters.* The two halves of the label are separated by two long bars in the center of the label that are called the *center guard pattern.* The UPC guard pattern is 01010; therefore, the two long bars are separated by a space in between and to either side of the bars, as illustrated in Figure 6-7(b) and (c).

The first of the 12 numbers encoded is referred to as the *UPC number system character.* The number system character identifies how the UPC symbol is used. For example, a number system character of 5 implies that the item is for use with a coupon. Table 6-14 lists the 10 possible usage characters. The next 10 digits, five on each side, are data characters. Data characters specify the details of the product. The last digit, or twelfth digit, called the *check character,* is used for error detection. Note that the number system character is always printed in decimal to the left of the UPC label. On many UPC labels, the check character is printed in decimal to the right of the label.

Unlike Code 39, the width of the bars and spaces for UPC does not correspond to binary 1s and 0s. Instead, individual characters, 0 through 9, are encoded into a combination of two variable-width bars and two variable-width spaces, which occupy a total of seven *modules,* as shown in Figure 6-8. A left-hand 5 and a right-hand 5 are shown here. Bars and spaces making up the seven modules correspond to the seven 1s and 0s representing the decimal character. A single bar represents a binary 1, or up to four consecutive 1s (of the 7-bit code), as in the left-hand characters representing the decimal numbers 3 and 6. A single space represents a binary 0, or up to four consecutive 0s, as in the right-hand characters representing the decimal numbers

Left-hand character	Decimal number	Right-hand character
0001101	0	1110010
0011001	1	1100110
0010011	2	1101100
0111101	3	1000010
0100011	4	1011100
0110001	5	1001110
0101111	6	1010000
0111011	7	1000100
0110111	8	1001000
0001011	9	1110100

FIGURE 6-7(a)
UPC Version A character set.

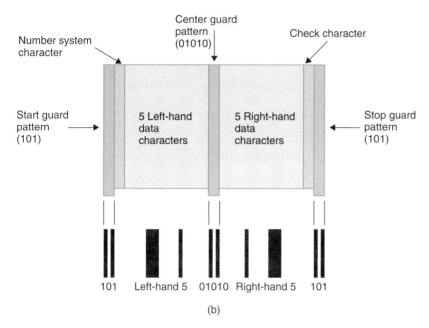

(b)

FIGURE 6-7(b)
UPC A label structure. (Courtesy of Hewlett-Packard Co.)

(c)

FIGURE 6-7(c)
UPC A label density. (Courtesy of Hewlett-Packard Co.)

3 and 6 (see the UPC character set in Figure 6-7[a]). A close look at the UPC character set will reveal that the 7-bit binary code representing each of the 10 decimal characters does, in fact, make up two bars and two spaces for each UPC character. In addition, the left-hand characters always have odd parity, so the number of modules that are bars are always odd whereas the parity for right-hand characters is always even.

TABLE 6-14
UPC Number System Characters

Character	Usage
0	Regular UPC Codes
1	Reserved
2	Random weight items that are symbol marked at the store level
3	National Drug Code and National Health Related Items Code
4	For use without code format restrictions and with check digit protection for in-store marking of nonfood items
5	For use on coupons
6	Regular UPC Codes
7	Regular UCP Codes
8	Reserved
9	Reserved

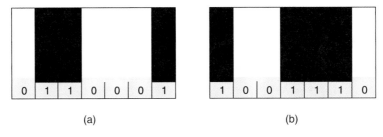

(a)   (b)

FIGURE 6-8
(a) Left-hand and (b) right-hand UPC Version A characters representing the digit 5.

Another distinction between Code 39 and UPC is that UPC is a *continuous code,* meaning that there are no intercharacter spaces between characters. Instead, characters are directly adjacent to each other.

6.9.5 Postnet

The *POSTNET* (*POST*al *N*umeric *E*ncoding *T*echnique) bar code was developed by the U.S. Postal Service to increase the sorting speed, accuracy, and delivery of mail based on ZIP codes. This includes business letters, advertisements, bulk mail, and more. Even your own personal letters can be prebar-coded to reduce mailing costs using a variety of software programs, including most word processors.

POSTNET is used to encode the standard 5-digit ZIP code, 9-digit ZIP+4, and 11-digit *Delivery Point Bar Code (DPBC)* that adds two digits to the 9-digit ZIP+4. The two additional digits represent the last two digits of a street address or post office box number. The 11-digit DPBC further automates the delivery of mail by eliminating the need for handsorting. Figure 6-9 illustrates a POSTNET 9-digit ZIP+4 bar code.

POSTNET (Postal Numeric Encoding Technique)
A *bar code* developed by the U.S. Postal Service to increase the sorting speed, delivery, and accuracy of mail based on ZIP codes.

Delivery Point Bar Code (DPBC)
An extension of the *POSTNET* bar code. The DPBC adds two more digits to the 9-digit ZIP+4 to represent the last two digits of a street address or P.O. box number.

Ilil.l.lil.ullIlll.ll.llil.lll.llllull.lll.l

FIGURE 6-9
POSTNET bar code for the 9-digit ZIP+4 number 89030-4296.

In contrast to most bar codes that are encoded by width or black and whites bars and spaces, POSTNET bar code symbols are encoded by height. That is, binary 1s and 0s are represented by tall vertical bars and short vertical bars. A logic 1 is a tall bar, and a logic 0 is a short bar.

6.9.5.1   POSTNET Bar Code Format   Each digit used to represent the standard POSTNET 5-digit ZIP code, 9-digit ZIP+4, or 11-digit DPBC can have a decimal value ranging from 0 to 9. As shown in Table 6-15, the bar code representing each of these 10 decimal digits (0 through 9) is comprised of five bars. Of the five bars, two are always tall bars (logic 1), and the remaining three are short bars (logic 0). With the exception of zero, the combination of tall and short bars forms a five-digit binary weighted word that is equivalent to the corresponding decimal digit.

Bar code numbers corresponding to any ZIP code are arranged in contiguous order to form the numeric portion of the bar code. A *check character* is appended to the end of the bar code, and the entire code is framed at the beginning and end with a tall start and stop framing bar. The check character is a single decimal digit that, when added to the sum of all bar code digits, causes the total number to equal the next multiple of 10.

Compute the check character for the 5-digit ZIP code 94086.

EXAMPLE
6.23

Solution:

Because 9+4+0+8 6 equals 27, the next multiple of 10 is equal to 30. A 3 must be added to 27 to equal 30; therefore, the check character is equal to 3.

TABLE 6-15
POSTNET Bar Code Truth Table

Decimal Number	Binary Code and Weighting of Each Digit 7 4 2 1 0	POSTNET Bar Code
0	1 1 0 0 0	
1	0 0 0 1 1	
2	0 0 1 0 1	
3	0 0 1 1 0	
4	0 1 0 0 1	
5	0 1 0 1 0	
6	0 1 1 0 0	
7	1 0 0 0 1	
8	1 0 0 1 0	
9	1 0 1 0 0	

EXAMPLE 6.24

Compute the check character for the 9-digit ZIP+4 code 89030-4296. The code is shown in Figure 6-9.

Solution:

Because 8+9+0+3+0+4+2+9+6 equals 41, the next multiple of 10 is equal to 50. A 9 must be added to 41 to equal 50; therefore, the check character is equal to 9. Note from Table 6-15 that the bar code for the digit 9 is 10100, or tall-short-tall-short-short. By looking closely at Figure 6-9, the check character of 9 can be seen just before the single tall stop bar.

PROBLEMS

1. Convert the following binary numbers to octal, decimal, and hexadecimal.
   a. 110101101_2.
   b. 1111000001010_2.
   c. 10101011101000111_2.
2. Convert the following decimal numbers to binary, octal, and hexadecimal.
   a. 46_{10}.
   b. 115_{10}.
   c. 773_{10}.
3. Convert the following octal numbers to binary, decimal, and hexadecimal.
   a. 17_8.
   b. 566_8.
   c. 7123_8.
4. Convert the following hexadecimal numbers to binary, decimal, and octal.
   a. $E4_{16}$.
   b. $88C_{16}$.
   c. $BD7A_{16}$.
5. Specify the following decimal numbers in BCD.
   a. 7.
   b. 123.
   c. 96.
6. Convert the following decimal numbers to BCD, and perform an arithmetic addition in BCD.
   a. 3 and 11.
   b. 789 and 165.
   c. 14 and 92.
7. Add the decimal numbers 9 and 8 in excess-3 code, and explain why the result is a valid BCD number.
8. Determine the Gray code for the following binary numbers.
   a. 1010111.
   b. 1100.
   c. 11101100.
   d. 10001.
9. Determine the binary code for the following Gray code numbers.
   a. 1101.
   b. 10000001.
   c. 10011110.
   d. 110011.

10. Write the sequence of Morse code characters for the message "TESTING 1 2 3 4. DO YOU READ ME?" Use adequate spacing to separate characters and words.

11. Draw the voltage waveform for the Baudot character "W." Include start and stop bits.

12. Refer to Figure 6-2. Draw the paper tape perforations that would be produced by a Teletype terminal for the same message as in problem 6.

13. How are upper- and lower-case letters distinguished from each other in EBCDIC?

14. What unique bit pattern is associated with EBCDIC decimal characters?

15. How many control characters are there in ASCII, and what can be said about their codes?

16. How many device control characters are there in ASCII, and what are their names?

17. Which ASCII control character is represented by a binary string of all zeros?

18. What is the ASCII code for "ACK" in binary, hexadecimal, and octal?

19. What are *format effectors,* and how are they used?

20. Name at least three applications of bar code.

21. Name two advantages and two disadvantages of bar code.

22. What is a *continuous* bar code?

23. What is a *discrete* bar code?

24. What is a *2D* bar code?

25. What is the binary word for the ASCII character "$" in Code 39?

26. What is the binary word for the ASCII character "R" in Code 39?

27. Draw the Code 39 bar code pattern for the ASCII character "R."

28. Draw the Code 39 bar code symbol for the ASCII character "$."

29. Draw the UPC A bar code symbol for a left-hand 7.

30. Draw the UPC A bar code symbol for a right-hand 8.

31. Draw the POSTNET bar code for the ZIP code 95147.

7

TERMINALS

The *terminal* has clearly become one of the most visible and readily identifiable pieces of computer-related equipment. They can be found in offices, laboratories, supermarkets and department stores, airport terminals, libraries, and virtually any other place with a need for data entry and display.

Thousands of different types of terminals have flooded the market over the years. Many are application specific; others are versatile enough to be reconfigured to various operating modes. Even our personal computers (PCs) can be configured to emulate the variety of terminals manufactured today. Most recently, the concept of a *network computer (NC)* terminal has emerged to simplify the complexity and power of the PC and relinquish it to a network server station.

The terminal, simply stated, is an input/output device used by an operator to communicate with a host computer on a network. It includes a keyboard that can generate an alphanumeric character set, a display (or printer) to monitor alphanumeric characters, and a communications interface, typically *network interface card (NIC)*. Terminals can also be electromechanical, such as a Teletype terminal (TTY), or a more sophisticated microprocessor-controlled video display terminal (VDT).

Advances in technology have brought a variety of new features to the terminal. These new features, coupled with technological advances in other segments of the computer market, have resulted in a great deal of confusion over what is best suited for a given application. Classifications of *dumb, smart, intelligent,* and *NC* terminals have surfaced to help define a terminal type. This chapter reviews some basic features of today's terminals and their classifications.

> **Terminal**
> An input/output (I/O) device used to communicate with a host computer. Typically includes a keyboard and a monitor.

7.1 TERMINAL CLASSIFICATIONS

In the midst of tough competition among manufacturers of PCs and graphics workstations, the terminal has taken on a new meaning. Terminal manufacturers have succumbed to the attitude "if you can't beat 'em, join 'em," with virtually all terminals manufactured today being microprocessor controlled. Computer-intensive applications for CAD/CAM (computer-aided design/computer-aided manufacturing), medical, research, and business continue to pressure manufacturers into pumping more power and capabilities into their terminals. Despite the continued growth in the terminal market, many of the resulting improvements have been subtle. Often, these improvements are needed only in specific installations. High-resolution graphics terminals and *ergonomically* improved displays and keyboards are often justified but not always necessary. The end result is an extensive range of terminals with varying degrees of features. It has, therefore, become necessary to classify terminals into four general categories that suit the end user's needs: the *dumb terminal,* the *smart terminal,* the *intelligent terminal* or *workstation,* and the *NC terminal.*

7.1.1   Dumb Terminals

There are literally millions of dumb terminals still being used today and still adequately serving the needs of their users. In the past, a dumb terminal was simply one that was not microprocessor controlled. Transmission parameters were manually set through the use of DIP (dual-in-line package) switches. Virtually all of today's terminals, including dumb terminals, are microprocessor controlled and sophisticated enough to offer programmable communications features, including self-test capabilities. Thus, what distinguishes the dumb terminal from other classes is not clear. A precise definition is subject to change over the years. Generally, the dumb terminal offers a limited number of features yet provides the essential input/output capability necessary to send and receive data from a host computer. A block diagram of Zentec Corporation's ADM-3A terminal is shown in Figure 7-1.

7.1.2   Smart Terminals

Smart terminals offer programmable features that require extensive memory, both read-only memory (ROM) and random access memory (RAM). In addition to the normal features of a dumb terminal, the distinguishing feature of the smart terminal is its capability to transmit *blocks* of data, or a *block mode* of operation. Other features include:

- Programmable communications setup
- Screen editing
- Display enhancement
- Alternative character sets
- Protocol emulation

7.1.3   Intelligent Terminals

Intelligent terminals or *workstations* are a third category of terminals. The typical workstation is a microprocessor-based multimedia computer station connected to a network. The workstation features a complete operating system with a high-resolution graphics display. Built-in communications protocols allow the interactive use of shared resources, including those of other workstations on a network. Microcomputing power with 32- or 64-bit architecture is necessary to obtain the highest level of workstation performance. High-resolution graphic displays, which are managed independently by a coprocessor, allow users to create visual aids that would otherwise be difficult, if not impossible, to understand. Bar graphs, pie charts, and line graphs, for example, are simple ways to make information readily understandable. Three-dimensional models can be created on the workstation for engineering, manufacturing, government, scientific, and educational applications. More complex applications performed by the workstation may involve *modeling* and *simulation;* an example could be the modeling and simulation of atmospheric and oceanic conditions

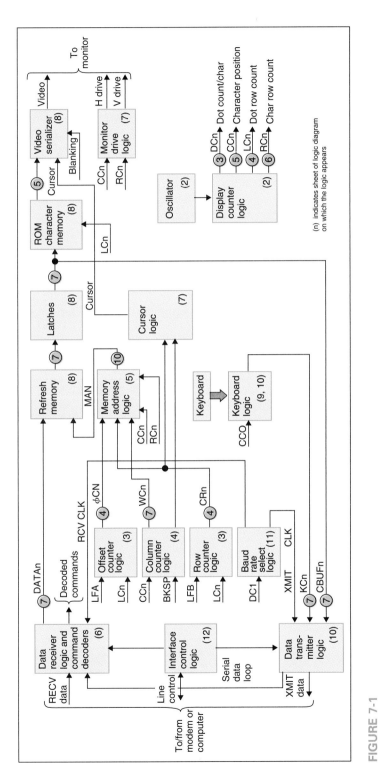

FIGURE 7-1
Block diagram of Zentec Corporation's ADM-3A terminal. (Reprinted with permission from Zentec Corporation.)

resulting from temperature changes. Other applications of the workstation include artificial intelligence (AI), computer-aided publishing, finance, and earth resources.

7.1.4 NC Terminals

As more and more stand-alone computer stations find themselves being networked together, the idea of an inexpensive, disk-free computer that can "surf the net" as well as perform routine application programs makes sense. Thus, a new breed of computer terminals has evolved in recent years. These terminals are classified as *network computers,* or simply *NCs.* Figure 7-2 illustrates the concept behind the NC terminal. NCs take advantage of high-powered, state-of-the-art workstations called *servers,* which are located elsewhere on the network. Unlike a PC, data are not kept locally in the NC terminal. Instead, the NC user's application program runs directly on the remote server. Keyboard and mouse data are sent through high-speed connections to the network, and the resulting outputs are sent over the network back to the NC terminal for display.

Because the NC terminal runs its applications on remote servers, hardware upgrade costs are minimized. Instead of upgrading all users, only the host computer running the applications program is upgraded. Thus, NC terminals have a longer life expectancy than the typical 3 years of a PC.

The major disadvantage of the NC terminal is that it relies entirely on the host computer or server. If an organization's server fails or becomes bottlenecked with service requests, NC users can be out of work or experience significant delays. Herein

> **NC Terminal**
> A diskless workstation designed to connect to a server on a network.

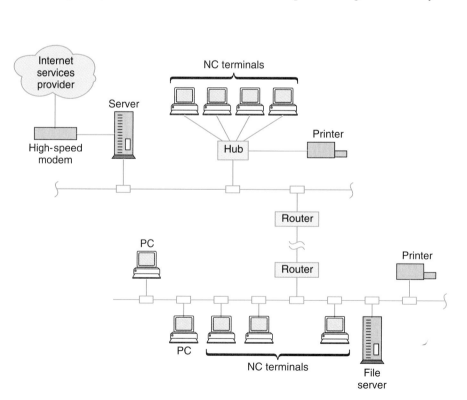

FIGURE 7-2
NC terminals configured on a network.

lies the advantage of PCs on the network: users of conventional PCs can be doing work locally while the network server is down, whereas NC users are temporarily out of commission. Nevertheless, experts believe NC terminals will become more prevalent, particularly in two kinds of organizations: those with highly centralized management that want total control over the applications of their users, and those that want to minimize future hardware-upgrade costs.

7.2   ERGONOMICS

During the last decade, considerable attention has been given to the science of *ergonomics,* which is the study of people in adjusting to their working environments. This environment includes everything from equipment, layout, temperature, lighting, and sound levels to the atmosphere and social context of the task. Ergonomics seeks ways to improve the working conditions within this environment.

> **Ergonomics**
> The study of people adjusting to their working environment. Ergonomics seeks ways to improve the working environment.

For the millions of people who work day in and day out on VDTs, terminal manufacturers are considering more seriously the ergonomics of terminal design. Consider the following:

- Keyboard layout
- Thickness and size of keys
- Sculptured key caps
- Variable phosphor color displays
- Mouse/joystick/data tablet entry
- Color graphic displays
- Slope of keyboard
- Keyboard detachability
- Key click intensity
- Independent numeric keypads
- Swivel/tilt display mounts
- Touch and light pen data entry
- Reflection free screens
- Clock/calendar function

Numerous studies have been conducted by ergonomic specialists on the human factors involved in use of terminals. These include keyboard and display discomforts, lighting and glare control, eye strain, and radiation effects. Some studies indicate that keyboards should be flat; others contend that they should be pitched from front to back and from center to side. Studies on phosphor colors have indicated that some colors may strain the eyes more than others. Amber, for example, may be better for your eyes than green; however, some reports indicate that green produces fewer headaches. Questions raised about whether VDTs possibly emit unsafe levels of radiation have led to several investigations on radiation emissions. One such study, performed by the American Council on Science and Health, reports that no scientific evidence indicates that VDTs cause birth defects or miscarriages.*

Ultimately, terminal manufacturers have decided that the ergonomic design of terminals is largely a matter of personal preference. For this reason, many terminals are equipped with multicolor modes, swivel mounts for the display, detachable key-

---

Health and Safety Aspects of VDTs, 2nd ed., a report by the American Council on Science and Health, 1985.

FIGURE 7-3
Wyse Technology's WY-60 ASCII terminal. (Courtesy of Wyse Technology.)

boards, and a number of keyboard layout designs to choose from. Wyse Technology's popular WY-60, as shown in Figure 7-3, includes many of the latest ergonomic design features.

7.3 THE ASCII TERMINAL

American Standard Code for Informational Interchange (ASCII)
A 7-bit alphanumeric code used extensively in data communications. A parity bit is often added to the 7-bit code for error detection.

Most terminals manufactured today are alphanumeric or *ASCII* character terminals used for data entry. Although the number of features built into these terminals continues to grow, most manufacturers adhere to the standard functional guidelines set forth in ANSI (American National Standards Institute) standards.

7.3.1 Alphanumeric Display

Cathode Ray Tube (CRT)
A vacuum tube designed to direct an intense electron beam to a fluorescent screen for displaying electrical signals.

The display most often used for the ASCII terminal is the *cathode-ray tube (CRT)*. High-voltage and sweep circuits are contained within the CRT display section. A raster scan deflection system is used to control an electron beam that is swept horizontally across the screen from top to bottom. The procedure is similar to that used by a television set. Characters are formed by a series of line segments and dots that are produced by turning the CRT's beam on and off at the appropriate time as it traverses the screen. For many terminals, characters are represented by a 5×7 or 7×9 dot matrix pattern on a display of typically 12 to 17 in. (diagonal measurement). Included in the matrix is two-dot spacing between characters, both horizontally and vertically. Figure 7-4 depicts the formation of upper-case letters for a 5×7 dot matrix pattern.

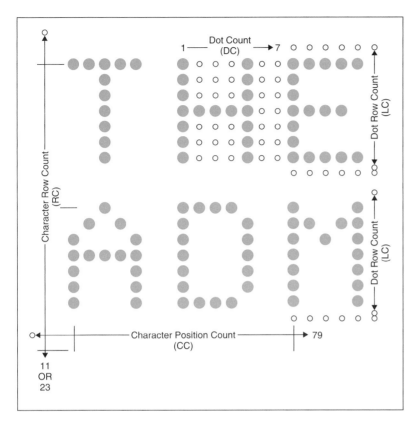

FIGURE 7-4
CRT display formation of a 5 × 7 dot matrix pattern. (Reprinted with permission from Zentec Corporation.)

7.3.2 Screen Capacity

A terminal's screen capacity is the maximum number of characters that can be displayed. Characters are typically arranged in a 24-row by 80-column format for a screen capacity of 1920 characters (24 × 80 = 1920). More recent terminals offer 24 rows by 132 columns, for a screen capacity of 3168 characters. Figure 7-5 illustrates the standard 1920-character format.

7.3.3 Keyboard Layout

The keyboard is the user's direct link to the computer. It is by far the most common input device to a computer. The placement of keys and their respective spacing are of major concern to the operator, who spends a great part of the day entering data. Keys are typically sculptured to fit the shape of the user's fingertips. Alphabetical and numeric keys have been standardized to the layout of a typewriter. Also, the popular numeric keypad has been designed into most terminal keyboards to offer the same rapid data entry found with adding machines and calculators.

Digital Equipment Corporation's VT300 series keyboard layout is shown in Figure 7-6. Introduced in 1986, the VT320 almost instantly assumed its role as a standard. We will use the VT320 keyboard layout to describe the functions of each key.

FIGURE 7-5
Screen capacity arranged in the standard 24-row by 80-column (1920-character) format. The 24-row by 132-column (3168-character) format is also becoming popular. (Courtesy of Digital Equipment Corporation.)

7.3.4 Function Keys

Function keys and their definitions are listed in Table 7-1. They are used to command the terminal's microprocessor to perform special functions based on programs stored in firmware. Figure 7-7 illustrates their relative locations on the main keypad.

7.3.5 Special Function Keys

The *special function keys* are located at the top row of the keyboard, as depicted in Figure 7-8. Most of these keys are defined by the software in use. They may also be programmed by the user. Each key is, therefore, capable of performing multiple functions, ranging from communications control setup to editing commands. These keys are tremendous time-savers for the user, because a series of instructions or keystrokes can be executed with the touch of a single key.

There are 15 special function keys for the VT300 series terminals (**F6** through **F20**). They may be programmed by the user to store and recall text and commands applicable to a given program. Up to 256 characters per function key can be programmed and saved in the terminal's nonvolatile memory. When defined by the user, these keys are referred to as *user-defined keys (UDKs)*. They are also referred to as *soft keys*.

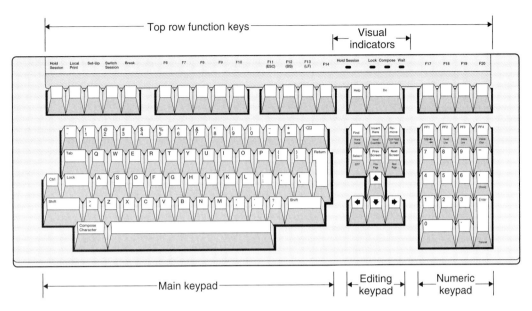

FIGURE 7-6
Keyboard layout for Digital Equipment Corporation's VT300 series video display terminal (North American/United Kingdom version). (Reprinted with permission from Digital Equipment Corporation.)

7.3.6 Editing Keypad

The editing keypad is illustrated in Figure 7-9(a). This dedicated keypad is used exclusively for editing text. It includes four arrow keys that may be used for cursor movement in the direction indicated by the arrow. Six additional editing keys are defined by the user's software.

7.3.7 Numeric Keypad

The numeric keypad is shown in Figure 7-9(b). The numbers on the keypad are arranged in standard calculator format for ease of numeric data input. The numeric keypad can also have special functions assigned by an applications program. For example, the keys **PF1** through **PF4** (programmed function 1–4) may be used for performing commands related to a spreadsheet or word-processor program. The applications manual must be referred to in this case. Often, a rubber or plastic template that fits over the numeric keypad is provided. The template defines the newly assigned functions for each key.

The **ENTER** key normally acts as a carriage return. It can also serve as a **TRANSMIT** key when the terminal is set up for block mode of operation.

7.3.8 Baud Rate Selection

A terminal's *baud rate* is the rate at which its characters are transmitted in bits per second. This form is illustrated in Figure 7-10. The character shown includes a *start bit, 7-bit data word, parity bit,* and a *stop bit.* The duration of each bit, the

---

Baud Rate
The rate at which a signal is changed or modulated. Directly proportional to the number of bits transmitted per second.

Start Bit
The first bit used to frame an asynchronously transmitted character. Always a logic 0 or Space.

7-Bit Data Word
Typically, an ASCII character represented with a 7-bit binary word.

Parity Bit
A single bit typically used to make the total number of 1 bits, either even or odd.

Stop Bit
The last bit used to frame an asynchronously transmitted character. Always a logic 1 or Mark.

TABLE 7-1

Definition of Function Keys

Key	Description
Tab	Generates a horizontal tab that normally moves the cursor and the text following it to the next stop setting.
CTRL	When pressed in combination with another key, the CTRL key causes the terminal to transmit a code that has a special meaning to your system.
Lock	When pressed, the LOCK key makes the alphabetical keys generate upper-case characters. When the LOCK key is pressed again, the alphabetical keys generate lower-case characters.
Shift (two keys)	When either the right- or left-side SHIFT key is pressed, the upper-case function of all keys is enabled. If a key does not have an upper-case function, the SHIFT key will be disregarded. In some cases, this key is used in combination with another key to generate a predefined control function.
Return	Transmits either a carriage return (CR) code or a carriage return (CR) and linefeed (LF) code. In some cases, it moves the cursor to the next line when editing text. If NEW LINE was selected in Set-Up mode, RETURN can be a signal to the applications program that a particular operation is finished.
Delete	Pressing this key generates a DE character. Normally, this erases one character to the left of the cursor.
Compose Character	This key is used to create special characters that do not exist as standard keys on your keyboard. Use of this key and compose character sequences are described in detail in the *VT220* and *VT240 Owner's Manual*.

Source: Digital Equipment Corporation.

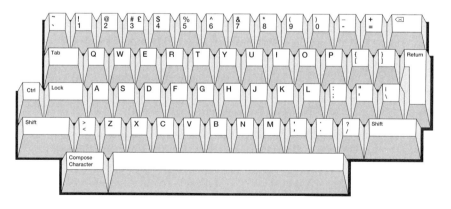

FIGURE 7-7

Main keypad for the VT300 series terminal. (Reprinted with permission from Digital Equipment Corporation.)

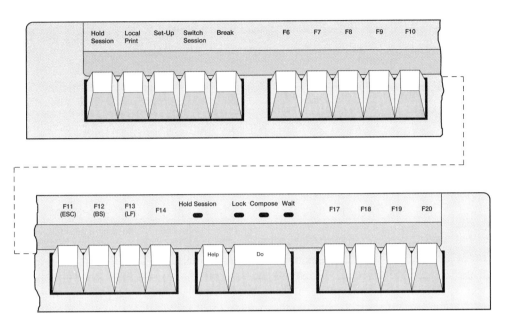

FIGURE 7-8
VT320 special function keys. (Reprinted with permission from Digital Equipment Corporation.)

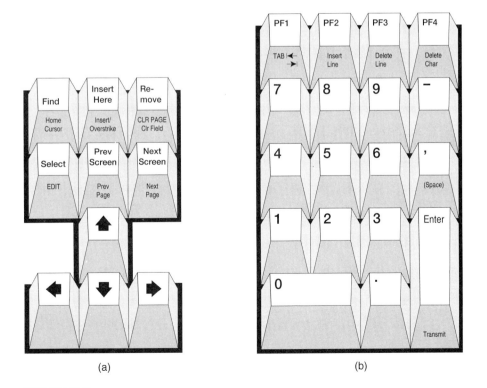

(a)   (b)

FIGURE 7-9
(a) Editing keypad for the VT300 series terminal; (b) numeric keypad for the VT300 series terminal. (Reprinted with permission from Digital Equipment Corporation.)

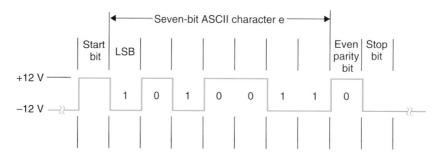

FIGURE 7-10
Asynchronously transmitted character from a terminal.

Bit Time
The length of time required to transmit 1 bit.

bit time, may be found mathematically by taking the reciprocal of the baud rate. A baud rate of 1200, for example, has a bit time of 833 μs (1/1200). Baud rate is selectable either through the terminal's soft keys or through hardware switches provided by the terminal manufacturer. Most terminals offer standardized baud rate settings. (Chapter 13 shows that baud rate and bit rate have different meanings in terms of transmission speed.) Table 7-2 lists the standard baud rates used in data communications.

Even Parity
When a terminal is configured for *even parity,* the transmitted or received ASCII character's parity bit is set or reset to make the total number of 1-bits an even number.

7.3.9 Parity

Parity is a simplified method of error detection. When an operator types a key, an asynchronous character is transmitted by the terminal to a remote device, such as a computer. A single bit, called the *parity bit,* is added to the transmitted 7-bit ASCII character.

The logic level of the parity bit depends on the number of 1 bits set within the transmitted character. When parity is enabled on a terminal, it can be set to either *even* or *odd.* For even parity, a terminal's transmitter section sets the parity bit to a level making the total number of 1 bits (including the parity bit itself) an even number. The opposite is true for odd parity. Consider the following examples of even and odd parity:

Odd Parity
When a terminal is configured for *odd parity,* the transmitted or received ASCII character's parity bit is set or reset to make the total number of 1-bits an odd number.

TABLE 7-2
Standard Terminal Baud Rates

75	9600
110	19,200
150	38,400
300	57,600
600	115,200
1200	230,400
2400	921,600
4800	

Even parity generation:

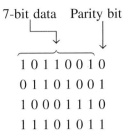

7-bit data   Parity bit

1 0 1 1 0 0 1 0
0 1 1 0 1 0 0 1
1 0 0 0 1 1 1 0
1 1 1 0 1 0 1 1

Odd parity generation:

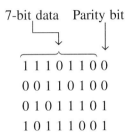

7-bit data   Parity bit

1 1 1 0 1 1 0 0
0 0 1 1 0 1 0 0
0 1 0 1 1 1 0 1
1 0 1 1 1 0 0 1

Enabling parity on a terminal also enables the receiver section of the terminal to perform a parity check on the received character transmitted from a remote device. The terminal's parity setting must be equivalent to that of the remote device. An agreement is decided on beforehand. If the number of 1 bits for the received character does not match with the parity setting, a transmission error has occurred. A special character is displayed in place of the received character. Each manufacturer has its own unique character. Digital Equipment Corporation's terminals use the checkerboard character: (▓▓).

Parity is an optional feature on a terminal. It can be enabled or disabled by an operator via the special function keys on the terminal or by hardware switches provided by the terminal. If parity is disabled, the bit following the 7-bit data word will be the (first) stop bit. If the terminal has been configured for 8-bit data with no parity, a logic 0 is typically transmitted in place of the parity bit. Some terminals allow the feature of forcing this bit, the eighth bit, to a logic 1 or a logic 0.

7.3.10   Transmission Modes

There are essentially two modes of terminal operation: *character mode,* and *block mode.* Most terminals are set up to operate in character mode.

7.3.10.1   Character Mode
When a terminal is in its character mode, characters are sent to the host computer only when a key is typed by the operator. The character is said to be transmitted *asynchronously;* that is, there is no synchronism with the operator's keystrokes. When the operator is not typing, the terminal is said to be in its *idle* state. Conversely, when the computer sends a character to the terminal, the character is displayed at the current position of the cursor. If the character is a nonprintable character (CR, LF, BEL, and the like), the terminal will act accordingly.

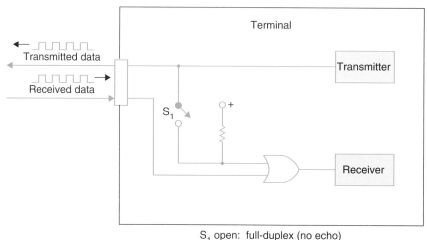

S₁ open: full-duplex (no echo)
S₁ closed: half-duplex (echo)

FIGURE 7-11
Half-duplex versus full-duplex operation.

Half-Duplex versus Full-Duplex   A terminal operating in its character mode must be configured for either *half-duplex* or *full-duplex* operation (Figure 7-11). In half-duplex, characters typed are transmitted and internally *echoed* back to the receiver section. The echoed character is displayed for the operator to see what has been typed. This echoed character is referred to as a *local echo.* In *full-duplex,* the characters typed are transmitted only. The characters are not displayed unless they are received by a remote device and echoed back. An echo generated from a remote location is referred to as a *remote echo.*

When remote echoes are displayed as a result of typing, an operator can be assured that the transmission link has been properly connected. Much of the associated hardware and software of the sending and receiving stations must function successfully for echoed characters to appear on the display. Echoed characters are, therefore, a test measure for the system beyond just the terminal itself.

Occasionally, a terminal will display duplicate characters as they are typed. In this case, the terminal must be reconfigured from half-duplex to full-duplex. What has happened is that a local echo and a remote echo have been received by the terminal. The first of the two characters displayed is the local echo, and the second character is the remote echo generated from the remote computer.

7.3.10.2 Block Mode   Smart terminals can be configured to operate in either character mode or block mode. In block mode, characters are *not* transmitted as they are typed. Instead, the operator works locally with the information displayed on the screen. Characters are stored in a buffer rather than transmitted as they are typed. In the meantime, the host computer can be servicing one of several other terminals that are part of a *multidrop* communications system. When the operator is satisfied with the information displayed on the screen, the **ENTER** (or **TRANSMIT**) key of the terminal is depressed and the buffer contents are transmitted in accordance with the given communications protocol.

When a terminal is operating in block mode, every character position on the display is assigned into one of two *fields:* a *protected field,* or an *unprotected field.* Protected fields are areas of the display that cannot be written to. Unprotected fields can be written to in the normal manner. These fields are defined by software through the use of *escape sequences.* (Escape sequences are discussed in Section 7-5.) Figure 7-12 depicts the two fields. Using the editing features that the terminal has been programmed for, characters, words, and lines are inserted and deleted throughout the unprotected fields of the display. When the end of an unprotected field is written to, the cursor moves to the beginning of the next unprotected field. The terminal's tab function can be used to move the cursor from one unprotected field to the next, skipping over the protected fields. If a character is typed within a protected field, the character will be displayed in the first position of the next unprotected field.

The maximum block size usually depends on the requirements of the computer. Unlike character mode, whereby characters are transmitted asynchronously, in block mode the entire block is sent synchronously; that is, each character is sent in contiguous order. The block of data may include several hundred contiguous bytes, including framing, control, and error-detection information. Start and stop bits are eliminated from each character in addition to any idle time between characters. Hence, transmission efficiency is greatly improved in block mode operation. Block mode terminals are much more expensive than character mode terminals due to the supporting hardware and software that are necessary.

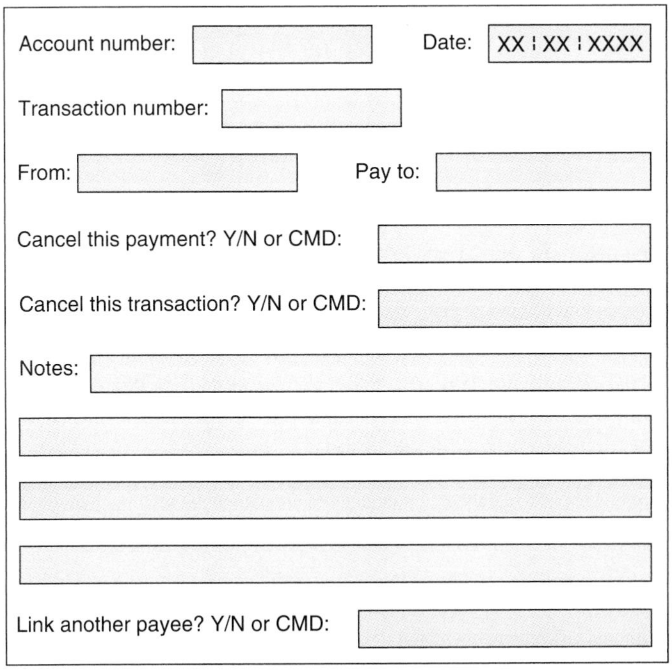

FIGURE 7-12
Block mode operation showing protected and unprotected fields of the display.

7.4 USING THE CONTROL (CRTL) KEY

Most ASCII characters are represented by dedicated terminal keys. Control characters, excluding the format effectors CR, LF, HT, and the like, are an exception. These characters are listed in the first two columns of Table 6-11. To transmit control characters, ASCII terminals provide the operator with a *control (CTRL) key.* The CTRL key allows an operator to send control characters, similar to the manner in which the SHIFT key is used to send an upper-case letter. The CTRL key is simply depressed, followed by one of the noncontrol characters listed in column 4 or 5 of Table 6-11. The transmitted ASCII control character is equal to 40H subtracted from this character (in software, 40H is masked with the character). For example, if an operator wanted to transmit the ASCII code for the BEL character, the CTRL key, followed by G, would be depressed. Because 40H subtracted from 47H, a G, is equal to 07H, the ASCII code for BEL is generated. Another example that perhaps many PC owners are familiar with is CTRL Q and CTRL S, which generate the ASCII control characters XON and XOFF, respectively:

$$\text{CTRL-Q} = 51H - 40H = 11H \text{ DC1 (XON)}$$
$$\text{CTRL-S} = 53H - 40H = 13H \text{ DC3 (XOFF)}$$

CTRL Q and CTRL S, as many of us know, are used to control the *flow* of data transmitted from a computer to a VDT or printer. A large directory file is often transmitted to a VDT that is either too fast for one to read, or the directory is larger than the screen capacity. As the screen fills, typing a CTRL S: DC3 (XOFF) turns the transmitter section of the computer off. Printing of the directory file on the display halts, thus allowing one to read the text before it scrolls off the screen. Once it is read by the operator, a CTRL Q: DC1 (XON) turns the transmitter section of the computer back on, and the directory file continues to be printed on the display from where it left off. This sequence of key strokes is repeated until the entire directory file has been read.

7.5 ESCAPE SEQUENCES

Most ASCII terminals today offer an entire set of commands and control functions that can be performed through the use of the ASCII character *escape (ESC).* As defined in Chapter 6, ESC, followed by a single character or a string of characters, is called an *escape sequence.* Escape sequences are used to perform special command and control functions, most of which are not immediately apparent to the operator. Clearing the screen, for example, or positioning the cursor to a specific location on the screen can be performed through an escape sequence.

The escape sequence begins with ESC ($1B_{16}$ or 033_8) and ends with the final character for the sequence. Any subsequent characters after the escape sequence are interpreted as normal ASCII text. Table 7-3 lists common escape sequences used by various manufacturers.

Escape sequences are normally sent to a terminal from a remote computer. An operator, however, can test an escape sequence for its effect, independent of the computer, by simply configuring the terminal to its half-duplex mode. Recall that in half-duplex a local echo is produced within the terminal. The ESC key can be typed, followed by the appropriate character(s) to perform the escape sequence. For example, some terminals (DEC VT52, HP2648) use **ESC A** and **ESC B** to position the cursor

TABLE 7-3
Common Escape Sequences Used by Various Manufacturers

Command Function	ANSI/ AT&T4410	DEC VT52	DEC VT100	Hazeltine 1420	HP 2648	IBM 3101	Lear-Siegler ADM3/5	Televideo 910
READ CURSOR POSITION	ESC[6n	N/A	ESC[6n	ESC CTRL E	ESC · DC1	ESC5	ESC ?	ESC ?
CURSOR UP	ESC[pn A	ESC A	ESC[Pn A	ESC CTRL L	ESC A	ESC A	CTRL K	CTRL K
CURSOR DOWN	ESC[pn B	ESC B	ESC[Pn B	ESC CTRL K	ESC B	ESC B	CTRL J	CTRL V
CURSOR RIGHT	ESC[pn C	ESC C	ESC[Pn C	CTRL P	ESC C	ESC C	CTRL L	CTRL L
CURSOR LEFT	ESC[pn D	ESC D	ESC[Pn D	CTRL H	ESC D	ESC D	CTRL H	CTRL H
HOME CURSOR	ESC[H	ESC H	ESC[H	ESC CTRL R	ESC H	ESC H	CTRL	CTRL ^
CLEAR TO END OF PAGE	ESC[J	ESC J	ESC[O J	ESC y	ESC J	ESC J	ESC y	ESC y
CLEAR TO END OF LINE	ESC[K	ESC K	ESC[O K	ESC t	ESC K	ESC I	ESC t	ESC T
LINE INSERT	ESC[L	N/A	N/A	ESC CTRL Z	ESC L	ESC N	ESC E	ESC E
LINE DELETE	ESC[M	N/A	N/A	ESC CTRL S	ESC M	ESC O	ESC R	ESC R
CHARACTER INSERT	ESC[@	N/A	N/A	ESC Q	ESC Q	ESC P	ESC Q	ESC Q
CHARACTER DELETE	ESC[P	N/A	N/A	ESC W	ESC P	ESC Q	ESC M	ESC W
POSITION CURSOR	ESC[n;pnH	ESC Y r + 31 c + 31	ESC[Pn; PnH	N/A	ESC&a #r#c	ESC Y xy	ESC = rc	ESC = rc
CLEAR ALL	ESC[2J	N/A	ESC[2 J	ESC CTRL L	ESC g	ESC ;	ESC*	ESC*
UNDERSCORE	ESC[4m	N/A	ESC[4m	N/A	ESC &d D	N/A	N/A	ESC G8
BLINK	ESC[5m	N/A	ESC[5m	N/A	ESC &d A	ESC 3 I	N/A	ESC G2
REVERSE VIDEO	ESC[7m	N/A	ESC[7m	N/A	ESC &d B	ESC 3 E	N/A	ESC G4
BLANK VIDEO	ESC[7m	N/A	N/A	N/A	ESC &d S	ESC 3 M	N/A	ESC G1
132 COLUMN MODE	ESC[?3h	N/A	ESC[?3h	N/A	N/A	N/A	N/A	N/A
80 COLUMN MODE	ESC[?3l	N/A	ESC[?3l	N/A	N/A	N/A	N/A	N/A
HORIZONTAL TAB SET	N/A	N/A	ESC H	ESC 1	N/A	ESC 0	ESC 1	ESC 1
LOCK KEYBOARD	N/A	N/A	N/A	ESC CTRL U	N/A	ESC :	ESC #	ESC #
UNLOCK KEYBOARD	N/A	N/A	N/A	ESC CTRL F	N/A	ESC ;	ESC "	ESC "
NEXT PAGE	N/A	N/A	N/A	N/A	ESC V	N/A	N/A	N/A
PREVIOUS PAGE	N/A	N/A	N/A	N/A	ESC U	N/A	N/A	N/A
PROTECT ON	N/A	N/A	N/A	ESC CTRL Y	ESC &dJ	ESC 3C	ESC)	ESC& ESC)
PROTECT OFF	N/A	N/A	N/A	ESC CTRL _	ESC &d@	ESC 3B	ESC (	ESC'ESC (
RESET DEVICE	N/A	N/A	ESC c	N/A	ESC E	N/A	N/A	N/A

Note: The letters n, r, c, pn, Pn, and xy represent a number used to specify a row, column, or the number of times to perform a sequence.

up or down, respectively. **ESC H** followed by **ESC J** (clear the screen from cursor on) will clear the entire screen.

Cursor up:

ESC	A	
1B	41	(hex)
033	101	(octal)

Cursor down:

ESC	B	
1B	42	(hex)
033	102	(octal)

Clear screen:

ESC	H	
1B	48	(hex)
033	110	(octal)
ESC	J	
1B	4A	(hex)
033	112	(octal)

Numerous other escape sequences can be performed beyond just cursor positioning. Consider the following:

- Local echo on/off
- Interrogate current cursor position
- Set/clear tabs
- Initialization of data communications test
- Inverse video
- Lock keyboard
- Caps mode
- Click on/off
- Block mode on/off
- Define block size
- Display data communications menus
- Display soft key labels
- Define character sets
- Define datacomm/printer ports
- Definition of protected and unprotected fields
- Definition of function (soft) keys
- Initialization of terminal self-test

Because escape sequences vary among terminal manufacturers, application programs must be tailored to suit a given terminal type. It is essential that the programmer refer to the manufacturer's operating manual to make use of the terminal's available escape sequences.

Escape sequences can also be sent by a terminal to command and control computers and peripheral devices such as printers, plotters, and modems. Here, again, the operating manual of each device must be referred to. (A more detailed explanation is given in subsequent chapters.)

7.6   TERMINAL INTERFACES

Many of today's terminals support more than one interface standard. Aside from the usual interface to a host computer, modems, printers, plotters, and even local area networks (LANs) are being directly connected to.

7.6.1   RS-232 Interface

Virtually all terminals offer the standard EIA (Electronics Industries Association) RS-232 interface. RS-232 is a serial interface standard that includes the electrical, mechanical, and functional specifications for interconnecting data communications equipment. The voltage specification for a logic 1 is -3 to -15 V, whereas a logic 0 is $+3$ to $+15$ V. In addition, ± 12V is typically used for terminals. The maximum data transfer rate is 20 kbps for a 15-m cable. A 25-pin, D-type connector is used to connect the interfacing cable. (In Chapter 8, the RS-232 interface standard is discussed in greater depth.)

7.6.2   RS-449, RS-422-A, and RS-423-A Interface

In 1977, EIA published the RS-449 standard. This new serial interface standard addresses the mechanical and functional specifications of an enhanced version of RS-232. A 37- and 9-pin connector interface are used. A year later, in 1978, EIA derived two new and improved electrical interface standards designed to work with RS-449: RS-422-A, and RS-423-A. The intent was to improve on the transmission characteristics (speed, noise immunity, and so on) of the existing RS-232 standard. RS-422-A defines the electrical characteristics for balanced line drivers and receivers. RS-423-A is for unbalanced line drivers and receivers. Valid logic levels are $+200$ mV to $+6$ V for a logic 0 and -200 mV to -6 V for a logic 1. Higher transmission speeds are attainable through these two interfaces. For a 10-m cable, 10 Mbps can be achieved. (RS-422-A and RS-423-A are discussed in greater depth in Chapter 8.)

7.6.3   PCMCIA

Common to most portable computers such as laptops, notebooks, and handheld computers is the *Personal Computer Memory Card International Association (PCMCIA)* interface standard. The PCMCIA standard, more recently known as the *PC Card Standard,* defines the 68-pin, credit card–size peripheral device and the PC Card slot in which it is plugged. In addition to the electrical, physical, and functional interface, the PC Card standard also defines the software architecture to provide plug-and-play (PnP) capabilities for a wide range of peripheral devices. Many of the PCMCIA standards that have evolved over the years are also used in the *Japan Electronic Industry Development Association (JEIDA)* standard developed in 1985. Today, PCMCIA is an international standards body consisting of representatives from more than 300 companies. A myriad of PC Card products are currently available as well, and they include the following:

- RAM memory
- Sound cards

Personal Computer Memory Card International Association (PCMCIA)
The international standards body that has defined and standardized the 68-pin, credit card–size peripheral device and PC Card slot into which it is plugged. Also referred to as the *PC Card* standard.

Japan Electronic Industry Development Association (JEIDA)
Established in 1958 as a nonprofit organization interested in contributing to Japan's economic prosperity by stimulating development in the electronics industry.

- MPEG video cards
- Fax/modems
- Floppy and hard disk controllers and drives
- CD-ROMs
- Ethernet token ring and wireless LAN adapters
- ISDN interface cards
- Data acquisition
- Digital cameras
- Cell phone interface
- SCSI (small computer systems interface) controllers
- Television and radio tuners
- GPS (global positioning system) cards

7.6.3.1 History of PCMCIA The PCMCIA stnadard was developed in 1989 by a small group of companies in San Jose, California, also known as "the heart of Silicon Valley." These technology-based companies wanted to standardize the development of memory cards used in portable computers in lieu of floppy disk drives. The original standard was designed exclusively for memory cards; however, PCMCIA has expanded its specifications to meet the market's demands for interfacing to computer peripheral devices. The ability to put input/output (I/O) capabilities on a card soon became the main attraction for adopting the technology. Addition of a PCMCIA card slot would allow mobile computers to have an easily accessible, bus expansion capability.*

By 1995, the PCMCIA standard became known as the *PC Card Standard,* and what was referred to as a PCMCIA card was not referred to as a *PC Card.* Enhancements to the PC Card standard include a 32-bit, 133-Mbps interface called *Card Bus* and a *Zoomed Video* bus that permits video data to be written to a VGA controller. Other enhancements include DMA (Direct Memory Access), power management, low-voltage operation at 3.3 V, and *plug-and-play (PnP)* or *hot swappable* capability, which permits the PC card to be plugged in or pulled out of the PC Card socket without having to power down the computer. Various layers of software specifications have also been added to the standard, thereby providing specific guidelines for equipment manufacturers to incorporate into their PC Card products. Table 7-4 lists the PCMCIA/PC Card Standard release history.† Detailed information on PCMCIA can be found at the PCMCIA Web site (http://www.pc-card.com) or from the PCMCIA International Headquarters (2635 N. 1st St., San Jose, CA 95131 408-433-CARD [2237]).

Plug-and-Play (PnP)
A hardware and software specification developed by Intel that permits PnP adapter cards to automatically configure themselves via a computer's PnP BIOS (Basic I/O System) or the PnP software provided by an adapter card's vendor.

Hot Swappable
A term used to denote that a device can be removed or installed in a computer without powering down or rebooting the system.

7.6.3.2 PCMCIA Card Types The PC Card Standard currently specifies three physical types of PC Cards: *Type I, Type II,* and *Type III.* These are shown in Figure 7-13 and listed in Table 7-5. All three card types measure the same length (85.6 mm) and width (54.0), and all three utilize the same 68-pin connector. Only their thicknesses differ. A thinner card can be used in a thicker slot, but a thicker card cannot be used in a thinner slot.

Type I PC Cards are 3.3-mm thick and the original cards used for memory such as static and dynamic RAM and flash memory (high-speed memory). Type II PC Cards, which are currently the most widely used, measure 5-mm thick and are used

---

*http://fortezza-support.com, *PC Card Standard Overview,* February 8, 1999.
†http://www.pc-card.com, *Detailed Overview of the PC Card Standard,* 1998, PCMCIA.

TABLE 7-4
PCMCIA Release History

Date	Release	Description
June 1990	1.0/JEIDA 4.0	The original release defines the electrical and physical specifications for memory cards. It includes the 68-pin interface and Type I and Type II (*Type* refers to the thickness of the PC Card) form factors originally defined by JEIDA.
September 1991	2.0/JEIDA 4.1	I/O interface definitions were included in this release. Other additions include support for dual-voltage memory cards, BIOS-type Socket Services, Card Information Structure (CIS) enhancement, and environmental and test methods.
November 1992	2.01	New in this release are the PC Card ATA specification, Auto-Indexing Mass Storage (AIMS) for digital images, Type III PC Card definition, enhancements to Socket Services, and the initial version of Card Services.
July 1993	2.1/JEIDA 4.2	Enhancement of Card and Socket Services, CIS, and electrical and physical sections of previous releases.
February 1995	PC Card Standard (no release no.)	32-Bit bus mastering interface (Card Bus), low-voltage (3.3-V) operation, power management interface (APM), Direct Memory Access (DMA), and multiple function cards.
May 1995	PC Card Standard, Second Printing	Power-up/power-down timing changes and updates.
November 1995	PC Card Standard, Third Printing	Custom Interfaces and Indirect CIS Addressing.
May 1996	PC Card Standard, Errata Update	Zoomed Video (ZV) Interface Specification and Flash Translation Layer (FTL).
March 1997	PC Card Standard Volumes 1–13, First Printing	Thermal Rating system, Power Management, ISDN Function, Hot Dock/Undock Software Support, and Physical Socket Naming.

in several I/O applications, including fax/modems, LAN adapters, sound and video cards, GPS (Global Positioning System), and many more. The thickest PC Card is Type III, which measures 10.5-mm thick and is used for rotating mass storage devices such as miniature hard disk drives. Table 7-6 lists the PC Card and Card Bus pin assignment.

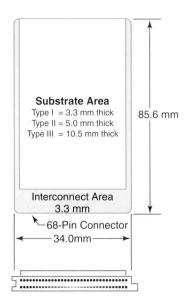

Substrate Area
Type I = 3.3 mm thick
Type II = 5.0 mm thick
Type III = 10.5 mm thick

85.6 mm

Interconnect Area
3.3 mm

68-Pin Connector
34.0mm

FIGURE 7-13
PCMCIA standard dimensions for Types I, II, and III PC Cards.

7.6.4 Ethernet Interface

The IEEE 802.3 Ethernet standard was developed in 1980 as a baseband LAN protocol that addresses the physical and data link layers of the ISO/OSI Seven-Layer Model. The standard has become so prevalent in networks that PC terminals can readily be equipped with Ethernet adapter cards or *network interface cards (NICs)*. These interface cards are designed to plug into ISA (Industry Standard Architecture), MCA (Micro Channel Architecture, or EISA (Extended Industry Standard Architecture) bus expansion slots available on a computer's motherboard. They can also be plugged into notebook computers with PCMCIA slots. Serial data transfer to and from the terminal is at a 10-Mbps transmission rate. The typical connector interface for an Ethernet NIC can be a 50-Ω BNC connector (10Base2 or thinnet), twisted-pair wire (10BaseT), or a DB-15 pin AUI (Attachment Unit Interface) connector for interfacing to thicknet (10Base5) or other Ethernet LAN devices. A detailed description of the Ethernet standard is presented in Chapter 15.

7.6.5 Current Loop Interface

Some terminal manufacturers continue to offer the 20-mA current loop interface. This standard has evolved from the old electromechanical teletype, which used current to activate its relays. A logic 1 is represented by the presence of 20 mA in the interface loop. A logic 0 is represented by the absence of current in the loop. The same serial bit stream used to drive RS-232 circuits is used to drive the current loop circuit.

The General-Purpose Interface Bus (GPIB) Also known as the *IEEE-488* standard and the *HPIB* (*Hewlett-Packard Interface Bus*). Specifies a method of interconnecting test and measurement instruments for control and measurement.

7.6.6 IEEE-488 Interface Bus

The IEEE-488 Interface Standard was published in 1975. This standard specifies a method of interconnecting *digital programmable measurement instruments (DPI)* via an 8-bit, bidirectional, asynchronous parallel bus. Hewlett-Packard Corporation developed the original standard, *HP-IB* (Hewlett-Packard interface bus), on which the IEEE-488 standard is based. The bus has also become known as the *general-purpose interface bus (GPIB)*. Many terminals have adopted the IEEE-488 interface for

TABLE 7-5
PC Card Types

PC Card Type	Length (mm)	Width (mm)	Thickness (mm)	Applications
I	85.6	54.0	3.3	Memory cards: RAM, DRAM, Flash, and so on
II	85.6	54.0	5.0	I/O Cards: fax/modems, LAN, sound and video cards, SCSI, and so on
III	85.6	54.0	10.5	Hard Disk drives, CD-ROMs

TABLE 7-6
PC Card and Card Bus Pin Assignment

Pin No.	Memory	I/O and Memory	32-Bit Card Bus	Pin No.	Memory	I/O and Memory	32-Bit Card Bus
1	GND	GND	GND	35	GND	GND	GND
2	D3	D3	CAD0	36	CD1*	CD1*	CCD1*
3	D4	D4	CAD1	37	D11	D11	CAD2
4	D5	D5	CAD3	38	D12	D12	CAD4
5	D6	D6	CAD5	39	D13	D13	CAD6
6	D7	D7	CAD7	40	D14	D14	RSRVD
7	CE1*	CE1*	CCBE0*	41	D15	D15	CAD8
8	A10	A10	CAD9	42	CE2*	CE2*	CAD10
9	OE*	OE*	CAD11	43	VS1*	VS1*	CVS1
10	A11	A11	CAD12	44	RSRVD	IORD*	CAD13
11	A9	A9	CAD14	45	RSRVD	IOWR*	CAD15
12	A8	A8	CCBE1*	46	A17	A17	CAD16
13	A13	A13	CPAR	47	A18	A18	RSRVD
14	A14	A14	CPERR*	48	A19	A19	CBLOCK*
15	WE*	WE*	CGNT*	49	A20	A20	CSTOP*
16	READY	IREQ*	CINT*	50	A21	A21	CDEVSEL*
17	Vcc	Vcc	Vcc	51	Vcc	Vcc	Vcc
18	Vpp1	Vpp1	Vpp1	52	Vpp2	Vpp2	Vpp2
19	A16	A16	CCLK	53	A22	A22	CTRDY*
20	A15	A15	CIRDY*	54	A23	A23	CFRAME*
21	A12	A12	CCBE2*	55	A24	A24	CAD17
22	A7	A7	CAD18	56	A25	A25	CAD19
23	A6	A6	CAD20	57	VS2*	VS2*	CVS2
24	A5	A5	CAD21	58	RESET	RESET	CRST*
25	A4	A4	CAD22	59	WAIT*	WAIT*	CSERR*
26	A3	A3	CAD23	60	RSRVD	INPACK*	CREQ*
27	A2	A2	CAD24	61	REG*	REG*	CCBE3*
28	A1	A1	CAD25	62	BVD2	SPKR*	CAUDIO
29	A0	A0	CAD26	63	BVD1	STSCHG*	CSTSCHG
30	D0	D0	CAD27	64	D8	D8	CAD28
31	D1	D1	CAD29	65	D9	D9	CAD30
32	D2	D2	RSRVD	66	D10	D10	CAD31
33	WP	IOISI6*	CCLKRUN*	67	CD2*	CD2*	CCD2*
34	GND	GND	GND	68	GND	GND	GND

interconnecting to thousands of different types of laboratory instruments, data acquisition devices, and other peripherals.

Four basic functional elements are used to organize and manage information among IEEE-48 interconnecting devices:

Controller: A device that can address other devices to control their transmission or reception of data and their operating functions. The controller is typically the host computer.

Talker: A device that can be addressed by an interface message to transmit data to other devices on the bus. Examples include frequency counters, voltmeters, spectrum analyzers, and terminals.

Listener: A device that can be addressed by an interface message to receive data from other devices on the bus. Examples include terminals, printers, and plotters.

Talker/listener: A device that can be addressed by an interface message to act as a talker or a listener.

TABLE 7-7
IEEE-488 Signal Definition

Signal Name	Group	Description	Pin Number
DI01-DI08	Data bus	Bidirectional data transfer lines	1–4 and 13–16
DAV	Handshake lines	Data Valid indicates that data on DIO lines are valid. DAV is issued by a talker.	6
NRFD		Not Ready For Data indicates the readiness of a listener to accept data.	7
NDAC		Not Data Accepted indicates whether or not a listener has accepted data from the bus.	8
ATN	Interface management	Attention is issued by a controller to indicate whether information on the bus is data or an interface control message.	11
IFC		Interface Clear is used by a controller to reset the complete interface system into its quiescent state.	9
SRQ		Service Request is used by a device to indicate to the bus controller that it requires attention.	10
REN		Remote Enable is used by a controller to provide selection between two sources of device programming data.	17
EOI		End or Identify is issued by a talker to indicate the end of a multiple-byte transfer.	5
		EOI is also used by a controller with ATN to initiate a polling sequence.	

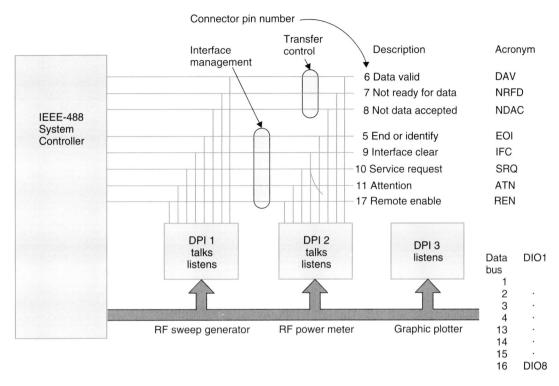

FIGURE 7-14
IEEE-488 bus interface setup. (From *PET and the IEEE 488 Bus [GPIB]* by Eugene
Fisher and C. W. Jensen. Copyright © 1980 McGraw-Hill, Inc.)

The *controller* assigns which device (or devices) on the bus will be a *listener,* that
is, receiver, or a *talker,* the transmitting device. Only one device may transmit on the bus
at any one time. The transmitting device can be the controller itself or an assigned talker.

Sixteen lines make up the IEEE-488 bus. Their functions are divided into three
groups, as shown in Table 7-7. Figure 7-14 depicts an IEEE-488 interface between a
system controller and DPIs. Figure 7-15(a) illustrates the standard IEEE-488, 24-pin
shielded connector pin-out assignment. The connector features a plug on one end and
a receptacle on the reverse or flip side so that it may be "piggy-backed" in parallel
with other IEEE-488 connectors. Figures 7-15(b) and (c) illustrate how this is done
in a linear and a star configuration, respectively.

Data transactions between devices occur via the 8-bit bidirectional data bus lines
DI01 through **DI08.** A *master/slave* relationship is used to transfer data bytes between
two devices. Three lines are used for handshaking the data: **NRFD** (Not Ready For
Data), **NDAC** (Not Data Accepted), and **DAV** (Data Valid). The remaining five control lines are **ATN** (Attention), **IFC** (Interface Clear), **SRQ** (Service Request), **REN**
(Remote Enable), and **EOI** (End Or Identify). Figure 7-16 illustrates the handshaking sequence for an 8-bit data transaction between a talker and a listener.

7.6.7   SCSI Interface

The *Small Computer Systems Interface (SCSI),* pronounced "scuzzy," was originally
developed by Shugart Associates during the late 1970s as an I/O interface to IBM's

> **Small Computer
> Systems Interface
> (SCSI)**
> Pronounced "scuzzy."
> This is a parallel I/O (in-
> put/output) interface
> bus used to connect
> as many as eight SCSI
> peripheral devices.

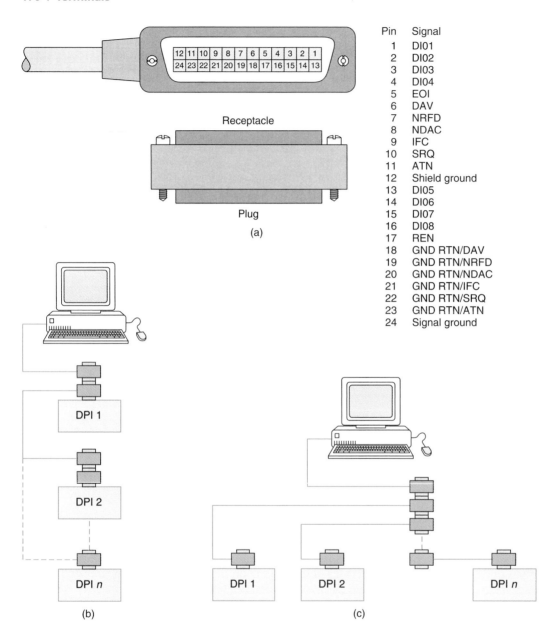

Pin	Signal
1	DI01
2	DI02
3	DI03
4	DI04
5	EOI
6	DAV
7	NRFD
8	NDAC
9	IFC
10	SRQ
11	ATN
12	Shield ground
13	DI05
14	DI06
15	DI07
16	DI08
17	REN
18	GND RTN/DAV
19	GND RTN/NRFD
20	GND RTN/NDAC
21	GND RTN/IFC
22	GND RTN/SRQ
23	GND RTN/ATN
24	Signal ground

Receptacle

Plug

(a)

DPI 1

DPI 2

DPI *n*

(b)

DPI 1   DPI 2   DPI *n*

(c)

FIGURE 7-15

IEEE-488 connector interface: (a) connector pin-out diagram; (b) linear configuration; (c) star configuration.

(International Business Machines) numerous peripheral devices and host computers over a single bus. At the time, it was called the Shugart Associates Standard Interface (SASI). The ANSI standards organization adopted SASI and began refining it, and in 1982, its X3T9.2 subcommittee proposed a newly revised standard called SCSI. The SCSI standard was eventually approved by ANSI in 1986 (X3.131) and, since then, has become one of the most popular computer interfaces in the computer industry.

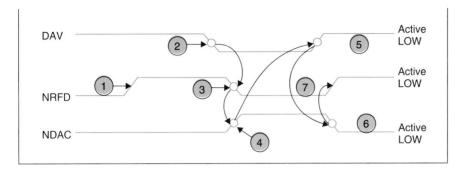

FIGURE 7-16
IEEE-488 handshaking sequence between talker and listener. (From *PET and the IEEE 488 Bus [GPIB]* by Eugene Fisher and C. W. Jensen. Copyright © 1980 McGraw-Hill, Inc.)

Three SCSI standards have evolved over the years: SCSI-1, SCSI-2, and SCSI-3. The original SCSI standard, or SCSI-1, specifies the physical and electrical definitions of an 8-bit, parallel I/O bus used to connect computers and peripheral devices in a daisy-chain manner. These peripheral devices today include scanners, hard disk and magnetic tape drives, CD-ROM drives, high-speed printers, and more.

As illustrated in Figure 7-17, as many as eight devices can be connected to the SCSI bus, one of which must be a *Host Bus Adaptor (HBA)*. The HBA is also referred to as a *SCSI controller* and typically plugs into the motherboard of a computer. Each SCSI device has a SCSI ID, 0–7, where the HBA has an ID of 7, or the highest priority. Jumpers or switches are used on SCSI peripheral devices to select the SCSI ID. Note that the HBA and the very end device in the SCSI chain must be terminated to prevent echoes on the bus. Most SCSI devices have built-in terminators that a user can switch on or off depending on its position in the chain.

The SCSI-2 standard, which was formally adopted by ANSI in 1991, is the most popular of the SCSI standards. It offers a considerable improvement in the electrical, mechanical, and functional specification over the old SCSI-1 standard. Major improvements include the following:

> **SCSI Controller**
> Typically plugs into the motherboard of a computer and controls the SCSI peripheral devices on the bus. Has the highest priority of the SCSI devices on the bus. Also known as a *Host Bus Adaptor (HBA)*.

- Definition of a comprehensive command set to promote standardization and interchangeability across peripheral devices of the same type. This command set is called the *Common Command Set (CCS)*.

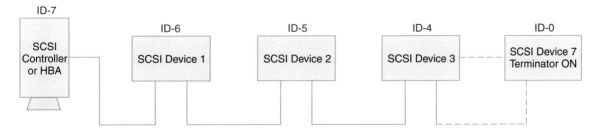

FIGURE 7-17
As many as eight SCSI devices can be daisy-chained together. One of the eight devices includes the HBA.

TABLE 7-8
SCSI Trade Association (STA) Endorsed Terms and Terminology

STA Terms	Maximum Bus Speed (Mbps)	Bus Width (bits)	Maximum Bus Lengths (m)[a]			Maximum Device Support
			Single-Ended	LVD	HVD	
SCSI-1[b]	5	8	6	—[c]	25	8
Fast SCSI[b]	10	8	3	—[c]	25	8
Fast Wide SCSI	20	16	3	—[c]	25	16
Ultra SCSI[b]	20	8	1.5	—[c]	25	8
Ultra SCSI[b]	20	8	3	—	—	4
Wide Ultra SCSI	40	16	—	—[c]	25	16
Wide Ultra SCSI	40	16	1.5	—	—	8
Wide Ultra SCSI	40	16	3	—	—	4
Ultra2 SCSI[b,d]	40	8	—[d]	12	25	8
Wide Ultra2 SCSI[d]	80	16	—[d]	12	25	16
Ultra3 SCSI[e]	160	16	—[d]	12	—[d]	16

[a]The listed maximum bus lengths may be exceeded in point-to-point and engineered applications.

[b]Use of the word *narrow* preceding SCSI, Ultra SCSI, or Ultra2 SCSI is optional.

[c]Low-voltage differential (LVD) was not defined in the original SCSI standards for this speed. If all devices on the bus support LVD, then 12-m operation is possible at this speed. If, however, any device on the bus is singled-ended only, then the entire bus switches to single-ended mode and the distances in the single-ended column apply.

[d]Single-ended is not defined for speeds beyond Ultra.

[f]High-voltage differential (HVD) is not defined for speeds beyond Ultra2.

[e]After Ultra2 all new speeds are wide only.

Courtesy of STA Executive Director L. Bue.

- Increased bus speed from 5 Mbps, called *Standard SCSI,* to 10 Mbps, called *Fast SCSI.*
- Expansion of the bus width from 8 bits, called *narrow SCSI,* to an optional 16 or 32 bits, called *wide SCSI.*
- Connector-type definition.
- Optional *low-voltage differential (LVD)* and *high-voltage differential (HVD)* signaling over the SCSI-1 *single-ended* signaling.

The SCSI-3 standard is a collection of documents that enhances the SCSI-2 standard. It provides an optional *Fast SCSI* speed of 20 MBps and a 16-bit *Ultra SCSI* speed of 40 MBps. One of the more popular aspects of SCSI-3, and one that has been widely adopted, is the ability for wide SCSI to control as many as 16 devices on the SCSI chain.* Table 7-8 lists the SCSI Trade Association (STA) endorsed terms and terminology for the SCSI standard. Figure 7-18 illustrates the common SCSI bus connectors. For more information on the SCSI standard, visit the STA Web page at http://www.scsita.org.

*Michael Meyers, *All-In-One A+ Certification Exam Guide,* 2nd ed. (New York: McGraw-Hill, 2000) p. 385.

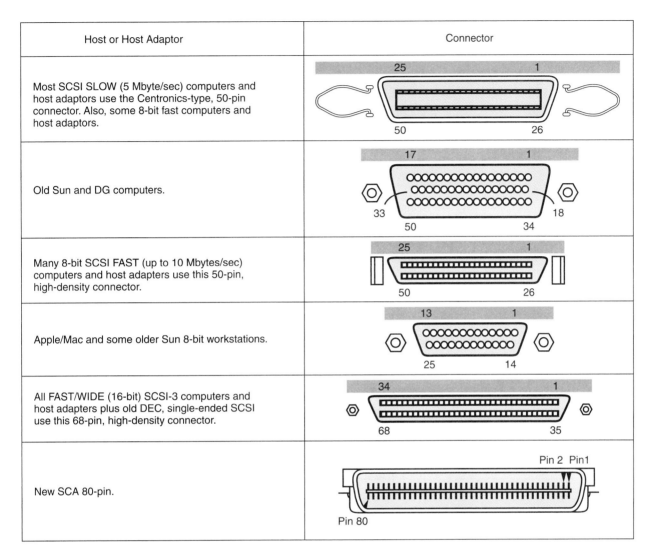

Host or Host Adaptor	Connector
Most SCSI SLOW (5 Mbyte/sec) computers and host adaptors use the Centronics-type, 50-pin connector. Also, some 8-bit fast computers and host adaptors.	
Old Sun and DG computers.	
Many 8-bit SCSI FAST (up to 10 Mbytes/sec) computers and host adapters use this 50-pin, high-density connector.	
Apple/Mac and some older Sun 8-bit workstations.	
All FAST/WIDE (16-bit) SCSI-3 computers and host adapters plus old DEC, single-ended SCSI use this 68-pin, high-density connector.	
New SCA 80-pin.	

FIGURE 7-18
Visual guide to SCSI connectors. (Courtesy of Parlan Corp. and Quantum Corp.)

PROBLEMS

1. What primary feature distinguishes a smart terminal from a dumb terminal?
2. Define *ergonomics*.
3. Name three applications for a workstation.
4. Name five ergonomic features of a terminal.
5. What is the typical screen capacity for a standard ASCII terminal?
6. Name the function keys of the main keypad for the VT300 series terminal.
7. What are special function keys used for?
8. A terminal is programmed for a baud rate of 4800. What is the bit time associated with the transmitted character?

9. Determine the parity bit for the following data words:

Odd parity

1 1 0 1 0 1 0 _____

0 0 1 1 0 1 0 _____

1 1 1 0 0 0 0 _____

1 0 1 1 0 1 0 _____

Even parity

0 0 1 1 0 1 0 _____

1 0 1 0 1 1 0 _____

1 1 1 1 0 0 0 _____

0 0 1 1 0 1 0 _____

10. Explain the difference between block mode and character mode.
11. Is a local echo produced in half-duplex or full-duplex mode?
12. Explain how a character is displayed when typed at a terminal that is set for full-duplex operation.
13. What happens when a terminal is set for half-duplex and a remote echo is returned to the terminal as a result of typing a key?
14. How may the CTRL key be used to generate the ASCII character BEL?
15. What is an escape sequence?
16. Explain how a terminal's cursor may be moved up by a remote device.
17. Name three types of terminal interfaces.
18. What does *PCMCIA* stand for?
19. State the length, width, and thickness dimensions for Type I, II, and III PC Cards.
20. What does *SCSI* stand for?
21. What is the maximum number of SCSI devices that can be connected together?
22. For what four functions may IEEE-488 devices be programmed?
23. What is the term for a DIP that can receive data only?
24. What are the names of the IEEE-488 handshake lines?

SERIAL INTERFACES

On May 24, 1844, Samuel F. B. Morse transmitted the famous message *"What hath God wrought."* The message was transmitted from the U.S. Supreme Court in Washington, D.C., to the city of Baltimore. It was translated by a receiving party and returned. A short conversation followed. Morse, inventor of the telegraph, had successfully demonstrated to the U.S. Congress that messages could be sent in excess of 10 miles by transmitting electrical impulses down a wire. The apparatus used for the demonstration included a telegraph key, conductive wire, a battery, and an electromagnetic relay. By manually opening and closing the telegraph key, Morse was able to activate the remote electromagnetic relay acting as the receiving device. The relay opened and closed accordingly. A series of *clicks* was transmitted and received in accordance with his specially devised code.

Morse's historical event paid tribute to many pioneers of electricity and marked perhaps the first electrical transmission of serial data. His serial communications link was capable of transmitting a few words per minute. Little did he realize that serial transmission of data would evolve into today's enormous transmission rates over the *public switched telephone network (PSTN)*.

The PSTN still remains the largest and most common facility for the transmission of serial data. Due to its vastness in size and complexity, data transfer rates are still limited to the bandwidth constraints of existing facilities. Although the original intent of the PSTN was for analog voice communications, it has evolved today as a standard medium for the Internet and data communications. Binary serial data are converted from parallel format to a serial bit stream used to modulate carrier frequencies that are compatible with the characteristics of the PSTN. Although the transmission of the original information from one point to another is less expedient in this manner, there is an enormous savings in hardware, and existing communications facilities of the PSTN can be utilized for long-distance communications. This chapter looks at some of the fundamental concepts, rules, and regulations regarding the format of serial data and how data are transferred between devices.

> **Public Switched Telephone Network (PSTN)**
> A dial-up telephone network. Also referred to as *TELCO* (short for *telephone company*).

8.1 SYNCHRONOUS VERSUS ASYNCHRONOUS SERIAL TRANSMISSION

The transmission of serial data between two devices needs to be coordinated regarding the manner in which it is sent. The receiver must synchronize with the incoming data to interpret the orderly sequence in which it was transmitted. The set of rules that govern the manner in which the data are both transmitted and received is called a *protocol*.

Transmitted serial data can be classified into two categories: *synchronous,* and *asynchronous*. We begin our discussion with asynchronous serial transmission. The term *asynchronous* literally means *lack of synchronism*. An example of an asynchronous event is a person typing characters at a video display terminal (VDT). Each time a character is typed, a serial bit stream representing the character typed is transmitted by the terminal. The person can proceed to type at any speed and pause for any length of time between characters. There is no synchronism to the manner in which the characters are typed. The transmitted characters, therefore, lack synchronism. Because characters are typed in a more-or-less random fashion, VDTs are well suited for synchronous serial transmission. How widespread is asynchronous serial transmission? Think of the millions of people who work on a daily basis typing at a terminal.

8.1.1   Asynchronous Serial Link Protocol

The lack of synchronism in asynchronous transmission is solved by having the transmitting device insert *framing* bits at the beginning and end of each transmitted character. These framing bits are referred to as the character's *start bit* and *stop bit* (Figure 8-1). The start bit is always a logic 0, and the stop bit is always a logic 1. A character's start and stop bits mark the beginning and end of the character, thereby allowing the receiving device a means of achieving frame sync with each character. The character can then be sent at any time. The time interval between characters is referred to as the *idle time*. This time varies between characters depending on the speed of the typist. Because there will always be at least one stop bit between characters, the receiver simply searches for the occurrence of the next start bit to synchronize and detect additional serial characters. The stop bit is verified to ensure frame sync. Framing is said to occur on a *character-by-character basis for asynchronously transmitted serial data*.

8.1.2   Synchronous Serial Link Protocol

Synchronous transmission of serial data involves the high-speed transmission of data in the form of *blocks*. A block of data can represent a contiguous series of data bytes. In contrast to asynchronously transmitted characters, the idle time between characters as well as the start and stop bits are eliminated, making it possible to send data at higher rates. Synchronization of data is performed on a *block-by-block* basis. The transmitting device often provides a separate clock pulse that is in sync with the cen-

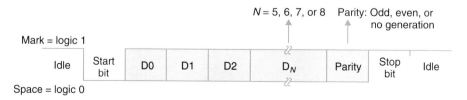

FIGURE 8-1

Format of an asynchronous serial character.

ter of each transmitted data bit. The synchronizing clock is carried on a line separate from the transmitted data line. (See the discussion of RS-232 circuits DA, DB, and DD in Section 8.4.6.) For long-distance communications via the telephone system, the synchronizing clock on a separate circuit becomes impractical. In this case, the clock is encoded with the data by a device called a *modem*. The modem modulates a carrier frequency with this information and sends it down the telephone lines. The receiving modem demodulates the synchronous clock along with the corresponding data. The clock is separated from the data and used to sample the data at the center of each bit, thus determining the state of each bit. Figure 8-2 illustrates these two methods of synchronous transmission.

Another method of achieving synchronization with the transmitted data is to insert a unique bit pattern at the beginning and end of each block. The receiver can synchronize with the data block by recognizing the occurrence of the unique bit pattern. This eliminates the need for a separate clock. This unique bit pattern and the number of bits contained in the block are a function of the synchronous serial link protocol. In some protocols, this special synchronizing bit pattern is referred to as the *sync character;* in others, it is referred to as the *opening flag* and *closing flag.* The synchronous receiver *hunts* for the sync character or opening flag until a recognition has been made. When the receiver has recognized this unique bit pattern, it goes into *sync-lock* with the data block that has been transmitted. More than one sync character can be sent in succession as an added measure of ensuring sync-lock. Figure 8-3

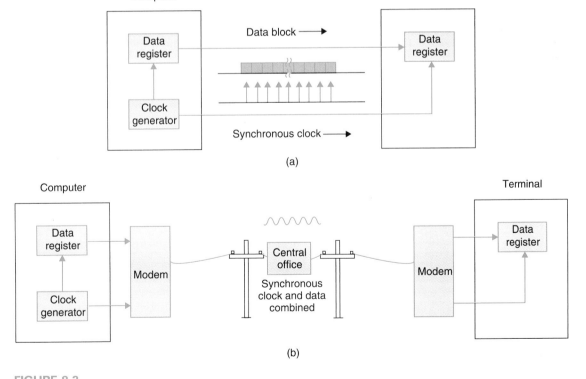

FIGURE 8-2
(a) Synchronous data transmitted with a separate clock; (b) synchronizing clock encoded with data and transmitted together.

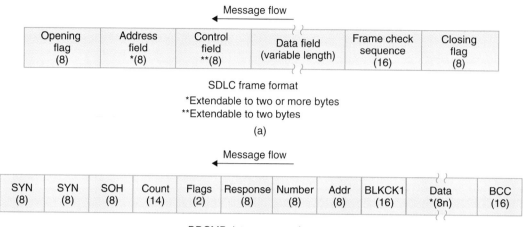

FIGURE 8-3
(a) SDLC frame format; (b) DDCMP message format.

illustrates two examples of synchronous protocols that are commonly used: IBM's *Synchronous Data Link Control (SDLC)*, and Digital Equipment Corporation's *Digital Data Communications Message Protocol (DDCMP)*.

Many different synchronous serial link protocols are used today. They have been developed by several manufacturers and standards organizations. A detailed discussion of these protocols is presented in Chapter 14. Some of the more common synchronous serial link protocols used today are:

> **BISYNC or BSC:** Binary Synchronous Communications
> **DDCMP:** Digital Data Communications Message Protocol
> **HDLC:** High-level Data Link Control
> **SDLC:** Synchronous Data Link Control

8.1.3   Protocol Efficiency

One often considers the relative advantages and disadvantages of serial data transmission protocols in terms of *efficiency*. The efficiency of a protocol can be thought of as the maximum transfer of data in a minimal amount of time, that is, with the least likelihood of getting garbled during the interim. In asynchronous serial link protocols, a significant amount of time is expended by including the start, stop, and parity bits with the actual data. A 7-bit ASCII character transmitted in asynchronous format may include one start bit, as many as two stop bits, and a parity bit, as illustrated earlier in Figure 8-1. If only one stop bit is used, the total composite character is 10 bits. The *protocol overhead* in this case is 30%, or three overhead bits and seven data bits. In is now apparent why asynchronous serial transmission is often thought of as *inefficient:* the overhead is high. Protocol overhead for serial transmission of data can be computed by the following equation:

Protocol Overhead
A measure of how much redundancy is added to a message stream for framing, flow control, and error detection.

$$\text{Protocol overhead} = \left(1 - \frac{N}{N + C}\right) \times 100\% \qquad \textbf{(8-1)}$$

where N represents the number of data bits transmitted and C the number of control bits transmitted.

Compute the protocol overhead for a DDCMP message block. The message block in this example will include the maximum allowable number of data bytes: 16,384 (2^{14}).

EXAMPLE 8.1

Solution:
Refer to Figure 8-3.

$$\text{Protocol overhead} = \left(1 - \frac{131,072}{131,072 + 96}\right) \times 100 = 0.074\%$$

where N = 16,384 bytes $\times$ 8 bits/byte = 131,072 bits and C = 96 bits.

The overhead for a DDCMP synchronous data block in this case is less than one-tenth of 1%! It is apparent that synchronous transmission of data is much more efficient than asynchronous transmission. The example here, however, uses the maximum allowable bytes in the DDCMP data field. The data field within the DDCMP message format can be anywhere between 0 and 16,384 bytes. What would be the case if a DDCMP message block were sent with only two bytes?

Compute the protocol overhead for a DDCMP message block containing two data bytes in the data field.

EXAMPLE 8.2

Solution:

$$\text{Protocol overhead} = \left(1.0 - \frac{16}{16 + 96}\right) \times 100 = 85.7\%$$

where N = 2 bytes $\times$ 8 bits/byte = 16 bits and C = 96 bits.

The overhead for synchronous transmission is very high for small messages. The number of small DDCMP message blocks should, therefore, be kept at a minimum. Likewise, if an error occurs in synchronous transmissions, the entire message block may have to be retransmitted. This can be very time consuming for large DDCMP message blocks. With asynchronous transmissions, if an error occurs, only one character may be lost, because each character is individually synchronized with its own start and stop bits.

As we can see, there are advantages and disadvantages to both synchronous and asynchronous transmission of data. They are listed in Table 8-1.

8.2 DEVELOPMENT OF THE MODEM

With the advent of the computer and the increasing need to render its services from a remote location, a device called a *modem* was developed in the early 1960s. The term *modem* is a contraction of the words *modulator–demodulator*. Telephone companies refer to a modem as a *data set*. The modem, which has become a household word, would make it possible to communicate serial binary data between computers and terminals via the telephone lines. Data could be sent in either synchronous or asynchronous form.

> **Modem**
> Converts digital signals to analog, and vice versa, for transmission over phone lines. A contraction of the words *modulator–demodulator*.

TABLE 8-1
Characterizing Synchronous and Asynchronous Serial Transmission

	Asynchronous	Synchronous
Advantages	Suitable for ASCII terminals and data entry	High-speed transmission
	Minimal hardware to implement	Maximum throughput
	Bit errors can readily be seen as erroneous characters displayed	Low overhead
	Low-speed transmission means fewer errors	Error-detection methods are extremely reliable
	Suitable for electromechanical teletype	
Disadvantages	Slow and inefficient	Expensive to implement
	High overhead due to start and stop bits	Communication protocols must be compatible
		Entire blocks may need to be retransmitted if a single bit error occurs
		Cannot be used with electro-mechanical teletype

A modem simply utilizes the computer's digital pulse streams to *modulate* an analog carrier frequency compatible with the communications facilities of the telephone system. The modem also performs the reverse task of *demodulating* an analog carrier frequency (generated from a remote via the telephone system) into digital pulse trains for the computer; hence, the name *mod*ulator–*dem*odulator or modem was derived (Figure 8-4). (A detailed discussion of the modem will be presented in Chapter 13).

It is necessary at this time to define two new very important data communication terms: *DTE,* and *DCE.*

> **Data Terminal Equipment (DTE)**
> In data communications, an end user or terminating circuit or device (typically a terminal or computer).

DTE *Data terminal equipment* corresponds to a device that transmits or receives binary digital data. DTE acts as the primary source or destination of transmitted or received data. Examples of DTE include VDTs, printers, and computers when the computer is interfaced to a modem.

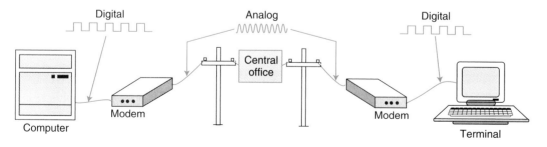

FIGURE 8-4
Diagram depicting the operation of a modem.

DCE   *Data communications equipment* corresponds to devices that *transfer* binary digital data between two transmission mediums. The binary digital data can be represented as an analog or digital signal. In either case, signal processing (modulation, demodulation, encoding, or decoding) is necessary for DCE to transfer the data between the two mediums. An example of DCE is a modem or data set. The two transmission mediums in this case would be the telephone lines and an RS-232 interface. A computer can also be DCE. Take, for example, when it is connected to the printer. The printer is DTE. It is the primary destination of the transmitted data, and the computer, DCE in this case, transfers the data from disk drive or memory to the terminal.

> **Data Communications Equipment (DCE)**
> Typically a modem or data set used to interface a terminal or computer to the telephone lines.

8.3   A NEED FOR STANDARDIZATION

Within a short period of time after the invention of the modem, computers and business machines within the same room, different buildings, and different cities were exchanging data over the phone lines. Eminent problems surfaced as the need to communicate continued to grow by orders of magnitude. Signal names and functions were incompatible between computers, modems, and other related equipment. Transmit and receive voltage varied between modems. When one business machine was in the process of sending data, the remote business machine was not ready to receive it and, subsequently, data were lost. In addition, connectors between devices varied. Special interfacing cables were necessary. These cables were adaptable only to a given situation. A standard was necessary to ensure compatibility between DTE and DCE. The standard would ensure that interfacing devices met the following criteria:

- The transmitted and received voltage levels must fall within a specified region.
- Electrical characteristics of the transmission line, including source and terminating loads, must meet specification, thus setting limitations on maximum data transfer rates.
- Interfacing cables between DTE and DCE must include cable connectors at each end that are compatible in size and pin number for all DTE and DCE.
- The electrical function of signals between DTE and DCE must be compatible.
- The function of each electrical signal must have common names and pin numbers.

8.4   EIA RS-232 INTERFACE STANDARD

A serial interface standard was developed that encompassed the preceding criteria. This standard, known as *RS-232* was developed and published in 1969 by the Electronics Industries Association (EIA), a U.S. organization of electronics manufacturers that establishes and recommends industrial standards. RS-232 conforms to the V.24 standard set within the European countries by the Consultative Committee on Telegraphy and Telephony (CCITT), now known as *ITU-TS*.

> **RS-232**
> A serial interface standard that specifies the electrical, functional, and mechanical interface specification between data communicating devices.

The RS-232 defines the electrical, mechanical, and functional interface between *data terminal equipment*, **DTE,** typically a computer terminal or computer, and *data communications equipment*, **DCE,** typically a modem or data set, employing serial binary data interchange. The standard has been universally observed throughout the world and has evolved as a standard not only for connecting computers and terminals

FIGURE 8-5
RS-232 communications interface.

to modems but also for connecting computers to printers, plotters, PROM programmers, and many other peripherals. Virtually all mainframe computers, personal computers, and microprocessor-based communication systems have provisions for an
RS-232 interface to associated peripherals. Figure 8-5 depicts a typical RS-232
interface.

The RS-232 specification is comprised of three parts:

1. Electrical signal specification
2. Mechanical specification
3. Functional specification

8.4.1 Electrical Signal Specification

The RS-232 electrical specification defines the complete electrical characteristics that
DTE and DCE shall adhere to. Figure 8-6 illustrates a model of the interchange equivalent electrical circuit.

- V_o is the open-circuit voltage presented by the driver.
- R_o is the internal resistance of the driver.
- C_o represents the equivalent capacitance associated with the driver and cable
  measured at the interface point.

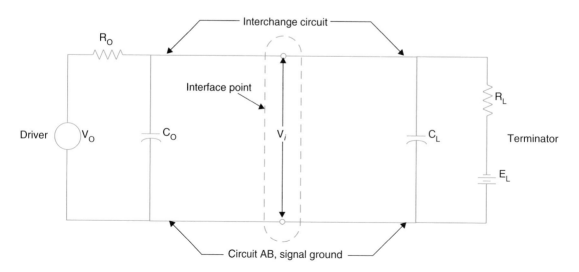

FIGURE 8-6
RS-232 equivalent circuit.

- V_i is the voltage measured at the interface point.
- C_L is the equivalent capacitance associated with the terminating load and any cable capacitance to the interface point.
- R_L is the terminating DC load resistance.
- E_L is the open-circuit terminator voltage presented by any DC bias associated with the terminating circuit.

The interfacing parameters associated with the electrical specification apply to both synchronous and asynchronous serial binary data communication systems. These parameters are intended to set limits on the impedances and voltages to which each interchange circuit must adhere. Some of the most useful parameters are summarized as follows:

1. V_o and V_i may not exceed ± 25 V with respect to signal ground.
2. The short-circuit current between any two or more pins or conductors within the interface may not exceed 0.5 A.
3. The total effective capacitance of the interchange circuit may not exceed 2500 pF.
4. $3000\ \Omega < R_L < 7000\ \Omega$.
5. $5\ \text{V} < V_i < 15\ \text{V}$ when $E_L = 0$ V.
6. $-15\ \text{V} < V_i < -5\ \text{V}$ when $E_L = 0$ V.
7. Data signaling rates must be in the range from zero to a nominal upper limit of 20,000 bps.
8. The driver slew rate must be less than 30 V/μs.
9. Cable length should be kept under 50 ft.

The RS-232 specification includes limits that define the voltage range of a logic 1, a MARK, and a logic 0, a SPACE. A logic 1 at the driver output must be between -5 and -15 V. A logic 1 at the terminating load must be between -3 and -15 V. A logic 0 at the driver output must be between $+5$ and $+15$ V. A logic 0 at the terminating load must be between $+3$ and $+15$ V. Figure 8-7 illustrates these ranges. Note that the voltage levels for a logic 1 and logic 0 are inverted from what we normally

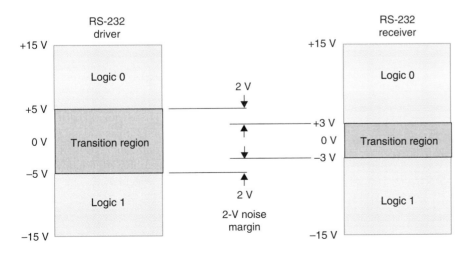

FIGURE 8-7
RS-232 logic levels.

think of in terms of HIGH and LOW. The driver and receiver circuits for the interchange will have to be buffered and level translated to be compatible with TTL, ECL, and other logic families.

8.4.2   Noise Margin and Noise Immunity

An implied *noise margin* of 2 V (the difference between 3 and 5 V or -3 and -5 V) exists between the driver and the terminator (Figure 8-7). Noise margin is a quantitative measure of a circuit's ability to tolerate noise transients inherent within the driving and receiving circuit or induced by external sources. If a circuit's noise margin is high, it is said to have a high *noise immunity.* Noise immunity is the general term associated with the same concept. If an RS-232 signal is received with a voltage swing of ± 5 V, a noise transient in excess of 2 V_P will fall into the transition region, as depicted in Figure 8-8. There is no guarantee that the voltages in this region are interpreted as the original logic level. If an RS-232 signal were to be transmitted by the driving circuit at ± 5 V, the noise margin would be less than 2 V at the receiving end due to the voltage (IR) dropped across the interfacing cable. The noise margin can be increased simply by increasing the output voltage swing of the driver up to the limits of the specification.

8.4.3   An Asynchronous RS-232 Transmitted Character

The asynchronous protocol used to transmit serial data has been established since the days of the electromechanical Teletype terminals. These electrical signals must conform to the RS-232 electrical specifications outlined earlier. The order in which the transmitted data is sent under this convention is reversed from what is customarily thought of as correct. Normally, we think of a structured group of characters, numbers, or letters as being read from left to right. ASCII characters coded in binary are transmitted in reverse order, so that the *least* significant bit is transmitted *first.* The remaining bits are transmitted in the order of their increasing significance. Figure 8-9 illustrates examples of asynchronous RS-232 characters transmitted at the output

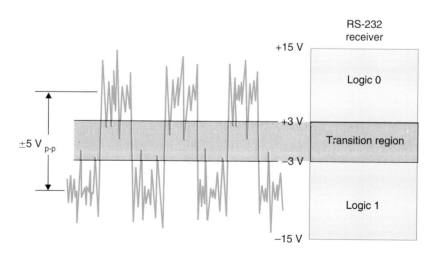

FIGURE 8-8
Excessive noise on a signal causes data to fall into the transition region.

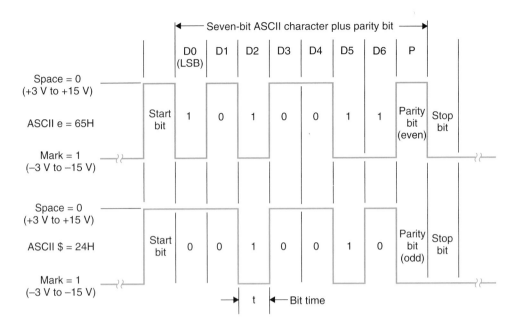

FIGURE 8-9
Examples of asynchronous RS-232 transmitted characters.

of a VDT, pin 2, *Transmitted Data.* The waveforms appear as they would on an oscilloscope if the given ASCII characters e or $ were typed.

Note that other bits have been inserted as part of the total character length. Before sending the first bit of the character, or LSB, an additional bit has been inserted. This bit is referred to as the *start bit*. The start bit indicates to the receiving device that it should initialize its circuitry to receive a data character. This occurs the moment the start bit is asserted. The start bit is always a logic 0. In effect, it is acting as a control bit to the receiving device. The last bit sent is referred to as the character's *stop bit*, which acts as a controlling indicator to the receiving device that it is the end of a character. The stop bit is always a logic 1, *opposite* that of the start bit. The time durations of the start and stop bits are each equivalent to that of a data bit. This discrete amount of time for each bit is referred to as the character's *bit time*. Once the stop bit has been transmitted, the logic level of the transmitting device remains in an *idle* state, which has the same logic level as the stop bit, a logic 1. The advantage to this technique is that it allows characters to be sent in an asynchronous fashion; that is, the time difference between characters can vary. A typical case would be a person typing characters at a terminal. The typist can proceed to type at any speed and can pause for any length of time between the characters being typed. The (odd or even) *parity* bit is inserted just before the stop bit. Its logic level depends on the number of binary 1-bits sets within the data character. The parity bit can be set to a logic 1 or a logic 0 by the transmitting device depending on the character itself. When a character is received, the receiving device checks the number of 1-bits set in the received character against the level of the corresponding parity bit. If they do not agree, the receiving device can exercise its option of flagging an error to the operator. Parity is perhaps the most fundamental of all error-checking schemes.

Start Bit
The first bit used to frame an asynchronously transmitted character. Its logic level is a 0 (space).

Stop Bit
The last bit used to frame an asynchronously transmitted character. Its logic level is a logic 1 (mark).

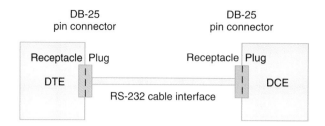

FIGURE 8-10
RS-232 connector assignment.

8.4.4 Mechanical Specification

> **Plug**
> The male portion of a connector.

> **Receptacle**
> The female portion of a connector.

The RS-233 mechanical specification states that the interface circuit must consist of a *plug* on one end to connect to DTE and a *receptacle* on the opposite end to connect to DCE. This implies that to connect the interfacing cable, DTE must have a receptacle and DCE must have a plug. Figure 8-10 illustrates the connector interface.

The RS-232 standard does not specify the type of mechanical connector to use; however, the DB-25 pin connector illustrated in Figure 8-11 has become almost universally accepted and associated with the standard itself. Detailed mechanical dimensions have been shown here for both plug and receptacle.

8.4.5 Functional Specification

The complete connector pin assignment for the RS-232 interface standard is listed in Table 8-2, with an unofficial abbreviation for each circuit that has been adopted as

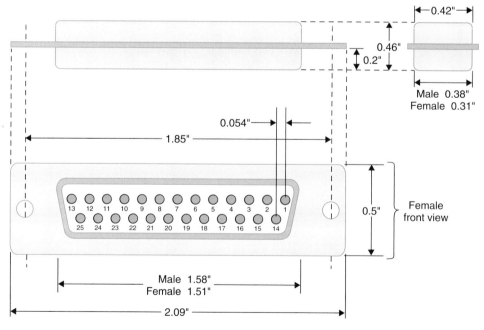

FIGURE 8-11
DB-25 pin connector.

TABLE 8-2
RS-232 Interchange Circuits

Pin No.	Interchange Circuit	C.C.I.T.T. Equivalent	Description	Gnd	Data From DCE	Data To DCE	Control From DCE	Control To DCE	Timing From DCE	Timing To DCE
1	AA	101	Protective ground	X						
7	AB	102	Signal ground/common return	X						
2	BA	103	Transmitted data			X				
3	BB	104	Received data		X					
4	CA	105	Request to send					X		
5	CB	106	Clear to send				X			
6	CC	107	Data set ready				X			
20	CD	108.2	Data terminal ready					X		
22	CE	125	Ring indicator				X			
8	CF	109	Received line signal detector (CD)				X			
21	CG	110	Signal quality detector				X			
23	CH	111	Data signal rate selector (DTE)					X		
23	CI	112	Data signal rate selector (DCE)				X			
24	DA	113	Transmitter signal element timing (DTE)							X
15	DB	114	Transmitter signal element timing (DCE)						X	
17	DD	115	Receiver signal element timing (DCE)						X	
14	SBA	118	Secondary transmitted data			X				
16	SBB	119	Secondary received data		X					
19	SCA	120	Secondary request to send					X		
13	SCB	121	Secondary clear to send				X			
12	SCF	122	Secondary rec'd line signal detector				X			

part of the standard. Each pin has a reference designator (AA, BA, and so on) that identifies its *circuit* name. The first letter of each circuit name designates the functional category to which that circuit belongs. For example, circuit CA, Request to Send, pin 4, is a control circuit. Its circuit name begins with the letter C. There are five functional categories, as shown in the table.

8.4.6 Functional Definition

The following material contains extracts from the Electronics Industries Association RS-232 Standard. The extracts include the functional specification for each interchange circuit listed in Table 8-2. The definitions of some circuits have been summarized, whereas others are written in their entirety. A complete listing of the specification can be obtained from the Electronic Industries Association (Engineering Department, 2001 Eye Street, N.W., Washington, D.C. 20006).

Pin 1, Circuit AA: Protective Ground, PG   The conductor shall be electrically bonded to the machine or equipment frame. It may be further connected to external grounds as required by applicable regulations.

Pin 7, Circuit AB: Signal Ground or Common Return, SG   This conductor establishes the common ground reference potential for all interchange circuits except pin 1, Protective Ground.

Pin 2, Circuit BA: Transmitted Data, TD (or TxD)   Signals on this circuit are generated by DTE and transmitted to DCE. DTE shall hold this line in the MARK condition between characters or words and at all times when no data are being transmitted. In all systems, DTE shall not transmit data unless an ON condition is present on all of the following four circuits:

1. Pin 4, Circuit CA: Request to Send, RTS
2. Pin 5, Circuit CB: Clear to Send, CTS
3. Pin 6, Circuit CC: Data Set Ready, DSR
4. Pin 20, Circuit CD: Data Terminal Ready, DTR

Pin 3, Circuit BB: Received Data, RD (or RxD)   The signals on this line are transmitted from CDE to DTE. DCE shall hold this line in the MARK condition at all times when pin 8, Circuit CF, Received Line Signal Detector, is in the OFF state. In half-duplex operation, this line shall be held in the MARK condition when pin 4, RTS, is in the ON condition and for a brief interval following the ON to OFF transition of RTS to allow for the completion of transmission and the decay of line reflections.

Pin 4, Circuit CA: Request to Send, RTS   This circuit is turned ON by DTE and is used to indicate to DCE that it is ready to transmit data. In the half-duplex mode, this line is used to control the direction of data transmission of DCE. RTS is used as a handshake line with Clear to Send, CTS, pin 5. When RTS is asserted by DTE, DCE responds when it is ready to accept the transmitted data from DTE by asserting CTS. When DTE turns RTS from ON to OFF, it is an instruction to DCE that it has completed the transmission of its data on pin 2, Transmitted Data. DCE responds (after a brief period of time to allow all the transmitted data to be received) by turning OFF its CTS line. DCE is then prepared to respond to any subsequent RTS signals from

DTE. When RTS is turned OFF, it shall not turn ON again until CTS is turned OFF by DCE. It is permissible for DTE to turn on RTS at any time DCE's CTS is OFF regardless of the condition of any other interchange circuit.

Pin 5, Circuit CB: Clear to Send, CTS   Signals on this circuit are generated by DCE to indicate whether DCE is ready to transmit the data from DTE onto the communications channel (the telephone system). The ON condition of CTS is a handshake to the ON condition of Request to Send, RTS, pin 4, and Data Set Ready, DSR, pin 6. The OFF condition of CTS is an indicator to DTE that it should not send data across the interchange circuit on Transmitted Data, TD, pin 2.

Pin 6, Circuit CC: Data Set Ready, DSR   The signal on this circuit is sent from DCE to DTE as a status line indicating the condition of the local data set (the local modem). Data Terminal Ready, DTR, pin 20 of DTE, is assumed to be in the ON condition indicating its readiness. The ON condition of DSR is presented to indicate the following:

1. The local DCE equipment is connected to the communications channel, for example, the *off-hook* condition of the telephone network.
2. The local DCE equipment is not in test (local or remote) mode, talk (alternate voice), or dial mode.
3. The local DCE has completed where applicable:
   (a) Any timing functions required by the switching system (telephone system) to complete call establishment.
   (b) The transmission of any discrete answer tone, the duration of which is controlled solely by the local data set.

The OFF condition shall appear at all other times and should serve as an indicator to DTE to disregard signals appearing on any other interchange circuit except for circuit CE, Ring Indicator, RI, pin 22. If DSR is turned OFF while DTR is still ON, DTE shall interpret this as a lost or aborted connection to the communications channel and take action to terminate the call.

Pin 20, Circuit CD: Data Terminal Ready, DTR   This line is turned ON by DTE, indicating that it is ready to transmit or receive data from DCE. DSR is a response to DTR. Both DTR and DSR work in conjunction with each other and indicate equipment readiness.

Pin 22, Circuit CE: Ring Indicator, RI   The Ring Indicator, RI, is sent from DCE to DTE. This circuit indicates that a ringing signal is being received on the communications channel. Its ON–OFF duration should be approximately coincidental with the ON–OFF duration of the ringing signal received from the communications channel.

Pin 8, Circuit CF: Received Line Signal Detector, RLSD (or Carrier Detect, DC) The ON condition of this circuit is presented by DCE when it is receiving a carrier signal from the remote DCE that meets its suitability criteria. These criteria are established by the DCE manufacturer. The OFF condition of this circuit indicates to DTE that no signal is being received that is suitable for demodulation. DCE shall clamp its Received Data, RD, pin 3, signal to the MARK condition. On half-duplex channels, CD is held in the OFF condition whenever Request to Send, RTS, pin 4, is in the ON condition and for a brief interval of time following the ON-to-OFF transition of RTS.

Pin 21, Circuit CG: Signal Quality Detector, SQ Signals on this circuit are sent by DCE to DTE. They are used to indicate whether there is a high probability of an error in the received data. An ON condition indicates there is no reason to believe that an error has occurred. An OFF condition indicates a high probability of an error. It may be used in some instances to call automatically for the retransmission of the previously transmitted data.

Pin 23, Circuit CH (DTE) or Circuit CI (DCE): Data Signal Rate Selector, SS. Circuit CH This signal is sent from DTE to DCE and is used to select between one of two data signaling rates in cases where two are offered. The ON condition selects the higher of the two rates.

Circuit CI This circuit is similar to Circuit CH, except that it is sent from DCE to DTE.

Pin 24, Circuit DA: Transmitter Signal Element Timing (DTE), TSET Signals on this circuit are sent from DTE to DCE to provide the transmitting signal converter with signal element timing information. The ON-to-OFF transition shall nominally indicate the center of each signal element on Transmitted Data, TD, pin 2. When implemented in DTE, DTE shall normally provide this timing information if in the power ON condition.

Pin 15, Circuit DB: Transmitter Signal Element Timing (DCE), TSET Signals on this circuit are sent from DCE to DTE to provide signal element timing information. DTE shall provide a data signal on Transmitted Data, TD, pin 2, in which the transition between signal elements nominally occurs at the time of the transitions from the OFF to ON condition of the signal on this circuit. When implemented in DCE, DCE shall normally provide this timing information if in the power ON condition.

Pin 17, Circuit DD: Receiver Signal Element Timing (DCE), RSET Signals on this circuit are sent from DCE to DTE to provide received signal element timing information. The transition from the ON to OFF condition shall nominally indicate the center of each signal element on pin 3, Received Data. Timing information on this circuit shall be provided at all times when Received Line Signal Detector (Carrier Detect), CD, pin 8, is in the ON condition. It may, but need not, be present following the ON to OFF transition of pin 8, Received Line Signal Detector.

Pin 14, Circuit SBA: Secondary Transmitted Data, (S)TD This circuit is equivalent to Transmitted Data, TD, pin 2, except that it is used to transmit data via the secondary channel. When the secondary channel is usable only for circuit assurance or to interrupt the flow of data in the primary channel, this circuit is normally not provided, and the channel carrier is turned ON or OFF by means of Secondary Request to Send, (S)RTS, pin 19. Carrier OFF is interpreted as an interrupt condition.

Pin 16, Circuit SBB: Secondary Received Data, (S)RD This circuit is equivalent to Received Data, RD, pin 3, except that it is used to receive data on the secondary channel from DCE. When the secondary channel is usable only for circuit assurance or to interrupt the flow of data in the primary channel, this circuit is normally not provided.

Pin 19, Circuit SCA: Secondary Request to Send, (S)RTS   This circuit is equivalent to Request to Send, RTS, pin 4, except that it requests the establishment of the secondary channel instead of requesting the establishment of the primary data channel. Where the secondary channel is used as a backward channel, the ON condition of RTS shall disable this circuit, and it shall not be possible to condition the secondary channel transmitting signal converter to transmit during any time interval when the primary channel transmitting signal converter is so conditioned.

When the secondary channel is usable only for the assurance or to interrupt the flow of data in the primary data channel, this circuit shall serve to turn ON the secondary channel unmodulated carrier. The OFF condition of this circuit shall turn OFF the secondary channel carrier and, thereby, signal an interrupt condition at the remote end of the communication channel.

Pin 13, Circuit SCB: Secondary Clear to Send, (S)CTS   This circuit is equivalent to Clear to Send, CTS, pin 5, except that it indicates the availability of the secondary channel instead of indicating the availability of the primary channel. This circuit is not provided where the secondary channel is usable only as a circuit assurance or an interrupt channel.

Pin 12, Circuit SCF: Secondary Received Line Signal Detector, (S)RLSD or (S)CD (Secondary Carrier Detect)   This circuit is equivalent to Carrier Detect, CD, pin 8, except that it indicates the proper reception of the secondary channel line signal. Where the secondary channel is usable only as a circuit assurance or an interrupt channel, this circuit shall be used to indicate the circuit assurance status or to signal the interrupt. The ON condition shall indicate circuit assurance or a noninterrupt condition. The OFF condition shall indicate circuit failure (no assurance) or the interrupt condition.

Recall that the RS-232 interface was written with the intention of interfacing DTE (a terminal or computer) to DCE (a modem) for long-distance data communications over the telephone network. The intention at that time was certainly not to satisfy the interface requirements of today's communications between microcomputers, printers, ROM blasters, and the like, all of which did not even exist when the standard was originally published! Nevertheless, the standard has adapted itself to this date as, perhaps, the most widely recognized data communication interface standard.

To improve our understanding of some of the circuits most commonly used, attention will be focused on building a typical RS-232 interface. For purposes of clarification, we will part from the two-letter (or three-letter) designator assigned for each circuit in the standard. Instead, the circuit descriptive name listed in Table 8-2 will be used.

8.5   INTERFACING DTE TO DCE

The minimal amount of wires necessary to establish a two-way communications link between DTE and DCE is depicted in Figure 8-12. The interfacing cable includes only three interconnecting lines: pin 2, pin 3, and pin 7. For many applications today, this is desirable, because it greatly simplifies the RS-223 cable alone.

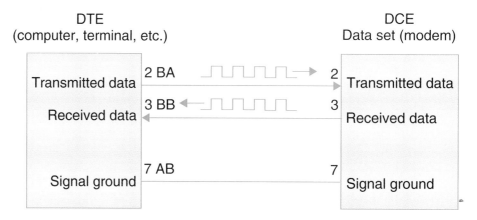

FIGURE 8-12
Minimal interface between DTE and DCE.

The RS-232 specification states that pin 2 of DTE will be used for **Transmitted Data,** TD (or TxD), to DCE. From our diagram in Figure 8-12, this implies that pin 2 of DCE *receives* the transmitted data from DTE. Pin 3 of DTE is **Received Data,** RD (or RxD), from DCE. Pin 3 of DCE is, therefore, transmitted data to DTE. Pin 7 of both DTE and DCE are **Signal Ground,** SG. It all seems so simple, no wonder so many of today's RS-232 interfaces include only three interconnect lines. The setup described is certainly acceptable, because it is functional. That is, it works and does so with a minimal amount of hardware. It does, however, leave much to be desired in terms of control. The following assumptions are made: Interconnecting devices are ready to transmit and receive data; the communications channel has been established through the telephone company; carrier frequencies of both modems are idling at their correct frequencies; interrupting of the transmitted and received data will not occur; and so on. A much more intelligent interface is often needed. The resulting interface would include the RS-232 *control circuits* (circuits that begin with C) for regulating and controlling the flow of data across pins 2 and 3.

8.5.1   A Complete RS-232 Interface

Figure 8-13 illustrates a complete RS-232 interface between DTE and DCE. The diagram depicts the most commonly used circuits compared to those that are not often used. Note that some of the control circuits that are included in the most commonly used group have nothing to do with an RS-232 interface between a computer and printer. Circuits such as **Ring Indicator** and **Received Line Signal Detector** or **Carrier Detect** are superfluous as far as a printer is concerned. These circuits, however, must be considered in *any* RS-232 interface. Even though some devices, such as printers, may not implement many of the circuits depicted in Figure 8-13, other devices may. Any attempt to interface two devices employing a different number of circuits will inevitably result in *floating* inputs and signals with a lost cause.

8.5.2   RS-232 9-Pin Serial Port Connector

When IBM developed its AT (advanced technology) line of personal computers in the 1980s, the standard RS-232, 25-pin connector was appended with a 9-pin, D-type

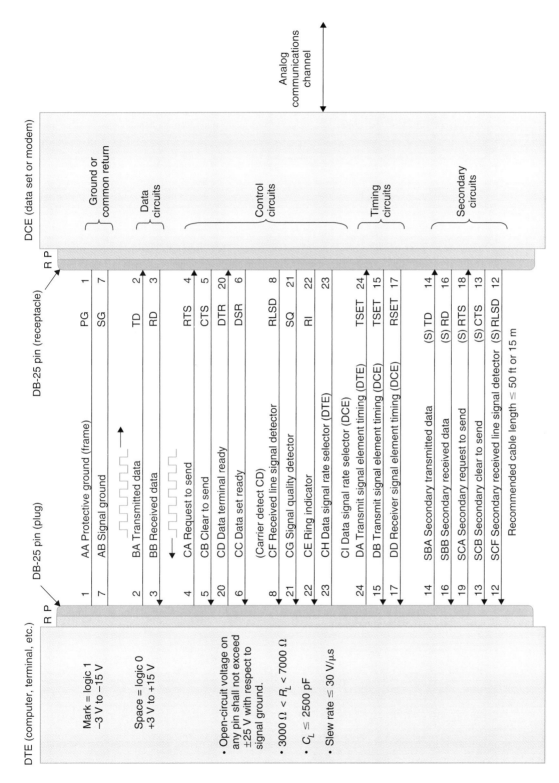

FIGURE 8-13
Complete RS-232 interface.

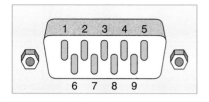

9-Pin	25-Pin	Interchange Circuit	Description
1	8	CD	Carrier detect
2	3	RD	Received data
3	2	TD	Transmitted data
4	20	DTR	Data terminal ready
5	7	SG	Signal ground
6	6	DSR	Data set ready
7	4	RTS	Request to send
8	5	CTS	Clear to send
9	22	RI	Ring indicator

FIGURE 8-14
9-Pin RS-232 serial port connector diagram.

connector as part of the serial interface between DTE and DCE. Only nine of the most commonly used RS-232 signals are included in the interface. Virtually all personal computers manufactured today include the 9-pin connector interface. Figure 8-14 illustrates the connector diagram and a listing of signal names for both 9- and 25-pin connectors.

8.6 HANDSHAKING

> **Handshaking**
> A signalling process that regulates and controls the flow of data between two devices.

The regulation and control of data between DTE and DCE is performed by a process called *handshaking.* The process stems from the literal meaning itself. When two people shake hands, they are communicating. The communication can range from a simple acknowledgment of one's presence to an agreement. The process is much the same in the interactive control of data between two devices, DTE and DCE. To illustrate the concept of handshaking, refer to Figure 8-15. Handshaking is said to occur

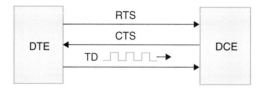

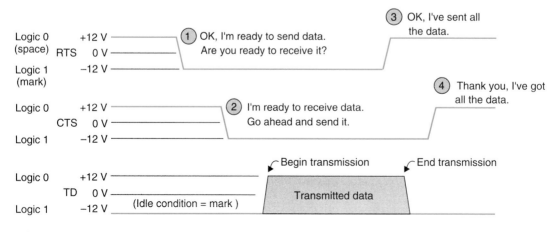

FIGURE 8-15
Timing diagram illustrating the handshaking process.

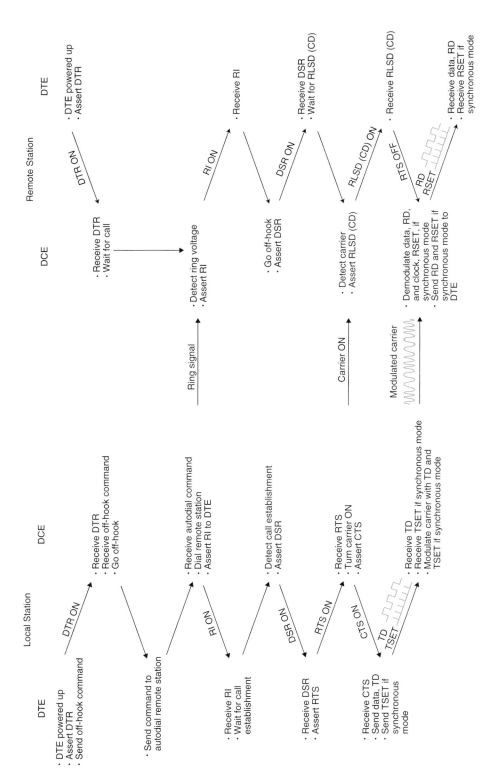

FIGURE 8-16
RS-232 half-duplex control sequence.

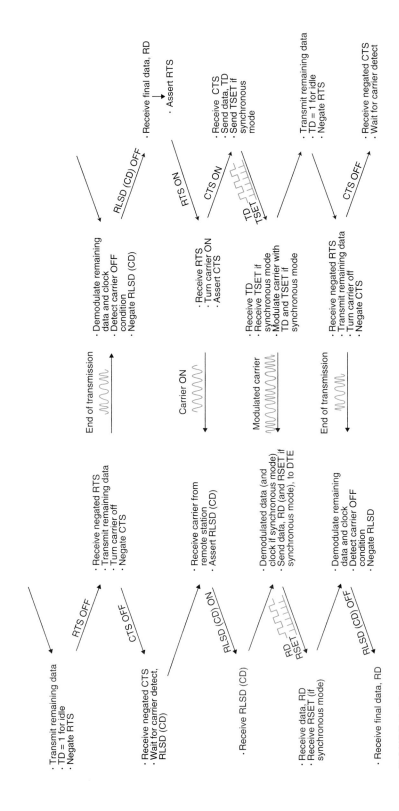

FIGURE 8-16
(*continued*)

between DTE's **RTS** and DCE's **CTS.** The entire process is a series of inquiries and acknowledgments between DTE and DCE, ultimately resulting in the successful transmission of data between the two devices. Let us now consider a complete RS-232 control sequence. The half-duplex communications link shown in Figure 8-16 is used for simplicity.

Suppose that DTE and DCE in Figure 8-16 are both powered up with **Data Terminal Ready** and **Data Set Ready** both ON. The ON condition of both of these circuits indicates that DCE has dialed a number and completed call establishments to a remote data set. When DTE is ready to transmit data, it turns ON its **Request to Send** signal. When the modem receives **Request to Send** from DTE, it will turn its carrier frequency (MARK condition) ON. The modem is now ready to transmit data from DTE. It informs DTE of its readiness by asserting its **Clear to Send** signal. During the course of this action, the remote modem has sensed the local modem's carrier frequency and, consequently, activates its **Carrier Detect** line. The local DTE can now begin to transmit its data on its **Transmitted Data** line. DCE in turn modulates its carrier frequency with the transmitted data. The resulting signal is transmitted over the communications channel and demodulated at the remote data set. The demodulated data are sent on the **Received Data** circuit of the remote DTE. Once the local DTE has completed its transmission of data, it turns its **Request to Send** line OFF and **Transmitted Data** is left in its quiescent state (MARK condition). The transition of **Request to Send** from ON to OFF is an instruction to the local DCE to complete the transmission (onto the communications channel) of the last data sent from DTE. The local DCE responds by completing the transmission and turning OFF its carrier frequency and **Clear to Send** line. Because the control sequence is half-duplex, the carrier frequency is turned OFF to allow the remote station to transmit data in return on the same frequency. The process is now repeated in the reverse order as depicted. Any subsequent data to be transmitted will follow the same procedure.

8.7   RS-232 INTERFACE TO DEVICES OTHER THAN A MODEM

Although the procedure just outlined may seem comprehensive and systematic, it has caused a great deal of confusion among those of us who have attempted to connect DTE to DCE. The underlying problem is that the RS-232 standard was never really intended to satisfy the interfacing requirements of today's microcomputers and peripheral devices. Computers, for example, may be interfaced in one situation as DTE and in another as DCE. For instance, in the previous example, the computer is DTE, interfaced to a modem, DCE; however, what would be the case if the same computer were interfaced to a printer? The printer, acting as the *terminating* device, or DTE in this case, would be interfacing with the computer as DCE. Computer manufacturers today are left with the dilemma of having to decide whether to configure their RS-232 ports as DTE or DCE or to provide the option of both. Figure 8-17(a) shows the seemingly inevitable situation that arises, that is, two devices that transmit and receive data on the *same* pin numbers. The output drivers for control and data are in conflict with each other. Communications obviously cannot exist in this situation. One solution to this problem is to simply reverse the wires on our RS-232 interface cable, as shown in Figure 8-17(b). A cable configured as such is referred to as a *null modem.* Null modems are also used to test two DTEs.

> **Null Modem**
> A cable that replaces the modem interface, allowing two DTE devices to communicate with each other without use of DCE. Connector wires are crossed over to achieve this.

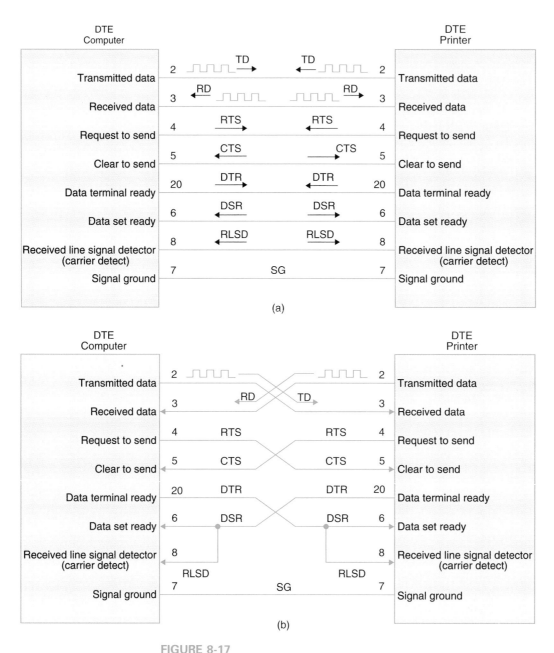

FIGURE 8-17

(a) Two devices that have been configured as DTE cannot communicate; (b) a null modem.

Obviously, we have deviated from the standard. As mentioned earlier, signal names like **Carrier Detect** and **Ring Indicator** have nothing to do with printers, programmable read only memory (PROM) programmers, and many other devices on the market that boast RS-232 compatibility. The fact of the matter is that many of the RS-232 circuits discussed so far are either emulated, cross-connected, or in some cases, not even used. Figure 8-18 illustrates several tricks-of-the-trade nonstandard

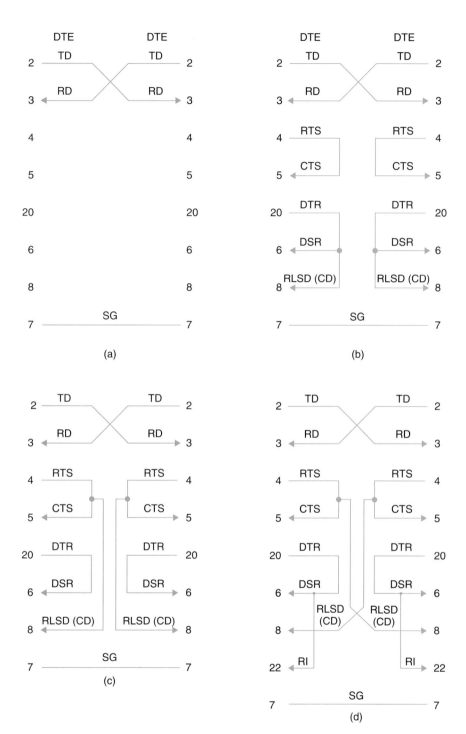

FIGURE 8-18
Nonstandard interface cable techniques.

connector configurations that are commonly employed to successfully interface the so-called RS-232 compatible devices of today.

8.8 EIA RS-449, RS-422-A, AND RS-423-A

Despite its shortcomings, RS-232 has allowed most computer manufacturers to consolidate their efforts toward standardization of serial interfaces. Without such formalities, the computer industry could very well face a deluge of incompatible products. The RS-232 standard is here and is likely to be around for awhile. Several related standards have since evolved for which RS-232 has served as a predecessor and a basis on which those standards to improve.

8.8.1 Improving the Old Standard

In November 1977, the EIA published a new and improved serial interface standard: EIA RS-449. The EIA RS-449 addresses the mechanical and functional specification of an enhanced version of RS-232. The new standard is stated as follows:

EIA Standard RS-449   General Purpose 37-Position and 9-Position Interface for Data Terminal Equipment and Data Circuit–Terminating Equipment Employing Serial Binary Interchange.

New semiconductor interfacing products have given more reason to improve on the old standard's electrical specification. Two additional standards immediately followed the publication of RS-449. *RS-423-A* and *RS-422-A* directly address the enhancement of the electrical characteristics of RS-232. These two additional standards are stated as follows:

EIA Standard RS-423-A   Electrical Characteristics of Unbalanced Voltage Digital Interface Circuits, September 1978.

EIA Standard RS-422-A   Electrical Characteristics of Balanced Voltage Digital Interface Circuits, December 1978.

8.8.2 EIA Objectives in Setting the New Standards

RS-449, together with RS-422-A and RS-423-A, is intended to gradually replace RS-232 as the specification for the interface between DTE and DCE. The new specifications meet the following objectives:

- Maintain compatibility with existing RS-232 equipment.
- Derive a new and more meaningful set of circuit names and mnemonics to differentiate between RS-232 and RS-449.
- Increase the data transmission rate beyond 20 kbps.
- Increase the transmission distance over twisted-pair wires.
- Specify a standard connector type that can be used without the use of a special tool.
- Provide a separator connector to carry secondary interchange circuits.
- Improve on the cross-talk characteristics of the signal lines.
- Provide for differential signal lines for transmitted and received data.

- Provide for loopback testing.
- Utilize the latest advances in semiconductor technology to improve on performance and reliability.

8.8.3   RS-449 Interchange Circuits

Table 8-3 is a complete listing of the RS-449 interchange circuits. The table includes RS-232 equivalent circuits where applicable. Note that RS-449 circuit names and mnemonics are more readily identifiable with their associated functions.

8.8.3.1   Category I and Category II Circuits
A main objective set forth by EIA in the establishment of RS-449 is to maintain compatibility with the existing RS-232 standard. To fulfill this objective, EIA has divided the new interchange circuits into two categories: *category I,* and *category II.* Category I includes those signals that are functionally compatible with RS-232. The remaining signals are category II signals. Category I and II circuits and their equivalent RS-232 circuits are shown in Tables 8-4 and 8-5.

Category I circuits can be implemented with either RS-422-A balanced drivers and receivers or RS-423-A unbalanced drivers and receivers (see Section 8.8.5 for balanced versus unbalanced circuits). The transmission data rates should be less than 20 kbps (the upper limit of RS-232) if RS-423-A is used. At greater than 20 kbps, category I circuits should always be implemented under RS-422-A. Note in Table 8-4 that category I circuits have been allotted two adjacent pins per signal function to allow for the option of either balanced or unbalanced circuits. Category II circuits are always implemented under RS-423-A, because these circuits provide the interconnection of only unbalanced drivers.

8.8.3.2   RS-449 Functional Specification for New Circuits
There are 10 functionally new interchange circuits in RS-449 that differ from its predecessor, RS-232. A brief definition of these new functions are as follows:

Pin 37, Circuit SC, Send Common   This circuit acts as a common signal return line for unbalanced signals transmitted from DTE to DCE.

Pin 20, Circuit RC, Receive Common   This circuit acts as a common signal return line for unbalanced signals transmitted from DCE to DTE.

Pin 28, Circuit IS, Terminal in Service   This circuit is used to indicate to DCE whether or not DTE is operational.

Pin 34, Circuit NS, New Signal   This circuit is used primarily for multipoint applications where two or more terminals or computers share a common communications channel. In this mode, DCEs are operating in a switched carrier mode. A control DTE polls other DTEs for messages to be sent to DCE. The ON state of this signal is an indicator to DCE from the control DTE that a message from a remote DTE is completed and a new one is about to begin.

Pin 16, Circuit SE, Select Frequency   This circuit is used primarily for multipoint applications where DTE selects the transmit and receive frequencies used by its connecting DCE.

TABLE 8-3
RS-449 and RS-232 Equivalent Interchange Circuits

EIA RS-449 37-Pin Connector			EIA RS-232 DB-25 Pin Connector		
SG	Signal	19	AB	Signal ground	7
SC	Send common	37			
RC	Receive common	20			
IS	Terminal in service	28			
IC	Incoming call	15	CE	Ring indicator	22
TR	Terminal ready	12, 30	CD	Data terminal ready	20
DM	Data mode	11, 29	CC	Data set ready	6
SD	Send data	4, 22	BA	Transmitted data	2
RD	Receive data	6, 24	BB	Received data	3
TT	Terminal timing	17, 35	DA	Transmitter signal element timing (DTE source)	24
ST	Send timing	5, 23	DB	Transmitter signal element timing (DCE source)	15
RT	Receive timing	8, 26	DD	Receiver signal element timing	17
RS	Request to send	7, 25	CA	Request to send	4
CS	Clear to send	9, 27	CB	Clear to send	5
RR	Receiver ready	13, 31	CF	Received line signal detector	8
SQ	Signal quality	33	CG	Signal quality detector	21
NS	New signal	34			
SF	Select frequency	16			
SR	Signal rate selector	16	CH	Data signal rate selector (DTE source)	23
SI	Signal rate indicator	2	CI	Data signal rate selector (DCE source)	23
LL	Local loopback	10			
RL	Remote loopback	14			
TM	Test mode	18			
SS	Select standby	32			
SB	Standby indicator	36			

9-Pin Connector					
	Shield	1	AA	Protective ground	1
SG	Signal ground	5	AB	Signal ground	7
SC	Send common	9			
RC	Receive common	2			
SSD	Secondary send data	3	SBA	Secondary transmitted data	14
SRD	Secondary receive data	4	SBB	Secondary received data	16
SRS	Secondary request to send	7	SCA	Secondary request to end	19
SCS	Secondary clear to send	8	SCB	Secondary clear to send	13
SRR	Secondary receiver ready	6	SCF	Secondary received line signal detector	12

TABLE 8-4
Category I Circuits

RS-449	RS-232 Equivalent Circuit
SD Send data (4,22)	BA Transmitted data (2)
RD Receive data (6,24)	BB Received data (3)
TT Terminal timing (17,35)	DA Transmitter signal element timing (24)
ST Send timing (5, 23)	DB Transmitter signal element timing (15)
RT Receive timing (8, 26)	DD Receiver signal element timing (17)
RS Request to send (7, 25)	CA Request to send (4)
CS Clear to send (9, 27)	CB Clear to send (5)
RR Receiver ready (13, 31)	CF Received line signal detector (8)
TR Terminal ready (12, 30)	CD Data terminal ready (20)
DM Data mode (11, 29)	CC Data set ready (6)

TABLE 8-5
Category II Circuits

RS-449
SC Send common (37)
RC Receive common (20)
IS Terminal in service (28)
NS New signal (34)
SF Select frequency (16)
LL Local loopback (10)
RL Remote loopback (14)
TM Test mode (18)
SS Select standby (32)
SB Standby indicator (36)

Pin 10, Circuit LL, Local Loopback   This circuit is used by DTE to request from DCE a local loopback test. When asserted by DTE, DCE loops data and control signals back to DTE to verify the functionality of the local DTE and DCE.

Pin 14, Circuit RL, Remote Loopback   This circuit is used by DTE to request from DCE a remote loopback test. When asserted by DTE, data and control signals generated by the local DTE are routed through the local DCE to the remote DCE and back to the local DTE. This, in effect, verifies the functionality of the local DTE, DCE, the communications channel, and the remote DCE.

Pin 18, Circuit TM, Test Mode   This circuit is used by DCE to inform its DTE that a test condition has been established.

Pin 32, Circuit SS, Select Standby   This circuit is used by DTE to request the use of standby equipment in the event of failure of primary equipment.

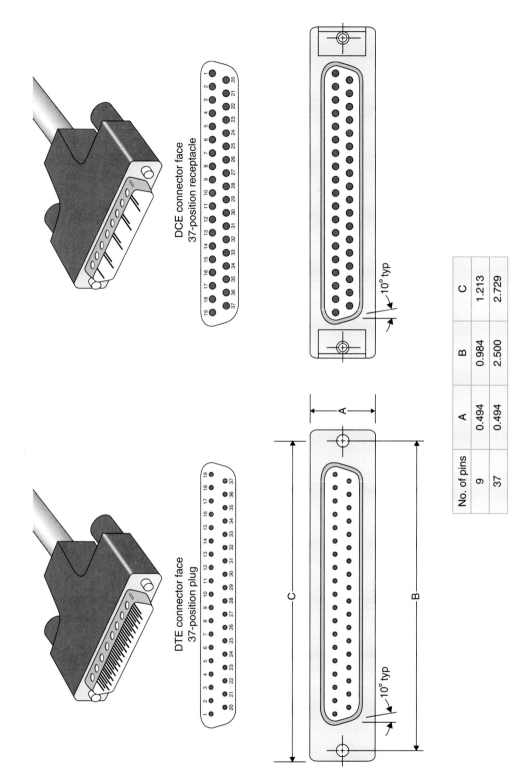

DCE connector face
37-position receptacle

DTE connector face
37-position plug

10° typ

10° typ

No. of pins	A	B	C
9	0.494	0.984	1.213
37	0.494	2.500	2.729

FIGURE 8-19
EIA RS-449 37- and 9-position connectors.

Pin 36, Circuit SB, Standby Indicator   This circuit is intended to be used as a response to circuit SS. In the event of an equipment failure, when standby equipment has replaced the failure, this circuit informs DTE of that replacement.

8.8.4 EIA RS-449 Mechanical Specification

With the addition of 10 new circuit functions, a larger connector type than the RS-223 DB25-pin connector was necessary. EIA decided to use a 37-pin connector to accommodate the new signals along with the basic existing signals and a 9-pin connector to separately carry the secondary interchange circuits. Figure 8-19 shows both connector types.

The new connectors permit latching and unlatching of the interfacing connector without the use of a special tool. Anyone who has experience with connecting RS-232 cables knows the numerous problems encountered: screws and standoffs preventing the plug and receptacle from being inserted, the absence of a proper screwdriver, incorrect match, and so on.

8.8.4.1 EIA RS-449 Cable Length   Because higher data transfer rates over longer distances are supported by the new standard, it was necessary for EIA to establish guidelines pertaining to the maximum cable length. The maximum cable length is primarily a function of the data transfer rate to be used. In general, the higher the data transfer rate, the shorter the cable length should be. Figure 8-20 has been provided by EIA as a guideline toward establishing the maximum cable length versus signal rate in bits per second.

8.8.5 EIA RS-422-A and RS-423-A: Balanced Versus Unbalanced Circuits

The RS-422-A and RS-423-A electrical standards are intended to support the mechanical and functional specifications of EIA-449. RS-422-A specifies the electrical characteristics of a balanced interface, whereas RS-423-A specifies the electrical characteristics for an unbalanced interface. Let us consider the meaning of *balanced* versus *unbalanced* circuits.

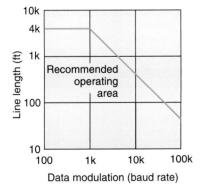

FIGURE 8-20
EIA graph depicting data signaling rate versus cable length.

Balanced Electrical Circuit   EIA RS-422-A specifies the use of balanced electrical interface circuits. A balanced electrical circuit is one in which the transmitted signal propagates on two signal paths (Figure 8-21). Both signal paths appear to the transmitting device as having the same impedances with respect to signal ground. For this reason, they are said to be *balanced*. The transmitted signals are the *difference* in the outputs of a differential amplifier or differential line driver. If the signal to be transmitted is digital in nature, then the output waveforms for the two signal paths are *complemented* with each other, as depicted in Figure 8-21.

> **Balanced Electrical Circuit**
> A circuit with two signal paths in which the transmitted signal propagates on. Each signal path has the same impedance with respect to signal ground. These circuits use double-ended amplifiers.

The receiving device at the terminating end is referred to as a differential line receiver. The line receiver is capable of amplifying the *difference* in signal levels between the two signal paths. Because the circuit is said to be balanced, both outputs of the transmitting device must have the same output impedances. Likewise, the receiving device must have the same input impedances for both signal paths. Transmitting and receiving devices operating in this mode are said to be *double-ended* amplifiers.

Unbalanced Electrical Circuit   EIA RS-423-A specifies the use of unbalanced electrical interface circuits. The unbalanced electrical circuit is shown in Figure 8-22. The transmitted signal propagates down a single transmission line accompanied by its signal return or common reference line typically shared by other signals. Unlike the balanced electrical circuit, the transmitting device has only one output that is connected to a single impedance: the impedance of the interface with respect to signal ground. The receiving device receives the transmitted signal referenced to the same signal ground. These two lines are said to be *unbalanced*, because their impedances are different. The transmitting device can still be a differential amplifier. Only one output is used in this case. The receiving device can also be a differential amplifier. One of

> **Unbalanced Electrical Circuit**
> A circuit in which the transmitted signal propagates down a single transmission line accompanied by its signal return line or common. Unbalanced electrical circuits use single-ended amplifiers.

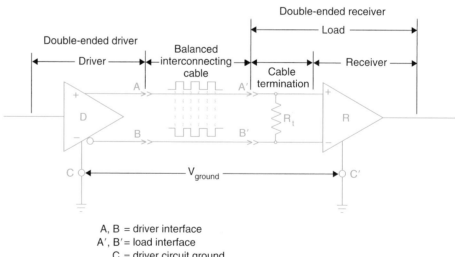

A, B = driver interface
A', B' = load interface
C = driver circuit ground
C' = load circuit ground
V_{ground} = ground potential difference
R_t = optional cable termination resistance/receiver input impedance

FIGURE 8-21
EIA RS-422-A balanced electrical interface circuit.

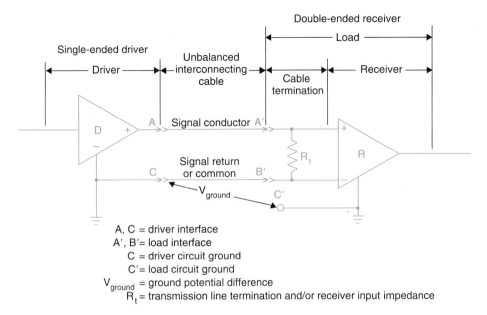

A, C = driver interface
A', B'= load interface
C = driver circuit ground
C'= load circuit ground
V_{ground} = ground potential difference
R_t = transmission line termination and/or receiver input impedance

FIGURE 8-22
EIA RS-423-A unbalanced electrical interface circuit.

its inputs is simply tied to signal ground. Amplifiers operating in this mode are said to be *single-ended* amplifiers.

Figure 8-23 depicts the RS-232 electrical interface circuit. Note that this circuit, similar to RS-423-A, is also unbalanced. The major advantage of the electrical circuits for RS-422-A and RS-423-A are their *differential receivers*. RS-232 does not employ differential receivers, a device that greatly enhances the noise immunity characteristics of the circuit.

8.8.6   RS-422-A and RS-423-A Common-Mode Rejection

One significant feature of the differential amplifier is its ability to cancel or reject undesirable signals that are *common* to both differential inputs of the receiver. Typically, in data communications employing RS-422-A or RS-423-A, a signal transmitted on a balanced or unbalanced circuit uses twisted-pair wire as the transmission medium. There are good reasons for the selection of twisted-pair wire. For one, the transmitted signal on each wire of the twisted-pair passes through the *same* electrical environment. Any noise induced by adjacent circuits will be approximately equal in amplitude and phase on both wires. This interference is *common* to both inputs of the receiving amplifier. This is the major advantage over RS-232. The differential amplifier employed as a receiver in an RS-449 interface amplifies the *difference* between its two inputs and rejects signals that are common to both inputs. A measure of this rejection of signals common to both inputs of the differential amplifier is called the *common-mode rejection ratio (CMRR)*. CMRR is given as

$$CMRR = \frac{AA_{vd}}{A_{vcm}} = \frac{V_{od}/V_{id}}{V_{ocm}/V_{icm}} \qquad \textbf{(8-2)}$$

> **Common-Mode Rejection Ratio (CMRR)**
> A measure of a differential amplifier's ability to reject signals common to its input pair of lines.

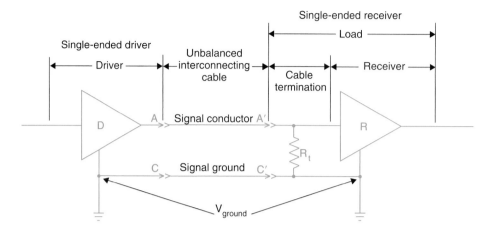

A, C = driver interface
A′, C′= load interface
C = driver signal ground
C′= load signal ground
V$_{ground}$ = ground potential difference
R$_t$ = transmission line termination and/or receiver input impedance

FIGURE 8-23
RS-232 electrical interface circuit.

where

A_{vd} = Differential gain voltage gain
A_{vcm} = Common mode voltage gain
V_{od} = Differential output voltage
V_{id} = Differential input voltage
V_{ocm} = common mode output voltage
V_{icm} = common mode input voltage

In decibels, CMRR is given as

$$CMRR \text{ (db)} = 20 \log CMRR \tag{8-3}$$

EXAMPLE 8.3

Compute the CMRR (dB) for the differential amplifier shown:

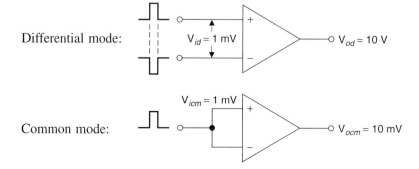

Differential mode: $V_{id} = 1$ mV, $V_{od} = 10$ V

Common mode: $V_{icm} = 1$ mV, $V_{ocm} = 10$ mV

Solution:
The differential voltage gain is

$$A_{vd} = \frac{V_{od}}{V_{id}} = \frac{10 \text{ V}}{1 \text{ mV}} = 10,000$$

The common mode voltage gain is

$$A_{vcm} = \frac{V_{ocm}}{V_{icm}} = \frac{10 \text{ mV}}{1 \text{ mV}} = 10$$

$$\text{CMRR (dB)} = 20 \log \frac{A_{vd}}{A_{vcm}} = 20 \log \frac{10,000}{10} = 60 \text{ dB}$$

The effect of CMRR is best when using both outputs of the line driver as specified in RS-422-A. The differential signal at the receiver is much greater in this case (because the signals are complemented with each other) than when the signal is transmitted unbalanced, as in RS-423-A.

8.8.7 RS-422-A and RS-423-A Voltage Specification

The voltage specifications for RS-422-A and RS-423-A are shown in Figure 8-24. Note the voltage swing for a logic 1 and a logic 0 are considerably less, at ± 6 V, than the RS-232 specification of ± 15 V. Also, the noise immunity for both specifications is different from RS-232. RS-422-A has a noise margin of 1.8 V, whereas RS-423-A has a noise margin of 3.8 V, more than twice as much as RS-422-A. The larger noise margin has been allotted for RS-423-A to compensate for the unbalanced circuit specification.

Distances as great as 4000 ft can be achieved with RS-422-A. A maximum data transfer rate of 10 Mbps is specified. In addition, the differential line drivers are intended to support full-duplex operation with a capability of driving up to a maximum of 10 modules sharing a common receive-line pair.

8.8.8 RS-485

A more recent standard is RS-485, which employes the same signal levels as RS-422. The RS-485 drivers and receivers are of better quality than their RS-422 counterparts, so you can expect to achieve maximum hardware performance over distances as great as 4000 ft at rates of 10 Mbps. As many as 32 devices can share the same connection. RS-485 cannot generally be interfaced to RS-422, however, because RS-485 has only one differential pair signal path and is limited to half-duplex operation, where only one device transmits at a time. Because there are no communications protocols, traffic on the bus must be controlled by software. Table 8-6 compares RS-232, RS-422-A, and RS-485.

8.8.9 RS-530

A data communications standard designed to supersede RS-232 and RS-449 is the RS-530 standard. This serial interface standard defines the electrical and mechanical interface between DTE and DCE and uses the same DB25-pin connector as specified in the RS-232 standard. Transmission rates are specified of as great as 2 Mbps over

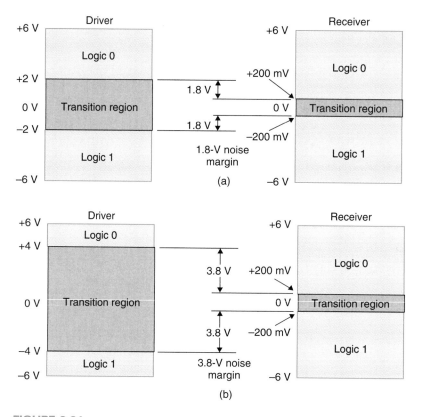

FIGURE 8-24
(a) RS-422-A and (b) RS-423-A logic levels.

TABLE 8-6
Summary Table for RS-232, RS-422, and RS-485

	RS-232	RS-422-A	RS-485
Mode of operation	Single-ended	Differential	Differential
Number of drivers and receivers allowed on line	1 Driver 1 Receiver	1 Driver 10 Receivers	32 Drivers 32 Receivers
Maximum cable length (ft)	50	4000	4000
Maximum data rate (bps)	20k	10M	10M

TABLE 8-7
RS-530 Signal Names and Corresponding Pin Numbers For DB25-Pin Connector

Pin Number	Signal Name	Pin Number	Signal Name
1	Shield (a)	14	Transmitted data (b)
2	Transmitted data (a)	15	Transmitter signal element timing DCE (a)
3	Received data (a)	16	Received data (b)
4	Request to send (a)	17	Receiver signal element timing DCE (a)
5	Clear to send (a)	18	Local loopback
6	DCE ready (a)	19	Request to send
7	Signal ground	20	DTE ready (a)
8	Received line signal detector (a)	21	Remote loopback
9	Receiver signal element timing DCE (b)	22	DCE ready (b)
10	Received line signal detector (b)	23	DTE ready (b)
11	Transmitter signal element timing DTE (b)	24	Transmitter signal element timing DTE (a)
12	Transmitter signal element timing DCE (b)	25	Test mode
13	Clear to send (b)		

a balanced or unbalanced RS-422 or RS-423 electrical interface respectively. Table 8-7 lists the signal names and pin numbers for the RS-530 interface.

8.9 TWENTY- AND SIXTY-MILLIAMPERE CURRENT LOOP STANDARDS

In the 1960s, mechanical Teletype (TTY) printers were interfaced to computers using 20- and 60-mA current loops. The currents were used to drive electromechanical relays in conjunction with the printing action of the terminals. A typical setup between the computer and Teletype includes two current loops: one for the computer to receive characters from the Teletype, and one for the computer to transmit characters to the Teletype. Figure 8-25 illustrates how the Intel 8085A microprocessor can be interfaced to a Teletype terminal using a 20-mA current loop. ASCII characters are represented by sequential combinations of current ON (MARK) and current OFF (SPACE) intervals, similar to the manner in which voltage levels are used in RS-232. The 8085A SID and SOD serial interface lines are used to send and receive TTL levels from the 20-mA current loop buffers.

Teletype terminals typically include built-in modems interfaced to the telephone lines for long-distance communications. Due to advances in technology, the Teletype is rapidly becoming extinct. The 20-mA current loop standard, however, has been adapted to many of today's terminals and high-speed printers. Instead of electromagnetic relays, these devices utilize *optocouplers* to interface to the current loop transmitter and receiver. Optocouplers, or *optoisolators,* are devices used to isolate high voltage and noisy circuits (found in printers and display terminals) from their respective controlling circuit. The optocoupler consists of a sealed infrared emitter and photodetector completely isolated from each other. The 20-mA current loop driver and receiver circuit can, therefore, run completely isolated from high-voltage and noisy circuits. Figure 8-26 depicts how the optocoupler is used in Zentec Corporation's ADM-3A Video Display Terminal. The circuits shown are bidirectional (current can flow in either direction) and operate over the range 16 to 24 mA.

> **Optocoupler**
> A sealed infrared emitter and photodetector used to couple an electrical signal by light. Isolates high voltage and noisy circuits from their respective controlling circuit.

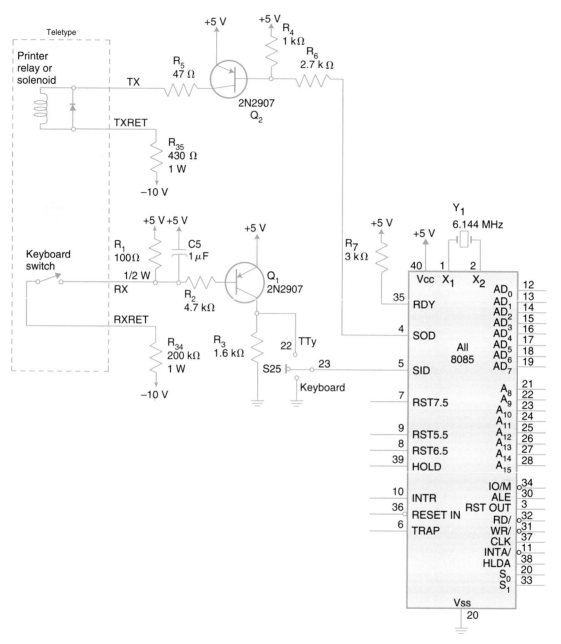

FIGURE 8-25
8085A current loop interface to a Teletype. (Courtesy of Intel Corporation.)

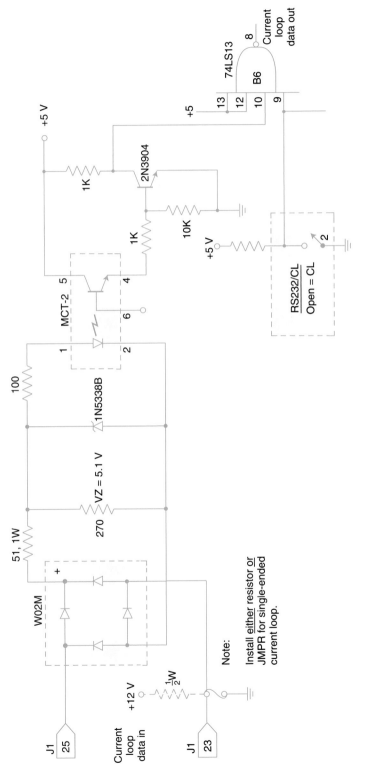

FIGURE 8-26

Twenty-milliampere current loop circuits for Zentec Corporation's ADM-3A employing optocouplers. (Courtesy of Zentec Corp.)

213

PROBLEMS

1. Define *protocol*.
2. What are the logic levels of the start and stop bits of an asynchronous serial character?
3. Compute the protocol overhead for a 7-bit ASCII character that includes a parity bit, a start bit, and two stop bits.
4. Compute the protocol overhead for a DDCMP message block that includes 512 bytes in its data field.
5. What does *modem* stand for?
6. Define *DTE* and *DCE*.
7. Is a printer considered DTE or DCE?
8. The RS-232 specification can be divided into which three categories?
9. What is the maximum recommended RS-232 cable length?
10. Compute the noise margin for an RS-232 transmitted signal that has an output voltage of ±9 V.
11. Draw the asynchronous serial RS-232 waveforms for the ASCII characters y, 3, and ;. Include one stop bit and even parity generation for each character.
12. What RS-232 signal informs DTE that it is ready to accept data?
13. What types of signals are specified for the EIA-449 nine-pin connector?
14. Specify whether the following EIA specifications use balanced or unbalanced electrical interface circuits:
    a. EIA RS-232.
    b. EIA RS-422-A.
    c. EIA RS-423-A.
15. A differential amplifier has a CMRR of 92 dB. If the differential gain is given as 13,500 and the common mode input voltage as 2 mV, compute the common mode output voltage.
16. Repeat problem 15 for a common mode input voltage of 10 instead of 2 mV.
17. What is the maximum data transfer rate specified for RS-422-A?
18. What is the maximum data transfer rate specified for RS-485?

9

THE UART

Data terminal equipment (DTE) such as terminals and host computers must transmit digital information over a single transmission line. To perform this operation, DTE uses a device called a *universal asynchronous receiver/transmitter (UART)*. The UART (Figure 9-1) is a peripheral device; that is, it operates external to the central processing unit (CPU). It is an essential component within terminals, computers, and many other serial communications devices. The UART must be programmed by the CPU to communicate between two devices. For *synchronous* communications, a USART, or *universal synchronous asynchronous receiver/transmitter* must be used. This chapter considers asynchronous communications.

> **Universal Asynchronous Receiver/Transmitter (UART)**
> A programmable device used to convert parallel data from a CPU to a serial data stream for transmission. Can also receive serial data and convert it back to parallel format for a CPU to read.

9.1 UART INTERFACE

The UART can accept a data character from the CPU in parallel format and convert it into a serial data stream. Likewise, the UART can receive a serial data stream and convert it to a parallel data character for the CPU. These two fundamental tasks of the UART can be performed simultaneously, because its internal receiver and transmitter sections operate virtually independently of each other.

Consider the case of the UART transmitting a character in serial format to a video display terminal (VDT). In the setup shown in Figure 9-1, decoding is necessary to enable the UART. The decoded output port enables the UART to receive a parallel word sent by the CPU via its data bus. The UART then begins its internal procedure to send the parallel word, bit by bit, as a serial bit stream to the terminal. Conversely, the UART must be enabled by the CPU whenever a character from the terminal has been received in serial format by the UART and is ready to be input by the CPU as a parallel data word.

The CPU can establish if the UART is ready to send a character, or has a character available by addressing the device through its decoded port. This will enable the UART and allow the CPU to read a complete status of the device at any time. The internal registers that are accessed contain specific information, such as transmitter and receiver ready flags and error-checking flags. External output pins are also provided by the UART for indicating its readiness to send or receive data. They may be used to interrupt the CPU for interrupt-driven programs.

Now that we have developed a fundamental idea of what the UART does, the complexities of the internal logic necessary to perform these tasks becomes increas-

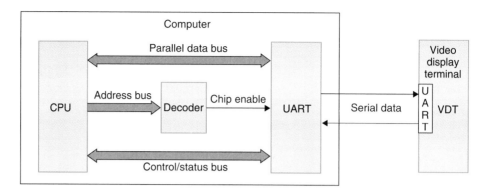

FIGURE 9-1
Block diagram of the UART interface.

ingly apparent. As in any complex device used as a building block, it behooves the technician and design engineer to investigate and understand the internal functions of that device. On this premise, the device is said to be best selected, utilized, and maintained with its associated hardware.

9.2 UART RECEIVER SECTION

The primary task of the receiver section of the UART is to convert a serial bit stream to a parallel data word for the CPU to read. This process includes the following functions:

- Start bit detection
- Synchronization of data bit cells
- Shift register timing and control
- Serial-to-parallel conversion
- Stop bit detection
- Error detection
- Status

The basic components of the receiver section are illustrated in Figure 9-2. When a character is transmitted from a terminal, it is received by the UART receiver section as Serial Data In. The signal levels at this point have been level translated from RS-232 format to TTL. The TIMING GENERATOR and CONTROL LOGIC provide the RECEIVER SHIFT REGISTER with the necessary clock pulses and control signals to shift the serial character in. It is then loaded into the RECEIVER HOLD REGISTER, where further processing such as error detection and status operations are performed. The CPU is notified by the Receiver Ready signal, RxRdy, that a parallel–formatted character is ready to be read from the UART's RECEIVER HOLD REGISTER.

9.2.1 Double Buffering the UART Receiver

Why not do away with the RECEIVER HOLD REGISTER all together and process the parallel character directly out of the RECEIVER SHIFT REGISTER? This is pos-

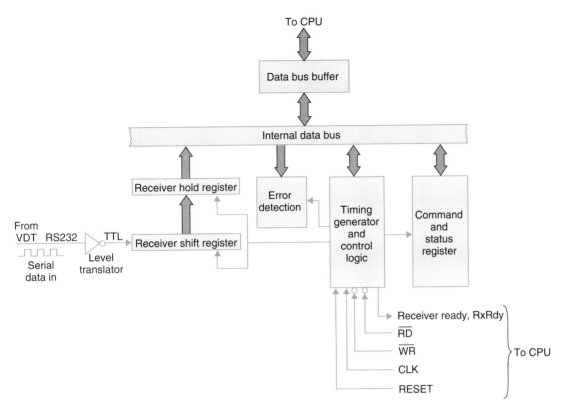

FIGURE 9-2
Block diagram of the UART receiver section.

sible; however, the CPU would have to read the character immediately following its last bit shifted in. This would ensure that serial characters sent to the UART in direct succession to each other would not write over each other before the CPU has a chance to read them. Often, it is not convenient for the CPU to input the character as soon as it is available, as in the case when it is performing other, more pertinent tasks. Holding the character in the RECEIVER HOLD REGISTER allows ample time for the CPU to input the character, whereas the UART can be shifting a new character in. This process is referred to as *double buffering*.

> **Double Buffering**
> The process of using two registers to store data: one to hold the data, and one to process it.

9.2.2 Composite Serial Character

If a character received from DTE by the UART were the ASCII character A, it would appear as the waveform illustrated in Figure 9-3. The composite serial data stream that the UART receives is comprised of 10 bits:

- One start bit
- Seven data bits
- One parity bit
- One stop bit

The number of bits per character can vary depending on the data character length, parity, and the number of stop bits for which the DTE has been configured. Ten bits

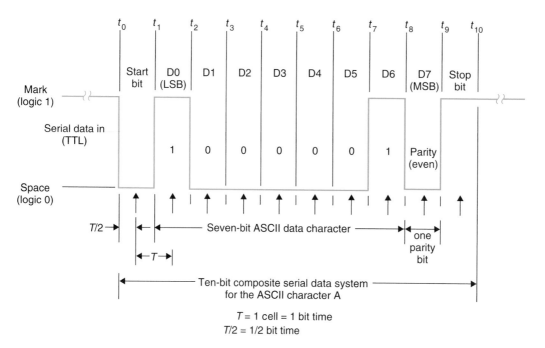

FIGURE 9-3

Composite serial data stream for the ASCII character A = 41H.

---

is commonly used in serial communication. Each of the 10 bits illustrated in Figure 9-3 has a fixed interval of time. This interval of time is referred to as the *bit time*. The reciprocal of the bit time results in what is referred to as the character's *baud rate*, or the number of bits transmitted per second. If the character shown in Figure 9-3 were transmitted or received from DCE, a modem, the baud rate would equal the transmission rate in bits per second *only* if the modulation rate of the DCE onto the communications channel were to vary at this same rate. Chapter 13 considers cases where the baud rate does not equal the number of bits transmitted per second. For now, however, we assume that the UART is transmitting or receiving serial data from a terminal.

In Figure 9-3, if the bit times were measured to be 833 μs, the baud rate would equal 1200 (1/833 μs = 1200). Furthermore, if there are 10 bits per character, dividing the baud rate by 10 will establish the character rate or maximum number of characters that can be sent or received per second:

$$\text{Baud rate} = \frac{1}{\text{bit time}} \quad \text{(bps)}$$

$$\text{Maximum character rate} = \frac{\text{baud rate}}{\text{bits per character}} \quad \text{(characters per second)}$$

EXAMPLE 9.1

Compute the baud rate and the number of characters transmitted per second given a bit time of 104.16 μs and a character length of 10 bits.

Solution:

$$\text{Baud rate} = \frac{1}{\text{bit time}} = \frac{1}{104.16 \ \mu s} = 9600 \text{ bps}$$

$$\text{Maximum character rate} = \frac{\text{baud rate}}{\text{bits per character}}$$

$$= \frac{9600}{10}$$

$$= 960 \text{ characters per second}$$

9.2.3   Receiver Timing

The character shown in Figure 9-3 is represented as a 7-bit ASCII character transmitted with an even parity bit. Its level has been translated from RS-232 format to TTL. Because the character has been transmitted by another device asynchronous to the UART's timing, the UART has the initial task of searching for the occurrence of the start bit. Ideally, this is precisely that instant in time, t_0, in which the signal changes from its idle condition of a MARK, a logic 1, to a SPACE, a logic 0. The terms *MARK* and *SPACE* are synonymous to a logic 1 and a logic 0 in the field of communications. A delay of $T/2$, referenced to t_0, is necessary before the first *sample* of Serial Data In is taken by the UART's RECEIVER SHIFT REGISTER. We will define a sample as that instant in time in which the RECEIVER SHIFT REGISTER is clocked. All bits within the register shift one bit position. It is at this instant in time, $T/2$, that the UART's hardware checks the level of the data bit sampled. It must be a SPACE, further confirming that the start bit of a character has been detected. If this were not the case, presumably a noise transient, otherwise known as a *glitch,* may have occurred. If sampling of the remaining bits were to continue, the data shifted into the RECEIVER SHIFT REGISTER would be erroneous. The process of seeking the start bit would be repeated in this case. If the data are in fact a SPACE at $T/2$, then the remaining bits are sampled. As depicted by the arrows shown in Figure 9-3, the sampling of each bit continues at a delay of $T,$ the bit time, until all bits have been shifted into the register.

> **Glitch**
> An undesirable noise transient coupled into a circuit or transmission line.

9.2.4   Start Bit Detection

The UART's task of shifting serial data into its RECEIVER SHIFT REGISTER is rudimentary and lends itself to further discussion. Whenever serial data into a shift register is being sampled by a clock that runs asynchronous to the serial data, the center of each bit that is being sampled can only be *approached.* Further discussion is necessary to find out why.

As stated earlier, the initial task of the UART receiver is the detection of the start bit. The timing necessary for shifting the serial data into the RECEIVER SHIFT REGISTER will rely on the detection of the start bit at t_0. A flip-flop can be used to perform this task (Figure 9-4). When Serial Data In changes from a MARK to a SPACE, the start bit detection flip-flop will SET, indicating t_0, the beginning of the start bit. Once SET, the output of the flip-flop can be used to enable the sampling of Serial Data In.

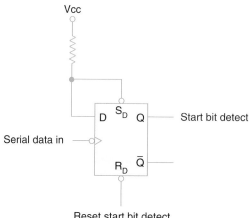

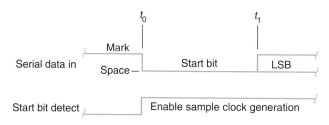

FIGURE 9-4
Detection of the start bit with a flip-flop.

9.2.5 Receiver Sample Clock Generation

A *sample clock* pulse must be generated at the center of each bit of the incoming serial data, including the start bit. Figure 9-5 illustrates the development of the sample clock and how it is used to shift Serial Data In into the UART's RECEIVER SHIFT REGISTER.

With respect to t_0, a delay of $T/2$ is necessary before the first sample clock is generated and a delay of T for samples thereafter (see Figure 9-3). Because the baud rate of the UART must be programmed before its operation, a PROGRAMMABLE DIVIDER is initially preset to half the number of receiver clock pulses that occur within the duration of a single bit. This will result in the initial delay of $T/2$ when the PROGRAMMABLE DIVIDER is allowed to count down to zero.

For many UARTs, a typical number of receiver clock pulses per bit time is 16. This is shown in Figure 9-5 to illustrate the relative occurrence of the sample clock for the RECEIVER SHIFT REGISTER. At t_0, the counter is enabled by our start bit detection flip-flop to begin its countdown sequence from its preset value of 8, that is, half the full count of 16. When the counter has counted down to zero, a sample clock pulse out of the PROGRAMMABLE DIVIDER is generated. At this time, the center of what is perceived to be the start bit occurs and gets shifted into the first flip-flop internal to the RECEIVER SHIFT REGISTER. The PROGRAMMABLE DIVIDER continues its division of the receiver clock by 16, producing the sample clock pulses necessary to shift the remaining bits into the RECEIVER SHIFT REGISTER.

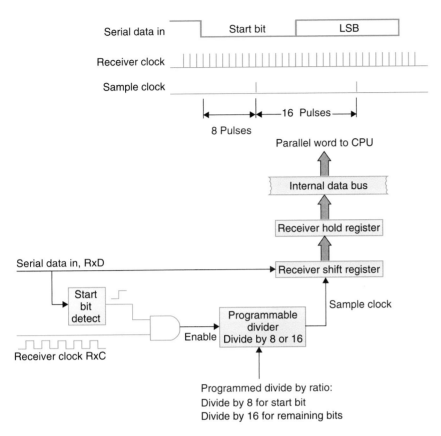

FIGURE 9-5
Developing the UART's sample clock.

Because the receiver clock runs asynchronous to Serial Data In, the timing of the resulting sample clock pulse shown in Figure 9-5 may not be precisely at the center of the start bit as we would want it. By observing the timing of the sample clock pulse out of the PROGRAMMABLE DIVIDER in relation to Serial Data In, this anomaly would be apparent.

To illustrate the asynchronous nature of the situation, consider the effect of a receiver clock frequency of 4×, 8×, and 32× the rate of Serial Data In. Figure 9-6 shows the resulting sample clock produced by the PROGRAMMABLE DIVIDER for these three frequencies. As mentioned earlier, the PROGRAMMABLE DIVIDER is preset initially to half its full count. In the three examples shown, this would be either 2, 4, or 16. When START BIT DETECT becomes active at t_0, the receiver clock is gated to the PROGRAMMABLE DIVIDER, which in turn counts its preset value down to zero. The resulting sample clock pulses shown in each example do not sample Serial Data In at the *ideal* center of the cells. The PROGRAMMABLE DIVIDER continues with its count of either 4, 8, or 32, producing the same relative *sampling error* for the remaining bits.

Note that the sampling error is greatly reduced with higher receiver clock frequencies. A conclusion may be drawn from this resulting effect: the higher the receiver clock frequency is relative to the baud rate, the greater the resolution of actual

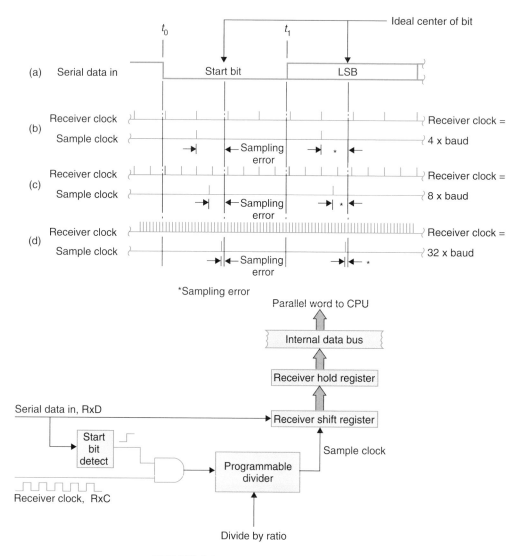

FIGURE 9-6
Timing diagram illustrating the effect of the receiver clock frequency on generation of the sample clock: (a) serial data in; (b) receiver clock of 4× the baud rate; (c) receiver clock of 8× the baud rate; (d) receiver clock of 32× the baud rate.

Serial Data In. To approach the ideal center of each bit, the receiver clock frequency would have to approach an infinite rate. Unfortunately, due to the frequency limitations of TTL devices (or of all devices for that matter), the speed of the clock must be a practical value. The ratio of the UART's clock frequency to the baud rate of the incoming serial data is a factor that must be considered in the recovery of the received character.

For the three examples depicted in Figure 9-6, a *worst-case* condition exists for each in terms of accuracy in detecting the center of each bit. The maximum error for any case would be the *period* the receiver clock used. A character's start bit may become active precisely at a time when the active edge of the receiver clock occurs. A race condition exists here between Serial Data In and the receiver clock pulse, because they are running asynchronous to each other. If the PROGRAMMABLE DIVIDER (enabled through the start bit) misses this first receiver clock pulse, it will have to wait until the next receiver clock pulse to begin its count. This would be the worst-case condition in which the sample clock pulse shown in Figure 9-6 would be off by the period of the receiver clock. If, on the other hand, the race condition allows the PROGRAMMABLE DIVIDER to count this first clock pulse, then the resulting sample clock pulse would be generated at the ideal center of each bit (within a propagation delay of the PROGRAMMABLE DIVIDER). This would be the most desirable condition. It is purely random and is as likely to happen as the worst-case condition. The sample clock will shift between both extremes with each new character sent from DTE.

As a rule, when a given concept has been realized through hardware implementation, the worst-case condition must always be considered a factor in the analysis of the design. In this case, the period of the receiver clock has been considered. If the period of the receiver clock is a significant percentage of the bit time, as is the case with the example of $4\times$ baud in Figure 9-6, it is apparent that the data sent from the DTE may be sampled too close to the boundaries of each cell. The margin for error is minimal. An appreciable amount of distortion that a character picks up en route from the DTE will likely be sampled and shifted by the UART at an erroneous time.

9.2.6 False Start Bit Detection

Earlier, we discussed provisions for checking the state of Serial Data In at $T/2$ to ensure that a SPACE condition was clocked into the RECEIVER SHIFT REGISTER. It is possible for a noise glitch to have occurred, falsely triggering the Start Bit Detection flip-flop. If a noise glitch falls below the maximum input LOW condition, $V_{IL\ MAX}$ as depicted in Figure 9-7, it will inadvertently trigger the Start Bit Detection flip-flop. Typically, this value is specified as 0.8 V for TTL. Noise transients generally have a duration in microseconds. The duration that actually causes the false start has elapsed by the time the first sample clock is generated at $T/2$; consequently, a MARK instead of a SPACE is shifted into the first flip-flop internal to the RECEIVER SHIFT REGISTER. This being the case, our counter is simply preset to eight and the Start Bit Detection flip-flop is reinitialized. The process of seeking the start bit of a character is repeated. If a SPACE occurs at $T/2$, the PROGRAMMABLE DIVIDER is allowed to continue its count, dividing the receiver clock by 16 and generating

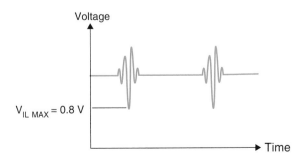

FIGURE 9-7
Noise transients that can cause false detection of the start bit.

sample clock pulses as illustrated in Figure 9-5. Most UARTs manufactured today have a *false start bit detection* feature.

9.2.7   Flowcharting the Operation of the Receiver

The foregoing material can be presented in a flowchart, thus providing an overview of the operation of the receiver (Figure 9-8). Note that error detection, an essential task of the receiver, has been included in the chart.

Once all the bits associated with a character have been shifted into the RECEIVER SHIFT REGISTER and stored in the RECEIVER HOLD REGISTER, error checking can be performed. The parity bit is checked in accordance with the number of data bits set in the character. If the UART's hardware detects an inconsistent result, even or odd depending on how it has been programmed by the user, the parity error bit is set in the UART's status register. A framing error is detected if the last bit sampled (see Figure 9-3) is not a MARK; that is, the end of the character, the stop bit, should always be a MARK. A framing error will occur if the baud rate is incorrect or the transmission of a character is incomplete. The overrun error flag is set if the CPU does not read a character before the next one is available. The UART will continue updating its receiver buffer with the latest character unless otherwise programmed. The previous overrun character is lost. (Detailed examples of parity, framing, and overrun errors are given in Chapter 10.)

The preceding error conditions do not inhibit the operation of the UART. The programmer must take the necessary steps to handle the error condition specified by the status register. The UART's error flags will remain active until the UART is either internally reset through a command or has undergone a power-up initialization sequence.

9.3   UART TRANSMITTER SECTION

The transmitter section of the UART includes the hardware to convert a parallel-formatted word from the CPU into a composite serial word. The transmitter's timing is virtually independent of its receiver counterpart. There is no need to search for a start bit or to create a delay of $T/2$ in search of the center of each bit. The basic functions of the UART transmitter section include:

- Start bit generation
- Shift register timing and control
- Parallel-to-serial conversion
- Stop bit generation
- Status
- Parity

Note that we have not included error detection as a part of the transmitter. Error detection is generally associated with the receiver section of a UART. Some UARTs have provisions for testing transmitter overrun and underrun errors. Chapter 14 looks at the interaction of both the transmitter and receiver in terms of an error that has been detected and followed by a retransmission request. The basic components of the transmitter section are illustrated in Figure 9-9.

The composite serial data stream is output to the Serial Data Out pin, TxD. The UART must effectively insert the start bit, parity bit, and the programmed number of stop bits as part of this data stream.

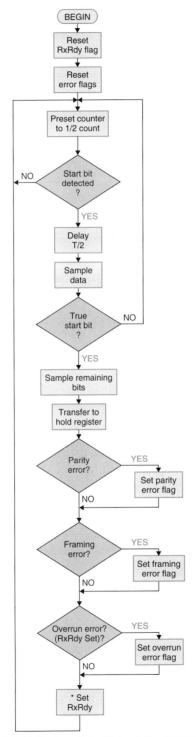

* RxRdy flag is reset after CPU reads the character.

FIGURE 9-8
Flowchart of the UART's receiver operations.

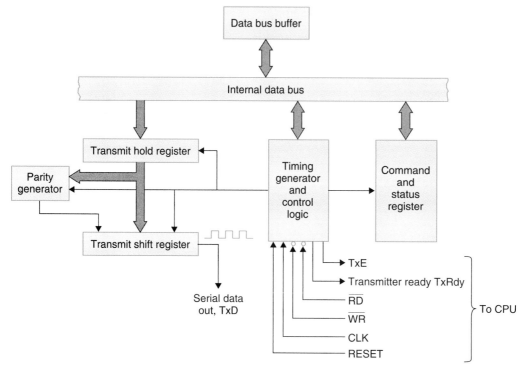

FIGURE 9-9
Block diagram of the UART transmitter section.

9.3.1   Transmitter Composite Character

The timing generator and control logic of the UART monitors the $\overline{\text{WR}}$ signal from the CPU. When $\overline{\text{WR}}$ becomes active, the UART loads the parallel data on the bus into its TRANSMIT HOLD REGISTER and generates the necessary timing pulses for transmitting the data in serial format. Note in Figure 9-9 that the Timing Generator and Control Logic accepts signals and issues signals from the CPU both internally and externally to accomplish this task.

Processing the parallel data word from the CPU is accomplished by loading the output of the TRANSMIT HOLD REGISTER into the TRANSMIT SHIFT REGIS-TER. It is here where the start bit, a logic 0, the stop bit, a logic 1, the programmed number of stop bits, and parity, if enabled, are inserted. The format of the entire composite serial data character is depicted in Figure 9-10. The DATA CHARACTER and the STOP BITS are shown here to be variable in length. Both are programmed by the user.

For the variable-length STOP BIT(S) illustrated in Figure 9-10, the programmer is typically provided with the option of controlling the number of stop bits, consequently increasing the overall length of time it takes to send the serial character. For example, the length of time it would take for a character to be sent with one stop bit would be one bit time less than the length of time it would take to send that same character programmed for two stop bits. Programming the variable-length Data Character to 5, 6, or 7 bits has the same effect.

CPU byte (5 to 8 bits/character)

Assembled serial data output (TxD)

Start bit	Data character	Parity bit	Stop bit/s

FIGURE 9-10
Transmitted composite serial character format.

9.3.2   Transmit Shift Clock Generation

The transmitter section of the UART includes a PROGRAMMABLE DIVIDER similar to the receiver section. There is no need to preset the divider with half the divide-by ratio in search of the center of a bit. As illustrated in Figure 9-11(a), the divider is simply programmed to a value that allows the external transmitter clock, TxC, to be divided down to a value equal to the programmed baud rate. The output of the PROGRAMMABLE DIVIDER is the Transmit Shift CLK. The Transmit Shift CLK has a period equal to the bit time of the transmitted character.

9.3.3   Transmitter Timing

Figure 9-11(b) depicts the timing sequence that the transmitter section of the UART undergoes while transmitting characters. Initially, the TIMING GENERATOR and CONTROL LOGIC's Transmit Ready line, TxRDY, is active, indicating to the CPU that the UART transmitter is ready for a parallel word. TxEMPTY, when HIGH, implies that the transmitter has no further characters to send. This occurs when the TRANSMIT HOLD and TRANSMIT SHIFT REGISTERS are both empty. A $\overline{\text{WR}}$ can be issued by the CPU to output a parallel word to the UART via the data bus. In the timing diagram of Figure 9-11(b), TxRDY immediately becomes inactive after the first byte has been written by the CPU to the Transmit Hold Register. The UART is now busy. The parallel word is loaded into the TRANSMIT HOLD REGISTER, and TxEMPTY becomes inactive. That is, both buffers are NOT empty. The TIMING GENERATOR and CONTROL LOGIC will provide the signals for loading the TRANSMIT HOLD REGISTER into the TRANSMIT SHIFT REGISTER. This occurs when the TRANSMIT SHIFT REGISTER is empty and the TRANSMIT HOLD REGISTER is NOT empty. The start bit, parity, and stop bits are inserted in the TRANSMIT SHIFT REGISTER. The Transmitter CLK, TxC, after getting divided down by the PROGRAMMABLE DIVIDER, will begin its procedure to shift the composite serial data stream out of the Serial Data Out, TxD output pin. The foregoing sequence of events occurs immediately following the first $\overline{\text{WR}}$ from the CPU.

A closer look at the timing in Figure 9-11(b) reveals an additional $\overline{\text{WR}}$ pulse immediately following the first $\overline{\text{WR}}$ pulse. It is justified by the preceding TxRDY pulse. How is this possible in the middle of a serial data stream that is being shifted out? This is the concept of *double buffering* spoken of earlier with regard to the

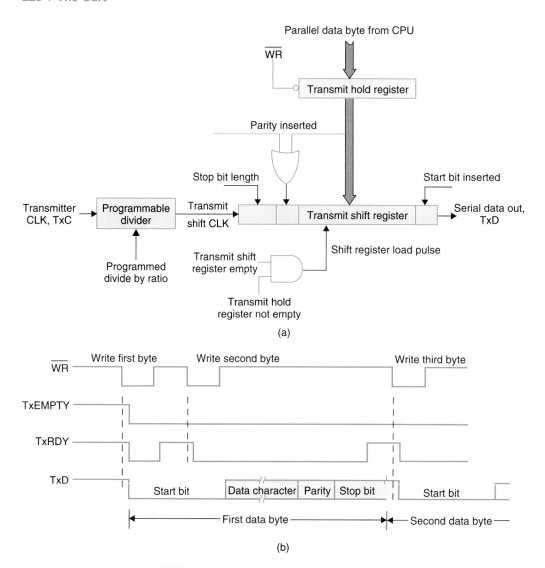

FIGURE 9-11
(a) Generation of transmitted serial data out, TxD; (b) transmitter timing sequence.

UART's receiver section. Double buffering is an essential part of the transmit section of the UART also. Its purpose here is to *hold* the current data word sent by the CPU while processing and sending the previous one. Note that after the second $\overline{WR}$ pulse occurs, both the TRANSMIT HOLD and TRANSMIT SHIFT REGISTERS are full. TxRDY is inactive until the first BYTE has been completely shifted out of the TRANS-MIT SHIFT REGISTER. At this time, the second BYTE, held in the TRANSMIT HOLD REGISTER, is transferred into the TRANSMIT SHIFT REGISTER. TxRDY becomes active again, signaling the CPU that the UART is ready for a third BYTE. At this time, the second BYTE sent to the UART begins its process of getting shifted out of the TRANSMIT SHIFT REGISTER. TxEMPTY remains inactive all the while. It will remain LOW until the UART has no further characters to transmit. Both buffers in this case would be empty, and TxEMPTY would become active again.

9.3.4   Implementing the Transmit Hold and Shift Registers

The concept of serial transmission may be further reinforced by implementing the hardware for a simplified TRANSMIT HOLD and TRANSMIT SHIFT REGISTER (Figure 9-12). The D-type flip-flops are used here to implement both registers. BD0 through BD7 represent the buffered data byte from the CPU. The buffered data byte gets parallel loaded into the TRANSMIT SHIFT REGISTER when $\overline{WR}$ becomes active. If the TRANSMIT SHIFT REGISTER is empty, a Shift Register Load Pulse generated by the UART's TIMING GENERATOR and CONTROL LOGIC will cause a *jam entry* via the direct set, $\overline{S_d}$, and direct reset, $\overline{R_d}$, inputs of the register. Without a Load Pulse, the AND gates depicted in the diagram remain inactive and a jam entry cannot occur. The flip-flops of the TRANSMIT SHIFT REGISTER can now serve as a shift register, providing a Shift CLK is generated.

> **Jam Entry**
> In digital circuits, when data are immediately loaded into a register via its direct set and direct reset inputs.

The composite serial data stream begins as soon as the jam entry propagates to the output of the START BIT flip-flop. This is the Transmitted Serial Data Out, TxD. Note that the first bit to get shifted out of the register is the START BIT. This first flip-flop is always jam loaded with a logic 0, a SPACE, via the direct reset input, $\overline{R_d}$. The transmitted Serial Data Out changes at this time from a MARK, or IDLE condition, to a SPACE, that is, the beginning of the transmitted character's start bit. The Shift CLK, occurring at the programmed baud rate, is generated one bit time after the Load Pulse. This will allow the START BIT to remain LOW at the output of the first flip-flop for one bit time.

Because all flip-flops share the same Shift CLK, the data present at each of their D inputs will be shifted to their Q outputs. The START BIT has elapsed at this time, and the LSB of the data character is present at the serial output pin, TxD. The process will continue until all bits have been shifted out of the TRANSMIT SHIFT REGISTER. The last bit shifted out is the STOP BIT. A closer look at the shift register's most significant flip-flop will reveal a pull-up resistor at its D input. The logic HIGH produced by the pull-up resistor will ensure that on the *ninth* Shift CLK pulse (the jam entry held for one bit time accounts for the tenth bit) that this HIGH will have been shifted through all flip-flops and will be present at the TxD output pin. This marks the beginning of the STOP BIT at this time. Continued clocking of the TRANSMIT SHIFT REGISTER will allow the length of the STOP BIT to be controlled. Once the Shift CLK is discontinued, the output of the TRANSMIT SHIFT REGISTER will remain a logic HIGH, which is the idle state.

9.3.5   Inserting Parity

The circuit in Figure 9-12 does not include provisions for inserting the parity bit. The preceding circuit would suffice. However, the generation of parity would depend on the software control of the MSB, BD7; that is, BD7 from the CPU *is* the parity bit. It can be set to even or odd parity by the program. It can also be simply set to zero at all times in cases when parity is deemed to be unnecessary. Parity generation by the UART is *disabled* through the command register.

If parity has been enabled through a command to the UART, the transmitter section must override the MSB of the data character and provide for the insertion of the parity bit. The circuit of Figure 9-13 depicts a method for doing this. If the parity enable, P.E., signal is active (LOW), BD7 would be inhibited and PARITY would be gated to the input of the next flip-flop. Conversely, if P.E. is inactive (HIGH), then the parity bit would be disabled and BD7 from the CPU would be gated to the next

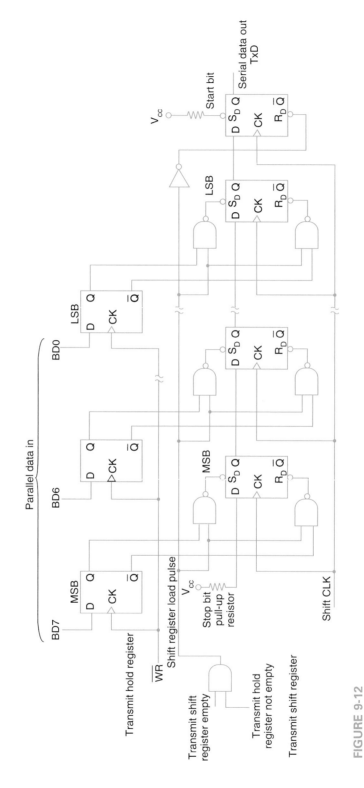

FIGURE 9-12
Implementing the TRANSMIT HOLD and TRANSMIT SHIFT REGISTERS.

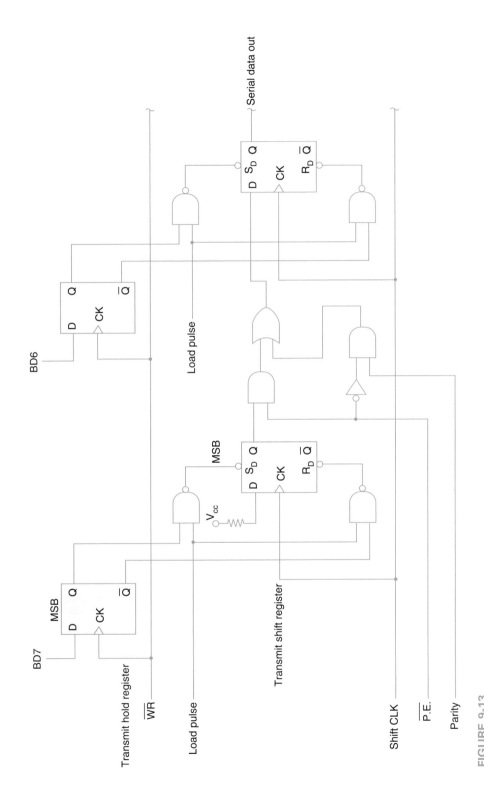

FIGURE 9-13
Inserting PARITY into the TRANSMIT SHIFT REGISTER.

231

flip-flop. The UART's Timing and Control Logic will ensure that the $\overline{P.E.}$ line is asserted at the appropriate time. (Parity-generation and error-checking circuits are considered in Chapter 17.)

PROBLEMS

1. Define *double buffering*.
2. What UART signal informs the CPU that a character is available and ready to be read from its RECEIVER HOLD REGISTER?
3. A character transmitted by a UART has a bit time of 104.16 μs.
    a. Compute its baud rate.
    b. If the character's length is 11 bits (7-bit data, parity, start bit, and two stop bits), compute the maximum number of characters that can be transmitted per second.
4. What are the logic levels for the following conditions?
    a. Mark.
    b. Idle.
    c. Space.
    d. Start bit.
    e. Stop bit.
5. Refer to Figure 9-6. Compute the maximum sampling error (in seconds) for the three receiver clock frequencies shown in Figure 9-6(b), (c), and (d). Assume a bit time of 104.16 μs.
6. Explain false start bit detection.
7. What UART signal informs the CPU that it is ready to accept a parallel word to be transmitted in serial format?
8. Refer to Figure 9-11(b). How is it possible for two $\overline{WR}$ pulses to occur before the first character is even sent by the UART?
9. For the circuit shown in Figure 9-13, what are the logic levels necessary for the signals P $\overline{P.E.}$ and PARITY to enable and set the parity bit to a logic LOW?
10. Explain how a logic 1 can be loaded into the MSB of the TRANSMIT SHIFT REGISTER shown in Figure 9-13.

THE UART INTERFACE

Interfacing a microprocessor to a peripheral device can be a difficult task without a reasonably in-depth functional understanding of both the processor and the device itself. Often, this level of understanding is beyond what the student can get out of manufacturers' specification data sheets. Chapter 9 presented the UART in a manner that was intended to give the student this functional insight. Now that we have developed this understanding, we are in a much better position to interface with it. This chapter discusses implementation of an asynchronous serial interface between the 8085A microprocessor and 8251A USART. An introduction to the high-speed 16550A UART also is presented.

10.1 INTERFACING THE USART

Figure 10-1 depicts how the 8085A microprocessor and 8251A USART are interfaced together to transmit and receive serial data to and from a video display terminal (VDT). The circuit diagram is complete except for the microprocessor, depicting only that portion of the hardware required to interface to the USART. Both the 8251A and the 8085A have been widely accepted as industry standards in the field of data communications and processor applications. On this basis, we have selected these two fundamental devices for our discussion.

10.1.1 Level Translation

Because the 8251A USART is a TTL device, its levels must be translated to standard RS-232 levels for the exchange of serial data to occur between the terminal and USART. The device we have selected for this purpose is the single-chip MAX232 level translator.* Internal to the MAX232 are two TTL-to-RS-232 level translators and two RS-232-to-TTL level translators. Note in Figure 10-1 that it operates from a *single* +5 V power supply, unlike conventional level translators, which require multiple supplies. An internal charge pump generates ±10 V output swings for TTL level signals in. The acceptable RS-232 voltage range for a logic 1 is −3 to −15 V. For a

> **Level Translation**
> The process of translating one family of logic levels to another.

---

*The MAX232 is manufactured by the MAXIM Corporation. Four external capacitors are required for operation. A MAX233 is available (at a higher price) that requires no external components for operation.

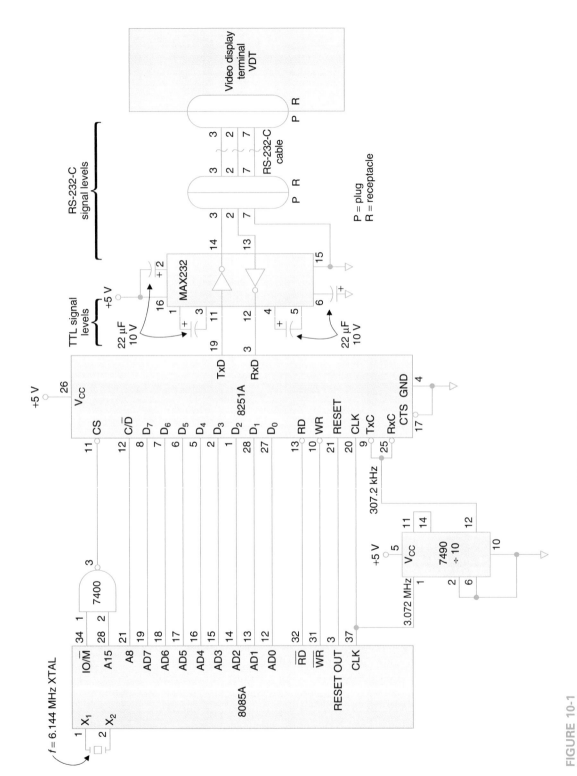

FIGURE 10-1
Interfacing the 8085A microprocessor and 8251A USART to a VDT.

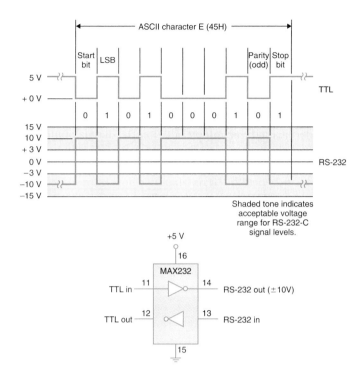

FIGURE 10-2
Level translation from TTL to RS-232 for the ASCII character E.

logic 0, it is +3 to +15 V. The ±10 V output swing from the MAX232 is well within the limits of the RS-232 convention. The MAX232 is also capable of translating RS-232 levels to TTL. Figure 10-2 illustrates the ASCII character E in asynchronous format. It is translated by the MAX232 from TTL to RS-232 levels. The shaded zone indicates acceptable levels in RS-232 format for a logic 1 and logic 0. Note that the voltage levels are inverted by the MAX232. Logic levels, however, remain the same; that is, a TTL logic 1 into the MAX232 is also a logic 1 out. Only its *voltage level* has been translated.

10.1.2 RS-232 Interface to a Terminal

The interface cable depicted in Figure 10-1 uses the standard RS-232 DB25 pin connector. A minimal interface (see Section 8.5) of three RS-232 circuits will be used in this example:

Signal ground	AB	Pin 7
Transmitted data	BA	Pin 2
Received data	BB	Pin 3

The cable length selected must conform to the specifications outlined in Section 8.4.1. We have included the connector's sex in our illustration, denoted by P, male plug, and R, female receptacle. A direct connection from the level translator to the terminal can also be used; however, a cable assembly will allow us to interconnect to other RS-232 terminals.

10.1.3   USART Transmit and Receive Clock

The selection of the USART's Transmit and Receive Clock frequency is not arbitrary. See inputs TXC and RXC of the 8251A shown in Figure 10-1. Careful attention must be given in selecting a frequency that is compatible to the features of the USART. The 8251A, for example, is capable of program dividing the Transmit and Receive Clock frequency by 1, 16, or 64. The resulting frequency is the data transmission rate, which must be compatible in speed to the interfacing device.

An external oscillator can be used to generate the Transmit and Receive Clock for the 8251A. This is not necessary in our case. Instead, we will use the available CLK output of the 8085A microprocessor. Its frequency was intentionally selected for this purpose by using a 6.144-MHz crystal, shown in Figure 10-1, for the X1 and X2 inputs of the 8085A. Internally, the processor divides the crystal frequency by 2. The CLK frequency out of the 8085A is, therefore, 3.072 MHz (6.144 MHz/2). A 7490 Decade Counter has been configured to further divide this frequency by 10. The resulting frequency of 307.2 kHz will be used as our Transmit and Receive Clock. The 8251A USART can now be programmed to further divide this frequency by 16 or 64, resulting in a baud rate of 19.2 kbaud or 4800 baud, respectively. Lower baud rates can easily be attained by simply dividing the CLK output of the 8085A by a value greater than the 10 that we are using. Several single-chip integrated circuits (IC) are available on the market to perform this task if desired.

10.1.4   Addressing the USART

Partial-Address Decoding The decoding of only a portion of a microprocessor's address bus to enable an I/O (input/output) port.

For circuit simplicity, *partial-address decoding,* or the decoding of less than the total number of address bits, is used for port selecting the 8251A. The 7400 NAND gate depicted in Figure 10-1 enables the 8251A for communication. Because port duplication occurs on the upper and lower address bits of the 8085A during an IOR or IOW machine cycle, the upper address bits can be used for decoding. By logically ANDing IO/M and A15 on an IN or OUT instruction to port 80H or above, we can enable the 8251A. This will occur on the *third* machine cycle (M_3) of instructions OUT 80H (or above) or IN 80H (or above), where IO/M and A15 are both a logic HIGH.

Figure 10-3 illustrates the timing produced by the 8085A for an IOR or IOW machine cycle. The timing input for the address decoder circuit is also illustrated. Note that IO/M and A15 are both HIGH throughout the entire machine cycle. This will enable the 8251A by activating its Chip Select, CS, input pin. Because RD or WR, depending on whether the machine cycle is an IOR or IOW, both occur within this time frame, the 8251A can be commanded or its status may be read by outputting or inputting from port 80H or above.

If one other address bit from the microprocessor is decoded, a distinction can be made by the 8251A as to whether it is being enabled for Control and Status or Data. Address bit A8, the LSB of our duplicated port address, is used for this purpose. It is connected to the Control/Data (C/D) input pin of the 8251A. Addressing ports 80H and 81H enables the 8251A for two separate functions:

1. Port 80H: Data
2. Port 81H: Control and Status

When C/D̄ of the 8251A is HIGH (addressing port 81H) and W̄R̄ is active, the Control Register of the 8251A is addressed. When C/D̄ is HIGH and R̄D̄ is active, the Status

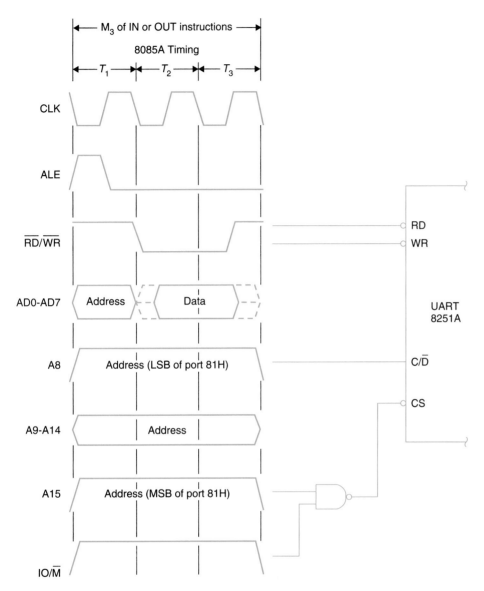

FIGURE 10-3
Timing for 8085A IOR/IOW cycle with partial address decoding to enable the 8251A.

Register of the 8251A is addressed. C/$\overline{\text{D}}$ when LOW (addressing port 80H) allows access to the Data Register for sending and receiving data to and from the 8251A. Table 10-1 summarizes the effect of control signals sent to the 8251A as a result of executing the 8085A instructions: IN 80H, or OUT 80H.

Because *full-address decoding,* or the decoding of all eight port address bits, is not used in our address decoding scheme, a little thought will reveal that the ports we have selected, 80H and 81H, can be replaced in Table 10-1 with ports F0H and F1H, respectively, or E0H and E7H, and so on. In either case, the active state of the MSB and LSB of the addressed port must be considered when enabling the 8251A for communication.

Full-Address Decoding
The decoding of a microprocessor's entire address bus to enable an I/O (input/output) port.

TABLE 10-1

Summary of 8085A Control Signals to Enable the 8251A

$\overline{CS}$	$\overline{WR}$	$\overline{RD}$	Instruction	A15	A8, C/$\overline{D}$	IO/$\overline{M}$	Action
0	0	1	OUT 81H	1	1	1	Send control word to 8251A
0	1	0	IN 81H	1	1	1	Receive status from 8251A
0	0	1	OUT 80H	1	0	1	Send data to 8251A
0	1	0	IN 80H	1	0	1	Receive data from 8251A

10.2 8251A BLOCK DIAGRAM AND PIN CONFIGURATION

A block diagram and pin assignment for the 8251A are shown in Figure 10-4. The internal functions of the 8251A can be grouped into the following categories:

1. Data bus
2. Read/write control logic
3. Transmitter section
4. Receiver section
5. Modem control

Table 10-2 lists the function of each of the 8251A's 28 pins by pin number and group.

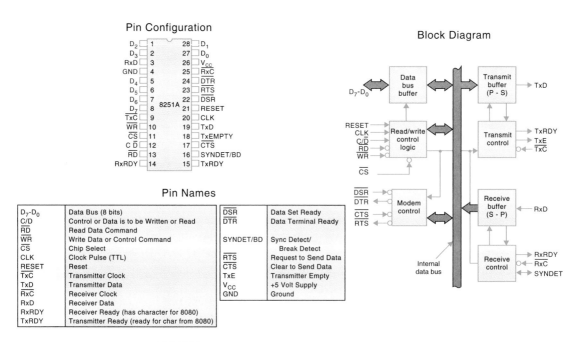

FIGURE 10-4

Block diagram and pin configuration for the 8251A. (Courtesy of Intel Corp.)

TABLE 10-2
Description of 8251A Pins

Pin Name	Pin No.	Group	Function
D7-D0	8, 7, 6, 5, 2, 1, 28, 27	Data bus	Eight-bit bidirectional data bus used for control, status, and data.
RESET	21	Read/write control logic	A HIGH on this line resets the 8251A to its idle mode. Internal registers and flags are cleared.
CLK	20		**Clock input:** Used to control the read/write timing between microprocessor and 8251A.
C/$\overline{\text{D}}$	12		**Control/data input:** When HIGH, data written to the 8251A are interpreted as **Control.** Data read are interpreted as **Status.** When LOW, data written and read from the 8251A are transmitted and received data, respectively. $\overline{\text{CS}}$ must be active with C/$\overline{\text{D}}$.
$\overline{\text{RD}}$	13		**READ:** A LOW on this line allows the CPU to read parallel data or status from the 8251A in accordance with the level of C/$\overline{\text{D}}$.
$\overline{\text{WR}}$	10		**Write:** A LOW on this line allows the CPU to write a control word or data word to the 8251A for serial transmission in accordance with the level of C/$\overline{\text{D}}$.
$\overline{\text{CS}}$	11		**Chip select:** A logic LOW on this pin enables the 8251A for communication.
TxD	19	Transmitter section	**Transmit data:** The transmitted serial data are output on this pin.
TxRdy	15		**Transmitter ready:** This line becomes active when the 8251A is ready to accept a data character from the CPU. It can be used for polling or interrupt I/O. TxRdy is reset when a byte is written to the Transmit Hold register.
TxE	18		**Transmit empty:** TXE will go HIGH when the 8251A has no further characters to transmit; that is, both the Transmit Hold and the Transmit Shift Registers are empty. TxE can be used to indicate the end of a transmission in half-duplex mode.
TxC	9		**Transmitter clock:** The frequency of this clock controls the baud rate of the serial data transmitted. The 8251A may be programmed to divide this clock frequency by 1, 16, or 64 to establish the desired baud rate.
RxD	3	Receiver section	**Receiver data:** Serial data are received on this pin.
RxRdy	14		**Receiver ready:** This line becomes active when the 8251A's Receiver Hold Register has a parallel data character ready for the CPU to read. It can be used by the CPU for polling or interrupt I/O. RxRdy is reset when the character is read by the CPU.

(continued)

TABLE 10-2
(continued)

Pin Name	Pin No.	Group	Function
RxC	25		**Receiver clock:** The frequency of this clock is a direct multiple of the baud rate of serial data in. The 8251A may be programmed to divide this clock by 1, 16, or 64 to equal the baud rate of serial data in.
SYNDET/BD	16		**Sync detect/break detect:** Used in the synchronous mode only. It is used as an input or output pin as programmed through the Control Word. As an output pin, a HIGH indicates that the receiver has detected the SYNC character and character sync has been achieved. As an input pin, a rising edge on this pin causes the 8251A to start assembling data characters on the next rising edge of the Receiver Clock pulse, RxC.
$\overline{\text{DSR}}$	22	Modem control	**Data set ready:** This input is normally used to indicate the readiness of a modem or data set. Its condition can be tested by the CPU through a Status Read operation (bit D7 of the status word).
$\overline{\text{DTR}}$	24		**Data terminal ready:** This output is normally used to indicate to a data set or modem the readiness of the DTE. It can be set LOW by programming bit D1 of the command instruction word.
$\overline{\text{CTS}}$	17		**Clear to send:** This input signal is normally used to test if a modem is ready to receive and transmit a character from the 8251A to a communications channel. A LOW on this pin from a modem enables the 8251A to transmit serial data if the TxEN bit in the command word is set.
$\overline{\text{RTS}}$	23		**Request to send:** This output signal is normally used to request sending of serial data to a modem. $\overline{\text{RTS}}$ is the handshake line to $\overline{\text{CTS}}$. It can be set LOW by programming bit D5 in the command instruction word.
V_{CC}	26	Power	+5-V supply.
GND	4		Ground.

10.3 INITIALIZING THE 8251A USART FOR COMMUNICATION

The 8251A must be programmed with a set of control words before transmitting or receiving serial data in either asynchronous or synchronous format. The control words define the complete functional definition of the 8251A and must be programmed immediately following an internal or external RESET.

The control words are split into two separate bytes that make up the Control Register within the Read/Write Control Logic block (Figure 10-5). These two bytes

Control Register	
Mode instruction (8)	Command instruction (8)

FIGURE 10-5
Control register format.

are referred to as the 8251A's *Mode Instruction* and *Command Instruction.* Both the Mode and Command Instructions must follow a specific sequence for proper communication to occur. This sequence is listed in Figure 10-6. Note that C/D = 1 for all control words. Recall that our address decoding scheme discussed earlier uses the LSB of the port address for the 8251A's C/D input. Writing to PORT 81H enables the 8251A for accepting a command from the CPU, because C/D = 1 when addressing PORT 81H.

After a RESET (internal or external), a Mode Instruction must then be written as the *first* command instruction to the 8251A. The 8251A automatically interprets this first word, after a RESET, as a Mode Instruction. It is the Mode Instruction that determines whether the 8251A is used for asynchronous or synchronous communications. If the Mode Instruction has been programmed for asynchronous communication, a Command Instruction must immediately follow it. If, however, the Mode Instruction is programmed for synchronous communication, one or two SYNC CHARACTERS must be written to the 8251A before a synchronous Command Instruction is issued. In each case, the 8251A's WR must be active and C/D = 1.

Mode Instruction
A control word sent to a *UART* that determines the baud rate factor, data character length, parity, and number of stop bits.

Command Instruction
A control word sent to a *UART* that enables or disables its transmitter and receiver section. Also used for flow control and resetting the UART.

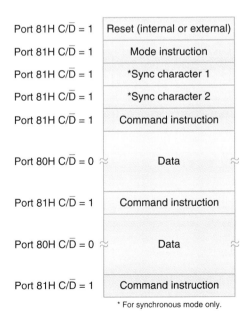

Port 81H C/D̄ = 1	Reset (internal or external)
Port 81H C/D̄ = 1	Mode instruction
Port 81H C/D̄ = 1	*Sync character 1
Port 81H C/D̄ = 1	*Sync character 2
Port 81H C/D̄ = 1	Command instruction
Port 80H C/D̄ = 0	Data
Port 81H C/D̄ = 1	Command instruction
Port 80H C/D̄ = 0	Data
Port 81H C/D̄ = 1	Command instruction

* For synchronous mode only.

FIGURE 10-6
Command sequence for the 8251A. (Courtesy of Intel Corp.)

10.3.1 Mode Instruction Definition for Asynchronous Communication

For asynchronous communication, the Mode Instruction word has the format illustrated in Figure 10-7(a). Note that the Mode Instruction determines the *baud rate factor, character length, parity,* and *number of stop bits.* Also, the least significant two bits of the Mode Instruction, D0 and D1, cannot be programmed LOW. If both bits are LOW, the synchronous mode is programmed. Figure 10-7(b) illustrates the data format of an asynchronous serial character.

10.3.2 Mode Instruction Definition for Synchronous Communication

For synchronous communication, the Mode Instruction has the format illustrated in Figure 10-8(a). The least significant bits, D0 and D1 here, are both LOW, indicating to the 8251A that this instruction is to be interpreted as a *synchronous* Mode Instruction. The remaining bits define the synchronous *character length* and *PARITY,* whether *syndet is internal or external,* and the *number of sync characters* (one or two). Figure 10-8(b) illustrates the data format of a synchronous serial character.

10.3.3 Command Instruction Definition

Once the 8251A's functional definition has been programmed by a Mode Instruction (and SYNC character/s have been loaded if the synchronous mode has been pro-

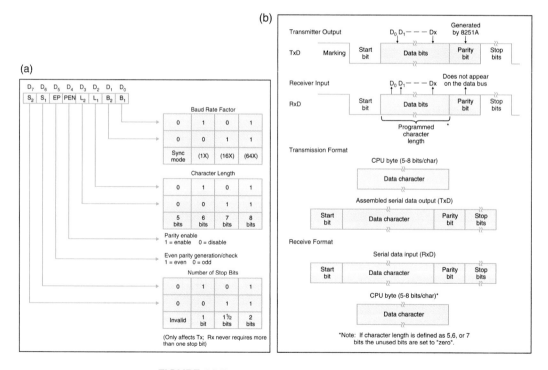

FIGURE 10-7

(a) Mode instruction format, asynchronous mode; (b) data format for an asynchronous serial character. (Courtesy of Intel Corp.)

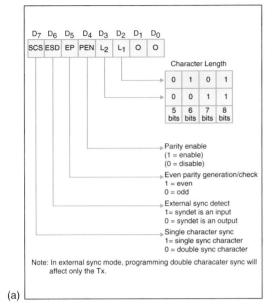

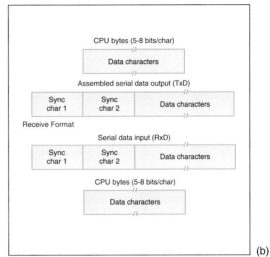

(a)

(b)

FIGURE 10-8
(a) Mode instruction format, synchronous mode; (b) data format for a synchronous serial character.

grammed), the Command Instruction is issued by the CPU. The Command Instruction format is the same for asynchronous and synchronous data communications (Figure 10-9). All control words written to the 8251A after the first Mode Instruction (and sync character if synchronous mode has been programmed) are interpreted by the 8251A as Command Instructions. Functions of the Command Instruction can, therefore, be changed at any time simply by outputting a new byte to port 81H.

What happens if the baud rate, character length, or any other function of the Mode Instruction needs to be changed? Referring to Figure 10-9, bit D6 of the Command Instruction is the Internal Reset Bit, IR. Because the 8251A can accept a Command Instruction at any time after the Mode Instruction, an Internal Reset can be issued at any time. This will allow us to send a new Mode Instruction, because the next command *after* a RESET is interpreted as such.

Once the Mode (and SYNC characters if synchronous mode has been programmed) and Command Instructions have been sent to the 8251A, serial transmission of data can occur by writing or reading to the 8251A from port 80H. In this case, $C/\overline{D} = 0$.

10.3.4 Status Read Definition

In data communication systems, it is often necessary to determine the status of the transmitting and receiving device. The 8251A USART can be polled at any time to ascertain if error or other conditions that may require processor intervention exist. To accomplish this function, the CPU issues a Status Read command to PORT 81H; that is, $C/\overline{D} = 1$ and $\overline{RD} = 0$. A status word is put onto the bus for the CPU to read. The Status Read word definition is listed in Figure 10-10.

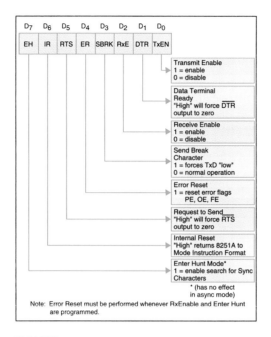

FIGURE 10-9

FIGURE 10-9
Command instruction format. (Courtesy of Intel Corp.)

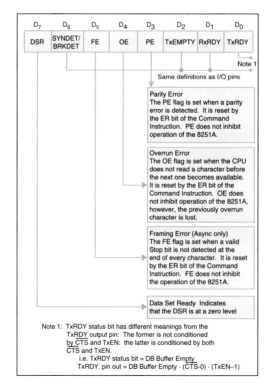

FIGURE 10-10
Status read format. (Courtesy of Intel Corp.)

10.4   ASYNCHRONOUS 4800-BAUD COMMUNICATION PROGRAM FOR THE 8251A USART

A program will now be developed to transmit asynchronous serial data from the 8251A USART to a terminal at 4800 baud. The setup discussed in Figure 10-1 will be used. Before we begin, however, we must first define the tasks of the program.

10.4.1   Program Task

1. Write an 8085A assembly language program to transmit your first and last name repeatedly to a terminal. The hardware setup is illustrated in Figure 10-1. Your name should occur on the display terminal once per line.
2. PORT 80H is to be used for data, and PORT 81H is to be used for Control and Status.
3. The program should be written under program Control I/O. Monitor the TxRdy bit of the Status Word for this task.
4. The following parameters should be specified in the initialization program:
   a. 4800 baud.
   b. 7-bit data character.
   c. One stop bit.
   d. Even parity generation.
5. Assume that RAM exists for your program from 2000H to 20FFH (256 bytes). ORG your program at location 2000H. Store ASCII characters that represent your first and last name (including carriage return and line feed) starting at memory location 2040H. Use a NULL BYTE 00H to terminate the end of your name.
6. Accompany your program with a flowchart. Be sure to construct your flowchart before you begin your program.

10.4.2   Mode Word Format

The *Mode Word* is 7BH. Bits D0 = 1 and D1 = 1 specify the asynchronous mode of operation with a baud rate factor of 64× the period of the CLK input: 1/[64 × (1/307.2 kHz)] = 4800. An easier approach is simply to divide the 8251A CLK input frequency by 64: (307.2 kHz)/64 = 4800. Bits D2 = 0 and D3 = 1 specify a 7-bit ASCII character. By setting D4 = 1 and D5 = 1, even parity will be generated for the parity bit. By setting D6 = 1 and D7 = 0, one stop bit will be sent with each character.

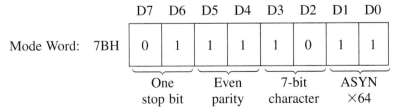

	D7	D6	D5	D4	D3	D2	D1	D0
Mode Word: 7BH	0	1	1	1	1	0	1	1

One stop bit   Even parity   7-bit character   ASYN ×64

10.4.3   Command Word Format

The format of the Command Word has been configured to enable the transmitter section of the 8251A to send data. This is accomplished by setting bit D0 = 1 of the Command Word. Because our program task does not include use of the receiver section of the 8251A, the receiver will be disabled, D2 = 0. This being the case, there is no need to monitor error-checking flags FE, OE, and PE of the Status Word. The Error Reset bit, D4 = 1, will be set as a precautionary measure to clear these flags. These flags are defined in Section 10.4.4.

D6, the Internal Reset bit, will initially be set in our program to internally reset the 8251A and to ensure that the first command sent to the 8251A is interpreted as a Mode Word. If this bit is always set, the Command Word will never be interpreted by the 8251A. Instead, a Mode Word will always be expected. Assuming that the 8251A has already been reset, we will set D6 = 0.

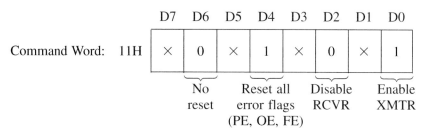

10.4.4 Status Word Format

The Status Word can be read into the 8085A accumulator by the instruction IN 81H (see Table 10-1). Once the 8251A has been initialized, our program must monitor the Transmit Ready bit, TxRDY, of the Status Word. When this bit is a logic HIGH, the transmitter section of the 8251A is ready and a parallel word can be sent from the 8085A to the 8251A. By outputting a data word to PORT 80H, our decoding circuit will enable the 8251A to accept the data word from the 8085A. The 8251A will then begin its internal procedure to transmit the character in serial form. The character will be transmitted serially in accordance with the Mode Word previously sent. Until the 8251A is ready to accept another character from the 8085A, TxRDY will remain a logic LOW. Our program can wait in an idle loop, continuously testing the state of the TxRDY bit, or it can be off performing other tasks, periodically testing the status of TxRDY. This concept is referred to as *polling*. In either case, the 8085A is under *program control I/O;* that is, the program is under the control of the peripheral device, in this case the USART. The flowchart and program to accomplish our overall task are illustrated in Figure 10-11. Directives (END, DB, and so on) should be added to the program if an assembler is used.

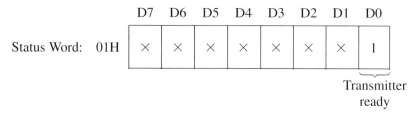

10.5 ERROR DETECTION: PE, OE, AND FE

The Status Word in our program has been masked of all bits, except for D0, the TxRDY bit. The remaining bits are not checked. If our program task were to include the reception of characters from the terminal, we might want to check for the detection of

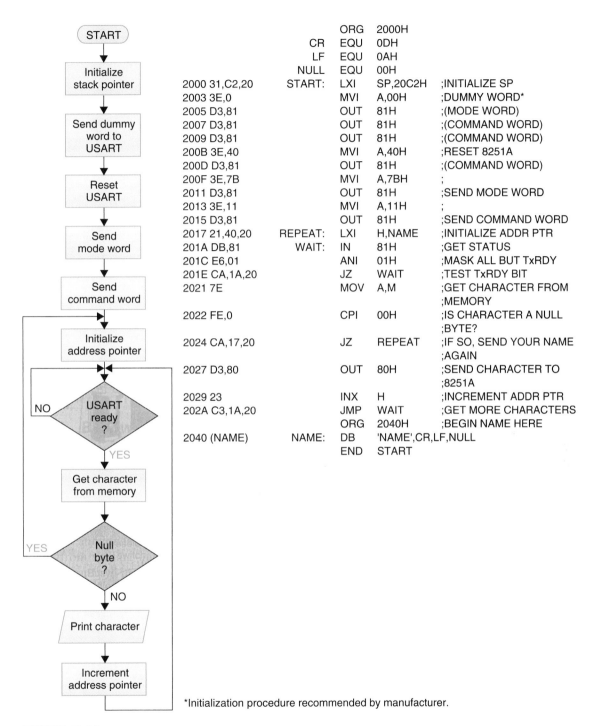

```
                                ORG    2000H
                          CR    EQU    0DH
                          LF    EQU    0AH
                          NULL  EQU    00H
2000 31,C2,20   START:    LXI    SP,20C2H    ;INITIALIZE SP
2003 3E,0                 MVI    A,00H       ;DUMMY WORD*
2005 D3,81                OUT    81H         ;(MODE WORD)
2007 D3,81                OUT    81H         ;(COMMAND WORD)
2009 D3,81                OUT    81H         ;(COMMAND WORD)
200B 3E,40                MVI    A,40H       ;RESET 8251A
200D D3,81                OUT    81H         ;(COMMAND WORD)
200F 3E,7B                MVI    A,7BH       ;
2011 D3,81                OUT    81H         ;SEND MODE WORD
2013 3E,11                MVI    A,11H       ;
2015 D3,81                OUT    81H         ;SEND COMMAND WORD
2017 21,40,20   REPEAT:   LXI    H,NAME      ;INITIALIZE ADDR PTR
201A DB,81      WAIT:     IN     81H         ;GET STATUS
201C E6,01                ANI    01H         ;MASK ALL BUT TxRDY
201E CA,1A,20             JZ     WAIT        ;TEST TxRDY BIT
2021 7E                   MOV    A,M         ;GET CHARACTER FROM
                                             ;MEMORY
2022 FE,0                 CPI    00H         ;IS CHARACTER A NULL
                                             ;BYTE?
2024 CA,17,20             JZ     REPEAT      ;IF SO, SEND YOUR NAME
                                             ;AGAIN
2027 D3,80                OUT    80H         ;SEND CHARACTER TO
                                             ;8251A
2029 23                   INX    H           ;INCREMENT ADDR PTR
202A C3,1A,20             JMP    WAIT        ;GET MORE CHARACTERS
                          ORG    2040H       ;BEGIN NAME HERE
2040 (NAME)     NAME:     DB     'NAME',CR,LF,NULL
                          END    START
```

*Initialization procedure recommended by manufacturer.

FIGURE 10-11
An 8085A communications program to transmit your name to a VDT.

error conditions. Problem 10, at the end of the chapter, includes a task to check error flags. A definition of these flags can be found in the Status Read Format of Figure 10-10. Additional clarification of these flags is necessary at this time to complete problem 10.

10.5.1 PE: Parity Error

Perhaps the most simplified method of error checking is parity. Although it is not 100% accurate, it does allow some assurance that the transmitted data are equivalent to the received data. Parity can be set to either *even* or *odd* by a transmitting device. The receiving device must set itself accordingly. For even parity generation, the transmitter section of the 8251A sets the parity bit to a level that makes the total number of 1s in the character *even* (not including the start and stop bits). The opposite is true for odd parity. Consider the examples of both even and odd parity generation shown in Table 10-3.

In our example program in Figure 10-11, the Mode Word was set for odd parity. The 8251A will generate an odd parity bit for all characters transmitted to the terminal. Programming the 8251A for odd parity also enables the receiver section of the 8251A to perform an odd parity check on characters received from the terminal. Whether we are sending or receiving characters to or from the terminal, it is necessary to set the terminal features (baud rate, stop bit length, parity, and so on) to be compatible to what the 8251A has been programmed for.

The PE, *parity error,* flag will set if the 8251A receives a character whose parity bit does not correspond to the number of 1s set in the character. The PE flag can be monitored by reading the 8251A Status Word, bit D3. If an error has been detected, that is, PE = 1, the program must take the necessary steps to notify the operator of the error condition. The 8251A will otherwise continue with its operations. PE can be reset through a Command Instruction to the 8251A. SETTING the ER *(error reset)* bit, D4, of the Command Word and outputting it to port 81H will accomplish this. Chapter 17 looks closer at the advantages and disadvantages of parity checking.

If a program were written to receive characters from a terminal (or DTE) and perform a parity check, an error condition should be forced to test if the error-checking capability of the 8251A is functioning. This can be accomplished by setting the parity of the terminal *opposite* to that for which the program is testing. If the 8251A has been programmed for odd parity and the terminal is set for even parity, a character received from the terminal will be tested for the number of 1 bits set. The parity bit of the received character will then be tested against this number of odd parity.

> **Parity Error**
> Indicates that the total number of 1 bits in a received character disagrees with the even or odd parity bit sent with the character.

TABLE 10-3
Examples of Even and Odd Parity

	Start Bit	7-Bit Data	Parity Bit	Stop Bit
Odd parity	0	1 0 1 1 0 0 1	1	1
	0	0 1 0 0 1 0 1	0	1
Even parity	0	1 1 1 0 1 0 0	0	1
	0	0 0 1 1 0 1 0	1	1

Its state will be opposite the state for which the 8251A is testing (assuming that the received character has an even number of 1 bits). As a result, the 8251A SETS its PE flag.

10.5.2   OE: Overrun Error

When a serial character is received by the 8251A from the DTE, the processor is notified when the character has been assembled into parallel format and is ready to be read. This can occur by interrupting the processor with the 8251A's RxRDY pin or through the program's polling procedure whereby the 8251A's RxRDY, bit D1, or the Status Word is monitored. If the processor does not read the available character before the next one is available, an *overrun error* occurs, and the previous character is destroyed. The 8251A will SET its OE flag, bit D4, of the Status Word.

Overrun Error
When a CPU does not read an available character from a buffer before the next one is available. The previous character is destroyed.

Suppose that the 8251A were programmed to receive characters from DTE at a baud rate of 4800. Then, the maximum number of characters per second (cps) that can be sent by DTE is 480, assuming a 10-bit character length, is:

$$4800 \text{ bps} \times \frac{1 \text{ character}}{10 \text{ bits}} = 480 \text{ cps}$$

The characters, in this case, would have to be sent in a contiguous manner; that is, the start bit of the next character must directly follow the stop bit of the preceding character. RxRDY would have to be polled at least every 2.083 ms (1/480 = 2.083 ms), or a character from DTE would be lost. Reading the character before the next one is available, however, will prevent OE from setting. A read will also reset the 8251A's RxRDY pin and status bit, D1, of the Status Word. This will allow the 8251A to inform the CPU when the next character is available.

The 8251A's OE bit of its Status Word can also be intentionally set for testing this error-checking feature. This can easily be accomplished by programming the 8251A to receive serial data from DTE and taking longer to read it than it takes DTE to send it. An example, using the setup described in Figure 10-1, would be to initialize the 8251A to receive data from the terminal. Once the initialization portion of the program is complete, a breakpoint or a delay loop can be executed. The 8251A, operating independently of the CPU at this time, will continue its operation, seeking characters typed in from the terminal. Because the CPU is not reading the available character before the next one has been assembled by the 8251A, OE will set. The Status Word can be checked at this time to verify if the overrun error condition has been detected. OE does not inhibit the operation of the 8251A but will remain set until it is cleared through a Command Instruction to the 8251A.

10.5.3   FE: Framing Error

Chapter 9 described how the UART's receiver section samples serial data sent from DTE to determine the level of each bit. The baud rate must be known beforehand for the receiver to sample the serial data at the center of each bit. The last bit sampled is the stop bit. Because the state of the stop bit (and start bit) is already known, the question may arise as to why this last sample is even necessary. The purpose of checking this last bit is to ensure that the character has been properly *framed*. Framing of an asynchronous character occurs when a UART's receiver section has synchronized with the start and stop bits of the character. If the state of the last bit is not a logic 1,

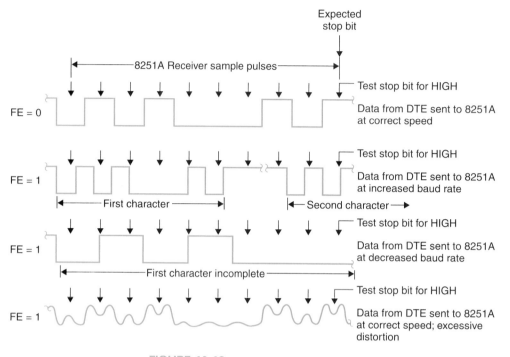

FIGURE 10-12
Conditions that will cause a FRAMING ERROR.

| Framing Error |
| When a receiver loses sync with the incoming data. |

opposite that of the start bit, a *framing error*, FE, has occurred. The 8251A will set its FE flag, bit D5, of its Status Word.

Framing errors can occur in several situations, many of which the 8251A is capable of flagging. Let us consider some of these conditions:

- The data sent by the DTE are faster than what the 8251A has been programmed to receive.
- The data sent by the DTE are slower than what the 8251A has been programmed to receive.
- The transmitted data from DTE becomes distorted en route to the 8251A.
- The 8251A's receiver clock, RxC, frequency is off.

Figure 10-12 illustrates conditions that result in a framing error, FE. Bit D5 of the Status Word would be set. The occurrence of FE does not inhibit the operation of the 8251A. Here, again, it is up to the program to take immediate steps to notify the operator of the error condition. FE can be reset through a Command Instruction by setting the ER bit (error reset), D4, of the Command Word and outputting it to PORT 81H.

10.6 INTRODUCTION TO THE 16550A HIGH-SPEED UART

Higher transmission rates, compatibility requirements, and increased independence of CPU intervention have influenced new UART designs. Like most other peripheral devices, UARTs have become faster, more integrated, and less expensive. For example, today's high-speed modems and serial interfaces operating at 28.8 kbps and higher require a UART with improved performance beyond the 8251A UART discussed earlier. The industry standard that meets the minimum requirement for transmission rates today is the 16550A UART. Advanced features of the 16550A UART have enabled it to maintain compatibility with the latest CPU technology and the thousands of PC-based programs that are continually being offered.

10.6.1   The 16550A UART Features

From a functional standpoint, the 16550A is equivalent to the 8251A UART discussed earlier. The following features have been retained:

- Microprocessor compatible
- Programmable baud rate, parity, data word size, and number of stop bits
- Transmit and receive buffering
- Framing, parity, and overrun error detection
- Complete status reporting
- Interrupt reporting
- False start bit detection
- Modem control (RTS, CTS, DTR, DSR)
- Independent receiver clock

The original UART installed in the first IBM PC was the 8250. It can be found in IBM PCs and XTs. The chip was upgraded to A and B versions to eliminate timing and interface problems. Transmission speed was limited to 9600 baud. The 8250 was eventually replaced by the 16450 UART, which retained the same architecture but featured programmable baud rates of up to 38,400. The 16450 UART can be found in IBM AT systems. The 16550A is an improved version of the 16540 and is capable of driving RS-232 and RS-422A interfaces at baud rates up to 256 kbaud using an 8-MHz crystal for its clock circuit. In addition to the features stated earlier, the 16550A includes new features not offered by its predecessors:

- Baud rate generation from 50 to 256 kbaud
- Sixteen-byte transmit and receive FIFO (First-In-First-Out) buffers
- DMA (Direct Memory Access) signaling
- Decreased access intervention time between CPU and UART
- Improved interrupt structure

The FIFO buffers are two 16 bit deep–by–8 bit wide (16 bytes) memory sections embedded in the 16550A's transmit and receive architecture. The transmit FIFO holds data for the transmitter, and the receive FIFO holds data for the receiver. Their purpose is to reduce the number of interrupts presented to the CPU. The concept is similar to the double-buffering action discussed for the transmit and receive sections of the 8251A. The difference is that the FIFO buffers for the 16550A can hold up to 16 characters instead of two used for double buffering.

The interrupt architecture of the 16550A, like the 16540, includes an interrupt enable register. Five types of UART interrupts can be enabled or disabled through software control: Receiver Error Flag, Received Data Available, Timeout (FIFO mode only), Transmit Hold Register Empty, and Modem Status. The five interrupts are fully prioritized. The advantage of the 16550A's interrupt architecture over those of its predecessors is built-in, time-saving features that minimize CPU intervention when an interrupt occurs.

To further reduce CPU interventions, the 16550A provides a *direct memory access (DMA)* request feature included in its predecessors. DMA permits the UART to

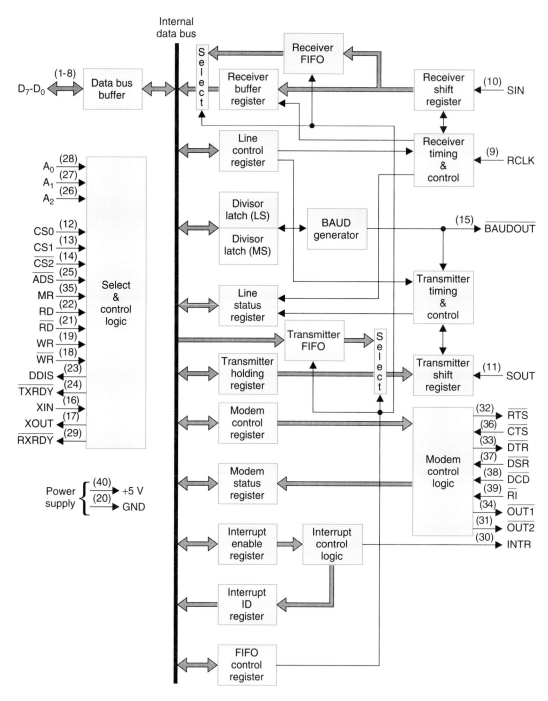

Note: Applicable pin-out numbers are included within parenthesis.

FIGURE 10-13

Block diagram of National Semiconductor's NS16550AF UART. (Courtesy of National Semiconductor Corp.)

Dual-In-Line Package

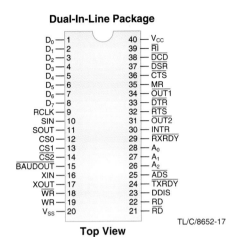

TL/C/8652-17

Top View

Order Number NS16550AFN
See NS Package Number N40A

Chip Carrier Package

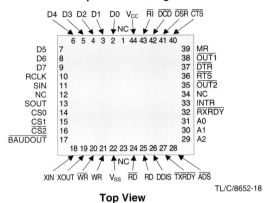

TL/C/8652-18

Top View

Order Number NS16550AFV
See NS Package Number V44A

TABLE I. UART Reset Configuration

Register/Signal	Reset Control	Reset State		
Interrupt Enable Register	Master Reset	**0000**	0000	(Note 1)
Interrupt Identification Register	Master Reset	0000	0001	
FIFO Control	Master Reset	0000	0000	
Line Control Register	Master Reset	0000	0000	
MODEM Control Register	Master Reset	**0000**	0000	
Line Status Register	Master Reset	0110	0000	
MODEM Status Register	Master Reset	XXX	0000	(Note 2)
SOUT	Master Reset	High		
INTR (RCVR Errs)	Read LSR/MR	Low		
INTR (RCVR Data Ready)	Read RBR/MR	Low		
INTR (THRE)	Read IIR/Write THR/MR	Low		
INTR (Modem Status Changes)	Read MSR/MR	Low		
OUT 2	Master Reset	High		
RTS	Master Reset	High		
DTR	Master Reset	High		
OUT 1	Master Reset	High		
RCVR FIFO	MR/FCR1•FCR0/ΔFCR0	All Bits Low		
XMIT FIFO	MR/FCR1•FCR0/ΔFCR0	All Bits Low		

Note 1: Boldface bits are permanently low.
Note 2: Bits 7–4 are driven by the input signals.

FIGURE 10-14

Pin-out diagram for the NS16550AF UART. (Courtesy of National Semiconductor Corp.)

This shows the basic connections of an NS16550AF to an 8088 CPU

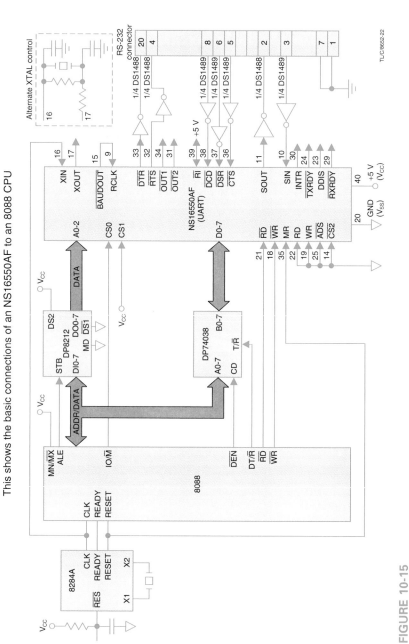

FIGURE 10-15

Basic connection of the NS16550AF UART to an 8088 microprocessor. (Courtesy of National Semiconductor Corp.)

communicate directly with memory without CPU intervention. Two DMA modes are supported: *single-mode transfer,* and *multiuser transfer.* These modes allow the UART to interface to higher performance DMA units that can interleave their transfers between CPU cycles or execute multiple byte transfers.*

A block diagram of National Semiconductor's NS16550AF is shown in Figure 10-13 on page 252. Figure 10-14 shows the pin-out diagram, and Figure 10-15 shows an example of a basic connection of the NS16550AF UART to an 8088 microprocessor.

A detailed discussion of the NS16550AF UART can be found in National Semiconductor's *Data Communications, Local Area Networks, and UARTs Handbook* (1990, pp. 4–58). For increased FIFO buffering and even higher baud rates, the 16560 is now available.

PROBLEMS

1. Draw the TTL waveform for the ASCII character @ as it would appear on an oscilloscope at the input and output of a TTL to RS-232 level translator such as the MAX232 IC. Label all voltage levels. Use odd parity.
2. Define *partial-address decoding.*
3. What function does the 8251A perform when its $\overline{C/D}$ line is:
   a. A logic HIGH?
   b. A logic LOW?
4. After resetting the 8251A, what is the first instruction that is necessary to condition the USART for communications?
5. What type of instruction is necessary to command the 8251A for asynchronous operation?
6. What type of instruction is necessary to command the 8251A for receiving data only?
7. Given the circuit shown in Figure 10-1, determine the mode word format for programming the 8251A for the following conditions: two stop bits, odd parity, 7-bit data, and 19.2 kbaud.
8. Given the circuit shown in Figure 10-1, what command word format would be necessary to enable both the transmitter and receiver sections of the 8251A and reset all error flags?
9. Explain why the internal reset bit is contained within the Command Word instead of the Mode Word.
10. For the program listed in Figure 10-11, what modifications would be necessary to halt the processor if a framing, parity, or overrun error occurred?
11. Define *framing error, overrun error,* and *parity error.*
12. Determine the parity bit ($\times$) for the following data words:
    a. 110101 $\times$ (odd)
    b. 100110 $\times$ (odd)
    c. 111000 $\times$ (even)
    d. 101110 $\times$ (even)
13. What are the minimum and maximum baud rates that the 16550A UART can be programmed for?
14. How many bytes does the 16550A UART's F1F0 memory store?

Data Communications, Local Area Networks, and UARTs Handbook (National Semiconductor Corp. 1990) pp. 4–58.

11

THE TELEPHONE SET AND SUBSCRIBER LOOP INTERFACE

Alexander Graham Bell, inventor of the telephone, once theorized that if an electrical current could be made to vary in intensity precisely as the air waves vary in density during the production of speech, then speech could be transmitted over electrical wires. Bell, a Scotsman who emigrated to Canada, set out to invent such a device, called the *telephone.* In 1876, he transmitted a complete sentence to his assistant located in another room. Since then, the telephone set has emerged as one of the most widely used electrical devices in the world. It is estimated more than 1 billion telephone sets are in operation worldwide today.

This chapter presents the fundamental principles governing the theory and operating specifications of the telephone set and subscriber loop interface. An in-depth look at caller ID (identification) signaling specifications and line conditioning is also presented.

11.1 BASIC FUNCTIONS OF THE TELEPHONE SET

Before discussing the operation of the telephone set, let us consider some of the basic functions that it serves:

1. The telephone set must notify the user of an incoming call through an audible tone such as a ring or bell.
2. The telephone set must transduce a caller's speech to electrical signals. Conversely, electrical signals must be transduced to audible speech signals.
3. A method of dialing subscriber numbers must be incorporated into the telephone set. This may be accomplished through dial pulses or tones.
4. The telephone set must regulate the speech amplitude of the calling party by compensating for the varying distances to the local telephone company, also known as the *central office.*
5. The telephone set must gain the attention of the central office when a user requests service by lifting the handset.

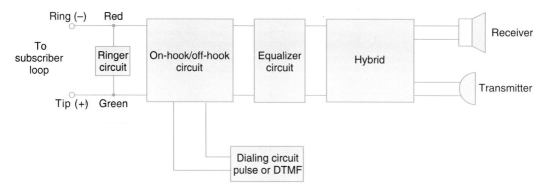

FIGURE 11-1
Block diagram of the telephone set.

6. The telephone set must provide a nominal amount of feedback from its microphone to its speaker so that a user can hear himself or herself speaking. This feedback is called *sidetone.* Sidetone regulates how loudly one speaks.
7. When the telephone set is not in use, an open-circuit DC path must be provided to the central office.
8. In addition to receiving voice, the telephone set should also be capable of receiving call progress tones (busy, ringing, and so on) from the central office.

A block diagram of the conventional telephone set is shown in Figure 11-1. The dialing circuit shown is used to dial the person with whom the caller wishes to speak. A standard rotary dial switch or the more modern *dual-tone multifrequency (DTMF)* keypad is used. When placing or answering a call, the telephone is lifted off of its cradle and the on-hook/off-hook circuit engages the telephone set to the telephone system. Power for the telephone set is derived from a −48 V DC supply located at the central office. The power is delivered to the telephone set via the *subscriber loop.* Because most subscriber loops are two-wire pairs, a *hybrid* circuit is necessary to transform the two-wire transmission line into four wires, thus separating the telephone set's transmitted and received signals. Full-duplex operation is made possible. To compensate for the varying lengths of wire between the central office and its subscribers, *equalizer* circuits are incorporated into the telephone set to regulate voice amplitudes.

11.1.1 Telephone Transmitter

The transmitter for the telephone set is essentially a microphone. It is the part of the handset into which the person speaks. The function of the transmitter is to convert acoustical energy generated from speech into electrical energy, which is transmitted onto the subscriber loop. Figure 11-2 illustrates a cross-sectional view of the transmitter.

The DC current provided by the telephone system is passed through two electrodes separated by thousands of carbon granules. One electrode is attached to a diaphragm that vibrates in response to the acoustical pressures of sound. The opposite electrode is supported by the handset molding. Vibration of the diaphragm causes the contact resistance between the two electrodes to vary inversely with pressure. As the resistance varies, the current varies inversely, thereby translating the acoustical mes-

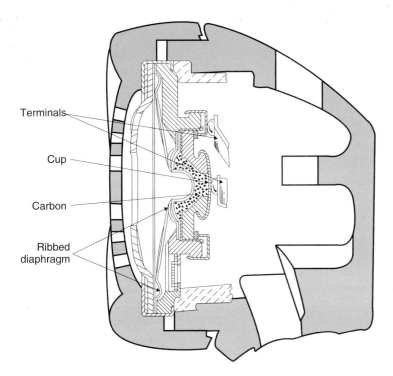

FIGURE 11-2
Cross-sectional view of the telephone transmitter. (Courtesy of Bell Laboratories.)

sage into the electrical signal that is transmitted to the central office. The central office, in turn, routes the electrical signal to its destination.

11.1.2   Telephone Receiver

Figure 11-3 is a cross-sectional view of the telephone set's receiver. The receiver is
essentially a speaker used to transduce a voice-generated AC signal back to sound. A
permanent magnet is used to produce a constant magnetic field. Insulated wire is
wound around the permanent magnet to form a coil, which passes the AC signal. The
magnetic field produced by the varying AC signal aids and opposes the existing permanent magnetic field. The resulting force causes the metallic diaphragm to vibrate.
The vibrating diaphragm produces sound waves corresponding to the original sound
waves delivered to the transmitter.

11.1.3   Telephone Ringer

The function of the *ringer* is to alert the party of an incoming call. The audible tone
generated by the ringer must be loud enough for the party to hear from a distance.
Several variations of ringers are used in today's telephone sets. The most popular type
is the conventional bell type shown in Figure 11-4. Buzzers, horns, lights, and more
recently, semiconductor sound generators with driven speakers are also used as ringers.
In the United States, telephone companies will *ring* the called party with an AC
ringing signal, typically 90 V_{rms} at 20 Hz. The ring signal is superimposed on the

> **Ringer**
> The ringing device on
> a telephone used to
> alert the party of an in-
> coming call. Activated
> by a 90 V_{rms} signal sent
> by the central office.

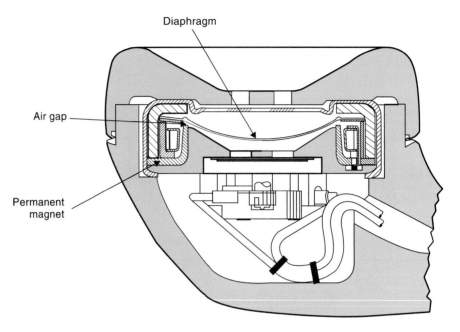

Diaphragm

Air gap

Permanent magnet

FIGURE 11-3
Cross-sectional view of the telephone receiver. (Courtesy of Bell Laboratories.)

existing −48 V DC signal. Figure 11-5 illustrates the ring signal. The two coils shown in Figure 11-4 are wound in a manner that causes the pivoting hammer to strike each bell on alternate parts of the cycle. Two dissimilar metals are used for each bell to produce the familiar ringing sound. A capacitor is used to block DC current and pass the AC ringing current. Its value, combined with the coil inductance, is selected to provide a high impedance to voice frequencies.

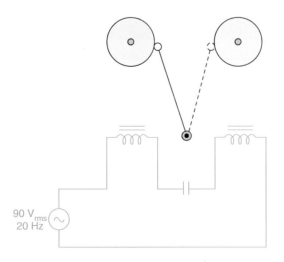

90 V$_{rms}$
20 Hz

FIGURE 11-4
Telephone ringer.

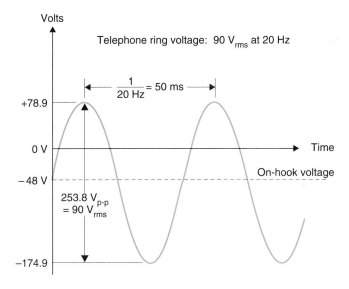

FIGURE 11-5
Ringing voltage for the telephone set.

11.1.4   Telephone Hybrid

The telephone set's *hybrid* is used to interface the transmitter and receiver's individually paired wires to a single pair for the subscriber loop. A multiple winding transformer is wound in a manner to electrically separate the transmitted and received signals. This permits simultaneous transmission and reception of speech, or what is more commonly referred to as *full-duplex operation.*

11.1.4.1   Sidetone   A balancing network included in the hybrid circuit allows the manufacturer to adjust a small amount of feedback from the telephone set's transmitter to its receiver. This feedback is called *sidetone.* Sidetone allows the person speaking into the handset to hear himself or herself talking. Tests have shown that when the sidetone is adjusted properly, a person can determine how loudly to speak based on the level of the sidetone presented to the receiver. If the sidetone is adjusted too small, the person talking tends to speak too loudly to compensate for the lack of hearing himself or herself at the receiver. Conversely, too much sidetone causes the speaker to lower his or her voice, making it difficult for the receiving party to hear what is being said.

> **Hybrid**
> The balancing circuit in a telephone used to separate the transmit (mic) and receiver (speaker) signals onto the two-wire subscriber loop.

> **Full-Duplex Operation**
> Simultaneous transmission and reception.

> **Sidetone**
> The small amount of signal fed back from a telephone's mic to its speaker that allows the callers to hear themselves while speaking.

11.2   ROTARY DIALING WITH THE BELL 500 TELEPHONE

The Bell 500 telephone was first introduced in 1951 and for more than four decades has been an industry standard. Although it is slowly being replaced by DTMF-type telephones, it remains one of the most widely used telephones throughout the world. Figure 11-6 illustrates the Bell 500 model and its schematic diagram.

Switches S1 and S2 are the on-hook/off-hook switches that open and close when the handset is engaged and disengaged from its cradle. The two switches work in

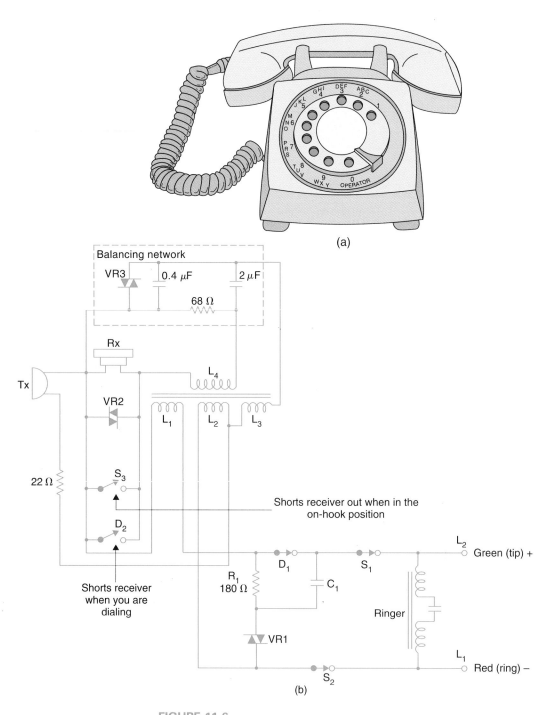

Balancing network

VR3 0.4 μF 2 μF

68 Ω

Rx

Tx

L₄

VR2

L₁ L₂ L₃

22 Ω

S₃

Shorts receiver out when in the
on-hook position

D₂

Shorts receiver
when you are
dialing

R₁
180 Ω

D₁

C₁

S₁

L₂
○ Green (tip) +

Ringer

VR1

L₁
○ Red (ring) −

S₂

(b)

FIGURE 11-6

(a) Bell 500 telephone set; (b) schematic diagram of the Bell 500 telephone set.

unison with each other. When the phone is resting in its cradle, the two switches are *open*. This is called the *on-hook condition*. Note that the ringer circuit is connected to the telephone system, whereas the telephone set itself is disconnected. When a call is placed, the handset is lifted off its cradle and S1 and S2 *close*. This is called the *off-hook condition*. The normal −48 V DC on-hook voltage supplied by the telephone company drops to approximately −5 to −8 V DC due to the impedance that the telephone set presents to the line. The DC current begins to flow in the subscriber loop as a result of going off-hook. This current flow is detected by the central office, which, in turn, sends a dial tone to the caller indicating that service is available and a number may be dialed. The subscriber loop current can range anywhere from 20 to 120 mA, depending on loop length and the impedance of the telephone circuit.

The rotary dial has 10 finger positions and a finger stop. Each position on the dial is represented by a number or group of letters. With the exception of 0, the dialing process generates pulses equal to the number being dialed. Dialing a 1, for example, generates one pulse; dialing a two generates two pulses; and so forth. Dialing a 0 produces 10 pulses. Pulses are generated by *making* and *breaking* contact with the line with switch D1.

Dialing is accomplished in the off-hook condition with the rotary dial switch, D1. Initially, D1 is closed. Going off-hook causes switches S1 and S2 to close and S3 to open. A current path is established to the receiver and transmitter, and a dial tone can be heard. Rotating the dial wheel to the finger stop winds a spring within the dialing assembly. Switch D2 closes during the process. This shorts the receiver out and prevents clicking noise from being heard at the receiver. Dial pulses are not generated at this point. When the dial wheel is released from the finger stop, the internal spring unwinds, rotating the dial back to its original rest position. During this release time, the dial pulses are generated. A cam, driven by gears turned by the revolving dial shaft, opens switch D1 for 60 ms (on-hook equivalent) and closes it for 40 ms (off-hook equivalent), thus creating a dial pulse. The number of times that the switch opens and closes is equal to the digit dialed or the number of dial pulses generated. A speed *governor* is included in the dial assembly to maintain a constant angular velocity as the dial returns to its rest position. This regulates the period of each pulse at 100 ms or a 10-Hz rate. Switch D2 opens at this time, activating the receiver until the next digit is dialed. Figure 11-7 illustrates the pulses generated when the number 6 is dialed. Nominal values for both current and voltage are shown. The idle time between digits is called the *interdigit time*. Phone companies limit the caller to approximately 10 seconds before the next digit must be dialed.

> **On-Hook Condition**
> The condition when a telephone set's hand piece is hung up. No current flows in the subscriber loop line in this condition.

> **Off-Hook Condition**
> The condition when a telephone set's handpiece is lifted off of it's cradle. Current then flows in the subscriber loop line, notifying the central office of the need for dial tone.

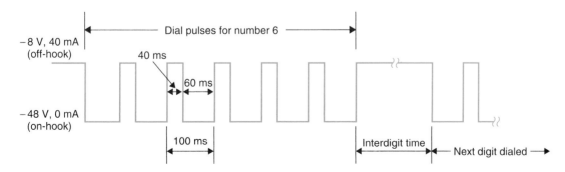

FIGURE 11-7
Dial pulses generated for the number 6.

11.2.1 Telephone Gain Control

Virtually every telephone set connected to the central office has a different subscriber loop length. As a result, a large variation in line resistance exists between each customer. Because each telephone is sourced from the same supply voltage at the central office, subscriber loop currents can range anywhere from 20 mA for longer loops to 120 mA for shorter loops. The telephone set must compensate for this variation by employing some type of gain-controlling mechanism; otherwise, the signal amplitude at the telephone set's receiver would diminish with increasing distance from the phone company.

To maintain constant transmit and receive amplitudes, *varistors* VR1 through VR3 are used. The varistor is a semiconductor device whose resistance varies *inversely* with current. By placing the varistor across the receiver line and balancing network as shown in Figure 11-6, large signals transmitted and received from shorter loop lengths are shunted through the varistor. For weak signals resulting from longer loop lengths, the varistor acts as a high impedance, thus permitting most of the signal to flow either through the receiver or out to the line.

The varistor also acts as a transient suppressor for excessive voltage spikes generated each time the dial switch makes and breaks contact with the line during dialing. These transients are produced by the interruption of line current through the ringer coil [$e_l = L(di/dt)$]. Capacitor C_1 and resistor R_1 further suppress the transients and prevent sparking across the dial contacts. This portion of the telephone circuit is often referred to as an *antitinkle* circuit, because without it, a tinkling noise produced by the high-voltage spikes across the ringer can be heard when dialing.

11.3 ELECTRONIC PULSE DIALING TELEPHONE

Many of the circuits discussed thus far are gradually being replaced with semiconductor integrated circuits (ICs). Single-chip ICs are now available that perform dialing and ringing functions and more. Memory and control circuits are included in these ICs for storing and automatically dialing telephone numbers. The *electronic pulse dialing telephone* incorporates much of this technology. This type of telephone is compatible with electromechanical switching facilities at the central office. Instead of a rotary dial switch, a keypad is used to enter the telephone number to the controlling IC. Although numbers can be rapidly entered with a keypad, the dial pulses generated are identical to those produced by the rotary dial switch (see Figure 11-7).

Electronic ringing circuits have replaced the old electromechanical bell with piezoelectric transducers driven by oscillators. These circuits are less costly and take up considerably less space. A major disadvantage, however, is that the ringing intensity produced by some of the transducers are significantly less than that of the conventional bell type. To bolster the electronic ringer, some manufacturers have equipped telephones with multitone oscillators and power amplifiers that drive speakers.

Memory within the IC permits the *redial* function. This function is useful when a line is busy and the caller wants to redial at some later time the last number entered, even if the phone has been placed back on-hook. By depressing the redial key, the telephone automatically redials the last phone number entered.

11.4 DUAL-TONE MULTIFREQUENCY

A much more efficient means of providing the dialing function of the telephone set is through the use of *dual-tone multifrequency (DTMF)*. DTMF is also known as *Touch Tone*. Most central offices are equipped to handle both Touch Tone and dial pulses.

Varistor
A semiconductor device, whose resistance varies inversely with current, used as a gain-controlling mechanism (in telephones) to maintain constant transmit and receive amplitudes.

Electronic Pulse Dialing Telephone
Recent electronic telephones using semiconductor devices to generate dial pulses equivalent to the old rotary dial telephone.

Dual-Tone Multifrequency (DTMF)
The signal generated by depressing any of the key pads on a telephone set. More commonly referred to as "touch tone."

In a Touch Tone telephone, a push-button keypad is provided for entering digits instead of a rotary dial. The arrangement of the keypad is shown in Figure 11-8. There are 12 keys corresponding to the numbers 0 through 9 and the characters * and #. Some keypads include four additional keys, A through D, for special control functions. Four rows and four columns of keys form a frequency matrix consisting of a *low band* and a *high band* of frequencies. The frequencies for each row and column are separated by a difference of approximately 10%, whereas the two bands of frequencies are separated by a difference of approximately 25%.

When a key is depressed, two tones are generated and sent to the telephone company for processing: one from the low band of frequencies, and one from the high band. The digit 6, for example, generates a 770-Hz tone and a 1477-Hz tone. Figure 11-9 illustrates the waveform generated by the electrical sum of these two tones. Frequency tolerances are specified at ±1.5% for the telephone set's DTMF generator and ±2% at the receiving central office. These stringent tolerances prevent the telephone company from detecting erroneous digits or characters. For the same reason, DTMF frequencies have been carefully selected so that they are not *harmonically* related to each other. The second and third harmonics for the digit 1, for example, include the following low- and high-band frequencies:

	Fundamental	Second Harmonic	Third Harmonic
High-band frequency (Hz)	1209	2418	3627
Low-band frequency (Hz)	697	1394	2091

Note that the harmonics are not equal to the tones generated by other keys, nor are they equal to any call progress tones generated by the phone company that may get cross-coupled into the line and misinterpreted as a digit.

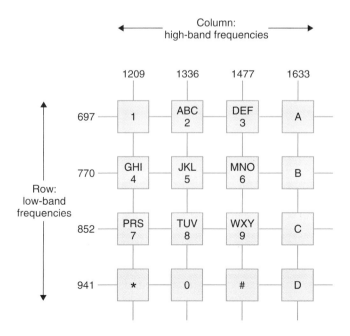

FIGURE 11-8
DTMF frequency and keypad layout.

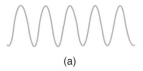

(a)

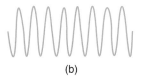

(b)

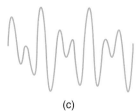

(c)

FIGURE 11-9
DTMF waveforms: (a) 770-Hz, low-band frequency; (b) 1336-Hz, high-band frequency; (c) electrical sum of the low- and high-band frequency producing the DTMF tone for the digit 5.

The major advantage of Touch Tone dialing over rotary dialing is speed and control. Keys need only be depressed for a minimum of 50 ms for telephone companies to detect and decode the digit. The minimum interdigit time is also 50 ms. Each digit can, therefore, be sent in 100 ms. A seven-digit telephone number can be sent in less than 1 second, whereas on a rotary dial phone, to dial the number 0 alone would take 1 second (100 ms/pulse × 10 pulses). This does not include the time that it would take to rotate the dial to its finger stop position.

11.5 THE LOCAL LOOP

For individual telephones to be useful, they must be interconnected to other telephones to establish a communications link. Figure 11-10 illustrates a simplistic method of interconnecting six parties together. The noticeable problem here is the overwhelming number of interconnecting lines necessary for each party to have the ability to call any one of the other parties. To provide service for *n* parties, the number of lines required for this method of interconnection is governed by the following equation:

$$\text{Number of interconnecting lines} = \frac{n(n-1)}{2}$$

where *n* is the number of parties. For the six parties illustrated, the number of interconnecting lines is 15:

$$\text{Number of interconnecting lines} = \frac{6(6-1)}{2} = 15$$

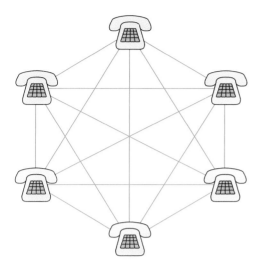

FIGURE 11-10
Method for interconnecting six telephone parties. Each party has access to any of the other five.

Each telephone in this setup must have the ability to switch to any of the other five. Imagine a telephone network of this type having to provide service to 50,000 subscribers! This would be quite impractical. Furthermore, it is not necessary for telephone systems to assume that every telephone connected to the network is in use 100% of the time. Normally, fewer than 10% are. Clearly, an alternative method for providing telephone service is needed.

11.5.1 A Need for Centralized Switching

Given the situation just presented, it makes sense to devise a centralized form of switching that can establish a temporary connection between two parties wishing to communicate with each other. This, indeed, has been the established method since the days of the first telephone networks, only the manner in which the connection is made has become more sophisticated. Each telephone subscriber is connected to a *central office* through a twisted pair of wires used as the transmission medium. This pair of wires is referred to as the *subscriber loop* or *local loop* and is illustrated in Figure 11-11. It is here at the central office where a temporary connection is made between parties.

   The first telephone networks used a *switchboard* to terminate subscriber loops. Switching was actually performed at the switchboard by a telephone operator who manually connected two subscriber loops together. Telephones were individually powered with batteries and were part of a system referred to as the *local battery system*. The calling party signaled the operator for service by cranking a magneto (a hand generator) located within the telephone set. The resulting AC signal activated a lamp at the switchboard, notifying the operator that a connection was desired. The operator, shown in Figure 11-12(a), then determined from the caller which party to contact. A *patch cord* was used to interconnect the two parties' subscriber loops. The patch cord, shown in Figure 11-12(b), is made up of two telephone jacks separated by a cord. The *tip* and *ring* contacts of the jack, on each end of the cord, connect the two subscriber loop lines.

> **Central Office**
> The local telephone company that connects your telephone lines.

> **Subscriber Loop**
> The pair of tip and ring wires that connects your telephone set to the central office. Also known as the *local loop*.

> **Local Battery System**
> The old telephone system, now obsolete, in which telephones had battery sets to power the telephone and run the generator to ring the operator.

> **Tip and Ring**
> The two lines that make up the subscriber or end loop and connect your telephone to the central office.

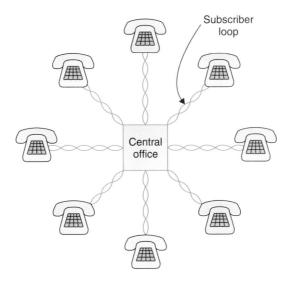

FIGURE 11-11
Central office.

A major drawback with the local battery system was having to maintain the condition of the battery. Phone calls could not be made on weak or dead batteries. Other inherent problems associated with local battery systems were the lack of privacy and also having to staff the switchboard 24 hours a day.

Today's telephone sets receive power from the central office for signaling. This is referred to as *common battery*. Switching is performed automatically. For traditional reasons, the names *tip* and *ring* are still used today to identify the two-wire subscriber loop lines.

11.5.2 The Local Feeder Network

Figure 11-13 illustrates how telephone lines or subscriber loop pairs are distributed to a community from the central office through a *feeder network*. The feeder network consists of thousands of twisted-pair wires that are brought out to the community in bundled cables and are fanned out to a number of servicing areas. The number of subscriber loop pairs is planned ahead of time to exceed the number of subscribers in a service area; this is to allow additional customers to be serviced at a later time.

Feeder network cables are manufactured in bundled increments of 25 pairs of twisted-pair copper wires. Their sizes are referred to by the total number of pairs they contain, for example, 25-pair, 50-pair, 75-pair, 100-pair, and so forth. Cable sizes can range from medium-size cables consisting of 75 to 600 pairs to larger cables with as many as 900 to 6,000 pairs. Wire sizes of each pair range from 19- to 26-gauge copper wire insulated with color-coded plastic. Figure 11-14 illustrates a standard feeder network cable. The bundles of twisted-pair wires in this cable are surrounded with a plastic wrapper, an aluminum shield that is earth grounded, and a polyethylene plastic jacket.

The feeder network cable is connected at the central office's main distribution frame (MDF) or *demarcation point,* the point at which all outside-plant cable pairs are terminated and fused for overvoltage and current protection. At the opposite end of the feeder network cable, subscriber loop pairs ultimately end up at the demarcation point between the central office and the customer. For residential customers, de-

Common Battery System
Today's telephone switching exchange that provides battery voltage at the central office instead of the user's telephone.

Feeder Network
The network of *subscriber loop* cables consisting of tip and ring lines that feed the community.

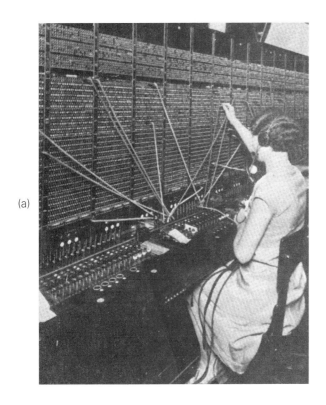

(a)

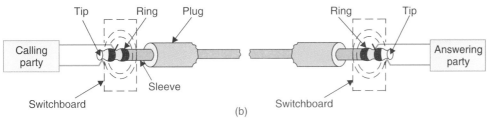

(b)

FIGURE 11-12
(a) Telephone switchboard operator; (b) patch cord. (Courtesy of AT&T Archives.)

marcation is the point where the outside telephone lines terminate and connect with the inside wiring of the home. A demarcation box, called a *network interface device (NID)*, is typically mounted on the outside of the home. Like the central office demarcation, the NID includes overvoltage and current protection.

11.5.3 Telephone Cable Color Codes

It would be an enormous task for a cabling technician to troubleshoot a 3,000-pair feeder network cable whose wires were not color coded in accordance with some standard. Each individual pair would have to be toned out and labeled to find an open or a shorted wire. Telephone cable manufacturers have, therefore, adopted a standardized color-coding sequence to track individual tip and ring wire pairs.

Ten colors are used to identify tip and ring wire pairs in all telephone cables, large and small. They are listed in Table 11-1. Five colors are used to designate the tips of the pairs, and five are used to designate the rings. The five tip and ring colors

> **Network Interface Device (NID)**
> The demarcation box typically mounted on the outside of the home. Includes overvoltage and current protection on the customer's tip and ring lines.

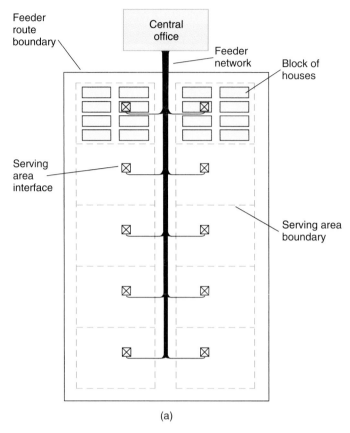

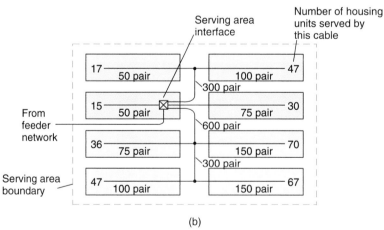

FIGURE 11-13

Feeder network distributing service to a community: (a) local distribution area; (b) detail of a serving area. (Courtesy of Bell Laboratories.)

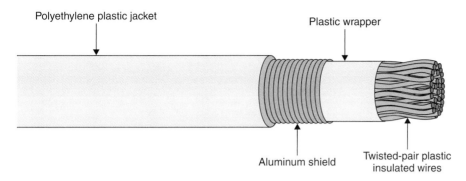

FIGURE 11-14
A feeder network cable.

form a permutation of 25 (5 × 5) color-pair combinations that form the basic *binder unit* or binder group. Cables larger than 25 pairs utilize the same 25-pair color coding; they are simply bound together with additional groups of 25 pairs and wrapped with an equivalent color coding. For the 25 pairs listed in Table 11-2, note the color coding and abbreviation for the standard 25-pair binder unit.

> **Binder Units**
> In telephone feeder network cables, binder units identify groups of 25-pair lines.

Cabling technicians are required to memorize the color coding sequence for the standard 25-pair binder unit, and various memory aids can be used. For example, some technicians use the color-coding matrix shown in Table 11-3 along with the following memory aid:

Tip: white-red-black-yellow-violet. *"Washington-Redskins-Bring-You-Victory."*
Ring: blue-orange-green-brown-slate. *"But-Oakland-Gets-Bigger-Scores."*

11.5.3.1 Determining the Pair Number from Wire Colors Cable technicians often determine the pair number based on the wire-pair colors. Using the matrix shown in Table 11-3, the tip and ring colors are assigned the following numeric values:

Tip Colors	Ring Colors
White = 0	Blue = 1
Red = 5	Orange = 2
Black = 10	Green = 3
Yellow = 15	Brown = 4
Violet = 20	Slate = 5

TABLE 11-1
Telephone Cable Standard Color Code

	Tip	Ring
	White (W)	Blue (Bl)
	Red (R)	Orange (O)
	Black (Bk)	Green (G)
	Yellow (Y)	Brown (Br)
	Violet (V)	Slate (S)

TABLE 11-2
Color Coding for the Standard 25-Pair Binder Unit

Pair No.	Pair Colors	Abbreviation
1	White-Blue	W-Bl
2	White-Orange	W-O
3	White-Green	W-G
4	White-Brown	W-Br
5	White-Slate	W-S
6	Red-Blue	R-Bl
7	Red-Orange	R-O
8	Red-Green	R-G
9	Red-Brown	R-Br
10	Red-Slate	R-S
11	Black-Blue	Bk-Bl
12	Black-Orange	Bk-O
13	Black-Green	Bk-G
14	Black-Brown	Bk-Br
15	Black-Slate	Bk-S
16	Yellow-Blue	Y-Bl
17	Yellow-Orange	Y-O
18	Yellow-Green	Y-G
19	Yellow-Brown	Y-Br
20	Yellow-Slate	Y-S
21	Violet-Blue	V-Bl
22	Violet-Orange	V-O
23	Violet-Green	V-G
24	Violet-Brown	V-Br
25	Violet-Slate	V-S

TABLE 11-3
Color-Coding Matrix for the Standard 25-Pair Binder Unit

			RING		
	Blue	**Orange**	**Green**	**Brown**	**Slate**
White	(1) W-Bl	(2) W-O	(3) W-G	(4) W-Br	(5) W-S
Red	(6) R-Bl	(7) R-O	(8) R-G	(9) R-Br	(10) R-S
Black	(11) Bk-Bl	(12) Bk-O	(13) Bk-G	(14) Bk-Br	(15) Bk-S
Yellow	(16) Y-Bl	(17) Y-O	(18) Y-G	(19) Y-Br	(20) Y-S
Violet	(21) V-Bl	(22) V-O	(23) V-G	(24) V-Br	(25) V-S

TIP

The numeric value of the wire pair is determined by adding the tip color to the ring color. For example, the wire-pair number for a pair of wires having the colors of yellow-green is 18, because 15 (yellow) + 3 (green) = 18.

EXAMPLE
11.1

Determine the pair numbers for wires with the following color pairs:

    (a) White-slate.   (b) Black-orange.   (c) Violet-brown.

Solution:

    (a) 0 (white) + 5 (slate) = pair 5
    (b) 10 (black) + 2 (orange) = pair 12
    (c) 20 (violet) + 4 (brown) = pair 24

11.5.3.2 25-Pair Binder Units   Once the 25-pair, color-coding standard has been mastered, it can be applied toward cables larger than 25 pairs. The colors are simply repeated again within the next binder unit. For example, a 75-pair cable consists of three 25-pair binder units, which are referred to as Binders 1, 2, and 3. The three binder untis are identified by colored mylar wrapping that uses the same color-coding sequence as the wire pairs. Binder 1 contains the first 25 pairs, or 1 through 25, which are boundled together and wrapped with a **white-blue** wrapping. Binder 2 contains pairs 26 through 50 and is wrapped with a **white-orange** wrapping. Binder 3 contains pairs 51 to 75 and is wrapped with a **white-green** wrapping, and so forth. Table 11-4 lists the color-coded binder wrappings for a 300-pair cable, and Figure 11-15 illutrates a cross-sectional view of a 300-pair cable consisting of 12 binders.

    Because the color sequencing remains the same within each binder unit, any wire-pair number can be determined by the color of its insulation and the color of its binder wrapping. The following equation can be used:

    Wire-pair no. = (Binder no. − 1) × 25 + wire-pair no. in a 25-pair binder

TABLE 11-4
Binder units for a 300-Pair Cable

Binder Number	Wrapping Color	Pair Numbers
1	White-Blue	1–25
2	White-Orange	26–50
3	White-Green	51–75
4	White-Brown	76–100
5	White-Slate	101–125
6	Red-Blue	126–150
7	Red-Orange	151–175
8	Red-Green	176–200
9	Red-Brown	201–225
10	Red-Slate	226–250
11	Black-Blue	251–275
12	Black-Orange	276–300

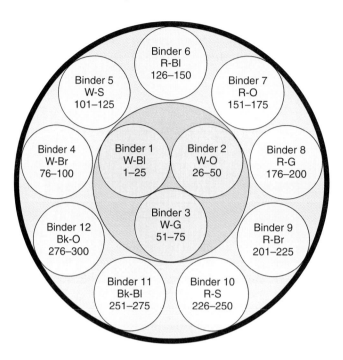

FIGURE 11-15
A cross-sectional view of a 300-pair feeder network cable consisting of twelve 75-pair binders.

EXAMPLE 11.2

Determine the wire-pair number for a yellow-green wire pair in the ninth binder of the 300-pair cable shown in Figure 11.15.

Solution:

Using the numerical color sequence discussed earlier, the wire number in a 25-pair binder is computed first:

$$15 \text{ (yellow)} + 3 \text{ (green)} = \text{pair } 18$$

The wire-pair number in the ninth binder can now be computed:

$$\begin{aligned}
\text{Wire-pair no.} &= (\text{Binder no.} - 1) \times 25 + \text{wire-pair no. in a 25-pair binder} \\
&= (9 - 1) \times 25 + 18 \\
&= 218
\end{aligned}$$

11.5.4 Operating Specifications and Call Procedures

The central office supplies −48 V DC (typical) to the ring and ground to the tip side of each loop, as shown in Figure 11-16. A negative voltage is used to minimize *electrolytic corrosion* of the subscriber loop wires. Signaling the central office is performed in one of two ways: DTMF signaling, or pulse dialing. Connection to the calling party is done automatically through computers and relays.

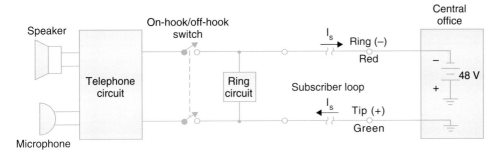

FIGURE 11-16
DC connection to the central office.

When a caller goes off-hook by lifting the handset off its cradle, a DC current path is provided by the telephone circuit. Current, I_s, flows from the central office, through the telephone, and returns via the subscriber loop. The amount of current that flows depends on such factors as wire size and type, length of the subscriber loop, and telephone impedance. Typical subscriber loop currents, I_s, range from 20 to 80 mA, and subscriber loop resistances range from 0 to 1300 Ω, as shown in Table 11-5. Telephone impedance ranges from 500 Ω to 1 kΩ. The loop current is, therefore, directly affected by several variables.

Current initially flowing in the subscriber loop as a result of a caller going off-hook is an indicator to the central office that service is required. A dial tone is sent to the caller to acknowledge the connection. A phone number may then be dialed.

TABLE 11-5
Subscriber Loop Operating Parameters

Parameter	Typical U.S. Values	Operating Limits	Typical European Values
Common battery voltage	−48 V DC	−47 to −105 V DC	Same
Operating current	20 to 80 mA	20 to 120 mA	Same
Subscriber loop resistance	0 to 1300 Ω	0 to 3600 Ω	
Loop loss	8 dB	17 dB	Same
Distortion	−50 dB total	NA	
Ringing signal	20 Hz, 90 V_{rms}	16 to 60 Hz, 40 to 130 V_{rms}	16 to 50 Hz, 40 to 130 V_{rms}
Receive sound pressure level	70 to 90 dBsp[a]	130 dBspl	Varies
Telephone set noise		<15 dBrnC[b]	

[a]dBspl = dB sound pressure level.
[b]dBrnC = dB value of electrical noise referenced to −90 dBm measured with C message weighting frequency response.

Source: From *Understanding Telephone Electronics,* 3rd edition, copyright © 1991. Published by SAMS Publishing, a division of Prentice Hall Computer Publishing. Used by permission of the publisher.

The central office translates and processes the dial pulses or DTMF tones sent by the caller. If current is flowing in the subscriber loop of the party being called, a *busy tone* is sent to the party placing the call. The caller terminates the procedure and attempts to place the call at a later time. If, however, no current is flowing in the subscriber loop of the party being called, its phone is on-hook. An AC *ring signal* of 90 V_{rms} at 20 Hz is sent by the central office to alert the called party that a call is waiting. At the same time that the ring signal is being sent, a ring tone is sent back to the original caller as an indicator that the central office is ringing the requested party. Both ring signals are sent until either current flow has been detected in the called party's loop, that is, the phone has gone off-hook and has been answered, or the caller simply hangs up. The central office then interconnects the two parties for service. The connection is made until one of the parties goes on-hook (hangs up). Some central offices will release the line only when the calling party hangs up. These are merely a few of the many tasks that the central office performs.

> **Ring Signal**
> The signal sent by the central office to ring your telephone and alert you to an incoming call. A 90 V_{rms} signal with a ring frequency of 20 Hz.

11.5.5   Call Progress Tones

Many of the signals received by the telephone set are acknowledgments and status indicators for the calling process. It is necessary for the caller to be able to recognize the sound of these tones to place a call properly. Most of these tones are frequency pairs that are turned on and off at varying rates. They are listed in Table 11-6. *Dial tone,* for example, is a composite of 350- and 440-Hz sine waves that are electrically summed together and sent by the central office to the caller. It acknowledges the caller going off-hook and informs the caller that service is available and a phone number may be dialed. To minimize costs, the central office presents dial tone to a caller for a limited amount of time, typically 20 seconds. A telephone number must be entered within this time frame, or a recorded help message is played.

> **Dial Tone**
> A tone sent by the central office when you go off-hook, notifying you that service is available and the phone number you wish to dial can be entered.

The *ring-back* signal informs the caller that the dialed party is being rung. This signal is often mistaken for the actual ringing signal (90 V_{rms} at 20 Hz) used to ring a caller's bell. They are two separate signals entirely. The ring-back signal may not necessarily be in sync with the ringing signal. Because of this, the situation may arise where the party being called may answer the phone before the caller even hears the ring-back tone.

> **Ring Back**
> When dialing another person, the ring-back signal is the ringing tone you hear on your telephone when the party you are calling is being rung.

The *busy tone* indicates that the party being called is off-hook and the party's line in use. The phone company can determine this by the DC current flowing in the called party's line.

TABLE 11-6
Telephone Call Progress Tones

Tone	Frequency (Hz)	On Time (sec)	Off Time (sec)
Dial	350 + 440	Continuous[a]	
Busy	480 + 620	0.5	0.5
Ring back	440 + 480	2	4
Congestion	480 + 620	0.2	0.3
Receiver off-hook	1400 + 2060 + 2450 + 2600	0.1	0.1

[a]Dial tone is presented to the customer for a limited amount of time, typically 20 seconds.

During peak periods of the day, the central office can become overburdened with calls. This generally occurs around 8:00 A.M. to 10:00 A.M. and 3:00 P.M. to 5:00 P.M. When this happens, *a congestion tone* is sent to the caller. This tone sounds the same as the busy tone except that its on-off rate is twice as fast. The call is said to be *blocked.* (Blocking is discussed further in Chapter 12).

The *receiver off-hook* signal creates a very loud tone at the telephone receiver. Its purpose is to alert the customer that the telephone's handset has accidentally gone off-hook and must be placed back onto its cradle. The tone is loud enough to hear from a distance (across the room) and lasts approximately 40 seconds. Usually, a voice-recorded help message is sent to the caller before this tone is generated.

11.5.6 Caller ID

Throughout the United States, Canada, and many other countries, *caller ID* (identification) service is now available to telephone customers. Caller ID enables a customer to see the caller's telephone number, name, and time and date of call on a display as the telephone is ringing. These data are stored in the caller ID telephone's memory section and can be displayed with previous callers, even if the customer chooses not to answer the telephone call. The service was originally conceived by AT&T Bell Laboratories in the late 1970s; since then, it has become universally available for a small fee. Circuits designed to decode the caller ID signal can be found in telephones with built-in displays, remote display panels, cellular telephones, PCS (personal communication services) devices, RS-232–to–PC interface devices, and even talking caller ID boxes.

11.5.6.1 Caller ID Theory of Operation   For subscriber loop connections to the central office, the caller ID signal is sent to the customer as a 1200-baud FSK (frequency-shift keying) signal burst transmitted between the *first* and *second* rings of the 90 V_{rms} − 20 Hz ring signal (Figure 11-17). Because the caller ID signal is inserted between the first and second rings, the telephone handset should not be picked up before the beginning of the second ring. Otherwise, the central office will abort the transmission of the signal and the data will be lost.

The caller ID FSK signal is similar to the Bell 202 standard discussed in Chapter 13 (Modems), in which a MARK (logic 1) equals 1200 Hz and a SPACE (logic 0) equals 2200 Hz. Each tone is transmitted at 1200 baud. Therefore, the bit rate is simply the reciprocal of 1200, or 833.33 μs per bit.

After the first ring, a delay of 500 ms occurs, followed by a string of alternating 0s and 1s (300 bits) that make up the *Channel Seizure* field. The duration of the channel seizure field is 250 ms. It is followed by the *Conditioning Signal* field that is comprised of a 150-ms string of 1s (180 bits). The next two words are the *Message Type* and *Message Length* fields. They precede the *Data Field,* and they indicate the type of message and number of words in the Data Field, respectively. Each word in the Message Type, Message Length, and Data Field are asynchronous, 8-bit characters that are framed by a start and stop bit. The final byte is called the *Checksum,* which is used for error detection. For the caller ID signal, the checksum is defined as the 2s complement of the modulo (divide by) 256 sum of all previous words beginning with the Message Type word and ending with the last byte in the Data Field. It does not include the Channel Seizure and Conditioning Signal fields.

The first two bytes of the Data Field are the month (01 through 12), with leading zeros for the months of January (01) through September (09). The next two bytes

Congestion Tone
A fast busy tone sent to you when you dial a number and the central office is overburdened with calls. Your call is blocked, and you must redial later, when traffic is lighter.

Receiver Off-Hook Tone
A loud, repetitive tone designed to alert you that your telephone handset is off-hook and has not been properly hung up or placed in its cradle.

Caller ID
Sends you information about the person calling you, typically including the caller's name, date, and time they called. The caller ID signal is sent between the first and second rings.

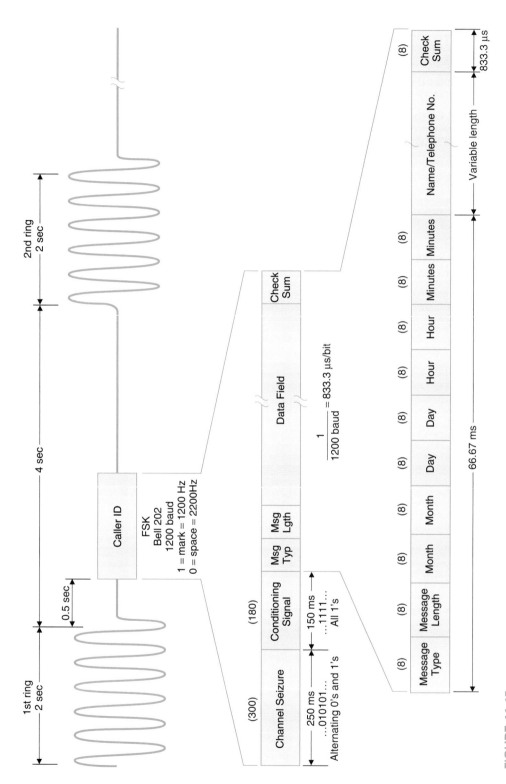

FIGURE 11-17
Caller ID signaling format.

specify the day of the month (01 through 31), and the two bytes following those specify the hour of the day and are followed by two more bytes that specify the minutes. Thus, the month, day, and time (in hours and minutes) of the call are data specified by the first eight bytes of the Data Field. The remaining data represents the calling party's name and telephone number. If the caller chooses to be anonymous, a ***67** can be dialed before dialing the telephone number. This results in blocking the caller's name and telephone number from being displayed. The telephone company simply replaces that portion of the Data Field that normally includes the caller's name and telephone number with data corresponding to the message: **PRIVATE NUMBER.** Other messages, such as **UNKNOWN NUMBER** (e.g., from cellular callers) or **OUT OF AREA** (e.g., from areas that do not have caller ID implemented), can also be displayed in special cases.

11.6 LINE CHARACTERISTICS

The quality of communications over the PSTN (Public Switched Telephone Network) is determined by several factors, such as bandwidth, impedance, transmission media, and line length. In the past, these line characteristics were considered primarily in terms of their effect on speech between two parties. The PSTN, as a result, has been tailored toward voice-grade communications. Because there are literally millions of miles of existing voice-grade lines, it is necessary to study these line characteristics to better understand their effects on voice as well as the limitations they impose on transmission of data.

11.6.1 Bandwidth Constraints

Voice includes frequency components ranging from approximately 100 Hz to as high as 8 kHz. Most of one's voice energy is distributed in frequencies ranging from 400 to 600 Hz, with a nominal voice frequency of 500 Hz. Figure 11-18 illustrates these characteristics. Extensive studies on human speech have indicated that the relative importance of voice-frequency components in terms of intelligibility is distributed differently

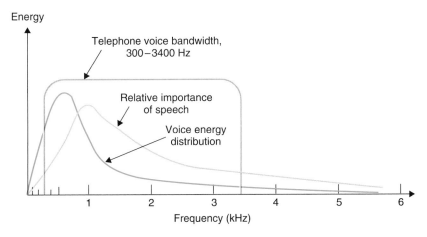

FIGURE 11-18
Telephone system bandwidth versus voice characteristics.

from their energy distribution. Note that voice frequencies less than approximately 200 Hz and greater than 2 kHz play only a minor role in determining intelligibility. The telephone lines used for subscriber loops have been tailored to capture these characteristics with a *bandwidth* ranging from 300 to 3400 Hz. At the same time, these bandwidth constraints limit the noise originating from 60-Hz lines, dial pulses, thermal and shot noise, and the like that would otherwise degrade the quality of reception.

> **Bandwidth**
> The range of frequencies that a transmission medium can pass without excessive distortion.

11.6.2 Loop Resistance

The subscriber loop resistance is governed primarily by the type of wire used. Typically, copper wire is used in sizes ranging from 19 to 26 gauge. For 26-gauge copper wire, the attenuation is approximately 3 dB/mile. However, for 19-gauge copper wire, the attenuation is approximately $1\frac{1}{4}$ dB/mile. Thus, roughly twice the transmission distance can be attained with the larger-diameter wire. Attenuation is generally kept at a value of less than 8 dB in the subscriber loop, with a maximum permissible loop resistance of 1300 Ω. The loop resistance also includes the resistance of the telephone, typically on the order of 120 Ω. The smallest wire used for the subscriber loop is 26 gauge, which has a DC resistance of 40.8 Ω at 68°F per 1000 ft. For 1300 Ω, less the resistance at the telephone, this is just more than 6 miles (3-mile pair). The average customer loop is approximately 2 miles; thus, 26-gauge wire satisfies the needs of most subscriber loops.

Figure 11-19 illustrates the model of a transmission line. The distributed values of L, R, and C make it more evident why there are signal losses and distortion in wire transmission media. The model can be used to represent the subscriber loop. Because the values of L, R, and C can be measured at any point along the subscriber loop, experiments have been conducted to determine methods to improve the transmission characteristics of the phone lines. The most practical method has been found to be adding *series inductance* to the line at various intervals between the subscriber and the central office. This is referred to as *loading*. The *loading coil* is depicted in Figure 11-20. The effect of loading increases the line impedance, consequently decreasing the overall attenuation. Longer distances can, therefore, be achieved through loading, at the same time preserving the DC characteristics of the line. Loading also results in the sharp cutoff frequency at approximately 3.4 kHz. This is undesirable for high-speed digital transmission.

> **Loading Coil**
> Inductive coils at specific intervals in the subscriber loop line to optimize line impedance.

Table 11-7 depicts how telephone cable pairs are labeled. The letters H and B correspond to series inductance added to the line every 6000 or 3000 ft, respectively. The designator, D, is also used for inductances added every 4500 ft. The value of the

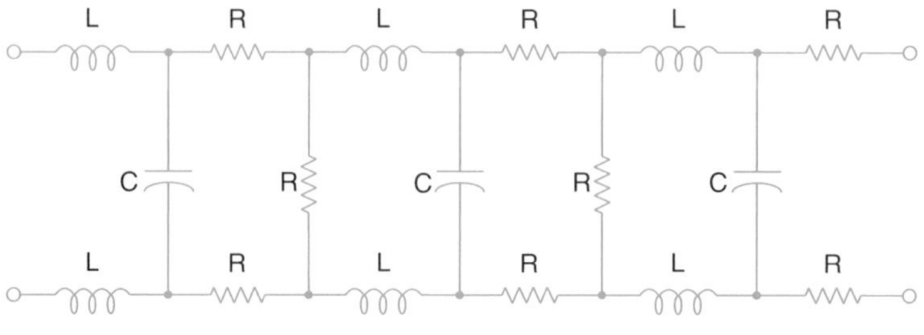

FIGURE 11-19
Model of a transmission line.

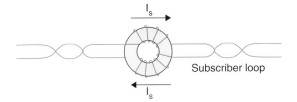

FIGURE 11-20
Loading coil in the subscriber loop.

loading coil in millihenrys (mH) is also specified. Typical values are 135, 88, 44, 22, and 7.5 mH. For example, a 26-gauge cable pair with loading coils of 88 mH every 6000 ft is labeled 26H88. Most cable pairs use 88-mH coils with a spacing of 6000 ft.

Table 11-8 lists the electrical characteristics for common wire sizes used by the PSTN. A comparison of nonloaded versus H88-loaded cables is made. Note, under the attenuation column, that the decibel per mile specification is reduced considerably through the use of loading coils.

11.6.3 The Private Line

Of the millions of telephone lines connected to the central office, the overwhelming majority are two-wire, twisted-pair loops. These subscriber loop lines, which connect our homes to the central office, are referred to by telephone companies as *switched* or *dial-up* lines, because they require the switching services of the central office.

The two-wire loop can also be a dedicated *leased* or *private* line. These types of lines are direct, hard-wired connections between two locations through the central office, offering 24-hour service. The switching matrix at the central office is bypassed; hence, no digits need to be dialed. The private line can also be a four-wire circuit offering full-duplex data transmission on dedicated pairs. There are several advantages that the private line has over the two-wire switched lines:

> **Switched or Dial-Up Lines**
> The standard voice-grade telephone lines.

- Line characteristics are consistent, because the same signal path is used at all times.
- The line is less prone to impulse noise generated from central office switching circuitry.

TABLE 11-7
Loading Coil Designation

Designation[a]	Nominal Cutoff Frequency, f_c	Use
H88	3500–4000	Message trunks and long subscriber lines
H44	5000–5600	Certain data circuits
B22	10,000–11,200	Program networks

[a]The letter designates the spacing: $H = 6000$ ft., $B = 3000$ ft. The number gives the inductance of each loading coil in millihenrys.

Source: Fink, Donald G. and John M. Carroll, *Standard Handbook for Electrical Engineers,* 10th ed. (New York: McGraw-Hill, 1969), pp. 25–49.

TABLE 11-8

Electrical Characteristics of Exchange-Type Cables at 68°F[a]

	Primary Constants (at 1000 Hz)				Secondary Constants (at 1000 Hz)						Characteristic Impedance		Midsection Image Impedance			
						Attenuation		Phase Shift							Cutoff Frequency	Speed of Propagation
Gauge (AWG)	C (μF/mi)	R (Ω/mi)	L (mH/mi)	G (S/mi)		dB/mi	Np/mi	rad/mi	deg/mi	R(Ω)	X(Ω)	R(Ω)	X(Ω)	(Hz)	(mi/s)
19	0.084	86	0.886	1.219	Nonloaded	1.27	0.146	0.156	8.9	296	−276				40,000
					H88-loaded	0.42	0.049	0.519	29.8			1013	−93	3440	12,000
22	0.082	173	0.870	1.190	Nonloaded	1.81	0.208	0.214	12.3	417	−403				29,000
					H88-loaded	0.79	0.091	0.519	29.7			1035	−180	3480	12,000
24	0.084	274	0.950	1.219	Nonloaded	2.31	0.266	0.272	15.6	516	−503				23,000
					H88-loaded	1.21	0.140	0.536	30.7			1045	−272	3440	12,000
26	0.079	440	0.995	1.146	Nonloaded	2.85	0.329	0.332	19.0	671	−660				19,000
					H88-loaded	1.79	0.206	0.542	31.0			1121	−425	3540	12,000

[a]Np = neper = 0.5 ln A_V (Np)

dB = decibel = 10 log A_V (dB)

1dB = 8.69 Np, or 1Np = 0.115 dB

Source: Fink, Donald G. and John M. Carroll, *Standard Handbook for Electrical Engineers*, 10th ed. (New York: McGraw-Hill, 1969), pp. 25–50.

- Line conditioning is available to improve on signal attenuation and delay distortion.
- There are higher data transfer rates with lower error rates.
- A private line is less expensive than a switched line if utilization is high.
- Unlike the unbalanced switched line, the private line is a balanced circuit, thus making it more suitable for line conditioning.

11.7   LINE CONDITIONING

Although the standard public switched lines are used primarily for voice, they may also be used for the transmission of data provided that special modulation techniques are used. These switched lines are classified by telephone companies as the *basic 3002 voice-grade lines*. The FCC has set tariffs governing the amount of distortion allowed on voice-grade lines. To compensate for this distortion, the PSTN offers private line services for an additional cost. These lines may be specially treated or *conditioned* to improve on the quality of transmitted data. Higher transmission rates with a reduced number of errors are achieved through line conditioning.

> **Basic 3002 Voice-Grade Lines**
> The technical name given to the standard switched *dial-up lines*.

11.7.1   Unconditioned Voice-Grade Lines

The standard public switched telephone lines are classified as 3002 unconditioned voice-grade lines. As described earlier, the bandwidth is limited to approximately 3 kHz (300–3400 Hz). For data transmission, these lines are normally used for speeds ranging from 300 to 9600 bps. Speeds beyond 9600 bps are now possible over unconditioned voice-grade lines; however, they are not guaranteed by the phone company.

Voice and data transmission can be impaired by the switched lines, because the signal path is not fixed through central and toll offices. Signal paths established during one call are likely to be different at another time between the same two parties; hence, line characteristics differ for each connection. For this reason, switched lines cannot be conditioned by telephone companies beforehand.

Two important electrical parameters that must be considered, particularly in the transmission of data, are *envelope delay distortion* and *attenuation distortion*. The propagation time for a signal to travel across a transmission medium varies with frequency. Some frequencies of the transmitted signal arrive ahead of others. This phase distortion is not readily noticeable for voice. For data, however, it may well render the voice channel completely unusable. The same is true for amplitude variations across the passband of the channel. Attenuation distortion and envelope delay distortion are particularly severe at the breakpoints of the channel's passband. Figure 11-21 illustrates a typical response curve for a 3002 unconditioned voice-grade line. Envelope delay and attenuation distortion are defined as follows:

> **Envelope Delay Distortion**
> The phase delay distortion over the passband of the telephone lines. The envelope of an AM test wave is used to measure this distortion.

> **Attenuation Distortion**
> The frequency response of the telephone lines.

Envelope Delay Distortion   Envelope delay distortion is the phase variation that occurs as a function of frequency over the passband of a given transmission medium. This specification is determined by measuring the *propagation delay time* or *phase delay* of the *envelope* of an AM wave measured throughout the medium's passband. Ideally, a linear or flat response is desired. In this case, the time that it would take for the signal to propagate from source to destination would be the same for all frequencies. Envelope delay distortion is measured in microseconds.

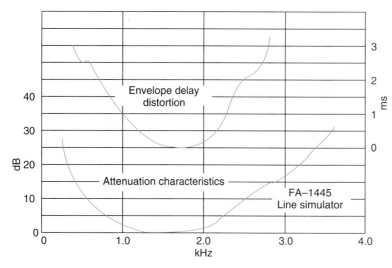

Because different frequencies encounter different amplitude-attenuation and propagation-delay times through the telephone network, not all of the bandwidth can be utilized for transmission of digital data. These differences are largely immaterial in voice communication but can be detrimental to data transmission, particularly at speeds faster than 2400 bps.

ENVELOPE DELAY DISTORTION AND ATTENUATION

FIGURE 11-21
Envelope delay and attenuation distortion characteristics for the 3002 unconditioned voice-grade line. (Reprinted with permission from Racal-Vadic.)

Attenuation Distortion   Attenuation distortion is the frequency response of the transmission medium. Amplitude variations throughout the medium's passband must not exceed specified limits. These limits are relative to the gain measured at the approximate center of the medium's passband. Ideally, a linear or flat response is desirable so that all frequencies throughout the passband encounter the same gain. Attenuation distortion is measured in decibels (dB).

11.7.2   Conditioning the Private Line

The permanent connection of the private line allows telephone companies to compensate for some of the distortion characteristics mentioned earlier. Phase and amplitude *equalizer* circuits are placed in individual leased lines. These circuits contain inductors and capacitors that are adjusted to flatten or *equalize* the line characteristic for envelope delay and attenuation across the band. Figure 11-22 illustrates the effect of line conditioning, which is the process of equalizing the line. Signal attenuation and propagation delay are made relatively constant for all frequencies within the passband.

11.7.2.1   C- and D-Type Line Conditioning   Two types of line conditioning are offered by telephone companies: *C type*, and *D type*. A customer can request one or both types at an extra monthly fee. C-type line conditioning sets the maximum limits on the amount of attenuation distortion measured on the line. FCC Tariff No. 260 describes these limits for private line services in North America. These limits are referenced to the channel gain at a standardized frequency of 1004 Hz. C-type conditioning is available in five types: C1 through C5. In general, C-type conditioning is

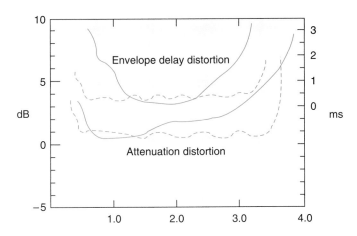

FIGURE 11-22
Effect of line conditioning through the use of equalizer circuits. The solid lines are before equalization, and the dashed lines are after equalization. (Reprinted with permission
from Racal-Vadic.)

used for frequency-shift keying (FSK) and phase-shift keying (PSK) modulation.
Specifications are shown in Table 11-9.

   D-type conditioning is a more recent type of conditioning introduced by AT&T
for 9600 bps over voice-grade lines. Limits are set on the amount of *signal-to-C-
notched noise ratio* and harmonic distortion measured on the line. C-notched noise is
a standard measurement used to determine the channel background noise power level.
D-type conditioned lines meet the following specifications:

$$\text{Signal-to-C-notched noise ratio} = 28 \text{ dB}$$
$$\text{Signal-to-second harmonic ratio} = 35 \text{ dB}$$
$$\text{Signal-to-third harmonic ratio} = 40 \text{ dB}$$

11.7.3   Equalization

For high-speed data transmission, compensation for amplitude and phase delay distortion encountered on telephone lines can now be performed within the modem
through the use of phase and amplitude equalizer circuits. A *compromise equalizer*
provides *pre-equalization* of the signal. It is implemented in the transmitter section
of the modem. An *adaptive equalizer* provides *post-equalization* of the signal and is
implemented in the receiver section of the modem. These circuits are standard features in modem designs and have become internationally recognized by ITU-TS modem recommendations.

   Pre-equalization is best suited when the characteristics of the line are fixed and
known beforehand. Because the private line offers this advantage, the compromise
equalizer can be manually adjusted to compensate for the given line condition. In
switched voice-grade lines, however, line characteristics are unpredictable, because
the signal path is subject to change with each call. Post-equalization with adaptive
equalizers is more effective in this situation.

Compromise Equalizer
A portion of a modem's
transmitter circuit that
provides pre-equaliza-
tion of the telephone
lines by compensating
for amplitude and
phase delay distortion
in the lines.

Adaptive Equalizer
A portion of a modem's
receiver circuit that provides post-equalization
of the telephone lines
by compensating for
amplitude and phase
delay distortion in
the lines.

TABLE 11-9

C1- Through C5-Type Line Conditioning for Private Leased Lines

Conditioning Type	Envelope Delay Distortion		Attenuation Distortion	
	Frequency Range (Hz)	Specification Limits (μs)	Frequency Range (Hz)	Specification Limits (dB)
C1	1000–2400	1000	300–2700	−2 to +6
			1000–2400	−1 to +3
C2	500–2800	3000	300–3000	−2 to +6
	600–2600	1500	500–2800	−1 to +3
	1000–2600	500		
C3 (access lines)	500–2800	650	300–3000	−0.8 to +3
	600–2600	300	500–2800	−0.5 to +1.5
	1000–2600	110		
C3 (trunks)	500–2800	500	300–3000	−0.8 to +2
	600–1600	260	500–2800	−0.5 to +1
	1000–2600	260		
C4	500–3000	3000	300–3200	−2 to +6
	600–3000	1500	500–3000	−2 to +3
	800–2800	500		
	1000–2600	300		
C5	500–2800	600	300–3000	−1 to +3
	600–2600	300	500–2800	−0.5 to +1.5
	1000–2600	100		

PROBLEMS

1. What part of the telephone circuit interfaces the two-wire subscriber loop to the four-wire transmit and receive circuit?
2. Explain the mechanism used in the telephone set to convert acoustical signals to electrical signals.
3. Explain how electrical signals are converted by the telephone set to acoustical signals.
4. What is the ring potential and the frequency sent by the central office to ring the telephone set?
5. Why is the telephone ring voltage superimposed on −48 V DC?
6. Define *sidetone.*
7. What is the difference between a ringing signal and a ring-back signal?
8. What frequencies are associated with a busy tone, and what is its on-off rate?
9. Refer to Figure 11-6(b).
   a. What is the purpose of D1?
   b. What is the purpose of D2?
   c. When the telephone is said to be on-hook, what are the conditions of switches S1 and S2?
   d. Which components are used to regulate voice amplitude?
10. For a rotary or electronic-pulse dial-type telephone, how many pulses are generated when the digit 0 is dialed?
11. What is the pulse width, period, and repetition rate for a dial pulse?

12. Assume that the off-hook DC potential is measured to be -5 V DC. Draw the waveform that would appear on an oscilloscope if the digit 8 were dialed.
13. Define *interdigit time.*
14. What are the DTMF frequencies for the digit 7?
15. Refer to Figure 11-10. How many lines would be necessary to interconnect 50 telephone parties using this method?
16. Name the five tip and five ring colors used to identify wire pairs in a telephone feeder network cable.
17. Determine the wire-pair numbers for wires having the following colors:
    a. Red-brown.
    b. Yellow-green.
    c. Violet-orange.
18. Determine the wire-pair number for a violet-blue wire pair in the seventh binder of a 300-pair feeder network cable.
19. Determine the wire-pair number for a red-green wire-pair in the eleventh binder of a 300-pair feeder network cable.
20. What is the tip-to-ring potential for a telephone in its on-hook position?
21. What is the nominal tip-to-ring DC subscriber loop current?
22. Describe the *busy* signal in terms of frequency and on-off times.
23. Describe the *receiver off-hook* tone.
24. The caller ID signal occurs between which rings?
25. Explain what would happen, in terms of caller ID, if a caller picked up the handset before the beginning of the second ring.
26. Over what range of the caller ID signal does the checksum perform in a 2s complement of the modulo sum words?
27. What is the bandwidth of the switched telephone lines?
28. What is the nominal voice frequency?
29. Refer to Table 11-8. Given a cable pair labeled 19H88:
    a. What is the attenuation in dB/mi?
    b. Compute the AC resistance for a 5-mile loop length.
    c. What is the cutoff frequency?
30. Assume that a subscriber loop has a total DC resistance of 950 Ω. This includes a telephone resistance of 130 Ω. Compute the following (assume 68°F):
    a. Subscriber loop current.
    b. Off-hook DC potential measured at the telephone.
    c. Distance to the central office for 19-AWG copper wire having a DC resistance of 8.33 Ω per 1000 ft at 68°F.
31. Repeat problem 26 for a subscriber loop having a total DC resistance of 800 Ω and a telephone resistance of 142 Ω.
32. Explain the difference between envelope delay distortion and attenuation distortion.
33. Refer to Table 11-9. A private line uses C4-type conditioning. For a 600-Hz to 3-kHz test tone:
    a. What is the maximum envelope delay distortion that could occur?
    b. What is the maximum attenuation distortion that could occur?
34. Explain the difference between a compromise equalizer and an adaptive equalizer.

12

THE TELEPHONE NETWORK

The invention of the telephone in 1876 led to an explosive outgrowth of engineering developments. These developments continue to thrive to this date. This proliferation, through what has become known today as "the largest industry in the world," has led to the existing informational era in which we live. Despite the Bell System divestiture (breakup) on January 1, 1983, the telecommunications industry still exists, employing millions of people. Divestiture has clearly established a distinction between the principal entities or segments of the telecommunications industry. More than 1400 independent telephone companies exist today, making up what has become known as the *public switched telephone network (PSTN)*.

The PSTN has been dubbed the "world's most complex machine." It is truly one of the modern wonders of the world. In the United States alone, the PSTN interconnects hundreds of millions of telephones through the largest network of computers in the world. Despite its electrical and mechanical sophistication, even the most unskilled person can utilize its services. At the touch of a dial, any two people, virtually anywhere in the world, can communicate with each other in a matter of seconds. This chapter examines the basic structure of the PSTN and how it has evolved over the years. The most recent technological advances are introduced as well.

12.1 THE PUBLIC SWITCHED TELEPHONE NETWORK

Since the invention of the telephone, the PSTN has grown proportionately with the increased demands to communicate. Switching services beyond metropolitan areas were soon developed, increasing the size and complexity of the central office. New methods of switching were required to interconnect central offices through the use of *interoffice trunks* and *tandem trunks*. Figure 12-1 depicts how today's central offices are connected through the use of trunks. In largely populated areas, a *tandem office* is used to minimize the number of trunks that a call must be routed through to reach its destination. Outside the local area, *toll trunks* are used to connect the central office to *toll centers*. Toll centers may be located in adjacent cities outside the local area. To achieve even longer distances, toll centers are interconnected by *intertoll trunks* as shown in Figure 12-1.

Public Switched Telephone Network (PSTN)
The dial-up telephone network. Also referred to as *Telco* (*tele*phone *co*mpany).

Interoffice Trunk
A trunk circuit that connects central offices.

Tandem Trunk
A trunk circuit that connects a *tandem office* with a central office.

Tandem Office
A switching office used to minimize the number of trunk circuits a call must be routed through to reach its destination in a heavily populated area.

Toll Trunk
A trunk circuit that connects a central office to a *toll center*.

Intertoll Trunk
A trunk circuit that connects toll centers together.

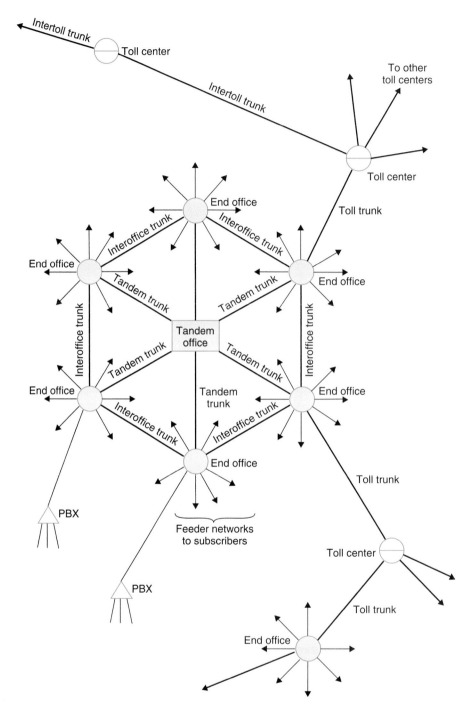

FIGURE 12-1
Interconnection of switching exchanges in North America.

12.1.1 Switching Hierarchy of North America

A hierarchy of switching exchanges evolved in North America to accommodate the demand for longer-distance connections. The PSTN has classified these exchanges into five *levels* of switching, as depicted in Table 12-1. At the lowest level, class 5, is the central office or *end office*. A large metropolis may require several end offices for service, whereas a single end office is usually sufficient in a rural area. When calls are made outside the local area, they are routed through class 4 centers, *toll centers*, and possibly higher levels of switching depending on the destination of the call and the current traffic volume within the PSTN. To aid in the volume of traffic between toll centers, *primary centers, sectional centers,* and *regional centers,* or classes 3, 2, and 1, respectively, are used. Figure 12-2 illustrates the possible routes that a toll call can take throughout the switching hierarchy. The best route is the shortest route or the route utilizing the smallest number of switching centers. A call may not always take this route, however. It depends on the availability of trunk circuits when the call is placed. Several alternative routes can be taken up and down the switching hierarchy. The selection of a route is under program control at the switching center.

Typically, trunks used to interconnect higher levels of switching are designed for high-speed transmission using the multiplexing techniques that are described in Section 12.2. These higher levels of switching make up the *long-haul network*. Calls placed onto the long-haul network are subject to toll fees. Figure 12-3 illustrates the long-haul network. To sustain higher transmission rates within the long-haul network, wideband trunk media are used. This includes coax, microwave ground and satellite links, and fiber-optic cables. Figure 12-4 illustrates the distribution of switching centers throughout the United States.

> **End Office**
> A Class 5 switching center. Also known as a *central office.*

> **Long-Haul Network**
> A trunk circuit that spans long distances by interconnecting toll centers. Calls placed on a long-haul network are subject to toll fees.

12.1.2 Two-Wire Versus Four-Wire Circuits

In two-wire circuits, whether the line is switched or private, the transmitted and received signals share the same two lines. When two parties talk at the same time, their signals are superimposed on each other. Although each party hears one another, they probably do not understand what is being said. Intelligent voice transmissions on two-wire circuits from this standpoint can be regarded as half-duplex.

TABLE 12-1
Hierarchy of Switching Exchanges in North America

Class 1	Regional center	□
Class 2	Sectional center	△
Class 3	Primary center	○
Class 4	Toll center	⊖
Class 5	End office	●

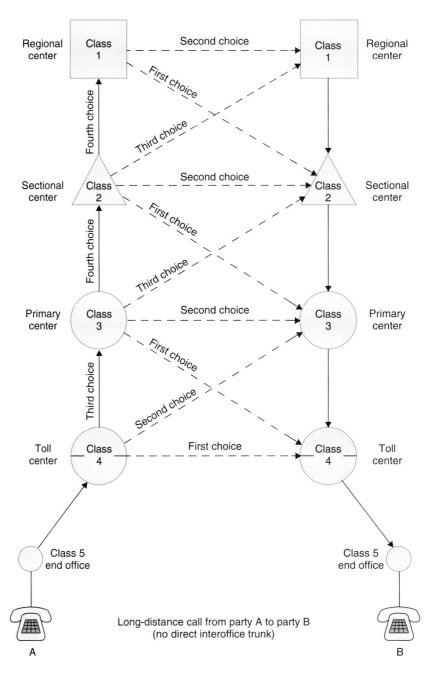

FIGURE 12-2
Long-distance switching hierarchy within the PSTN depicting possible routes to complete a call between parties A and B.

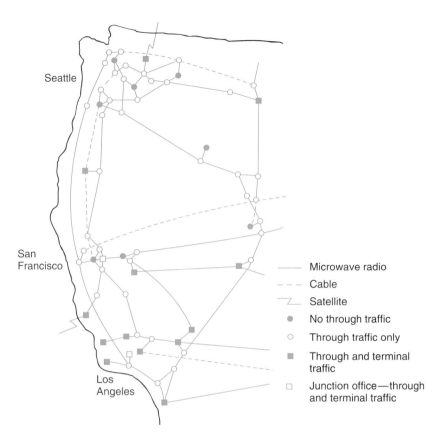

FIGURE 12-3
Long-haul network depicting various trunk media. (Courtesy of Bell Laboratories.)

For data communications, this presents a serious problem unless a modulation technique is used to separate full-duplex signals.

Another inherent problem with the two-wire circuit is providing consistent transfer characteristics for bidirectional signal flow, because energy from a transmitting source falls off (as in any transmission medium) with distance. Telephone signals transmitted beyond more than a few miles must be amplified and restored to their original condition. A bidirectional amplifier is not a practical solution. It is much more desirable to physically separate transmitted and received signals by employing a four-wire line so that directional amplifiers may be used in each signal path.

The PSTN uses a variety of transmission mediums to interconnect switching centers. These interconnecting links are referred to as *trunks*. Trunks normally carry multiple telephone signals, often several thousand simultaneously. Class 5 switching centers are typically linked with *four-wire circuits* for trunks. As shown in Figure 12-5, four-wire circuits allow the transmitted and received signals to propagate on physically separate pairs of wires. This allows the use of *repeaters* in each direction. Repeaters amplify and condition the signals for longer transmission distances. The multiplexing techniques discussed in Section 12.4 are best performed on transmitted and received signals that are physically separate from each other.

Four-wire circuits may not always mean four physical wires. Two physical wires can also serve as a four-wire circuit by partitioning the transmitted and received

> **Four-Wire Circuits**
> Trunk circuits that permit transmit and receive signals to propagate on physically separate lines.

> **Repeater**
> An electronics circuit used to filter, condition, and amplify signals for long-distance transmission.

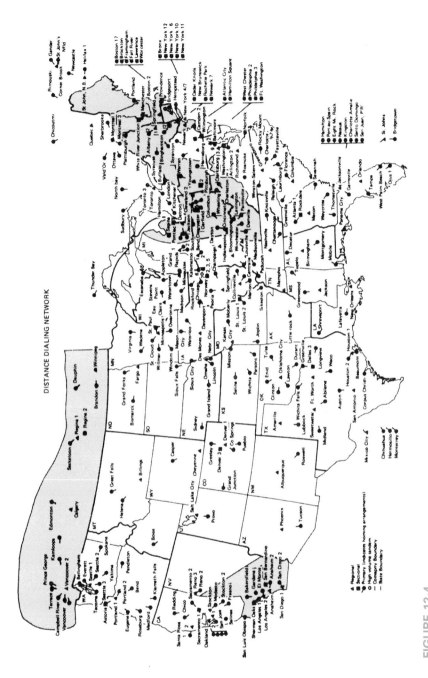

DISTANCE DIALING NETWORK

FIGURE 12-4
Switching centers throughout the United States. (Courtesy of Bell Laboratories.)

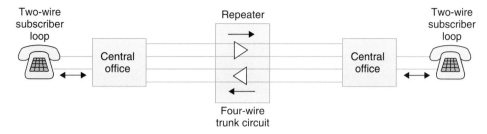

FIGURE 12-5
Four-wire trunk circuit with separate amplifiers for each direction.

signals into separate frequency bands. Full-duplex operation is made possible by transmitting on one band of frequencies and simultaneously receiving on the other. This is referred to as a *derived four-wire circuit.* In most cases, however, four physical wire circuits are used for interoffice trunks.

12.1.3   Hybrids

The two-wire subscriber loop connection at the central office must be converted to a four-wire circuit for interfacing to a trunk circuit. This conversion is performed by the *hybrid circuit,* which, as illustrated in Figure 12-6, consists of two separate amplifier circuits. The top amplifier circuit amplifies signals traveling in the west–east direction. The bottom amplifier amplifies signals traveling in the opposite direction from east to west. The hybrid coil is a balanced, cross-coupled transformer assembly with equal windings in each coil. Signals in the east–west direction are canceled in the west–east direction, and vice versa. A *balancing network* is used to properly match the subscriber loop impedance to that of the hybrid. When precisely matched, maximum power is transferred in the appropriate direction and no portion of the

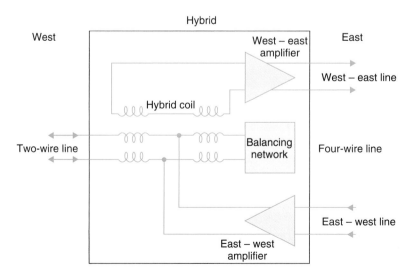

FIGURE 12-6
Hybrid two- and four-wire terminating circuit.

transmitted signal is returned to its source. The splitting of signal power causes a 3-dB (half-power) signal loss. Amplifiers within the hybrid make up for this loss.

12.1.4 Echo Suppressors and Echo Cancellers

Long-distance transmission of signals over the PSTN often suffers from impedance mismatches. This occurs primarily at the hybrid interface. Balancing networks within the hybrid can never perfectly match the hybrid to the subscriber loop due to temperature variations, degradation of transmission lines, and other variables. As a result, a signal transmitted in the east–west direction does not completely cancel itself in the secondary of the hybrid coil. A small portion of the signal is returned in the west–east circuit. This returned signal is known as an *echo*. In general, for distances of less than 1000 miles between two parties, echoes are unnoticeable. In fact, if strong enough, they can serve the same purpose as a telephone's sidetone, reinforcing the caller's own voice. When the round-trip delay time between two parties exceeds about 45 ms, an echo of one's voice can be heard. For transcontinental and international calls, the round-trip delay time can be several hundred milliseconds. Telephone calls via satellite links can take up to as much as a half-second. The resulting echoes are extremely annoying, making it difficult to converse.

To circumvent the problem of echoing in long-distance communications, *echo suppressors* are used. Figure 12-7 illustrates the echo suppressor. In most cases, two people conversing do not talk at the same time. The operation of the echo suppressor relies on this principle. When a caller from the west begins to speak, the speech detector for the west–east direction is activated, which, in turn, causes the logic control circuit

> **Echo**
> Any transmitted signal reflected back to the source where it was generated.

> **Echo Suppressor**
> An electronic circuit used in the central office to suppress echoes by disabling the returned amplifier circuit.

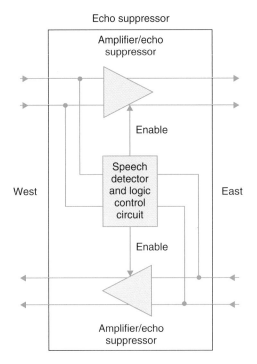

FIGURE 12-7
Echo suppressor.

to disable the amplifier for the east–west direction. The returned echo is effectively *suppressed* by approximately 60 dB. Likewise, when a caller from the east begins to speak, the speech detector for the east–west direction becomes activated, thus causing the logic control circuit to disable the amplifier in the return west–east channel. Echo suppressors are used in cases where the round-trip delay time of the signal exceeds 45 ms. Geosynchronous satellites are positioned 22,300 miles above Earth, and the round-trip delay time for satellite communications in this case is nearly a quarter of a second (22,300 miles × 2/186,000 miles/s). Echo suppressors are required in this case.

What happens if two long-distance parties talk at the same time when echo suppressors are employed? You may want to attempt this experiment the next time you are talking long distance beyond a few thousand miles. Echo suppressors in *both* directions are enabled, and you will not be able to hear each other. Only one person can talk at a time; thus, long-distance communication is half-duplex.

To achieve full-duplex operation with voice or data, more modern devices called *echo cancellers* are used. Echo cancellers eliminate the return echo by electrically subtracting it from the original signal rather than disabling the return amplifier circuit. This allows both speakers to talk and listen simultaneously.

> **Echo Canceller**
> An electronic circuit used in the central office to cancel echoed signals by electrically subtracting them from the original signal.

Echo suppressors present a problem when data are transmitted over the PSTN in both directions simultaneously (full-duplex mode). The data are lost as the echo suppressors are enabled. Telephone companies have equipped echo suppressors with a means of disabling themselves. On receiving a tone within the frequency range of 2010 to 2240 Hz for a duration longer than 400 ms, the echo suppressor disables itself. The disabling tone can be sent from either direction. No other signal should be present during this interval. Once disabled, both amplifiers within the echo suppressor circuit remain active as long as signal energy is within the frequency range of 300 to 3000 Hz. An interruption of more than 50 ms will automatically enable the echo suppressor to its normal mode of operation.

12.1.5 Analog Companding

One of the characteristics of voice is the wide dynamic range over which its power varies. This range can be as high as 60 dB. A signal with such a large dynamic range is difficult to transmit over long distances because of the required use of several repeaters and amplifiers. Large signals tend to saturate amplifiers en route, and small signals eventually get lost in the amplified noise. The problem can be overcome through the use of a *compandor.*

A compandor is a circuit that performs two functions: *com*pressing a signal's amplitude range before it is transmitted, and ex*panding* a signal's amplitude range back to its original condition when it is received. The overall process is referred to as *companding.* The compandor circuit includes logarithmic amplifiers (log amps) with nonlinear transfer characteristics.

> **Compandor**
> An electronic circuit used to *com*press a signal transmitted and ex*pand* a signal received. Improves signal-to-noise (SNR) ratios.

A comparison between transmission systems with and without companding is shown in Figure 12-8. The diagram depicts power loss versus transmission distance. A 20-dB repeater is used to amplify the signal between the transmitting and receiving stations. No companding is used in the system shown in Figure 12-8(a). The SNR (signal-to-noise ratio) is degraded from 80 to 55 dB for peak amplitudes. Low-level amplitudes, originally at 20 dB SNR, eventually fall below the amplified noise power to −5 dB SNR. Improved SNR and a reduction in the likelihood of saturating amplifiers are attained through the process of companding. This is shown in Figure 12-8(b). Strong and weak signals are *compressed* from a 60- to a 30-dB dynamic range at the

> **Companding**
> Compressing a signal transmitted and expanding a signal received. *Compandors* perform this function.

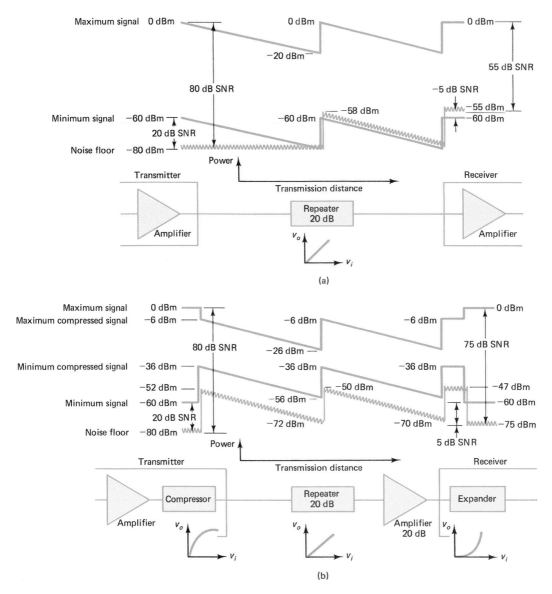

FIGURE 12-8
Comparison between a transmission system with and without companding. The diagram depicts signal strength versus transmission distance: (a) transmission system without companding; (b) transmission system with companding.

transmitter and restored to 60 dB at the receiving end. The SNR is maintained above unity throughout the transmission system.

The preferred method of transmission onto trunk circuits today is to convert the analog voice signal to digital form. Before the conversion process, voice signals are first compressed by compandors. In the United States, the μ-*law* is used for companding. The μ-law is governed by the following equation:

$$v_o = \frac{\ln(1 + \mu|v_i|)}{\ln(1 + \mu)} \qquad 0 \le |v_i| \le 1$$

where   ln = natural log
      v_o = output voltage
      v_i = input voltage
      μ = mu, compression factor (typically 100 or 255 used in U.S. PSTN)

Figure 12-9(a) depicts a graph of the μ-law equation for various values of μ. Note that the gain, v_o/v_i, is much larger for lower-amplitude signals than for higher-amplitude signals. This is the nonlinear characteristic of the compandor. As μ is increased, the degree of compression is increased. A value of $\mu = 0$ corresponds to linear amplification.

In Europe, voice signals are companded in accordance with ITU-TS (International Standards Union-Telecommunications Standardization Sector, formerly CCITT) *A-law* for companding and is governed by the following equation:

$$v_o = \frac{A \, |v_i|}{1 + \ln A}, \qquad 0 \le v_i \le \frac{1}{A}$$

$$= \frac{1 + \ln (A \, |v_i|)}{1 + \ln A}, \qquad \frac{1}{A} \le v_i \le 1$$

where A is the compression factor (ITU-TS recommendation: $A = 87.6$). As shown in Figure 12-9(b), there is very little difference between μ-law and A-law companding, except that at low amplitudes, the gain is greater for μ-law companding. A compression factor, A, of 87.6 is recommended by ITU-TS.

12.2 TRANSMISSION MEDIA FOR TRUNKS

Several types of transmission media are used for trunk circuits, ranging from twisted-pair wire to coaxial and fiber-optic cable. Satellite communication is also used as a transmission medium for trunk circuits. In each case, the purpose of the trunk is to interconnect switching centers to achieve longer-distance communications. Trunk circuits carry multiple voice channels, and in many cases, particularly with the latest fiber-optic technology, thousands of voice channels are multiplexed together and sent over a single cable. Various trunk media and their characteristics are considered here.

12.2.1 Open-Wire Pairs

Open-wire pairs were used in the early years of the telephone system. Although they are still used in some rural communities and older sections of towns, for the most part they have become part of our historical past.

A pair consists of two *open wires* suspended on telephone poles. The wires are separated by approximately 1 ft to minimize capacitance. Glass insulators mounted on wooden crossbeams of the telephone pole suspend the wires between poles. Open wire is usually made of steel coated with copper. Steel is used for the strength necessary to withstand varying weather conditions and to withstand the suspension weight of the wire between poles. Because most AC flows on the outer portion of a conductor due to *skin effect,* coated copper, the better of the two conductive metals, carries the electrical signals.

Distances as great as 50 km can be achieved with open-wire pairs before repeaters are necessary. Several disadvantages of open-wire pairs have caused it to become obsolete. It is unsightly and bulky, subject to crosstalk, and severely affected by weather conditions.

> **Skin Effect**
> The tendency for AC (alternating current) to flow on the outer portion of a conductor, especially at high frequencies.

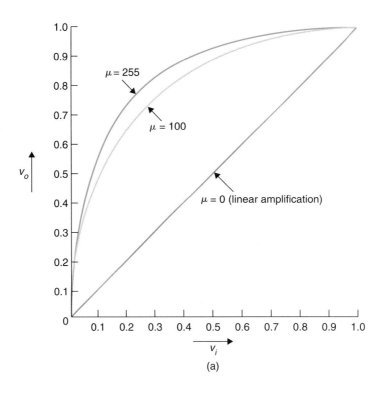

(a)

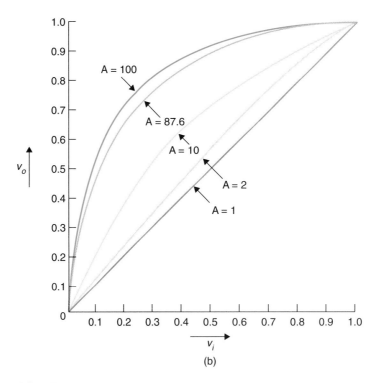

(b)

FIGURE 12-9
(a) μ-Law used for companding in the United States; (b) A-law used for companding in Europe.

12.2.2   TWISTED-PAIR WIRES

Twisted-pair wires are insulated pairs of copper wire that have been bundled together and insulated to form a single cable. Individual pairs of wires are twisted together to minimize crosstalk. Cables can contain several hundreds of twisted pairs, ranging from 19- to 26-gauge copper wire. The cables are laid throughout cities in underground tunnels. Because the twisted pairs are bound so closely together, they suffer from crosstalk even more so than open-wire pairs. Due to the small diameter of the wires, resistance contributes significantly to signal loss. The use of repeaters every 3 to 4 miles is required. Twisted pairs are used for short-haul trunks, typically with 12 or 24 multiplexed voice channels per twisted pair.

12.2.3   Coaxial Cable

At frequencies above 1 MHz, it becomes desirable to use coaxial cable. Radiation losses and adjacent channel interference are virtually eliminated by coaxial shielding. The greater available bandwidth offered by coax over wire pairs makes it much more suited for high-capacity trunk circuits used between cities and states and for national trunk routes. Coaxial cable also has a high propagation velocity rating, with excellent phase delay response.

Coax is manufactured with a hollow, cylindrical copper tube used for the shield. Insulating material (dielectric) separates the conductive tube from the copper center conductor. Several individual coaxial tubes are often bound together with insulating material and steel reinforcement to produce a high-capacity trunk cable. Each coaxial tube can carry several thousands of voice channels.

12.2.3.1   The Bell System L5 Coaxial Carrier   The Bell System *L5 carrier* is a long-haul trunk that includes 22 coaxial tubes bound together to form a single cable. Figure 12-10(a) illustrates a cross-sectional view of the L5 carrier. A total of 108,000 simultaneous two-way voice conversations can be carried by the cable. Ten tubes carry 108,000 voice channels in one direction, and 10 tubes are for the opposite direction. Two coaxial tubes are for backup spares. Repeaters for the L5 system are spaced at 1-mile intervals, maintaining an overall system bandwidth of 58 MHz. The DC power required for the repeaters is supplied through the cable. Power supply stations spaced at 120 km (75 repeaters apart) feed the adjoining cable with a DC potential of 1350 V. To minimize the possibility of arcing across the insulation, $+675$ V is supplied by a station to one end of the cable and -675 V by the adjacent station. Figures 12-10(b) through 12-10(d) illustrate the cable laying of the L5 carrier system.

12.2.4   Microwave Links

An alternative to coaxial cables for high-capacity long-haul trunks are microwave radio links. Several thousand voice channels are modulated onto microwave carrier frequencies and transmitted to repeater stations spaced 20 to 30 miles apart. Repeater antennas are typically perched on towers, hilltops, and huge skyscrapers so that no obstructions are in the *line-of-sight* transmission path between two repeater stations. Figure 12-11 illustrates the Bell System's distribution of broad-band microwave routes throughout the United States. A single microwave link interconnecting Cape Charles to Norfolk is shown in Figure 12-11(b).

(a)

(b)

(c)

(d)

FIGURE 12-10
(a) Cross-sectional view of the Bell System L5 coaxial carrier system, capable of carrying 108,000 simultaneous two-way voice conversations; (b) to (d) laying of the L5 carrier system. (Courtesy of AT&T Archives.)

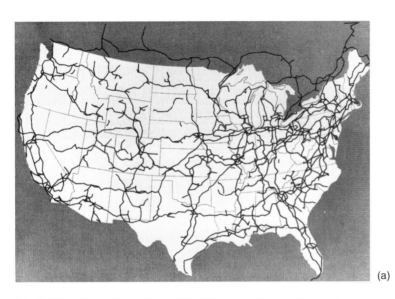

(a)

(b)

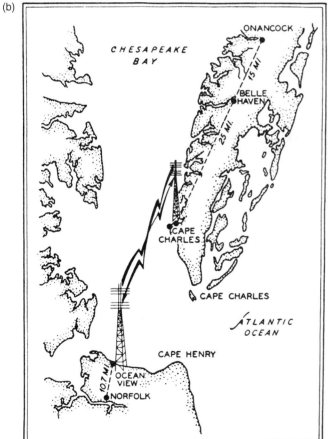

FIGURE 12-11

(a) The Bell System's broad-band microwave routes across the United States;
(b) microwave route linking the Cape Charles to Norfolk radio telephone system.
(Courtesy of AT&T Archives.)

Microwave radio links are expensive; however, the costs over coaxial media are offset by several advantages:

- Fewer repeaters are necessary for amplifying signals
- Distances between switching centers are shorter
- Underground facilities are not necessary
- Multiple channels can be transmitted over a single link
- Minimal delay times
- Minimal crosstalk
- Fewer repeaters mean increased reliability and less maintenance

Because both coaxial media and microwave links are well suited for high-capacity trunks, additional factors must be considered in determining which is best suited for a given application. Whereas coaxial cable is less prone to RF (radio frequency) interference, microwave radio links rely on the absence of physical as well as electrical obstructions between transmitting and receiving stations. Microwave antenna beam widths can be as narrow as 1 degree. Trees, buildings, mountains, and even airplanes can interfere with signal transmission. Varying weather conditions such as rain and intense heat can alter the direction of the beam, thus causing the signal to fade.

Over the years, the telecommunications highways through the air have become heavily congested with electrical signals. Microwave beams in large metropolitan areas often intersect with each other, causing interference. Frequency channels allocated by the FCC are limited in the amount of skyway traffic that can be handled.

12.2.5   Submarine Cables

The transmission of voice signals overseas has become possible through the use of submarine cables. Submarine cables are coaxial cables specially designed to withstand the rugged oceanic floor conditions throughout the world. It took nearly a century of progress before the first voice-grade cable was laid across the Atlantic Ocean floor in 1956. The TAT-1 (Transatlantic) Cable System, developed by AT&T, spanned a distance of 2200 nautical miles. The construction of the cable includes several layers of insulation and armored steel reinforcement surrounding the conductor to protect it from corrosion, temperature changes, and leakage. Repeaters are constructed in a similar manner to prevent the damage of internal circuitry. Figure 12-12 shows an undersea repeater unit. DC power for the repeater, as in coaxial trunk media used on land, must also be housed within the cable.

A considerable amount of engineering, testing, and oceanic research was performed before and during the laying of intercontinental submarine cables. Consider some of the major factors involved in this engineering feat:

- The cable must be protected from saltwater corrosion and leakage
- Suboceanic terrain conditions and ocean depth must be considered
- Temperature and pressure changes from sea level to ocean floor must be determined
- The weight of cable material and rate of descent to the oceanic floor are critical parameters
- Off-coast trenches must be dug in shallow waters to bury and protect the cable from fishing trawlers and anchors
- Electrical circuits must be environmentally tested at temperature extremes exceeding those of the ocean floor

FIGURE 12-12
Construction of the submarine repeater unit.

- Repeater units must be x-ray tested for faulty welds and leaks
- Performance tests must be exercised constantly while laying cable to determine immediately the location of a fault

The first-generation submarine cables laid during the mid-1950s carried 48 voice channels on two separate conductors with a diameter of 0.62 in. Vacuum tube amplifiers were used within the repeater units. Repeaters were separated by a distance of 39 nautical miles. The overall bandwidth for the 2200-nautical mile TAT-1 cable was 164 kHz. The latest generation of coaxial submarine cables span distances as great as 4000 miles, interconnecting every continent in the world. Solid-state amplifiers are used for repeater units. By decreasing the separation between repeater units and increasing conductor size, overall bandwidths of 28 MHz have been achieved. As many as 4000 voice channels are carried on center conductors with a diameter of $1\frac{1}{2}$ in.

In recent years, AT&T has installed the TAT-8 SL (Submarine Lightwave) cable shown in Figure 12-13(a). The single fiber-optic cable doubles the number of existing transatlantic cable circuits that are available. Figure 12-13(b) compares the TAT-8 and the coaxial copper cable used for the TAT-7. The fiber cable shown is half the size and one-third the weight of the TAT-7 coaxial copper cable.

12.2.6 Satellite Communications

In 1965, the first commercial satellite used for telecommunications was launched into space from Cape Kennedy.* The Intelsat I (called Early Bird) was designed to handle an average of 240 voice channels. Since then, several generations of satellites have been deployed throughout space. A dramatic increase in the number of TV and voice channels has occurred with each generation, consequently lowering the cost of this transmission medium. Satellite communication has become a major facet of the telecommunications industry. Thousands of long-distance transoceanic telephone calls are now placed throughout the world via the satellite link.

The satellite is essentially a microwave relay station placed in orbital space. Telephone and television broadcast signals are beamed up to the satellite from an

*James Martin, *Telecommunications and the Computer,* 2nd ed. (Englewood Cliffs, N.J.: Prentice-Hall, 1976), p. 280.

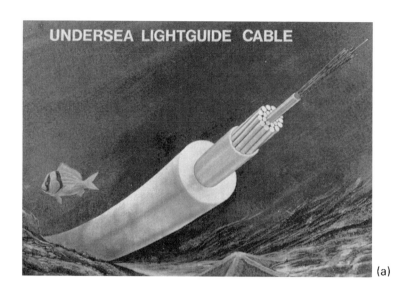

(a)

(b)

FIGURE 12-13
(a) AT&T's TAT-8 SL (submarine lightwave) fiber-optic cable more than doubles the previously laid transatlantic cable circuits. (b) TAT-8 SL compared with the older, larger TAT-7. (Courtesy of AT&T Archives.)

earth station through a large, highly directive microwave dish antenna that is synchronized to the position of the satellite. A device called a *transponder* is used on board the satellite to receive the weak microwave signal, amplify and condition it, and retransmit the signal back to another earth station at a different location on the planet.

To prevent the transponder's strong transmitted signal from interfering with the earth station's weak received signal, most commercial satellite links separate, transmit, and receive carrier frequencies by approximately 2 GHz. Earth stations typically transmit their signals to satellites on carrier frequencies in the 6-GHz band, ranging from 5.92 to 6.43 GHz. These frequencies are called the *up-link frequencies*. The satellite's transponder down-converts these signals to a 4-GHz band, ranging from 3.7 to 4.2 GHz. These frequencies are referred to as the *down-link frequencies*. Earth station receivers are tuned to these frequencies.

Modern telecommunication satellites are positioned in orbit at an elevation of approximately 22,300 miles above the equator (Figure 12-14). This is referred to as *geosynchronous* or *geostationary orbit*. In this orbit, the satellite is made to travel at

Transponder
Used on board satellites to receive a weak microwave signal, amplify and condition it, and retransmit it to another earth station at a different location.

Up-Link Frequencies
Satellite carrier frequencies in the 6-GHz band (5.92–6.43 GHz).

Down-Link Frequencies
A 4-GHz band of frequencies (3.7–4.2 GHz) to which earth station receivers are tuned.

Geosynchronous Orbit
Also known as *geostationary orbit*. Satellites positioned 22,300 miles above the Earth, thus maintaining a fixed position relative to a point on the planet.

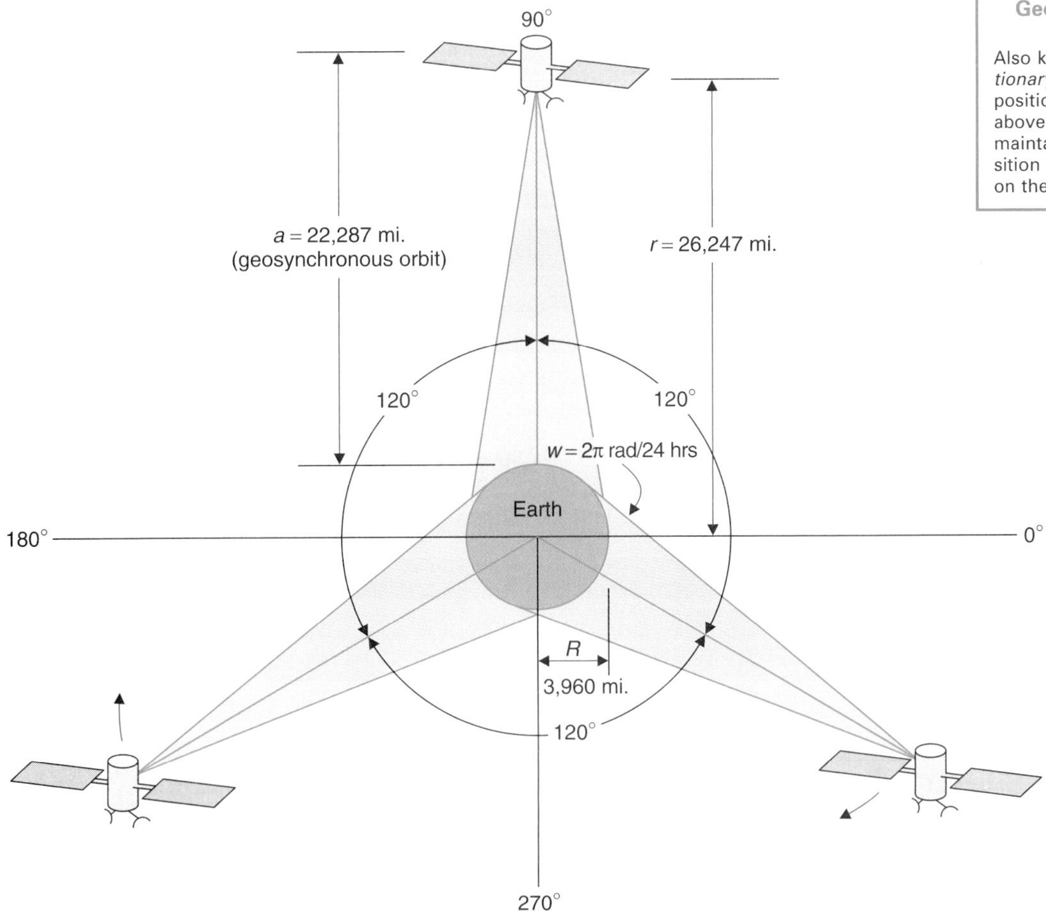

FIGURE 12-14
Three satellites in geosynchronous orbit spaced 120° apart can provide full coverage of the Earth, with the exception of the polar caps.

a velocity necessary to maintain a fixed position relative to a point above the equator (i.e., it rotates radially with the surface of the Earth and, therefore, remains fixed in the sky 24 hours a day). See Example 21.1. At an altitude of 22,300 miles, 40% of the Earth is exposed. The satellite's antenna is designed to emit a radiation pattern that covers this entire *exposed* portion. Satellites positioned in geosynchronous orbit, 120° apart from each other, can cover the entire surface of the earth, with the exception of the polar caps. Hence, the advantage to geosynchronous orbit is that it permits line-of-sight tracking by earth stations 24 hours a day. Earlier satellites had elliptical orbits and were useful for only short periods of the day. Figure 12-15 depicts the Telstar Models I and II communications satellites and a tracking microwave dish antenna.

EXAMPLE 12.1*

A satellite is to be launched into a geosynchronous orbit over the equator (i.e., it should rotate at the same rate as the Earth so that it remains over a fixed point on the surface). Compute the distance between the center of mass of the satellite and Earth, r, and the altitude of the geosunchronous satellite, A. See Figure 12-14.

Constants needed:

g = 32.2 ft/s^2 = gravitational acceleration at sea level
R = 3960 miles = radius of the earth
M = mass of the Earth (data not needed)
G = universal gravitation constant (data not needed)
F = gravitational force of attraction between two bodies

Solution:

Newton's law of universal gravitation states that the gravitational force between the Earth, of mass M, and a body, of mass m, is $F = GMm/r^2$, where r is the distance between the centers of mass of the masses. When $r = R$, however, then at sea level, $F = mg$. Therefore, $GMm/R^2 = mg$ and, hence,

$$GM = gR^2$$

(*Note:* This formula makes it unnecessary to look up G and M.) Therefore, we have

$$F = \frac{GMm}{r^2} = \frac{gR^2m}{r^2} = gm\,\frac{R^2}{r^2}$$

Now, for rotational motion, the acceleration is $\omega^2 r$, where ω equals angular velocity, so

$$F = ma = m\omega^2 r = gm\,\frac{R^2}{r^2}$$

Solving for r^3 gives

$$r^3 = g\,\frac{R^2}{\omega^2}$$

---

*The geosynchronous altitude problem as derived and presented by Ron Fischer, Mathematics Department instructor and Center Coordinator for Evergreen Valley College, San Jose, Calif.

(a)

(b)

(c)

FIGURE 12-15

(a) Half of Bell Laboratories "telephone terminal to outer space" at Crawford Hill, Holmdel, N.J.; (b) complete Telstar Model I satellite on worktable; (c) the Telstar III is capable of relaying tremendous amounts of information: up to 94,000 simultaneous two-way telephone conversations, or 360 video teleconferences, or 24 color television programs, or billions of bits per second of high-speed data and facsimile signals. The Telstar III satellite will operate longer than any of its predecessors—10 years instead of 7 years. (Courtesy of AT&T Archives.)

Now all quantities must be placed in consistent units. To get r in miles, we need g in miles/hr^2, R in miles, and ω in rad/hour.

$$g = 32.2 \, \frac{\text{ft}}{\text{s}^2} \cdot \frac{1 \text{ mile}}{5280 \text{ ft}} \cdot \frac{(3600)^2 \text{s}^2}{1 \text{ hr}^2} = 79,036.36 \text{ mi/hr}^2$$

$$\omega = \frac{2\pi \text{ rad}}{24 \text{ hr}} = (\pi/12) \text{ rad/hr}$$

Therefore,

$$r^3 = g \, \frac{R^2}{\omega^2} = (79,036.36) \, \frac{(3960)^2}{(\pi/12)^2} = 1.8083 \times 10^{13} \text{ mi}^3/\text{rad}^2$$

or $r = 26,247.83$ miles. The altitude, A, is then

$$r - R = 26,247.83 - 3960 = 22,287.83 \text{ miles}$$

(*Note:* In solving for r using dimensional analysis, the rad^2 term in the denominator is dimensionless and, therefore, disregarded.)

12.3 CENTRAL OFFICE SWITCHING SYSTEMS

Switching at the central office is necessary to establish a connection between two parties. For common battery systems, this is performed *automatically*. Common battery switching systems are classified into three basic categories:

1. Step by step
2. Crossbar
3. Electronic switching system

12.3.1 Step-by-Step Switching

By the 1920s, reliance on switchboard operators within the PSTN eventually reached the point where the services provided did not meet the needs of the general public. Alleged eavesdropping and suspicion of business malpractice on the part of telephone companies led to the invention of the first automatic switch. Alman B. Strowger, an undertaker concerned that the telephone company may have been diverting his business calls to competitors, invented an automatic dial switch that became the basis of telephone switching for the next 70 years. The *Strowger switch,* depicted in Figure 12-16, is a step-by-step (SXS) system that performs switching in two dimensions: *vertically,* and *horizontally.* The switching action is a direct result of the dial pulses generated by the rotary dial telephone. The switch shown here has 10 rows and 10 columns, thus making it possible for a caller to connect to 100 other subscribers with two dialed numbers. Strowger switch exchanges are still being used throughout the world today. Many are currently being replaced with more modern computerized switching exchanges.

Figure 12-17 illustrates a simplified version of a 10,000-line SXS central office switch. There are 10,000 subscribers that can be represented here by the numbers 0000 through 9999. When a caller goes off-hook, current is detected in the subscriber loop and the *preselector* switch becomes active. The preselector switch advances to a level that seizes an idle line and sends a dial tone to the caller. Let us assume that the party being dialed is **5831.** When the number **5** is dialed, the resulting electrical impulses cause the electromechanical relay of a *selector switch* to step in the vertical

Strowger Switch
Invented by Alman B. Strowger, an electromechanical step-by-step switch used in older central office switching systems.

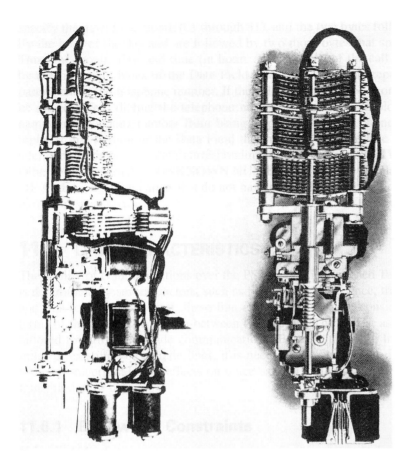

FIGURE 12-16
Strowger switch. (Courtesy of AT&T Archives.)

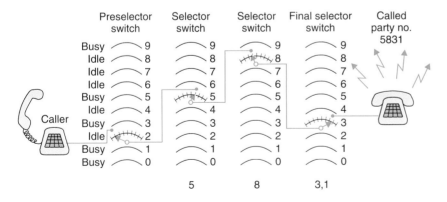

FIGURE 12-17
Simplified SXS call procedure to subscriber 5831.

direction to a level equal to 5. The wiper then advances, step by step, in the horizontal direction until it seizes an idle line available on the next selector switch. The movement of the wiper contact is similar to the way in which a television's channel selector switch operates. An **8** is then dialed, and the procedure is repeated with the next selector switch. The connection is further advanced to its final destination. The *final selector switch* is capable of handling the last two digits, **3** and **1.** When the **3** is dialed, the final selector switch advances vertically to the third level and horizontally to the first position. The called party at **5831** is tested for a busy condition, and the ring potential is applied if the party line is idle. Once the party answers, the lines are further supervised until the conversation is terminated. Additional switches can be used to extend the procedure, thus increasing the sophistication of the network.

12.3.2 Crossbar Switch

Crossbar Switch
An electromechanical switch used in older central offices. The crossbar switch was an upgrade to the *Strowger switch.*

It was not long after the Strowger switch came into use before a faster and more sophisticated system was developed. This system is called the *crossbar switch.* Crossbar switches are still serving several metropolitan and rural areas throughout the world. The crossbar switch, as its name implies, is a lattice of crossed bars that make and break contact. Figure 12-18 shows the crossbar switch.

Crossbar switches, like Strowger switches, are electromechanically activated and rely on moving parts. A detailed view of the crossbar switch is shown in Figure 12-19. The switch contains sets of contact points or *crosspoints* with three to six individual contacts per set. Magnets cause vertical and horizontal bars to cross each

FIGURE 12-18
Crossbar switch. (Courtesy of AT&T Archives.)

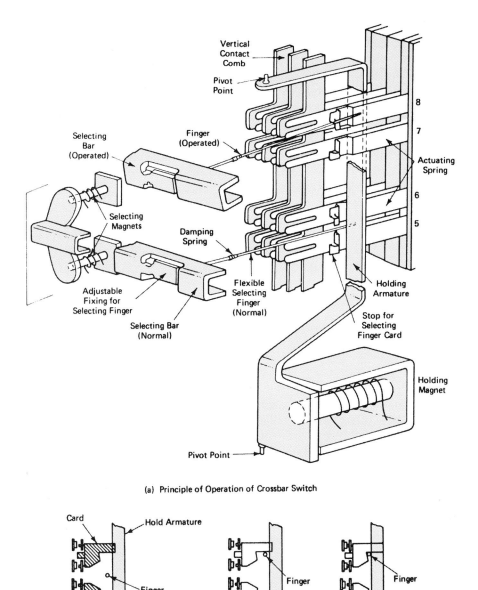

(a) Principle of Operation of Crossbar Switch

(b) Finger Action

FIGURE 12-19
Detailed views of the crossbar switch: (a) principle of operation; (b) finger action.
(Courtesy of Northern Telecom.)

other and make contact at coordinates determined by the number being called. Each switch typically has either 100 or 200 crosspoints. The lattice structure of the cross-bar switch has 10 *horizontal select bars* and either 10 or 20 *vertical hold bars*. The horizontal and vertical hold bars are activated by magnets. Any individual crosspoint within the matrix can make contact by activating one horizontal select bar and one vertical hold bar, similar to a rectangular coordinate system.

12.3.2.1 Blocking By combining crossbar switches, the number of possible signal paths can be increased, consequently lessening the likelihood of a signal path being blocked. As mentioned earlier, in most cases less than 10% of all telephones are in use at the same time. It is, therefore, not economical to provide a signal path between every subscriber. *Blocking* occurs during heavy traffic volume when the central office switches are fully utilized. A distinctive busy tone is sent to the caller from the central office if the connection cannot be made. The blocked call has nothing to do with the party being called and whether that line is busy or idle. The call will have to be postponed until a later time, when traffic subsides. The busiest times of the day are from 8 A.M. to 10 A.M. and 3 P.M. to 5 P.M. Holidays such as Christmas and New Year's Day are also peak operating times for phone companies, when one is likely to experience blocking. Blocking has also been known to occur during emergency situations involving entire communities, such as earthquakes and fires.

Figure 12-20 illustrates a simplified matrix with 25% blocking. Callers 4 and 7, 2 and 8, and 5 and 6 are on line with each other. When caller 3 attempts to make a call to 1, it is blocked. All available lines are used in the switching arrangement. This is referred to as 25% blocking; that is, one out of four calls is blocked.

> **Blocking**
> Occurs when a central office switch is overburdened with more calls than it can handle.

12.3.3 Electronic Switching System

The computer revolution has brought forth major developments within the central office. These developments have carried the industry forward toward much faster and more reliable switching systems capable of handling more calls and offering new customer services. Although this progress has been slow due to the enormous size and complexity of the PSTN, eventually all existing electromechanical switching systems will be replaced with computerized switching systems. These switching systems are referred to as *ESS*, an acronym for *electronic switching system.*

> **Electronic Switching System (ESS)**
> A solid-state, computer-controlled switching system used in the central office.

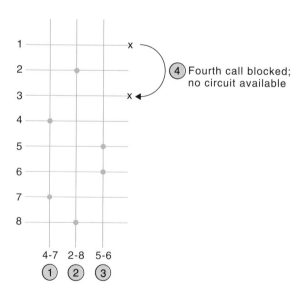

FIGURE 12-20
Crossbar switch with 25% blocking.

12.3.3.1 No. 1 ESS In 1965, the Bell System introduced the first computer-controlled switching system to be used in the PSTN. The *No. 1 ESS* digital computer uses *stored program control (SPC)* to perform switching, signaling, and administrative tasks. Customer service with the No. 1 ESS has proved far superior to the conventional techniques of the crossbar and SXS switching facilities. The No. 1 ESS can handle from 10,000 to as many as 70,000 subscribers. Several metropolitan areas currently use the No. 1 ESS. It has served as a steppingstone to more advanced ESS models developed over the years. The control panel for the No. 1 ESS system is shown in Figure 12-21. Switching and memory are described as follows:

No. 1 ESS Switching The switching arrangement for the No. 1 ESS is made up of *sealed dry* reed switches that are activated or deactivated by a 300-μs current pulse. The magnetic material within the reed relay is called a *ferreed.* No power is consumed by the switch while it is in its quiescent state of either opened or closed. The current pulses determine the remanent state of the switch.

No. 1 ESS Memory Two types of memory are used for the No. 1 ESS: *twistor memory,* and *ferrite sheet memory.* Twistor memory is superpermanent memory that stores the control program and any data that are not likely to change. Memory is, thus, *read-only (ROM)* and nonvolatile. Power failures and read errors cannot alter the twistor memory contents. Only an operator can change its contents by manually extracting the card and reprogramming its contents with a special device. The twistor memory card is shown in Figure 12-22.

FIGURE 12-21
Front panel control for the No. 1 ESS. (Courtesy of AT&T Archives.)

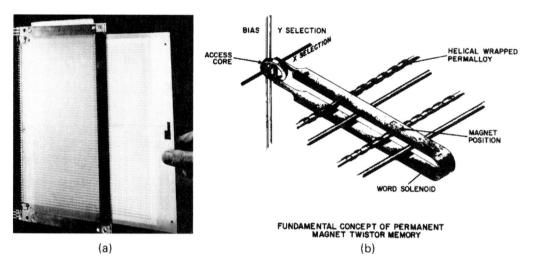

(a)   (b)

FIGURE 12-22
(a) Twistor memory card; (b) the No. 1 ESS semipermanent twistor memory, which operates as follows: Information is stored in the vicalloy magnet next to the intersection of the twistor wire and the copper solenoid. A current pulse sent through the x and y wires will cause the ferrite core to send a pulse through the copper "word" solenoid. If the magnet at the intersection of the solenoid and the twistor is not magnetized, the pulse will reverse the direction of the magnetic field that links the intersection and generate a "read-out" pulse in the twistor wire. If the magnet at the intersection is magnetized, its field will prevent the reversal at the intersection and no significant voltage will be produced in the twistor wire. (Courtesy of AT&T Archives.)

The twistor memory card is made of aluminum sheets measuring approximately 11 by $6\frac{1}{2}$ in. Each sheet contains rows of magnetic spots that are either magnetized or demagnetized before installation. The magnetic state of each spot represents one bit of stored data. Each card stores 64 words that are 24 bits in length. The state of each bit is determined by sending a pulse down an *interrogating loop* of wire. Permalloy magnetic tape is spirally wound around copper sensing wires placed over the magnetic spots. The interrogating loop intersects the magnetic spot and sensing wire at right angles. If the spot has not been magnetized, the interrogating pulse will cause the permalloy magnetic tape to become magnetized for the duration of the interrogating pulse. This results in a small current that is sensed by amplifiers. When the spot is already magnetized, no current is produced.

Ferrite sheets are used for temporary storage of data (read–write memory) related to the processing and administration of a call. The ferrite sheet, shown in Figure 12-23(a), consists of 256 perforated holes on a 1-in.-square board. Ferrite material surrounds each hole. Three lines are threaded through each hole to allow reading and writing to each hole in a manner similar to *core memory*. Each hole acts as a core and stores one bit of information. The ferrite sheets are stacked in a module, and four modules make up a *Call Store*, each holding 196,608 bits of read–write information. Figure 12-23(b) depicts one module of ferrite sheet memory. An office of about 10,000 lines generally requires two or more Call Stores (eight modules). A 65,000-line office with a high calling rate may contain 40 Call Stores. The No. 1 ESS can address over 1 million bits of memory.

(a)

(b)

FIGURE 12-23
(a) Ferrite sheet memory card; (b) ferrite sheet memory module.

12.3.3.2   No. 2 ESS   The No. 2 ESS is capable of handling 1000 to 10,000 lines. Although its capacity to handle several lines is not as great as the No. 1 ESS, its attractiveness lies in its ability to provide extremely reliable service to smaller communities at an economical cost. Also, the No. 2 ESS is fully operational from a remote location. Many rural areas employ the No. 2 ESS, whereby traffic volume, maintenance requirements, and performance of administrative tasks are monitored and achieved in a more populated area. An upgrading of logic, from the diode–transistor logic (DTL) used in the No. 1 ESS to resistor–transistor logic (RTL), has increased the speed and reduced the size of the control circuitry.

12.3.3.3 No. 3 ESS

In the 1970s, LSI technology brought forth further enhancements to the ESS. The No. 3 ESS employs bipolar LSI ROMs for microprogram control. Under microprogram control, the SPC is executed from a unique set of *microinstructions* stored in ROM. The No. 3 ESS was designed for small offices serving rural communities and small cities of 100 to 1000 subscribers.

12.3.3.4 No. 4 ESS

The No. 4 ESS was first installed within the PSTN in 1976. It was the first all-electronic exchange with digital circuit technology employed in its computerized control and switching matrix. Over 10,000 trunk circuits can be handled by the No. 4 ESS, which uses a combination of *time-division multiplexing (TDM)* and *space-division multiplexing (SDM)* (see Section 12.4).

In TDM, incoming analog voice signals are digitized and converted to PCM (pulse code modulation) signals. PCM signals from several voice channels are multiplexed together and loaded into a memory buffer. From here, the stored program control selects an available path through the SDM switch. The multiplexed signal is then routed through the outgoing buffer to the appropriate line.

12.3.3.5 No. 5 ESS

The No. 5 ESS is the most advanced and versatile central/toll switching unit developed in the Bell System ESS product line. It uses the latest technology in integrated circuits, fiber optics, and software design. Metropolitan areas with as many as 100,000 subscribers can be serviced as well as rural areas with as few as 1000. A fully remote controlled unit, the ESS No. 5A, has been developed to serve as an economical central office that can be operated by a host No. 5 ESS system from as far as 100 miles away. As many as 4000 subscribers per unit can be serviced remotely over digital T1 carrier facilities.

The hardware design of the No. 5 ESS relies heavily on LSI technology specifically designed to handle high-voltage potentials up to 500 V. Testing of ringing functions can, therefore, be performed without the large risks of damaging components. The addition of new technology to the No. 5 ESS was kept in mind by Bell Laboratory's design engineers. A modular design concept was followed that permits rapid growth of the switching system as well as ensuring that the system fits smoothly into the Bell System's existing facilities.

Software technology incorporated into the No. 5 ESS was also designed to permit the rapid addition of new features as the hardware technology advances. Most of the controlling software for the No. 5 ESS are written in a language called *C*, developed by Bell Labs. The operating system, *UNIX,* also developed by Bell Labs, provides an abundance of tools specifically tailored to support software design and testing. Figure 12-24 illustrates the No. 5 ESS. Listed here are some of the custom calling features of the No. 5 ESS.*

Call Forwarding: Transfers a call automatically to where you can be reached.

Call Waiting: Acts as a home or business second line. While you are using the phone, a short tone warns you of an incoming call. The dial switch can be pressed and released to answer the second caller. The same action allows you to switch back and forth between callers.

---

*Compiled from the *Sprint Central Telephone—Nevada First Source Phone Book,* Area Code 702 Las Vegas Telephone Directory. Reuben H. Donnelley and Centel Directory Company, July 1993.

FIGURE 12-24
No. 5 ESS. (Courtesy of AT&T Archives.)

Cancel Call Waiting: Allows you to cancel Call Waiting so that you can enjoy un-interrupted or important calls.

Call Within: Allows you to use internal telephones within your household as an in-expensive intercom. By dialing your own number and hanging up, all the phones con-nected to the same line will ring and you may talk to other members that answer.

Speed Call: Allows you to program several telephone numbers that can be dialed by pressing a one- or two-digit code. A two-digit access code is typically dialed first to enable Speed Call.

Three-way Calling: Allows you to call two other parties and have a three-way conversation.

Return Call: If you cannot get to your telephone when it is ringing, Return Call will allow you to dial a special code and the telephone network will announce the last number that called you, unless it is a private number.

Redial Call: Allows you to redial the last number you called whether the call was answered, unanswered, or busy.

Call Trace: Call Trace allows you to trace the last call that you received. By acti-vating the trace with a special code number entered from your Touch Tone keypad, the telephone company will store the calling number, your own number, and the date and time the last call took place. This feature should only be used for threatening or obscene phone calls. Only an authorized agency is provided with trace results.

Caller ID: Allows you to screen your calls by viewing a special telephone number display that shows you the telephone number of the person calling you. You can choose to answer or not depending on the number being displayed. Caller ID is available in some states but not in others for privacy and other reasons.

Caller ID Block: Allows you to prevent your telephone number from appearing on a Caller ID display device when you are making a call. Instead, the party you are calling will see "Private Number" on their display when their telephone is ringing.

12.4   MULTIPLEXING

> **Multiplexing**
> Combining of two or more signals and transmitting them onto a single transmission line.

In communications, *multiplexing* is the process of combining two or more signals and transmitting them over a single transmission link. *Demultiplexing* is the reverse process of separating the multiplexed signals at the receiving end of the transmission link. The link can be any of the transmission media discussed earlier. Multiplexing results in the efficient use of the communications link. Trunk circuits within the PSTN use multiplexing techniques to combine several signals. The number of signals that can be multiplexed together is directly related to available *space, time,* and *bandwidth.* Space is required for the medium to exist in, and time is required for multiple signals to be transmitted and received. Perhaps the single most important factor in multiplexing is bandwidth. Bandwidth is necessary to accommodate the related frequency components of the multiplexed signals. The greater the bandwidth, the greater the number of signals that can be multiplexed. For digital signals, transmission speed is directly related to the available bandwidth. Wideband transmission media such as coaxial cable, microwave, and fiber-optic links, for example, have the capacity to multiplex several thousand voice signals together. There are three fundamental classifications of multiplexing:

> **Demultiplexing**
> Separating *multiplexed* signals received on a single transmission line and distributing them to several individual circuits.

1. Space-division multiplexing (SDM)
2. Frequency-division multiplexing (FDM)
3. Time-division multiplexing (TDM)

Multiplexing has become an essential part of the communication system today. It is necessary for us to understand the concept of multiplexing and how it results in efficient use of the communications channel.

12.4.1   Space-Division Multiplexing

> **Space-Division Multiplexing (SDM)**
> Multiplexing that utilizes physical space to combine multiple signals into a single, bundled transmission cable.

Space-division multiplexing (SDM) is simply the combining of physically separate signals into a bundled cable. It would not make sense to have a unique set of telephone poles or underground trenches for each telephone subscriber. Subscriber loop and trunk circuits are, therefore, combined. The shared use of space is attained in SDM. Because large volumes of space are not always available to contain cables, TDM or FDM are often combined with SDM.

12.4.2   Frequency-Division Multiplexing

> **Frequency-Division Multiplexing (FDM)**
> Multiplexing that utilizes the frequency domain to send multiple signals simultaneously over a channel's available bandwidth.

Frequency-division multiplexing (FDM) utilizes a channel's available bandwidth to send multiple signals simultaneously. By modulating several subcarriers with independent telephone signals, a composite signal can be generated and modulated onto a main carrier. The carrier is then transmitted onto a channel. SDM is consequently minimized. Figure 12-25(a) depicts FDM of three sine waves: 1, 2, and 3 kHz. Three

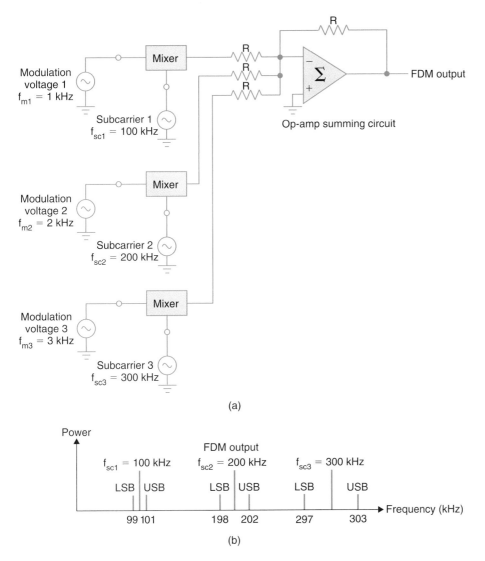

FIGURE 12-25
(a) Three independent sine waves mixed with subcarrier frequencies to produce the FDM output; (b) frequency spectrum of the FDM output signal.

subcarriers (100, 200, and 300 kHz) are mixed with the three independent modulating voltages. The output of each (nonlinear) mixer is electrically summed together to produce the given FDM output. The resulting frequency spectrum is shown in Figure 12-25(b).

12.4.2.1 Hierarchy of the Bell System's FDM Groups To standardize the telecommunications highways of the world, the Bell System has formed a hierarchy of *groups* that classify the number of voice channels that are multiplexed together before they are sent onto a trunk circuit (Figure 12-26). The trunk circuit may be microwave, fiber, or coax. Groups may also be multiplexed together to form higher groups in the hierarchy before transmission. The 300- to 3400-Hz telephone voice

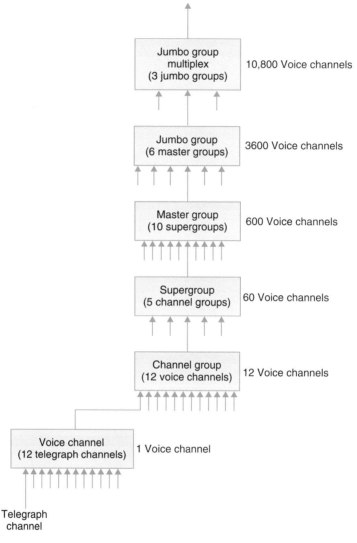

FIGURE 12-26
Hierarchy of the Bell System FDM groups.

channel is regarded as the fundamental building block of the hierarchy. A single voice channel can be further divided into 12 telegraph channels.

At the bottom of the hierarchy is the *telegraph channel*. A telegraph channel contains messages sent by telegraph equipment such as a Teletype terminal. The electrical impulses from the Teletype are used to frequency modulate a tone. As many as 12 tones can be modulated by 12 independent Teletypes to produce a composite signal that is sent over a single voice channel. The composite signal has no frequency components outside the voice-grade channel of 300 to 3400 Hz.

Twelve voice channels make up a *channel group*. By multiplexing five channel groups, a total of 60 voice channels is combined to form a *supergroup*. Ten supergroups form a *master group* containing 600 voice channels. Six master groups form a *jumbo group* of 3600 voice channels. At the top of the hierarchy is the *jumbo-group multiplex*. The jumbo-group multiplex is formed by multiplexing three jumbo groups together for a total of 10,800 voice channels. The Bell System L5 Carrier discussed earlier contains 20 coaxial tubes, each tube carrying a jumbo-group multiplex signal. Ten are used for transmitted signals, and 10 are for received signals. Thus, 108,000 (10 transmit and 10 receive jumbo-group multiplex signals) simultaneous telephone calls are possible through a combination of both SDM and FDM on the L5 carrier.

Figure 12-27(a) illustrates how 12 voice channels are frequency-division multiplexed together to form the basic channel group of composite signals. Each voice channel is mixed by a balanced modulator with subcarriers separated by 4 kHz. This technique is referred to as *single-sideband suppressed carrier (SSBSC)*; 4-kHz bandpass filters are used to separate adjacent voice channels and filter the lower sideband (LSB) of each signal. This prevents sidebands from spilling into adjacent channels. The 12 lower sidebands are electrically summed together and further filtered to produce the FDM channel group output. A *pilot tone* of 104.08 kHz is sent with the channel group output signal for monitoring and demodulation purposes at the receiving end.

> **Single-sideband Suppressed Carrier (SSBSC)**
> An amplitude modulation (AM) technique that suppresses the carrier frequency and one of the sidebands. Realizes a significant power savings.

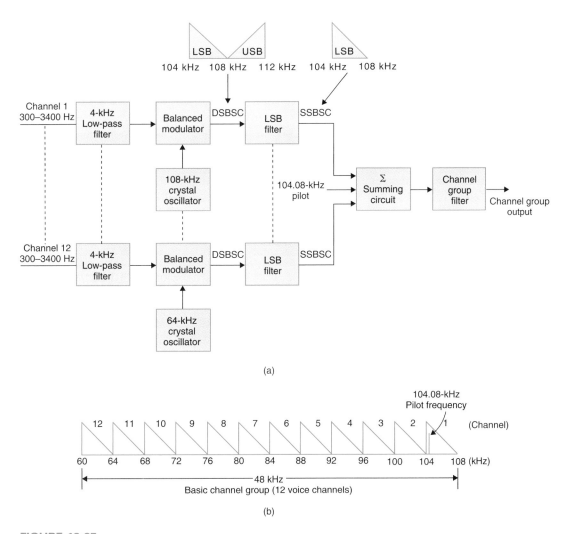

(a)

(b)

FIGURE 12-27
(a) Formation of the Bell System's channel group; (b) frequency distribution of the channel group.

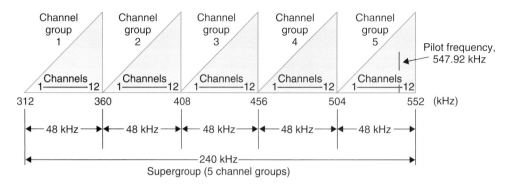

FIGURE 12-28
Frequency distribution of the Bell System supergroup.

The distribution of frequencies for the channel group is shown in Figure 12-27(b). A triangle is typically used to denote the distributed frequency spectrum as a result of mixing. The triangle, when facing as shown, denotes the selection of the LSB signals. LSB signals are said to be *inverted sidebands;* that is, the higher frequencies of the voice channel become the lower frequencies of the translated frequency spectrum.

Figure 12-28 illustrates the frequency distribution of signals for the supergroup. Five channel groups that make up a supergroup are translated to a frequency band occupying the range from 312 to 512 kHz, a bandwidth of 240 kHz (5 channel groups × 48 kHz each). The FDM process is repeated here. The upper-sideband (USB) frequencies are selected in the formation of a supergroup. Note that the triangle for the supergroup is opposite that of the channel group due to the selection of the USB. Higher frequencies appear at the higher end of the distributed spectrum.

12.4.3 Time-Division Multiplexing

Time-Division Multiplexing (TDM)
Multiplexing that utilizes the time domain to interleave multiple signals onto a single transmission line.

Analog-to-Digital Converter (ADC)
Used to convert an analog signal to a digital signal through quantization.

Pulse-Code Modulation (PCM)
Modulation technique that converts an analog signal into a digital bit stream for transmission.

A third form of multiplexing is called *time-division multiplexing (TDM).* Before 1960, telecommunications was predominantly analog transmission, with FDM serving as the major form of multiplexing. Since then, time-division multiplexed PCM (pulse-code modulation) has dominated the scene and become the preferred method of transmission onto PSTN trunk circuits.

In contrast to FDM, TDM involves the distribution of multiple signals in the *time domain,* whereas in FDM, these signals are distributed in the *frequency domain.* Another major distinction between these two forms of multiplexing is that FDM is an analog process, whereas TDM is a digital process. In TDM, several analog signals are sampled and converted to digital bit streams through the use of *analog-to-digital (A/D) converters.* The process of converting the analog signal into an encoded digital value is referred to as *pulse-code modulation (PCM).* In TDM, signals from several sources are digitized and *interleaved* to form a PCM signal. The time-division multiplexed PCM signal is then transmitted onto a single channel. When the digital bit stream is received, the reverse process is performed. The bit stream is *demultiplexed* and converted back to the original analog signals, and the analog signals are routed to their final destination.

Figure 12-29 illustrates the concept of TDM. Four analog signals are contiguously sampled and digitized by an 8-bit A/D converter. The interleaved binary serial

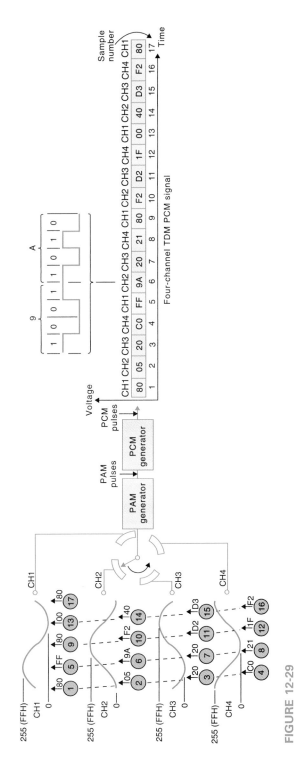

FIGURE 12-29
Simplified diagram illustrating TDM.

bit stream is transmitted onto the communications channel. One of CH2's sampled and digitized values has been extracted to depict the binary signal actually transmitted.

12.5 NORTH AMERICAN DIGITAL MULTIPLEX HIERARCHY

T-Carrier System
A hierarchy of TDM/PCM signals used in most telephone trunk circuits today.

Before its divestiture, the Bell System established one of the most widely used time-division multiplexed PCM systems in Northern America. This transmission system is known as the *T-carrier system*. A hierarchy of this TDM PCM structure is shown in Figure 12-30. Table 12-2 lists the characteristics of each T-carrier signal. T-carriers are used in most major trunk circuits today.

12.5.1 The Bell System T1 Carrier

T1 Carrier
Fundamental building block of the *T-carrier system*. The T1 carrier, also known as a DS-1 (Digital Signal-1), consists of 24 TDM/PCM channels and one framing bit. The transmission rate is 1.544 Mbps.

Because Bell System *T1 carrier* is the fundamental building block of the TDM multiplex hierarchy, we limit our discussion to the T1 carrier. In 1984, more than 120 million voice miles were transmitted on T1 carriers in the United States alone. Your telephone conversations today, beyond the local loop or class 5 switching centers, have most likely been digitized, encoded into a PCM signal, and multiplexed onto a T-carrier together with several other callers.

The T1 carrier consists of 24 voice channels that are sampled, digitized, and encoded into a TDM PCM signal. Each sample is encoded into an 8-bit digital word (sign plus 7-bit data) that represents the voice amplitude at the time of the sample. Coding of the PCM signal for a single sample is shown in Figure 12-31, and the T1 carrier frame format is shown in Figure 12-32.

Framing Bit
The synchronization bit used in a T1 frame: one framing bit per frame, and 12 bits per superframe.

The transmission rate onto the T1 carrier is 1.544 Mbps (million bits per second). DS-1 (digital signal 1) is the designation for the signal number and its transmission rate. The 1.544–Mbps transmission rate is established by sampling each of the 24 voice frequency channels contiguously at an 8-kHz rate. Twenty-four channels at eight bits per sample yield a total of 192 bits.

T1 Carrier Frame
A frame consisting of 192 bits plus one framing bit.

Because the sampling sequence of a single sweep of all 24 channels occurs in a predetermined order, the receiving equipment must employ a method of synchronizing with the serial bit stream. For this purpose, a *framing bit (F-bit)* is added to the beginning of the 192 bits to make up the *T1 carrier frame*. The T1 carrier frame, therefore, consists of 193 bits. The time duration of a frame is 125 μs ($\frac{1}{8}$ kHz); 193 bits $\times$ 8 kHz results in the bit rate of 1.544 Mbps.

TABLE 12-2
North American Digital Multiplexing Hierarchy

Line Type	Digital Signal No.	Number of TDM Voice Channels	Transmission Rate (Mbps)	Transmission Media
T1	DS-1	24	1.544	Wire pair
T1C	DS-1C	48 (2 T1 lines)	3.152	Wire pair
T2	DS-2	96 (4 T1 lines; 2 T1-C lines)	6.312	Wire pair, fiber
T3	DS-3	672 (28 T1 lines; 7 T2 lines)	44.736	Coax, microwave fiber
T4	DS-4	4032 (168 T1 lines; 6 T3 lines)	274.176	Coax, microwave fiber
T5	DS-5	8064 (336 T1 lines; 2 T4 lines)	560.160	Coax, fiber

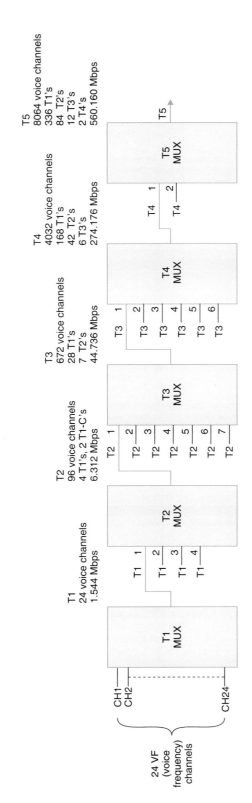

FIGURE 12-30

Block diagram of the North American digital multiplexing hierarchy.

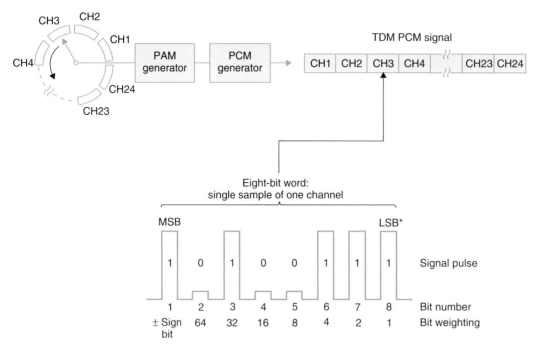

FIGURE 12-31
Coding for the T1 carrier PCM signal.

T1 carrier frames are transmitted in groups of 12. Twelve frames make up a *superframe*. The PCM receiver synchronizes to an alternating pattern of 1s and 0s (101010) transmitted as framing bits in *odd*-numbered frames within the superframe. Even-numbered frames within the superframe have a framing bit pattern of 001110. The format of the T1 carrier frame and its relationship to the superframe are shown in Figure 12-33.

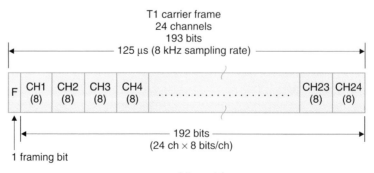

FIGURE 12-32
T1 carrier frame format.

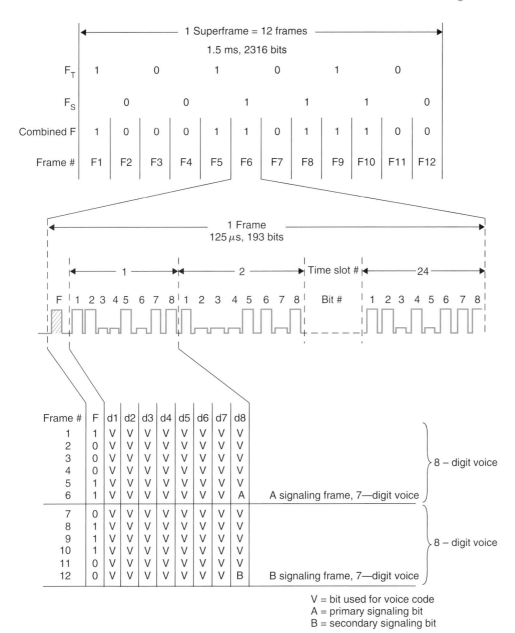

FIGURE 12-33
Frame structure for a T1 carrier frame and superframe. (From Bell System Technical Reference Publication 62411, *High Capacity Digital Service Channel Specification*, Sept. 1983.)

Signaling information, such as on-hook/off-hook condition or ringing, must also be transmitted between digital channel banks. This is accomplished by *robbing* the 65B position of each channel's 8-bit word. To keep distortion to a minimum, this is performed *only* in the sixth and twelfth frames, as shown in Figure 12-33. In all other frames, the LSB position conveys the normal voice data.

Extended Super Frame (ESF)
A TDM/PCM signal that extends the DS-1 (T1 Carrier) superframe signal from 12 to 24 frames.

The preferred framing format for all new designs of DS-1 rate terminals or equipment utilizes the *extended superframe (ESF)* format.* ESF extends the DS-1 superframe structure from 12 to 24 frames (4632 bits) and divides the 8-kbps, 193rd bit position pattern (F-bits) previously used for basic frame and robbed bit signaling synchronization into a number of subchannels.

12.5.2   Digital Channel Banks

The PSTN uses *digital channel banks* to perform the sampling, encoding, and multiplexing of 24 voice channels for the basic DS-1 signal. Digital channel banks are designated D1 through D5, in accordance with the respective technology used over the years. D1 channel banks, the first of the channel banks, employed discrete components. A 7-bit data word (sign plus 6-bit data) was originally used to represent the sampled voice. The eighth bit was used exclusively for signaling. As technology advanced, new specifications were written to meet the improved performance resulting from integrated-circuit technology. D3 channel banks incorporated SSI (small-scale integration) technology. Most of today's channel banks are D4 and D5, which use custom-designed LSI technology. Eight-bit data words are used to represent voice, thus improving on the SNR. For the most part, D1 channel banks have become obsolete. D2 and D3 channel banks are slowly being replaced with more recent equipment as well.

12.5.3   Pulse Train for the T1 Carrier

The PCM signal discussed so far has been presented as a *unipolar pulse train;* that is, the pulses are positive. Although these pulses are regenerated, occasionally an error is made. These errors have been known to produce clicks in the received telephone signal. Fewer errors are produced if the PCM signal is converted from a unipolar to a *bipolar pulse train,* in which the polarity of each consecutive pulse must be reversed (Figure 12-34). The bipolar DS-1 pulse train is the actual signal presented to the T1 carrier line. Note that the bipolar pulse train must maintain a 50% duty cycle whenever a pulse is present. If a pulse is present within a time slot, positive or negative, it represents a 1-bit. If there is no pulse present within a time slot, it represents a 0-bit.

12.5.4   B8ZS Coding

Bipolar with 8 Zero Substitution (B8ZS)
A self-clocking encoding technique for synchronization of *T-carrier signals.* Ensures adequate signal energy by substituting any string of eight consecutive zeros within the serial bit stream with a specific 8-bit code.

For receivers to maintain synchronization to the DS-1 bipolar signal, there must be an adequate amount of energy in the signal at any given time. This is true for many synchronous serial transmission links. The problem arises when an excessive number of 0s are transmitted. For the DS-1 bipolar pulse train shown in Figure 12-34(b), suppose the line is quiet (all 0s). No alternating pulses (representing 1s) would be present for the receiver to synchronize to. To circumvent this problem within the T1 network, common carriers require a minimum number of 1-bits within a given amount of time or within a given number of bits transmitted. One technique used for ensuring compliance with pulse density requirements for synchronization is called **B8ZS** *(bipolar with 8 zero substitution)* **coding.** B8ZS coding ensures adequate signal energy by substituting any string of eight consecutive zeros within the serial bit stream

---

*Bell Communications Research, Inc., 1985, *The Extended Superframe Format Interface Specification.*

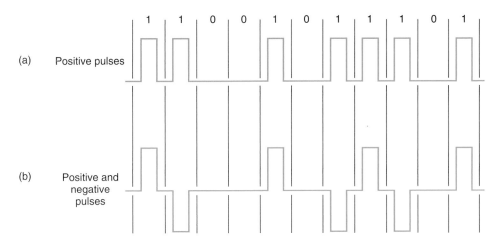

FIGURE 12-34
(a) Unipolar pulse train; (b) bipolar pulse train.

with a specific 8-bit code. There are two 8-bit replacement codes. They are inserted as follows:

1. If the pulse preceding the string of eight consecutive 0s is a positive one pulse, the inserted 8-bit code is $0\ 0\ 0\ +\ -\ 0\ -\ +$. For example,

	1	2	3	4	5	6	7	8
Original word:	0	0	0	0	0	0	0	0
Substituted word:	0	0	0	+1	−1	0	−1	+1

Transmitted bit stream:

2. If the pulse preceding the string of eight consecutive 0s is a negative 1 pulse, the inserted 8-bit code is $0\ 0\ 0\ -\ +\ 0\ +\ -$. For example,

	1	2	3	4	5	6	7	8
Original word:	0	0	0	0	0	0	0	0
Substituted word:	0	0	0	−1	+1	0	+1	−1

Transmitted bit stream:

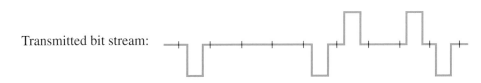

The receiver, on receiving either of the two substituted bit streams, simply replaces the B8ZS code with the original string of eight zeros. The obvious question now arises: How does the receiver distinguish between the B8ZS code and eight bits

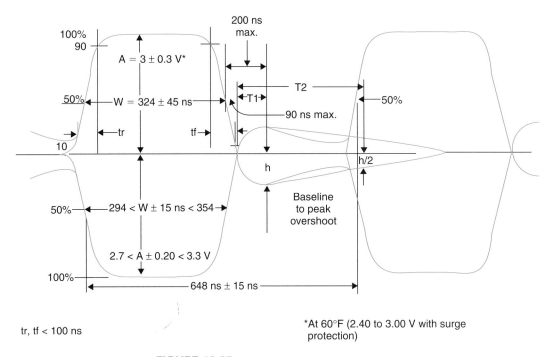

FIGURE 12-35

Output pulse characteristic for the DS-1 signal. (From Bell System Technical Reference Publication 62411, *Addendum 1 M24—Digital Data Throughput,* June 1985.)

of data that happen to be the same sequence? A close look at the *transmitted bit stream* for either of the B8ZS codes presented earlier will reveal that *bipolar violations* occur in the **fourth** and **seventh** bit positions. (See preceding pulses to these bit positions.) A bipolar violation occurs in a T1 signal whenever two consecutive pulses occur with the *same* polarity, regardless of the number of zero bit times that separate the two pulses. Each pulse, or 1-bit, must be alternating in polarity, as shown in Figure 12-34(b). The receiver now has a mechanism for distinguishing between eight bits of data that should be replaced with zeros and eight bits that should be left alone as part of the message stream.

If 16 or more zeros occur in the bit stream, two or more consecutive B8ZS codes are inserted into the transmitted serial bit stream. This is possible, because the eighth bits of both B8ZS codes are positive and negative logic 1 pulses that will precede the next B8ZS code under the same rules. Figure 12-35 depicts the pulse characteristics of the bipolar DS-1 signal.

PROBLEMS

1. What types of trunks are used to interconnect the following?
   a. Central offices.
   b. Tandem office to a central office.
   c. Central office to a toll center.
   d. Toll center to toll center.

2. How many classes of switching exchanges are used in North America, and what are their names?
3. Name five advantages that a private leased line has over a switched or dial-up line.
4. What is the name of the device used by switching offices to convert the two-wire subscriber loop to a four-wire circuit?
5. Compute the minimum round-trip delay time for a signal to propagate between two telephones separated by 2900 miles. Assume the speed of light in free space. Would an echo suppressor or an echo canceller be necessary?
6. What is the name of the process for compressing a signal at the transmitter and expanding it at the receiver?
7. What major parameter is improved as a result of the process in problem 6?
8. Name five types of transmission mediums used for trunk circuits.
9. Explain what happens when a call is blocked.
10. Name four customer services that an ESS system provides.
11. What are the three classifications of multiplexing? Briefly define their differences.
12. Derive the bit rate for the T1 carrier system.
13. Compute the following:
    a. Bit time for the T1 carrier system.
    b. Frame rate for the T1 carrier system.
    c. Length of time to transmit a superframe.
14. What special bit pattern is used in the T1 carrier system for frame synchronization?
15. What is the primary difference between a *superframe* and an *extended superframe*?
16. Refer to Figure 12-34. Draw both a unipolar pulse train and a bipolar pulse train for the serial bit stream 1011101011.
17. What does the acronym *B8ZS* stand for?
18. Draw the B8ZS transmitted bit stream for a string of eight consecutive 0s assuming that the pulse preceding the eight 0s is a negative 1 pulse.
19. Repeat problem 19 assuming that the pulse preceding the eight 0s is a positive 1 pulse.

MODEMS

It is often necessary for computers, like people, to communicate with each other beyond rooms and buildings. Normally, a direct connecting would suffice. For longer distances, it becomes economical to use the existing PSTN. Because telephone circuits are analog carriers and computers use digital signals, a device is necessary to interface the two. This device is called a *modem*.

The term *modem* is a contraction of the words *mo*dulator and *dem*odulator. These are the two principal functions that the modem performs. A computer's digital serial bit stream is used by the modem to modulate a carrier tone suitable for transmission over the phone lines. The modem at the receiving end demodulates the carrier tone, thus restoring the signal to its original digital form.

This chapter discusses various types of modems and their signal characteristics. Some of the standard techniques used to enhance communications via the modem interface are also discussed. These include line conditioning, data compression, and error control.

> **Modem**
> A contraction of the words *modulator-demodulator*. The modem converts a computer's digital bit stream into an analog signal suitable for the telephone lines, and vice versa.

13.1 MODEM FEATURES

To meet the demands of the communications field, today's modems have become extremely sophisticated. Most are preinstalled in a computer's motherboard. These are referred to as *internal modems*. Some users prefer an external modem, as shown in Figure 13-1. Consider some of the features offered by internal and external high-speed modems:

- Autodial, autoanswer, and autoredial
- Synchronous and asynchronous operation
- 14,400-bps ITU-TS Group III send/receive FAX
- Error detection and correction
- Adaptive phase equalization
- Data compression
- Caller ID
- Phone number storage
- Speed conversion from 300 bps to 56 kbps
- Self-test
- Analog and digital loopback test

FIGURE 13-1
U.S. Robotics Sportster external data/fax modem. (Courtesy of U.S. Robotics.)

- Protocol management
- On-screen help menu
- ASL (Adaptive Speed Leveling)*

13.2 INTERFACE TECHNIQUES

Modems are connected to the phone lines either through an *indirect connection* or a *direct connection*. An indirect connection is made by *acoustically coupling* the modem to the line. A direct connection to the line involves a hard-wired connection directly to the line, usually through a switch, internal to the modem.

13.2.1 Acoustically Coupled Modems

> **Acoustically Coupled Modem**
> A low-speed modem (1200 baud or less) that connects indirectly to telephone lines through an *acoustic coupler.* Two rubber, cup-size sockets are used to mount a telephone set's handpiece to the coupler.

An acoustically coupled modem provides a method of coupling a modem's transmitted and received data to the phone lines through the use of transducers. The modem's transducers convert sound energy to electrical energy, and vice versa. Figure 13-2 illustrates the *acoustically coupled modem.* Two rubber, cup-sized sockets on the modem are used to mount the handpiece of the telephone set. Inside one of the cups is the modem's speaker, and in the other is the modem's microphone. The spacing of each rubber cup is such that the mic and speaker of the handset can be seated snugly into the appropriate socket; that is, the modem's mic is seated against the telephone handset's speaker. Conversely, the modem's speaker is seated against the telephone handset's mic. The modulated carrier tones representing the transmitted data are made audible through the audio amplifier section of the modem. These audible tones can

*ASL is a registered trademark of U.S. Robotics.

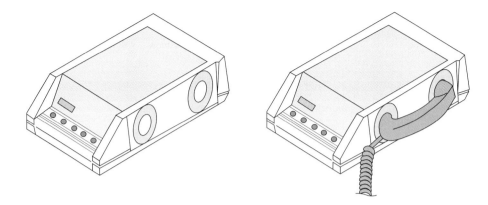

Another common form of connection to the switched network is the acoustically coupled modem, or acoustic coupler. Acoustic couplers were first introduced in 1967 from a design originating at the Stanford Research Institute. Three types of couplers are available. Two are 103- and 202-compatible devices, the third is the VA3400-compatible coupler operating at 1200 bps full duplex.

FIGURE 13-2
Acoustically coupled modem. (Reprinted with permission from Racal-Vadic.)

be heard at the modem's speaker. They are transduced from sound energy to electrical energy in the same manner as voice by the microphone of the telephone set. Received data are acoustically coupled from the telephone handset's speaker to the microphone of the modem.

With an acoustically coupled modem, data can be transmitted and received from any location with a standard telephone set. To transmit or receive data, a call is manually dialed in the usual manner. The user listens for ringing and the off-hook condition. When an answer tone is heard, acknowledging a connection, the telephone is placed in the modem's rubber fittings, carrier signals are exchanged, and data communication begins.

Transmission speeds of acoustically coupled modems are typically limited to less than 1200 bps due to the limitations of bandwidth and noise immunity. Even with the modem's rubber fittings, tightly sealed to the telephone handpiece, ambient noise can leak through. Following approval by the FCC to permit modems to be directly connected to the PSTN, acoustically coupled modems have become virtually extinct.

13.2.2 Direct-Connect Modems

In the past, telephone installations required a service call to the local telephone company to connect a phone to an existing line. After divestiture of the Bell System, modular telephones and connections have become standardized, making it possible for anyone to install a phone. Likewise, modems registered (FCC Part 68) and approved (FCC Part 15) by the FCC are permitted to be connected to the line directly. A standardized cable is used to interconnect today's telephones and modems to the telephone network. One of the most common connectors used is the RJ11C voice jack module shown in Figure 13-3. Other common voice and data jacks used with today's modems are the RJ41S and RJ45S.

> **Direct-Connect Modem**
> A modem that can electrically connect directly to telephone lines.

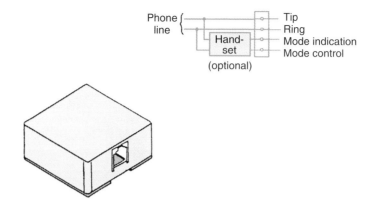

Modems registered as "permissive" devices are most commonly
connected to an RJ11C voice jack. This connection is used to
connect a standard telephone to the telephone line. Permissive
devices must limit the amplitude of the signal presented to the
telephone line to a maximum of −9 dBm.

FIGURE 13-3
Common modem voice and data jacks. (Reprinted with permission from Racal-Vadic.)

Modems are designed to accept the same cable and connector used for the telephone set, thus allowing direct connection to existing telephone jacks. Switching between normal telephone use and the modem is controlled either by commands generated by a user from DTE or by a manual switch located on the modem. Figure 13-4 illustrates the direct connection.

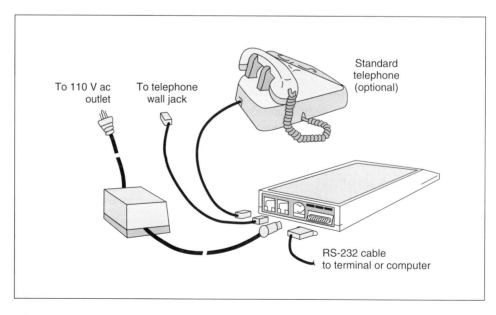

FIGURE 13-4
Typical direct-connection installation. (Reprinted with permission from Racal-Vadic.)

13.3 MODULATION TECHNIQUES

Because the frequency spectrum of a pulse train consists of an infinite number of related harmonics, the limited bandwidth of the telephone network, approximately 3 kHz, does not lend itself to transmitting a computer's digital pulses. The filtering loss of high-frequency components inherent in the pulse train causes serious degradation to the pulse train's shape. A modem is necessary to convert the digital signal into analog form, which is suited for the telephone lines. To perform this task, four basic modulation techniques are employed by modems. They are illustrated in Figure 13-5. The technique used depends on the data transmission rate. Generally, the higher the transmission rate, the more sophisticated the modulation technique must be to meet the passband requirements of the phone lines. The basic modulation techniques are described next.

Frequency Shift Keying (FSK)   FSK is used in low-speed asynchronous transmission from 300 to 1800 bps. The carrier frequency of the modem is shifted between two discrete frequencies in accordance with the logic levels of the digital signal. The higher of the two frequencies represents a mark (logic 1), and the lower frequency represents a space (logic 0). Mark and space frequencies lie within the 300- to 3400-Hz passband of the PSTN. Bell 103/113-type modems utilize FSK.

Amplitude Shift Keying (ASK)   ASK is a form of AM in which the amplitude of the carrier frequency is turned on and off in accordance with the digital data. ASK is also referred to as OOK, which stands for *on-off keying*. The reverse channel of Bell 202-type modems use ASK for error control. Secondary RS-232 and RS-449 circuits are

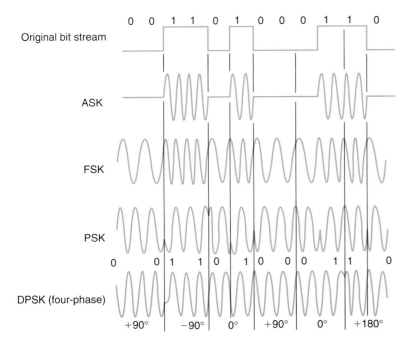

FIGURE 13-5
Modulation techniques employed by modems.

used as the driver and receiver interface. Transmission speeds for this application are generally limited to 5 bps due to noise problems and bandwidth constraints.

Phase Shift Keying (PSK)   PSK is a modulation technique in which the carrier frequency remains the same and its phase is in accordance with the digital data. When only two phases are used, this is referred to as *binary phase shift keying (BPSK).*

Differential Phase Shift Keying (DPSK)   DPSK is a variation of PSK employed by modems with data transmission rates of 1200 bps or greater. Multiple phases are used to encode groups of bits called *dibits, tribits, quadbits,* and so on. This reduces the number of phase changes that the carrier frequency undergoes, thus allowing the data transmission rate to be increased. Figure 13-5 illustrates four-phase DPSK. Two bits, or *dibits,* are encoded into one of four phase changes. The advantage of DPSK over PSK is that an absolute phase reference is not necessary for demodulation of the data. Phase shift is *differential,* meaning that it is referenced to the phase of the carrier during the previously encoded interval. Although DPSK is more costly to implement, it is the most efficient modulation technique used by modems in terms of bandwidth utilization. Several bits can be encoded into a single phase change using DPSK. The Bell 212A employs four-phase DPSK to achieve 1200 bps. Bell 208-type modems use eight-phase PSK to achieve 4800 bps.

Quadrature Amplitude Modulation (QAM)   QAM is a combination of ASK and PSK. It is used to achieve higher transmission rates than PSK alone. The Bell 209A modem, for example, operates at a transmission rate of 9600 bps. The QAM signal is comprised of 16 carrier states and three different amplitudes. Data rates of 14,400, 16,800, 19,200, and 28,800 bps are possible using the QAM technique. As many as 64 carrier states are required at these speeds.

13.4   MODEM TRANSMISSION MODES

Three transmission modes of operation are used by modems: *simplex, half-duplex,* and *full-duplex.*

Simplex   When a modem is configured for simplex operation, data are sent or received in one direction only.

Half-Duplex   In half-duplex mode, the communications channel is shared between sending and receiving stations. The transmission and reception of data are performed in an alternating manner. Before a change in transmission direction can occur, the transmitter at one end must be turned off while the other end is turned on. The time that it takes for transmission directions to change between two stations is referred to as *modem turnaround time.*

Full-Duplex   Modems capable of operating in full-duplex can transmit and receive data simultaneously. In two-wire telephone circuits, this is performed by using frequency-division multiplexing (FDM), whereby two separate frequency channels, a *low band* and a *high band,* are allocated within the passband of the telephone lines. One modem transmits on the low band and receives on the high band. The other modem transmits on the high band and receives on the low band, thus allowing full-duplex operation. In private or leased lines, four-wire circuits are often used, whereby the transmit and receive circuits are physically separate from each other. The entire frequency band can be utilized by each modem in this case since the channel is not shared. Another technique is called *echo cancelling,* which allows both modems to transmit simultaneously on the same frequency.

When operating in full-duplex mode over a single channel, an agreement between the two stations is typically made beforehand as to which bands will be used to transmit and receive data on. This eliminates the problem of both stations transmitting and receiving on the same frequency band. Communications cannot occur in this case unless echo cancelling is used. Historically, full-duplex modems have been designated to operate in one of two modes:

1. Originate mode
2. Answer mode

A modem configured for the *originate mode* is the station that originates the call. In the originate mode, transmission occurs on the low band of frequencies and reception on the high band of frequencies. The station that answers the call must be configured for the *answer mode.* In the answer mode, transmission occurs on the high band of frequencies and reception on the low band of frequencies. When a host computer services several remote terminals, the interfacing modem to the host computer is set to the answer mode; that is, it answers the calls placed by the remote terminal's modems that have been configured for the originate mode.

> **Originate Modem**
> The modem that initiates the telephone call for data communication.

> **Answer Modem**
> The modem that answers a call initiated by an *originate modem.*

13.5 THE BELL FAMILY OF MODEMS

The Bell System, historically, has dominated the modem market. Operating specifications of the various types of Bell modems have become de facto standards and have evolved into international standards set forth by the ITU-TS (and formerly CCITT). Some of the most common types of modems are discussed here.

13.5.1 Bell 103/113 Modem

The Bell 103/113 modem is an asynchronous modem designed to operate full-duplex over switched or leased lines. Transmission speed is limited to 300 bps. To operate in the full-duplex mode, the Bell 103/113 modem employs FDM within the 300- to 3400-Hz bandwidth of the switch phone lines (Figure 13-6). FSK is the modulation technique used. The 3-kHz passband has been divided into two separate frequency channels: a *low band,* and a *high band.* The low band includes the FSK mark and space frequencies of 1270 and 1070 Hz, respectively. Mark and space frequencies for the high band are 2225 and 2025 Hz, respectively. The Bell 113A/D operates in the originate mode only. The Bell 113B/C operates in the answer mode only.

13.5.2 Bell 202 Modem

A disadvantage with the Bell 103-type modem is having to divide the existing bandwidth of the phone lines in half to obtain two frequency channels for full-duplex operation. Transmission speed is sacrificed in this case. The Bell 202 modem operates in the half-duplex mode. Because transmission occurs in only one direction at a time between modems, the entire band width can be utilized by the transmitted signal. A

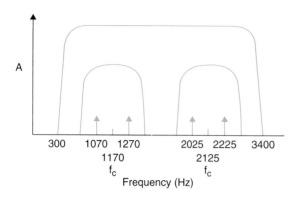

Specifications

Data:

Serial, binary, asynchronous, full-duplex

Data Transfer Rate:

0 to 300 bps

Modulation:

Frequency shift-keyed (FSK) FM

Frequency Assignment:

	Originate	Answer
Transmit	1070-Hz SPACE; 1270-Hz MARK	2025-Hz SPACE; 2225-Hz MARK
Receive	2025-Hz SPACE; 2225-Hz MARK	1070-Hz SPACE; 1270-Hz MARK

Transmit Level:

0 to −12 dBm

Receive Level:

0 to −50 dBm simultaneous with adjacent channel transmitter at as much as 0 dBm.

Specifications and channel assignments for the full-duplex 300-bps asynchronous Bell 103/113 modem are shown in this illustration.

FIGURE 13-6

Bell 103/113 frequency assignment. (Courtesy of Racal-Vadic.)

higher transmission rate is achieved. For switched lines, the transmission rate is 1200 bps, whereas for leased lines with C2 conditioning, 1800 bps is used. FSK is the modulation technique employed. A mark is represented by 1200 Hz, and a space is represented by 2200 Hz. Figure 13-7 illustrates the frequency assignment for the Bell 202 modem.

Handshaking is performed by the Bell 202 modem through the use of RS-232 interface control circuits: RTS, and CTS. When data are to be transmitted by DTE, RTS is activated. RTS causes DCE to turn its carrier frequency ON and inhibit its receiver section. The remote DCE detects the carrier and turns its CD line ON. When DCE is ready to transmit data onto the phone lines, CTS is sent to DTE and DTE transmits its data to DCE. When all of DTE's data have been transmitted, it turns RTS OFF. This instructs DCE to complete the transmission of the remaining data onto the communications channel and turn its carrier OFF. DCE inhibits CTS. The channel is quiet at this time. Once the remote DCE detects that the carrier is gone, CD is turned OFF and the remote station begins its transmission using the same procedure.

The process of changing the direction of transmission in half-duplex operation is called *modem turnaround time*. For long-distance communications, echo suppressors in the line must have sufficient time to *turn around* once the local carrier is turned off and the remote carrier is turned on. The turnaround time of an echo suppressor can be as high as 100 ms. Additional time is also necessary for echoes to subside and for the local receiver to turn on its CD signal on receiving the return carrier frequency. A 150- to 200-ms delay is inserted between RTS and CTS for this purpose. Modem turnaround time is a significant factor to consider in the transfer of files back and forth. Short files requiring numerous turnarounds can reduce the *throughput* of data considerably. (See Sections 13.14 and 13.16 for a definition of throughput.)

Specifications

Data:

Serial, binary, asynchronous, half duplex on two-wire lines

Data Transfer Rate:

0 to 1200 bps — switched network

0 to 1800 bps — leased lines with C2 conditioning

Optional 5-bps AM reverse channel transmitter and receiver available for switched-network units

Modulation:

Frequency-shift keyed (FSK) FM

Frequency Assignment:

MARK 1200 Hz; SPACE 2200 Hz

Transmit Level:

0 to –12 dBm

Receive Level:

0 to –50 dBm switched network
0 to –40 dBm leased network

Specifications and channel assignments for the half-duplex 1200-bps asynchronous Bell 202 modem are shown in this illustration.

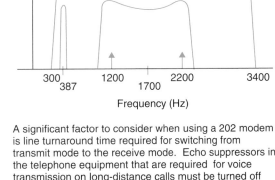

A significant factor to consider when using a 202 modem is line turnaround time required for switching from transmit mode to the receive mode. Echo suppressors in the telephone equipment that are required for voice transmission on long-distance calls must be turned off by the modem to transmit digital data. The modem must provide a 200-ms signal to the line to turn off the echo suppressors every time it goes from transmit to receive mode; hence, if short records are being transmitted, the turnaround time can slow the throughput considerably. In addition, many terminals and computers do not have the capability to control the Request To Send lead on the Bell 202 interface and can only support full-duplex 103-line discipline.

FIGURE 13-7
Bell 202 frequency assignment. (Courtesy of Racal-Vadic.)

13.5.2.1 Pseudo Full-Duplex Operation   Although the Bell 202 is generally considered a half-duplex modem, *pseudo full-duplex* operation is possible through a FDM low-speed, ASK, 5-bps *reverse channel.* The reverse channel is supported by RS-232 secondary interface circuits, as depicted in Figure 13-8. A 387-Hz carrier frequency is amplitude shift keyed at a low enough rate to prevent the resulting AM sidebands from spilling into the passband of the main channel. The reverse channel is used primarily to indicate that a remote station is connected to the interface. It is also used as a feedback signal requesting the retransmission of data in the event of a detected error.

13.5.2.2 Disabling the Echo Suppressors   For full-duplex operation, echo suppressors must be disabled in the long-distance trunk facilities. The PSTN has set provisions for disabling echo suppressors by applying a tone within the range of 2010 and 2240 Hz for 350 ± 50 ms. The tone must be presented at a time when the channel is quiet. The tone may be generated from either direction. Typically, the answer modem will apply this done during a call setup procedure before shifting to its idle frequency. The echo suppressor will remain disabled as long as one of the interconnecting modems continues to assert a signal within the range 300 to 3400 Hz. They will become enabled again if there is any period as long as 100 ms without any signal on the line. In relation to the Bell 202 modem, another purpose of its reverse channel is to hold echo suppressors, disabled in pseudo full-duplex operation.

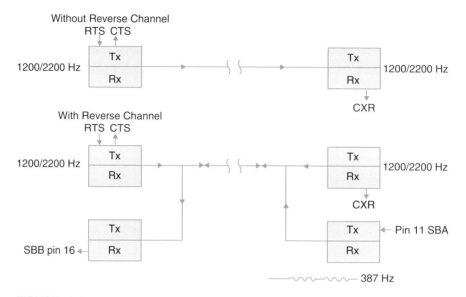

FIGURE 13-8
Bell 202 reverse channel operation. (Courtesy of Racal-Vadic.)

There are several versions of the Bell 202 modem. Later versions have upgraded the reverse channel transmission rate to 75 and 150 bps through the use of FSK. Mark and space frequencies for the reverse channel FSK signal are 390 and 490 Hz, respectively. ITU-TS' V.23 international standard is very similar to the BELL 202 specification. The forward channel rate is the same, at 1200 bps. The reverse channel FSK rate is 75 bps, with mark and space frequencies of 390 and 450 Hz, respectively.

13.5.3 Bell 212A Modem

The Bell 212A is a two-speed modem that operates full-duplex and supports asynchronous or synchronous transmission modes over the switched lines. The low-speed asynchronous mode operates in accordance with the BELL 103 specification with a 300-bps data transfer rate and FSK employed as the modulation technique. Transmit frequencies for the originate mode are 1070 Hz (space) and 1270 Hz (mark). Receive frequencies for the originate mode are 2025 Hz (space) and 2225 Hz (mark). In the answer mode, the opposite frequencies are used to permit full-duplex operation.

In the high-speed mode, characters can be transmitted synchronously or asynchronously at 1200 bps. Four-phase DPSK is used to phase shift a 1200-Hz tone for the originate mode and a 2400-Hz tone for the answer mode. Figure 13-9 illustrates the Bell 212A frequency assignment for the high-speed mode. A mark and a space are not represented by two discrete frequencies, as is the case with FSK. Instead, each consecutive two bits of the serial binary data sent to the 212A modem are encoded into a single phase change of the carrier frequency. The encoded *two* bits are called *dibits*. Because a dibit represents two bits, there are four possible phase changes that

> **Dibit Encoding**
> The encoding of 2 bits per baud.

Specifications*
    Data: Serial, binary, asynchronous, full duplex
    Data transfer rate: 0 to 1200 bps
    Modulation: Differential phase shift keying (DPSK)
    Originate frequency: 1200 Hz
    Answer frequency: 2400 Hz
*Also see Bell 103 specification (Figure 9-6) for Bell 212A
    low-speed mode.

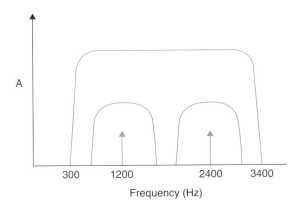

FIGURE 13-9
Bell 212A frequency assignment for the high-speed mode. Frequency assignment for
the low-speed mode is identical to the Bell 103 specification (see Figure 13-6).

the carrier frequency can undergo. This is shown in the phasor diagram of Figure
13-10. Note that the encoded bits are Gray coded. Four-phase DPSK is also referred
to as *quadrature PSK (QPSK)*.

13.5.3.1 M-ary   When PSK or QAM is used as a modulation technique, the term
M-ary, derived from *bi-nary*, is used to denote the number of encoded bits used to
modulate the carrier frequency. M-ary is governed by the equation

$$M = \log_2 n \tag{13-1}$$

where M is the number of encoded bits used to represent a carrier stage, M-ary, and
n is the number of state changes that the carrier can undergo represented by n bits.

> **M-ary**
> Derived from the word
> *bi-nary*, denotes the
> number of encoded bits
> used to modulate a car-
> rier frequency.

The Bell 208 modem employs eight-phase DPSK as its modulation technique.
Compute the M-ary.

**EXAMPLE
13.1**

Solution:

$$M = \log_2 n$$
$$= \log_2 8$$
$$= 3$$

Therefore, M-ary $= 3$ bits.

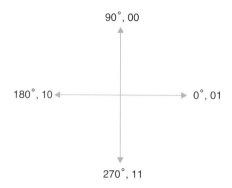

FIGURE 13-10
Phasor diagram for the Bell 212A modem.

13.5.3.2 Baud Rate Versus Bit Rate   When more complex modulation techniques are employed by modems to achieve higher data transfer rates, a distinction must be made between the transmitted signal's *bit rate* and its *baud rate*. They are not always equal. Bit rate and baud rate are defined as follows:

Baud Rate   A signal's baud rate is defined as the rate at which the signal changes per unit time. For modems, it is the actual *modulation rate* of the carrier frequency as it is transmitted or received via the communications channel. Baud rate is also referred to as *signaling rate*.

Bit Rate   A signal's bit rate is the actual number of binary bits transmitted per second (bps) onto the communications channel.

   Bell 212A modems have a modulation rate of 600 baud when operating in the high-speed mode. This is equal to half its bit rate of 1200 bps, because its carrier frequency is phase shifted at dibit intervals ($1200 = 2 \times 600$). In its low-speed mode, however, the baud rate and bit rate (300) are equal; that is, the carrier is frequency shifted at the same rate as the binary serial data stream.

13.5.4   Bell 201B/C Modem

The Bell 201 family of modems is designed to operate at a fixed data transfer rate of 2400 bps over the basic, unconditioned, 3002-type line or two- or four-wire private line. The Bell 201A is an obsolete 2000-bps modem. The Bell 201B is for private or leased line applications, and the Bell 201C is for switched or leased line application. Each modem is designed for half-duplex operation over the switched line or full-duplex operation over the four-wire private line. Four-phase DPSK is the modulation technique employed to achieve 2400 bps. The phasor diagram for the Bell 201B/C is shown in Figure 13-11.

13.5.5   Bell 208A and 208B Modems

Bell 208A and 208B modems are designed for synchronous transmission and reception of data at 4800 bps over four-wire private leased lines and switched lines, respectively. Eight-phase DPSK is employed on a 1800-Hz carrier frequency. Each con-

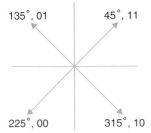

FIGURE 13-11
Phasor diagram for the Bell 201B/C modem.

secutive *three* bits, called *tribits,* of the binary serial input data are encoded into a single phase change of the carrier frequency. The encoding of three bits into a tribit allows the representation eight possible phase changes of the carrier frequency. A transmission rate of three times the baud rate of 1600 is achieved ($4800 = 1600 \times 3$). Figure 13-12 depicts the phasor diagram for the Bell 208A modem. Note that here, again, a Gray code is used.

> **Tribit Encoding**
> The encoding of 3 bits per baud.

13.5.6 Bell 209A Modem

Data transfer rates can be increased further by encoding additional bits into a greater number of phase changes. *Four* bits, or a *quadbit,* for example, can be encoded into 16 possible phase changes (M-ary = 4). The phase differential between adjacent phasors would amount to $22.5°$ ($360°/16 = 22.5°$). The problem here, however, is that any phase jitter in excess of $11.25°$ would result in the detection of erroneous data. This amount of phase jitter is not uncommon in long-haul networks that utilize regenerative repeaters and digital multiplexers. For this reason, 16-phase PSK is generally not used.

> **Quadbit Encoding**
> The encoding of 4 bits per baud.

   To avoid the problem of phase jitter, the Bell 209A modem employs a combination of ASK and PSK called *quadrature amplitude modulating (QAM).* QAM, pronounced "Kwamm," is a modulation technique that uses 12 different phases and three different amplitudes to represent 16 possible carrier states. Susceptibility to phase jitter is effectively reduced by increasing the separation between adjacent phasors. The phasor diagram for the Bell 209A QAM signal is shown in

> **Quadrature Amplitude Modulation (QAM)**
> A modulation technique employed in high-speed modems. A combination of ASK and DPSK encodes 4 bits into one of 16 signaling state changes.

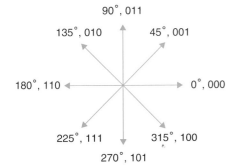

FIGURE 13-12
Phasor diagram for the Bell 208A modem.

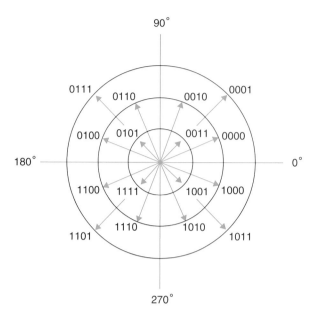

FIGURE 13-13
Phasor diagram for the Bell 209A modem depicting 9600-bps QAM.

Figure 13-13. Each state is represented by one of 16 possible quadbits. By employing QAM, 9600-bps full-duplex synchronous communications is achieved using a baud rate of 2400 (9600 = 4 × 2400) over private four-wire lines with D1 conditioning. The Bell 209A also has provisions for multiplexing multiples of 2400 bps into 9600 bps.

13.6 ITU-TS MODEMS AND RECOMMENDATIONS

Data transmission standards outside the United States are set by ITU-TS (formerly CCITT), which is headquartered in Geneva, Switzerland. Standards V.21, V.23, and V.26 describe modems similar to the Bell 103, 202, and 201, respectively. V.22 describes modems similar to the Bell 212A, and V.29 is similar to the Bell 209A specification. Table 13-1 lists ITU-TS modems and recommendations.

13.6.1 ITU-TS Modem Recommendation V.22bis

ITU-TS' V.22bis (*bis* means *second revision* in French) specification provides for 1200- and 2400-bps synchronous full-duplex communication over switched and two-wire leased lines. Four-phase DPSK is employed as the modulation technique for modem operation at 1200 bps. QAM is used to achieve a data transfer rate of 2400 bps. Modulation rate is specified at 600 baud for both operating speeds. Full-duplex operation is achieved by phase and amplitude shift keying a low-channel carrier frequency of 1200 Hz and a high-channel carrier frequency of 2400 Hz.

Phase and amplitude assignment for dibit (1200 bps) and quadbit (2400 bps) encoding is depicted by ITU-TS as a *16-point signal constellation* rather than a phasor diagram. They are essentially the same. Figure 13-14 illustrates the signal con-

> **Signal Constellation**
> A constellation of dots, each representing an amplitude and phase state of a sine wave.

TABLE 13-1
ITU-TS Modems and Recommendations

Recommendations	Description
V.21	0 to 200 (300) bps (similar to Bell 103). Defined for FDX switched network operation.
V.22	1200 bps, FDC, switched, and leased line network operation.
V.22bis	1200/2400 bps, FDX, switched, and leased line network operation.
V.23	600/1200 bps (similar to Bell 202). Defined for HDX switched network operation. Optional 75 bps reverse channel.
V.24	Definition of interchange circuits (similar to EIA RS-232).
V.25	Automatic calling units (similar to Bell 801).
V.25bis	Serial interface autocalling.
V.26	2400 bps (identical to Bell 201B). Defined for four-wire leased circuits.
V.26bis	2400/1200 bps (similar to Bell 201C). Defined for switched network operation.
V.26ter[a]	2400 bps over the switched network using echo cancelling.
V.27	4800 bps (similar to Bel 208A). Defined for leased circuits using manual equalizers.
V.27bis	4800/2400 bps with autoequalizers for leased lines.
V.27ter	4800/2400 bps for use on switched lines.
V.28	Electrical characteristics for interchange circuits (similar to RS-232).
V.29	9600 bps FDX (similar to Bell 209). Defined for leased circuits.
V.32	9600 bps FDX for switched or leased-line circuits using echo cancelling.
V.32bis	14,400 bps FDX for switched or leased-line circuits using echo cancelling.
V.42	Error-correction procedures for DCEs using asynchronous to synchronous conversion.
V.42bis	An extension of V.42 that defines data compression for use with V.42.
V.34	(V.FAST) ITU-TS 28,800 bps standard.
V.90	ITU-TS 56 kbps standard.

[a]In French, *ter* means *third revision*.

stellation for the V.22bis specification. For 1200-bps operation, the data stream is divided into groups of two consecutive bits, or dibits. Each dibit is encoded into a quadrant phase change relative to the preceding phase of the carrier frequency. This is shown in Table 13-2. For 2400-bps operation, the data stream is divided into groups of four consecutive bits, or quadbits. The two least significant bits of the quad bit are encoded into a quadrant phase change in the same manner as for 1200-bps operation. The most significant two bits of the qaudbit define one of four signaling elements associated with the new quadrant.

13.6.2   ITU-TS Modem Recommendation V.29

ITU-TS' V.29 specification is the first internationally recognized standard for 9600-bps communications. This standard provides for synchronous data transmission over four-wire leased lines. The same 16-point QAM signal constellation used for V.22bis is used for the V.29 specification. The higher data transfer rate is made possible by

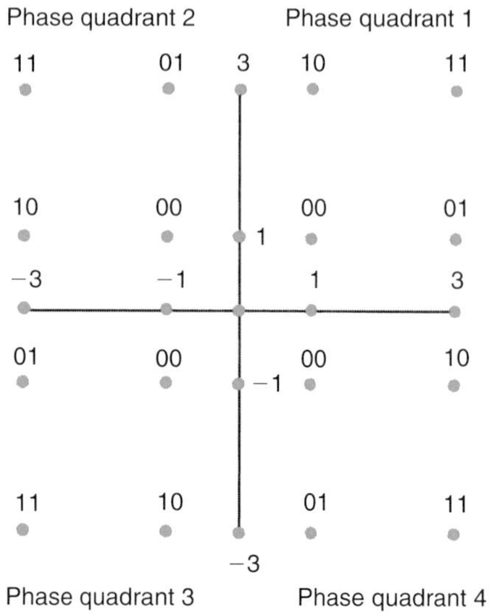

FIGURE 13-14
V.22bis 16-point signal constellation.

using a single carrier frequency of 1700 Hz and increasing the baud rate from V.22bis' 600 to 2400 baud. The entire bandwidth is utilized. Some modem manufacturers have elected to use V.29-compatible modems in half-duplex mode over the switched lines. Pseudo full-duplex operation over the switched lines is also performed by one of two techniques: *ping-pong,* or *statistical duplexing.* These are described next.

Ping-Pong   Ping-pong is a method of simulating full-duplex operation between two modems. Data sent to each modem by DTE are buffered and automatically exchanged over the link. By rapidly turning carriers on and off in a successive fashion (hence the name *ping-pong*) through flow control procedures, full-duplex operation is simulated.

Statistical Duplexing   Statistical duplexing uses a low-speed, 300-bps reverse channel, similar to the manner in which the Bell 202 operates in pseudo full-duplex. The intent of the reverse channel is to allow keyboard data entry from an operator while, at the same time, receiving a file from a remote station. By monitoring the modem's data buffers, the direction of the data transaction can be sensed and high- and low-speed channels reversed to suit the desired condition.

13.6.3   ITU-TS Modem Recommendation V.32

ITU-TS' V.32 recommendation is intended for the use of 9600-bps synchronous modems on connections to switched and leased lines. The recommendation also specifies signaling rates of 2400 bps (based on V.26ter) and 4800 bps. QAM is the modulation technique employed on a carrier frequency of 1800 Hz. V.32 is very similar to V.29, except that an optional encoding technique called trellis encoding is specified.* Trellis encoding divides the data stream to be transmitted into groups of five

---

*For further details on trellis encoding, refer to ITU-TS Recommendation V.32, 1984.

TABLE 13-2
V.22bis Line Encoding

First Two Bits in Quadbit (2400 bps) or Dibit Values (1200 bps)	Phase Quadrant Change
00	$1 \rightarrow 2$ $2 \rightarrow 3$ $3 \rightarrow 4$ $4 \rightarrow 1$ 90°
01	$1 \rightarrow 1$ $2 \rightarrow 2$ $3 \rightarrow 3$ $4 \rightarrow 4$ 0°
11	$1 \rightarrow 4$ $2 \rightarrow 1$ $3 \rightarrow 2$ $4 \rightarrow 3$ 270°
10	$1 \rightarrow 3$ $2 \rightarrow 4$ $3 \rightarrow 1$ $4 \rightarrow 2$ 180°

consecutive bits or *quintbits*. This unique encoding technique results in superior signal-to-noise ratios. A 32-point signal constellation is achieved (M-ary = 5). Figure 13-15 depicts the 32-point trellis signal constellation.

13.6.3.1 Echo Cancellation One principal characteristic outlined in the V.32 standard is to provide for a 9600-bps modem with true full-duplex operation over the switched lines. Through the advanced technology of digital signal processors (DSPs), full-duplex operation is achieved by a technique called *echo cancellation*. Echo cancellation is performed by adding an *inverted* replica of the transmitted signal to the received data stream. This permits the transmitted data from each modem to use the same carrier frequency and modulation technique simultaneously. The two clashing signals are separated by the receiver section of each modem.

Echo Cancellation
A technique used by high-speed modems to achieve true full-duplex operation over switched lines. An inverted replica of the transmitted signal is added to the received signal to eliminate interference.

13.6.4   ITU-TS Modem Recommendation V.32bis and V.32 terbo

In 1991, the V.32bis standard created a new benchmark in the industry, allowing modem speeds of 14,400 bits per second (bps), 50% faster than the V.32 9600-bps modem standard at the time. Instead of using a 16-point signal constellation (4 bits per baud) as in the V.32 standard, V.32bis uses a 64-point signal constellation (6 bits per baud) and maintains the same 2400 baud rate as V.32. Thus, 14,400 bps (6 × 2400 = 14,400), full-duplex operation over the two-wire switched lines is achieved. Another improvement of V.32bis over V.32 is the inclusion of *automatic fall forward*, or the ability to return to a higher transmissions speed when the line

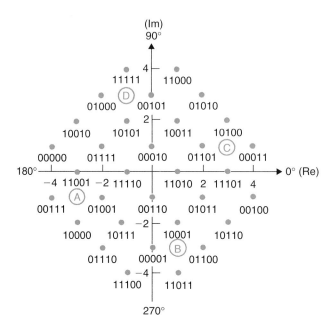

32-point signal structure with trellis coding for 9600 bps and states A B C D used at 4800 bps and for training

FIGURE 13-15
V.32 trellis 32-point signal constellation.

quality improves. V.32bis modems can also *fall back,* or quickly slow down to 12,200, 9600, or 4800 bps, if line quality degrades. Most V.32bis modems also support Group III fax. Group III fax is a standard for fax communication that specifies the connection procedure between two fax machines or fax modems and the data compression procedure that will be followed during the transmission.

In August 1993, U.S. Robotics announced a major evolution to its product line: the **V.32 terbo** protocol with its proprietary *Adaptive Speed Leveling** technology, which boosts modem speeds to 21.6 kbps. These new features fall into three new categories: increased data rates, FAX enhancements, and high-end features.[†] V.32 terbo is the new 19.2-kbps data transmission rate developed by AT&T. It is designed to deliver a 33% increase in speed over the 14,400-V.32bis standard.

13.6.5   ITU-TS Modem Recommendation V.33

The ITU-TS V.33 Recommendation is designed for modems that will operate over point-to-point four-wire leased lines. It is similar to V.32 except that it encodes a redundant bit and six information bits to produce a transmission rate of 14,400 bps at 2400 baud. The carrier frequency is also 1800 Hz. The V.33 128-point signal constellation is shown in Figure 13-16.

ASL is a trademark of U.S. Robotics.

[†]*U.S. Robotics News,* U.S. Robotics, Skokie, Ill.

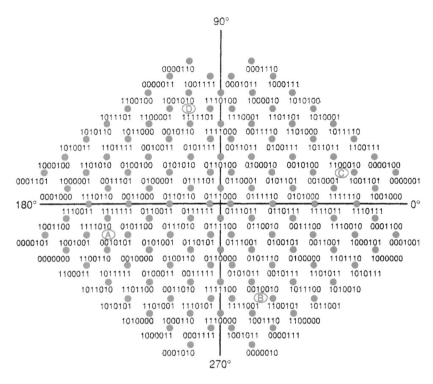

FIGURE 13-16
V.33 128-point signal constellation.

13.6.6 ITU-TS Modem Recommendation V.42

A modem protocol adopted in 1988 by ITU-TS is the V.42 standard: *Error Correcting Procedures for DCEs.* The V.42 standard is designed to address asynchronous-to-synchronous conversions, error detection and correction, and modems without such protocols. V.42's main impetus revolves around a new protocol called *Link Access Procedure for Modems (LAP M).* LAP M is similar to the packet-switching protocol used in the X.25 standard. An alternative procedure developed by Microcom has also been adopted by the V.42 standard. This procedure is called *Microcom Networking Protocol (MNP).* Both MNP and LAP M are discussed later in this chapter.

13.6.7 ITU-TS Modem Recommendation V.42bis

To enhance the performance of error-correcting modems that implement the V.42 standard, ITU-TS adopted the V.42bis standard, which addresses *data compression for DCEs using error-correcting procedures.* Modems employing data compression have significant throughput performance over their predecessors. The V.42bis standard can achieve 3:1 to 4:1 data compression ratios for ASCII text. The algorithm specified by the standard is British Telecom's *BTLZ* technique. In 1990, the ITU-TS Study Group XII voted to include Microcom's *MNP 5* and *MNP 7.* These two new revisions to the standard are data compression and advanced data compression algorithms, respectively. Throughput rates up to 56,600 bps can be achieved by today's modems that employ V.42bis data compression.

13.6.8   ITU-TS Modem Recommendation V.34

The ITU-TS established the TR-30 Group (formerly SGXVII) to work on a recommendation for the next generation of modem speed: *V.fast*. V.fast was officially adopted in June 1994 and has been designated V.34. The new standard's speed is 28,800 bps *without* data compression. With data compression, the new modems will be able to send asynchronous data two to three times as fast, thus dramatically reducing telephone costs. V.34 will automatically adapt to line conditions and adjust its speed up or down to ensure data integrity.

Increasing both complexity and speed does not come easy, however. There are definite boundaries for both, and V.34 pushes these limits. A number of innovations enable V.34 to go faster*:

- **Nonlinear coding** combats the effects of nonlinearities, such as harmonic distortion and amplitude proportional noise.
- **Multidimensional coding** and **constellation shaping** give the data greater immunity to noise in the channel.
- **Reduced complexity decoding** makes it possible to use more complex codes. A 64-state, four-dimensional code is now feasible with this technology. Without it, this code would increase the computations 40%.
- **Precoding** allows more of the available channel bandwidth to be used, which means more symbols can be sent further. With older standards, the symbols were sent closer to the middle of the bandwidth. The outer limits of the bandwidth are where amplitude attenuation and phase distortion are most severe.
- **Line probing** is a scheme that quickly looks during the training sequence at the line for impairments that might be encountered. It then attempts to select the best solution to counteract the circuit problems.

Inside the V.34 modems, look for more sophisticated hardware elements. For example, high resolution sigma-delta converters lower self-generated receiver front end noise. V.34 algorithms chew up memory, so they'll need larger and faster SRAMs. Finally, a doubling of modem-to-modem speed means that the modem-to-computer speed will also escalate, at the most to 115,200 bps.

13.6.9   ITU-TS Modem Recommendation V.34+

In 1996, ITU-TS drafted an enhanced specification for V.34 called *V.34+*. The specification adds two speeds to the V.34 standard: 31.2 kbps, and 33.6 kbps. Like previous modem standards, many vendors said they were pushing the data transfer limits over the standard analog telephone lines, which have a limited bandwidth of 3 kHz. Although V.34+ is 17% faster than its counterpart, according to ITU-TS it was not a significant enough speed enhancement to append V.34 with V.34bis. Furthermore, unless the V.34+ modems were connected to extremely clean lines, a throughput of 33.6 kbps without data compression was difficult to achieve.

V.90 Specification
Based on U.S. Robotics' X2 and Lucent and Rockwell's 56K*flex* technologies. After ratification, V.90 became the new 56-kbps standard.

13.6.10   ITU-TS Modem Recommendation V.90

In February 1998, the ITU-TS agreed on the technical specification for 56-kbps modems. This recommendation was the *V.90 specification*, based on the proprietary

*Dale Walsh, U.S. Robotics Vice President, Advanced Products, " 'V.fast' The modem's next generation," *U.S. Robotics: The Intelligent Choice in Data Communications*, 1993.

and competing technologies of U.S. Robotic's X2 technology and Lucent and Rockwell's 56K*flex* technology. These two technologies were incompatible, causing Internet Service Providers (ISPs) to provide support for both technologies. Shortly after the V.90 specification was ratified, modems were upgraded to the new 56-kbps standard.

A V.90 modem differs from conventional modems of the past, because it transmits and receives data asymmetrically. That is, the upstream transmission rate (from your computer to the ISP) and downstream transmission rate (from your service provider to your ISP) are not the same. Upstream data are transmitted in accordance with the V.34 standard at a maximum transmission rate of 33.6 kbps. The downstream data, however, differ by overcoming the theoretical limit of 34 kbps. Herein lies the difference.

Recall that in Chapter 2, we stated the channel capacity of a transmission medium is typically governed by *Shannon's Law,* which states that the maximum theoretical speed at which data can be transmitted over a bandwidth-limited transmission line is based on the signal-to-noise (SNR) ratio and the bandwidth of the transmission medium. Using a 3-khz bandwidth and an optimum SNR of 35 dB, both of which are typical of values over the PSTN, the channel capacity, C, is computed as follows:

> **Shannon's Law**
> A fundamental law used in telecommunications to compute *channel capacity.*

$$C = \text{BW} \log_2(1 + \text{SNR})$$
$$= 3 \text{ kHz} \log_2(1 + 3163) \quad (Note: 35 \text{ dB has a power gain of } 10^{35/10} = 3163)$$
$$= 3 \text{ kHz} \log_2 3164$$

Dividing both sides by 3 KHz, we have

$$C/3 \text{ kHz} = \log_2 3164$$

and taking the antilog, we have

$$2^{C/3 \text{ } kHz} = 3164$$

Now, take the common log of both sides and solve for C:

$$\log_{10} 2^{C/3 \text{ } kHz} = \log_{10} 3164$$
$$C/3 \text{ kHz} \log_{10} 2 = \log_{10} 3164$$
$$C = 3 \text{ kHz } 3 \text{ kHz} \cdot \log_{10} \left(\frac{3164}{\log_{10} 2} \right)$$

V.90 modems exceed this theoretical limit by utilizing the digital server connections that ISPs use at their end to connect to the PSTN. Figure 13-17 illustrates the difference between a V.34 and a V.90 modem. V.34 modems are optimized for the situation in which both ends connect by analog lines to the PSTN. Even though most of the network is digital, V.34 modems treat it as being entirely analog. In contrast, V.90 modems eliminate the need for analog-to-digital conversion (ADC) in the download direction (ISP to user). An SNR of nearly 20 dB is gained by eliminating the quantization noise resulting from the ADC conversion process, and this almost doubles the data rate capability of the line.*

It should be noted that most V.90 or 56K modems operate between 40 and 53 kbps. The name *56K* is a misnomer for several reasons:

---

*Edmundo E. Martínez, "56Kbps Modem Technology," *Western Polytechnic Institute,* Worcester, MA (http://www.ece.wpi.edu).

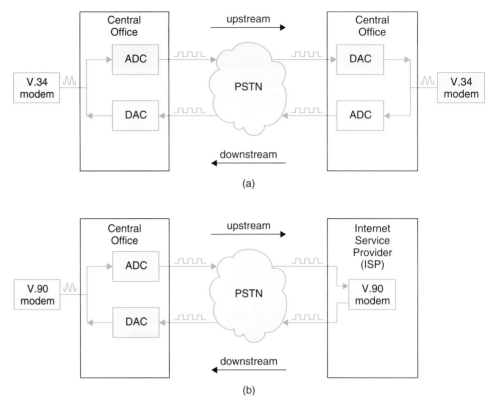

FIGURE 13-17

Comparison of a V.34 and V.90 modem connection: (a) V.34 connection showing analog-to-digital conversions in both directions; (b) V.90 connection to an ISP showing only one analog-to-digital conversion.

- FCC transmission speed limitation to 53 kbps (to minimize crosstalk in feeder cables)
- FCC power limitations to −12dBm (to minimize crosstalk in feeder cables)
- Distance from the central office
- Quantization noise
- Line impairments in the subscriber loop
- T-carrier logged bits

13.7 ISDN MODEM

Terminal Adapter (TA)
A modem that permits users to transmit and receive voice, video, and data over a single *digital* connection between the central office and the users. Also referred to as an *ISDN modem* or a *digital modem.*

Our discussion to this point has been limited to *analog* modems, or modems that convert a binary serial bit stream to an analog signal compatible with the phone lines, and vice versa. In recent years, modem manufacturers have developed the *ISDN modem.* The ISDN modem is also referred to as a *terminal adapter (TA)* or *digital modem.* Unlike its predecessors, the ISDN modem permits a user to transmit and receive voice, video, and data over a single *digital* connection between the central office and users. This all-digital connection is tied into a digital telephone network called the *Integrated Services Digital Network (ISDN),* which has taken nearly 15 years for the PSTN to deploy. The upsurge of the Internet and its highly graphical content has driven ISDN technology to the forefront. It has become a preferred choice for desktop connection to the Internet, video conferencing, and local area network (LAN) interface.

There are two types of ISDN digital lines: a *Basic Rate Interface (BRI)* line, and a *Primary Rate Interface (PRI)* line. The BRI delivers ISDN services to a subscriber via two 64-kbps B (Bearer) channels for voice, data, or video and one 16-kbps D (Delta) channel for control and packet switching. The PRI delivers 23 B channels and one D channel and used to deliver ISDN services to digital PBXs, host computers, and LA systems. The ISDN modem requires a BRI connection to the local telephone company. It is possible to make this connection using the existing twisted-pair copper wires; however, it must meet specific noise and length requirements set forth by the local phone company. For example, the two conductors separating the ISDN modem and the central office must not exceed a length of 18,000 feet. The two 64-kbps B channels can be *bonded* together to form a single 128-kbps data channel. Bonding stands for **B**andwidth **ON D**emand **IN**teroperability **G**roup. It is the multiplexing protocol that combines the two 64-kbps B channels, resulting in a transmission rate over four times that of a 28.8-kbps analog modem. (More details on ISDN can be found in Chapter 16.)

Figure 13-18 illustrates Motorola's *BitSURFR Pro-EZ* ISDN terminal adapter modem and its connection to the central office. It includes two RJ11 jacks for connection to two analog devices such as a telephone and FAX machine, a DB25 connector for an EIA RS-232 interface to a computer, and an RJ45 jack for connection to the ISDN network.

> **Basic Rate Interface (BRI)**
> Delivers ISDN services to subscribers over a standard twisted-pair telephone wire.

> **Primary Rate Interface (PRI)**
> A trunking technology delivering ISDN services to digital PBXs, host computers, and LANs.

13.8   CABLE MODEM

The growing demand for Internet access has given birth to another new modem technology: the *cable modem*. The cable modem is designed to provide high-speed Internet access and video services, including picturephone to the millions of subscribers already connected to the cable TV (CATV) network.

There are basically two types of cable modems: *upstream,* and *downstream.* The upstream modem is installed at the subscriber's home, whereas the downstream modem resides at the CATV network's *headend.* The headend is the originating point of the CATV audio, video, and data signals that are distributed to the subscribers via the process of downstream transmission. Upstream transmission is the process of forwarding signals from the local subscriber to the headend for processing. Figure 13-19 shows the cable modem with Internet access via the CATV system. The modulation techniques employed by the cable modem include QPSK, QAM, and VSB. The cable modem frequency assignments are*:

> **Headend**
> The part of a broadband communication network serving as the origin and destination of all RF signals to and from devices connected to the network.

Upstream modem (CATV subscriber to headend):
  Transmit frequency: 5–40 MHz
  Receive frequency: 250–850 MHz

Downstream modem (headend to CATV subscriber):
  Transmit frequency: 250–850 MHz
  Receive frequency: 5–40 MHz

The input and output frequency range and bandwidth can be programmed with 250-kHz steps and a data channel bandwidth of 250 kHz to 6 MHz. Because the cable system's downstream bandwidth is much greater than its upstream bandwidth (due

---

*Paul J. Fung, "Designing the Cable Modem," *Communication System Design,* July 1996, pp. 44–46.

(a)

Specifications

Data rates
300 to 230,400 bps asynchronous

B-channel protocols
- MLPPP (multi-link point-to-point protocol)
- PPP (point-to-point protocol)
- V.120
- AIMux (asynchronous inverse multiplexing)

ISDN interface
U interface

ISDN standards
National ISDN-1, Northern Telecom DMS-100, AT&T 5ESS

Phone interfaces
Two standard RJ11 jacks for analog devices

Command set
AT compatible

Computer interface
Standard RS-232E, DB-25, ITU-T V.24 (cable required)

Size
6.4 in. wide, 5.3 in. deep, 1.5 in. high; weight 10.5 oz.

Line requirements
Requires an ISDN Basic Rate line (order from your telephone company). BitSURFR Pro EZ is compatible with North American telephone networks.

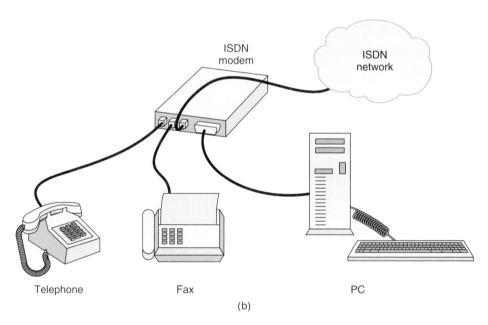

| Telephone | Fax | PC |

(b)

FIGURE 13-18
(a) Motorola's *BitSURFR ProEZ*™ ISDN modem and specifications (Courtesy of Motorola Inc.); (b) ISDN terminal adapter modem connection to an ISDN network.

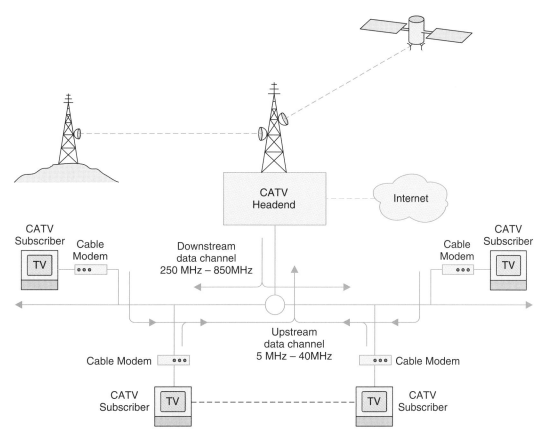

FIGURE 13-19
Cable modem setup in relation to CATV system.

to the distribution system), download capabilities range from 10 to 30 Mbps, with a reverse upload data rate of 19.2 kbps to 3.0 Mbps. Thus, cable modems are said to be "asymmetric" in their transmission and reception capabilities.

Although cable modems are still in their trial stages, the cable modem is destined to become a success, particularly when considering the robust bandwidth advantage of CATV coaxial and fiber-optic cables over the switched analog lines currently used to connect most modems. Residential users, who represent the largest potential market for cable modems, stand to benefit the most from this new technology.

13.9 ADSL MODEM

In 1989, Bellcore Laboratories (now Telcordia Technologies, Inc.) developed the *Asymmetric Digital Subscriber Line (ADSL),* which is a digital subscriber line (DSL) technology that allows high-speed data transmission over the POTS (Plain Old Telephone Service) copper lines. This is the interface between the central office and the customer's home, also known as the *customer premises.* The prime motivator of Bellcore's ADSL research was the application of video-on-demand, not the Internet. In 1995, the American National Standards Institute (ANSI) approved the first issue of the ADSL T1.413 standards. Left dormant for some years by the phone

Asymmetric Digital Subscriber Line (ADSL)
A digital subscriber line (DSL) technology allowing high-speed data transmission using older copper lines.

Customer Premises
The communication network customer's home.

companies, the technology has recently been revived in response to the deployment of cable modems for high-speed Internet access.* In Chapter 16, we discuss other DSL technologies; here, we introduce the ADSL modem.

The ADSL modem delivers high-speed voice and data simultaneously over twisted-pair telephone wires up to approximately 18,000 feet, 3.4 miles, or 5.5 kilometers. The asymmetry in ADSL stems from the difference in transmission speeds between the customer premises and the central office. The ANSI T1.413 standard specifies *upstream rates* (customer to central office) to 640 kbps and *downstream rates* (central office to customer) to 6.144 Mbps. This asymmetry, as with V.90 modems, takes advantage of the asymmetric flow of data to and from the Internet. That is, most users send short bursts of upstream data, consisting of keyboard entries and mouse clicks. The downstream data from the Internet is where the enormous amounts of data are requested and sent to the home computer.

Figure 13-20 illustrates the ADSL modem connection. Note that the subscriber loop line enters the home via the *Network Interface Device (NID),* which is attached to the outside of the home. The NID includes current and overvoltage protection for the tip and ring lines. For ADSL service, a *POTS splitter* is installed either internal or external to the NID and separates the low-frequency voice signals from the high-frequency ADSL signals. Telephones and fax machines are connected to the low-frequency interface of the POTS splitter. The ADSL modem is connected between the

Upstream Rates
Transmission rates from the customer to the central office.

Downstream Rates
Transmission rates from the central office to the customer.

Network Interface Device (NID)
Attached to the outside of the home, where the subscriber loop line enters.

POTS Splitter
Separates low-frequency voice signals from high-frequency ADSL signals.

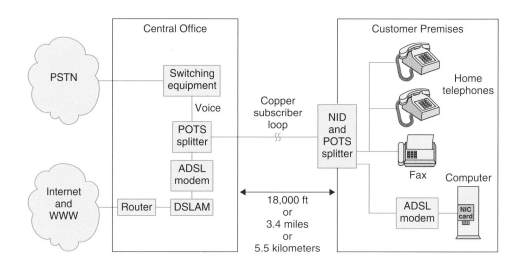

DSLAM: Digital Subscriber Line Access Multiplexer
POTS: Plain Old Telephone Service
NID: Network Interface Device
NIC card: Network Interface Card
PSTN: Public Switched Telephone Network
WWW: World Wide Web

FIGURE 13-20
ADSL (digital subscriber line) modem connection.

*Amitava Dutta-Roy, "A Second Wind for Wiring," *IEEE Spectrum,* September 1999, pp. 52–60.

POTS splitter's high-frequency interface and the network interface card (NIC) installed in the home or business computer.

The central office is set up in a similar manner. Voice signals are separated from ADSL signals by the POTS splitter, then routed in the normal manner to and from the central office switching equipment. ADSL signals are routed to and from a *Digital Subscriber Line Access Multiplexer (DSLAM).* The DSLAM (pronounced "dee-slam") includes several racks of multiplexing cards that function like ADSL modems, only they communicate with one another. Data packets from customers are multiplexed together by the DSLAM and routed to various ISPs over a high-speed backbone to the Internet. The DSLAM also demultiplexes high-speed signals from the Internet and forwards them to the appropriate individual ADSL connections.

> **Digital Subscriber Line Access Multiplexer (DSLAM)**
> Multiplexes and routes data packets from subscribers to the Internet, and demultiplexes and routes data packets from the Internet to subscribers.

In terms of performance, the major difference between ADSL and cable modems is that ADSL modems provide each customer with a dedicated, point-to-point connection to the Internet. Cable modems share the use of a network cable. Thus, even though the downstream transmission rate for cable modems is 10 Mbps, the bandwidth is shared among all users of the cable. This effectively lowers the throughput, causing network performance to vary dramatically with the amount of traffic on the cable network.

Figure 13-21 illustrates the frequency spectrum utilized by the ADSL modem. Note that frequency-division multiplexing (FDM) is employed. Voice and fax frequencies occupy the lower spectrum to approximately 4 kHz. The upstream ADSL signal occupies frequencies ranging from 25 to 138 kHz, and the downstream ADSL signal occupies the frequencies ranging from 200 kHz to 1.1 MHz.

In Chapter 11, we learned that loading coils were placed in the standard, voice-grade telephone lines to optimize the bandwidth for voice and not data. This bandwidth ranges from 300 Hz to 3400 Hz. Because the ADSL signal includes frequency components above 1 MHz, the question arises; How does this get through the limited bandwidth of the telephone lines? The solution is not simple. The bandwidth of the subscriber loop must be extended to 1.1 MHz. To achieve this, some of the following line impairments must be removed from the subscriber loop:

- Loading coils
- *Bridged taps* (splices into existing wires that are left open on one end)
- Poor splices
- Wet cable

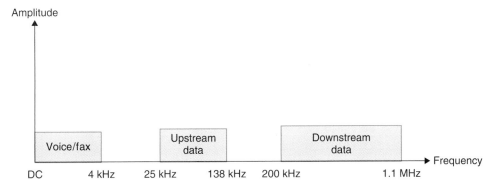

FIGURE 13-21
The ADSL modem uses frequency-division multiplexing (FDM) in the subscriber loop.

- Nontwisted wire
- Wire gauge variations

Carrierless Amplitude Phase (CAP)
A modulation or line-coding technique in ADSL modems using quadrature amplitude modulation (QAM).

Discrete Multitone (DMT)
A modulation or line-coding technique in ADSL modems dividing the frequency spectrum into 256 subchannels.

Analog Loopback Test (ALB)
Used by a transmitting and receiving device to verify operation by internally looping the transmitter's analog signal back to its own receiver section.

Digital Loopback Test (DLB)
Used to verify the transmitter and receiver sections of a local and remote station in which a command issued by the local station is sent to the remote station to loop back the detected digital data.

Two types of modulation or line-coding techniques are used in ADSL modems: *Carrierless Amplitude Phase (CAP),* and *Discrete Multitone (DMT).* CAP uses quadrature amplitude modulation (QAM) and has a signal constellation of as many as 1024 symbols, whereas DMT divides the 1.1 MHz frequency spectrum into 256 subchannels, each approximately 4 kHz wide. Both modulation techniques have merits, but DMT is specified in the ANSI T1.413 standard and is employed in most recent ADSL modems.

13.10 ANALOG LOOPBACK TEST

Among the standard features of today's modems are self-test, remote test, and loopback test capabilities. These test capabilities permit fault isolation down to the modem, customer facilities, or the telephone facilities. An *analog loopback test (ALB)* is a test feature that verifies the operation of the local modem and its connection to the DTE. The modem's transmitter section, normally connected to the telephone channel, is *looped back* to its own receiver section, as illustrated in Figure 13-22. A character typed from a terminal is, therefore, modulated onto the carrier frequency of the modem in the normal process. The analog signal that has been looped back is demodulated by the receiver section of the modem and sent back to the terminal for display. If the character typed is not displayed, a faulty modem should be considered.

13.11 DIGITAL LOOPBACK TEST

The *digital loopback test (DLB)* permits data generated from a terminal to be sent between two modem interfaces, thus testing the transmit and receive sections of both modems, the interconnecting telephone lines, the central office, and the terminal itself.

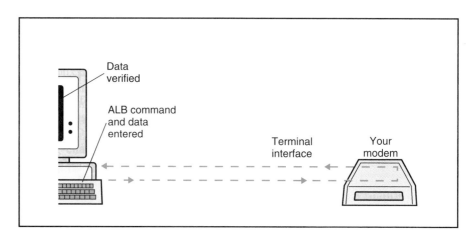

FIGURE 13-22
Analog loopback test setup. (Reprinted with permission from Racal-Vadic.)

A *local* DLB uses data from a remote terminal to test each modem and the interconnecting telephone lines. This is shown in Figure 13-23(a). The data are said to be looped back *locally*. A command must be initiated and sent by the local terminal to the locally attached modem to begin the test. An operator at the remote station is necessary to send and verify that characters typed at the remote terminal are looped back by the local modem, back through the telephone facilities, and displayed by the remote terminal.

A *remote* DLB, as shown in Figure 13-23(b), performs the same test as a local DLB, except that the *remote* operator initiates the DLB test and the local modem loops back the data typed by an operator at the remote terminal. No local operator is required for this test. In either test, if the data do not match what has been typed (assuming that the terminal and its interface to the modem is functioning), a problem exists either in the telephone lines or one of the modems. An ALB test should then

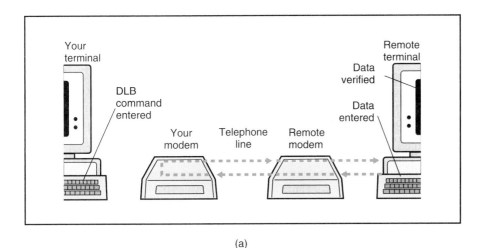

(a)

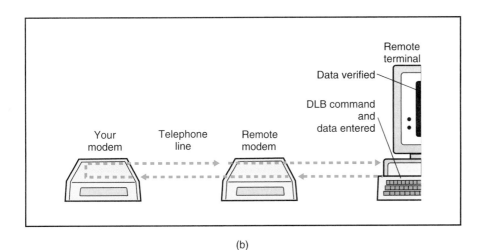

(b)

FIGURE 13-23
(a) Local DLB test setup; (b) remote DLB test setup. (Reprinted with permission from Racal-Vadic.)

be performed on each modem. If the ALB test is successful for both modems, this indicates that the telephone facilities have failed.

13.12   MODEM SYNCHRONIZATION

Modem receivers are classified into two categories: *coherent,* and *noncoherent.* Coherent receivers extract and recover the carrier frequency of the received signal. The recovered frequency is phase locked to the original carrier frequency and used in the demodulation process. High-speed modems that utilize multiphase PSK or QAM contain a coherent receiver section. In contrast, noncoherent receivers do not require carrier synchronization for the purpose of demodulation. The carrier frequencies of the transmitting and receiving modems are independent of each other. Data are recovered by detecting the *shape* of the carrier frequency. Envelope detectors are often used in noncoherent receivers.

13.13   SCRAMBLING AND DESCRAMBLING

To extract the carrier frequency in modems with coherent receivers, phase-locked loop (PLL) technology is employed. A PLL circuit is a feedback-controlled circuit. Its basic components include a voltage-controlled oscillator (VCO), a low-pass filter, and a phase comparator. The output of the VCO is phase compared with the incoming signal. Any difference between the two produces an error voltage which is used to raise or lower the VCO's frequency to maintain phase lock. The frequency spectrum of the digital signal usually contains spectral energy at the carrier frequency (or symmetrical about) in which the PLL can achieve phase lock. If a bit pattern of all 1s or 0s is transmitted by the modem for a prolonged period of time, carrier synchronization can be lost, and demodulation cannot occur. This is due to the lack of carrier spectral energy in the received signal necessary to maintain phase lock. To prevent this, high-speed modems typically scramble their data with a *scrambling* circuit to produce an optimum bit pattern for the receiving modem to achieve phase lock to. The data stream is scrambled in accordance with a defined mathematical algorithm before modulation of the carrier frequency. At the receiving end, the detected data stream is unscrambled by a *descrambler* circuit.

ITU-TS' V.22bis recommendation specifies that self-synchronizing scrambler and descrambler circuits be included in the transmitter and receiver sections of the modem. The transmitted data stream is scrambled by dividing it by the polynomial given by

$$1 + X^{-14} + X^{-17} \tag{13-2}$$

The coefficients of the quotients of this division, taken in descending order, form the data sequence at the output of the scrambler. This sequence is equal to

$$D_s = D_i \oplus D_s * X^{-14} \oplus D_s * X^{-17} \tag{13-3}$$

The demodulated data stream is descrambled by multiplying it by the polynomial given by equation (13-2). The coefficients of the recovered data sequence, taken in descending order, form the output data sequence given by

$$D_o = D_R (1 \oplus X^{-14} \oplus X^{-17}) \tag{13-4}$$

where
D_s = data sequence at the output of the scrambler
D_i = data sequence applied to the scrambler
D_R = data sequence applied to the descrambler
D_o = data sequence at the output of the descrambler
$\oplus$ = modulo 2 addition
$*$ = binary multiplication

13.14   MODEM FILE TRANSFER PROTOCOLS

Historically, file transfers over the PSTN were error prone. Errors occurring in text messages were tolerable, because the messages could still be interpreted by users. Recently, however, there has been growing concern over the integrity of interactive asynchronous data communications over the PSTN. Some studies estimate that more than 90% of users communicate asynchronously in an interactive mode with a personal computer (PC) or mainframe linked to various bulletin board services (BBS) and other mainframes and PCs. Many of these applications make speed and error control a necessity rather than a luxury. Software developers have hastened to fill the need for efficient file transfer protocols. As a result, an array of protocols are available to suit our needs for uploading and downloading files to and from other terminals. A brief discussion of the most widely used file transfer protocols offered by BBS systems will now be given.

13.14.1   Xmodem

When the first computer BBS went on line, there was an obvious need for an error-controlling mechanism that would allow program files to be reliably exchanged among users of PCs. Xmodem was one of the first software data communications protocols designed to meet this need. Xmodem is sometimes referred to as the *Christensen protocol* after its designer, Ward Christensen. It has become a de facto standard since the late 1970s for modem file transfer verification between PCs.

Xmodem is an ACK/NAK alternating protocol that operates in half-duplex mode. This means that when a packet of data is transmitted and received without error, a positive acknowledgment (ACK) control packet is sent back to the transmitter. In the event of an error, a negative acknowledgment (NAK) control packet is returned to the transmitter. The packet is retransmitted in this case. Packets must be acknowledged before communications can resume. This form of error control is referred to as *automatic repeat request (ARQ)*. As shown in Figure 13-24, 128 bytes are used in the data

| SOH | Packet no. | Packet no. cmpl. | Data field (128 bytes) | BCC |

SOH	Start of header (beginning of packet)
Packet no.	Sequential packet number
Packet no. cmpl.	Sequential packet number complement
Data field	Fixed length data field of 128 bytes
BCC	Block check character, 8-bit checksum

FIGURE 13-24
XMODEM packet format.

field of the Xmodem packet. An 8-bit checksum is appended to the data field as the block check character (BCC).

A variation of Xmodem is Xmodem/CRC. Xmodem/CRC uses a 16-bit cyclic redundancy check (CRC) of the binary data within the packet instead of an 8-bit checksum. The 16-bit CRC used as a BCC is much more reliable in terms of detecting errors.

13.14.2 1K-Xmodem

This file transfer protocol is identical to Xmodem, except that the block size has been increased from 128 bytes in the data field to 1024 (1K), hence the name *1K-Xmodem*. For relatively quiet telephone lines, 1K-Xmodem is faster than its counterpart. A smaller number of blocks is necessary to transfer the same amount of data; therefore, fewer blocks need to be checked for errors.

13.14.3 1K-Xmodem/G

Another variation of Xmodem is *1K-Xmodem/G*. This protocol also uses a 1-kilobyte data field. The "/G" denotes the use of MNP (Microcom networking protocol), a protocol that resides in the modem's hardware (see the detailed discussion of MNP later). For modems that support MNP, 1K-Xmodem/G offers a very fast and efficient file transfer protocol. Unlike many protocols that perform a block-by-block handshake for error control, the use of MNP allows multiple frames to be transmitted before an acknowledgment is required. This ability increases the overall throughput.

13.14.4 Ymodem

The unique advantage of *Ymodem* is that it is a *multiple file transfer protocol*. It was developed by Chuck Forsberg of Omen Technology, Inc. A maximum of 99 files can be uploaded (transmitted from the local terminal to the remote terminal) or downloaded (transmitted from the remote terminal to the local terminal) in succession. Block sizes are typically 1K bytes in length, and the BCC is CRC-16, a 16-bit CRC algorithm standard.

13.14.5 Ymodem/G

A very fast and efficient protocol that supports multiple file transfers is *Ymodem/G*. This protocol, like 1K-Xmodem/G, requires a modem with MNP residing in its hardware. Most of the latest 9600-bps or faster modems utilize MNP. Data compression is also performed in the modem's hardware. Both error control and data compression, residing in the modem's hardware, adhere to ITU-TS V.42 and V.42bis standards. For communication sessions requiring large file transfers at high data rates (9600, 14,400, 19,200, or 38,400 bps), Ymodem/G, or *Zmodem* (discussed later), is among the recommended choices.

13.14.6 Zmodem

One of the most widely used file transfer protocols is *Zmodem*. Some statistical surveys indicate that Zmodem is utilized in more than 70% of BBS file transfers. This high-performance and high-reliability protocol was also developed by Chuck Forsberg.

Zmodem uses a 32-bit CRC to reduce the number of undetected errors. Error checking of this degree is accurate to 99.9999%. Multiple file transfers and variable block sizes of data are supported. MNP hardware is not necessary with Zmodem, and if connecting links do not support Zmodem, it can step down to Ymodem.

Zmodem does not wait for acknowledgments from the receiving device. Instead, it assumes that data have been received without error unless a repeat request is sent for a specific block. Zmodem also has the unique capability to resume file transfers that have been aborted for some reason and, thus, only partially completed. This is called *crash recover.** For overall performance and reliability, Zmodem is recommended as one of the best file transfer protocols.

13.14.7 Kermit

Another commonly used protocol is Kermit, developed at Columbia University. It is used extensively with PCs, minicomputers, and mainframes. Like Xmodem, Kermit is an ACK/NAK alternating protocol that uses ARQ for error correction. Figure 13-25 illustrates the format of the Kermit packet. Although the data field of the packet is shorter than that of Xmodem, a length field (LEN) offers the flexibility of varying the packet size to a maximum of 94 bytes. Small buffers can be accommodated, and the final packet in a transmission is not restricted to a fixed number of bytes.

13.14.8 Microcom Networking Protocol

Unfortunately, the move to higher data transfer rates over the switched telephone lines involves the trade-off of increased errors. To maintain the same error rate, a V.22bis compatible modem operating at 2400 bps requires a SNR several decibels higher than a Bell 212A-compatible modem operating at 1200 bps. A Massachusetts-based company called Microcom has developed a method of controlling these errors. This method is MNP, an acronym for *Microcom networking protocol;* it offers far more capability than the protocols discussed thus far.

MNP resides in the modem's hardware. This relieves the user's DTE from the burden of controlling errors via software-based protocols such as Xmodem. The CPU

> **Microcom Networking Protocol (MNP)**
> An error-correction protocol for modems designed by Microcom, Inc.

SOH	LEN	SEQ	TYPE	Data field	BCC

SOH	Start of header
LEN	Specifies the length of the data field. A maximum of 94 characters can be used
SEQ	Packet sequence identifier
TYPE	Specifies the type of packet, control, or data
Data field	ASCII data up to 94 characters
BCC	Typically 16-bit CRC

FIGURE 13-25
Kermit packet format.

---

*This information was downloaded from the *Wildcat BBS*. A more detailed description of Zmodem can be downloaded from many BBS services under the file name of *ZMODEM8.ZIP*.

"GO BACK N"

Basic MNP frame

FIGURE 13-26
MNP frame structure.

is left to perform other tasks, thus increasing system productivity. MNP formats ASCII data sent from DTE into an SDLC frame, similar to that used on larger mainframe systems. The basic frame structure is shown in Figure 13-26. By using a synchronous format, MNP is capable of reducing the number of bits in the user's data. Once the data have been converted, MNP will calculate a check sum or CRC for the number of bits in the data. This CRC is then sent with the data. At the receiving modem, the CRC is removed from the frame and a new CRC is computed. This new CRC is then compared with the CRC originally received from the transmitting modem. If the new check sum matches the original CRC computed by the transmitting modem, the data are passed on to the user's DTE in its original asynchronous format. If the two do not match, the frame is in error.

An advantage of MNP over other ACK/NAK protocols is that multiple frames can be transmitted without having to wait for an acknowledgment from the receiver for each individual frame. Throughput is increased. This is possible through a technique called *Go Back N*. Should any frame be in error using this technique, an ARQ control frame is sent back to the transmitting modem. The transmitting modem must then go back and retransmit the frame in error, including all other frames that followed.

Figure 13-27 illustrates the Go Back N technique. A typical number of frames that may be transmitted in succession by a modem that features MNP may be five. Modem A has transmitted five frames of data. Frame number 3 contains an inaccurate CRC calculation. Modem B requests a retransmission of frames 3 through 5. This scheme results in a total number of eight frames that have been transmitted in order to send five frames of data.

MNP has been disseminated within the data communications industry through licensing agreements with Microcom. It has become a de facto standard for a number of manufacturers and service providers, such as Racal-Vadic and GTE Telenet to name just two.* To date, there are nine designated classes of MNP. Each is designed to reduce data errors and optimize throughput over varying line conditions. The nine MNP classes are listed in Table 13-3. Classes 1 through 4 have become part of the ITU-TS V.42 recommendation.

13.14.9 Link Access Procedure

Another widely used data communications protocol recognized by the ITU-TS V.42 (Error Correction Procedures for DCEs) standard is link access procedure (LAP).

---

*A Primer on MNP, from Racal-Vadic.

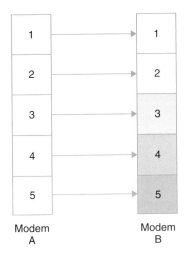

"Go Back N" MNP Scheme

Should any frame be errored
the transmitting modem must
retransmit the bad frame and
all frames that follow.

Example:
Modem A has transmitted 5
frames of data. Frame 3
contains an inaccurate CRC
calculation. Modem B requests
a retransmission of frames
3 through 5. This scheme results
in a total of 8 frames that
have been transmitted in order
to send 5 frames of data.

Modem
A

Modem
B

FIGURE 13-27
MNP's "Go Back *N*" technique. (Courtesy of Racal-Vadic.)

TABLE 13-3
The Nine Designated Classes of MNP

Class 1	Half-duplex asynchronous character-based error control (Bell 202 types of modems). Frame size is a maximum 260 octets (bytes).
Class 2	Full-duplex asynchronous character-based error control (Bell 212A types of modems). Frame size is a maximum 64 octets.
Class 3	Full-duplex synchronous block-based error control (Bell 212A or ITU-TS V.22bis types of modems). Frame size is a maximum of 64 octets. Frame size is determined during initial call setup negotiations.
Class 4	Enhancement to class 3, adaptive packet lengths. Increases throughput to 120%. Frame size is extended to a maximum of 256 octets (V.22bis modems at 2400 bps).
Class 5	Data compression. Uses a real-time adaptive algorithm to compress data. The algorithm continually analyzes the data and adjusts its compressing parameters. Increased throughput up to 200% (2400-bps modems and above).
Class 6	Universal link negotiation. This procedure links at 2400 bps and then looks for a higher-speed protocol such as ITU-TS V.29 or V.32.
Class 7	Enhanced data compression. Utilizes an adaptive real-time algorithm like class 5 to compress data. Also, a predictive algorithm is used to predict the probability of characters in the data stream. Increased throughput up to 300% (2400-bps modems and above).
Class 8	Enhanced data compression with V.29 fast train, HDX.
Class 9	Enhanced data compression with V.32 modem engine, FCS.

Several variations of LAP have been written to meet specific applications of the X.25 standard. LAP B, for example, is the link-level protocol used for the X.25 public data networks. LAP D is the link-level protocol for use in ISDN. For modems, LAP M has been designed specifically as the link access protocol. LAP M is an error controller such as MNP. AT&T, Hayes, the United Kingdom (led by British Telecom), and Japan support LAP M. This raises the issue of compatibility between modems employing MNP versus LAP M. Currently, modems compatible with the ITU-TS V.42 standard will query the other modem and use LAP M only if it is compatible. If one of the modems is not equipped with LAP M but has MNP capability, both modems will default to communications using MNP.

13.15 IMPROVING MODEM PERFORMANCE

Increasing the data transmission speeds of modems has brought about extensive hardware and software options that seriously affect the performance of today's modems. Several standards have been written to utilize this performance and achieve uniformity, particularly among high-speed modems.

Three parameters must be controlled by the high-speed modem: *error detection and correction, data compression,* and *throughput.* They are defined as follows:

Error Detection and Correction   The mechanism used to reduce the number of errors that may occur between a transmitting and a receiving modem.

Data Compression   The mechanism used to reduce the number of data bits that is normally used to express a given amount of information.

Throughput   A measure of transmission rate based on the time that it takes to successfully transmit and receive a maximum number of bits, characters, or blocks per unit time. This includes the added time for acknowledgments, framing, and error control. Throughput is measured in one direction.

In data communication systems, these three parameters are of major concern to the user. Consider, for example, an electronic banking transaction. A sudden burst of noise induced into the communications channel from an external source can cause errors in the data bit stream. These errors *must* be detected and corrected, which takes additional system time. If the error is not corrected or goes undetected, the results could be catastrophic. The customer, therefore, expects prompt and error-free communications. We now consider some of the basic principles regarding these three parameters.

13.16 MODEM ERROR CONTROL

Several techniques are used to detect if there are errors in a data stream. Typically, the transmitted data stream is formatted in accordance with a communications protocol that inserts additional bits into the data stream for error control purposes. In asynchronous transmission, the parity bit is used for error detection purposes. For synchronous transmission, blocks of data can include several hundred contiguous characters sent in succession. The block is framed with redundant information, called the *preamble* and *postamble.* The postamble of the block typically includes a block check character (BCC) used for error detection. The BCC is the result of some mathematical or logical operation performed on the transmitted data bits and inserted in the postamble of the block during transmission. The receiver performs the same mathematical or logical operation on the received data block. A comparison is made to the BCC received from the transmitter. If there is a difference, an error has been detected. Generally, the receiving station requests a retransmission of the block in error. If communications is simplex (one way), a request for retransmission is impossible. Special techniques must be employed in the receiver to correct the detected errors. (Chapter 17 covers error detection and correction in depth.)

13.17   THROUGHPUT

The *throughput* of a communications channel is of major concern in applications requiring intensive data transfer rates. A user being charged by the minute for downloading information from a data bank would no doubt benefit from the increased throughput of a 33.6-kbps modem over a 1200-bps modem. Many defense- and medical-related situations often require immediate demand for data.

Several factors govern the throughput of a system: the bit rate; the electrical characteristics of the channel, such as bandwidth and phase and amplitude distortion; the occurrence of errors; block size; communications protocol; and data compression.

Throughput is not to be confused with the absolute maximum instantaneous bit transfer rate. An asynchronously transmitted character from a terminal, for example, may have a bit time associated with a terminal setting of 9600 bps. However, the duration between the transmitted character and when the next character is typed is wasted in terms of channel utilization. Throughput, in this case, depends primarily on the speed of the typist, which may be slower than a few characters per second in this mode of operation. Even if the asynchronous characters are transmitted in succession, throughput is lowered by the overhead included in each character for framing and error control (start and stop bits and parity). Ideally, maximum throughput is obtained by transmitting as many characters as possible in a given period of time without having to include redundancy for framing, error control, and other overhead requirements.

For synchronous transmission, throughput is reduced in the preamble and postamble of the transmitted block. The smaller the block size, the greater the amount of time that is spent transmitting redundant information relative to the actual data within the block. Block size should, therefore, be maximized to increase throughput. Maximum block size is governed by the synchronous communications protocol used.

Several methods are commonly used to compute system throughput. One such formula commonly used by system designers is TRIB, an acronym for *transmission rate of information bits*. TRIB is given by the equation

$$\text{TRIB} = \frac{B(L - C)(1 - P)}{(BL/R)} \text{ bps} \tag{13-5}$$

where B = number of information bits per character
   L = total number of characters (or bytes) in the block
   C = average number of noninformation characters in the block
   P = probability of an error occurring in the block
   R = modem transmission speed (bps)
   T = interval of time between blocks

Opening flag (8)	Address (8)	Control (8)	Data field (256 bytes)	Frame check sequence (16)	Closing flag (8)

FIGURE 13-28
HDLC frame for computing the throughput of a communications system.

EXAMPLE 13.2

A 2400-bps modem transmits five contiguous blocks of HDLC information frames with no idle time between blocks. Each block contains 256 bytes of raw data. The format of each block is given in Figure 13-28. Prior tests indicate that an average of three blocks in every 100 contains an error. Compute the TRIB.

Solution:

$$\text{TRIB} = \frac{8(262 - 6)(1 - 3/100)}{[8 \times 262)/2400] \times 0} = 2275 \text{ bps}$$

This example illustrates how throughput is reduced by protocol overhead and errors. The parameter T was assumed to be zero for the full-duplex HDLC link. If a half-duplex protocol such as BISYNC were used, T must be considered in the equation for acknowledgments of individual blocks.

Throughput is clearly improved by increasing the block size and transmission rate of the modem. At some point, however, the percentage of errors will diminish this effect. An optimum block size can, therefore, be established for any given communication system. System designers must conduct random tests to ascertain this information. Modeling by computer simulation is often used. Many programs are available for this.

13.18 DATA COMPRESSION

One method of drastically increasing system throughput is through the process of *data compression.* Data compression can increase system throughput by a consistent 4:1 margin. It is employed in many of today's high-speed modems. A 2400-bps modem, for example, can now communicate at an effective 9600 bps without any modifications to the modem's transmitter and receiver sections.

The term *data compression* refers to the ability of a data communication system to remove redundant bits from a transmitted data stream, thus reducing the total number of transmitted bits necessary to convey the *same* information. The bandwidth constraints of the telephone lines are indirectly avoided. To accomplish this, data compression takes advantage of the fact that characters transmitted within a block of data do not occur with equal probability of use. Some vowels, for example, are used much more frequently than some of the consonants in the alphabet. Many ASCII and EBCDIC punctuation and control characters are rarely used in text files, yet they are still represented by 8 bits. This is also true with files containing graphic and numeric data. Spreadsheets and graphs typically include numerous repeated characters, such as lines, dots, and spaces. In addition, the probability of groups of characters statistically dependent on each other exists in many cases. The letter *q,* for example, is almost always followed by the letter *u* in the English language, or a *t* is often followed by the letter *h*. For these reasons and more, it is well known that for any specific application, a more efficient encoding scheme is desirable.

13.18.1 Huffman Encoding

Huffman encoding is one of the oldest data compression techniques. It has been used for more than 20 years and has served as a predecessor for more advanced techniques. The theory behind Huffman encoding is to reduce the number of bits representing those characters that have a high frequency of occurrence.

> **Huffman Encoding**
> Used to reduce the number of bits that represent frequently occurring characters.

For example, the letter *e* is the most common letter in the English text and the letter *z* the least common. Huffman encoding takes this probability of occurrence into account, encoding the most probable characters with fewer than eight bits and the least probable characters with more than eight bits. The average word length after compression is much less than eight bits.

In the previous paragraph, there are 38 lower-case *e*'s and one lower-case *z*. It is easy to see the benefit of re-encoding the letter *e* as a 3-bit word and the letter *z* as a 16-bit word. This is precisely the strategy behind a Huffman-based compression technique. Figure 13-29 is a graph of the frequency of occurrence of each character in the preceding paragraph.

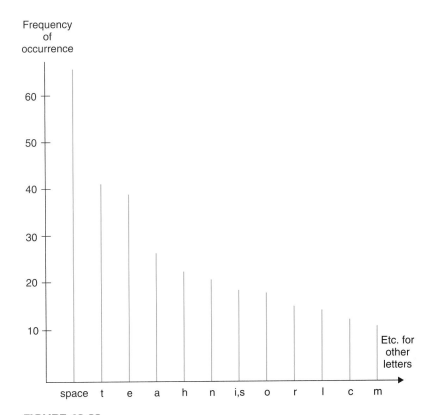

FIGURE 13-29
Graph depicting the frequency of occurrence of the characters used in the boldface paragraph above. (Reprinted with permission from Concord Data Systems, *All About Adaptive Data Compression for Asynchronous Applications*.)

Table 13-4 illustrates an example of how a Huffman encoding table might look. The table is used to represent 256 possible characters of an alphanumeric character set, such as ASCII or EBCDIC. Three *fields* are used to divide the character set into a code based on each character's frequency of use. The right of the table shows how the 256 characters are grouped into one of three categories that are represented by a 3-bit code, a 7-bit code, or a 15-bit code.

Seven of the most frequently used characters, space and vowels for example, are represented at the top of the table by a 3-bit *character code* (CHAR CODE). The 15 next most frequently used characters are encoded into a 7-bit code, where the first 3 bits are a special noncharacter (NO-CHAR) code, and the remaining 4 bits represent the 15 characters in descending order of frequency. The 3-bit NO CHAR code indicates to software to look in the second CHAR CODE field for the actual character code. Seven bits are still an improvement over the original encoded 8-bit character.

If the character to be transmitted is not one of the 22 (7 + 15) most frequently used characters, it is represented by a 15-bit code. This includes the remaining 234 entries (256 − 15 − 7), with the least frequently used character occupying the 234th entry. Although 15 bits used to represent these characters are greater than the original 8 bits, the average transmitted word length after Huffman compression is much less than 8 bits.

TABLE 13-4
Huffman Table[a]

	Huffman Anticipates Characters		
	3	7	15
	Bit Boundaries		
CHAR CODE			
CHAR CODE			
CHAR CODE			7 CHARS
CHAR CODE			
CHAR CODE			
"NO-CHAR"	CHAR CODE		
"NO-CHAR"	CHAR CODE		
"NO-CHAR"	CHAR CODE		15 CHARS
"NO-CHAR"	CHAR CODE		
"NO-CHAR"	CHAR CODE		
"NO-CHAR"	"NO-CHAR"	CHAR CODE	
"NO-CHAR"	"NO-CHAR"	CHAR CODE	
"NO-CHAR"	"NO-CHAR"	CHAR CODE	234 CHARS
"NO-CHAR"	"NO-CHAR"	CHAR CODE	
"NO-CHAR"	"NO-CHAR"	CHAR CODE	
"NO-CHAR"	"NO-CHAR"	CHAR CODE	

Number of characters in table segment

[a]**The Huffman table** is organized from top to bottom in descending order of frequency. Each entry could consist of, say, 15 bits divided into three fields of 3, 4, and 8 bits. Seven characters can be represented in the field containing 3 bits (plus the "noncharacter" code). Fifteen characters can be represented in the field containing 4 bits (plus the noncharacter code).

Source: Reprinted with permission from Telcor Systems Corporation.

Huffman tables may be either static or dynamic.* A static table is one in which the frequency of each character in the message is assumed, so the order of the character in the table is determined ahead of time. That order is fixed so that even if the actual frequency changes, the software will continue using the same table. Obviously, both the sender and the receiver will have created identical tables before transmission to enable proper interpretation of the message codes.

In a dynamic Huffman model, a frequency algorithm determines which characters are represented at which levels in the table. Every time a character is used, its position in the table is exchanged for the position of the character immediately above it. The bit patterns in the table themselves do not actually change. What changes is the assignment of the bit patterns within a table entry to represent a particular character. An exchange is always made after the code currently assigned is sent across the line. This ensures that both sender and receiver can update their respective copies of the table in sync.

For example, suppose that a data stream shifted from using upper-case and lower-case letters to all upper case. In the first instance, the lower-case *e* might be the most frequently used character and at the top of the table. Upper-case *E,* on the other hand, could very well be at the bottom. Once the shift to all upper-case occurred, every time *E* was used its table assignment would be swapped to the next-higher level, until it reached the top. Along the way, it would cross the boundary between 15- and 7-bit representation and then the boundary between 7- and 3-bit representation.

Typical performance for Huffman-based data compression is approximately a 2:1 ratio, depending on the statistics of the data being sent. The primary advantage of the Huffman encoding technique is its simplicity and that it does not require a large amount of memory to implement.

More advanced data compression techniques are currently being used by modem manufacturers. Huffman encoding is based on the *statistical independence* of characters. In other words, a character's probability of occurrence does not take into account what the preceding character is. More advanced data compression techniques do. They are also *adaptive* to the data being sent. In the English language, a *q* is most likely to be followed by a *u,* or a *t* is likely to be followed by an *h.* In addition, characters used in spreadsheets and graphs often repeat themselves (e.g., spaces, dots, dashes, and so on). Rather than sending a repeated string of these characters, the data can be encoded into a word indicating the number of repeated characters that follow. This is referred to as *run-length encoding.* Several sophisticated algorithms employ these techniques, achieving as much as a 4:1 compression ratio. The disadvantage is that this added complexity requires dedicated processors and extra money. Within time, however, the added cost will certainly decline.

PROBLEMS

1. Define *modem.*
2. Explain the difference between a direct-connect modem and an acoustically coupled modem.
3. Why are acoustically coupled modems limited to speeds of less than 1200 bps?

---

*Francis Bacon (Telcor Systems Corporation), "How to Quadruple Dial-Up Communications Efficiency," *Mini-Micro Systems,* Feb. 1988: *Technology Forum.*

4. If the bit stream shown in Figure 13-5 were changed to 101110100010, draw the waveforms resulting from the following modulation techniques: ASK, FSK, PSK, and DPSK.
5. Define *dibit*.
6. What Bell modem standard utilizes tribit encoding as a modulation technique?
7. What is the transmitting MARK frequency for a Bell 103 modem operating in the answer mode?
8. What is the transmitting originate frequency for a Bell 212A modem?
9. Explain the differences between simplex, half-duplex, and full-duplex transmission modes for a modem.
10. What range of frequencies is used by modems to disable echo suppressors? How long must the tone be present?
11. A 4800-bps modem uses tribit encoding to represent eight phases of a DPSK signal. Compute its baud rate.
12. A 9600-bps modem uses QAM for its modulation technique. Compute its baud rate.
13. Compute the M-ary for the 9600-bps modem in Problem 12.
14. What do *bis* and *ter* mean?
15. Using Shannon's Law, compute the channel capacity for a medium with a bandwidth of 1.1 MHz and an SNR of 35 dB.
16. What is an *NID?*
17. What is an *POTS splitter?*
18. What is a *DSLAM?*
19. What is the range of frequencies for an ADSL's downstream data?
20. Explain the difference between an ALB test and a DLB test.
21. What is the number of data bytes used in the data field of Xmodem?
22. Explain the difference between Xmodem and 1K-Xmodem/G.
23. How accurate, in terms of error detection, is Zmodem's 32-bit CRC?
24. What error-controlling technique is used to allow multiple frames to be transmitted without having to wait for an acknowledgment for each frame?
25. Refer to Figure 13-28. A 4800-bps modem transmits four contiguous HDLC blocks with the format shown. There is no idle time between blocks. An average of 2.5 blocks out of every 100 sent are received in error. Compute the transmission rate of information bits (TRIB) using equation (13-5).
26. Repeat problem 25 for a 9600-bps modem.
27. Define *data compression.*
28. What is a typical compression ratio that can be achieved with a Huffman-based data compression technique?

14

SYNCHRONOUS PROTOCOLS

In data communications, a *protocol* is defined as a set of rules and procedures developed for purposes of communicating between devices. A multitude of protocols has been documented. They range from specifying the type of connector and voltage levels to be used by a device, EIA RS-449 for example, to the management of software used to control the signaling sequence necessary for communications.

> **Protocol**
> A set of rules or procedures for communication between devices.

Rapid technological advances have forced the standardization of protocols in recent years to become more revolutionary and anticipatory rather than evolutionary and documentary as in the past. As a result, there has been widespread concern among manufacturers and buyers whether the more recent standards will adapt themselves as *accepted* standards in the industry. Manufacturers and buyers both benefit in this case in terms of costs, compatibility, and application. On this premise, the discussion of protocols and their classification is limited here to those universally observed as an accepted standard.

14.1 STANDARDS ORGANIZATIONS FOR DATA COMMUNICATIONS

A consortium of standards organizations, vendors, and users of data-communicating devices meets on a regular basis to establish guidelines and standards for communications between two or more devices. A brief look at some of the major organizations that have contributed to the success of the telecommunications industry is presented here. These organizations continue to develop and refine standards concurrent with the technological trends in communications.

ISO: The International Standards Organization (ISO) is *the* Standards Organization. ISO creates the Open Systems Interconnection (OSI) protocols and standards for graphics, document exchange, and related technologies. ISO endorses and coordinates work with other groups, such as CCITT, ANSI, and IEEE.

CCITT: The Consultative Committee for International Telephony and Telegraphy (CCITT) was founded more than 100 years ago. It is now an agency of the United

Nations. CCITT develops the recommended standards and protocols for telecommunications. The group consists of many government authorities and representatives of the public switched telephone network (PSTN). CCITT has developed the V series specifications for modem interface, the X series for data communications, and the I and Q series for Integrated Services Digital Network (ISDN). CCITT is now known as ITU-TS, the International Standards Union–Telecommunication Standardization Sector.

ANSI: The American National Standards Institute is the official U.S. agency and voting representative for ISO. ANSI has developed information exchange standards above 50 Mbps. The institute is involved with coordinating manufacturers through the Computer and Business Equipment Manufacturers Association.

IEEE: The Institute of Electrical and Electronic Engineers is a professional organization consisting of over 300,000 electronics, communication, and computer engineers from more than 135 countries. The IEEE is a leading authority in setting standards in areas ranging from communications to aerospace, biomedical technology, and power control.

EIA: The Electronic Industries Association (EIA) is a U.S. organization of manufacturers that establishes and recommends industrial standards. EIA has developed the RS *(recommended standard)* series for data and telecommunications.

ITU-TS: See CCITT.

IETF: The Internet Engineering Task Force is an international organization of Internet researchers, designers, and vendors who recommend and coordinate the operation of the Internet. The IETF is split up into several working groups. Each working group is assigned to a particular Internet topic, such as routing and transport protocols, security, etc.

14.2 ISO-OPEN SYSTEMS INTERCONNECT SEVEN-LAYER MODEL

Previous chapters focused on fundamental interfacing techniques and devices used for serial communications. The electrical, mechanical, and functional aspects of serial interfacing were considered. In summary, we have been dealing with the elements of data communications on a *hardware* level. This is by no means the whole of data communications but, rather, a crucial aspect of the overall requirement for a system or network of systems. Consider, for example, the software necessary for handling error conditions resulting from the transmission loss of data. Also consider how data may be interpreted by a computer on a bus in determining whether they are data that should be attended to or passed on to another device on the bus. For informational resources to be shared among users who are either centrally located, as in a business building, or remotely located throughout the world, the necessary hardware and software must be adapted to standardized guidelines. Worldwide networks that currently exchange enormous amounts of data on a 24-hour basis all follow stringent sets of defined and documented protocols. All the aforementioned standards organizations have collaborated in the development of these standards.

With the ever-increasing need for standards and dependence on standards, the combined efforts of ANSI, ITU-TS, EIA, IEEE, ISO, and others have led to the development of a hierarchy of protocols, called the *Open Systems Interconnect (OSI)* model. This model encourages an open system by serving as a structural guideline for exchanging information between computers, terminals, and networks. Figure 14-1 depicts the OSI model, which categorizes data communications protocols into seven levels. The hierarchy of each level is based on a *layered* concept. Each layer serves a defined function in the network and depends on the lower adjacent layer's functional interaction with the network. If level 1, the physical layer, for example, were to experience complications, all layers above would be affected. On the other hand, because each layer serves a defined function, that function may be implemented in more than one way. In other words, more than one protocol can serve the function of a layer, thus offering the advantage of flexibility.

> **Open Systems Interconnect (OSI)**
> A heirarchy of protocols encouraging an open system by providing a structure for exchanging information between networks and devices.

Physical Layer   The lowest layer of the OSI model defines the electrical and mechanical rules governing how data are transmitted and received from one point to another. Definitions such as maximum and minimum voltage and current levels are made on this level. Circuit impedances are also defined in the physical layer. An example would be the RS-232 serial interface specification.

Data Link Layer   This layer defines the mechanism in which data are transported between stations to achieve error-free communications. This includes error control, formatting, framing, and sequencing of the data. IBM's BISYNC and SDLC are examples that fall into the data link layer.

Network Layer   This layer defines the mechanism in which messages are broken into data packets and routed from a sending node to a receiving node within a communications network. This mechanism is referred to as *packet switching*. Individual packets representing the original message may take various routes throughout the network to arrive at their final destinations. The order in which they are received may or may not be the same order in which they were sent.

Transport Layer   The transport layer of the OSI model ensures the reliable and efficient end-to-end transportation of data within a network. It is the highest layer in

7	Application
6	Presentation
5	Session
4	Transport
3	Network
2	Data link
1	Physical

FIGURE 14-1
Seven-layer OSI model.

terms of communications. Layers above the transport layer are no longer concerned about the technological aspect of the network. The upper three layers address the software aspects of the network, whereas the lower three layers address the hardware. The functions served by the transport layer are ensuring the most simplified and efficient service, error detection and recovery, and multiplexing of end-user information onto the network.

Session Layer When a user interacts with a computer within a network, it is often referred to as a *session*. A session is initiated and terminated by a user during log-in and log-out procedures. The session layer concerns itself with the management of a session. This includes the recognition of a user's request to use the network for communications as well as terminating the user's session. If a break occurs during the session, this layer addresses the full recovery of the session without any loss of data.

Presentation Layer The services provided on this level address any code or syntax conversions necessary to present the data to the network in a common format for communications. This includes alphanumeric code sets (ASCII and EBCDIC), data encryption, data compression, file formats, and so on.

Applications Layer The applications layer is the highest ISO/OSI layered protocol. The specific applications program that performs the end-user task is defined at this level. This includes, for example, database management programs, word processing, spreadsheets, banking, and electronic mail.

14.3 BIT-ORIENTED PROTOCOLS VERSUS BYTE-ORIENTED PROTOCOLS

We have learned that protocols are a set of rules that govern the orderly flow of information between two parties. In serial communications, the information can be transmitted in either synchronous or asynchronous format. As the communications system becomes more complex, the need for speed and efficiency rises. Synchronous transmission is used. A closer look at synchronous transmission methods and protocols that serve the function of the data link layer (level 2) is necessary to understand the development and maintenance of data communication systems.

Synchronous data link protocols can be subdivided into two categories: *bit-oriented* protocols, and *byte-oriented* protocols.

Bit-Oriented Protocols In bit-oriented protocols, special groups of uniquely defined bit patterns are used to control the framing, error checking, and flow of data between devices. The data in bit-oriented protocols may be of any content and may not necessarily represent an encoded character set such as ASCII or EBCDIC. An example would be raw data from an A/D converter. Special transmission schemes must be employed so that the receiver can distinguish between the actual control characters for framing and error control versus the raw data patterns from the A/D converter that may coincidentally take on the same bit pattern as the control character.

Byte-Oriented Protocols In byte-oriented protocols, the transmission of data blocks is controlled by ASCII or EBCDIC control characters such as SYN, SOH, and ETX.

Like the data characters, control characters are uniquely defined as part of the ASCII or EBCDIC character set. They are placed at the beginning and end of the transmitted data block for purposes of framing and error control. Because the actual data within the block are typically ASCII or EBCDIC, the receiving device can distinguish between data and control.

14.4 BISYNC

BISYNC stands for *binary synchronous communications protocol*. BISYNC is also referred to as BSC. Developed in 1964 by IBM, BISYNC was one of the most widely used synchronous protocols until recent protocols made it relatively slow and inefficient in comparison. Many systems that have been installed with BISYNC hardware and software are still being used to this date. The BISYNC data link protocol has served as a predecessor for more recent protocols to improve on.

BISYNC is a byte-oriented synchronous serial communications protocol. It is designed for half-duplex operation between two or more stations connected in a *point-to-point* or *multipoint* configuration. Figure 14-2(a) illustrates two computers configured for point-to-point operation. Point-to-point can also be a direct connection between computers or computer and terminal without the use of a modem. Figure 14-2(b) illustrates a computer connected to several terminals in a multipoint (or multidrop) configuration. Several terminals are shown here sharing a private line through the use of modems.

Binary Synchronous Communications (BISYNC)
A byte-oriented, synchronous serial communications protocol. Also referred to as *BSC protocol*.

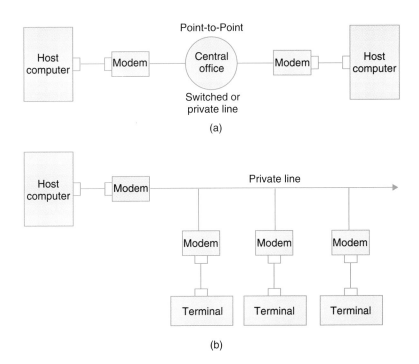

FIGURE 14-2
(a) Computers connected point-to-point; (b) computer connected to several terminals in a multipoint (or multidrop) configuration.

14.4.1   BISYNC Message Block Format

Figure 14-3 illustrates the format of a BISYNC message block. Note that the block contains *data link control* characters. Data link control characters are used for framing and management of the data between devices. A complete list of BISYNC control characters is given in Table 14-1. These control characters are included in the ASCII and EBCDIC code sets. The components of the BISYNC message block are defined as follows:

SYN: The message block begins with the framing control character, SYN. Two SYN characters precede the message. The USART in Chapter 10 can be programmed to enter the SYNC HUNT mode in a search for these characters. Once found, the remaining fields of the block can be interpreted in their respective order.

SOH: The start of header is the control character used to introduce the header field to the receiving device.

HEADER: The header is a variable-length field that is typically used for addressing, that is, selecting a device or polling a device. It is an optional field.

STX: Start of text is a framing control character used to inform the receiving device that text will immediately follow.

TEXT: This is a variable-length field that generally includes ASCII or EBCDIC characters.

FIGURE 14-3
BISYNC message block format.

TABLE 14-1
BISYNC Data Link Control Characters

ACK	Affirmative acknowledgment
DLE	Data link escape
ENQ	Enquiry
EOT	End of transmission
ETB	End of transmission block
ETX	End of text
ITB	End of intermediate transmission block
NAK	Negative acknowledgment
SOH	Start of header
STX	Start of text
SYN	Synchronous idle
WACK	Wait before transmit positive acknowledgment

ETX or ETB: End of text or end of text block is a framing control character that identifies the end of the text field.

BCC: The block check character immediately follows ETX or ETB. It is computed by the transmitting device and inserted at the end of a message block that includes a TEXT field. All characters following STX are computed in the BCC. The length of the BCC is typically 8 to 16 bits. It can be a simple LRC character or a 16-bit CRC character.

14.4.2 Transparent Text Mode

A problem is encountered in BISYNC when the message block contains data that are normally restricted within the TEXT field. These would be data that do not conform to the given standard code set, EBCDIC or ASCII. Take, for example, a block of A/D converter data. Several binary bit patterns within the block's TEXT field are likely to be equivalent to the control characters mentioned earlier. To prevent the receiver from interpreting the raw binary data within the TEXT field as control characters, the transmitting device must somehow inform the receiver that the following data are *transparent*. Any bit patterns that happen to be equivalent to control characters are to be disregarded by the receiver in terms of its normal control procedures. BISYNC uses the data link control character DLE (data link escape) followed by STX (start of text) to enter the *transparent text mode*. To exit the transparent text mode, DLE followed by ETX (end of text) or ETC (end of text block) is used. Figure 14-4 illustrates the format of a BISYNC transparent message block. On receiving DLE followed by STX (start of text), the receiver interprets the following data within the block as *transparent data.*

> **Transparent Text Mode**
> In synchronous serial communications, when any received bit patterns, equivalent to control characters, are disregarded by the normal control procedures.

This raises an obvious question: How does the receiver know when the end of the block occurs? The problem is solved by the transmitter inserting a second DLE whenever an equivalent DLE bit pattern is to be sent within the transmitted TEXT field. The receiving device, in turn, disregards one of the two DLE bit patterns in a detected *pair* of DLEs as shown in Figure 14-4. When it receives only one DLE after the beginning of a defined transparent block (by the first DLE), it returns to the normal mode of operation, and the next character is to be interpreted as a control function, for example, ETX. Any data within the TEXT field can now be issued by the transmitting device once the transparent text mode has been started. Table 14-2 lists BISYNC DLE control sequences used in the transparent text mode.

> **Transparent Data**
> Data, sent by transparent text mode, that are disregarded by the normal control procedures of the receiving device.

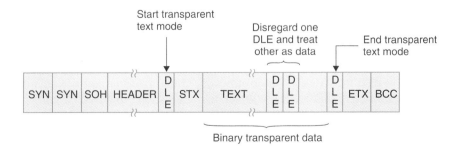

FIGURE 14-4
BISYNC transparent text mode format.

TABLE 14-2
BISYNC DLE Control Sequences Used in the Transparent Text Mode

DLE STX	Data link control characters for beginning the transparent text mode.
DLE DLE	When a bit pattern equivalent to DLE occurs within the transparent data, a second DLE is sent in succession. The receiver disregards one DLE, and the other is treated as data.
DLE ETX	Terminates the transparent text mode, returns the data link to normal mode, and calls for a reply.
DLE ETB	Terminates a block of transparent text, returns the data link to normal mode, and calls for a reply.
DLE SYN	Used to maintain SYNC or as time-fill sequence for transparent mode.
DLE ENQ	Indicates "disregard this block of transparent data" and returns the data link to the normal mode.
DLE ITB	Terminates an intermediate block of transparent data, returns the data link to normal mode, and does not call for a reply. BCC follows DLE ITB. Transparent intermediate blocks may have a particular fixed length for a given system. If the next intermediate block is transparent, it must start with DLE STX.

14.4.3 BISYNC Point-to-Point Line Control

Computers often need to transfer large files of data between each other. These files are broken into blocks of data using the format we have just discussed. Take, for example, two computers that are configured point-to-point as illustrated in Figure 14-2(a). To ensure the integrity of the data transferred between computers, they are broken into blocks, framed, and sent with a block check character. The size of the block can vary depending on several factors:

- Transmission media
- Message content
- System noise
- Transmission distance
- Overhead
- Baud rate
- Probability of error
- Retransmission time

If the block size is large, the probability of an error increases and retransmission time must be considered. However, the data are transferred in the most expedient manner if no errors occur. If the block size is small, the overhead increases and the relative time to transmit data increases. If an error occurs in the transmission of a small block, retransmission time is shorter. There are certainly trade-offs involved. A nominal block size of 256 bytes is commonly used in BISYNC and other protocols.

14.4.3.1 Handshaking Blocks of Data   BISYNC uses a system of *handshaking* blocks of data from one computer to another. The following BISYNC data link control characters are used for this purpose:

ACK 0 and *ACK 1* (acknowledgment):   ACK is an acknowledgment that a block has been received successfully. ACK 1 always acknowledges the reception of the first message block of data that was received and all odd-numbered blocks thereafter. ACK 0 is used to acknowledge all even-numbered blocks received.

ENQ (enquiry):   ENQ is used by a device to gain control of the line for transmitting data. It is also used to enquire with the receiving device why there was no acknowledgment of the previously transmitted block.

NAK (negative acknowledgment):   NAK indicates to the transmitting device that the previous block was received in error (checksum error). A retransmission is typically performed. NAK is also used as a "not ready" indicator.

WACK (wait before transmit positive acknowledgment):   WACK is used as a temporary "not ready" indicator to the transmitting device. It can be sent as a response to a test or heading block, line bid, or an identification (ID) line bid sequence.

The method of handshaking blocks of data is called ACK ALTERNATING, whereby the data link control characters ACK 0 and ACK 1 are sequentially used to acknowledge even- and odd-numbered blocks that are received successfully. Figure 14-5 depicts a typical BISYNC, point-to-point, half-duplex line control sequence using ACK ALTERNATING. Assuming that both stations shown here are equal contenders for use of the line, the transmitting station is the station that *bids* for the line first. This is achieved by asserting ENQ. If both stations assert ENQ at the same time, a *collision* occurs: two transmitters are transmitting at the same time on the half-duplex link. An agreement is made beforehand as to which system has priority, in which case the other system backs down and acts as the receiving station. This process is referred to as *line contention*. (A closer look at line contention is presented in Chapter 15).

Framing control characters have been left off for purposes of clarification. Note the receiving station's acknowledgment, ACK 0, of the transmitting station's bid for the line first. ACK 1 is an acknowledgment to the first message block and all odd-numbered blocks thereafter. ACK 0 is an acknowledgment to all even-numbered blocks received without any errors. The block check character BCC is not used unless a text field is included in the message block.

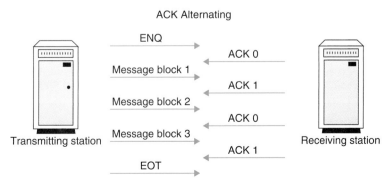

FIGURE 14-5
BISYNC point-to-point line control sequence.

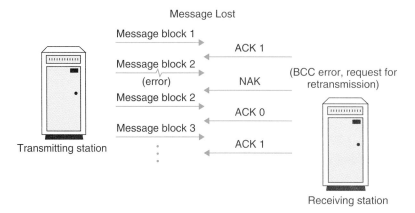

FIGURE 14-6
An error condition encountered causes the receiving station to request a retransmission.

14.4.3.2   Encountering a BCC Error   Figure 14-6 illustrates an example of a block that gets garbled en route as a result of impulse noise. The receiving station receives the block; however, the computed BCC does not agree with the BCC that was sent. The receiving station issues a NAK to the transmitting station. NAK is a request for retransmission of the second block. The transmitting station, on receiving NAK (instead of ACK 0), retransmits the previous even-numbered message block, and the handshaking process continues.

14.4.3.3   A Time-Out Error   When two devices are handshaking data between one another, a limited amount of time must be imposed on the receiving device to acknowledge the reception of the transmitted data. If this were not the case and the receiving device failed to acknowledge the received data, all further transmissions would cease pending the acknowledgment. Both systems would "hang" until an operator attends to the problem. Computers incorporate, in either hardware or software, what is referred to as a *time-out error*. A time-out error occurs when a device fails to respond to a message within a given period of time. It may be a few microseconds to several seconds.

> **Time-Out Error**
> When a device fails to respond to a message within a given period of time.

In BISYNC, if the transmitting station does not receive ACK within an agreed period of time, a time-out error will occur (Figure 14-7). Presumably, the last message block was received but the receiving station's ACK was lost. The transmitting station then issues an ENQ. ENQ, in this case (when not bidding for the line), is an enquiry to the receiving station to see if it received the last message block. An ACK 0 or NAK in return will allow the transmitting station to determine whether the last message was received. In Figure 14-7, ACK 0 is the response to ENQ. It is, therefore, presumed that Message block 2 was received and the previous ACK 0 was lost.

14.4.4   BISYNC Multipoint Line Control

Thus far, we have discussed the format of a BISYNC message block and the method of handshaking data blocks in a point-to-point configuration. In a point-to-point configuration, it is certain where the data are going to and coming from, because there are only two devices in question. In multipoint operation, the process is similar in terms of transmitting messages between individual stations. The difference is that a

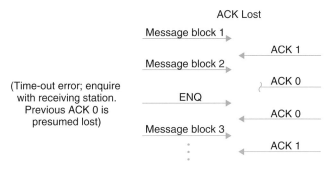

FIGURE 14-7
Acknowledgment, ACK, lost en route to the transmitting station.

method of addressing is needed in multipoint operation to determine which station is transmitting and receiving the data blocks. We now discuss this addressing method.

14.4.4.1 Device Polling and Selecting

There is no bidding for the use of the line in multipoint operation. One station is designated as the *host computer,* and the remaining stations on the line are designated as *tributaries* (Figure 14-8.) The host computer supervises all activity on the line by a method called *device polling* and *device selecting.*

Device Polling Each tributary on the line has a unique *polling address.* The host computer sequentially *polls* (addresses) each tributary with its address followed by ENQ to enquire if it has any data to be sent. If the tributary has data for the host computer, it is handshaked in the same manner as discussed under point-to-point operation. If no data are available, a corresponding EOT message is sent to the host and the next device in sequence is polled. Device polling is used when data are sent from the tributary to the host computer.

Device Selecting *Device selection* is used when data are to flow from host computer to tributary. Each tributary on the line has a unique *select address.* A tributary's select address is different from its polling address. This allows the device to send or receive data from the host on receiving one of its two addresses. A tributary is selected by the host computer by asserting its *select address* followed by ENQ. If the device is ready to receive data that the computer has for it, it responds with ACK 0. Data are then handshaked between the host and tributary in the same manner as point-to-point operation. If a tributary is not ready for data from the host, it asserts WACK in response to being *selected.* The host responds to WACK with EOT and checks for readiness at a later time.

14.4.4.2 BISYNC Multipoint Communications Between Host Computer and Several Terminals

Figure 14-9 depicts several terminals that have been configured for multipoint operation. In this mode, internal and external switch settings or the terminal's software are configured for block mode operation. When an operator is ready to transmit his or her buffer of data, the ENTER key is depressed. Data are not sent immediately to the host computer. The operator's terminal must wait for its turn to be polled before it can begin to transfer its blocks of data.

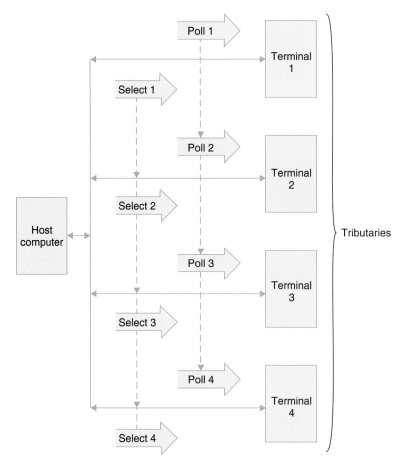

FIGURE 14-8
Host computer poll and selecting a device for transmitting data in a multipoint setup.

Each terminal in this example has been assigned a unique polling address and select address. The host computer begins by polling terminal 1, address P1, for possible message blocks. Terminal 1 responds with three message blocks that are acknowledged by the host. After the data are interpreted, the host sends a one-block message to the terminal as a response. The terminal is first selected with its select address, S1. The select enquiry is acknowledged by ACK 0, indicating its readiness for the message block. The block is then transferred to terminal 1 and acknowledged. EOT is sent to terminal 1, thus terminating the exchange.

Terminal 2 is then polled for any possible messages. An EOT is sent to the host, indicating that there are no pending data at this time. The host computer, however, has a message block to send to terminal 2. Its select address, S2, along with ENQ, is asserted by the host. Terminal 2, however, is not ready to receive the message block, so it responds to the selection with WACK. The host computer terminates the handshaking process with terminal 2 by sending EOT, and its readiness to receive a message will be checked at a later time.

When terminal 3 is polled at its polling address, P3, its returned messaged block is garbled en route to the host computer. The computed BCC is in conflict with the BCC sent with the data. As a result, the host computer sends NAK to terminal 3; a

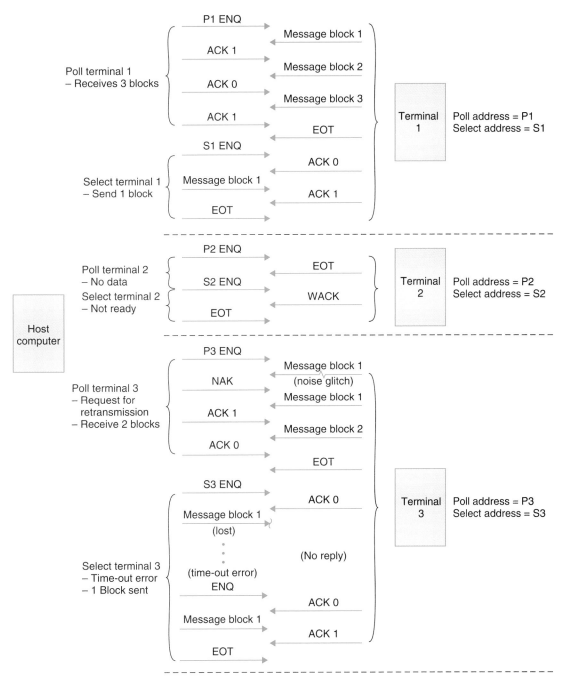

FIGURE 14-9
BISYNC multipoint operation between a host computer and several terminals.

request for retransmission. The message block, as shown in Figure 14-9, is transmitted again by terminal 3. The host computer this time successfully receives the message and, consequently, responds with ACK 1, acknowledging the first message block. The second block is then transferred to the host, and the transaction is terminated with EOT. The computer at this time has a message for terminal 3. S3 ENQ is asserted to test for terminal 3's readiness. On receiving ACK 0 (ready for data), message block 1 is transmitted. During the transmission, the message block is lost due to an intermittent connector contact. After a 3-second time-out, there is still no responding acknowledgment to the message block sent to terminal 3. The host computer enquires at this time by asserting ENQ. ACK 0 from terminal 3 is an indicator to the computer that message block 1 was lost rather than the acknowledgment, ACK 1, from the receiving device. Message block 1 is, therefore, retransmitted by the host computer. The message is received this time and acknowledged. The host computer has no further messages for terminal 3. The transaction is terminated with EOT.

14.5 TELECOMMUNICATION SWITCHING FACILITIES

Point-to-Point
A communications link connecting two stations.

Section 14.4 discussed the BISYNC protocol and its *point-to-point* and *multipoint* or *multidrop* interface connection. Many of the first connections between computers and terminals were interfaces of this type. As computer systems and telecommunication switching facilities grew, the need for new and more sophisticated methods of ensuring data integrity and end-to-end connectivity grew. Traditionally, there have been three switching technologies utilized by the PSTN for data transmission:

Multipoint
A communications link between a host computer and several terminals configured for block mode operation.

1. Circuit switching
2. Message switching
3. Packet switching

14.5.1 Circuit Switching

Circuit Switching
A switching technology that permits DTE to establish temporarily an immediate, full-duplex connection to another station.

Circuit switching is a method of allowing data terminal equipment (DTE) to establish an immediate full-duplex connection to another data station on a temporary basis. Once the connection is established, exclusive use of the channel and its available bandwidth is provided by the switching network until the channel is relinquished by one of the stations (e.g., the standard PSTN voice-grade switched line service). Figure 14-10 illustrates an example of a circuit-switched network. Circuit switching has its advantages over message and packet switching services. The switched connection is dedicated for the entire communication session, and no time buffering is necessary. Thus, it is highly efficient in cases when relatively high data transfer rates occur throughout the session. Addressing information occurs only once during the call setup procedure by the network. A circuit switched channel can also be full-duplex and provide interactive communication between stations.

A subcategory of circuit switching is called *channel switching*.* Channel switching provides the ability to modify multiplexers and network configurations remotely in response to outages or time-of-day traffic variations or to accommodate growth and organizational changes.

---

*Joseph Pecar, Roger O'Conner, and David Garbin, *Telecommunications Factbook* (New York: McGraw-Hill, 1993), p. 225.

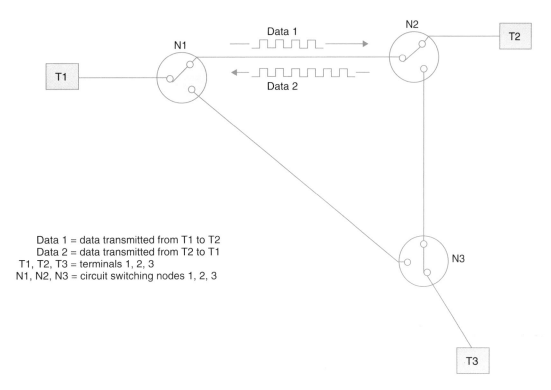

Data 1 = data transmitted from T1 to T2
Data 2 = data transmitted from T2 to T1
T1, T2, T3 = terminals 1, 2, 3
N1, N2, N3 = circuit switching nodes 1, 2, 3

FIGURE 14-10
Circuit switching network.

The problem arises with the circuit-switched network when multiple stations require use of the switching facilities. The switch must support a wide range of transmission rates from all users simultaneously. Typically, these user rates are "bursty"; that is, peak periods of transmission are followed by periods in which no data at all are transmitted. This tends to be very inefficient in cases when the switch is overloaded. Other users could be transmitting at maximum rates during these idle periods. *Message switching* and *packet switching* systems have been devised to overcome this problem.

14.5.2   Message Switching

Many telephone companies offer automatic *message switching* services to their customers. Message switching (Figure 14-11) is a method of transferring messages between DTE by temporarily buffering or "storing" the message at the switching exchange and "forwarding" it to the next switching exchange acting as a successor. This occurs when traffic on the communications channel is favorable for transmission. The next successor, if necessary, repeats the process until the message is routed to its final destination. This message switching technique is known as *store and forward*. Because immediate connection between DTEs is not necessary, the telecommunications facilities can be shared among several users on a per-message basis. Efficiency of the switching network is increased as a result of this technique. An example of message switching that has been around for many years is the international *Telex* network: a *Western Union* worldwide Teletype exchange service that uses the PSTN.

> **Message Switching**
> A switching technology that permits message transfer between DTE by temporarily "storing" the message at one exchange and then "forwarding" it to the next.

> **Store and Forward**
> The principle of message switching on which e-mail transmission over the Internet is based.

> **Western Union**
> A worldwide Teletype exchange service using the PSTN.

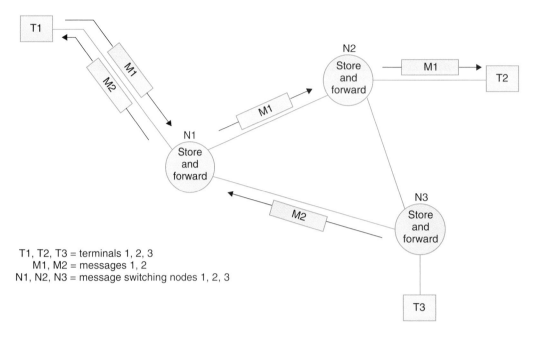

T1, T2, T3 = terminals 1, 2, 3
M1, M2 = messages 1, 2
N1, N2, N3 = message switching nodes 1, 2, 3

FIGURE 14-11
Message switching network.

A message switching system operation at 100% of design capacity will have substantial delays regardless of message length.* However, a message switching system operating at 80% capacity or less will have short delays provided no long messages are in the system that might block certain routing paths and delay other messages. Long messages should be broken up into "packets" and appended with address and control information; hence, *packet switching* should be considered.

14.5.3 Packet Switching

> **Packet Switching**
> A communications protocol in which messages are divided into discrete units and routed independently to their final destination.

> **Packet Assembler–Disassembler (PAD)**
> A device that assembles and disassembles discrete communications data packets.

Until recently, *packet switching* technology has been the most advanced and established data communications switching technology used for *wide area networks (WANs)*. Packet switching is a method of segmenting a user's message into discrete, variable-length units called *packets* (Figure 14-12). By limiting the length of the packets, other users can effectively share the use of the channel. Packets are assembled and disassembled by a *packet assembler–disassembler (PAD)*. Individual packets are appended with control information for routing, sequencing, and error detection. Packets are then routed to various switching nodes throughout the network depending on availability of the channel. Individual packets may not necessarily take the same switching route as other packets derived from the same message. In addition, they may not arrive at the terminating switching node in the same order in which they were transmitted. Eventually, all packets arrive at their destination node, where they

---

*John E. McNamara, *Technical Aspects of Data Communications,* 2nd ed. (Bedford, Mass.: Digital Press, 1982), p. 196.

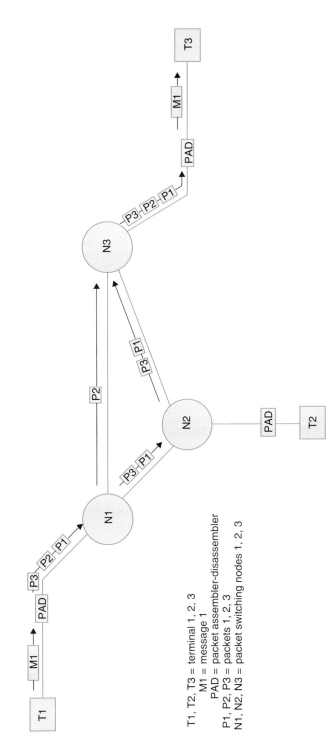

FIGURE 14-12
Packet switching network.

T1, T2, T3 = terminal 1, 2, 3
M1 = message 1
PAD = packet assembler-disassembler
P1, P2, P3 = packets 1, 2, 3
N1, N2, N3 = packet switching nodes 1, 2, 3

are disassembled by a PAD. Data are placed into their original message form and transported to their final destination.

Packet switching networks can be enormously large and complex, spanning the world and permitting many users to share the use of the communications facilities. For these reasons, the user's data in a packet-switched network are not highly time critical. Typical applications involve low-to-moderate data transfer rates of files containing banking information, electronic mail, airline reservation, ticket information, and so on. The packet-switched network can deliver this type of information in fractions of a second or a few seconds in cases when system loading, reliability, and propagation delays due to distance spans become a factor. *Telenet,* now called *Sprint Net,* and the *ARPANET* (Advanced Research Projects Agency Network) are examples of packet-switched networks.

The establishment of packet-switched networks throughout the world has created a need to produce a standard protocol that facilitates international internetworking. The ITU-TS recommended protocol for packet switching over public data networks is the *X.25 Protocol,* which was written in Geneva in 1976 and amended in 1980. It addresses the interface between data terminal equipment (DTE) and data circuit terminating equipment (DCE) operating in the packet mode on public data networks. With respect to the ISO-OSI seven-layer model discussed in Section 14.2, the X.25 protocol is a three-layer process: layers 1, 2, and 3, with most of its protocol complexity being defined in layer 2. The next section concentrates on the X.25 *Link Access Procedures (LAP)* for data exchange between DTE and DCE as recommended by ITU-TS and specified by the ISO.

14.6 HIGH-LEVEL DATA LINK CONTROL

> **High-Level Data Link Control (HDLC)**
> A bit-oriented protocol used to implement the X.25 packet switching network.

> **Synchronous Data Link Control (SDLC)**
> A bit-oriented protocol used in IBM's Systems Network Architecture (SNA).

High-level data link control (HDLC) is the standard communications link protocol proposed by the ISO. The HDLC protocol has been accepted internationally and used to implement the X.25 packet switching network. *Synchronous data link control (SDLC)* is a variation and predecessor to HDLC. SDLC was developed in 1974 by IBM. Unlike BISYNC, these two bit-oriented protocols are ideally suited for full-duplex communications. The two protocols are functionally identical. Because HDLC encompasses SDLC and HDLC has been internationally recognized as the proclaimed standard, our discussion focuses on HDLC. Any differences between the two protocols will be pointed out as needed.

14.6.1 HDLC Frame Format

The frame format for HDLC is shown in Figure 14-13. In HDLC, the term *frame* is synonymous with the term *block* used in BISYNC. For bit-oriented protocols, including HDLC, the framing structure is the same for all messages. There are no framing characters within the block, such as SYN, STX, and EOT, as there are in BISYNC, a character-oriented protocol. Framing is achieved by placing the unique bit pattern **7EH** (01111110) at the beginning and end of the HDLC frame. All fields within the frame consist of *bytes* (8 bits) or multiples thereof, with the exception of the information transfer field. In HDLC, a byte is also referred to as an *octet.*

14.6.1.1 Flag Byte and Bit Order of Transmission
The beginning and end of all frames are enclosed with the unique flag byte 7EH, or 01111110 in binary. The

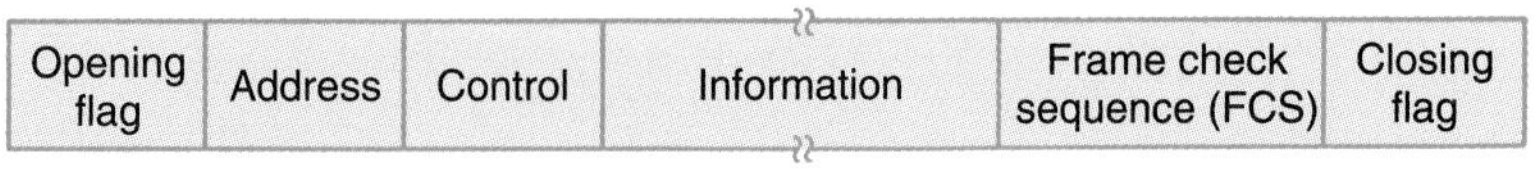

Opening flag	Address	Control	Information	Frame check sequence (FCS)	Closing flag

FIGURE 14-13
HDLC frame format.

flag byte is the only framing character used in HDLC. Figure 14-14 depicts the bit structure of the flag as well as the remaining HDLC fields.

The order of bit transmission is such that the low-order (LSB) bit, bit 1 (as defined in the X.25 protocol), is transmitted first for address, commands, responses, and sequence numbers. The order of bit transmission is not specified for the information field. The *frame check sequence (FCS)* field is transmitted to the line, commencing with the coefficient of the highest term of the 16-bit CRC character. Figure 14-14 depicts this order.

14.6.1.2 Address Byte   The address byte* indicates the address of the secondary station that the frame corresponds to. In multipoint operation, the address byte within the frame represents which secondary station the frame is either going to or coming from. No address represents the primary station, because it is controlling the communications.

In HDLC, the address byte can be extended to include multiple address bytes. The receiving device must, therefore, be able to discern between a single-address byte field and a multiple-address byte field. In HDLC, the LSB of the address byte is set to a logic 0 if the following byte is to be interpreted as an extension of the address field. The following byte conforms to the same rule. If the LSB of the address byte is a logic 1, that byte is the last byte of the address field (Figure 14-15).

14.6.1.3 Control Byte   The control byte[†] serves many of the same functions as data link control characters do in character-oriented protocols, for example, ACK, NAK, and EOT. It also serves to identify the *type* of HDLC frame that is being sent. There are three types, as defined by the low-order bits, D1 and D2, of the control byte. For each type, the control byte has a different format. The three types of HDLC frames are *information transfer, supervisory,* and *unnumbered.* Figure 14-16 illustrates the structure of the CONTROL BYTE for each type of HDLC frame. Control byte terms are defined as follows:

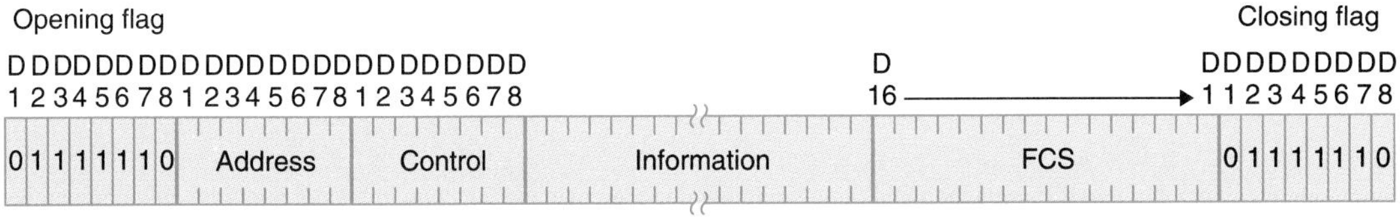

FIGURE 14-14
HDLC framing pattern and bit order of transmission.

---

*The address byte for SDLC does not offer extended addressing capability.

[†]The control byte for HDLC can be extended in the same manner as the address byte. It is limited to one extension byte only. SDLC does not offer extension of the control byte.

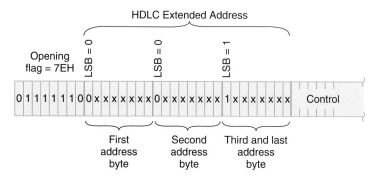

FIGURE 14-15
Extending the HDLC ADDRESS BYTE field.

NR (Receive Sequence Number)   NR acknowledges the number of frames that have been received successfully. It is included in information transfer and supervisory types of frames. NR is incremented by 1 with each frame received having no errors detected. The maximum number of frames that can be received without an acknowledgment is seven. The value of NR is an indicator of what the *next* received frame's NS value should equal. The value of NR can also be thought of as an indicator that

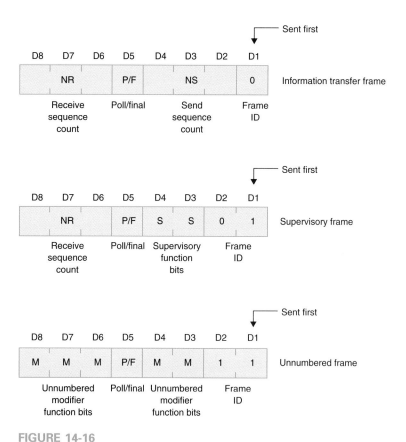

FIGURE 14-16
Format of CONTROL BYTE for information transfer, supervisory, and unnumbered HDLC frames.

the DTE or DCE sending the NR has correctly received all information frames numbered up to and including NR1.

P/F (Poll/Final Bit)   The P/F bit serves a dual control function. When set by the primary station, P (poll) is used to poll a secondary station for a response. The secondary station, designated by the address field of the given frame, is required to respond to the poll. When set by a secondary station, F (Final) is used to indicate the final frame that the secondary has for the primary. The primary is required to acknowledge the reception of the secondary's frames on receiving a frame with the F (Final) bit set. When the P/F bit is 0, P = 0 in a frame sent by the primary station. Thus, a secondary station shall not respond, because it is not a poll. When the P/F bit is 0, F = 0 and is sent in a frame from a secondary station to the primary station, and the frame sent from the secondary station is not the last frame. The primary station in this case shall not acknowledge the receptor of the secondary's frames.

NS (Send Sequence Number)   The NS field is unique to information transfer frames. NS is initialized to 0 for the *first* information transfer frame sent by a station and incremented by 1 with each information transfer frame sent thereafter. NS and NR work in conjunction with each other in terms of control and acknowledgment of the number of information transfer frames sent and received. The maximum number of frames that can be sent without an acknowledgment is seven.

Frame ID (Frame Identifier)   The least significant bits of the control byte identify the HDLC frame type as follows:

D2	D1	
(NS)	0	Information transfer frame
0	1	Supervisory frame
1	1	Unnumbered frame

S (Supervisory Function Bits)   The supervisory function bits (S) are used to further classify the supervisory frame into one of three different types: receiver ready (RR), receiver not ready (RNR), and reject (REJ). Bits D4 and D3 determine the supervisory frame type as follows:

D4	D3	
0	0	Receiver ready (RR): Used to indicate a primary or secondary station's readiness to receive an information frame. Used as an acknowledgment to receiving a frame.
0	1	Receiver not ready (RNR): Used for acknowledgments and to indicate that a station is busy.
1	0	Reject (REJ): Used for error control and requesting retransmission of a frame starting with the frame numbered NR.

M (Unnumbered Modifier Function Bits)   There are 5 bits within the control field of the unnumbered frame that serve as the unnumbered modifier (M) function bits: D8, D7, D6, D4, and D3. The state of these 5 bits determines the function of the unnumbered frame (Table 14-3).

TABLE 14-3
HDLC Unnumbered Frame Definition

Name	Binary Format $D_8 \cdots D_1$	Description
DISC	010 P 0011	Disconnect
DM	000 F 1111	Disconnect Mode
FRMR	100 F 0111	Frame Reject
RD	010 F 0011	Request Disconnect
RIM	000 F 0111	Request Initialization Mode
SIM	000 P 0111	Set Initialization Mode
SNRM	100 P 0011	Set Normal Response Mode
UA	011 P/F 0011	Unnumbered Acknowledgment
UI	000 P/F 0011	Unnumbered Information

HDLC Frame Types are defined as follows:

Information Transfer Frame   The information transfer frame carries data in the information field between the primary and secondary stations. It includes control for polling and data acknowledgment through the use of the P/F bit. This type of frame is identified by a logic 0 for the LSB, D1, of the control byte (Figure 14-17). Stations transmitting information transfer frames use the NS count to indicate the number of information transfer frames sent. The NR count is used to acknowledge the number of information transfer frames received.

Supervisory Frame   The supervisory frame is used for polling, data acknowledgment, and control. The control byte of this type of frame has a unique 2-bit supervi-

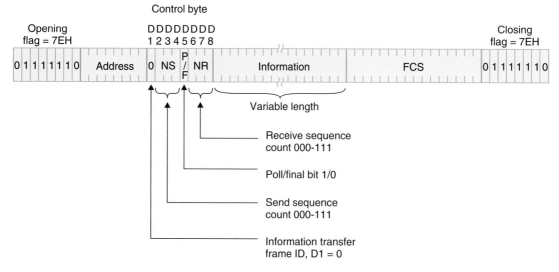

FIGURE 14-17
HDLC information transfer frame structure.

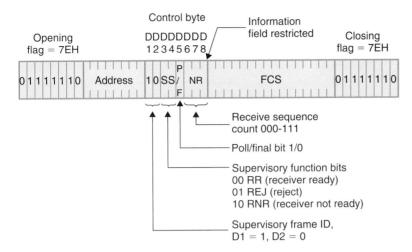

FIGURE 14-18
HDLC supervisory frame structure.

sory function (S) field that is used to indicate a station's readiness: RR (receiver ready), and RNR (receiver not ready). The 2-bit field is also used for requesting the retransmission of an information frame with REJ (reject). Figure 14-18 illustrates the format of the supervisory frame. Note that a supervisory frame cannot have an information field. The least significant two bits of the control byte identify the supervisory frame. D1 and D2 are a logic 1 and a logic 0, respectively.

Unnumbered Frame   This type of frame is identified by the lower two bits of the control byte. D1 and D2 both equal a logic 1 (Figure 14-19). The unnumbered frame is used for polling, testing between stations, initialization, and control of stations. The information field may or may not be present in this type of frame. Table 14-3 lists the various types of unnumbered frames with a description of each.

14.6.1.4 Information Field   The HDLC information field is a variable-length field that contains any number of bits. The vast number of applications, however, tend to use multiples of 8 bits. This field is always present in information transfer-type frames

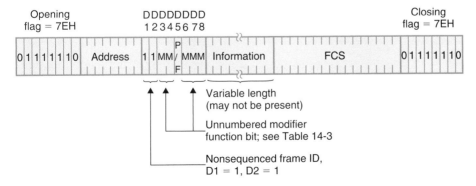

FIGURE 14-19
HDLC unnumbered frame structure.

and may be present in unnumbered-type frames. In supervisory-type frames, the information field does not exist. The code within this field is transparent to the receiver station. The size of the field is entirely left to the system designer. Here, again, the protocol overhead, system noise, distance between stations, and various other factors must be considered. Typically, 256 bytes are used.

14.6.1.5 Frame Check Sequence The FCS is a 16-bit CRC character computed by the transmitting device and checked by the receiving device. All bits within the frame, excluding the flag pattern, are used to compute the FCS character. Inserted, *zero bits* (discussed later) used to attain transparency are not included in the calculation. The mathematical polynomial used to compute the FCS has been documented by ITU-TS' V.41 specification.

14.6.2 Zero-Bit Insertion and Deletion

The information field in HDLC is said to be *transparent* to the receiver section. As with character-oriented protocols, a method of distinguishing between data and control within the frame is needed. HDLC is a bit-oriented protocol. Bit-oriented protocols do not identify groups as *characters.* In BISYNC, a character-oriented protocol, dedicated characters are used for framing and control as well as resolving the transparency problem. Transparency for bit-oriented protocols must be achieved in a different manner due to the absence of these dedicated characters.

Because 7EH is the *only* framing character used in HDLC, the transmitting device must ensure that this delimiting pattern does not exist *within* the boundaries of the frame itself. The receiving device would otherwise misinterpret the end of the frame. For purposes of discussion, we refer to this portion of the frame as the *data field* (Figure 14-20). This includes all HDLC fields, with the exception of the flags. The technique used to achieve transparency within the data field in HDLC (and other bit-oriented protocols) is referred to as *zero-bit insertion* or *bit stuffing.* Zero-bit insertion occurs within the range of the data field as depicted in Figure 14-20.

Note that the 8-bit FLAG pattern, 01111110 (7EH), marking the beginning and end of the frame, includes a series of *six* consecutive 1-bits between 0-bits. In zero-bit stuffing, the transmitting device, *after* sending the opening flag, automatically inserts, or "stuffs," a binary 0-bit after any succession of *five* consecutive 1-bits. This will ensure that no pattern of the flag, 01111110, is ever transmitted within the data field. It is important to recognize that bit stuffing occurs *only* in the data field.

Figure 14-21 shows how the bit-stuffing technique works. Once the receiver detects the opening flag, it monitors for five consecutive 1-bits. If five consecutive 1-bits are received after the opening flag, the sixth bit is automatically deleted *if* it is a binary 0, thus resulting in the original bit pattern. If the six consecutive 1-bits are detected after the opening flag, then it is assumed to be the closing flag or an *abort character.* The 16 bits preceding it are taken to be the frame check sequence (FCS) character. Inserted zeros are not included in the calculation of FCS character.

14.6.3 HDLC Abort and Idle Condition

Another requirement for the receiving device is the detection of two other bit patterns: the *abort pattern,* and the *idle pattern.* The HDLC abort pattern* is *7 to 14* con-

---

Bit Stuffing
A technique used in bit-oriented protocols to achieve transparency of data. A 1-bit is "stuffed" by the transmitter after any five consecutive 1-bits that are sent. Also referred to as *zero-bit insertion.*

Abort Pattern
A pattern of 7 to 14 consecutive 1-bits without zero-bit insertion.

Idle Pattern
A pattern of 15 or more consecutive 1-bits without zero-bit insertion.

---

*IBM's SDLC Abort Pattern is eight consecutive 1-bits without zero-bit insertion. Seven contiguous 1-bits in SDLC are used for polling purposes.

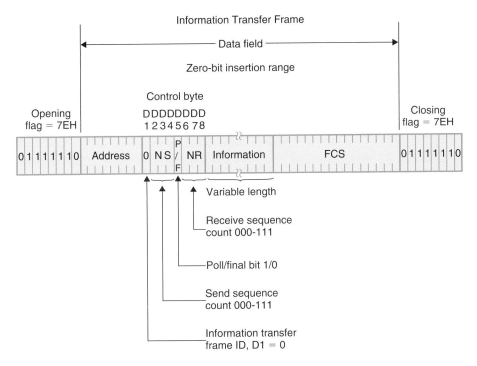

FIGURE 14-20
Zero-bit insertion range.

secutive 1-bits without zero-bit insertion (one bit more than the closing flag). The idle pattern is 15 or more consecutive 1-bits without zero-bit insertion.

When the abort pattern has been detected by the receiver, the current frame is prematurely terminated. That portion of the frame already received is disregarded. An example of an abort condition may be a computer's loss of its modem carrier frequency or of one of its control signals, such as CTS. The computer in this case may be in the process of transferring data to other computers or terminals. If the loss of its modem's carrier frequency or modem control lines occurs during a frame transfer, the transmitting device sends seven consecutive 1-bits without zero-bit insertion to the station that the frame is being transmitted to. The receiving station detects the abort pattern and invalidates the current frame.

A channel is defined in HDLC as being in an idle condition when the receiver detects 15 or more contiguous 1-bits on the line. The specific action to take on detecting the idle condition is up to the system designer.

14.6.4 Control and Information Exchange

In Figure 14-22, examples of HDLC frame sequences are shown between a host computer and three terminals; the same multipoint setup used earlier for BISYNC line control is used here. Although HDLC has virtually twice the informational transfer rate of BISYNC (because it is suited for full-duplex operation), a half-duplex control sequence is illustrated here for simplicity. The formats of the frames are depicted from left to right with their respective types, information, supervisory, or unnumbered, identified within each frame's control field.

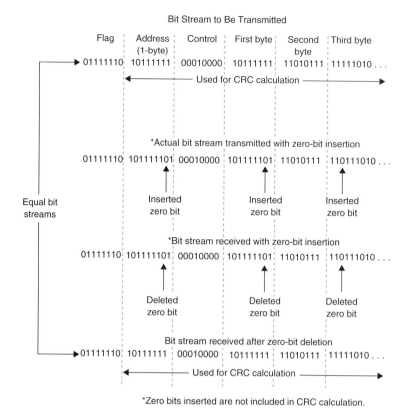

FIGURE 14-21
HDLC zero-bit insertion, bit-stuffing technique.

Step 1 Initially terminal A1 is polled by the host computer for possible information. See step 1 of Figure 14-22. NR, the number of frames received by the host, has been initialized to 0. P/F has been set to 1 to indicate that terminal A1 is being polled (P). The host computer is ready to receive data, RR.

Step 2 Terminal A1 responds to the poll by transmitting three information frames (NS = 0, 1, 2). NS, the number of frames sent, is incremented by 1 with each frame sent to the host starting with frame 0, NS = 0. Note the third and final (F) frame, P/F, is set to 1, indicating the last frame has been sent. The FCS character is sent with each of the three information frames, thus allowing the host to perform error checking on each individual frame.

Step 3 The host computer acknowledges the reception of terminal A1's three frames. The acknowledgment is a supervisory frame. NR in this frame is set to a value of 3 as an indicator to terminal A1 that no errors were detected in the three frames received. If an error were detected in one of the received frames, frame number 2 for example, then the value of NR would be set to 1, notifying terminal A1 that only one frame was *successfully* received. Terminal A1 in turn would retransmit the last two frames with NS = 1 and NS = 2, respectively.

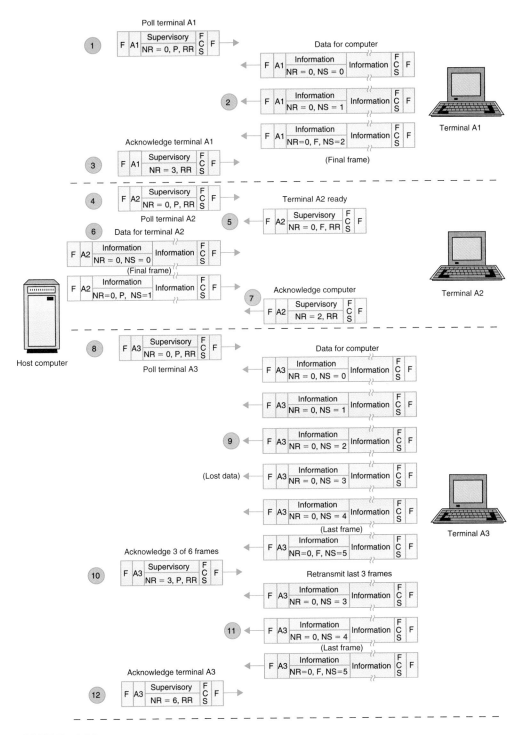

FIGURE 14-22
HDLC frame sequencing.

Step 4   A new sequence is initiated in step 4. Terminal A2 is polled (P), P/F = 1, for information and readiness to receive two frames that the host computer has for it.

Step 5   Terminal A2 has no information frames at this time for the host as indicated by the final (F) bit in this supervisory frame. P/F is set to 1. Terminal A2, however, is ready to receive data, RR.

Step 6   Two information frames are sent to terminal A2. In the first frame sent, NS = 0. In the second and final (P) frame sent, NS is incremented by 1 and P/F is set to 1 to poll terminal A2 for acknowledgment of the transmitted data.

Step 7   The two information frames sent by the host computer are successfully received, NR = 2, and acknowledged by terminal A2.

Step 8   The host computer polls terminal A3 (P), P/F = 1, for information.

Step 9   Terminal A3 responds to being polled by transmitting six consecutive frames (NS = 0 through NS = 5) to the host computer. The value of NS is incremented by 1 with each frame sent. A portion of the data within the fourth frame, however, is lost en route to the host due to an intermittence in the transmission line. The host computer will have to catch this error through the CRC check and request a retransmission of the fourth frame and all subsequent frames. The sixth and final (F) frame is identified by P/F = 1.

Step 10   As a result of an error detected in the fourth frame received from terminal A3, the host computer sets NR to a value of 3, because it successfully received three frames. It polls (P) terminal A3 with a supervisory frame, NR = 3 and P/F = 1 act as a request for retransmission of the last three information frames: NS = 3, NS = 4, and NS = 5. Note that the supervisory frame's NR value in this case serves the dual purpose of acknowledging the reception of three frames and, at the same time, requesting the retransmission of frames starting with NS = 3. The NR value sent by the host is also the value that it is anticipating in the NS field of the next frame sent from terminal A3. Because the host computer knows the total number of frames sent based on the NS value received, it can further anticipate the number of frames that must be retransmitted.

Step 11   Terminal A3 retransmits its last three frames: NS = 3, NS = 4, and NS = 5. The final (F) frame again is identified by P/F = 1.

Step 12   The host computer receives the three retransmitted frames from terminal A3. NR is incremented from 3 to 6 with the reception of each frame. A supervisory frame is sent to terminal A3 to acknowledge with NR = 6 that all six frames have been received without errors.

PROBLEMS

1. Define *protocol*.
2. Which standards organization is a member of the United Nations?
3. What are the seven layers of the ISO/OSI model? Briefly describe each layer's function.

4. Which of the seven ISO/OSI layers defines the type of error control method that is used for a given protocol?

5. Which of the seven ISO/OSI layers defines the maximum voltage level that can be used on a conductor?

6. Explain the difference between a byte-oriented protocol and a bit-oriented protocol.

7. What data link control character(s) is (are) used in BISYNC to:
   a. Enter the transparent text mode?
   b. Exit the transparent text mode?
   c. Tell the receiver to disregard the bit pattern of data in the text field that is equivalent to DLE?

8. Define *ACK alternating*.

9. When a time-out error occurs in BISYNC, what procedures do the transmitter and receiver go through?

10. What data link control character(s) is (are) used in BISYNC to enter the *transparent text mode*?

11. What data link control character(s) is (are) used in BISYNC to:
    a. Contend for the use of the line?
    b. Handshake blocks of data between a host and tributary?
    c. Indicate that a block has been received in error?

12. Define *time-out error.*

13. Define *tributary.*

14. Explain the difference between device polling and device selecting.

15. What are the names of the three switching technologies traditionally used with the PSTN?

16. What advantages does circuit switching have over other switching methods?

17. To what length is a circuit-switched connection limited?

18. Define *store and forward.*

19. The *Telex* network is an example of what type of switching technology?

20. What does *PAD* stand for.

21. What is the function of a *PAD*?

22. What international protocol is used for packet switching?

23. Is HDLC a byte- or a bit-oriented protocol?

24. What unique framing pattern is used in HDLC, and what is its name?

25. Refer to Figure 14-15. If an HDLC frame has a 2-byte address field, how is the receiver informed that the address is a multiple-byte field?

26. What are the names of the three HDLC frame types?

27. What is the name of the HDLC process used to achieve data transparency?

28. Explain what an HDLC transmitter does when it must transmit more than five consecutive 1-bits after sending the opening flag.

29. Explain what an HDLC receiver does when it encounters five consecutive 1-bits.

30. What is the difference between an HDLC abort pattern and an idle pattern?

31. Which HDLC frame types allow use of the information field?

32. Refer to Figure 14-22. Continuing from step 12, show how a fourth terminal, A4, would be polled and sent four information transfer frames from the host computer. Use the same frame format shown. Be sure to show the acknowledgment from terminal A4 to the host computer on receiving all four frames.

33. Repeat problem 32, but reverse the direction of the data. That is, show how four information transfer frames would be sent from the terminal to the host computer.

15

LOCAL AREA NETWORKS

In the last two decades, there has been an enormous outgrowth in the field of communications called *networking*. Networking involves the sharing of computers, peripheral hardware, software, and switching facilities, all interconnected with transmission media used to establish a connection between network users. The end result is the shared use of information and resources. The concept of a network is not new and can be understood by considering examples of those services that have been provided to us by the network for many years:

- Television
- Radio broadcast
- Public switched telephone network (PSTN)
- Airline passenger and flight information
- Computer time-sharing systems
- Banking services

In each example, the intention of the network is to distribute information to users requiring the network services. The structure of the network is not of importance to the end user. It is the services rendered by the network that are of value. In most cases today, the network is controlled by computers.

This chapter focuses on networking fundamentals such as topology, channel access schemes, and network cable and connector technology. Because of its popularity and widespread use, a close examination of the Ethernet standard is presented. Finally, the student is introduced to IBM's Token Ring standard.

15.1 THE LOCAL AREA NETWORK

Computers of the past were basically large, expensive, and complex mainframes that required a tremendous amount of space and specialized maintenance. A computer expert was required to run the machine for the various batch jobs that were submitted for execution. The results of programs were not immediately available. The programmer or scientist submitting the jobs was at the mercy of the computer specialist running the machine.

With advances in computer technology and supporting hardware, it has become economically feasible for industry, educational institutes, and the private sector to own and interactively operate computers directly from office desktops. A new form

Local Area Network (LAN)
A privately owned network of interconnecting data communicating devices that share resources within a local area, such as a room, building, or group of buildings.

of network has evolved from this breakthrough called the *local area network (LAN)*. A LAN is typically a privately owned network of interconnecting data communicating devices that *share* resources (software included) within a limited physical area: a *local area.* This can be a single room within a building to several floors within a building. A LAN can also encompass a building or cluster of buildings. Most LANs link equipment within less than a few miles of each other. Why a local area? Extensive studies of the working environment indicate that 80% of communications occur *within* the local environment, whereas the remaining 20% occur *outside* the local geographical area. A LAN offers the most effective means of handling local communicating tasks. A medium- to large-sized business, for example, may be flooded with intelligent computers and related products. A LAN can interconnect these resources in a manner that best suits the employee's needs for performing everyday communicating tasks. Ultimately, the company benefits from the efficient and cost-effective use of these resources. Let us consider some of these resources:

- Laser printer
- Graphics plotter
- Mass storage devices
- Application programs
- Facsimile machines
- Personal computers
- Mainframe computers
- High-speed modems
- Private branch exchange (PBX)
- Public switched telephone network (PSTN)

The percentage utilization of many of these resources is often too low, and the costs are too high to justify purchasing one for each office, department, or even, at times, a building. Within a large corporation, for example, several buildings can share the use of a mainframe computer's speed and sophisticated database for inventory control. Each building can have a shared facsimile machine that is tied into the same LAN. Several users with personalized workstations within each building can be tied into the LAN to gain access to the shared facilities provided by the LAN. Data can be exchanged between the mainframe computer and each user, and users can send each other messages at any time via electronic mail. Figure 15-1 illustrates a LAN setup.

15.2 LAN TOPOLOGY

Topology
The geometric physical pattern or logical configuration of intelligent devices in a LAN.

Node
An addressable device on a communications network. Also known as a *station.*

LAN *topology* refers to the geometric pattern or configuration of intelligent devices and how they are linked together for communications. The intelligent devices on the network are referred to as *nodes.* Nodes in a network are *addressable* units that are *linked* together. Nodes are also referred to by some manufacturers in their specifications as *stations.* The two terms are used interchangeably. The *link* is the communications channel. In the design of a LAN, topology is considered to best suit a particular environment. In other words, there are advantages and disadvantages to the various topologies used. Factors such as message size, traffic volume, costs, bandwidth, reliability, and simplicity are important. Let us consider some of the most common LAN topologies.

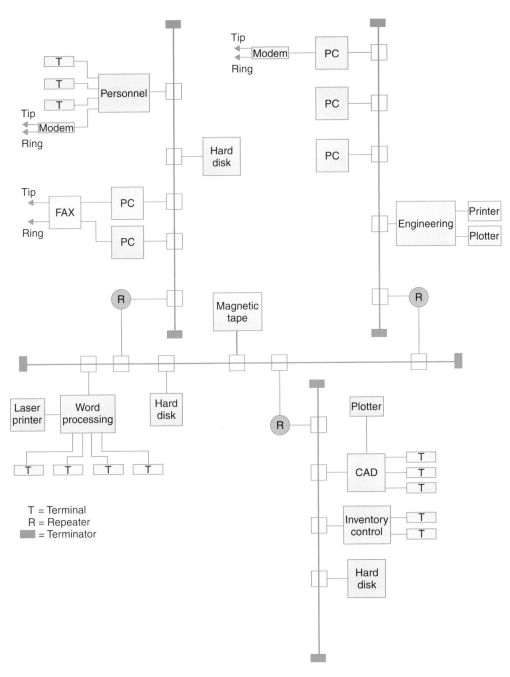

FIGURE 15-1
Typical LAN setup.

15.2.1   The Star

Figure 15-2 illustrates the *star* topology. The star topology is one of the oldest topologies used in networking. The telephone system was its first use. In recent years, it has become the most popular topology for all networks. The predominant feature of the

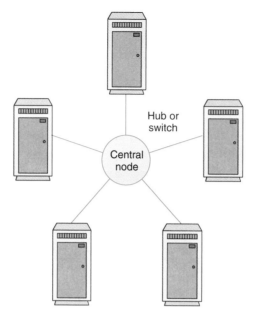

FIGURE 15-2
Star LAN.

star topology is that each node is radially linked to a *central node* in a point-to-point connection. The central node of the star topology is also referred to as *switch* or *hub*. In some cases the central node controls the communication on the LAN. In other cases, it acts as a multiport repeater. Any traffic between the outlying nodes must flow through the central node, which offers a convenient base for troubleshooting and network maintenance.

The star configuration is best utilized in cases where most of the communication occurs between the central node and outlying nodes. When communications traffic is extensive between outlying nodes, a burden is placed on the central node that can cause message delays. A PBX, for example, is configured as a star. In peak demand situations, the PBX may become overburdened with calls, in which case a busy signal is issued to the person requesting the use of the PBX. Older time-share systems linking several terminals needing the computational power of the central computer utilized the star topology. Most LANs today have evolved from other topologies, such as the bus and ring topologies, to the star as a result of new cabling and ring technologies and supporting hardware and software.

A disadvantage to the star topology is that the central node must carry the burden of reliability for all of the nodes connected to it. If the central node fails, the outlying nodes fail. If an outlying node fails, the remainder of the system will continue to operate independently of that node's failure. When the failure of any portion of the network is critical to the extent that it will disable the entire network, it is referred to as the *critical resource*. Thus, the central node in a star LAN is the critical resource. Communication systems with critical resources are often provided with *system redundancy*, which is a critical resource's backup protection in case of a failure. It can be hardware or software either built into the system or provided as an equivalent replacement to the device that failed. System redundancy can minimize the downtime of a network at the expense of cost and complexity.

Critical Resource
Any part of a LAN system that fails and, consequently, disables the entire system.

System Redundancy
Hardware or software built into a communication system as backup protection in case of failure by a critical resource.

15.2.2   The Bus

The *bus* topology is essentially a multipoint or multidrop configuration of interconnecting nodes on a *shared* channel. The original Ethernet LAN standard specifies the bus topology. Figure 15-3 illustrates the bus topology. Control over the communications channel is not centralized to a particular node, as with a star topology or a multipoint link with a host computer and its tributaries. The distinguishing feature of a bus LAN is that the control of the bus is *distributed* among *all* the nodes connected to the LAN. When data are to be transmitted from one node on the bus to another node, the transmitting station *listens* to the current activity on the bus. If no other stations are transmitting data, that is, the channel is clear, then it begins its transmission of data. All nodes connected to the bus are receivers of that transmission, typically a data packet. The function of each receiver is then to determine if the received data packet corresponds to its own address. If it does, then the data are acted on; if it does not, then the data are simply discarded. No routing or circuit switching is involved, nor is there any transferring of messages from one node to another. The overhead and time required to perform these tasks are eliminated with the bus LAN structure, hence one of its major attractions.

With heavy volumes of traffic on the bus, the likelihood of more than one station transmitting on the channel at the same time increases. A *collision* of data occurs between stations transmitting. A priority contention scheme is used to handle this problem. Typically, the stations attempting to gain access to the channel at the same time will *back off* for a random interval of time before attempting to access the channel again. This allows one of the stations to transmit its data while the others listen. Eventually, the traffic on the network subsides, and fewer collisions occur.

> **Collision**
> When two transmitters transmit at the same time over the same channel, destroying data.

Because the control of the bus LAN is not centralized, a node failure will not hinder operation of the remaining portion of the LAN. The critical resource in this case is not a node but rather the bus itself. A short or an open circuit along the bus can virtually cease all communications within the LAN. The degree of failure is not always fatal, however. It is possible for communications to continue between nodes up to the obstruction in the line. Once a short or break in the line occurs, the performance of the LAN is generally degraded due to the resulting reflections and standing waves.

The addition of nodes on a bus that has been previously routed within the local area necessitates gaining access to the bus cable. In some situations, this may be a cumbersome task. Typically, the bus cable is routed through walls and ceilings. A

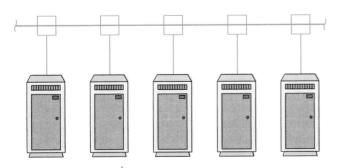

FIGURE 15-3
Bus LAN.

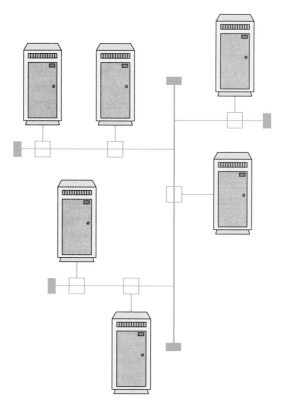

FIGURE 15-4
Bus tree LAN.

node may be tapped into the bus cable at any point provided that it meets manufacturer's specifications of minimum distance between taps. The bus may also be extended to additional areas. By branching off into other buses, a multiple bus structure called a *tree* is formed. Figure 15-4 depicts the tree structure. Section 15.7 looks at the *Ethernet* specification and how the bus topology can be extended with the use of *repeaters*.

15.2.3   The Ring

The *ring* topology, as its name implies, interconnects nodes point to point in a closed-loop configuration (Figure 15-5). The *Token Ring* standard uses this topology. A message is transmitted in simplex mode (one direction only) from node to node around the ring until it is received by the original source node. Each node acts as a repeater, retransmitting the message to the next node. Each node also shares the responsibility of identifying if the circulating message is addressed to itself or another node. In either case, the message is eventually received by the destination node and returned to the original source node. The source node then verifies that the message circulated around the ring is identical to the message that was originally transmitted. Acknowledgment bits within the message block are typically set by the destination node so that the source node has a way of verifying that the message was in fact received.

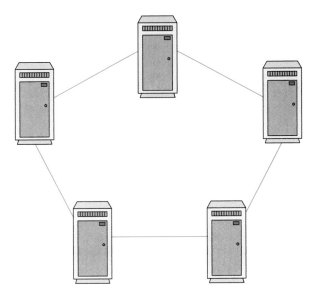

FIGURE 15-5
Ring LAN.

The critical resource in a ring topology is the interconnecting links and nodes. A node or link that malfunctions is typically replaced or bypassed. System redundancy is often included in the ring topology in case of a failure. This includes relays for bypassing a faulty node and additional cabling for faulty links, as shown in Figure 15-6. It can also include backup software or even backup nodes.

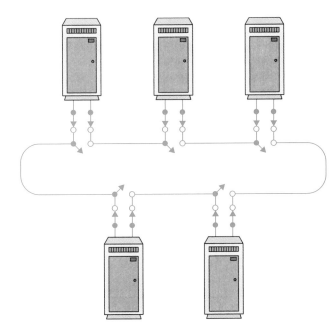

FIGURE 15-6
Ring LAN with bypass relays.

15.2.4 Extended Star and Star-Wired Ring

Coaxial cable systems used in many star and bus topologies developed in the 1980's have been slowly replaced with common household telephone cable, often referred to as *UTP (unshielded twisted-pair wire)*. Compared to coaxial cable, UTP provides a transmission medium that is inexpensive, easy to install, and conforms to new standards and equipment that have been developed for its support.

One such device is called a *hub,* or *concentrator,* which allows a bus topology to be collapsed into a physical star. The hub is essentially a multiport repeater that also serves as a central location for wiring. Figure 15-7(a) illustrates the *extended star-wired bus.* The physical star can readily be seen; however, the logical bus operations of the LAN are maintained. An Ethernet 10BaseT LAN system is an example of an extended star topology. The extended star is the most widely used networking topology today.

IBM's Token Ring architecture also has the physical resemblance to a star, as shown in Figure 15-7(b). Stations are linked together to a central connection point

> **Hub**
> The central node of a star topology. Also known as the *concentrator* or the *central control* or *switch.*

> **Multistation Access Unit (MAU)**
> A central connection point at which computer stations are linked.

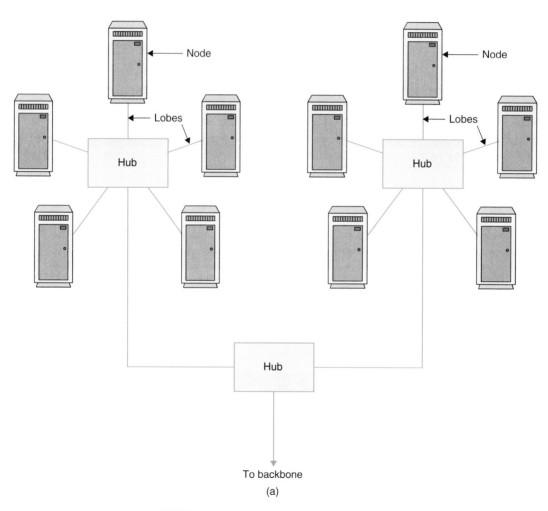

FIGURE 15-7
(a) Extended star-wired bus.

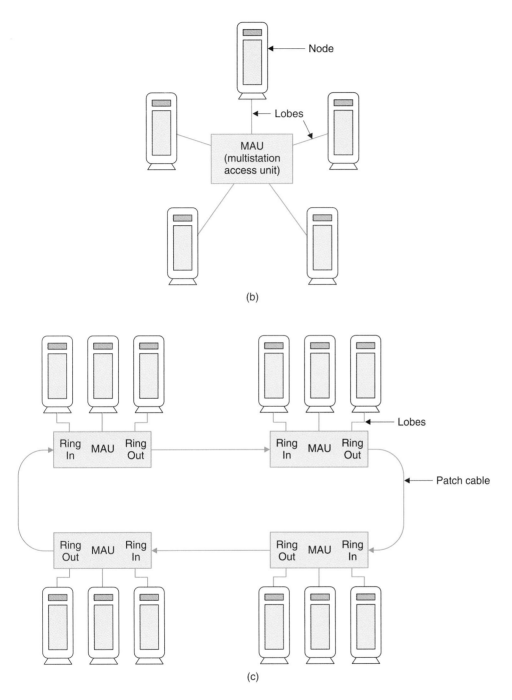

FIGURE 15-7 (continued)
(b) Star-wired ring showing MAU connection; (c) extended star-wired ring MAU connection.

called a *MAU (multistation access unit).* The MAU acts as the hub of the network and connects up to eight nodes or computers. They can also be linked together to extend the number of nodes on the network, as shown in Figure 15-7(c). The interface cable between the computer station and a MAU is called a *lobe,* and *patch cables* are used to interconnect MAUs together. Although the network topology here appears to be a star, a closer look at the internal connections of the MAU will reveal that the electrical ring is preserved. For these reasons, IBM's Token Ring topology is referred to as a *star-wired ring*.

15.3 CHANNEL ACCESS

The data link layer of the ISO/OSI seven-layer model defines the channel access protocol used by a node to gain the use of the communications channel. The following factors govern the selection of the channel access protocol used:

- Topology
- Physical size of the LAN
- Number of nodes
- Application

15.3.1 Polling

> **Polling**
> A communications control procedure in which a host computer systematically addresses one of several tributaries to enquire (ENQ) if it has any data to send.

Polling is a channel access technique whereby the host computer polls each tributary in a logical sequence for possible data. In the general sense of the word, it also includes the selection of each tributary for purposes of sending data from the host computer. The poll-select technique, discussed in Chapter 14, can also be applied to LANs. A node acting as the host can control the use of the channel by polling and selecting all other nodes within the LAN. The key to this technique is that only one host controls the use of the channel at all times. When a node has been granted use of the channel through a poll or select command from the host, its data are placed on the network and sent to their destination node either directly or indirectly through the routing of the host. Any of the topologies discussed thus far are suited for polling. The major disadvantage to this channel access technique is that communications is extremely time consuming due to the overhead required for controlling and acknowledging messages. Also, the critical burden of reliability is placed entirely on the host computer.

15.3.2 Contention

> **Contention**
> The process whereby multiple stations vie for use of the communications channel.

Contention is a channel access protocol whereby stations contend with each other for use of a single communications channel. A station desiring use of the channel asserts its message onto the channel. The message is received by a destination station on the same channel. When two or more stations inadvertently attempt to send their messages at the same time, a *collision* occurs between messages.

A common analogy used to describe contention is a *cocktail party*. At a cocktail party, when two or more people speak at the same time, their messages conflict with each other. Each person then backs off, listens for a moment, and attempts to talk again. The more crowded the party becomes, the more interference there is likely to be.

15.3.2.1 Aloha To share the use of a host computer located at the University of Hawaii on the island of Oahu, several surrounding islands interface their terminals to the host computer via a radio link. To minimize the costs of the network broadcasting equipment involved, all terminals share use of the communications channel. The communications channel is a pair of frequencies. One frequency is used by all remote stations to transmit to the host, and the other frequency is used exclusively by the host for acknowledgments and transmitted messages to the remote stations. The channel access protocol used is a contention scheme called *Aloha*. In Aloha, a station wishing to transmit a message simply does so at any time, running the risk of a collision from other stations. This is referred to as *pure Aloha:* talk whenever you want. An acknowledgment from the host computer verifies that the message was received without interference from messages transmitted by other stations that share the same frequency.

In pure Aloha, when a station transmits a message, a collision from another station can occur at any time during the interval of the transmission. Even after an entire message has been transmitted, a collision can occur, because the message takes time to arrive at its destination. Figure 15-8 depicts the Aloha contention scheme. When a collision occurs in Aloha, no acknowledgment is returned to any of the stations involved in the collision. All stations back off and wait for a predefined period of time before attempting another transmission. Studies indicate that when station activity on the network is greater than approximately 20%, performance is severely degraded due to the number of collisions. In spite of its shortcomings, the Aloha contention protocol is the predecessor to more sophisticated contention schemes.

15.3.2.2 Slotted Aloha   A more sophisticated approach to pure Aloha is *slotted Aloha*. In slotted Aloha, all stations on the network are time synchronized with each other and restricted to transmissions at predefined intervals of time called *slots*. A slot of time is based on the maximum allowable size of a message. A station desiring use

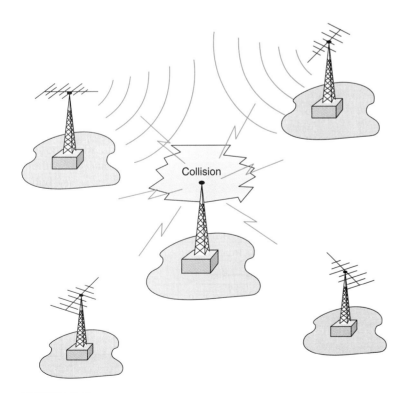

FIGURE 15-8
Aloha collision.

of the channel must begin its transmission at the beginning of a slot and finish before the end of the slot interval. Contention of the channel still exists in slotted Aloha; however, once a station has begun its transmission without a collision occurring at the beginning of the slot, that station is guaranteed the remainder of the slot time. In slotted Aloha, any collisions that would have otherwise occurred in pure Aloha are eliminated; overlapping messages cannot occur. All other stations must begin their transmissions during another time slot. Channel utilization is effectively doubled in slotted Aloha.

> **Carrier Sense Multiple Access with Collision Detection (CSMA/CD)**
> The channel access technique used in Ethernet LANs.

15.3.2.3 Carrier Sense Multiple Access with Collision Detection
One of the most widely used contention protocols for bus LANs is called *carrier sense multiple access with collision detection (CSMA/CD)*. In CSMA/CD, any node can send a message, or more specifically a packet, to any other node connected to the LAN as long as the transmission media are free of signals being transmitted by other nodes.

Carrier Sense   If we consider our earlier example of the cocktail party, the meaning of *carrier sense* in CSMA/CD would be analogous to people *listening* before talking. The interruptions in a conversation could be eliminated entirely if rules at our cocktail party ensured that, in politeness, no one speaks while another one is talking. Recall that in pure Aloha, interruptions can occur at any time during the course of a transmitted packet. The highly efficient CSMA/CD eliminates much of the wasted time that would otherwise be spent having to retransmit interrupted packets. The hardware used to monitor the activity on the channel simply senses the voltage level on the channel and compares it against a reference voltage. Above or below this reference voltage determines whether there is activity on the channel. Figure 15-9 illustrates the concept of carrier sensing.

Multiple Access   In CSMA/CD, the feature of *multiple access* allows any node on the network to access the channel at any time, provided that the channel is free. Packets are deferred if the channel is busy.

It is entirely possible for two or more nodes seeking use of the channel to sense that the channel is free at the same time. Furthermore, there is the propagation delay

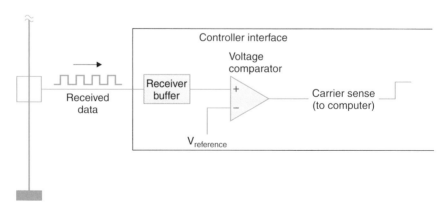

FIGURE 15-9
Carrier sensing in CSMA/CD.

time involved in the transmission of a packet from its source to its destination node. A node, for example, could have already begun transmitting a packet, and the channel, as sensed by other nodes, still appears to be inactive due to the propagation delay time before that packet arrives at other nodes. Technically, other nodes can begin transmitting their own packets onto the channel in this case. Collisions would then occur, hence the need for *collision detection.* Figure 15-10 illustrates a collision between packets transmitted by node B and node D.

Collision Detecting In addition to monitoring (listening) for activity on the channel prior to transmitting, each node in CSMA/CD has provisions for detecting collisions during the *course of a transmission.* If two or more packets collide, the energy level on the channel changes. *Collision detection* involves monitoring for this change in energy level. If a collision is detected during the course of a transmission, the transmitting node continues the transmission of its current packet, consequently *jamming* its packet onto the channel. The purpose of jamming is to ensure that the nodes involved in the collision detect that a collision has occurred. The jamming signal must be asserted for a length of time necessary to propagate to all nodes connected to the LAN. Transmitting nodes then *back off* for an interval of time before attempting to retransmit the packet again.

> **Collision Detection**
> Monitoring for the signal energy change resulting from collision on a communications channel.

It is important that node back-off times not be equivalent to each other; otherwise, collisions would continue to occur between the same transmitting nodes. The back-off time is, therefore, random. With regard to our cocktail party example, the analogy here could be two people, after noticing that no one is speaking, begin to talk at the same time. When this occurs, both are aware of the conflict and back off a random interval of time before attempting to talk again. There is, of course, the possibility of the same two people attempting to talk again at the same time. A similar event can occur in CSMA/CD. Repeated packet collisions from the same nodes are possible in spite of random back-off times. To remedy the possibility of repeated collisions from the same nodes, the mean value of the random back-off times is increased in an exponential fashion with each repeated collision. Thus, collisions involving the same nodes become even less probable.

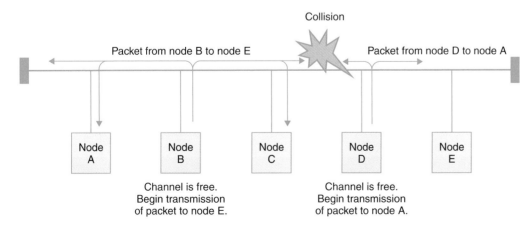

FIGURE 15-10
Two stations in CSMA/CD sense that the channel is free and begin their transmissions. A collision occurs between two packets.

Slot Time and Minimum Packet Size   There is a misconception among many of us in our early training that when a signal is transmitted, it is at the same time being received at its destination. This is especially true in cases when signals are confined to small spaces, such as circuit cards with their respective signals between gates or signals between nodes of a network separated by a few meters. In each case, there is always a definite period of time involved for the signal to propagate from its source to its destination. That length of time is often crucial to the success or failure of the system. Several factors govern this length of time, such as distance, transmission media, and temperature. It is possible in CSMA/CD for a packet of small length to be transmitted in its entirety and a collision to occur at some time later.

In Figure 15-11(a), a packet is transmitted from node A to node B, the farthest two nodes from each other on the LAN. Node A's packet size is small, and the length of time that it takes for node A to transmit its packet is *less* than the round-trip propagation delay time between the farthest two nodes in a LAN. This round-trip propagation time is defined as the *slot time*. Node B senses that the channel is free (node A's packet has not arrived yet) and begins to transmit its packet onto the channel. The collision occurs between the two packets. The collision here goes undetected by node A. Recall that collisions are monitored and reported during the *course of a transmission.* Node A thinks that its packet has been successfully transmitted, because no collision detect signal occurred during the course of transmitting its packet. A collision, in fact, has occurred. The collision return signal arrives at node A *too late.* As far as

> **Slot Time**
> The round-trip propagation time for a packet to travel between the farthest two nodes in a bus LAN.

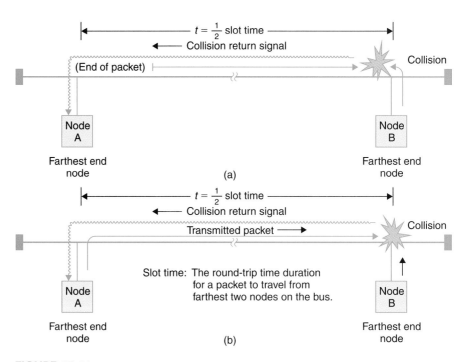

(a)

(b)

FIGURE 15-11
(a) A packet is transmitted from node A to node B whose length is less than the slot time. A collision occurs with node B's packet. The collision goes undetected by node A, because the collision return signal arrives at node A *after* it has transmitted its packet; (b) A packet must be transmitted for a minimum duration of the slot time for the transmitting station to detect a collision during the course of the transmission.

node A is concerned, the resulting collision detect signal is caused by a collision of packets from other nodes on the bus. To avoid this problem, a minimum size requirement in CSMA/CD is placed on all packet lengths transmitted by a node. This length is slightly larger than the slot time of the LAN, as depicted in Figure 15-11(b). This ensures that when a packet is transmitted by a node, it will have time not only to reach its destination but also to receive the change in energy level if a collision occurs. The packet can then be aborted and issued again at a later time. It follows that once a packet has been transmitted and the slot time has elapsed, all stations connected to the LAN are aware of the channel being used. No collisions can occur for the remainder of the transmitted packet. Transmitted packets in CSMA/CD are typically much larger than the slot time, hence the most efficient use of the channel with the least amount of contention.

15.3.3 Token Ring Passing

In ring-configured LANs, there is no contention over use of the channel. The discipline most often used to share the channel is called *token passing.* A *token* is a special bit pattern or packet that circulates around the ring from node to node when the channel is not being used (Figure 15-12[a]). A node desiring the use of the channel for communications takes possession of the token and *holds* it when its turn to receive it comes up. The node then transmits its packet onto the ring. The packet circulates to its destination node on the ring and returns to the transmitting node, where it is then verified that it was received. The token is passed forward to the next node. The token cannot be used twice, and there is a limitation on the length of time that the token can be held before it must be passed on. This prevents any one station from "hogging" the channel. In this manner, each node has the opportunity to use the channel. Possession of the token, therefore, guarantees exclusive rights to the channel. Without the token, a station can only receive and transfer packets.

> **Token**
> A special bit pattern or packet that circulates around a ring LAN from node to node.

15.3.3.1 Slotted Ring   A variation of token ring passing is *slotted ring.* In slotted ring, a fixed number of contiguous *time slots* are circulated around the ring, as shown in Figure 15-12(b). Each slot is fixed in size and contains positions in the slot for packet information. This includes source and destination address, control, data, and error checking. A *busy bit* is included at the beginning of each circulating slot that indicates the availability of the slot. A slot is either full or empty depending on the state of the busy bit. When a node wishes to transmit a packet, it waits for an empty slot. The empty slot is inserted with data in the appropriate place, and the busy bit is set before it is passed on. The full slot circulates around the ring until it arrives at its destination address. The receiving node, after identifying ownership of the packet, loads the data into its buffers and resets the busy bit to indicate that the slot is empty and available for subsequent nodes to use.

15.3.3.2 Token on a Bus   Token passing is also used in bus or tree topologies. Because the physical layout of a bus does not form a ring, an orderly sequence for passing the token from node to node must be established beforehand. This logical sequence does not have to be related to the physical placement of the nodes. The token, with its destination address, is simply passed in a virtual ring configuration, as shown in Figure 15-13.

Token passing is best suited for LANs that have few stations but frequent demands for communicating. Factory-oriented environments are examples where token passing

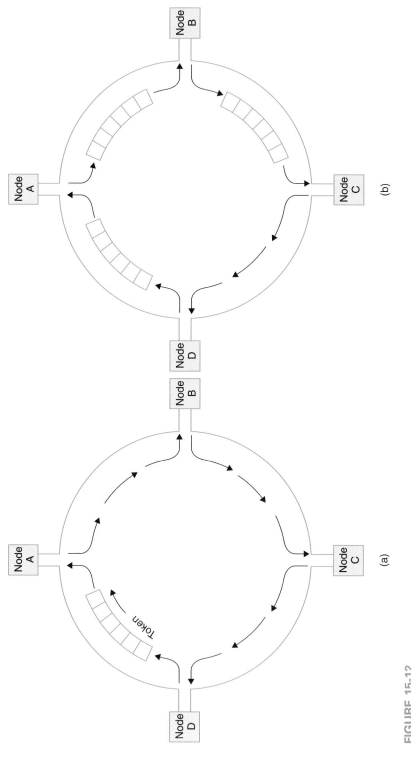

FIGURE 15-12

(a) Token passing on a ring; (b) slotted ring.

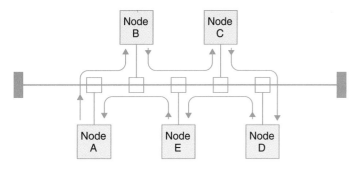

FIGURE 15-13
Token passing on a bus.

is used. One such protocol that uses this concept is called *manufacturing automation protocol (MAP),* which is based on the IEEE 802.4 token-passing specification.

15.4 LAN TRANSMISSION MEDIA

The *transmission media* or network cabling are the physical interconnections between nodes on a network. They provide the communications channel for the network. Some examples of transmission media are coaxial cable, twisted-pair wire, fiber optics, and free space or air waves in the case of wireless LANs. Table 15-1 list the various cable types and specifications for the IEEE 802.3 Ethernet standard that is discussed in Section 15.7. There are advantages and disadvantages in using each of these media. The selection of the medium to use for a LAN is governed by several factors, which will become apparent through our discussion of the various types of media. Consider the following:

> **Transmission Media**
> The physical interconnections, such as cabling, between nodes on a network.

- Topology
- Transmission protocol
- Bandwidth
- Size of the network
- Reliability
- Security
- Cost
- Installation, service, and repair

TABLE 15-1
IEEE 802.3 Cabling Specifications

	10BaseT	10BaseFL	100BaseT	100base FX
Transmission rate	10 Mbps	10 Mbps	100 Mbps	100 Mbps
Signaling type	Baseband	Baseband	Baseband	Baseband
Medial type	CAT5 UTP	Mutimode fiber (duplex)	CAT5 UTP	Multimode fiber (duplex)
Length specification	100 m	2000 m	100 m	400 m

15.4.1   EIA/TIA 568A Cabling Standards

During the 1980s, companies representing the telecommunications and computer industries were concerned about the lack of standards for telecommunications wiring systems. The evolution of a structured cabling system that would eventually support a multiproduct, multivendor networking environment began. By 1991, *EIA/TIA* (Electronic Industry Association/Telecommunications Industry Association) published the *EIA/TIA 568 Commercial Building Telecommunications **Wiring** Standard*. The revised standard is currently the ANSI/EIA/TIA 568A standard, and its new title is *Commercial Building Telecommunications **Cabling** Standard*. Representatives from various manufacturers, distributors, and customers in the networking industry make up the ANSI (American National Standards Institute), EIA, and TIA. Together, they form the central body responsible for the ANSI/EIA/TIA 568A standard. The following items are specified:

> **Electronics Industry Association/ Telecommunications Industry Association (EIA/TIA)**
> An American organization of manufacturers that establishes and recommends industrial standards.

- Minimum requirements for telecommunications cabling within an office environment
- Topology and distances
- Connectors and pin assignments to ensure interconnectivity
- Life expectancy of telecommunication cabling systems in excess of 10 years
- Electrical specifications for media and connectors

Most networks use a variety of cabling technologies, the choice depending primarily on the network's size, topology, and protocol. The EIA/TIA 568A standard provides guidelines for the connection of the various cabling technologies by dividing a network's wiring system into six unique subsystems; a summary of each subsystem follows.* For detailed information, refer to the 568A standard document.

1.   **Horizontal Cabling**   The horizontal cabling system, as shown in Figure 15-14(a), extends from the work area telecommunications outlet to the telecommunications closet. It includes the workstation outlet, mechanical terminations for the horizontal cable, the horizontal cable itself, and the cross-connections (patch cords and jumpers in the telecommunications closet).

Design requirements for Ethernet 10BaseT and 100BaseT include:

- Maximum distance for each run is 90 m (295 ft)
- Maximum horizontal cross-*connect* lengths are 6 m.
- Maximum patch cord length between telecommunications outlet and host computer is 3 m.
- Home run from the wiring closet to each outlet
- Star topology
- No bridge taps (open connections)

2.   **Backbone Cabling**   The backbone cabling, as shown in Figure 14-14(b), provides interconnection between telecommunications closets, equipment rooms, and entrance facilities. It consists of the backbone cables, intermediate and main cross-

---

Source: Anixter, Inc., *1995 Cabling System Catalog.* (Courtesy of Anixter, Inc.)

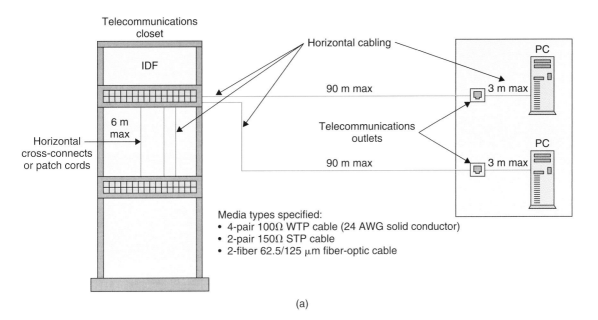

(a)

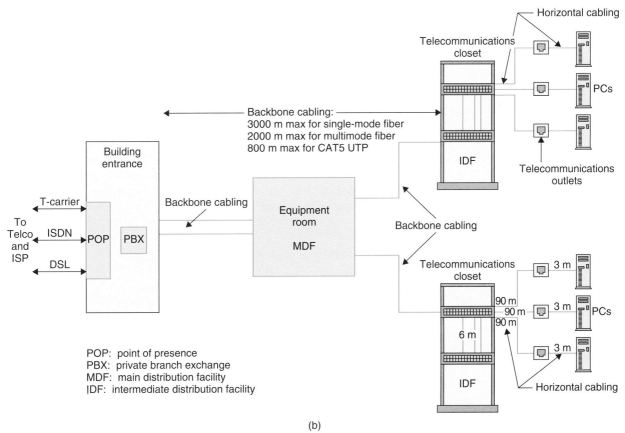

(b)

FIGURE 15-14
Horizontal versus backbone cabling specifications; (a) horizontal cabling; (b) backbone cabling.

connects, mechanical terminations, and patch cords or jumpers used for backbone-to-backbone cross-connection. These cross-connections include:

- Vertical connections between floors (risers)
- Tie cables between telecommunication (or riser) closets and satellite closets
- Cables between buildings (interbuilding)
- Cables between an equipment room and building cable-entrance facilities

Recognized cabling types and their maximum backbone distances are:

100-Ω unshielded twisted-pair (UTP) (24 or 22 AWG)	800 m (2624 ft)
150-Ω shielded twisted-pair (STP)	90 m (295 ft)
62.5/125-μm optical fiber (multimode)	2000 m (6560 ft)
Single-mode optical fiber	3000 m (9840 ft)

Other design requirements include:

- Star topology
- No more than two hierarchical levels of cross-connects
- Bridge taps are not allowed
- Main and cross-connect jumper or patch cord lengths should not exceed 20 m (66 ft)
- Avoid installing in areas where sources of high levels of electromagnetic interference (EMI)/radio frequency interference (RFI) may exist
- Grounding should meet the requirements as defined in EIA/TIA 607

3. Work Area The work area components extend from the telecommunications (information) outlet to the station equipment. It may consist of patch cords, connectors, adapters, baluns, and media filters.

4. Telecommunications Closet A telecommunications closet is the transition point between the horizontal and the backbone subsystems. It contains the intermediate distribution facility (IDF) termination hardware and cross-connect media (patch cords or jumper wire) necessary to connect the horizontal and backbone subsystems to each other or to the active telecommunications equipment located within the closet itself.

5. Equipment Room Equipment room, also known as the *main distribution facility (MDF)*, are considered to be distinct from telecommunications closets because of the nature or complexity of the equipment they contain. An equipment room provides a controlled environment to house telecommunications equipment, connecting hardware, splice closures, grounding and bonding facilities, and protection apparatus where applicable. From a cabling perspective, an equipment room contains either the main cross-connect or the intermediate cross-connect used in the backbone cabling hierarchy.

6. Building Entrance The entrance facility consists of the cables, connecting hardware, protective devices, and other equipment needed to connect the outside service facilities to the premise cabling. The building entrance also includes the telco demarcation hardware. This interface is also referred to as the *point of presence (POP)*.

Over the years, several important revisions have been added to the IEEE 802.3 standard to make Ethernet LAN architecture easier to implement and more cost-effective to manage and maintain. Most of these changes reflect the new cabling standards being used, particularly with UTP. From 1980 to approximately 1985, Ethernet systems used the thick RG8 coaxial cable technology known as *Thicknet.* Because of its bulkiness and overdesign for most applications, however, the cabling technology changed to the RG58-type coax and BNC connector technology described earlier. These systems are known as *Thin-net.* Ethernet LANs employing Thin-net dominated the market from 1985 to the early 1990s. Thicknet and Thin-net technology are still widely used today, particularly in larger LAN systems supporting many nodes. Most Ethernet LANs, however, currently use UTP cabling technology specified by the *IEEE 802.3 10BaseT* standard. Table 15-2 summarizes the Ethernet cabling standards that have evolved over the years. The most recent standard is the *IEEE 802.3u 100BaseT standard.* This standard is also known as *Fast Ethernet,* because it essentially increases Ethernet's speed from 10 Mbps to 100 Mbps. This is a speed increase of 10 times while maintaining the CSMA/CD access control protocol. As shown in Table 15-2, 100BaseT supports three types of cabling media: *100BaseT4,* which uses category 3, 4, or 5 UTP; *100BaseTx,* which uses category 5 UTP; and *100BaseFx,* which uses two-stranded fiber-optic cables. We now discuss these important cabling standards.

15.4.2   Twisted-Pair Wire

To explain this, one must consider the magnetic fields that exist when a signal is transmitted. When electrical current flows in a wire, it creates a magnetic field that surrounds the wire. Magnetic fields can interact with adjacent wires and induce undesirable signals in them. The direction and strength of the field depend on the magnitude and direction of the current. If the two wires carry electrical signals that are equal and opposite in phase, as illustrated in Figure 15-15(b), their magnetic fields will be equal and opposite in direction, resulting in a "cancellation" effect. Magnetic fields from other wire pairs also tend to be cancelled.

Twisted-pair wire is one of the oldest and most popular transmission media used for networking. Most of its growth and popularity stems from extensive use in the telephone system, including the PBX. It is also widely used in serial interface cables supporting RS-232, RS-449, RS-422, and RS-485. Its main advantage over other transmission media is that most industrial buildings, offices, and workplaces are prewired with twisted-pairs through feeder networks during construction for telephone usage.

TABLE 15-2
Evolution of IEEE 802.3 Cabling Standards

Years of Max. Use	Standard Number	Standard Name	Cabling Technology	Connector Type
1980–1985	IEEE 802.3	10Base5 (Thicknet)	RG8 thick coax	AUI (15-pin D), type-N
1985–1990	IEEE 802.3a	10Base2 (Thin-net)	RG58 thin coax	BNC
1990–present	IEEE 802.3i	10BaseT	CAT 3, 4, or 5	RJ-45
1995–present	IEEE 802.3u	100BaseTx	CAT 5; type 1	RJ-45, IBM Data Conn.
		100BaseT4	CAT 3,4,5; type 1	RJ-45, IBM Data Conn.
		100BaseFx	62.5/125-μm multimode fiber	ST or SC

These twisted-pair links are usually wired far in excess of the immediate demands for telephone use; consequently, links are available and conveniently installed as demand grows.

Today, twisted-pair wire has become the preferred transmission medium for LAN systems. It is easy to install, less expensive than coax and fiber-optic cable, and allows the Ethernet and Token Ring standards to be collapsed from a bus and ring topology to a star topology, thus allowing easier management.

As its name implies, *twisted-pair wire,* as shown in Figure 15-15(a), are two wires that have been twisted together to a transmission medium. The wires have been twisted so that the number of twists per unit length varies along the line. This helps to eliminate crosstalk, which is noise generated from adjacent channels that are capacitively or inductively coupled into the line.

Twisting the wires together also ensures a closeness so that *both* conductors are exposed to the same noise environment. Thus, any noise induced on one line is likely to be induced on its pair by the same amount. Differential amplifiers and receivers will amplify the differential signals traveling on the pairs and reject the common mode noise.

Figure 15-15(b) also illustrates the differential and common mode signals. Differential signals are transmitted and received 180° out of phase from each other using the *balanced electrical line drivers and receivers* discussed in Chapter 8. This effectively doubles the potential difference of the signal level, thereby making it easier to detect and allowing greater transmission distances. Because noise induced on one of the twisted-pair wires is likely to be induced by the same amount on its pair, it is said to be common mode.

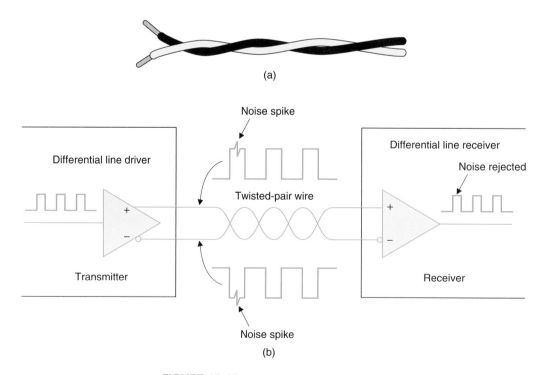

FIGURE 15-15

(a) Twisted-pair wire; (b) common mode noise induced on both twisted-pair wires is rejected by the differential line receiver amplifier.

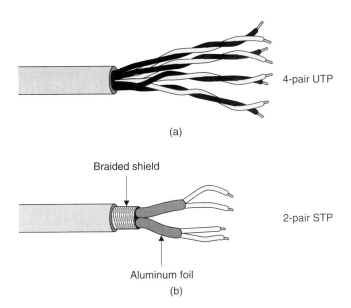

(a)

(b)

FIGURE 15-16
(a) Four-pair UTP LAN cable; (b) two-pair STP LAN cable.

A variety of twisted-pair cables are used in today's LAN systems. Two types of twisted-pair cables are specified by the EIA/TIA 568A standard for LAN cabling: *unshielded twisted-pair (UTP),* and *shielded twisted-pair (STP).* Figure 15-16 illustrates UTP and STP cable.

15.4.2.1   UTP Cable   Unshielded twisted-pair cable, also known as UTP cable, consists of solid 24 AWG (American wire gage) copper wire with PVC (polyvinyl chloride or some variation) insulation around each wire. Although 24 AWG is specified, 22 and 26 AWG are also used. The conductors are twisted at varying lengths to minimize crosstalk, with a minimum of two twists per foot. Any number of pairs can be specified for use within the cable, even up to thousands of pairs, depending on the application. For LAN cabling, typically two to six pairs are used. Surrounding the insulated pairs of wire is an insulation jacket, also typically made of PVC or some variation. The characteristic impedance of each pair is 100 Ω but typically ranges from 85 to 110 Ω. To meet the wide range of operational requirements for LAN system utilizing UTP, the EIA/TIA 568A specification classifies UTP into different *levels* and *categories* (Table 15-3). Categories 3 through 5 support Ethernet LAN systems.

15.4.2.2   STP Cable   Shielded twisted-pair cable, also known as STP, differs from UTP in that twisted pairs have aluminum foil surrounding them. This serves as a shield against EMI from external sources, including adjacent channel crosstalk. The number of twists per foot is increased to allow for higher transmission speeds. Surrounding each shielded pair is an additional braided shield used for EMI protection as well. Individual shields form a separate conductor that should be grounded at each end of the cable; the entire assembly is bound together with a PVC insulation jacket. Although the specification calls for 22 AWG, two-pair assembly with a characteristic impedance of 150 Ω, 24 and 26 AWG multipair cabling assemblies are also used as with

TABLE 15-3
TIA/EIA 568A UTP levels and categories.

Cable Type	Usage
Level 1	Voice and low-speed data applications
Level 2	Low-speed data to 4 Mbps and level 1 applications
Category 3	LAN applications to 10 Mbps and level 2 applications
Category 4	LAN applications to 20 Mbps and category 3 applications
Category 5	High-speed LAN applications to 100 Mbps
Category 6	High-speed LAN applications to 250 MHz (proposed)

its UTP counterpart. Because of its cost, STP is not as widely used as UTP, except in the case of Token Ring LANs.

15.4.2.3 Token Ring UTP and STP Cabling The *IBM Cabling System* is based on 150-Ω STP cable that is intended to support Token Ring LAN architectures. The IBM Cabling system complies with the EIA/TIA 568A standard and also specifies UTP and fiber. Table 15-4 lists the various types.

15.4.3 Coaxial Cable

Coaxial cable is another wire medium that has long been associated with the field of communications, particularly in RF applications. Coaxial cable has several advantages to offer over twisted-pair wire. Bandwidth, which means higher data transfer rates, noise immunity, and ruggedness are its main advantages.

The center conductor of coax is solid copper wire surrounded by a dielectric material made of PVC or Teflon. A braided conductor is woven over the dielectric to form a shield. The braid is usually made of copper or aluminum. The center conduc-

TABLE 15-4
IBM Cabling System

Type	Description
Type 1	Two-pair 22 AWG STP data-grade cable with IBM data connector and DB-9 connector. Token Ring Controller connector. Supports speed greater than 16 Mbps.
Type 2	Two-pair 22 AWG STP data cable with four-pair 26 AWG voice-grade wires added outside of the shielded data pairs.
Type 3	Four-pair 22 or 24 AWG Category 3, 4, or 5 UTP cable with RJ-45 modulator jacks. Typically supports 4-Mbps Token Ring networks. A *media filter* (low-pass filter) is required for type 3 cables to improve noise immunity and reduce RFI to meet FCC requirements.
Type 5	Token Ring 100/140-μm, two-pair fiber-optic cable used for inter-MAU connection.
Type 6	Two-pair 22 AWG STP data-grade cable used as a patch cable. Similar to type 1 but limited to two-thirds of its distance.

tor and the shield form a uniform concentric circle sharing the same center axis, hence the name *coaxial*. For the outer portion of the coax, a protective vinyl insulating sleeve forms a waterproof barrier. Coaxial cable serves in most cases as the predominant choice for transmission media used for LANs.

Coax is manufactured in a variety of different diameters and types. In addition to the flexible coax we have been discussing, there are also *rigid* and *semirigid* coax. These types of coax have solid copper material in place of the braid with no outer insulator. They are used primarily for RF applications. Coaxial cable is available in different impedances; typically, 50 or 75 Ω is used. Its frequency response ranges from DC to an upper limit of approximately 500 MHz. This lends itself ideally to LAN applications.

The IEEE 802.3 (Ethernet) 10Base5 and 10Base2 standards specify the use of two different types of coaxial cable. The 10Base5 standard, or *Thicknet*, uses a special coaxial cable specifically manufactured for Ethernet Thicknet applications. The Thicknet cable shown in Figure 15-17(a) is an extremely rugged design, consisting of several layers of insulation and shielding surrounding its center conductor. The outside insulating jacket has marker indicators every 2.5 m for the specific placement of the interconnecting device (transceiver) to the LAN. Thicknet cable is equivalent in design to the standardized RG-8 coax.

Before 1985, most Ethernet LANs employed Thicknet cable. Over the years, however, most technologists found that Thicknet cable was overbuilt and unnecessary in most applications. The LAN industry shifted to the 10Base2 standard, which uses the commercially available RG-58 cable illustrated in Figure 15-17(b). The 10Base2 standard is also known as *Thin-net*, because of its relative size in comparison to Thicknet. Table 15-5 lists the characteristics of Thicknet and Thin-net coaxial cable.

> **Thicknet**
> Another name for the original Ethernet 10Base5 standard.

> **Thin-net**
> Another name for the Ethernet 10Base2 standard.

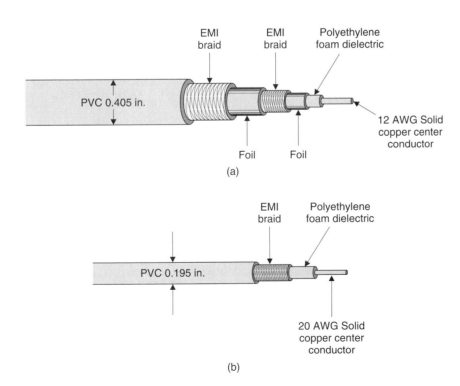

FIGURE 15-17
Coaxial LAN cable: (a) 10Base5 (Thicknet) RG8; (b) 10Base2 (Thin-net) RG-58.

TABLE 15-5
Coaxial Cable Specifications

Type	Characteristic Impedance, Ω	Velocity Factor, %	Capacitance, pF/ft	Conductor Size, AWG	Outside Dia., in.	Attenuation @ 10 MHz
RG58/A-AU	53	66	28.5	20	0.195	1.25
RG58 Foam	50	79	25.4	20	0.195	1.00
RG59/A-AU	73	66	21.0	20	0.242	1.13
RG59 Foam	75	79	16.9	20	0.242	0.875
RG8/A-AU	52	66	29.5	12	0.405	0.585
RG8 Foam	50	80	25.4	12	0.405	0.572

15.4.4 Fiber-Optic Cable

With the declining costs of fiber-optic cable and networking devices, fiber-optic technology continues taking over applications where wire media have long been established. Virtually every business, government, and educational entity has either integrated fiber into its network architecture or seriously thought about its benefits. Consider some of the advantages of fiber optics over wire media:

- Bandwidth up into the Gigahertz region
- Attenuation as little as 0.1 dB/km
- Noise immunity
- Size and weight
- Security

With all the advantages of fiber-optic technology over other transmission media, one may wonder why wire technology remains the dominant media used for networking. Currently, fiber-optic technology still has some drawbacks. Fiber-optic cables tend to be somewhat fragile and lack flexibility relative to copper wire. Coaxial cable and twisted-pair wire, as we know, can be pulled quite rigorously through conduits and walls. The same force exerted on a fiber-optic cable can cause damage, resulting in the need to splice fractured fibers. *Strength members,* as shown in Figure 15-18, are being included within the cables to overcome this problem. Splices and taps into the fiber-optic cable can amount to significant signal loss unless special equipment is used to perform this task. The substantial progress being made in fiber optics will soon resolve many of these problems. (Chapter 18 discusses fiber optics further.)

15.4.5 Wireless

An inherent shortcoming with the transmission media discussed thus far is the burden of installation. Cables packed in conduit, walls, and ceilings leave much to be desired by most network managers. "Digital wireless" communication systems are an attractive alternative for replacing solid cabling and the extensive planning and maintenance required. Digital wireless technology for telecommunication systems has risen dramatically in the past 5 years. Standards organizations are scrambling to acquire

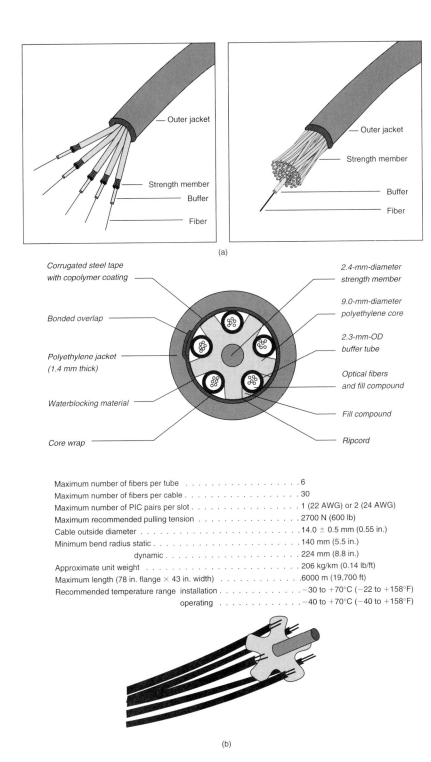

Maximum number of fibers per tube	6
Maximum number of fibers per cable	30
Maximum number of PIC pairs per slot	1 (22 AWG) or 2 (24 AWG)
Maximum recommended pulling tension	2700 N (600 lb)
Cable outside diameter	14.0 ± 0.5 mm (0.55 in.)
Minimum bend radius static	140 mm (5.5 in.)
dynamic	224 mm (8.8 in.)
Approximate unit weight	206 kg/km (0.14 lb/ft)
Maximum length (78 in. flange × 43 in. width)	6000 m (19,700 ft)
Recommended temperature range installation	−30 to +70°C (−22 to +158°F)
operating	−40 to +70°C (−40 to +158°F)

FIGURE 15-18
Fiber-optic cable. (Courtesy of Northern Telecom.)

433

portions of the available RF spectrum as the capacity of the air waves becomes increasingly congested. Wireless LAN systems employ RF and infrared (IR) transceivers on stations, thus eliminating the need for cabling. For LAN systems, one of two wireless methods is used: *infrared,* or *radiobased.*

IR-based systems employ one of three techniques for communicating between stations: *line-of-sight, scatter,* or *reflective.* Line-of-sight, as its name implies, uses optical transceivers that are aimed at each other. They offer high-speed connectivity between stations within ranges of 100 ft. Unfortunately, persons walking through the line-of-sight IR path will disrupt the signal; therefore, IR systems must be installed where the path will not be interrupted. Scatter IR systems employ transceivers at each station that transmit and receive IR that is "bounced" off walls and ceilings, similar to the manner in which light scatters, except that IR is invisible to the naked eye. Scatter IR systems are best for peripheral sharing covering distances up to approximately 100 ft. Reflective IR systems also have optical transceivers at each node. Each workstation's transceiver is aimed at a spot on the wall off which the IR signal is reflected. Reflective systems are best suited where there are high ceilings, typically 30 to 40 ft, where persons are unlikely to disrupt the IR communications path.

Radio-based systems use microwave and UHF frequencies to transmit and receive signals between nodes. Various protocols are used for communications. In some cases, a master control transceiver broadcasts and receives from a cluster of workstations. Other wireless radio-based LANs use an Ethernet-like contention scheme or Token Ring architecture where each node has its own wireless LAN card and plug-in antenna. The advantage of the radio-based system is that walls can be penetrated to some degree and the user does not have to worry about obstructing the path of the signal as with an IR system. (Chapter 19 discusses more details on wireless communications.)

15.5 LAN CONNECTORS

The interconnection of all networks demands the use of highly reliable connectors that are capable of coupling electrical and optical signals both to and from the transmission line without interference. Desirable features of a connector are:

- Easily connectable and disconnectable
- Low loss
- Durability
- Conforms to given standard

15.5.1 UTP Connectors

The standard connectors used for twisted-pair wire are the RJ-11 and RJ-45 connectors. They are illustrated in Figure 15-19 along with a color-coded chart for various connection standards and the corresponding eight-position (RJ-45) and six-position (RJ-11) modular cable jacks into which they plug. The Ethernet 10BaseT standard uses the RJ-45 connector with UTP wire, and the Token Ring standard uses both the RJ-45 and RJ-11 connectors. The RJ-11 connector can house up to six wires (three pairs), and the RJ-45 connector can house up to eight wires (four pairs). Most Ethernet connections use a four-pair category 3, 4, or 5 UTP cable consisting of four color-

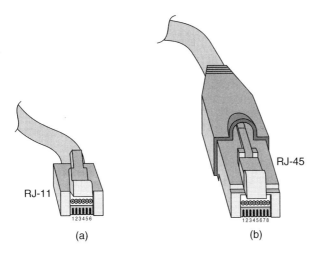

*Pin	(RJ-45) 10BaseT	(RJ-45) Token Ring	(RJ-45) TIA/EIA 568A	(RJ-45) TIA/EIA 568B	(RJ-11) USOC	(RJ-45) 10BaseT cross-over
1 (RD+)	WHT-ORN	NC	WHT-GRN	WHT-ORN	WHT-GRN	WHT-GRN
2 (RD−)	ORN	NC	GRN	ORN	WHT-BRN	GRN
3 (TD+)	WHT-GRN	WHT-ORN	WHT-ORN	WHT-GRN	WHT-BLU	WHT-ORN
4	NC	WHT-BLU	BLU	BLU	BLU	NC
5	NC	BLU	WHT-BLU	WHT-BLU	ORN	NC
6 (TD−)	GRN	ORN	ORN	GRN	GRN	ORN
7	NC	NC	WHT-BRN	WHT-BRN		NC
8	NC	NC	BRN	BRN		NC

(c)

FIGURE 15-19
UTP connectors: (a) RJ-11; (b) RJ-45; (c) pin-out listing for various standards and corresponding modular jacks. *Note: The Ethernet signals for received data (RD+; RD−) and transmitted data (TD+, TD−) are on pins 1, 2, 3, and 6 respectively.

coded pairs that include one solid color and one mixed color (solid color mixed with the color white). The color pairs are defined as:

Pair 1:   blue, white-blue
Pair 2:   orange, white-orange
Pair 3:   green, white-green
Pair 4:   brown, white-brown

15.5.2 STP Connectors

The standard connector used with STP cabling is the IBM data connector or universal data connector. The data connector is a black rectangular connector attached to

STP type-1 cable. If the data connector is attached to one end of the STP cable and a DB-9 connector is attached to the opposite end, this makes up a standard lobe cable. The data connector always snaps into the MAU port, and the DB-9 connection is made at the NIC (network interface card) or Token Ring controller card located in the personal computer (PC). If the data connector is attached to both ends of the STP, it is typically used as a patch cable to make a MAU-to-MAU connection. The IBM data connector is shown in Figure 15-20.

15.5.3 Coaxial Cable Connectors

There are two basic types of coaxial cable connectors used in networks: *standard BNC connector,* and *type-N connector.* The BNC connector is considered a bayonet mount and can be readily twisted on or off its mating connector. It is the standard connector used for Ethernet 10Base2 systems (Thin-net) and interfaces to RG-58 and RG-59 coax. In contrast, the type-N connector is a threaded connector that is screwed on and off of its connecting mate. It is the standard connector used for Ethernet 10Base5 terminators and cable splices. The BNC and type-N connectors and their adapters are shown in Figure 15-21.

15.5.4 D-Type Connector

Ethernet Transceiver
A device to which the Ethernet controller card residing in the computer must be interfaced.

Transceiver Cable
The cable used to interface between the Ethernet transceiver and host computer.

In the Ethernet 10Base5 standard, the Ethernet controller card residing in the computer must be interfaced to a device called an *Ethernet transceiver,* and the interfacing cable is called a *transceiver cable.* The connectors used to attach the transceiver cable from the controller card to the transceiver are called *AUI connectors* by the IEEE standards organization. AUI stands for *Attachment Unit Interface.* The AUI connector is a standard DB-15 connector. Figure 15-22(a) illustrates the AUI connector and its pin-out versus signal names for the Ethernet transceiver interface. The AUI connector has since become a standard interface connector for many networking devices.

Another popular D-type connector is the DB-9 connector. The DB-9 connector is the standard connector type for interfacing Token Ring LAN cables to the Token

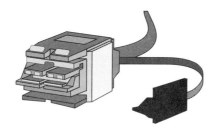

Data connector

FIGURE 15-20
IBM Data connector.

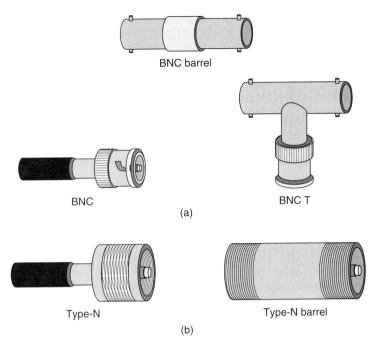

FIGURE 15-21
Coaxial cable connectors: (a) BNC connectors; (b) type-N connectors.

Ring controller card residing in the PC. The DB-9 connector is shown in Figure 15-22(b).

15.5.5   Fiber-Optic Connectors

There are several types of fiber-optic connectors, ranging from the military SMA connector to the DNP connector used for plastic fiber. The most widely used fiber-optic connectors for LANs are the ST and SCs, which are shown in Figure 15-23.

15.6   BASEBAND VERSUS BROADBAND TRANSMISSION

Data can be transmitted from one node to another within a LAN by several transmission techniques depending on factors such as media, transmission rate, distribution area, and the volume of data. The method by which the data are transmitted in a LAN is classified into two categories: *baseband,* and *broadband.*

15.6.1   Baseband

A LAN is classified as a *baseband* LAN when the entire bandwidth of its transmission medium is used as a single network data channel. Signals in the baseband are digital and are not converted to analog signals used to modulate carrier frequencies; that is, they remain as serial binary bit streams that are transmitted onto the channel in digital form. This makes the interface to the data channel simple since most data communications devices are inherently digital. Baseband LANs are typically optimized to transfer digital data from DC to 100 MHz. The most common media used

> **Baseband**
> Any digital signal that is not modulated onto a carrier frequency.

Transceiver Cable Electrical Connections

Connector pin assignment	Signal
Controller: 15-pin D (plug)	
Transceiver: 15-pin D (receptacle)	
Pin 1	Shield
2	Collision detect (+)
3	Transmitted data (+)
4	No connection
5	Received data (+)
6	Power return
7	No connection
8	No connection
9	Collision detection (−)
10	Transmitted data (−)
11	No connection
12	Received data (−)
13	Power
14	No connection
15	No connection
Connector shell	Shield

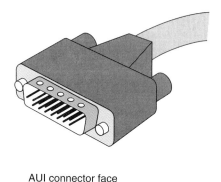

AUI connector face
15-position plug

(a)

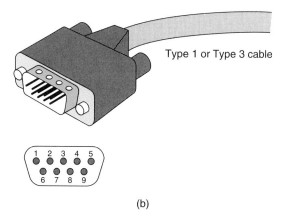

Type 1 or Type 3 cable

(b)

FIGURE 15-22

(a) DB-15 AUI connectors; (b) DB-9 Token Ring controller interface connector.

are coax cable and twisted-pair wire. The Ethernet and Token Ring protocols are examples of baseband LANs.

15.6.2 Broadband

> **Broadband**
> Any signal that requires modulation onto a carrier frequency.

In contrast to baseband LANs, *broadband* LANs use *frequency-division multiplexing (FDM)* to divide the bandwidth of a single transmission medium into multiple channels of analog signals. Each channel is a fixed band of frequencies that operates independently of each other, thus allowing various modulation techniques to be used simultaneously. These include AM, FM, and PM. The bands of frequencies allocated for various channels can vary in width depending on whether the intelligence that is modulated onto the channel carrier frequency is audio, video, or data.

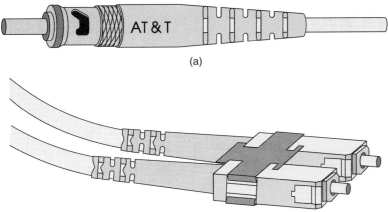

(a)

The **SC Connector** features a molded body and a push-pull locking system. It's perfect for the office, CATV, and telephone applications.

(b)

FIGURE 15-23
Fiber-optic connectors for LANs: (a) ST connector; (b) SC connector.

The evolution of broadband LANs can be attributed to a technology that has been around for some time called *community antenna television (CATV),* or *cable TV.* Many years of research and development have allowed the CATV industry to evolve into the successful communications medium that it is today. Parts, servicing equipment, terminology, and technology have long been established and are easily adaptable to broadband LANs.

CATV, until recently, has been unidirectional; that is, TV signals travel in one direction only. That direction is from the CATV station antenna, where it is conditioned by a unit called the *head end* and then forwarded to community subscribers. This is referred to as *downstream transmission.* Subscribers now have the option of transmitting in the reverse direction: *upstream transmission.* Figure 15-24 illustrates a small portion of the frequency spectrum that has been allotted for such transmission. Because most services are forwarded to the subscriber, the frequency allocation favors downstream transmission. Essentially, broadband LANs, apart from CATV, offer bidirectional communications in much the same way, only bandwidth is more equally split.

Community Antenna Television (CATV)
Another name for cable TV.

Head End
The part of a broadband communication network serving as the original and destination of all radio frequency signals distributed to and from the connected devices.

Downstream Transmission
A cable TV (CATV) signal's direction of travel from the CATV station antenna to community subscribers.

Upstream Transmission
A cable TV (CATV) signal's direction of travel from community subscriber to the CATV station antenna.

Return   Forward
5   32   54

0   50   100   150   200   250   300   350   400

	TV Low	FM	Mid	TV High	Super	Hyper

T7 — T-13 2   6   14   22 7   13 23   36 37   53

FIGURE 15-24
CATV frequency allocation with subsplit frequency assignment.

15.7 ETHERNET

Ethernet
A baseband LAN system employing a bus topology and using 10-Mbps transmission over coaxial cable.

A baseband network that has dominated the LAN scene over the years and become an accepted standard is *Ethernet,* which was developed in 1980 by the combined efforts of Xerox Corporation, Digital Equipment Corporation, and Intel Corporation. It has been accepted under the IEEE 802.3 specification. The Ethernet specification addresses the physical and data link layers of the ISO/OSI seven-layer model, as illustrated in Figure 15-25. To gain further insight into the details of a LAN, the Ethernet specification, due to its widespread use, has been chosen for a detailed discussion.

Ethernet's rise in popularity stems from its simplicity. It is easy to configure, flexible, and readily extendible. Because of its popularity and acceptance as a standard, many manufacturers provide capabilities for interfacing their devices to Ethernet. This includes a broad range of devices from mainframes and PCs to mass storage devices.

The Ethernet specification provides for a high-speed communications facility within a local area. By using CSMA/CD as access control, the need for complex routing or switching techniques as well as the substantial time involved in managing non-contention protocols are eliminated.

15.7.1 IEEE 802.3 10Base5 Thicknet Specification

The IEEE 802.3 *10Base5* specification is listed in Table 15-6. This is the original Ethernet specification. The 10Base5 name stands for "**10**" Mbps, "**Base**band" signaling, and a maximum segment length of "**5**00" meters. As illustrated in Figure 15-26, the Ethernet 10Base5 specification calls for the use of "thick," 50-Ω, RG-8, double-shielded coaxial cable with a solid copper 12 AWG center conductor for its transmission medium. For this reason, the original Ethernet standard is referred to today as *Thicknet.* The thick coaxial cable is routed through walls, ceilings, and floors in a manner that allows easy access to the cable for the addition of nodes. A *transceiver* taps into the Ethernet cable and connects to a node via a *transceiver cable.* The transceiver cable is attached to the Ethernet controller, which resides in the node. A maximum of 1024 nodes can be networked together on the bus.

Although the Thicknet standard was most widely used from 1980 to 1985, Thicknet LANs still exist today. The standard also serves as a basis for understanding the latest Ethernet standards.

7	Application layer		
6	Presentation layer		
5	Session layer		
4	Transport layer		
3	Network layer		
2	Data link layer	Ethernet	IEEE 802.3
1	Physical layer		

FIGURE 15-25
Ethernet specification in relation to seven-layer ISO/OSI model.

TABLE 15-6
Ethernet Specifications

Topology	Bus (branching nonrooted tree)
Access control	CSMA/CD
Message protocol	Variable packet size (see data encapsulation/decapsulation)
Transmission medium	Shielded coaxial cable
Signaling type	Baseband
Signal rate	10 Mbps
Maximum number of nodes	1024
Maximum node separation	2.8 km
Slot time	51.2 μs
Maximum segment length	500 m
Maximum number of nodes per segment	100
Minimum node separation	2.5 m
Maximum length of coaxial separation between two nodes	1500 m
Maximum segment separation with point-to-point link	1000 m
Maximum number of repeaters between any two nodes	2

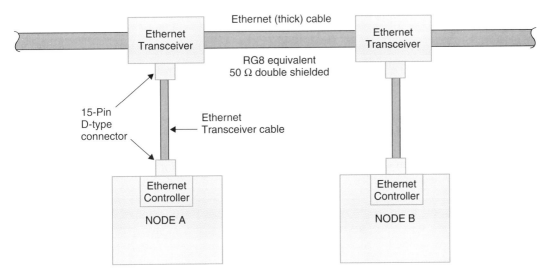

FIGURE 15-26
Ethernet 10Base5 connection.

15.7.2   The Ethernet Segment

Each coaxial cable within a network is referred to as a *segment*. A segment, as shown in Figure 15-27, can span a maximum of 500 m and include a maximum of 100 nodes. Each segment must be terminated at their ends with a 50-Ω terminator designed to

Segment
A coaxial or UTP cable link used in an Ethernet LAN.

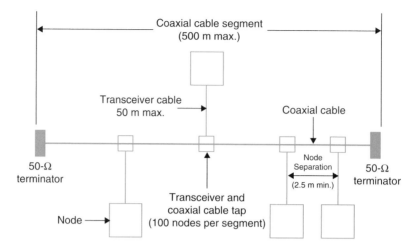

FIGURE 15-27
Small-scale Ethernet configuration. (Courtesy of Digital Equipment Corporation.)

match the characteristic impedance of the line. Nodes must be separated by a minimum of 2.5 m. When adding a node to a segment, the Ethernet cable must be tapped at multiples of 2.5 m from other nodes on the segment. This minimizes reflections and standing waves. For ease of identifying where taps may be placed for the addition of a node, the cabling manufactured for Ethernet is marked at 2.5-m intervals.

15.7.3 The Ethernet Repeater

The repeater is shown in the medium- and large-scale Ethernet configurations of Figures 15-27 and 15-28. The function of the repeater is to transmit signals from one segment to another without altering the integrity of the signal. Segments cannot be separated by more than 100 m: two 50-m transceiver cables separated by the repeater. The network can then be extended beyond 500 m by joining segments together. The repeater resides between segments and is connected to the segments via a transceiver cable. Note in both figures that the repeater's transceiver cables are tapped into the network as a node would be; that is, a repeater takes the position of a node and counts toward the maximum allowable 100 nodes. A repeater is not, however, a node, because it is not addressable. Once the repeater is activated, it becomes *transparent* to the network.

There are two types of repeaters: the *local repeater*, and the *remote repeater*. The local repeater is shown in Figure 15-28 and is indicated by a circle linking two segments together. The remote repeater is indicated by the two partial circles interconnected by a full-duplex fiber-optic link. Both types of repeaters serve the function of joining segments. The remote repeater, however, allows the network to be extended to a maximum of 1000 m via a fiber-optic link. Each unit of the remote repeater has its own independent, stand-alone AC power supply, thus allowing segments to be separated by the maximum 1000 m. The remote repeater is essentially identical to a local repeater, with the exception of the fiber-optic interface installed in the repeater unit.

Local Repeater
A repeater used in an Ethernet LAN employing a full-duplex communications link.

Remote Repeater
A repeater used in an Ethernet LAN with an independent, stand-alone power supply that can extend the range of the network.

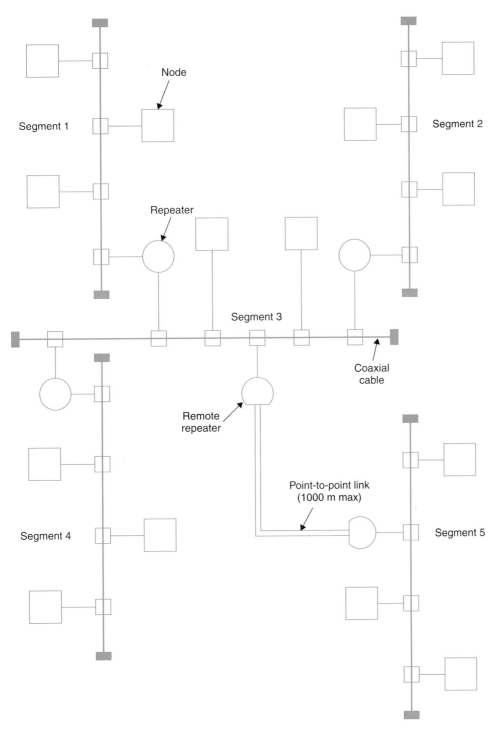

Node

Segment 1

Segment 2

Repeater

Segment 3

Coaxial
cable

Remote
repeater

Point-to-point link
(1000 m max)

Segment 4

Segment 5

FIGURE 15-28
Large-scale Ethernet configuration. (Courtesy of Digital Equipment Corporation.)

15.7.4 The Ethernet Transceiver Cable

The *transceiver cable* is used to interconnect the Ethernet transceiver to the Ethernet controller card that resides within a node. Figure 15-29 illustrates the interface. The transceiver cable consists of four twisted-pair wires that are shielded and protected with an insulating jacket. Fifteen-pin D-type or AUI connectors are used on both ends of the cable. A plug is used on the controller end, and a receptacle is used on the transceiver end.

The transceiver cable is specified for a maximum cable length of 50 m. Extending the cable length beyond this specification increases propagation delay time and results in collisions.

The transceiver cable includes the following signals:

- Power
- Transmitted data
- Received data
- Collision detection

The transceiver cable electrical connections are shown in Table 15-7.

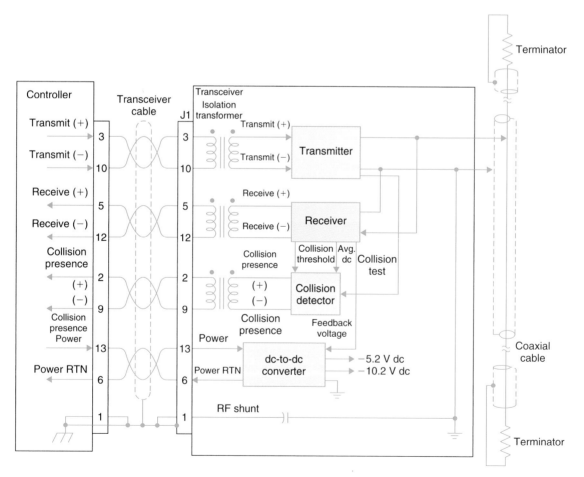

FIGURE 15-29

Ethernet transceiver interface. (Courtesy of Digital Equipment Corporation.)

TABLE 15-7
Transceiver Cable Electrical Connections

Connector Pin Assignment	Signal
Controller: 15-pin D (plug)	
Transceiver: 15-pin D (receptacle)	
Pin 1	Shield
2	Collision detect (+)
3	Transmitted data (+)
4	No connection
5	Received data (+)
6	Power return
7	No connection
8	No connection
9	Collision detection (−)
10	Transmitted data (−)
11	No connection
12	Received data (−)
13	Power
14	No connection
15	No connection
Connector shell	Shield

15.7.5 The H4000 Ethernet Transceiver

The Ethernet transceiver provides the physical and electrical interface to the Ethernet coaxial cable. Electrical circuits internal to the transceiver are powered via the transceiver cable connected to the Ethernet controller circuit card. On occasion, there is a need for the test engineer to install, test, or service the transceiver. A close look at the electrical and physical construction of the transceiver is necessary. The model selected for our discussion is the widely used H4000 Ethernet transceiver manufactured by Digital Equipment Corporation. Figure 15-29 depicts a functional block diagram of the H4000 transceiver.

15.7.5.1 H4000 Transceiver Physical Construction
The physical construction of the H4000 Ethernet transceiver is shown in Figure 15-30. A cutaway view shows the physical and electrical interface between the transceiver and the coaxial cable. The housing that contains the coaxial cable is removable. This allows the transceiver to be tapped into the cable if a node is added to the network. It also allows the transceiver to be easily serviced. The housing contains braid contacts and a center pin. When the Ethernet coaxial cable is secured by the housing, the braid contacts penetrate the coaxial cable outer insulating jacket and make contact with the coaxial shield. A hole is then drilled into the cable to clear the coaxial cable shield, thus allowing the center conductor pin to penetrate the dielectric material surrounding the center conductor of the cable. Contact is never actually made between the center conductor pin and the center conductor of the coaxial cable. Ethernet signals are *inductively coupled* between the transceiver and coaxial cable.

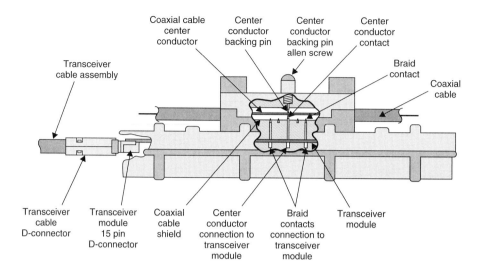

FIGURE 15-30

H4000 Ethernet transceiver manufactured by Digital Equipment Corporation. (Courtesy of Digital Equipment Corporation.)

15.7.5.2 H4000 Transceiver Circuit   A functional block diagram of the Ethernet transceiver is shown in Figure 15-31. Also shown is the relationship between the Ethernet bus cable, transceiver cable, and controller interface. The main functions of the transceiver are discussed next.

Transmitter   The transmitter's primary function is to buffer the signals TRANS-MIT(+) and TRANSMIT(−) from the transceiver cable and transmit them onto the Ethernet cable. Timing circuits in the transmitter limit the length of time that the transmitter may be on. This prevents signals from inadvertently getting stuck in the on condition beyond the maximum packet length. A circuit is also included in the transmitter to verify that the *collision detector* circuit is operational during the transmission. A protective circuit is included in the transmitter to prevent electrical damage between Ethernet and the transmitter.

Receiver   The receiver couples the signals from the Ethernet coaxial cable to the receiver buffer circuit. RECEIVE(+) and RECEIVE(−) are generated and sent to the transceiver cable pair provided that the signals on the Ethernet cable exceed the average DC threshold for a valid signal. The average DC value of the signal and a collision threshold are sent to the collision detector circuit. A protective circuit is included in the receiver to prevent electrical damage between Ethernet and the receiver interface.

Collision Detector   The collision detector circuit monitors the average DC value from the Ethernet coaxial cable indirectly through the receiver circuit. Two stations transmitting at the same time on Ethernet increase the average DC value beyond the collision threshold, thus turning on the collision detect signals: COLLISION PRESENCE(+), and COLLISION PRESENCE(−). These signals are sent onto the transceiver cable to notify the transmitting nodes of a collision. The collision detector circuit also responds to the collision test from the transmitter.

DC-to-DC Converter   The DC-to-DC converter circuit generates the required DC voltages used by the H4000 transceiver circuits. It is sourced by the POWER and POWER RETURN signal from a node via the transceiver cable.

15.7.6   The Ethernet Controller

A final link to the Ethernet interface is the Ethernet controller. The controller (Figure 15-31) resides as a plug-in unit in an Ethernet node. Typically, the controller card utilizes a microprocessor to perform three major functions:

1. Data encapsulation/decapsulation
2. Access control
3. Manchester encoding/decoding

As illustrated in Figure 15-31, the controller functions are implemented within the data link and physical link layers of the ISO/OSI seven-layer model.

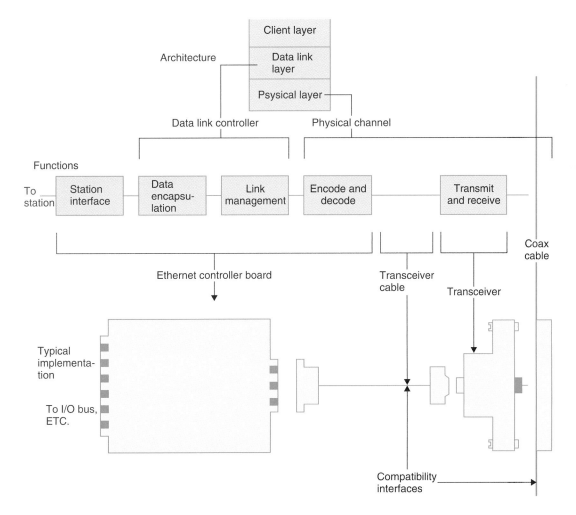

FIGURE 15-31
Ethernet controller layered functions. (Courtesy of Digital Equipment Corporation.)

15.7.6.1 Data Encapsulation/Decapsulation Data encapsulation/decapsulation refers to the task of assembling and disassembling the Ethernet frame structure depicted in Figure 15-32. Addressing and error detection are also included. The maximum frame size for an Ethernet packet is 1526 bytes (12,208 bits). The minimum packet size is 72 bytes (576 bits). For a data transfer rate of 10 MHz, this is equal to 57.6 μs (576 bits $\times \frac{1}{10}$MHz). This time is slightly larger than the Ethernet slot time, which is specified as 51.2 μs, or 512 bit times. Recall that the slot time is the round-trip propagation time of a signal to travel between the farthest two nodes on the Ethernet bus. For Ethernet, it is based on the specification for maximum separation between nodes of 2800 m. Let us now consider each field of the Ethernet frame.

Preamble   The Preamble consists of 7 bytes of alternating 1s and 0s (starting with 1 and ending with 0). This particular pattern produces a periodic waveform by the Manchester encoding circuit. It allows the receiver to achieve frame synchronization with the packet.

Start Frame Delimiter   The Start Frame Delimiter (SFD) is a 1-byte field that indicates the start of the packet. The SFD bit pattern is 10101011.

Destination Address   The Destination Address is a 2- or 6-byte field that specifies the destination address of the packet. Its size is determined by the manufacturer and must be the same size as the Source Address. The LSB is transmitted first for each byte.

Source Address   The Source Address is a 2- or 6-byte field that specifies the source address of the generated packet. Its size is determined by the manufacturer and must be the same size as the Destination Address. The LSB is transmitted first for each byte.

Length   The Length is a 2-byte field that specifies the number of data bytes in the Data field. The Length field is transmitted and received with the high-order byte first.

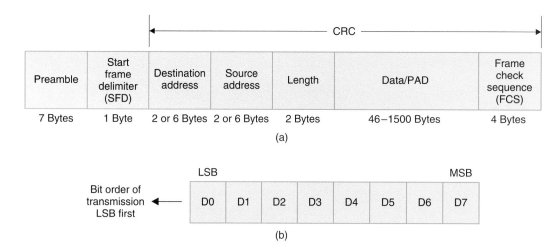

FIGURE 15-32
(a) Ethernet frame structure; (b) bit order at transmission. (LSB transmitted first).

Data/PAD   The Data field is a transparent, variable-length data field ranging from 46 to 1500 bytes. Data link control characters or bit stuffing are not used to achieve data transparency. Transparency is achieved by counting back from the Frame Check Sequence field. This is possible by knowing beforehand the number of bytes included in the data field. A total byte count of the packet is maintained by the receiving node once the packet has been taken in by the controller. Because a minimum frame size is required for correct CSMA/CD, it may be necessary to extend small data fields by appending extra bytes, called a *PAD*.

Frame Check Sequence   The Frame Check Sequence field is a 4-byte cyclic redundancy check (CRC) field of the Destination Address, Source Address, Length, and Data/PAD fields. It is used by the transmitter and receiver for error control. (Error control is discussed in Chapter 17.) The CRC check range is shown in Figure 15-32. The encoded CRC generator polynomials is defined as

$$G(x) = x^{32} + x^{26} + x^{23} + x^{22} + x^{16} + x^{12} + x^{11} + x^{10} + x^8 + x^7 + x^5 + x^4 + x^2 + x + 1$$

15.7.6.2 Access Control   One of the many tasks of the Ethernet controller is handling contention over use of the bus. The access control protocol used for Ethernet is CSMA/CD. When the controller is in the process of transmitting a packet and senses that a collision has been detected by the transceiver module, the collision is enforced by continuing the transmission of the remainder of the packet. This is referred to as *jamming* the channel. Jamming the channel ensures that all *transmitting* stations involved in the collision sense the collision. Other transmitting stations follow the same procedure. As discussed in Section 15.3.2.3, the stations involved back off a random interval of time before attempting another transmission of the packet.

> **Jamming**
> The process of completing the transmission of a packet onto a communications channel even though a collision has occurred with another packet.

During the course of a collision, all receiving stations on the network continue to receive in their normal fashion. The data packets involved in the collision are fragmented because of the collision. Generally, they do not meet the minimal 72-byte frame size requirement for a packet and are discarded.

15.7.6.3 Manchester Encoding/Decoding   Because the Ethernet bus is a single coaxial cable used for half-duplex synchronous serial communications, a method of synchronizing to the serial data is necessary. No separate clock is provided on a separate line. Instead, the transmitted baseband signal is *Manchester encoded* by the Ethernet controller (Figure 15-33). Note that each bit interval has at least one transition regardless of the data bit pattern. The center of each cell contains a state transition. A LOW-to-HIGH transition represents a logic 1, and a

> **Manchester Encoding**
> A method of encoding a binary serial bit stream so that each bit interval exhibits at least one signal-level transition regardless of the data bit patterns.

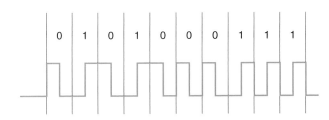

FIGURE 15-33
Manchester encoding.

HIGH-to-LOW transition represents a logic 0. Manchester encoding allows the receiving device to synchronize to the serial bit stream without the use of a separate clock. The synchronous serial bit stream is often referred to as *self-clocking*. Once the receiver has achieved synchronization with the bit stream, the serial data are then decoded.

> **Self-Clocking**
> Any digital signal that switches at least once with its bit rate, so that a separate clock is not required for synchronization.

15.8 IEEE 802.3a 10BASE2 THIN-NET SPECIFICATION

To reduce the cost of the Ethernet LAN system, the ANSI/IEEE 802.3 committee has defined alternative transmission media to the thick and expensive double-shielded coaxial cable specified in the original standard. The addendum to the standard, *IEEE 802.3a*, is the *10Base2* specification.

This standard widely used from 1985 to 1990, is also known as *Cheapernet, Thin-net*, or *Thinwire Ethernet*. The 10Base2 standard supports a 10-Mbps transmission rate and also uses Manchester encoding as its signaling technique. 10Base2 specifies the use of RG-58, 50-Ω characteristic impedance coaxial cable with the use of BNC-T-type connectors interfaced directly to the Ethernet controller *network interface card (NIC)* In contrast to 10Base5, the transceiver circuitry is built into the NIC card. This eliminates the expensive transceiver cable and module used in the traditional interface. It also eliminates the need to "tap" or drill into the coaxial Ethernet cable to install a network node.

> **Media Access Control (MAC) Address**
> A 48-bit address required for every device or node on a network. The MAC address resides in all NIC cards.

The NIC card, also used in 10BaseT, includes the *media access control (MAC)* address required for every device or node on the network. The MAC address, specified in *dotted hex notation*, is 48 bits (6 bytes) in length and has the structure shown in Figure 15-34. The first 3 bytes is the Vendor code, and the second three bytes is the serial number as given by manufacturers of the card. The IEEE standards organization issues the unique vendor code, and the manufacturer determines the value of the remaining 3 bytes. The combined 6 bytes produces a MAC address such that no two NIC cards on any network are duplicated. The MAC address is permanently stored in ROM (read-only memory) in every NIC card.

> **Dotted Hex Notation**
> A hexadecimal numbering notation that uses a dot or period to separate groups of hexadecimal characters.

Thin-net is extremely popular in the PC-based LAN environment. It uses the same 10-Mbps CSMA/CD protocol as the original Ethernet and offers the advantages of low cost per node, easy installation and maintenance, and ready availability of supporting hardware and software. Thin-net is a scaled-down version of Ethernet, however. Segment lengths are limited to 185 m instead of 500 m, and a maximum of 30 nodes can be placed on a segment instead of the 100 in Ethernet. Thin-net may also be more susceptible to noise than its 10Base5 counterpart, because its cabling technology and connection interface are not as robust. Still, there are a number of Thin-

FIGURE 15-34
The 48-bit MAC address format.

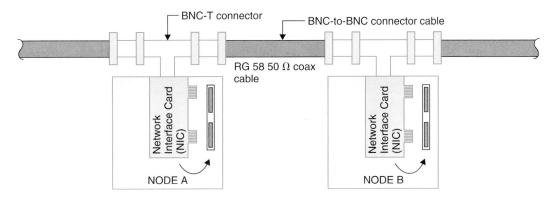

FIGURE 15-35
Ethernet 10Base5 Thin-net connection.

net LAN systems in use today, particularly in the office and laboratory environment. Figure 15-35 illustrates the 10Base2 Thin-net connection.

15.9   IEEE 802.3I 10BaseT SPECIFICATION

The most popular Ethernet connection standard today is 10BaseT. The "T" stands for *twisted-pair wire* (unshielded), or simply UTP. 10BaseT also conforms to the 10-Mbps CSMA/CD Ethernet protocol standard but uses a hub or switch that fans out the transmission media to its end-users in a star topology. The primary advantage of 10BaseT over 10Base5 and 10Base2 is that it uses inexpensive UTP cabling. Modular RJ45 telephone wall jacks and four-pair CAT (category) 3 through 5 UTP cabling wire are specified in the standard for interconnecting nodes to the LAN. The RJ45 connector plugs directly into the *network interface card (NIC),* which resides in the PC. Combinations of shielded twisted-pair wire (STP) and coax can also be combined. 10BaseT is ideally suited for stand-alone PC LAN systems. Advances in high-end technology are linking systems together and making 10BaseT much more appealing for LAN connectivity. Figure 15-36 illustrates the 10BaseT connection, and Table 15-8 compares the three specifications.

> **Network Interface Card (NIC)**
> An Ethernet or Token Ring adapter card designed to plug into a PC or notebook computer's bus expansion slot.

15.10   INTRODUCTION TO TOKEN RING

Due to the phenomenal growth of PC networking and internetworking, token ring networks like Ethernet have emerged as one of the most widely adopted media access and topologies today. Earlier in this chapter, we introduced the basic ring and star-wired ring topology (Figures 15-6 and 15-7). Figure 15-37 illustrates the ring topology showing the transmitter and receiver aspect of the node, and we now elaborate on the ring topology by presenting a short introduction to the *IBM Token Ring* standard.

15.10.1   Token Ring History

Although *Token Ring* has become synonymous with IBM, the IBM Corporation did not invent the concept of token passing on a ring topology. The token ring control principle was originally proposed by Professor E. Newhall in 1969 at the University

> **Token Ring**
> The LAN protocol that employs the passing of a token on a ring topology.

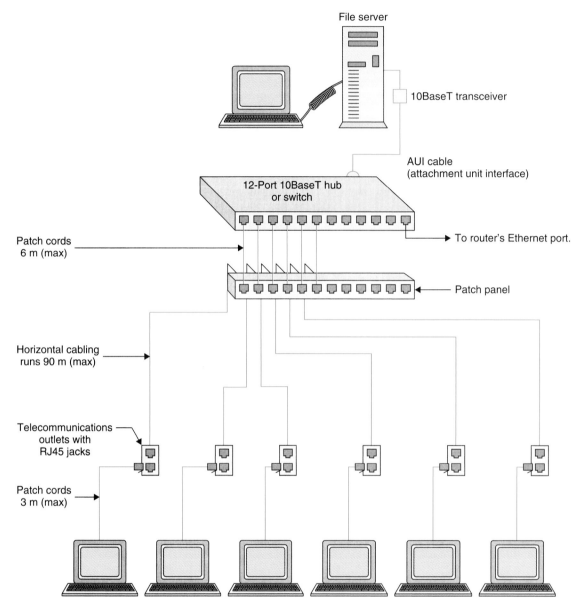

FIGURE 15-36
Ethernet 10BaseT Connection.

of Toronto. At the time, it was referred to as the *Newhall Ring.* The actual networking patent was filed by Olof Soderblom of the Netherlands.* Indeed, Soderblom was paid a large fee by IBM to clear the patent to make way for future development. It was not until 1985, however, more than a decade later, that IBM unveiled its high-speed *Token Ring* network. Its architecture is based on the Zurich Ring, which was developed at IBM's research facilities in Zurich, Switzerland. IBM representatives

---

*Frank J. Derfler, Jr., "Making Connections—The IBM Token-Ring Network," *PC Magazine,* January 13, 1987, pp. 227–241.

TABLE 15-8
Comparison of IEEE 802.3 Physical Specifications for 10Base5, 10Base2, and 10BaseT

	IEEE 802.3		
	10Base5 (Ethernet)	**10Base2 (Cheapernet)**	**10BaseT**
Access control	CSMA/CD	CSMA/CD	CSMA/CD
Topology	Bus (branching nonrooted tree)	Bus (branching nonrooted tree)	Star
Message protocol	Variable packet size	Variable packet size	Variable packet size
Signaling rate	10 Mbps	10 Mbps	10 Mbps
Signaling type	Baseband	Baseband	Baseband
Cable type	RG-8 thick double-shielded coax	RG-58 coax	CAT 5 UTP
Cable impedance	50 Ω	50 Ω	100 Ω
Minimum node separation	2.5 m	0.5 m	NA
Maximum segment length	500 m	185 m	100 m (PC to hub)
Maximum nodes per segment	100	30	1024 (per network)
Maximum number of segments	5	2	NA
Maximum station separation	2500 m	925 m	NA

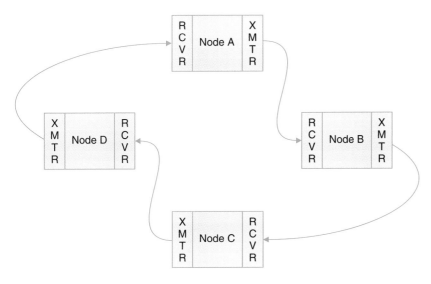

FIGURE 15-37
Basic token ring topology showing the transmitter and receiver sections of a node.

working in conjunction with IEEE and ISO committee representatives established the IEEE 802.5 and ISO 8802 Token Ring standard, which has become the most popular ring access technique used in the United States today.

When IBM introduced its Token Ring network, its objective was to produce an inexpensive, high-speed, baseband networking technology that would target the PC networking community supporting office communications, manufacturing, and computing centers. A 4-Mbps baseband transmission rate was specified in 1985. In 1989, IBM announced its 4- and 16-Mbps Token Ring. In addition to a major throughput improvement over the 4-Mbps version, the 16-Mbps Token Ring permits early release of the token and multiple frames to circulate the ring at the same time.

Several independent vendors began to supply Token Ring products to support the standard. The largest vendor today is *Proteon,* a U.S. manufacturer that produces a full range of Token Ring products.* Proteon develops Token Ring systems operating at 4, 10, 16, 80, and 100 Mbps. Proteon also sells a proprietary 10-Mbps Token Ring network, known as *ProNET-10* and a high-performance, 80-Mbps *ProNET-80* system that operates over optical fiber.** The IEEE 802.5 Token Ring specification calls for a baseband transmission rate of either 4 or 16 Mbps.

15.10.2 Token Ring Architecture

IBM's Token Ring architecture has a physical resemblance to a star. Stations are linked together to a central connection point, the *MAU* (multistation access unit), which acts as the hub of the network and connects up to eight nodes. The interface between the station and a MAU is called a *lobe*; that is, the connection forms a lobe. If more than eight nodes are used, the MAU must be connected to another MAU using its *Ring In* and *Ring Out* ports. The cable connecting two MAUs via its Ring In and Ring Out ports is called a *patch cable.* If the MAU to MAU connection runs throughout the building, the cable is called a *trunk cable.*

IBM specifies a maximum of 260 nodes using type 1 or type 2 cable. This means a maximum of 33 MAUs (8 nodes per MAU). If type 3 cable is used, no more than 72 nodes and nine MAUs is recommended. Although the network topology using MAUs appears to be a star, a close look at the internal circuitry of the MAU reveals that the electrical ring is preserved. For this reason, IBM's Token Ring LAN topology is referred to as a *star-wired ring.*

Figure 15-38 illustrates a 16-Mbps Token Ring network using type 1 cabling technology. The patch cables shown employ IBM data connectors at each end. The lobe cables employ IBM data connectors at the MAU interface and DB-9 connectors at the Token Ring controller card interface. The controller card is a plug-in card located in the PC.

Figure 15-39 illustrates a 4-Mbps Token Ring network using type 3 cabling technology. In contrast to the 16-Mbps system shown in Figure 15-38, the type 3 patch cables here use RJ11 jacks at the MAU interface. The lobe cables shown here have the recommended *media filters* built in-line to the type 3 cable. Medial filters are low-pass filters designed to reduce the noise on the line. They are recommended, because Type 3 cables are UTP and not STP (like type 1 cables).

Lobe
The interface cable between the computer station and a MAU in a Token Ring system.

Patch Cable
A UTP jumper cable used in Ethernet or Token Ring LANs.

Media Filters
Low-pass filters designed to reduce noise on the line in a Token Ring LAN.

---

*Hans-Georg Gohring and Franz-Joachim Kauffels, *Token Ring Principles, Perspectives and Strategies* (Addison-Wesley Publishing Company, 1992), pp. 58–59.

**John R. Abrahams, *Token Ring Networks Design, Implementation and Management* (Oxford, England: NCC Blackwell Limited, 1991), p. 13.

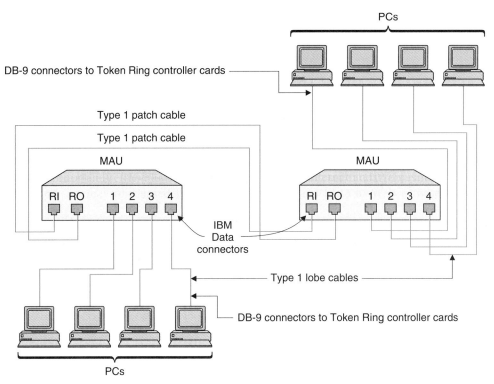

FIGURE 15-38
16-Mbps Token Ring LAN using type 1 cabling technology.

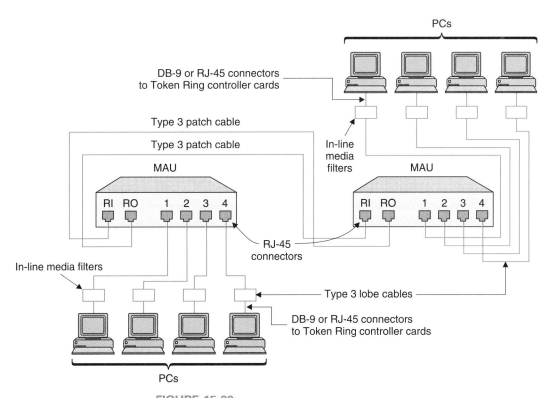

FIGURE 15-39
4-Mbps Token Ring LAN using type 3 cabling technology and media filters.

Starting delimiter (1 byte)	Access control (1 byte)	Ending delimiter (1 byte)

FIGURE 15-40
The 3-byte token format.

15.10.3   Token Ring Principle

The Token Ring architecture is based on the use of a single 3-byte frame or packet called a *token*. Figure 15-40 illustrates the token format. It consists of a *starting delimiter* byte, an *access control* byte, and an *ending delimiter* byte. The token circulates around the ring among stations when they are idle. When a station wishes to transmit data to another station on the network, it must wait until it receives the free token before it can transmit. On seizing the token, the station modifies the free token into a *dataframe*. This is done by setting a *busy bit* or, more specifically, the *T-bit* within the access control byte. Address, control, and data are appended to the new dataframe, and the dataframe is transmitted onto the ring and to the neighboring node. The dataframe circulates around the ring from node to node, with each node checking if the data has been addressed for it to receive. Once the intended node is reached, the receiving station copies the data from the dataframe into its memory bank and sets the *frame copied* bits (C-bits) within the *frame status (FS)* field, and then the dataframe is reasserted back onto the ring, where it circulates back to the original transmitting station. The structure of the dataframe is illustrated in Figure 15-41. Note that the dataframe also includes the starting delimiter, ending delimiter, and access control bytes used in the token.

Once the original transmitting station receives its own message back, it verifies that the station the message was intended for received it, and a new token is generated and asserted onto the network for the next station to use. If the message received is not the original message that was sent, however, an error has occurred. The message must be resent. Figure 15-42 shows an example of a message transmitted from node B to node D.

> **Differential Manchester Encoding**
> An encoding technique for binary serial bit streams in which a transition from a logic high to low or low to high occurs at the center of each cell, providing the self-clocking mechanism.

15.10.4   Differential Manchester Encoding

The signal coding technique used in Token Ring is called *differential Manchester encoding*. Differential Manchester encoding is an inherently reliable self-clocking technique. It differs from the Manchester encoding technique used in Ethernet in that it has the advantage of being differential. By this, we mean that it does not rely on the

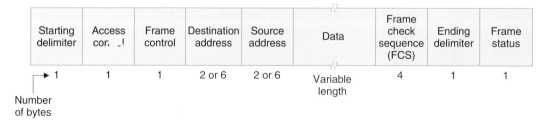

Starting delimiter	Access con__l	Frame control	Destination address	Source address	Data	Frame check sequence (FCS)	Ending delimiter	Frame status
1	1	1	2 or 6	2 or 6	Variable length	4	1	1

Number of bytes

FIGURE 15-41
The Token Ring dataframe format.

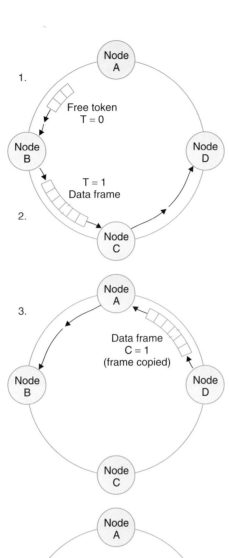

1. Free token circulating around ring. T = 0.

2. Node B seizes the free token so it may transmit dataframe to Node D.

3. Node D recognizes the addressed dataframe is intended for itself. It copies data into its buffer, sets the C bits to 1, and passes dataframe on.

4. Node B receives back its original dataframe and notes that its data was received by station D. It releases the free token for other stations to use the ring.

FIGURE 15-42
Token Ring example of node B transmitting a message to node D.

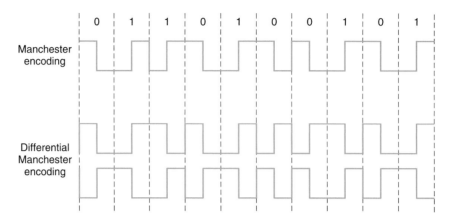

FIGURE 15-43
Manchester versus differential Manchester encoding.

absolute value of the signal level during the bit time of each cell. Instead, a logic level depends on whether a polarity change occurs at the beginning of the interval's cell boundary. A polarity change here represents a logic 0 for the next cell, and the absence of a polarity change represents a logic 1. This is illustrated in Figure 15-43, which also compares the difference between Manchester and differential Manchester encoding. Note that the differential Manchester encoded signal can be illustrated two ways, because it is a differential signal.

15.10.5 Token Structure

Because the token is used to regulate data transmission on the network, it is important to look at its structure so that we may better understand how stations on the network distinguish between the token and a dataframe. As stated, the token consists of 3 bytes: the starting delimiter, ending delimiter, and access control byte.

15.10.5.1 The Starting Delimiter Byte
The starting delimiter byte of the token and dataframe is shown in Figure 15-44. The two bits that most concern us are the *J* and *K* bits: positions 0, 1, 3, and 4. The remaining bits are a logic 0. The J and K bits are referred to as the *non-coded information bits* or *code violation bits*. Together, the J and K bits and their respective bit positions serve the unique function of identifying the beginning and end of the token. The J and K bits are also included in the ending delimiter byte. Because a dataframe also begins and ends with the starting and ending delimiter bytes, the dataframe is also readily identified.

D0	D1	D2	D3	D4	D5	D6	D7
J	K	0	J	K	0	0	0

FIGURE 15-44
The Starting Delimiter byte of the token and dataframe.

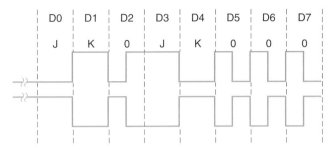

J: Positive code violation—no polarity change at beginning of cell
K: Negative code violation—polarity change at beginning of cell

FIGURE 15-45
The differential Manchester encoded starting delimiter bit stream illustrating the J and K code violation bits.

15.10.5.2   The J and K Code Violation Bits   A close look at the Manchester encoded signal shown in Figure 15-43 reveals a polarity change in the middle of each cell. Herein lies the key to identifying the beginning and end of the token and dataframe packet. For the cells representing the J and K bits within the starting and ending delimiters, there is no polarity change. This is called a *code violation,* hence the name *code violation bits* (or *non-coded information bits,* because do they do not represent data). More specifically, transmission of the J bit represents a *positive code violation,* where there is no polarity change at the beginning of the cell boundary. Conversely, the transmission of the K bit represents a *negative code violation,* where there is a polarity change at the beginning of the cell boundary. This is illustrated in Figure 15-45. In summary, the following rules apply to the differential Manchester encoded bit stream:

1. *Logic 0:* A polarity change at the beginning and center of the cell boundary.
2. *Logic 1:* No polarity change at the beginning of the cell boundary, and a polarity change at the center of the cell boundary.
3. *J:* No polarity change at the beginning or center of the cell boundary (positive code violation).
4. *K:* Polarity change at the beginning of the cell boundary, and no polarity change at the center of the cell boundary (negative code violation).

A code violation should occur only in the starting and ending delimiter's J and K bits; anywhere else results in an error condition the Token Ring system must correct. The beauty of this technique is that all receiving stations within the ring have a mechanism for framing the token and dataframe as well as for identifying a code violation error. Thus, the use for a special procedure, such as bit stuffing in High-Level Data Link Control (HDLC) or of data link escape characters (DLE) in BISYNC, is unnecessary.

15.10.5.3   The Ending Delimiter Byte   The structure of the ending delimiter byte of the token and dataframe is illustrated in Figure 15-46. Figure 15-47 illustrates the differential Manchester encoded bit stream. Note that the J and K code violation bits are included in the same bit positions as the starting delimiter byte. Two additional bits in the ending delimiter byte are not included in the starting delimiter byte; these include the *I* (intermediate frame bit) and *E* (error detected) bits. The I bit, when set,

D0	D1	D2	D3	D4	D5	D6	D7
J	K	1	J	K	1	I	E

FIGURE 15-46
The ending delimiter byte of the token and dataframe.

indicates to a receiving station that consecutive, related dataframes will follow the dataframe received. The E bit, when set, indicates to a receiving station that an error in the data stream has occurred, such as a code violation error. The station in the ring detecting the error sets the E bit.

15.10.5.4 The Access Control Byte

The third byte of the token is the *access control byte*. It is included in the dataframe as well. As its name implies, it is used for access and control of communications on the ring. Its format is illustrated in Figure 15-48.

There are four bits included in the access control byte's field: *P* (priority), *T* (token), *M* (monitor), and *R* (reservation). The three P bits in Figure 15-48 establish the priority of the token, and this permits eight levels of priority (2^3). Under the basic Token Ring priority scheme, a station wishing to transmit data to another station on the ring must wait for a token's priority level to be equal to or less than that of the dataframe it wishes to transmit. A station may also modify the priority bits depending on its application.

The T bit is simply used to identify if the received packet is a token or a dataframe. If the T bit is set, the packet is a dataframe; if the T bit is not set, the packet is a token. A station that seizes the token must set the T bit to a logic 1 before asserting its dataframe onto the ring. Once its dataframe circulates the ring to its destination and returns, it must reset the T bit to a logic 0 before releasing the token.

The M bit is used by the *ring monitor*. The ring monitor is a single station that monitors for error conditions in the ring. When the ring monitor receives a dataframe, it sets the M bit to a logic 1. If it receives a dataframe with the M bit set to 1, it means that the dataframe has circulated around the ring more than once and was not re-

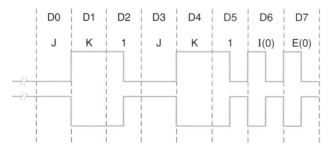

J: Positive code violation—no polarity change at beginning of cell
K: Negative code violation—polarity change at beginning of cell
 I: Intermediate frame bit (shown as 0).
E: Error detect bit (shown as 0).

FIGURE 15-47
The differential Manchester encoded ending delimiter bit stream.

D0	D1	D2	D3	D4	D5	D6	D7
P	P	P	T	M	R	R	R

P: Priority bits
T: Token bit
M: Monitor bit
R: Reservation bit

FIGURE 15-48
The access control byte of the token and dataframe.

moved. Under this condition, the ring monitor will purge the dataframe and create a new token to circulate around the ring.

The remaining three R bits may be used by stations to indicate the priority level of the next free token. A station may reserve a future token by setting the R bits within the received dataframe to a high priority. To do this, the received dataframe's reservation field must be less than the priority of the dataframe it wishes to transmit. In addition, the priority of the token that it receives must also be less than that of its own.

15.10.6 Dataframe Structure

When a station seizes the token for transmitting data to another station on a Token Ring network, the 3-byte token is appended with control and data and made into a dataframe, as shown earlier in Figure 15-41.* The starting delimiter, ending delimiter, and access control byte of the dataframe are identical to that of the token. The difference is six additional fields: the *frame control field, destination address, source address, data field, frame check sequence,* and the *frame status field.*

Frame Control   A 1-byte field that determines whether the dataframe is an *LLC* (Logical Link Control) frame or an *MAC* (Media Access Control) dataframe. The LLC and MAC are IEEE 802.2 specification layers that make up the data link layer of the ISO/OSI seven-layer model. An LLC frame is used to carry data, whereas a MAC frame is used for Token Ring control.

Destination Address   A 2- or 6-byte field that identifies the destination address of the dataframe.

Source Address   A 2- or 6-byte field that identifies the controller source of the dataframe.

Data Field   A variable-length data field with no preset size. It is limited by the system designer.

Frame Check Sequence   A 32-bit CRC code like Ethernet but using a different algorithm. It is used for error control and covers all fields except the Frame Status field.

---

*For a detailed explanation of the Token Ring priority scheme, see William Stallings, *Local and Metropolitan Area Networks,* 4th ed. (New York: Macmillan, 1993), pp. 196–200.

Frame Status   A 1-byte field that contains the A bit (address recognized) and C bits (2-frame copied bits). These bits indicate to the transmitting station that the address of the dataframe was recognized and data copied by the destination node.

15.11 THE LAN ENVIRONMENT

Most of our discussion of the LAN system thus far has been limited to the lower two layers of the ISO/OSI model: layer 1, the *physical layer*; and layer 2, the *data link layer*. Of equal importance are the upper layers of the OSI model and its relationship to the LAN environment. Layer 7, the *applications layer*, in particular, concerns it- self with the software that provides the end-user with applications programs. Layer 7 also addresses the end-user interface between applications, its supporting software, and the underlying hardware. Examples include DOS, OS/2, Windows NT, NetWare, VMS, and UNIX operating systems. Although it is not the intent of this book to ad- dress layer 7 and its relationship to the LAN, some fundamental concepts necessitate discussion. These include the LAN's software and hardware components in terms of network operating environments.

15.11.1 The LAN Server

In a LAN system, the *server* is typically a high-powered computer or workstation that shares its resources as a service to the network users, also referred to as *clients*. Resources can be hardware or software. The LAN relies on the server for virtually all communications. Therefore, the server in most LAN systems is dedicated to "serv- ing" the network. It cannot be used as a workstation. There are many types of servers. Figure 15-49 illustrates the LAN file server and print server.

> **File Servers**
> A program permitting users to access disk drives and other de- vices for storing and re- trieving common data- bases and applications.

Most network servers are *file servers*. A file server is a program that permits users to access disk drives and other mass storage devices for storing and retrieving common databases and applications programs.* Many servers can be configured on a LAN and do not necessarily have to reside within a dedicated workstation. A *print server*, for example, can be attached to the station designated as the file server, or it can be attached directly to the LAN or to any other computer on the network. Like the file server, the print server is a program that resides on the station or node that is associated with the service it renders. In this case, the service is providing the net- work users with shared access to the printing device. Other types of servers include terminal servers, FAX servers, high-speed modems (modem servers), compact discs or CDs (CD servers), and even *gateways* that provide services to other networks.** (Gateways are discussed in the next section.)

15.11.2 The LAN Client

> **Client**
> A station on the net- work permitting users to request the shared services provided by the network server.

A *client* is simply a station on the network that permits its user to request the shared services provided by the network server. Today's enormous number of PC users make up, by and large, the most common type of client on the network. Clients can also be multiple terminals connected to a terminal server.

---

*John E. McNamara, *Local Area Networks* (Burlington, Mass.: Digital Press, 1985), p. 93.

**Emilio Ramos, Al Schroeder, and Lawrence Simpson, *Data Communications and Network Fundamentals Using Novell Netware* (New York: Macmillan, 1992), p. 354.

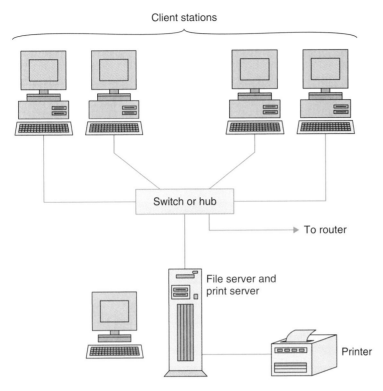

FIGURE 15-49
Client/server LAN system.

In a typical LAN, the client station does not have (nor does it need) the high-powered capacity of the workstation or mainframe computer used as the network server. Instead, the client utilizes the network server's hardware and software. Herein lies the advantage of the network. Clients need not have an expensive laser printer, CD-ROM drive, scanner, or plotter. The client station need not have the mass storage media of the LAN server for information retrieval. Instead of purchasing an applications program such as word-processing or computer-aided design (CAD) packages for each client station, a single network version of the program can be purchased with a site license for a predetermined number of client stations to use. The single program is then installed on the network's file server, thus making it available on the network. The client station sends a request for a particular applications program to the file server. In turn, the file server retrieves the program from disk and sends a working copy over the network to the client requesting the service. The process is transparent to the user, as if the user had a stand-alone copy of the program on his or her own disk. Clearly, the services provided by the LAN offer a much more cost-effective and efficient working environment.

> **Client/Server Network**
> A network in which the server is dedicated to serving the network clients and cannot be used as a workstation.

15.11.3   Client/Server Versus Peer-to-Peer Networking

There are basically two types of networks in terms of the network operating system: the *client/server network* and the *peer-to-peer network*. So far, our discussion has been

> **Peer-to-Peer Network**
> A network in which any workstation can be configured as a client, server, or both.

limited to the client/server network (Figure 15-49) in which the station acting as the file server is dedicated to running the network operating system and servicing the network. The server cannot be used as a workstation, which is a drawback. Another major drawback is that if the server on a client/server network fails, the service it provides to the network is no longer available to its clients. This could be catastrophic without some degree of fault tolerance built into the system.

An alternative approach to the client/server network is to have nondedicated servers. A workstation in this environment can be configured as a client, a server, or both a client and a server. This is referred to as a *peer-to-peer network.* Each station is said to have "peer" status. Figure 15-50 illustrates an example of a peer-to-peer network. Peer-to-peer networking is ideally suited for the small business or working environment and has gained tremendous popularity in recent years. For example, *LANtastic* is a peer-to-peer network operating system developed and marketed by Artisoft, Inc., of Tucson, Arizona. It is designed to support up to 300 PC stations on the network and operates over an IEEE 802.3 Ethernet LAN or a proprietary Artisoft system.* Another peer-to-peer network is Novell's *NetWare Lite,* which is designed to network from 2 to 25 PCs in a small business environment. NetWare Lite is also designed to operate over an Ethernet system. Any user can set up his or her station to share applications programs, directories, and printers. NetWare Lite is easy to administer, inexpensive, and does not require the extensive training and software installation task of a client/server-based system. However, one of the major drawbacks with peer-to-peer networks is security. Because the network can be managed from any PC on the network by virtually any user, files and directories can get corrupted as a result of poor management. Table 15-9 lists the advantages and disadvantages of the client/server network versus the peer-to-peer network.

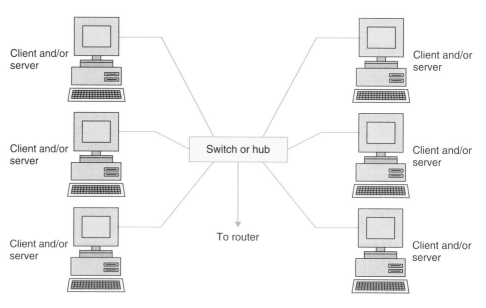

FIGURE 15-50
A peer-to-peer network system.

---

*Greg Nunemacher, *LAN Primer,* 2nd ed. (New York: M&T Publishing, 1992), p. 97.

TABLE 15-9
Client/Server Network versus Peer-to-Peer Network

Client/Server Network

Advantages	Disadvantages
—Security: Access rights to users and groups can be managed more effectively by a single system manager instead of several users on a peer-to-peer system.	—Critical Resource: If a server on a client/server system fails, clients may be without service.
—Accounting: User and group accounts can be managed much more effectively.	—Cost: Software, hardware, and training can be costly, especially for small systems.
—Cost: For large numbers of stations on the network and internetwork, client/server LANs are cost effective.	—Installation: The software installation is much more extensive than a peer-to-peer system.
—Fault Tolerance: In the event of a power failure, client/server software is designed to interact with an uninterruptable power supply (UPS) device for backup protection.	—Training: Extensive training is often required, including certification, to administer and maintain the network.

Peer-to-Peer Network

Advantages	Disadvantages
—Installation: Easy to install, with little or no training necessary. Intended for first-time PC network users.	—Security: Because the network is managed by its users, users may become careless and damage other users' files and directories. Servers are usually not in a remote and secure environment.
—Peer Status: Any client can be a file server and any server can be a client. Servers can be used as workstations and need not be dedicated servers to the LAN.	—Accounting: Several users administering the LAN may make accounting difficult to keep track of who gets rights and restrictions to the services of the LAN.
—Administration: Easy to administer without extensive training. The entire network can be managed from any PC.	—Speed: Not as fast as client/server-based systems, especially when a number of stations are requesting services from a single server.
—Shared Resources: Directories and files within directories for each station can be networked and readily shared. Printers and other peripherals on each station can also be readily shared.	

15.12 INTERNETWORKING THE LAN TO A WAN

In many cases, the resources shared among users of a LAN are either inadequate or can greatly be enhanced by internetworking with other LANs to form a WAN (wide area network), therefore, the goal of designing or upgrading many communication systems has been to extend the network beyond the LAN so that business employees, scientists, educators, students, and other users can be tied together in a common electronics workplace, regardless of geographic location.

An example of a WAN is the *Internet* and *World Wide Web,* a collection of thousands of computer networks spanning the globe linking universities, businesses, libraries, museums, government agencies, and more. *Internet service providers (ISPs)* such as *America Online, Prodigy, CompuServe,* and others provide an abundance of consumer services.

To link two or more LANs together for optimum performance, several factors need to be considered:

- Customer needs
- Bandwidth
- Protocol schemes
- Transmission media
- Applications
- Number of users
- Costs
- Future growth

It is necessary at this time to introduce the primary *internetworking devices* used to link LANs together. These include the *hub, bridge, switch, router,* and *gateway.* The function of each internetworking device can be best understood by considering its relationship with the ISO/OSI seven-layer model illustrated in Figure 15-51. Note that the bridge, router, and gateway encompass the layers below themselves and, therefore, serve multiple functions.

15.12.1 The Hub

The hub, also considered a *multiport repeater,* is the simplest internetworking device used to extend the LAN. As illustrated in Figure 15-51, the hub performs *physical layer* operations only. Its purpose is to prevent any ambiguity in the recognition of the transmitted bit stream by regenerating signals that have been attenuated and distorted, thus permitting the signal to be transmitted a greater distance. The hub does not perform any data link layer functions such as error control, addressing, or flow control. It can only be used to extend the network or link portions of the network that share the same architecture and channel access protocol.

Figure 15-52 illustrates how an Ethernet 16-port hub can be connected to form a small LAN. Signals sent to the hub from one of the host computers are regenerated and sent to all other ports on the LAN. Because the hub essentially collapses the Ethernet bus into a star topology, collisions can still occur when two or more hosts send data to the hub at the same time. Therefore, the entire network represents a single *collision domain.*

> **Collision Domain**
> An area on a network in which collisions are propagated throughout that area.

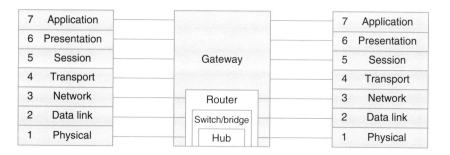

FIGURE 15-51
Functions of the repeater, bridge, router, and gateway in relation to the ISO/OSI seven-layer model.

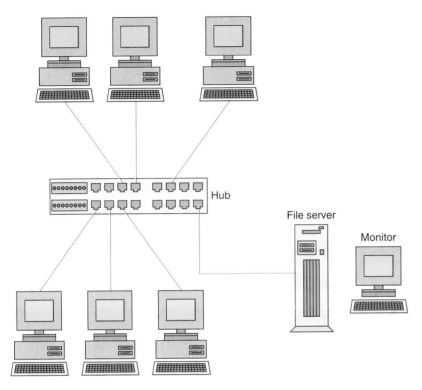

FIGURE 15-52
A small Ethernet network using a hub.

15.12.2 The Bridge

The *bridge* is an internetworking device that operates at the Data Link layer (layer 2) of the OSI model. Though becoming extinct in the wake of high-performance switches, the technology is still being used. The bridge is used to link LAN segments together that use the same protocol (e.g., two IEEE 802.3 Ethernet LAN segments). Figure 15-53 illustrates the bridge used to connect two local segments and two remote segments. Bridges operating remotely are typically connected by fiber-optic or wireless technology.

    Unlike the hub, which transmits frames to all connecting devices, the bridge filters frames based on their destination *MAC address*. This is the 48-bit address (see Figure 15-34) burned into the NIC card and used to uniquely identifiy the address of a host computer on the network. When a frame is transmitted on a local segment and its destination address is not on the same segment, the bridge will forward the frame to the connecting segment. This effectively reduces traffic on the network, thus providing better bandwidth utilization.

> **Bridge**
> A layer 2 internetworking device that links two or more LANs using the same protocol.

15.12.3 The Switch

The LAN *switch* has become increasingly important as an internetworking device. It operates at the Data Link layer (layer 2) of the OSI model. Like a bridge, a switch forwards frames based on MAC addresses. In fact, a switch is often referred to as a "multiport bridge." Each port on the switch, as shown in Figure 15-54, is a dedicated

> **Switch**
> A layer 2 or 3 internetworking device that switches packets from one port to another.

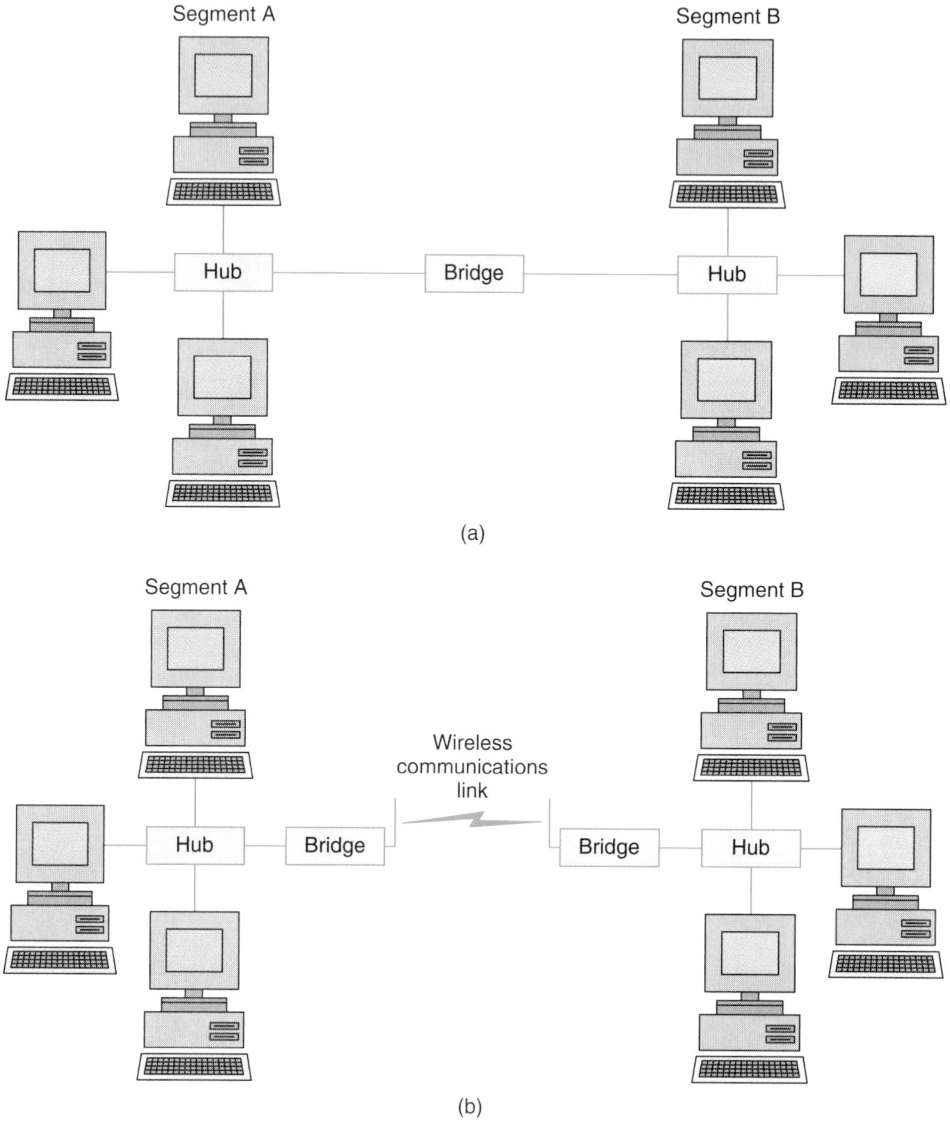

Segment A   Segment B

Hub — Bridge — Hub

(a)

Segment A   Segment B

Hub — Bridge — Wireless communications link — Bridge — Hub

(b)

FIGURE 15-53

The bridge connects LAN segments together and filters traffic based on destination MAC addresses: (a) local bridge; (b) remote bridges.

> **Microsegmentation**
> Each port on a switch being a dedicated 10-Mbps Ethernet segment.

10-Mbps Ethernet segment (or 100-Mbps Ethernet segment for 100-Mbps switches). This is referred to as *microsegmentation*. Five segments are shown here: Segments A through E. Each segment represents its own collision domain. With the exception of Segment E, all host computers connected to a switched port are collision-free, thereby offering 10-Mbps, full-duplex communication. Segment E is connected to a four-port hub. Because the hub is essentially a collapsed bus, the four host computers share Segment E and represent a single collision domain.

Switches perform their function by buffering or temporarily storing the incoming frame. Thus, memory is required along with a CPU. The switch is, therefore, programmable and menu-driven through a console port on the rear panel. As a frame enters a switch's port, its source and destination MAC addresses are read. The source address is time-stamped and stored in the switch's forwarding database called *content addressable memory (CAM)*. From these addresses, the switch learns each device on each port. The destination address is used to determine which port to send the frame. The system administrator can program the switch for three types of switching modes, which are defined as follows:

Content Addressable Memory (CAM)
The volatile memory in a switch that stores an incoming frame's source address and time stamp.

Store-and-Forward   In this switching mode, the entire frame is read by the switch and temporarily stored in its memory buffers so that a CRC (cyclic redundancy check) can be performed. The frame is discarded if there is an error; otherwise, it is forwarded to its destination port based on the frame's destination address and what the switch has learned from previous frames. This method of switching has the highest *latency* (propagation delay through the switch).

Latency
The propagation delay through a switch.

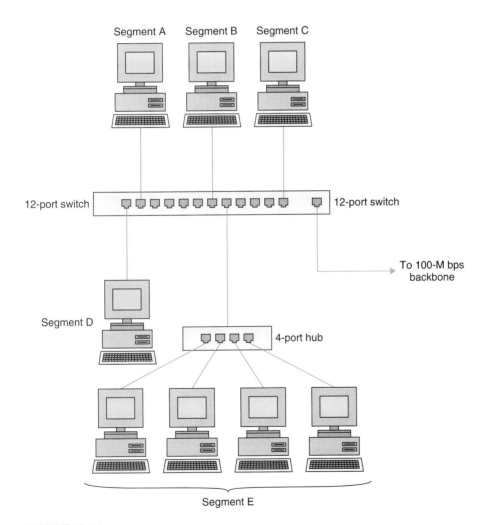

FIGURE 15-54
The Ethernet switch provides dedicated 10-Mbps (or 100-Mbps) bandwidth on each port and eliminates the impact of collisions through microsegmentation.

Cut-Through   In cut-through switching, the latency time through the switch is reduced. The switch accomplishes this by reading only the first 14 bytes of the Ethernet frame, as shown earlier in Figure 15-32. This includes the 7-byte Preamble, 1-byte Start Frame Delimiter (SFD), and the frame's 6-byte Destination Address. Once this information is received by the switch, the frame is immediately forwarded to the outgoing port based on the frame's destination address. The disadvantage with cut-through switching is that there is no CRC (error-control) check on the entire frame. Corrupted frames are forwarded to the output port of the switch. This includes frames with bit errors and *runt packets,* which are packets shorter than the minimum Ethernet frame size of 64 bypes and typically caused by collisions on the network.

> **Runt Packets**
> Packets shorter than the minimum Ethernet frame size of 64 bytes, typically caused by collisions on the network.

Fragment-Free   This mode of switching is a form of cut-through. Instead of reading the first 14 bytes of the frame, however, the first 64 bytes are read into the switch's buffer and immediately output to the appropriate ports. The theory behind this is that if a collision or runt packet is received by the switch, it will likely be within the first 64 bytes of the frame. Frames with less than 64 bytes are discarded by the switch. The latency time is slightly increased over cut-through switching but fragment-free switching offers the benefit of not forwarding runt packets onto the network and causing unnecessary congestion.

15.12.4   The Router

> **Router**
> An internetworking device linking two or more LANs using the same communications protocol.

The *router* adds another level of sophistication to internetworking equipment. It operates at the Network layer (layer 3) of the OSI model. Routers are used to connect two or more networks or subnetworks together, as illustrated in Figure 15-55. A *subnetwork,* or simply *subnet,* is a small network formed by dividing a larger network. This is commonly done to reduce network traffic, optimize the network performance, and simplify network management. Routers are configured by the network administrator to perform these tasks.

> **Subnet**
> A small network formed by dividing a larger network.

Because the router connects networks or subnets together, its must be capable of directing traffic on the network. The router uses various Layer 3 protocols to do this. Some of the more common ones are *IP (Internet Protocol),* Novell's *IPX, Appletalk,* and *DECNET.* These protocols are specifically called *routed protocols.*

> **Routed Protocols**
> Used to direct traffic on a network.

Another task of the router is to maintain routing tables between routers. Routing tables contain information on the best routes for passing information on the network. Protocols that maintain routing tables between routers are called *routing protocols.* Common routing protocols include *Routing Information Protocol (RIP), Open Shortest Path First (OSPF), Interior Gateway Routing Protocol (IGRP),* and *Enhanced Interior Gateway Routing Protocol (EIGRP).* The latter two are Cisco Systems proprietary protocols. Both routing protocols and routed protocols are typically configured by the network administrator via an RS-232 console interface on the rear panel of the router.

> **Routing Protocols**
> Used to maintain routing tables between routers.

15.12.5   The Gateway

> **Gateway**
> An internetworking device that interlinks LANs with different architectures.

The final component used for internetworking is the *gateway.* The gateway functions on all layers of the ISO/OSI seven-layer model by providing a complete hardware and software translation between networks that support entirely different architectures. It also permits the connection of a LAN to a host computer that supports a different protocol family. For example, a Novell-based PC network can be interconnected

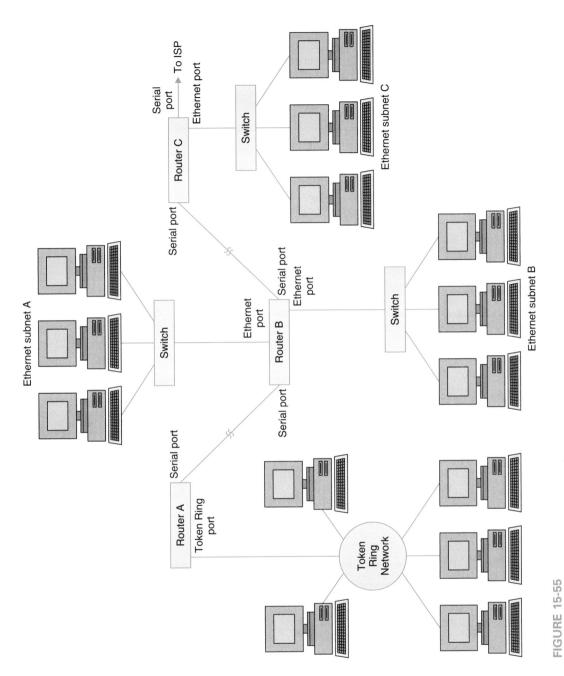

FIGURE 15-55

Routers are used to connect networks or subnetworks together. A Token Ring network is linked to three Ethernet subnetworks.

471

by a gateway to a network or a host computer system that supports IBM's proprietary SNA (Systems Network Architecture). Gateways are extremely complex devices but offer the most diversity in internetworking.

PROBLEMS

1. Define *LAN*.
2. Explain the function of a LAN.
3. Define *LAN topology*.
4. For a star LAN:
   a. What is the critical resource?
   b. How is this topology best utilized?
   c. What is a major disadvantage with this topology?
5. For a bus LAN:
   a. What is the critical resource?
   b. What is the distinguishing feature of this topology?
   c. What is a major disadvantage with this topology?
6. For a ring LAN:
   a. What is the critical resource?
   b. What is the distinguishing feature of this topology?
   c. What is a major disadvantage with this topology?
7. Explain a *collision*.
8. What is the advantage of slotted Aloha over pure Aloha?
9. Define *CSMA/CD*.
10. What is the purpose of jamming?
11. What is the round-trip propagation delay time between the farthest two nodes in a bus LAN referred to as?
12. When a token is passed in a ring LAN, why is a node limited in the length of time that it may possess the token?
13. In a slotted ring LAN, what is circulated around the ring instead of a token?
14. Distinguish between horizontal and backbone cabling.
15. Distinguish between a telecommunications closet and an equipment room.
16. Define *UTP*.
17. Define *STP*.
18. What are the five levels and categories of UTP cable?
19. Describe IBM type 1 cable.
20. What type of connector is used for 10BaseT?
21. What type of connectors are used with IBM's type 1 cable?
22. What are the connector types used for 10Base2 versus 10Base5?
23. What two methods of transmission are used in "wireless" LAN communications?
24. Explain the difference between a baseband LAN and a broadband LAN.
25. Define *CATV*.
26. What level of the ISO/OSI seven-layer model does Ethernet fall into?
27. For the original Ethernet 10Base5 standard:
    a. What is the topology used?
    b. What is the transmission rate?
    c. What is the maximum number of nodes that can be used?
    d. What is the maximum length of a segment?
    e. What is the slot time?
    f. What is the maximum length of a transceiver cable?
    g. How may a repeater be used to extend the length of the network?

28. Draw the Manchester encoded waveform if the bit pattern shown in Figure 15-33 were changed to 1011100101.

29. Repeat problem 28 for a bit pattern of 1100101011.

30. What is another name for 10Base2?

31. Explain what type of connector and transmission medium is used for Cheapernet.

32. What type of transmission medium is used for 10BaseT?

33. Explain the advantage of 10BaseT over 10Base5.

34. Define *MAU*.

35. What type of topology is used with IBM's Token Ring protocol?

36. What are the two transmission rates discussed for IBM's Token Ring protocol?

37. Explain the difference between a *client/server* network versus a *peer-to-peer* network.

38. What are the three switching modes on a switch?

39. What is a runt packet?

40. Explain at what layers of the ISO/OSI seven-layer model a repeater, bridge, router, and gateway operate.

16

THE INTERNET AND EMERGING TECHNOLOGIES

This chapter involves many of the concepts we have touched on previously so that we may expand our understanding of computer networking and internetworking and how it has evolved into the *Internet*. It establishes a basic understanding of the Internet, its history, and its evolution into the *World Wide Web (WWW)*. The *Internet protocol suite,* also know as the *TCP/IP (Transmission Control Protocol/Internet Protocol) protocol suite,* is also discussed. Finally, an introduction to emerging technologies is presented, emphasizing Asynchronous Transfer Mode (ATM), Integrated Services Digital Network (ISDN), and Synchronous Optical Network (SONET) technologies.

> **Internet**
> A collection of thousands of linked computer networks spanning the globe.

16.1 INTRODUCTION TO THE INTERNET

The Internet, a wide area network (WAN), is a collection of thousands of computer networks spanning the globe, thus making it possible for millions of users throughout the world to communicate with each other. Educational institutes, libraries, government agencies, research centers, on-line services, and businesses typify the kinds of networks that have been linked together throughout the world to form the Internet. The overwhelming growth of the Internet, now more than doubling in size each month, has resulted in the so-called "Information Superhighway." In addition to being an invaluable resource for researchers, educators, government officials, and librarians, the Internet has become an essential tool for individuals engaged in electronic mail, research, and virtually any activity involving the distribution and acquisition of information.

Millions of files, ranging from books and poetry to government archives and even compressed music and video, are now available over the Internet. Electronic mail, which has become one of the most popular uses of the Internet, can be sent to and received from virtually anyone around the world in a matter of seconds. The Internet has made it possible to develop professional contacts abroad, make new friends, and exchange information, thus forming new bonds that otherwise would have been difficult due to geographical barriers.

16.2 EVOLUTION OF THE INTERNET

ARPANET
Advanced Research
Projects Agency
Network, developed in
1969 by the U.S. Dept.
of Defense and to
which the origin of the
Internet can be traced.

The origin of the Internet can be traced to a U.S. Department of Defense (DOD) organization called the *Defense Advanced Research Projects Agency (DARPA)*, also known by its old acronym, *ARPA*. In 1969, ARPA developed a four-node packet-switched network called the *ARPANET (Advanced Research Projects Agency Network)*.* The network was intended to support military research on fault-tolerant computer networks. In the event of a nuclear war, the DOD wanted to ensure the reliable transmission of data even if parts of the network had been destroyed. The original transport layer protocol (layer 4 of the ISO/OSI seven-layer model) was called *NCP (Network Control Protocol)*. As the network grew in size, however, unreliable connections to the network prompted development of a new transport layer and network layer protocol called *TCP (Transmission Control Protocol)* and *IP (Internet Protocol)*, respectively. By 1978, the combination of these two protocols, called *TCP/IP*, became a DOD standard, and by January 1, 1983, TCP/IP was officially adopted on a network-wide basis. The ARPANET had become so successful that ARPA no longer considered it to be experimental and passed control of it over to the Defense Communications Agency (DCA). A mandate was issued by the DCA to split the ARPANET into two networks: *ARPANET*, for continued research; and *MILNET (Military Network)*, for unclassified military operations. The networks became available for academic research, government employees, and contractors. A geographical layout of the ARPANET is illustrated in Figure 16-1.

As local area networks became more and more prevalent during the late 1970s, the benefits of linking networks together for sharing resources became overwhelming. Many mainframe computers and supercomputers of that time were running

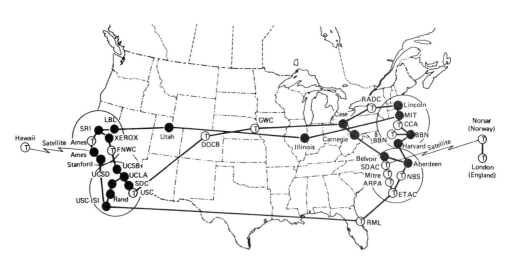

FIGURE 16-1

A geographical layout of the ARPANET in 1974. (From *Telecommunications and the Computer,* 2nd ed., by James Martin [Upper Saddle River, N.J.: Prentice-Hall, 1976], p. 90.) Reprinted with permission from the publisher.

*Smoot, Carl-Mitchell and John S. Quarterman, *Practical Internetworking with TCP/IP and UNIX* (Reading, Mass.: Addison-Wesley, 1993), p. 7.

UNIX,* a multiprograming, time-sharing operating system. Because the UNIX operating system supported the ARPANET's IP interface, host computers serving more co-ordinated networks were connected to the ARPANET and its rate of growth increased. Other internetworking entities began to form during the late 1970s and early 1980s. These included *UUCP* (Unix-to-Unix Copy Program), a worldwide UNlX-based communications network; *USENET* (User's Network); *CSNET* (Computer Science Network); and *BITNET* (Because It's Time Network).

It was not until 1986, however, that the dramatic growth of the Internet began. At that time, the *National Science Foundation (NSF),* which formed the *National Science Foundation Network (NSFNET),* linked five of its regional supercomputer centers together to provide a national high-speed backbone network across the United States. The world's fastest and most powerful computers were made available to the academic and scientific community. The NSFNET was based on the ARPANET's TCP/IP architecture. Now a user sitting at a terminal at Stanford University in California could log on to a host computer linked to the Internet and access a diverse collection of research archives at MIT (Massachusetts Institute of Technology). Hosts on the NSFNET provided gateways to other local and regional networks as well. The collection of these networks linked together to form an Internet was simply referred to as the "Internet." Each network's host computer shared (and still share) the common TCP/IP protocol suite. With time, the research work performed on the Internet replaced the role of the ARPANET, and in 1990, the ARPANET was officially decommissioned. Table 16-1 lists some of the major networks contributing to the growth of the Internet.

> **UNIX**
> A multiprogramming, time-sharing operating system.

TABLE 16-1

Major Networks Contributing to the Growth of the Internet

Acronym	Network Name	Year of Inception	Description
ARPANET	Advanced Research Projects Agency Network	1969	An experimental packet-switched network used to support military research for the DOD. The ARPANET was the precursor to the Internet. It served as the first transcontinental backbone network in the Internet before it was decommissioned in March 1990.
UUCP	UNIX-to-UNIX Copy Program	1978	A worldwide UNIX-based communications network used for sending data over a point-to-point connection using ordinary dial-up lines and a modem.
USENET	User's Network	1979	A network that provides a service called *network news*. News messages, called *articles,* are sent over USENET to all users subscribing to that particular subject or topic, called a *newsgroup.*

(continued)

---

*The UNIX operating system was developed in 1971 by Ken Thompson and Denis Ritchie at Bell Laboratories.

TABLE 16-1 *(continued)*

Acronym	Network Name	Year of Inception	Description
CSNET	Computer Science Network	1981	A network designed to facilitate the academic and research community using electronic mail. Ordinary dial-up lines and modems were used to connect to the network. CSNET was discontinued in 1991.
BITNET	Because It's Time Network	1981	A network that uses the NJE (Network Job Entry) protocol developed by IBM for its MV/370 operating system. Like the CSNET, BITNET supports the academic and research community with electronic mail and file transferring.
FidoNET	FidoNET	1983	A network invented to support personal computers running MS-DOS. Data is transmitted over a point-to-point connection using ordinary dial-up lines and a modem. The *Fido* (named after a dog) protocols are used for communications.
NSFNET	National Science Foundation Network	1986	The NSFNET is the most prominent of the Internet backbones providing connectivity to thousands of government, educational, and corporate networks throughout the world.
CREN	Corporation for Research and Education Networking	1989	An organization representing the merging of BITNET and CSNET
WWW	World Wide Web	1989	The birth of the World Wide Web is attributed to Tim Berners-Lee of the European Laboratory for Particle Physics (CERN) in Geneva, Switzerland.
NREN	National Research and Education Network	1991	A high-speed backbone network designed to provide U.S. academic and research institutes with supercomputer resources. Senator Al Gore sponsored a bill called the "High-Performance Computing Act of 1991." Signed into law in December 1991, the bill authorizes promotion of this high-speed network at Gbps speeds. The NSFNET is currently referred to as the *Interim NREN*.[a]
Intranet	Intranet	1996 to present	Emergence of *intranets* provides sites that link with corporate databases. An intranet is a corporate network infrastructure based on Internet standards. Its purpose is to link a company's employees and information together to improve productivity and information flow, (e.g., Human Resource policies, administrative functions, education, etc.).

[a]Tracey LaQuey and Jeanne C. Ryer, *The Internet Companion,* (Reading, Mass.: Addison-Wesley, 1993), p. 16.

16.3 INTERNET SEARCH TOOLS

A variety of Internet search tools have been developed to help one navigate the "Net." Although many of these tools have seemingly rendered themselves obsolete due to the advent of World Wide Web (WWW) "browsers," they are still extensively used as reference tools by the WWW. A brief explanation of some of the more popular tools follows.

File Transfer Protocol A program that allows its user to copy or transfer text, graphics, or video files from one computer to another across the Internet. The command structure for using file transfer protocol (FTP) requires a user to become familiar with its intricacies. Many FTP commands are similar to those used in the UNIX operating system, and they have been around for just as long. Table 16-2 lists some common FTP commands. Using an FTP file directory command, a user can enter directories on a remote computer and copy, delete, place, or modify existing files. To date, a broad range of databases and services can be accessed with FTP. A web browser can be used to access FTP sites by typing the URL (Uniform Resource Locator): *ftp://[ftp host site]*. For example, the National Center for Supercomputing Applications (NCSA) site address can be accessed from your web browser at *ftp://ftp.ncsa.uiuc.edu*

Anonymous FTP The use of FTP often requires a login name and password for the computer database located at the FTP site. Anonymous FTP allows a user to access public databases and archives without an account. When anonymous FTP is enabled at an FTP site, *anonymous* is given as the login name, and ftp will generally accept any string as a password. Usually, one enters their electronic-mail address for the password.

Telnet A terminal emulation protocol used to remotely log on to other host computers on the Internet. The host computer can be located in another city, state, or

TABLE 16-2
Common FTP Commands

Command	Description
account	Supply accounting or security information
ascii	ASCII mode (text-file transfers)
binary	Binary mode (binary-file transfers)
cd	Change directory on remote host
close	End FTP session, enter command mode
delete	Delete the named file on remote host
dir	List directory contents
get	Retrieve file from remote host
help	List available FTP commands
mget	Retrieve multiple files
name	User name
open	Connect to FTP host
password	User password
pwd	Print working directory
quit	End FTP session

country. Once a connection is made, it is as if you are directly connected. Telnet commands can be entered after the Telnet command prompt, which is the percent sign: %. Table 16-3 lists some common Telnet commands. Like FTP, Telnet requires that you log on to the remote computer and navigate through the various resources with UNIX-based commands. Telnet host servers can also be accessed via the WWW by using the URL: *telnet://[remote computer name]*. For example, the U.S. Government's Information Infrastructure Task Force can be accessed at the URL: *telnet://iitf.doc.gov*

Gopher   An information service program developed at the University of Minnesota, home of the "Golden Gophers." The Internet Gopher program was designed to "Gopher" things, hence the name *Gopher*. Gopher allows its users to access information databases throughout the world (often referred to as *Gopher space*) without having to use special names, addresses, or commands. Instead, Gopher is menu driven. To access a Gopher server, the system you are connected to must have a Gopher client program. The command *gopher* is simply typed in, and a main menu appears. Menu commands allow you to navigate Gopher space: some common Gopher commands are listed in Table 16-4. Gopher servers can also be accessed via the WWW using the URL: *gopher://[gopher server name]*. For example, information about the University of Minnesota Gopher server can be accessed at the URL: *gopher://gopher.tc.umn.edu*

Veronica   Veronica stands for *Very Easy Rodent-Oriented Net-wide Index to Computerized Archives.* It is a keyword search program designed at the University of Nevada and is used exclusively as a Gopher aid in searching through Gopher space. Veronica constructs a simplified indexed database from all of the Gopher site menus that have been accessed. Veronica itself is accessed through the Gopher menu. When an Internet search is made from a Veronica-generated database, the user is automatically connected to the Gopher server from which the choice was originally made.

Archie   A file and directory search program developed at McGill University in Canada. Archie automatically interrogates host servers across the Internet on a regu-

TABLE 16-3
Common Telnet Commands

Command	Description
close	Close current session
display	Display operating parameters
help	List available Telnet commands
logout	Logout user and close connection
mode	Character or line mode
open	Connect to host
quit	Exit Telnet
send	Transmit special characters
set	Set operating parameters
status	Display status information
toggle	Toggle operating parameters
z	Suspend Telnet
?	Display help information

TABLE 16-4
Common Gopher Commands

Command	Description
m	Mail file to yourself
n	Find next search item
q	Quit Gopher
Q	Quit Gopher unconditionally
s	Save current item to a file
u	Go up to previous menu
/	Search for item in menu
?	Help menu
<SP>	Advance one page

lar basis and updates its own database directory with files available on other Archie servers. Archie servers can be accessed via an Archie client or a Telnet connection—for example: *telnet archie.rutgers.edu*

WAIS   Pronounced "ways" or "wase," *Wide-Area Information Services* is based on the ANSI 739.50 standard for requesting bibliography information within the library and computing community. WAIS was developed jointly by Apple Computer, Thinking Machines Corporation, and Dow Jones.* It is a text-searching engine that allows you to search and retrieve text files, called *sources,* from the vast resources of the Internet. This includes scientific, government, and private databases as well as Usenet newsgroups. Unlike Gopher, you must have a computer running a WAIS client program to access a WAIS server on the Internet. WAIS can be accessed via Gopher or other Gopher information servers. The WAIS help screen typically offers information on how to navigate through the various directories, and UNIX editor commands are used for moving about the page.

16.4 DOMAIN NAME SYSTEM

The *Domain Name System* (*DNS*) is a method of mapping domain names and IP addresses for computers linked to the Internet. The system was developed in 1986 to replace a central registry of IP addresses used to identify host computers connected to the ARPANET. The DNS structure is an hierarchical tree consisting of *domains.* A domain is a node and its descendent nodes on a network. A *domain name* is the unique name of a particular node within the domain, and domain names are made up of *subdomains,* which are nodes leading to a particular node. Subdomains are separated by a period. For example, in the domain name *ncsa.uiuc.edu,* the host computer *ncsa* is located at the *uiuc* campus (University of Illinois at Urbana Champaign). The root node, *edu,* is at the top of the hierarchy. Table 16-5 lists various types of Internet domains used in the United States, and Table 16-6 lists various international domains.

> **Domain Name System (DNS)**
> A method of mapping domain names and IP addresses of computers linked to the Internet.

> **Domain Name**
> The unique name of a particular node within the domain.

---

*Mark Gibbs and Richard Smith, *Navigating the Internet* (Carmel, Ind.: Sams Publishing, 1993), p. 126.

TABLE 16-5
U.S. Internet Domains

Domain	Description
com	Commercial organization
edu	Educational institute
gov	Government organization (excluding military)
int	International organization
mil	Military organization
net	Network or service provider
org	General organization other than above

TABLE 16-6
International Internet Domains

Domain	Description	Domain	Description
af	Afghanistan	in	India
ao	Angola	ir	Iran
ar	Argentina	iq	Iraq
am	Armenia	ie	Ireland
au	Australia	il	Israel
at	Austria	it	Italy
be	Belgium	jp	Japan
bm	Bermuda	kp	North Korea
bo	Bolivia	kr	South Korea
br	Brazil	kw	Kuwait
ca	Canada	ly	Libya
cl	Chile	my	Malaysia
cn	China	mx	Mexico
co	Columbia	ma	Morocco
cr	Costa Rica	nl	Netherlands
cu	Cuba	nz	New Zealand
cz	Czechoslovakia	ng	Nigeria
dk	Denmark	no	Norway
ec	Ecuador	pk	Pakistan
sv	El Salvador	pa	Panama
et	Ethiopia	py	Paraguay
eg	Egypt	pe	Peru
fi	Finland	ph	Philippines
fr	France	pl	Poland
de	Germany	pt	Portugal
gr	Greece	pr	Puerto Rico
hk	Hong Kong	ro	Romania
hy	Hungary	su	Russia
lc	St. Lucia	tn	Tunisia

(continued)

TABLE 16-6   *(continued)*

Domain	Description	Domain	Description
sa	Saudi Arabia	tr	Turkey
sn	Senegal	ua	Ukraine
sg	Singapore	ug	Uganda
sk	Slovakia	ae	United Arab Emirates
sl	Slovenia	uk	United Kingdom
za	South Africa	us	United States
es	Spain	va	Vatican
lk	Sri Lanka	ve	Venezuela
se	Sweden	vg	Virgin Islands (British)
ch	Switzerland	vi	Virgin Islands (U.S.)
sy	Syria	vn	Vietnam
tw	Taiwan	yu	Yugoslavia
th	Thailand	zr	Zaire

16.5 ELECTRONIC MAIL

Electronic mail, more commonly referred to as *e-mail,* is the single most widely used application of the Internet. Most business associates, educators, and scientists have their e-mail addresses printed on their business cards. E-mail over the Internet permits you to converse with millions of people around the world without having to wait for your message to be sent and received via the postal system. With e-mail, users can send and receive text, program files, and even graphical images.

> **E-Mail**
> Allows users to send and receive text, program files, and graphics. Also known as *electronic mail.*

The transmission of e-mail over the Internet is based on the *store and forward* principle of message switching discussed in Chapter 14. An immediate connection between end-users is not necessary. Instead, e-mail messages are sent from one host computer on a network to another in a store-and-forward manner similar to the U.S. Postal Service. A letter sent via the U.S. Postal Service must have a correct address written on the envelope. It is then placed in a mailbox, where it is essentially stored until it is picked up by a postal worker and transported to the post office. Here, it is sorted by zip code and stored again for transport to a location closer to its destination. The procedure continues in a store and forward manner until the letter reaches its destination. In general, the farther its destination, the longer it takes for the letter to be sent. The same is true for e-mail.

Host computers or servers that are used for e-mail and file transfers are referred to as *application gateways.* They perform the process of connecting two different protocol suites (TCP/IP and IBM's SNA) so that messages are properly transported to their destination.

The underlying key to sending e-mail successfully is having the correct e-mail address. An e-mail address is an extension of the DNS system described earlier, and it is appended with a prefix that identifies the personal name of the end-user. The "at" symbol, @, is used to separate the end-user from the domain name. For example, the e-mail address of the author is *warren_hioki@ccsn.nevada.edu* where *warren_hioki* is the end-user and *ccsn.nevada.edu* is the domain name.

16.6 THE WORLD WIDE WEB

World Wide Web (WWW)
A global information system combining text, graphics, and sound on a series of user-friendly, computer-displayed documents.

The explosion in personal use of the Internet among millions of ordinary people all over the world can be attributed to that part known as the *World Wide Web (WWW),* or simply the *Web.* The Web was originally developed by Tim Berners-Lee in 1989 at the European Laboratory for Particle Physics (CERN) in Geneva, Switzerland. His original intent was aimed at the high-energy physics community: to develop a global information system that combined text, graphics, and sound on a series of computer-displayed documents called *web pages.* Embedded into the Web page are *hypertext* or *hypermedia* documents, which are underlined text or highlighted graphical icons. By simply pointing and clicking (with your mouse) on hypertext or hypermedia, a link is made to that particular resource document, which can also lead to the pathways of other hypertext links.

Web Page
A computer-displayed document to be read and used as a cross-reference to other documents on the WWW through hypertext or hypermedia links.

The concept of the Web became a major project at CERN with one major goal in mind: to develop a simplified, user-friendly network where information from many sources could be accessed from anywhere in the world with one universal program. The developers at CERN would eventually cause the Web to embrace most previously networked information systems such as FTP, Gopher, Archie, Veronica, and Usenet. *Web browser* programs like *Viola, Cello,* and *Lynx* added fuel to the fire. It was not until 1993, however, that the Web became widely accessible outside of the scientific and academic communities. In that year, Marc Andreesen of the National Center for Supercomputing Applications (NCSA) developed the first graphical interface web browser program, called *Mosaic.*

Hypertext
Highlighted, underlined text or icons embedded into a Web page providing links to other Web pages or information.

On July 7, 1994, in Cambridge, Massachusetts, a major international initiative to develop a universal computer framework for the global information society was announced by European and American governments and educational leaders.* The combined efforts of MIT and CERN were to further the development and standardization of the Web to make the world computer network easier to use for research, commercial, and future applications.

16.6.1 Navigating the World Wide Web

Navigating the Web requires the use of a program called a *client.* The client software provides the communications protocol to interface with the various host computers on the network. It must be installed in the computer that is used to access the Web. The host computer is called the *server,* and the server provides the documents requested by the client. Servers are connected to other clients and servers on the network, so a client-server relationship exists between a user, the client, and his or her connection to the Web (the server).

To fulfill a client's request for documents, the server communicates with other servers on the Internet until it finds the source of the requested document. The document is then retrieved and sent back to the client using *TCP/IP,* the communications protocol used by the Internet.

Internet Service Provider (ISP)
The Internet server to which a client is linked.

The Internet server that a client is linked to is called an *Internet Service Provider (ISP).* For a monthly or an hourly fee, ISPs provide users access to the Internet and

---

*The CERN/MIT Initiative, *International Initiative for Universal Framework for Information Web,* July 7, 1994, *http://www.lcs.mit.edu/lcs/consortium.html*

the Web. Some of the larger bulletin board systems (BBS), commonly referred to as *commercial on-line services,* also provide full Internet access via the client's modem connection. These include *Prodigy, CompuServe, America Online, Delphi, GEnie,* and others.

16.6.2 Web Browsers

The more common name for client software is called a *Web browser.* A Web browser is a program that permits its user to navigate the Web by accessing Web documents that have been coded in a language called *HyperText Markup Language (HTML).* HTML was invented by Tim Berners-Lee at CERN. Documents written in HTML are plain-text ASCII files that can be generated with a text editor. They reside on the Web server and can be identified with an *.html* or a *.htm* extension. The Web browser program translates the HTML document into a *Web page.* Several commercially available HTML editor programs can be used to simplify the generation of an HTML document. Several primers on HTML can be found at the U.S. Government URL: *http://www.ncsa.uiuc.edu* (type in *html* in the search window).

> **Web Browser**
> A program permitting users to navigate the WWW by accessing Web documents coded in HTML.

> **HyperText Markup Language (HTML)**
> The language used for coding Web pages.

Several Web browsers are used to navigate the Web. One of the most popular is *Netscape Navigator,* developed by Netscape Communication Corporation. Figure 16-2 illustrates the Netscape's home page. Netscape Navigator is the first commercial offshoot of Mosaic, the U.S. Government's (NCSA) Web browser. Netscape Navigator, like many Web browsers, is designed to provide full access to the Internet and the Web. This means that it can effectively load the requested data for displaying text or graphic still images, viewing animated video files, or listening to sound files. These types of files can be identified by the following extensions:

Text:

- .txt (Simple text)
- .asc (ASCII)
- .rtf (Rich Text Format)
- .src (WAIS source file)
- .pdf (Portable Document Format, Adobe)

Graphic still images:

- .gif (Graphics Interchange Format, CompuServe)
- .jpeg (Joint Photographic Experts Group)
- .tiff (Tagged Image File Format)
- .bmp (Bit-mapped, Microsoft Windows)
- .ps (PostScript)
- .eps (Encapsulated PostScript)

Audio files:

- .au (Audio file)
- .aiff (Apple sound file)
- .snd (Sound file)
- .ul (μ-Law)
- .wav (Waveform, Microsoft)
- .voc (Vocal file)

FIGURE 16-2

Netscape's home page: *http://home.netscape.com* (Courtesy of Netscape Communication).

Video files:

- .mpeg (Motion Picture Experts Group)
- .mpeg2 (Motion Picture Experts Group 2)
- .cgm (Computer Graphics Metafile)
- .dvi (Digital Video Interactive)

Web browsers can also be used to download files into your computer from remote servers around the world, send and receive e-mail, access USENET newsgroups, and search for and retrieve information over the entire Internet and Web using the latest *search engines* (discussed later). Some popular and historic Web browsers are:

- Lynx
- Mosaic
- Cello
- Viola
- MacWeb
- Microsoft Explorer
- IBM WebExplorer
- NetManage Chameleon
- Netscape Navigator

16.6.3   The Web Page

As stated, the Web page is designed to be read and used as a cross-reference to other documents on the Web through use of hypertext or hypermedia links. The term *page,* however, is a misnomer. Although it may resemble a magazine page with text, graphics, and even video animations, the Web page has no fixed size in length or width. These parameters are defined by the HTML document.

> **Home Page**
> A more specific Web page acting as an introductory page or home base for navigating the WWW.

A more specific type of Web page is called a *home page.* A home page acts as an introductory page or home base for navigating the Web. It is the principal page through which a person, business, educational institute, and so on wants to be represented on the Web. The home page typically includes links to other Web pages or sites.

There are two basic types of home pages: a *client home page,* and a *server home page.* A client home page is a document that first appears when you start up your Web client program, such as the Netscape Navigator home page.* It provides a home base for navigating the Web. A server home page typically represents the organization providing the service. Resources from its own database are provided to the client as well as links to other resources on the Internet using Internet and Web tools called *search engines.*

> **Uniform Resource Locator (URL)**
> The unique addresses of all Web pages and Internet resources allowing users to retrieve documents from the Internet server.

16.6.3.1   Uniform Resource Locator   All Web pages and Internet resources have a unique address called a *Uniform Resource Locator,* or *URL.* There are well over 50 million Internet URLs as of this writing. A URL is analogous to a card catalog number referencing a library book. It permits its user, through use of a client program, to

---

*Shannon R. Turlington, *Walking the World Wide Web* (Research Triangle Park, N.C.: Ventena Press, 1995), p. 9.

retrieve documents from the Internet server. Examples of URL Web documents include:

http://www.weather.com	(The Weather Channel)
http://www.media.mit.edu	(MIT Media Lab)
http://www.moma.org	(Museum of Modern Art)
http://www.sports.com	(Sports.Com)

The first part of the URL specifies the protocol *http,* which stands for *HyperText Transport Protocol.* This is the Web's main protocol for transporting HTML documents between clients and servers. The colon and two slashes follow the protocol. The *www* and remainder of the URL (after the two slashes) indicate you are accessing a Web server in search of a particular file and also its path, which is specified after any single slashes. The Library of Congress Home Page and URL is shown in Figure 16-3.

Telnet, Gopher, FTP, and USENET sites can also be addressed with a URL. Some examples include:

telnet://downwind.sprl.umich.edu.3000	(Univ. of Michigan Weather Underground Service)
ftp://ftp.ncsa.uiuc.edu	(NCSA's Anonymous FTP Server)
gopher://gopher.adrc.wustl.edu/	(The Alzheimer Gopher Site)
news:comp.infosystems.www.users	(USENET Newsgroup)

FIGURE 16-3

Library of Congress home page: *http://lcweb.loc.gov*

16.6.4 Web Search Engines

The most common tool used for navigating the Web is called a *search engine*. Search engines are programs used to search for virtually any form of intelligence imaginable. Whether you are seeking information on butterflies, cancer, Peruvian cooking, connector and cabling standards, employment opportunities, modern art, the address and telephone number of a long-lost friend or business, or any other imaginable subject, chances are you can find it with one of the thousands of available search engines.

> **Search Engine**
> The most common tool for navigating the WWW and search for intelligence.

Access to search engines are provided by ISPs and commercial on-line services. When a connection to the Web is first established, the home page typically has the ISP's proprietary search engine and may list links to other popular engines, such as *Yahoo, Lycos, Alta Vista,* and *WebCrawler,* to name a few. Table 16-7 lists some popular Web search engines; more search engines can be found by simply typing "search

TABLE 16-7
Popular Search Engines and Their URLs

Name	URL	Description
Alta Vista	*http://www.altavista.digital.com*	Keyword search engine for searching the Web or newsgroups
AT&T Toll Free Internet Directory	*http://www.tollfree.att.net*	Search for toll-free 800 numbers
Better Business Bureau	*http://www.econet.apc.org/cbbb/ webindex.html*	U.S. and Canadian business information search
Bible Gateway	*http://www.gospelcom.net/bible*	Bible search
Books On-Line	*http://www-cgi.cs.cmu.edu/cgi-bin/ book/titlesearch*	Database of books on-line
FedEx Airbill Tracking	*http://www.fedex.com/track_it.html*	Tracks FedEx shipments
FindLaw	*http://www.findlaw.com/index.html*	Search engine for legal text
Infoseek	*http://www.infoseek.com*	Web, Usenet newsgroups, select sites, site categories, e-mail addresses, Reuters news, and web FAQs keyword search
Library of Congress	*http://lcweb.loc.gov/harvest*	Search engine for Library of Congress Web pages and LC MARVEL Menus.
Lookup USA	*http://www.lookupusa.com*	People and businesses national directory, and classified directory. Has credit ratings for most business listings
Lycos	*http:/www.lycos.com*	Web keyword search
National Mortgage Loan Directory	*http:/www.mortgageloan.com*	Search for interest rates on the Internet
Nebula Search	*http://members.gnn.com/mochaman/ nebsearch.html*	Sci-fi search utility on the Internet

(continued)

TABLE 16-7 *(continued)*

Name	URL	Description
OncoLink	*http://oncolink.upenn.edu*	Search site of cancer-related subjects
PharmInfoNet	*http://pharminfo.com/search_pin.html*	Search for information on medicinal drugs
Security APL Quote Server	*http://www.secapl.com/cgi-bin/qs*	Get stock quotes by entering a ticker symbol
Sports.com	*http://www.sports.com*	Basketball, baseball, football, tennis, boxing, soccer, etc.
Switchboard	*http://www.switchboard.com*	A complete residential and business numbers U.S. directory
THOMAS.REGISTER	*http://www.thomasregister.com:8000*	U.S. companies search
U.S. Patent Database Access	*http://patents.cnidr.org:4242/access*	Searching interface of the U.S. Patent Database
USA Today	*http://167.8.29.8/plweb-cgi/ixacct.pl*	*USA Today* news search
WebCrawler	*http://www.webcrawler.com*	Web keyword search engine
Yahoo	*http://www.yahoo.com*	Search engine that is category oriented
Yahoo Finance	*http://finance.yahoo.com*	Get stock quotes
Yahoo Shopping	*http://shopping.yahoo.com*	Thousands of stores and millions of products for sale.

engine" on any category-oriented search engine's search field. Figure 16-4 illustrates Yahoo's search engine Web page.

Because of the vast amount of information available on the Web, using search engines can be a tiresome process. A particular subject may result in over 1 million matches from sites all over the world. Most search engines provide tips on how to search a particular subject more effectively. For example, using quotation marks around the subject or phrase can filter out many undesirable resources. Boolean logical operators can also be used to focus your search. In the following examples, the Boolean logic operators are capitalized for emphasis only; they do not need to be capitalized in your search.

Using quotation marks:	**"microprocessors"** will filter out resources on computer, data communications, and other technically unrelated subjects
Logical AND:	**italian AND french cuisine** will search for resources having both Italian AND French cuisine in their pages.
Logical OR:	**transistors OR transistor testers** will broaden your search to include resources with transistors OR transistor testers
Logical NOT:	**bees NOT honey** will limit your search to bees and filter out any resources on honey

16.7 CONNECTING TO THE INTERNET

There are several ways of gaining access to the Internet. Most businesses, educational institutes, and government agencies provide unlimited access to the Internet and the

FIGURE 16-4
Yahoo's Web page: *http://www.yahoo.com* (Reprinted with permission from Yahoo!)

Web for e-mail and business or educational correspondence. Because of the large volumes of data that are transferred to and from the Internet by these organizations, a high-speed communications link is necessary between the server and the local area network supporting its clients. Common layer 2 WAN protocols are used. They include ATM, BISDN, T-carrier, Frame Relay, and others.

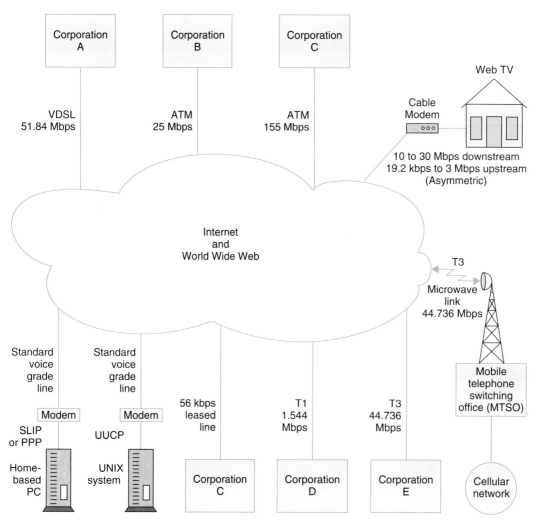

FIGURE 16-5
Common types of Internet connections.

Most home connections to the Internet use the standard voice-grade telephone lines connected to a modem and a personal computer. A commercial on-line service or ISP provides the Internet service for a monthly fee. In most cases, a *SLIP (Serial Line Internet Protocol)* or *PPP (Point-to-Point Protocol)* connection is necessary for the home connection. That is, the client software must support the SLIP or PPP communications protocol used to encapsulate IP datagrams or packets. The PPP is a more recent protocol that corrects many of the deficiencies in SLIP. Figure 16-5 illustrates various connections to the Internet.

> **TCP/IP**
> Transmission Control Protocol/Internet Protocol, which describe the movement of data between host computers.

16.8 INTRODUCTION TO TCP/IP

Since the development of the ARPANET, TCP/IP has emerged as a worldwide inter-networking communications architecture. It is implemented in computers of all sizes and makes, not only within the United States but throughout the world. It has become the language of the Internet.

TCP/IP is more than just the two protocols: *Transmission Control Protocol,* and *Internet Protocol.* These two protocols alone describe the movement of data between host computers on an Internet. The protocol in its entirety, however, is a *suite* consisting of a multitude of protocols that provide for reliable communications across the Internet and the Web. We now describe the TCP/IP protocol suite as an architectural development of *layers,* with each layer being responsible for a different facet of communication.

16.8.1   TCP/IP Layering

Networking protocols are typically described in layers, with each layer defining or categorizing some element of the communication process. A defined set of layers provides a model that serves as a common basis for the development and refinement of standards. It permits the designers of hardware and software systems to divide the complex task of developing reliable communication systems into smaller, more manageable elements. The interconnection of new and existing systems is greatly simplified as well. Equipment manufacturers can develop new products based on the overall layered reference model. Furthermore, because each layer decouples the function of the adjacent layers, a change in standards or technology will not dramatically affect existing users of the communication system.

The TCP/IP protocol suite is traditionally described as a five-layer communications system, although some models separate the *data link* and *physical layer,* thus making it a five-layer system. Like the ISO/OSI seven-layer model, each layer serves a different function and depends on the lower layer's functional interaction with the network. Figure 16-6 compares the TCP/IP protocol suite with the ISO/OSI seven-layer model. The two architectures are similar from the transport layer down. The differences are primarily in the upper layers, where TCP/IP architects have viewed the presentation and session layers as an integral part of the applications layer and combined them into one layer, called the *applications layer.*

Applications Layer   The TCP/IP applications layer defines the services that are suitable for various applications that make use of the network. These include some of the following protocols:

Lynx
Mosaic
Netscape Navigator
Telnet: remote login
FTP: File transfer protocol
SMTP: Simple mail transfer protocol
SNMP: Simple network management protocol
RLOGIN: Remote login protocol
NFS: Network file system
NTP: Network time protocol
BOOTP: Boot protocol
TFTP: Trivial file transfer protocol
DNS: Domain name system
LPR: Line printing protocol

7	Application
6	Presentation
5	Session
4	Transport
3	Network
2	Data link
1	Physical

(a)

4	Application and Process	Lynx, Mosaic, Netscape Navigator, Telnet, FTP, SMTP, SNMP, RLOGIN, NFS, NTP, BOOTP, TFTP, DNS, LPR, etc.
3	Transport	TCP, UDP
2	Internet	IP, ICMP, IGMP
1	Network Interface (Data link and physical layer)	Ethernet, Token Ring, Token Bus, ISDN, ATM, FDDI, Frame Relay, etc. (Various)

(b)

FIGURE 16-6
(a) ISO/OSI seven-layer model; (b) the TCP/IP Internet protocol suite.

Transport Layer   The transport layer for TCP/IP, like that in the ISO/OSI model, ensures reliable and efficient end-to-end transportation of data between host computers for the layer above it. Two different protocols are used in this layer:

TCP: Transmission control protocol
UDP: User datagram protocol

TCP provides for the reliable flow of data between host computers or two user processes. It is designed to provide for error control and recovery, time-outs for lost packets of data as well as connection setups and close-down between hosts, and segmenting the data passed to it from the applications layer into the appropriate format for the network layer below. In contrast, UDP provides the applications layer with a much more simplified service requiring less overhead. UDP simply arranges the data into packets called *datagrams,* and it tries to deliver the datagrams between hosts without any guarantee the data will reach its destination. In some environments, this is desirable. Reliability must be provided by the applications layer.

Internet Layer   The Internet layer is often referred to as the *Internet Protocol (IP) layer.* **IP** provides the basic datagram service of routing packets around the network and is implemented in all computers on the Internet. The main task of the IP is the addressing of computers as well as the fragmentation and reassembly of datagrams.

IP makes a "best effort" at moving data to its destination, but it contains no function for end-to-end message reliability. Four additional services are provided by the IP layer:

ICMP: Internet control message protocol
IGMP: Internet group message protocol
ARP: Address resolution protocol
RARP: Reverse address resolution protocol

ICMP and IGMP permit diagnostic, control, and error messages to be sent between Internet nodes; ARP and RARP are used to report error conditions and control network congestion.

Network Interface Layer   The TCP/IP *Network Interface Layer* includes the lower two layers of the ISO/OSI seven-layer model, the *Data Link Layer,* and the *Physical Layer.* They are defined as follows:

Data Link Layer   The TCP/IP data link layer defines the formatting, framing, and sequencing of data placed on the network by the network interface card (NIC). The TCP/IP protocol suite operates independent of the data link layer, thus enabling it to run on virtually any network, including the following:

- Ethernet
- Token Ring
- ISDN
- ATM
- Fiber Distributed Data Interface (FDDI)
- Frame Relay

Physical Layer   The physical layer defines the electrical and mechanical interface between hosts on the Internet. This includes the cabling system (fiber, copper, or wireless) and electrical signaling. TCP/IP has been designed to operate independent of the type of physical and electrical media used. Layers 1 and 2 are not defined by TCP/IP Requests for Comments.

16.8.2   Request for Comments

The official TCP/IP standards are based on publications for the Internet community called *Request for Comments (RFCs).* RFCs originated in the days of the ARPANET, when protocols were being developed and members were requesting and exchanging ideas. They are developed and published by the standards organizations listed in Table 16-8. E-mail is used to publish, exchange comments and ideas, and to update drafts of RFCs over the Internet. There are currently thousands of RFCs, all numbered in the order in which they are drafted. For example, *RFC 1157* specifies the *Simple Network Management Protocol (SNMP):* the standard Internet protocol for accessing common TCP/IP management information on network nodes. The size of an RFC can range from less than a page to several hundred pages. Not all RFCs are standards, however. They may be for informational purposes only. A detailed list of RFCs can be obtained at the URL: *http://www.cis.ohio-state.edu/hypertext/information/rfc.html*

> **Request For Comments (RFCs)**
> Publication for the Internet community on which official TCP/IP standards are based.

TABLE 16-8
TCP/IP Standards Bodies[a]

Acronym	Standards Body	Description of Body
ISOC	Internet Society	A professional, nonprofit international organization that promotes global use of the Internet for research and scholarly communication.
IAB	Internet Activities Board	The overall design and technical review board for the Internet. The IAB serves as the final editorial board for the publication of RFCs
IETF	Internet Engineering Task Force	A subgroup of the IAB that originates and develops the TCP/IP protocols and specifications for Internet standards.
IRTF	Internet Research Task Force	A subgroup of the IAB responsible for long-term Internet research projects.
IESG	Internet Engineering Steering Group	Designed to aid the IETF in recommendations and standards.
IRSG	Internet Research Steering Group	Designed to aid the IRTF in research.

[a]For a more detailed discussion of Internet standards bodies, see Smoot, Carl-Mitchell and John S. Quarterman, *Practical Internetworking with TCP/IP and UNIX* (Reading, Mass.: Addison-Wesley, 1993), pp. 23–36.

16.9 INTRANETS

Intranet
A corporate network infrastructure based on Internet standards.

An emerging network paradigm arising out of the enormous growth of the Internet is the *intranet.* An intranet is a corporate network infrastructure based on existing Internet standards.* The purpose of the intranet is to link a company's employees and information together to improve productivity through the efficient flow of information disseminated over the intranet. Figure 16-7 illustrates the concept of the intranet.

16.9.1 Common Uses of the Intranet

There are numerous justifications for an intranet. For example, most companies need to distribute vast amounts of internal documents to their employees. These include everything from personnel directories to Human Resource policies, newsletters, memorandums, department schedules, and even software upgrades. By making this information available to employees over the intranet, most hard-copy procedures and dissemination of information in the traditional manner is eliminated. That is, a "paperless workforce" is justified through cost savings and efficiency. Some common uses of intranets are:

- Department scheduling
- Education and Training
- Human Resource policies
- Job postings
- Company events

*http://ip.com/html_docs/info/found_intro.html, *What is an Intranet?* (Intranet Partners, 1-19-97).

- Purchasing
- Sales
- Annual reports
- Product literature
- Marketing
- Inventory control
- Software distribution/upgrades
- Company safety procedures
- Security/firewall protection

16.9.2 Firewalls

Though the premise of the intranet is to support sharing of corporate information within a limited or well-defined group, some information, such as products and services, are often shared with the general public over the Internet. Thus intranet sites have rapidly become commonplace over the Internet and World Wide Web.

Figure 16-7 shows that the distinguishing feature of the intranet is the information within itself is predominantly restricted to company employees. This is accomplished through the use of a *firewall*. A firewall is an intranet security system designed to limit Internet access to a companys' intranet. A firewall is analogous to a corporate "ambassador" acting between the intranet and Internet. It permits the flow of e-mail traffic, products and services, job postings, and so forth while restricting unauthorized access to private information residing on the intranet.

Unfortunately, the Internet is plagued with hackers and vandals that continually break into networks, stealing or destroying confidential files containing trade secrets and confidential information. Therefore, a corporate decision to connect its network to the Internet requires careful planning between the network administrator and corporate management. A firewall consultant is often required.

Firewalls are implemented with routers and *proxy servers*. A proxy server is a firewall component that controls how internal users access the outside world (the Internet) and how Internet users access the internal network. In some cases, the proxy blocks all outside connections and only allows internal users to access the Internet. The only packets allowed back through the proxy are those that return responses to requests from inside the firewall. In other cases, both inbound and outbound traffic are allowed under strictly controlled conditions.

> **Firewall**
> An intranet security system designed to limit Internet access to a company's intranet.

> **Proxy Server**
> A firewall component that controls how internal users access outside networks and how outside users access the internal network.

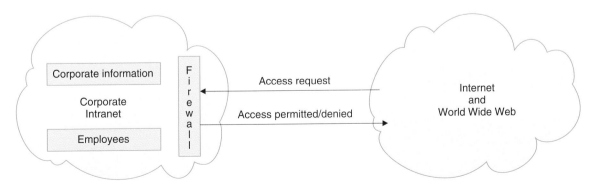

FIGURE 16-7
The intranet connection to the Internet and World Wide Web.

Screening Router
The most basic firewall, which uses access lists to permit or deny traffic.

Access List
A sequence of logical statements configured into the router.

The most basic firewall is implemented with a *screening router*, which operates at the Network and Transport layers of the OSI model. The screening router provides packet filtering through use of *access lists*, which are sequences of logical statements configured into the router by the system administrator. Access lists permit or deny traffic in and out of the router's I/O (input/output) ports based the IP address of the traffic and the type of application being transported.

Firewalls are also implemented with proxy servers acting as gateways that work at a higher level of the OSI model. The proxy-server gateway provides more opportunities for monitoring and controlling access between networks. It acts like a middleman, relaying messages from internal clients to external services. The proxy service changes the IP address of the client packets to, essentially, hide the internal client to the Internet, then acts as a proxy agent for the client on the Internet. Using proxies reduces the threat from hackers who monitor network traffic to glean information about computers on internal networks, because the proxy hides the addresses of all internal computers. Traditionally, using proxies has reduced performance and transparency of access to other networks. However, current firewall products solve some of these problems.*

No matter how sophisticated an organization's firewall, it can never offer 100% protection against hackers and traitors who operate from within the organization or outside of the organization. Furthermore, firewalls cannot keep out most viruses.

16.10 EMERGING TECHNOLOGIES

As scientists continue their research and development (R&D) of new technologies and refine existing technologies, the general public and private sectors reap the benefits from their labor. There are adverse effects to R&D, however. The technological growth it fosters continues to spawn new technologies, new standards, and new equipment that must adhere to these standards. No sooner does one technology achieve global acceptance before another, more advanced technology arrives with the potential to displace it. This global competition in the marketplace has left many industry leaders uncertain and cautious about emerging technologies. Furthermore, with technology changing so rapidly, working people must enhance their skills continuously to remain productive in the workforce. This will remain a way of life for many of us.

During the past decade, several emerging technological standards in telecommunications have gained the acceptance of equipment manufacturers serving the needs of the community. Each of these telecommunication standards has its unique advantages and disadvantages over one another, depending primarily on the user's application. There is no long-term assurance for any standard to prevail. Among the more widely recognized communication standards are:

- ATM
- ISDN
- SONET
- DSL
- FDDI
- Fibre channel
- Frame relay
- SMDS

---

*Tom Sheldon, "General Firewall White Paper," *tec.ref.com*, November 1996, *http://www.ntresearch.com/firewall.htm*

Together, these standards form an infrastructure that experts believe will provide a flexible, unifying set of communication protocols capable of carrying multimedia information at a wide range of speeds across a variety of communications platforms. These include *local area networks (LANs)* and *wide area networks (WANs).*

16.10.1 ATM

Most experts believe that in the forthcoming years, a new technology called *Asynchronous Transfer Mode (ATM)* will profoundly change the communication industry. In 1992, this new telecommunications technology exploded from virtual obscurity to one that will likely change the basic structure of the PSTN. Standards are currently being developed by ITU-TS (Study Group XVIII) to enable equipment manufacturers and local exchange carriers (LECs) to unleash several new ATM products and switching services.

> **Asynchronous Transfer Mode (ATM)**
> A high-speed form of packet switching.

16.10.1.1 The ATM Network ATM is a high-speed form of packet switching developed as part of the *Broadband Integrated Services Digital Network (BISDN).* It is intended to be carried on the *Synchronous Optical Network (SONET)* and serve needs that revolve around corporate private networking. Figure 16-8 illustrates a paradigm of an ATM network. Experts believe the ATM network will gradually displace private leased T1 facilities and customer switching equipment. Traditional analog or digital TDM switches used to route traffic through the network use a central processor (ESS) to establish the proper path through the switch. In contrast, ATM switches will be built using self-routing procedures in which individual *cells* consisting of user data will find their own way through the ATM switching network on the fly using their own address rather than having an external process establish a path.

ATM uses the concept of *virtual channels (VCs)* and *virtual paths (VPs)* to accomplish the routing of cells. A VC is a connection between communicating entities. It may consist of several ATM links between LECs. All communications occur on the VC, which preserves cell sequence. In contrast, a VP is a group of VCs carried between two points and may consist of several ATM links. Further details of ATM network operations and switching is far beyond the scope of this book. We will, however, introduce the format of the ATM cell for purposes of comparing structure and definition with the other protocols discussed.

16.10.1.2 The ATM Cell Header ATM transmits short, fixed-length packets called *cells.* As shown in Figure 16-9, each cell is 53 bytes in length and is comprised of two parts: a 5-byte *Header Field* containing address and control information, and a 48-byte *Information Field* containing the user's data. The Information Field can represent digitized voice, data, image, and video. Individual cells can be mixed together and routed to their destination via the telecommunications network.

ATM and its high transmission speeds will provide a boost to fiber-optic installation. Thus far, the transmission speeds agreed on by the *ATM Forum** are 45,

---

*The *ATM Forum* was founded in 1991 by Adaptive, Cisco, Northern Telecom, and Sprint. Its membership currently includes over 120 firms.

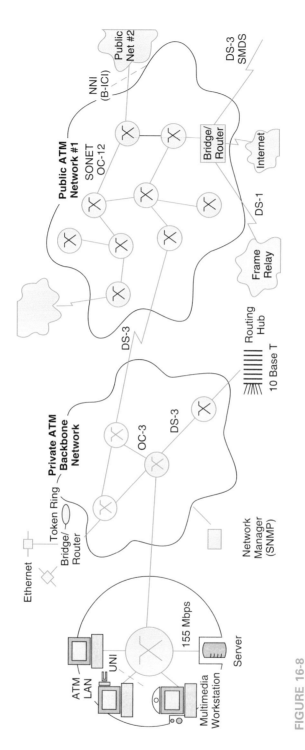

FIGURE 16-8

Paradigm of an ATM network. (Courtesy of Agile Networks, Inc.)

53-Byte ATM cell
Header field
(5 bytes)
Information field
(48 bytes)

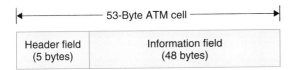

FIGURE 16-9
ATM cell structure.

100, and 155 Mbps, which matches the SONET OC-3 rate.* Transmission rates are currently used up to 622 Mbps and will continue to rise as computer speeds increase.

The heart of the ATM communications process lies in the content and structure of the cell. The ATM cell contains all of the network information for relaying individual cells from node to node over a pre-established ATM connection. The *Header Field* of the cell, which includes the first five bytes of the cell, has been designed for addressing and flow control. Its role is for networking purposes only. The format of the Header Field is illustrated in Figure 16-10, and its various fields are defined as follows:**

Generic Flow Control Field (GFC) The first four bits of the first byte controls the flow of traffic across the user-network interface (UNI) and into the network.

Virtual Path Identifier (VPI)/Virtual Channel Identifier (VCI) The next 24 bits, which include the second half of the first byte, the second and third bytes, and the first half of the fourth byte, make up the ATM address.

Payload Type (PT) The first three bits of the second half of the fourth byte specify the type of message in the payload. The 3-bit code is encoded into one of eight types ($2^3 = 8$) of payloads. Types 0 to 3 are reserved at this time for identifying the type of user data. Types 4 and 5 indicate management information, and types 6 and 7 are reserved for future definition.

Cell Loss Priority (CLP) The last bit of the fourth byte indicates the eligibility of the cell for discard by the network under congested conditions. The CLP bit is set by the user. If set, the network may discard the cell depending on traffic conditions.

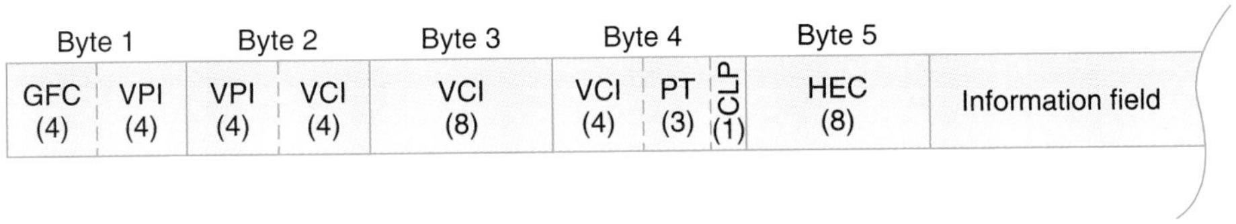

Byte 1
Byte 2
Byte 3
Byte 4
Byte 5
GFC (4)
VPI (4)
VPI (4)
VCI (4)
VCI (8)
VCI (4)
PT (3)
CLP (1)
HEC (8)
Information field

FIGURE 16-10
ATM 5-byte header field structure.

*Michael Fahey, "ATM: The Choice of the Future?" *Fiber Optic Product News,* May 1993, p. 21.

**The following cell information was compiled with permission from Jim Lane, *Asynchronous Transfer Mode: Bandwidth for the Future* (Norwood, Mass.: Telco Systems, 1992), pp. 18–20.

Header Error Control (HEC)   The fifth and final byte of the Header Field is designed for error control. The value of the HEC is computed based on the four previous bytes of the Header Field. The HEC is designed to detect header errors and correct single-bit errors within the Header Field only. This provides protection against the misdelivery of cells to the wrong address. The HEC does not serve as an entire cell check character.

16.10.1.3 The ATM Information Field

The 48-byte Information Field of the ATM cell contains the user's data. Insertion of the user's data into the cell is accomplished by the upper half of layer 2 of the ISO-OSI seven-layer model. This layer is specifically referred to as the *ATM Adaptation Layer (AAL)*. It is the AAL that gives ATM the versatility to carry many different types of services from continuous processes like voice to the highly bursty messages generated by LANs, all within the same format. Because most users' data require more than 48 bytes of information, the AAL divides this information into 48-byte segments suitable for packaging into a series of cells to be transmitted between endpoints on the network. There are five *types* of AALs:

Type 1: Constant Bit Rate (CBR) Services   This AAL handles T-Carrier traffic like DS0s, DS1s, and DS3s. This permits the ATM network to emulate voice or Digital Signal (DS) services.

Type 2: Variable Bit Rate (VBR) Timing-Sensitive Services   This AAL is currently undefined but reserved for data services requiring transfer of timing between endpoints as well as data (e.g., packet video).

Type 3: Connection-Oriented VBR Data Transfer   This AAL transfers VBR data (i.e., bursty data generated at irregular intervals) between two users over a pre-established connection. The connection is established by network signaling similar to that used by the PSTN. This class of service is intended for large, long-period data transfer, such as file transfers or backup, and provides error detection at the AAL level.

Type 4: Connectionless VBR Data Transfer   This AAL provides for the transmission of VBR data without pre-established connections. It is intended for short, highly bursty transmission as might be generated by LANs.

Type 5: Simple and Efficient Adaption Layer (SEAL)   This new and well-defined AAL offers improved efficiency over type 3. It serves the same purpose and assumes that the higher layer process will provide error recovery. The SEAL format simplifies sublayers of the AAL by packing all 48 bytes of the Information Field with data.

16.10.1.4 The Future of ATM

ATM is already beginning to find its way into LECs throughout the world. With most major players in the computer networking industry working on ATM products, the evolution of ATM looks promising, but not without obstacles. ATM technology as it stands today faces many of the bottlenecks that any new technology faces. These include the high initial costs of ATM equipment, installation, training, and more. Many analysts believe that the expense of converting to ATM technology will not be justified unless multimedia catches fire throughout the general public and private sectors. However, most of these obstacles are only because ATM is new. Prices are expected to come down dramatically in the next few years, which will speed the development of this revolutionary technology.

16.10.2 ISDN

ISDN stands for *Integrated Services Digital Network.* ISDN was developed in the 1970s by Bellcore (Bell Communications Research, Livingston, N.J.) and marketed by the seven Bell operating companies (BOC). It was progressively standardized by ITU-TS in 1984. Its purpose is to provide a set of standardized interfaces and signaling protocols for delivering integrated voice and data over a standard telephone line. By ordering ISDN services through the local telephone company, custom ISDN telephones, computers, FAX machines, and more can be used to send and receive digital signals simultaneously on dial-up to any accessible location in the world via the telephone network. As users of the PSTN become more and more committed to non-voice communications (i.e., computer data, facsimile, video, and graphics information), the all-digital network will soon prevail. This is the basic premise behind the major thrust toward ISDN.

> **Integrated Services Digital Network (ISDN)**
> An ITU-TS standard providing a standardized interface and signaling protocol to delivering integrated voice and data via the PSTN.

16.10.2.1 Architectural Overview Figure 16-11 compares the traditional data connection to the PSTN with the ISDN interface. In the traditional connection, data originating from terminal or host computer (DTE) must be transformed to an analog signal through the use of a modem. The analog signal is then transported to another end-user, whose modem reconverts the analog signal to digital data for computer and terminal use. A more efficient process is the ISDN connection shown. Here, the signals originating from digital sources remain digital throughout the network. Terminals and computers connect directly to an ISDN digital line. Even the analog voice signal is digitized by the ISDN telephone being placed on the network.

16.10.2.2 Equipping Subscriber Loops with ISDN Most major PBX (Private Branch Exchange) vendors offer ISDN interfaces that are used in business facilities today. However, the deployment of a standard ISDN interface to residential customers over the existing two-wire facilities has been slow, primarily due to the limited bandwidth of the telephone lines. These lines, by and large, have been designed to accommodate the analog voice signal only. ISDN signals are digital and require a greater

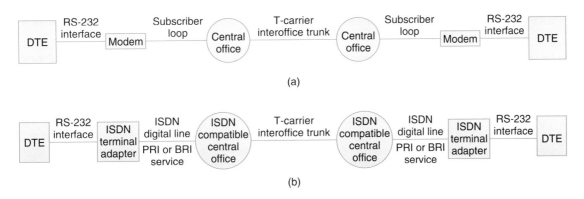

FIGURE 16-11
(a) Traditional and (b) ISDN data connection to the PSTN.

bandwidth than the 3.1 kHz (300–3400 Hz) available over the standard switched voice-grade lines. Unfortunately, the loading coils used in the subscriber loop that have been designed to minimize losses within this frequency range have an abrupt increase in loss above 3400 Hz. This loss plays havoc with phase and amplitude characteristics of the ISDN signal. To provide ISDN basic rate services to the home, existing subscriber loops must be modified in the following manner:

1. Loading coils must be removed in the loop.
2. Digital echo cancellers must be used on both ends of the loop.
3. High-grade, twisted-pair telephone cables must be used.
4. Central office amplifiers and repeater amplifiers should be designed for ISDN signals.

16.10.2.3   BRI Versus PRI   Figure 16-12 illustrates how the ISDN system provides end-to-end digital connectivity to a myriad of user services. There are two standard ISDN interfaces: the *Basic Rate Interface (BRI),* and the *Primary Rate Interface (PRI).* The BRI delivers ISDN services to the subscriber over a standard twisted-pair telephone line.* The BRI carries two 64-kbps B (Bearer)-channels for voice, data, or video and one 16-kbps, packet-switched, D (Delta)-channel that carries user packet data and call-control messaging. B-channels always operate at 64 kbps and carry end-user voice, audio, video, and data. The primary purpose of the D-channel is to exchange signaling messages necessary to request services on the B-channel. The D-channel is also used for packet switching and low-speed telemetry at times when no signaling is waiting.** For user services requiring additional bandwidth for high-speed transmission, *H-channels* are used. H-channels carry multiple B-channels at rates of 384 kbps (H0: 6 B-channels), 1536 kbps (H11: 24 B-channels), and 1920 kbps (H12: 30 B-channels). They are used for audio, video and graphics conferencing, business television, and other high-speed applications. Table 16-9 lists the various ISDN channel types, their transmission rates, and applications.

The PRI is an ITU-TS–defined ISDN trunking technology that delivers ISDN services to digital PBXs, host computers, and LANs. PRI interconnections illustrated in Figure 16-12 are made up of digital "pipelines" or "pipes" capable of carrying multiple trunk lines. A PRI has the bandwidth of a T1 link, carrying 23 B-channels, each at 64 kbps, and one D-channel for messaging, also at 64 kbps. The overall data rate is 1.544 Mbps. PRI can serve *customer premises equipment (CPE),* such as PBXs, LAN gateways, and host computers. PRI can also serve as an interoffice trunk (IOT). ISDN experts are hopeful that BRI and PRI services combined will some day extend beyond the PBX and into most homes.

16.10.2.4   ISDN Customer Premises   The customer premises segment of ISDN is defined by ITU-TS in terms of *functional groupings* and standard *reference points.* There are five functional groupings and four reference points designed to provide

---

Basic Rate Interface (BRI)
Delivers ISDN services over standard, twisted-pair telephone wires.

Primary Rate Interface (PRI)
Delivers ISDN services to digital PBXs, host computers, and LANS.

---

*David Moody, *ISDN,* Issue 2, Northern Telecom, 1991, p. vii.

**William Stalling, *Data and Computer Communications* (New York: Macmillan, 1988), p. 598.

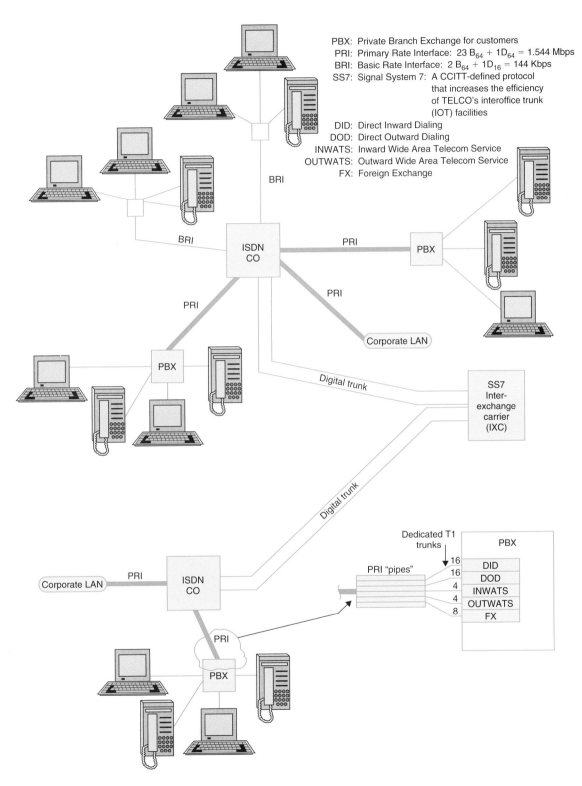

PBX: Private Branch Exchange for customers
PRI: Primary Rate Interface: $23 B_{64} + 1D_{64} = 1.544$ Mbps
BRI: Basic Rate Interface: $2 B_{64} + 1D_{16} = 144$ Kbps
SS7: Signal System 7: A CCITT-defined protocol
        that increases the efficiency
        of TELCO's interoffice trunk
        (IOT) facilities
DID: Direct Inward Dialing
DOD: Direct Outward Dialing
INWATS: Inward Wide Area Telecom Service
OUTWATS: Outward Wide Area Telecom Service
FX: Foreign Exchange

FIGURE 16-12
ISDN connection depicting BRI and PRI services.

505

TABLE 16-9
ISDN Channel Types

Channel Type	Transmission Rate	Switching Technology	Applications
B	Up to 64 kbps	Circuit switched, packet switched	Digital voice, FAX, e-mail, graphics, bulk data, interactive datacom, slow-scan video
D	16 kpbs (BRI), 64 kbps (PRI)	Packet switched (LAP-D)	Telemetry, remote alarms, energy management, e-mail, interactive datacom
H0	384 kbps	Channel switched	High-quality audio, high-speed digital information
H11	1536 kbps	Channel switched	Video/teleconferencing, high-speed digital information
H12	1920 kbps	Channel switched	Video/teleconferencing, high-speed digital information
H4	Up to 150 Mbps (approximate rate)	Channel switched	High-definition television, interactive video

interface specifications and facilitate access to the ISDN network. Figure 16-13 depicts the customer premises interface. ISDN functional groupings and reference points are defined as follows:

ISDN functional groupings:

NT1   Network Termination 1: Converts four-wire ISDN equipment lines to the two-wire ISDN-compatible subscriber loop line

NT2   Network Termination 2: Switches traffic between customer devices and NT1

TA   Terminal Adapter: Converts noncompatible ISDN signals to ISDN compatible signals.

TE1   Terminal Equipment Type 1: ISDN-compatible equipment

TE2   Terminal Equipment Type 2: Noncompatible ISDN equipment

ISDN reference points:

R   The R reference point is between TA and TE2. It provides a non-ISDN interface between non-ISDN customer premises equipment (CPE) and adapter equipment. It is recommended that this interface complies with ITU-TS' V and X series.

S   The S reference point is between a TA and NT2 or TE1 and NT2. It separates terminal equipment from network communications.

T   The T reference point is between NT1 and NT2. It defines the boundary between the CPE and the network provider's segment of the network.

U   The U reference point separates NT1 of the customer premises from the PSTN transmission line.

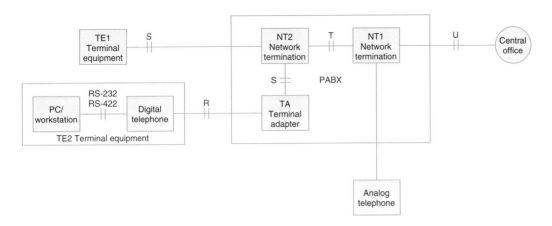

FIGURE 16-13
ISDN functional groupings and reference points for customer premises. (From TE&M, February 15, 1991, pp. 42–43.)

16.10.2.5   2B1Q Line Coding   The line-coding technique used by the ISDN BRI is called *2B1Q (2 Binary 1 Quaternary)*. It was originally designed as an enhancement to the AMI (alternate mark inversion)-encoding technique used in the T-Carrier system. The simplicity in 2B1Q is that only 2 bits per baud are encoded. As illustrated in Figure 16-14, two levels of amplitude are used: ±2.5 V, and ±0.8 V. This is referred to as *multilevel encoding*. The encoding voltages are defined as follows:

> **2B1Q**
> The line-coding technique used by the ISDN BRI. Also known as *2 binary 1 quaternary*.

- +2.5 V equals a 1 and 0
- −2.5 V equals a 0 and 0
- +0.8 V equals a 1 and 1
- −0.8 V equals a 0 and 1

16.10.2.6   Broadband ISDN   As new, bandwidth-intensive services such as *high-definition television (HDTV)* and ultrahigh-speed computer links are developed, *local area network (LAN), metropolitan area network (MAN),* and *wide area network (WAN)* services must fulfill the demand for high-speed data delivery. Standards organizations are now developing a *Broadband Integrated Services Digital Network (BISDN)* to address this need. Whereas ISDN applies mainly to the narrowband telephony world, the BISDN network will use fiber-optic transmission systems capable of transmitting at speeds ranging from 150 Mbps to 2.5 Gbps. BISDN will use the new multiplexing technique employed in ATM and SONET transport networks designed for BISDN facilities. The future of BISDN, like other new technologies, will depend on its ability to offer users the same or better services, features, and cost benefits.

> **Broadband ISDN (BISDN)**
> A broadband PSTN service supporting transmission speeds of 150 Mbps to 2.5 Gbps.

16.10.3   SONET

The culminating efforts of standards organizations have resulted in a worldwide standard for optical communications, *Synchronous Optical Network (SONET),* published by the American National Standards Institute (ANSI) in 1988 (ANSI T1.105). The SONET standard has also been incorporated into the *Synchronous Digital Hierarchy (SDH)* recommendations of ITU-TS. It has since emerged as a forerunner in today's leading telecommunications technologies. The major goal of SONET is to

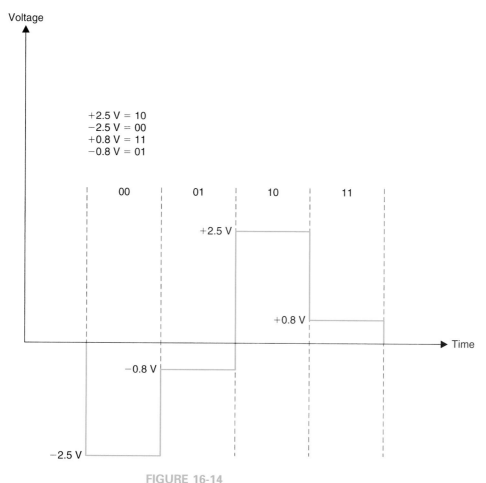

FIGURE 16-14
2B1Q (2 Binary 1 Quaternary) line coding.

standardize fiber-optic network equipment and allow the internetworking of optical communication systems from different vendors. Several telephone carriers have been aggressively deploying SONET equipment with hopes that it will reach its greater potential as a broadband switching network. There is sufficient flexibility designed into the SONET payload such that it will be used as the underlying transport layer for BISDN and ATM cells.

16.10.3.1   SONET Signal Hierarchy and Line Rates   In brief, SONET defines optical carrier levels and their equivalent electrical *synchronous transport signals (STS)* for a fiber-optic–based transmission hierarchy. Table 16-10 lists the standard transmission rates for SONET. Those rates that are marked with an *a* are the most widely supported by network vendors and providers.

The STS-1 rate of 51.84 Mbps is the basic building block for SONET optical line rates. Higher rates are integer multiples of this rate. For STS-N, only certain values of N are permitted. These values of N are 1, 3, 9, 12, 18, 24, 36, and 48. Higher rates than STS-48 may be allowed in future revisions, with a maximum of 255 under the current standard.

TABLE 16-10
SONET Optical Transmission Rates

Optical Carrier	Synchronous Transport Signal	Line Rate (Mbps)
OC-1[a]	STS-1	51.84
OC-3[a]	STS-3	155.52
OC-9	STS-9	466.56
OC-12[a]	STS-12	622.08
OC-18	STS-18	933.12
OC-24	STS-24	1244.16
OC-36	STS-36	1866.24
OC-48[a]	STS-48	2488.32
OC-96	STS-96	4976
OC-192	STS-192	9953

[a]Popular SONET physical layer interface.

16.10.3.2 The SONET Frame Format The transport system adopted in SONET utilizes a synchronous digital bit stream comprised of groups of bytes organized into a frame structure in which the user's data is filled. The basic STS-1 SONET frame format is illustrated in Figure 16-15. The frame format is typically depicted as a 9-row by 90-column matrix representing individual bytes of the synchronous signal. The frame is transmitted byte by byte starting with byte one and scanning from left to right and top to bottom for a total of 810 bytes (9×90) or 6480 bits (810×8). The entire frame is transmitted in 125 μs, which works out to be the STS-1 line rate of 51.84 Mbps (6480 bits/125 μs = 51.84 Mbps).

STS-1 frames are divided into two main areas: the *transport overhead (TOH)*, and the *synchronous payload envelope (SPE)*. The first three columns of the 90-column matrix is occupied by the TOH. The remaining 87 columns make up the SPE. The first column of the SPE is the *STS Path Overhead*, which contains payload specific data. These data do not change as the SPE traverses the network. The remaining 86 columns of the SPE are used to carry the payload or network traffic. The TOH and SPE are defined as follows.

TOH The *transport overhead* portion of the STS-1 frame is for alarm monitoring, bit error monitoring, and data communications overhead necessary to ensure the reliable transmission of the SPE between nodes in the synchronous network.

SPE The *synchronous payload envelope* is designed to transport a tributary's signal across the synchronous network from end to end. The SPE is assembled and disassembled only once, even though it may be transferred from one transport system to another on its route through the network. In most cases, the SPE is assembled at the point of entry to the synchronous network and disassembled at the point of exit from the network.*

Introduction to SONET Networks and Tests (Palo Alto, Calif.: Hewlett-Packard, 1992), pp. 36–38.

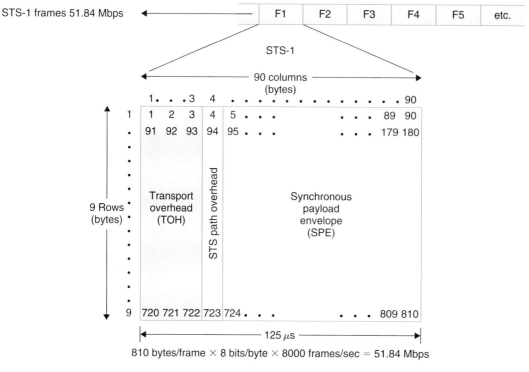

STS-1 frames 51.84 Mbps

| F1 | F2 | F3 | F4 | F5 | etc. |

STS-1

90 columns
(bytes)

Transport overhead (TOH)

STS path overhead

Synchronous payload envelope (SPE)

9 Rows (bytes)

125 μs

810 bytes/frame × 8 bits/byte × 8000 frames/sec = 51.84 Mbps

FIGURE 16-15
SONET STS-1 frame format.

16.10.3.3 STS-1 Payload The *payload* can be thought of as the revenue-producing traffic being transported and routed over the SONET network. Once the payload is assembled (or multiplexed as discussed later) into the SPE, it can be routed through the SONET network to its destination. The STS-1 payload has the capacity to transport the circuits (or equivalent of) listed in Table 16-11.

The 86 columns of the SPE that are designed to carry the payload are arranged in accordance with standard "mappings" or rules that are a function of the data services carried (e.g., DS1, DS2, etc.). The specific arrangement used is called a *virtual tributary* (*VT*). SONET specifies different sizes of VTs. For example, a VT1.5 is a frame consisting of 27 bytes structured as three columns of 9 bytes. With a 125-μs

TABLE 16-11
STS-1 Payload Capacity

Capacity	Signal Type	Signal Rate (Mbps)	Voice Circuits	T1s	DS3s
28	DS1	1.544	24	1	—
21	CEPT1	2.048	30	—	—
14	DS1C	3.152	48	2	—
7	DS2	6.312	96	4	—
1	DS3	44.736	672	28	1

frame time (8 kHz), these bytes provide a transport capacity of 1.728 Mbps and will accommodate the mapping of a DS1 signal at 1.544 Mbps. Twenty-eight VT1.5s may be multiplexed into the STS-1 SPE.

The SPE may not need a VT frame structure if the service occupies the entire SPE. The DS3 signal in Table 16-11 is an example. SONET's STS-1 SPE has been specifically designed to provide transport for a DS3 tributary signal. A DS3 signal occupies the entire SPE and does not need a VT frame structure.

16.10.3.4 SONET Multiplexing Higher levels of synchronous transport signals (STS) are created by a technique called *byte-interleaved multiplexing*. STS-N is constructed by byte-interleave multiplexing *N* STS-1 signals together. STS-3, for example, is three STS-1 signals multiplexed together as illustrated in Figure 16-16. The STS-3 frame, therefore, has 90×3, or 270, columns and nine rows for a total byte count of 2430 (270×9). Because the STS-3 (or STS-N) frame is also transmitted in 125 μs, the transmission line rate is three times that of the STS-1 rate (3×51.84 Mbps), or 155.52 Mbps. Note that the byte-interleaved process results in a matrix of multiplexed columns also. Thus, the first nine columns of the STS-3 frame are occupied by the TOHs of the three STS-1 signals. The remaining 261 columns are occupied by the SPEs of the three STS-1 signals.

16.10.4 Digital Subscriber Line (DSL)

One of the fastest growing Internet connection technologies is *DSL,* which stands for *Digital Subscriber Line.* This new, high-speed digital service is currently being deployed over the POTS (Plain Old Telephone Service) lines throughout Northern America, Europe, and Asia. Its rapid deployment and rise in popularity can be attributed primarily to the enormous demand for a high-speed, inexpensive connection to the Internet via the central office or local exchange company (LEC).

> **Digital Subscriber Line (DSL)**
> A high-speed, digital service using POTS lines.

There are nine types of DSL services: ADSL, ADSL *Lite* (also known as *G. lite*), HDSL, HDSL2, IDSL, RADSL, SDSL, UDSL, and VDSL. Combined, they are often referred to as *XDSL.* The *X* is used as a designator representing the entire family DSL technologies. Each technology can deliver simultaneous voice and data over an "always on" subscriber loop connection to the central office. Therefore, there is no dialing, busy signals, and call setup procedures as with analog or ISDN modems. Also, the point-to-point connection from the customer premises to the central office is dedicated and not shared, as with cable modem, where all residents on a coaxial segment connection contend for use of the line. Table 16-12 lists the XDSL family and their respective characteristics.

The type of DSL service available to the customer depends on factors such as LEC (local exchange carrier) or CLEC (competitive local exchange carrier), distance to the central office, condition of your telephone lines, geographical area, and other factors. The most critical factor is distance. In Chapter 13, the ADSL modem and its connection (see Figures 13-20 and 13-21) to the central office was introduced. We noted that the maximum distance from the customer premises to the central office as 18,000 feet (3.4 miles or 5.5 kilometers). This may be true for ADSL, but other DSL technologies are limited to shorter lengths. That is, DSL performance is distance and transmission rate-dependent. Figure 16-17 depicts the maximum theoretical transmission rate under ideal conditions. Note that the longer the cable run, the lower the transmission rate.

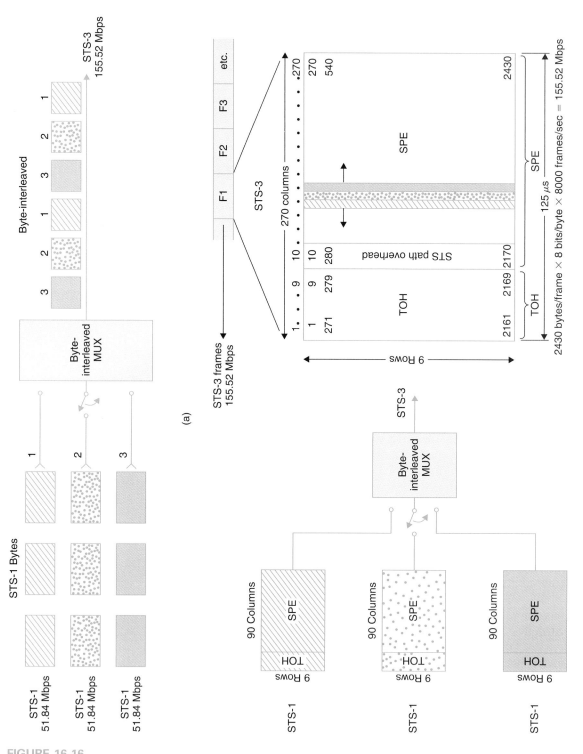

FIGURE 16-16

Byte-interleaved multiplexing of an STS-3 frame: (a) byte-interleave process; (b) STS-3 frame format.

TABLE 16-12
The XDSL Family

XDSL Technology	Max. Distance	Max. Upstream/Downstream Transmission Rate (< 5000 ft).	Modulation Type	Description
ADSL (Asymmetric DSL)	18,000 ft.	1 Mbps/9 Mbps	DMT	ADSL is the most common DSL technology. It is called asymmetric because upstream and downstream transmission full-duplex rates are at different speeds.
ADLS Lite (G. Lite)	18,000 ft.	128 Kbps/1 Mbps	DMT	Also known as G. lite. ADSL Lite is a slow-speed version of ADSL. Phone companies do not need to install a POTS splitter at the customer premisses.
HDSL (High-bit-rate DSL)	12,000 ft.	1.544 Mbps/1.544 Mbps	2B1Q/CAP	A symmetrical service that delivers T1 speeds in both directions (high-bit-rate DSL) under ideal conditions. Like a trunk circuit, four wires are used (two pairs).
HDSL2 (HDSL version 2)	12,000 ft.	1.544 Mbps/1.544 Mbps	2B1Q/CAP	A new version of HDSL offering the same T1 speeds over a single-wire pair.
IDSL (ISDN DSL)	18,000 ft.	144 Kbps/144 Kbps	2B1Q	A symmetrical service that delivers ISDN like speeds of 128 kpbs in both directions under ideal conditions. In contrast to ISDN, IDSL is an "always on" connection.
RADSL (Rate-adaptive DSL)	18,000 ft.	1 Mbps/12 Mbps	CAP	An asymmetric service that can reach 12 Mbps downstream and 1 Mbps upstream under ideal conditions. Rates are adaptive to the existing line condition and are negotiated between the modem and central office's DSLAM.
SDSL (Symmetric DSL)	10,000 ft.	1.1 Mbps/1.1 Mbps	2B1Q/CAP	A symmetrical DSL service over a single-wire pair that tops out at 1.1 Mbps.
UDSL (Universal DSL)	18,000 ft.	2 Mbps/2 Mbps	DMT	A symmetrical DSL service over a single-wire pair that tops out at 2 Mbps.
VDSL (Very high-speed DSL)	4500 ft.	51.84 Mbps/2.3 Mbps (<1000 ft.)	QAM/DMT	Designed to support SONET rates and subrates up to 1000 ft over a single twisted-pair wire. VDSL is projected to become as defined as ADSL. It is the only DSL technology converted from copper to fiber at the customer premisses and sent to the central office.

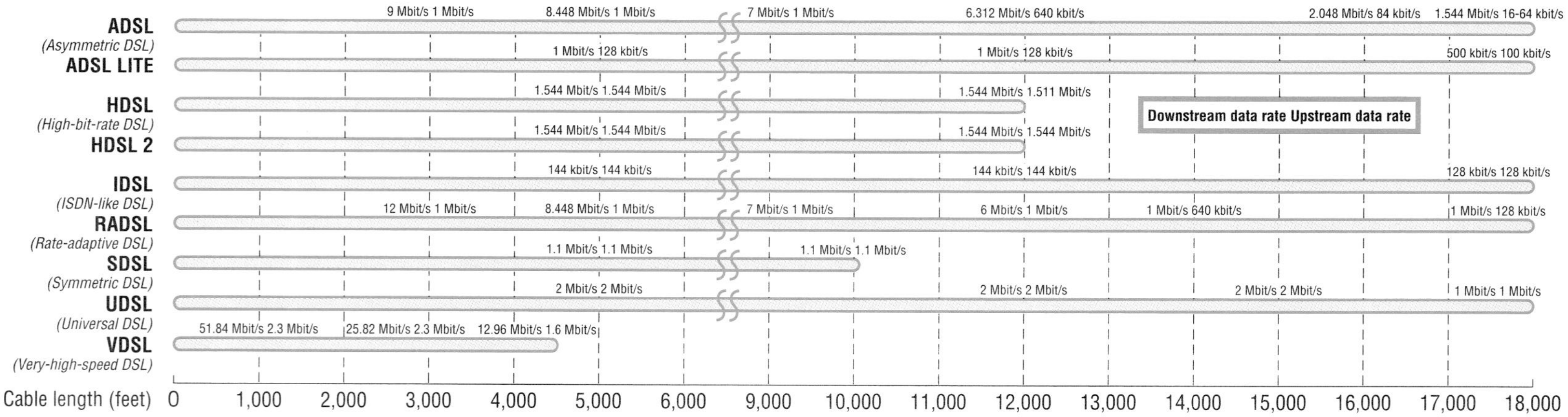

FIGURE 16-17

Maximum theoretical transmission rates versus distance for the various DSL technologies. (Source: *Data Communications Magazine*, April 21, 1998, pp. 44–45. Reprinted with permission from CMP, Inc.)

16.10.4.1 DSL Modulation Techniques   Because DSL is a relatively new technology still in its trial stages, standards are continually being worked on in all areas, including definition of the best-suited modulation technique for a respective DSL family. Table 16-11 lists four different types of modulation or line-coding techniques used on the DSL line. A brief definition is given as follows:

Carrierless Amplitude Phase (CAP)   CAP is a variation of QAM (Quadrature Amplitude Modulation). The phase and amplitude of two sinusoids whose frequenices are within the passband of the phone lines are varied in accordance with a defined signal constellation. The data rate is divided in two and modulated onto the two carriers before being filtered, combined, and fed to a digital-to-analog converter (DAC) before being transmitted. DMT has become the selected standard for most DSL technologies, but CAP was implemented in nearly all ADSL deployments worldwide and has become a de facto standard.

Discrete Multitone (DMT)   DMT differs from CAP in that it uses a combination of frequency-division multiplexing (FDM) and QAM. The entire usable bandwidth from DC to 1.1 MHz is separated into 256 frequency bands or subchannels of 4.3 KHz each. The lower six subchannels are used for the voice band, and the remaining channels are used for upstream and downstream data. Within the center of each subchannel, a subcarrier frequency undergoes QAM with as many 15 bits per baud (signal change). DMT offers a significant improvement of signal-to-noise ratio (SNR), power efficiency, and flexible transmission rates over its counterparts.

2 Binary 1 Quaternary (2B1Q)   2B1Q is the line-coding technique used with the BRI ISDN standard. It was originally designed as an enhancement to the AMI encoding techniques used in the T-Carrier system. Both HDSL and IDSL use 2B1Q. The simplicity in 2B1Q is that only two bits per baud are encoded. (See Figure 16-14.)

Quadrature Amplitude Modulation (QAM)   QAM (pronounced "kwamm") is a method for encoding data onto a single carrier frequency. It is the dominant modulation technique employed for high-speed, voice-band modems. QAM encodes groups of data bits as discrete phase and amplitude changes of a carrier frequency. As many as 10 bits can be encoded into a single phase and/or amplitude change of the carrier frequency, that is, 10 bits per baud. Each phase and amplitude variation of the carrier frequency (baud) is represented by a vector or phasor. The vectors are arranged in a pattern of points called a signal constellation (see the V.33 128-point signal constellation in Figure 13-16) from which the transmitted point is selected based on the data to be sent. The modem sends the symbols as abrupt changes in phase and amplitude.

16.10.5 Fiber Distributed Data Interface

As our demand for information increases, the telecommunication system becomes increasingly more complex. First-generation network standards such as Ethernet and Token Ring cannot handle the enormous volumes of data that users are demanding today, particularly over longer-distance spans. The lack of bandwidth on existing transmission media is the bottleneck. With the evolution of fiber-optics technology, bandwidth is virtually unlimited; hence, the *Fiber Distributed Data Interface (FDDI)* standard was conceived.

> **FDDI**
> An ANSI standard to enhance LAN technology with fiber optics. Also known as *Fiber Distributed Data Interface.*

The ANSI committee has developed the FDDI standard (X3T9.5) to support users who require the flexibility, reliability, and speed provided by fiber-optic technology. The standard specifies a 100-Mbps transmission signaling rate with up to 2 km between stations. A dual counter-rotating ring structure is used for the high-speed, token-passing network.

The relatively high cost of fiber-optic transmission media for FDDI has kept the 100-Mbps standard from dominating the personal computer and workstation LAN market. The ANSI X3T9.5 committee continues to work on an alternative to the standard to lower the cost. The alternative is to attain 100 Mbps over copper wire, both *shielded twisted-pair (STP)* and *unshielded twisted-pair (UTP)*. In addition, several vendors have combined their efforts to unite the benefits of FDDI with those of copper: a transmission medium that is less expensive than fiber and likely to already be installed in the user's facility.

16.10.6   Fibre Channel

Fibre Channel
An ANSI standard for transmission speeds as fast as 1 Gbps using fiber-optic media.

Although the FDDI standard has alleviated much of the communications bottleneck resulting from limited transmission speeds, many commercial, educational, and scientific environments are looking for performance beyond the 100-Mbps FDDI transmission rate. The emerging *Fibre Channel Standard,* being developed by the ANSI X3T9.3 committee, is a high-performance standard designed to transfer data at speeds up to 1 Gbps over distances of 10 km using fiber-optic transmission media. In addition, Hewlett-Packard, IBM, and Sun Microsystems Computer Corp. have announced the *Fibre Channel Systems Initiative,* which is a joint effort to advance the Fibre Channel as an affordable, high-speed interconnection standard for workstations and peripherals. The primary goals of the initiative are to advance high-speed interconnections for workstations and systems, promote open systems for distributed computing, and propose selected sets of Fibre Channel options for manufacturers to build conforming products.

The Fibre Channel defines a matrix of switches, called a *fabric,* that performs network switching functions similar to that of a telephone system. Each computer system attaches to the fabric with dedicated send and receive lines designed for point-to-point, bidirectional serial communications. The switch can route any incoming signal to any output port.

The Fibre Channel is one of the key technologies of the 1990s that will provide high-speed performance at an affordable cost. It is expected that a significant share of the workstations and servers will be using the Fibre Channel interface by the end of the decade.

16.10.7   Frame Relay

A technology that has gained acceptance in the LAN and WAN community is *Frame Relay,* a *fast-packet* switching protocol that supports a variable-length frame structure of as many as 4096 bytes. Frame Relay began as a concept of a simple packet mode access to ISDN. It is defined by ITU-TS Recommendation I.122 as *Framework for Additional Packet Mode Bearer Services.* In contrast to the conventional packet switching discussed earlier, fast-packet protocols such as Frame Relay are used in operating environments that include digital broadband systems. Frame Relay's high through-

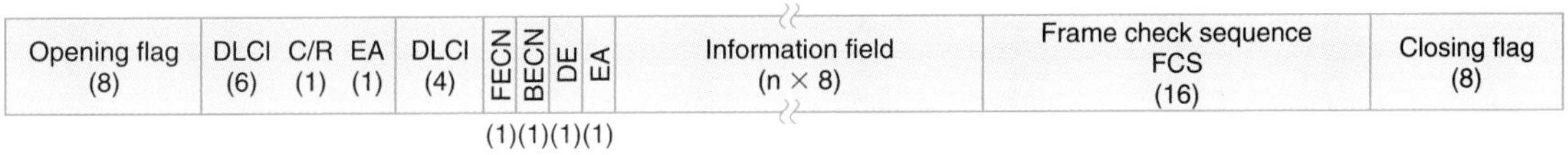

Opening flag (8)	DLCI (6)	C/R (1)	EA (1)	DLCI (4)	FECN	BECN	DE	EA	Information field (n × 8)	Frame check sequence FCS (16)	Closing flag (8)

(1)(1)(1)(1)

DLCI = data link connection identifier
C/R = command/response
EA = address extension
FECN = forward explicit congestion notification
BECN = backward explicit congestion notification
DE = discard eligibility indicator
n = number of octets up to 4096

FIGURE 16-18
Frame format for frame relay.

put of 64 kbps to 2 Mbps makes it suitable for LAN and WAN data and imaging network traffic but less satisfactory for voice and real-time video. It is far more efficient than X.25 packet technology due to its simplistic architectural framework. Roughly two-thirds of the protocol complexity of X.25 is eliminated.

The frame format for Frame Relay is shown in Figure 16-18. Note that the structure of the frame has been designed similar to that of HDLC and SDLC. This permits data encapsulation and decapsulation of these frames. The opening flag is followed by a 2-byte control field used for network addressing and control. The information field of the frame is variable length up to 4096 octets (bytes). A 16-bit FCS is used for error control followed by an 8-bit closing flag.

16.10.8   Switched Multimegabit Data Service

As its name implies, *Switched Multimegabit Data Service (SMDS)* is a *service* offered by several major telephone companies or LECs. SMDS is designed to offer efficient and economical connectivity between LAN and WAN systems over the PSTN. Any organization that needs to transmit large amounts of data via the PSTN to several locations at different times should consider SMDS as a viable service.

SMDS is currently designed to operate over the standard North American PCM Multiplex Hierarchy at DS1 and DS3 (Digital Signal 1 and 3). In Europe, E1 and E3 are used. These transmission rates for telephone trunk lines are 1.544 and 44.736 Mbps, respectively. Because these rates are standardized between central offices, SMDS lends itself to ubiquitous public connections.

Using SMDS is very much like using a telephone. Once the user establishes the called party's "SMDS telephone number," that number (in SMDS language) need only precede packets addressed to the called party.* The packet reaches its destination without further ado. This type of service makes it unnecessary to add remote ends in a private network, making it ideal for subscribers. A large bandwidth at a bargain price, with the ease of connection of a telephone, makes SMDS successful and ideally suited for users looking for a wide-bandwidth digital connection worldwide.

SMDS
A PSTN service offering efficient and economical connectivity between LAN and WAN systems. Also known as *Switched Multimegabit Data Service.*

*Alan J. Spiegleman, "What Is SMDS?" *Networking Management,* October 1992, p. 44.

PROBLEMS

1. In what year was the *ARPANET* formed?
2. In what year was the *NSFNET* formed?
3. Explain the difference between *FTP* and *Anonymous FTP.*
4. Give an example of how to *Telnet* a host computer at a remote location.
5. Give an example of how to use *Gopher.*
6. Explain the difference between *Veronica* and *Archie.*
7. What does *WAIS* stand for, and what is its function?
8. What is the domain name of your educational institute?
9. What is the domain of a government organization?
10. What is the domain for the country of Australia?
11. What is the domain for the country of the Netherlands?
12. What is the name of the message-switching principle on which e-mail is based?
13. Give an example of an e-mail address.
14. Who has been credited with inventing the *World Wide Web*?
15. What is *CERN*?
16. What is a *Web browser*?
17. Name at least one Web browser.
18. What does *HTML* stand for?
19. Define *home page.*
20. Define *URL.*
21. Give an example of a URL.
22. Give an example of how to use the Boolean logical operator "OR" in a Web search.
23. Give an example of how to use the Boolean logical operator "AND" in a Web search.
24. What does *TCP/IP* stand for?
25. What RFC specifies the SNMP protocol used in TCP/IP?
26. What is the distinguishing feature of an *intranet*?
27. Define what is meant by a *firewall.*
28. What does *ATM* stand for?
29. Define *VP* and *VC.*
30. What is the length of an ATM cell in bytes?
31. Draw the structure of an ATM cell, and briefly define its two fields.
32. Draw the structure of the ATM Header Field.
33. Briefly define each field within the Header Field of an ATM cell.
34. What does *ISDN* stand for?
35. What prevents ISDN services from being provided to residential customers?
36. Define *BRI* and *PRI.*
37. Explain the difference between ISDN B-channel and D-channel.
38. Name the five ISDN functional groupings for customer premises.
39. What are the four ISDN reference points for customer premises?
40. Draw the 2B1Q waveform for the binary bit stream 1 0 0 1 1 1 0 1 1 0 0 1. Label all voltages and encoded bits.
41. Repeat problem 40 for the bit stream 0 1 1 1 1 0 0 0 0 1 1.
42. What does *SONET* stand for?
43. Derive the 51.84-Mbps line rate for SONET's STS-1 signal.
44. What is a *virtual tributary* in SONET?
45. How many STS-1 SONET frames must be multiplexed together to form an STS-12 frame?
46. What is the maximum theoretical transmission rate for ADSL?
47. What three modulation or live-coding techniques are used for *XDSL*?
48. What does *FDDI* stand for?
49. What is the transmission rate for FDDI?
50. What does *SMDS* stand for?
51. What is the *Fibre Channel Systems Initiative*?
52. Draw the frame structure for Frame Relay.

ERROR DETECTION, CORRECTION, AND CONTROL

A major design criterion for all telecommunication systems is to achieve error-free transmission. Errors, unfortunately, do occur. There are many types and causes originating from various sources, ranging from lightning strikes to dirty switch contacts at the central office. A method of detecting and, in some cases, correcting for their occurrence is a necessity. To achieve this, two basic techniques are employed. One is to detect the error and request a retransmission of the corrupted message. The second is to correct the error at the receiving end without having to retransmit the message. The trade-off for either technique is the redundancy that must be built into the transmitted bit stream. This redundancy decreases system throughput.

Many of today's communication systems employ elaborate error-control protocols. Some of these protocols are software packages designed to facilitate file transfers between personal computers and mainframes. More recent error controllers are completely self-contained within a hardware module, thus relieving the central processing unit (CPU) of the burden of error control. The entire process is transparent to the user.

This chapter considers some of the most common methods used for error detection and correction, including error-controlling protocols specifically designed for data-communications equipment.

17.1 PARITY

Parity is the simplest and oldest method of error detection. Although it is not very effective in data transmission, it is still widely used due to its simplicity. A single bit, called the *parity bit,* is added to a group of bits representing a letter, number, or symbol. ASCII characters on a keyboard, for example, are typically encoded into bits, with an eighth bit acting as parity. The parity bit is computed by the transmitting device based on the number of 1 bits set in the character. Parity can be either *odd* or *even.* If odd parity is selected, the parity bit is set to a 1 or 0 to make the total number of 1 bits in the character, including the parity bit itself, equal to an odd value. If

> **Parity Bit**
> Added to a group of bits as an error-detection method.

TABLE 17-1
Even and Odd Parity for a 7-Bit Data Character

Data Character	Odd Parity Bit	Data Character	Even Parity Bit
1101000	0	1011101	1
0010111	1	1110111	0
1010110	1	0011010	1
1010001	0	1010111	1

even parity is selected, the opposite is true, and the parity bit is set to a 1 or 0 to make the total number of 1 bits, including the parity bit itself, equal to an even number. The receiving device performs the same computation on the received number of 1 bits for each character and checks the computed parity against what was received. If they do not match, an error has been detected. Table 17-1 lists examples of even and odd parity.

The selection of even or odd parity is generally arbitrary. In most cases, it is a matter of custom or preference. The transmitting and receiving stations, however, must be set to same mode. Some system designers prefer odd parity over even. The advantage is that when a string of several data characters are anticipated to be all zeros, the parity bit would be set to 1 for each character, thus allowing for ease of character identification and synchronization.

17.2 PARITY GENERATING AND CHECKING CIRCUITS

Parity generating circuits can easily be implemented with a combination of exclusive-OR gates. Figure 17-1 illustrates an even parity generating circuit for a 7-bit data word. Odd parity can be obtained by simply adding an inverter at the output of the given circuit. Additional gates can be included in the circuit for extended word lengths. The same circuit can be used for parity checking by adding another exclusive-OR gate to accommodate the received parity bit. The received data word and parity bit are applied at the circuit's input. For even parity, the output should always be low unless an error occurs. Conversely, for odd parity checking, the output should always be high unless an error occurs. Figure 17-2 depicts another design that can be used for parity generation and checking.

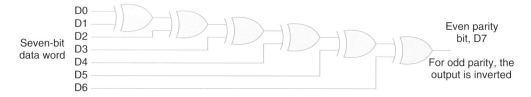

FIGURE 17-1
Even parity generating circuit. Odd parity generation is obtained by adding an inverter at the output.

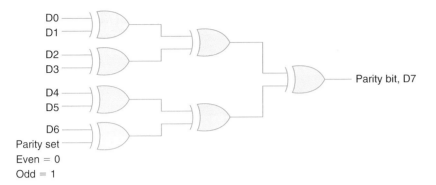

FIGURE 17-2
Even or odd parity generation is achieved in this circuit by setting the appropriate level at the parity set input.

17.3 THE DISADVANTAGE WITH PARITY

A major shortcoming with parity is that it is only applicable for detecting when one bit or an *odd* number of bits have been changed in a character. Parity checking does not detect when an *even* number of bits have changed. For example, suppose that bit D2 in Example 17.1 were to change during the course of a transmission for an odd parity system. Example 17.1 shows how the bit error is detected.

	Parity (odd)	D7	D6	D5	D4	D3	D2	D1	D0	EXAMPLE
Transmitted:	0	0	1	1	0	1	1	0	1	17.1
Received:	0	0	1	1	0	1	0	0	1	

Single bit error

The received parity bit, a 0, is in conflict with the computed number of 1 bits that was received: in this case, *four,* an even number of 1 bits. The parity bit should have been equal to a value making the total number of 1 bits odd. An error has been properly detected. If, on the other hand, bit D2 *and* bit D1 were both altered during the transmission, the computed parity bit would still be in agreement with the received parity bit. This error would go undetected, as shown in Example 17.2. A little thought will reveal that an even number of errors in a character, for odd or even parity, will go undetected.

	Parity (odd)	D7	D6	D5	D4	D3	D2	D1	D0	EXAMPLE
Transmitted:	0	0	1	1	0	1	1	0	1	17.2
Received:	0	0	1	1	0	1	0	1	1	

Errors: two bits or an even number of bits go undetected

Parity, being a single-bit error-detection scheme, presents another problem in accommodating today's high-speed transmission rates. Many errors are a result of impulse noise, which tends to be *bursty* in nature. Noise impulses may last several

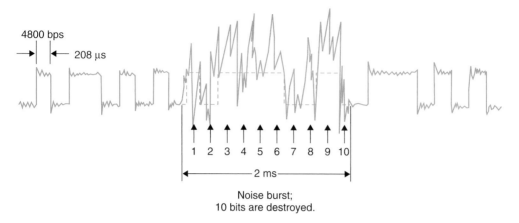

FIGURE 17-3
Effect of a 2-ms noise burst on a 4800-bps signal.

milliseconds, consequently destroying several bits. The higher the transmission rate, the greater the effect. Figure 17-3 depicts a 2-ms noise burst imposed on a 4800-bps signal. The bit time associated with this signal is 208 μs (1/4800). As many as 10 bits are affected. At least two characters are destroyed here, with the possibility of both character errors going undetected.

17.4 VERTICAL AND LONGITUDINAL REDUNDANCY CHECKS

Vertical Redundancy Check (VRC)
A parity check performed on a character basis.

Longitudinal Redundancy Check (LRC)
A parity check performed on an accumulation of the value of individual bit positions in a message stream.

Block Check Character (BCC)
The word resulting from an LRC and transmitted at the end of the message stream.

Thus far, the discussion of parity has been on a per-character basis. This is often referred to as a *vertical redundancy check (VRC)*. Parity can also be computed and inserted at the end of a message block. In this case, the parity bit is computed based on an accumulation of the value of each character's LSB through MSB, including the VRC bit, as shown in Figure 17-4. This method of parity checking is referred to as a *longitudinal redundancy check (LRC)*. The resulting word is called the *block check character (BCC)*.

Additional parity bits in LRC used to produce the BCC provide extra error-detection capabilities. Single-bit errors can now be detected and corrected. For example, suppose that the LSB of the letter *y* in the message in Figure 17-4 was received as a 0 instead of a 1. The computed parity bit for the LRC would indicate that a bit was received in error. By itself, the detected LRC error does not specify which bit in the row of LSB bits received is in error. The same is true for the VRC. The computed parity bit in the column of the character in error, *y*, would be a 1 instead of a 0. By itself, the detected VRC error does not specify which bit in the *y* column has been received in error. A *cross-check*, however, will reveal that the intersection of the detected parity error for the VRC and LRC check identifies the exact bit that was received in error. By inverting this bit, the error can be corrected.

Unfortunately, an even number of bit errors is not detected by either the LRC or VRC check. Cross-checks cannot be performed; consequently, bit errors cannot be corrected.

	H	a	v	e	sp	a	sp	n	i	c	e	sp	d	a	y	!	BCC (LRC)
LSB	0	1	0	1	0	1	0	0	1	1	1	0	0	1	1	1	0
	0	0	1	0	0	0	0	1	0	1	0	0	0	0	0	0	0
	0	0	1	1	0	0	0	1	0	0	1	0	1	0	0	0	0
	1	0	0	0	0	0	0	1	1	0	0	0	0	0	1	0	1
	0	0	1	0	0	0	0	0	0	0	0	0	0	0	1	0	1
	0	1	1	1	1	1	1	1	1	1	1	1	1	1	1	1	0
MSB	1	1	1	1	0	1	0	1	1	1	1	0	1	1	1	0	1
VRC	1	0	0	1	0	0	0	0	1	1	1	0	0	0	0	1	1

FIGURE 17-4
Computing BCC for a message block with VRC and LRC odd parity checking.

17.5 CYCLIC REDUNDANCY CHECKING

Parity checking has major shortcomings. It is much more efficient to eliminate the parity bit for each character in the block entirely and utilize the redundant bits at the end of the block.

A more powerful method than the combination of LRC and VRC for error detection in blocks is *cyclic redundancy checking (CRC)*. CRC is the most commonly used method for error detection in block transmission. A minimal amount of hardware is required (slightly more than LRC/VRC systems), and its effectiveness in detecting errors is greater than 99.9%.

CRC involves a division of the transmitted message block by a constant called the *generator polynomial*. The quotient is discarded, and the remainder is transmitted as the BCC. This is shown in Figure 17-5. Some protocols refer to the BCC as the *frame check sequence (FCS)*. The receiving station performs the same computation on the received message block. The computed remainder, or BCC, is compared to the remainder received from the transmitter. If the two match, no errors have been detected in the message block. If the two do *not* match, either a request for retransmission is made by the receiver or the errors are corrected through use of special coding techniques.

Cyclic codes contain a specific number of bits, governed by the size of the character within the message block. Three of the most commonly used cyclic codes are

> **Cyclic Redundancy Checking (CRC)**
> The most commonly used error-detection method in block transmission.

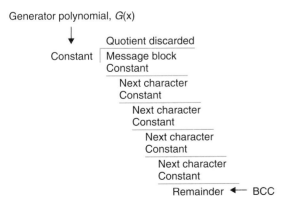

FIGURE 17-5
Computing the BCC of a message block using CRC.

CRC-12, CRC-16, and *CRC-CCITT.* Blocks containing characters that are 6 bits in length typically use CRC-12, a 12-bit CRC. Blocks formatted with 8-bit characters typically use CRC-16 or CRC-CCITT, both of which are 16-bit codes. The BCC for these three cyclic codes is derived from the following generator polynomials, $G(x)$:

CRC-12 generator polynomial: $\qquad G(x) = X^{12} + X^{11} + X^3 + X^2 + X + 1$

CRC-16 generator polynomial: $\qquad G(x) = X^{16} + X^{15} + X^2 + 1$

CRC-CCITT generator polynomial: $\quad G(x) = X^{16} + X^{12} + X^5 + 1$

A combination of multistage shift registers employing feedback through exclusive-OR gates is used to implement the mathematical function performed on the message block to obtain the BCC. Figure 17-6 depicts three CRC generating circuits for CRC-12, CRC-16, and CRC-CCITT. The BCC is accumulated by shifting the data stream into the data input of the register. When the final bit of the message block is shifted in, the register contains the BCC. The BCC is transmitted at the end of the message block, *LSB first.*

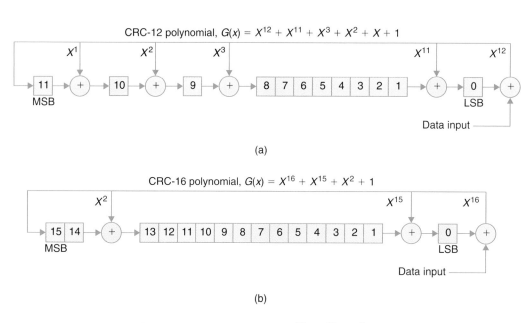

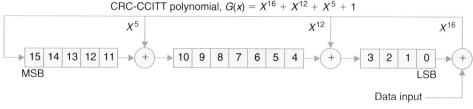

FIGURE 17-6
CRC generating circuits: (a) CRC-12; (b) CRC-16; (c) CRC-CCITT.

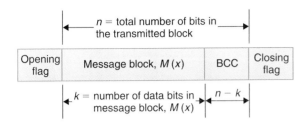

FIGURE 17-7
Format of a message block for computing the BCC in CRC.

17.5.1 Computing the Block Check Character

The generating polynomial, $G(x)$, and message polynomial, $M(x)$, used for computing the BCC include degree terms that represent positions in a group of bits that are a binary 1. For example, given the polynomial

$$X^5 + X^2 + X + 1$$

its binary representation is

$$100111$$

Missing terms are represented by a 0. The highest degree in the polynomial is one less than the number of bits in the binary code. The following discussion illustrates how the BCC can be computed using long division.

Referring to Figure 17-7, if we let n equal the total number of bits in a transmitted block and k equal the number of data bits, then $n - k$ equals the number of bits in the BCC. The message polynomial, $M(x)$, is multiplied by X^{n-k} to achieve the correct number of bits for the BCC. The resulting product is then divided by the generator polynomial, $G(x)$. The quotient is discarded and the remainder, $B(x)$, the BCC, is transmitted at the end of the message block. The long-division process is *not* accomplished in the usual manner through the subtraction process. Rather, an *exclusive-OR* operation is performed. As shown in the following examples, this will yield a BCC having a total number of bits *one* less than the number of bits in the generator polynomial, $G(x)$. This number is also equal to the highest degree of the generator polynomial. The entire transmitted block can be represented by the CRC polynomial

> **Exclusive-OR**
> A Boolean logic function of $A\bar{B} + \bar{A}B$

$$T(x) = X^{n-k}[M(x)] + B(x)$$

where $T(x)$ = total transmitted message block
X^{n-k} = multiplication factor
$B(x)$ = BCC

Consider the following examples:

EXAMPLE 17.3

In this example, the transmitted message block will include a total number of bits, n, equal to 14. Nine of the 14 bits are data, k. Therefore, the BCC consists of 5 bits ($n - k = 5$).

Given:

$$\text{Generator polynomial, } G(x) = X^5 + X^2 + X + 1$$
$$= 100111$$
$$\text{Message polynomial, } M(x) = X^8 + X^6 + X^3 + X^2 + 1$$
$$= 101001101$$

The number of bits in the BCC, $n - k = 5$ (the highest degree of the generator polynomial). Compute the value of the BCC and the transmitted message block, $T(x)$.

Solution:

1. Multiply the message polynomial, $M(x)$, by X^{n-k}:

$$X^{n-k}[M(x)] = X^5(X^8 + X^6 + X^3 + X^2 + 1)$$
$$= X^{13} + X^{11} + X^8 + X^7 + X^5$$
$$= 10100110100000$$

2. Divide $X^{n-k}[M(x)]$ by the generator polynomial, and discard the quotient. The remainder is the BCC, $B(x)$.

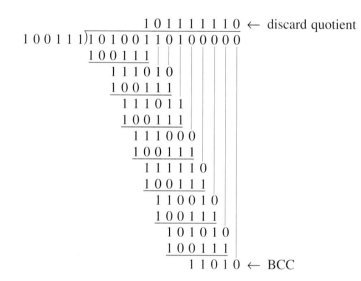

3. To determine the total transmitted message block, $T(x)$, add the BCC, $B(x)$, to $X^{n-k}[M(x)]$:

$$T(x) = X^{n-k}[M(x)] + B(x)$$
$$= 10100110100000$$

$$+ \quad \underline{\qquad\qquad 11010} \quad \text{BCC, } B(x)$$
$$10100110111010 \quad \text{transmitted message block, } T(x)$$

At the receiving end, the transmitted message block, $T(x)$, is divided by the same generating polynomial, $G(x)$. If the remainder is zero, the block was received without errors.

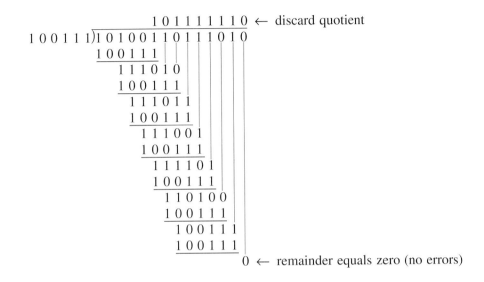

$$
\begin{array}{r}
1\;0\;1\;1\;1\;1\;1\;1\;0 \leftarrow \text{discard quotient}
\end{array}
$$

0 ← remainder equals zero (no errors)

EXAMPLE 17.4

For simplicity, a 16-bit message ($k = 16$) using CRC-16 will be used. Therefore, the total number of bits in the transmitted message block, n, is 32.
Given:

$$\text{Generator polynomial for CRC-16, } G(x) = X^{16} + X^{15} + X^2 + 1$$
$$\text{Message polynomial, } M(x) = X^{15} + X^{13} + X^{11} + X^{10} + X^7 + X^5 + X^4 + 1$$

The number of bits in the BCC, $n - k = 16$ (the highest degree of the generator polynomial). Compute the value of the BCC and the transmitted message block, $T(x)$.

Solution:
1. Multiply the message polynomial, $M(x)$, by X^{n-k}:

$$
\begin{aligned}
X^{n-k}[M(x)] &= X^{16}(X^{15} + X^{13} + X^{11} + X^{10} + X^7 + X^5 + X^4 + 1) \\
&= X^{31} + X^{29} + X^{27} + X^{26} + X^{23} + X^{21} + X^{20} + X^{16} \\
&= 10101100101100010000000000000000
\end{aligned}
$$

2. Divide $X^{n-k}[M(x)]$ by the generator polynomial and discard the quotient. The remainder is the BCC, $B(x)$.

```
                                                1100100011011100  ← discard quotient
1100000000000101)10101100101100010000000000000000
                 11000000000000101
                 11011001011001110
                 11000000000000101
                   1100101100101 1000
                   11000000000000101
                     10110010111010000
                     11000000000000101
                       1110010111010 1010
                       11000000000000101
                         10010111010111100
                         11000000000000101
                           1010111010 1110010
                           11000000000000101
                             11011101011101110
                             11000000000000101
                               1110101110101100  ← BCC
```

3. To determine the total transmitted message block, $T(x)$, add the BCC, $B(x)$, to $X^{n-k}[M(x)]$:

$$T(x) = X^{n-k}[M(x)] + B(x)$$
$$= 10101100101100010000000000000000$$

```
        +         1110101110101100  ← BCC, B(x)
        10101100101100011110101110101100  ← transmitted message block, T(x)
```

At the receiving end, the transmitted message block, $T(x)$, is divided by the CRC-16 generator polynomial, $G(x)$. The quotient is discarded, and the remainder is checked for zero, indicating that there are no errors in the received block.

```
                                                1100100011011100  ← discard quotient
1100000000000101)10101100101100011110101110101100
                 11000000000000101
                 11011001011001101
                 11000000000000101
                   11001011001000101
                   11000000000000101
                     10110010000000111
                     11000000000000101
                       1110010000000 0100
                       11000000000000101
                         10010000000000110
                         11000000000000101
                           10100000000000111
                           11000000000000101
                             11000000000000101
                             11000000000000101                  remainder equals
                                            00  ← zero (no errors)
```

17.6 CHECKSUMS

Another popular method of error detection is through use of the *checksum*. The checksum is basically a summation quantity that is computed from the data and appended to the transmitted block. Like CRC and LRC, the checksum serves as the BCC. It is transmitted at the end of the message block. Data, on arriving at their destination, undergo the same checksum computation by the receiving device. The resultant checksum is compared against the original checksum sent with the message block. If the two match, it can be assumed that the data block has been transmitted and received successfully. If the two do not match, an error has been detected (i.e., the transmitted and received data blocks are not the same, and the message has been corrupted). The necessary steps are then taken to correct the error.

It should be emphasized at this point that the purpose of the checksum process is merely to detect the occurrence of an error. It by no means identifies where in the message block the error is located. This is a much more complex task and is discussed in the next section.

Checksums are commonly used in large file transfers between mass storage devices.* They are easily computed in hardware or software and frequently are used when blocks of data are to be transported from one location to another. There are four primary types of checksums:

1. Single precision
2. Double precision
3. Honeywell
4. Residue

17.6.1 Single-Precision Checksum

The most fundamental checksum computation is the *single-precision checksum*. Here, the checksum is derived simply by performing a binary addition of each n-bit data word in the message block. Any carry or overflow during the addition process is ignored, thus the resultant checksum is also n bits in length. Figure 17-8 illustrates how the single-precision checksum is derived, transmitted as the BCC, and used to verify the integrity of the received data. For simplicity, a 4-byte data block is used. Note that the sum of the data exceeds $2^n - 1$ and, therefore, a carry occurs out of the MSB. This carry is ignored, and only the 8-bit (n-bit) checksum is sent as the BCC.

An inherent problem with the single-precision checksum is if the MSB of the n-bit data word becomes logically *stuck at 1* (SA1), the checksum becomes SA1 as well. A little thought will reveal that the regenerated checksum on the received data will equal the original checksum and that the SA1 fault will go undetected. A more elaborate scheme may be necessary.

17.6.2 Double-Precision Checksum

As its name implies, the *double-precision checksum* extends the computed checksum to $2n$ bits in length, where n is the size of the data word in the message block. For example, the 8-bit data words used in the single-precision checksum example above

Checksum
An error-detection method that computes the sum of data and appends this value to the end of a transmitted block.

Single-Precision Checksum
A most fundamental checksum, derived by a binary addition of each n-bit data word in the message block.

Double-Precision Checksum
Extends the computed single-precision checksum to $2n$ bits in length.

*For a more detailed discussion on checksums, refer to Barry W. Johnson, *Designs and Analysis of Fault Tolerant Systems* (Reading, Mass.: Addison-Wesley, 1989), pp. 98–103.

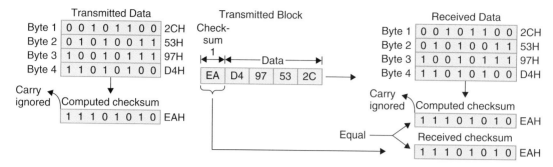

FIGURE 17-8

A *single-precision checksum* is generated and transmitted as a BCC at the end of a 4-byte block. The receiver verifies the block by regenerating the checksum and comparing it against the original.

would have a 16-bit checksum. Message blocks with 16-bit data words would have a 32-bit checksum, and so forth. Summation of data words in the message block can now extend up to modulo 2^{2n}, thereby decreasing the probability of an erroneous checksum. In addition, the SA1 error discussed earlier would be detected as a checksum error at the receiver. Figure 17-9 depicts how the double-precision checksum is derived, transmitted as the BCC, and used to verify the integrity of the received data. For simplicity, a 4-byte data block is used again. Hexadecimal notation is also used. Note that the carryout of the MSB position of the low-order checksum byte is not ignored. Instead, it becomes part of the 16-bit checksum result. Any carryout of the MSB of the 16-bit checksum is ignored.

17.6.3 Honeywell Checksum

> **Honeywell Checksum**
> An alternate double-precision checksum based on interleaving consecutive data words to form double-length words.

The *Honeywell checksum* is an alternative form of the double-precision checksum. Its length is also $2n$ bits, where n is again the size of the data word in the message block. The difference is that the Honeywell checksum is based on interleaving consecutive data words to form double-length words. The double-length words are then summed together to form a double-precision checksum. This is shown in Figure 17-10. The advantage of the Honeywell checksum is that *stuck at 1* (SA1) and *stuck at 0* (SA0)

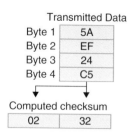
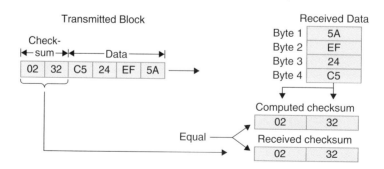

FIGURE 17-9

A *double-precision checksum* is generated and transmitted as a BCC at the end of a 4-byte block. The receiver verifies the block by regenerating the checksum and comparing it against the original.

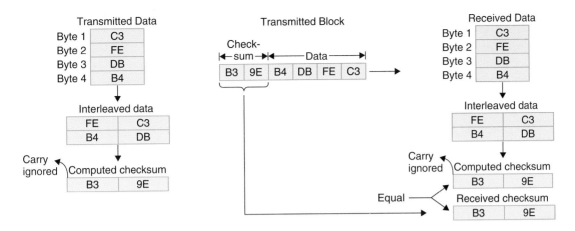

FIGURE 17-10
Structure of the *Honeywell checksum*. The checksum is generated and transmitted as the BCC at the end of a 4-byte block. The receiver verifies the block by regenerating the checksum and comparing it against the original.

bit errors occurring in the same bit positions of all words can be detected during the error-detection process, the interleaving process places the error in the upper and lower words of the checksum. At least two bit positions in the checksum are affected.

17.6.4 Residue Checksum

The last form of checksum in our discussion is the *residue checksum*. The residue checksum is identical to the single-precision checksum, except that any carryout of the MSB position of the checksum word is "wrapped around" and added to the LSB position. This added complexity permits the detection of SA1 errors that go undetected. This is illustrated in Figure 17-11.

> **Residue Checksum**
> Identical to the single-precision checksum, except any MSB carryout is "wrapped around" and added to the LSB.

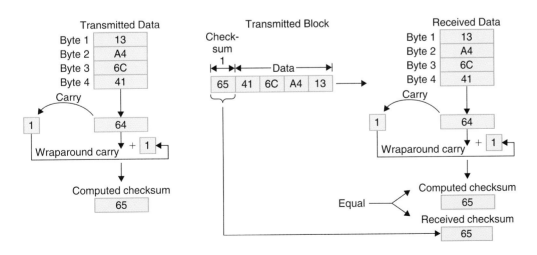

FIGURE 17-11
Structure of the *residue checksum*. The checksum is generated and transmitted as the BCC at the end of a 4-byte block. The receiver verifies the block by regenerating the checksum and comparing it against the original.

17.7 ERROR CORRECTION

Two basic techniques are used by communication systems to ensure the reliable transmission of data. They are shown in Figure 17-12. One technique is to request the retransmission of the data block received in error. This technique, the more popular of the two, is known as *automatic repeat request (ARQ)*. When a data block is received without error, a positive acknowledgment is sent back to the transmitter via the reverse channel. ACK alternating in BISYNC is an example of a protocol that uses ARQ for error correction. A second technique is called *forward error correction (FEC)*. FEC is used in simplex communications or applications where it is impractical or impossible to request a retransmission of the corrupted message block. An example might be the telemetry signals transmitted to an earth station from a satellite on a deep space mission. A garbled message could take several minutes or even hours to travel the distance between the two stations. Redundant error-correction coding is included in the transmitted data stream. If an error is detected by the receiver, the redundant code is extracted from the message block and used to predict and possibly correct the discrepancy.

> **Automatic Repeat Request (ARQ)**
> An error-correction method in which a receiver requests retransmission of a block received in error.

> **Forward Error Correction (FEC)**
> In simplex communication, an error-correction method that extracts a redundant code to predict and correct an error without retransmission.

17.7.1 Hamming Code

In FEC, a return path is not used for requesting the retransmission of a message block in error, hence the name *forward error correction*. Several codes have been developed to suit applications requiring FEC.* Those most commonly recognized have been

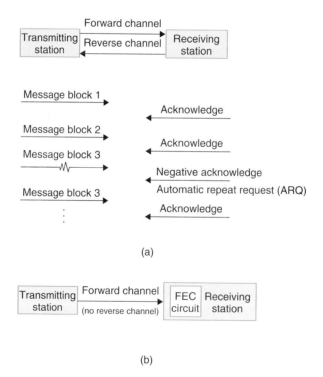

(a)

(b)

FIGURE 17-12

(a) Error correction using the ARQ technique; (b) error correction using FEC.

---

*For further details on Hamming codes, see Richard W. Hamming, *Coding and Information Theory*, 2nd ed. (Englewood Cliffs, N.J.: Prentice-Hall, 1986).

based on the research of mathematician Richard W. Hamming. These codes are referred to as *Hamming codes*. Hamming codes employ the use of redundant bits that are inserted into the message stream for error correction. The positions of these bits are established and known by the transmitter and receiver beforehand. If the receiver detects an error in the message block, the Hamming bits are used to identify the position of the error. This position, known as the *syndrome*, is the underlying principle of the Hamming code.

Hamming Codes
A redundant set of bits inserted into a message stream with which to perform FEC.

17.7.1.1 Developing a Hamming Code

We now develop a Hamming code for single-bit FEC. For simplicity, 10 data bits will be used. The number of Hamming bits depends on the number of data bits, $m_0, m_1, \ldots, m_n$ transmitted in the message stream, including the Hamming bits. If n is equal to the total number of bits transmitted in a message stream and m is equal to the number of Hamming bits, then m is the smallest number governed by the equation

Syndrome
Identifies the bit location of an error in a message stream in systems employing FEC.

$$2^m \geq n + 1$$

For a message of 10 data bits, m is equal to 4 and n is equal to 14 bits $(10 + 4)$:

$$2^4 \geq (10 + 4) + 1$$

If the syndrome is to indicate the position of the bit error, *check bits*, or Hamming bits, $C_0, C_1, C_2, \ldots$, serving as parity, can be inserted into the message stream to perform a parity check based on the binary representation of each bit position. How is this possible? Note in Table 17-2 that the binary representation of each bit position forms an alternating bit pattern in the vertical direction. Each column proceeding from the LSB to the MSB alternates at half the rate of the previous column. The LSB alternates with every position, the next bit alternates every two bit positions, and so forth.

Check Bit
A redundant parity bit inserted in a message stream with which to perform FEC.

TABLE 17-2

Check Bits Can Be Used as Parity on Binary Weighted Positions in a Message Stream

Bit Position in Message	Binary Representation	Check Bit	Positions Set
1	0001	C_0	1, 3, 5, 7, 9, 11, 13
2	0010	C_1	2, 3, 6, 7, 10, 11, 14
3	0011	C_2	4, 5, 6, 7, 12, 13, 14
4	0100	C_3	8, 9, 10, 11, 12, 13, 14
5	0101		
6	0110		
7	0111		
8	1000		
9	1001		
10	1010		
11	1011		
12	1100		
13	1101		
14	1110		
*	*		
*	*		
*	*		

To illustrate how the check bits are encoded, the 10-bit message 1101001110 is labeled m_9 through m_0, as illustrated in Figure 17-13. By inserting the check bits into the message stream as shown, the total message length n is extended to 14 bits. The binary-weighted bit positions 1, 2, 4, and 8 will be used for the check bits. Even or odd parity generation can be performed on the bit positions associated with each check bit. We will use even parity here. As discussed earlier, even parity can be performed by exclusive-ORing individual bits in a group of bits. For even parity, PE0 through PE3 can serve as weighted parity checks over the bit positions listed in Table 17-2. Exclusive-ORing these bit positions together with the data corresponding to the 14-bit message stream shown in Figure 17-13 produces the following:

$$\begin{array}{ccccccc} 13 & 11 & 9 & 7 & 5 & 3 & 1 \leftarrow \text{bit positions} \end{array}$$
$$PE0 = 0 = m_8 \oplus m_6 \oplus m_4 \oplus m_3 \oplus m_1 \oplus m_0 \oplus C_0$$
$$\begin{array}{ccccccc} 14 & 11 & 10 & 7 & 6 & 3 & 2 \leftarrow \text{bit positions} \end{array}$$
$$PE1 = 0 = m_9 \oplus m_6 \oplus m_5 \oplus m_3 \oplus m_2 \oplus m_0 \oplus C_1$$
$$\begin{array}{ccccccc} 14 & 13 & 12 & 7 & 6 & 5 & 4 \leftarrow \text{bit positions} \end{array}$$
$$PE2 = 0 = m_9 \oplus m_8 \oplus m_7 \oplus m_3 \oplus m_2 \oplus m_1 \oplus C_2$$
$$\begin{array}{ccccccc} 14 & 13 & 12 & 11 & 10 & 9 & 8 \leftarrow \text{bit positions} \end{array}$$
$$PE3 = 0 = m_9 \oplus m_8 \oplus m_7 \oplus m_6 \oplus m_5 \oplus m_4 \oplus C_3$$

To determine the value of the check bits C_0 through C_3, the equations above can be rearranged as follows:

$$\begin{aligned} C_0 &= m_8 \oplus m_6 \oplus m_4 \oplus m_3 \oplus m_1 \oplus m_0 \\ &= 1 \oplus 1 \oplus 0 \oplus 1 \oplus 1 \oplus 0 = 0 \\ C_1 &= m_9 \oplus m_6 \oplus m_5 \oplus m_3 \oplus m_2 \oplus m_0 \\ &= 1 \oplus 1 \oplus 0 \oplus 1 \oplus 1 \oplus 0 = 0 \\ C_2 &= m_9 \oplus m_8 \oplus m_7 \oplus m_3 \oplus m_2 \oplus m_1 \\ &= 1 \oplus 1 \oplus 0 \oplus 1 \oplus 1 \oplus 1 = 1 \\ C_3 &= m_9 \oplus m_8 \oplus m_7 \oplus m_6 \oplus m_5 \oplus m_4 \\ &= 1 \oplus 1 \oplus 0 \oplus 1 \oplus 0 \oplus 0 = 1 \end{aligned} \right\rbrace \text{even parity}$$

Thus, the check bits inserted into the message stream in positions 8, 4, 2, and 1 are:

$$C_3 = 1$$
$$C_2 = 1$$
$$C_1 = 0$$
$$C_0 = 0$$

Let us now look at how a bit error can be identified and corrected by the weighted parity checks. Suppose that an error has been detected in the transmitted message stream. Bit position 7 has been lost in the transmission:

$$1\ 1\ 0\ 1\ 0\ 0\ 1\ 1\ 1\ 1\ 0\ 0\ 0 \leftarrow \text{transmitted bit stream}$$
$$\downarrow \text{(lost in transmission)}$$
$$1\ 1\ 0\ 1\ 0\ 0\ 1\ 0\ 1\ 1\ 1\ 0\ 0\ 0 \leftarrow \text{received bit stream}$$
$$\uparrow \text{error in bit position 7}$$

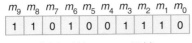

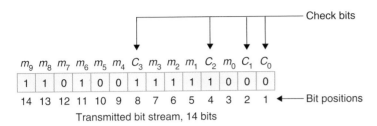

Original bit stream, 10 bits

Check bits

14 13 12 11 10 9 8 7 6 5 4 3 2 1 ← Bit positions

Transmitted bit stream, 14 bits

FIGURE 17-13
Check bits are inserted into a message stream for FEC.

The receiver performs an even parity check over the same bit positions as discussed earlier. Even parity should result for each parity check if there are no errors. Because a bit error has occurred, however, the syndrome (location of the error) will be identified by the binary number produced by the parity checks, PE0 through PE3, as follows:

$$14 \quad 13 \quad 12 \quad 11 \quad 10 \quad 9 \quad 8 \quad 7 \quad 6 \quad 5 \quad 4 \quad 3 \quad 2 \quad 1 \leftarrow \text{bit position}$$
$$1 \quad 1 \quad 0 \quad 1 \quad 0 \quad 0 \quad 1 \quad 0 \quad 1 \quad 1 \quad 1 \quad 0 \quad 0 \quad 0 \leftarrow \text{received bit stream}$$

Check 0: 13   11   9   7   5   3   1 = ← bit position
$$\text{PE0} = 1 \oplus 1 \oplus 0 \oplus 0 \oplus 1 \oplus 0 \oplus 0 = 1 \text{ (even parity failure) } 1$$

Check 1: 14   11   10   7   6   3   2 = ← bit position
$$\text{PE1} = 1 \oplus 1 \oplus 0 \oplus 0 \oplus 1 \oplus 0 \oplus 0 = 1 \text{ (even parity failure) } 1$$

Check 2: 14   13   12   7   6   5   4 = ← bit position
$$\text{PE2} = 1 \oplus 1 \oplus 0 \oplus 0 \oplus 1 \oplus 1 \oplus 1 = 1 \text{ (even parity failure) } 1$$

Check 3: 14   13   12   11   10   9   8 = ← bit position
$$\text{PE3} = 1 \oplus 1 \oplus 0 \oplus 1 \oplus 0 \oplus 0 \oplus 1 = 0 \text{ (correct) } \quad 0$$

syndrome = 0111 = 7

The resulting syndrome is 0111, or bit position 7. This bit is simply inverted, and the four parity checks will result in 0000 (correct). The check bits are removed from positions 1, 2, 4, and 8, thereby resulting in the original message. One nice feature of this Hamming code is that once the message is encoded, there is *no difference* between the check bits and the original message bits; that is, the syndrome can just as well identify a check bit in error.

17.7.1.2 An Alternative Method   Now that we have established the principle behind a Hamming code, an alternative method for correcting a single-bit error will be given here. The disadvantage with this method, however, is that it will not detect an error if it occurs in the Hamming bit. For simplicity, the same 10-bit message stream, 1101001110, will be used. Therefore, the number of Hamming bits, four, remains the same. The Hamming bits can actually be placed anywhere in the transmitted message stream as long as their positions are known by the transmitter and receiver. The procedure is outlined as follows:

1. Compute the number of Hamming bits m required for a message of n bits.

$$\text{Original message stream: } 1\ 1\ 0\ 1\ 0\ 0\ 1\ 1\ 1\ 0\ (10\text{ bits})$$
$$2^m \geq n + 1$$
$$2^4 \geq (10 + 4) + 1, \qquad m = 4,$$
$$n = 14$$

2. Insert the Hamming bits H into the original message stream. Transmitted message stream:

14	13	12	11	10	9	8	7	6	5	4	3	2	1	← bit position (14 bits)
1	H	1	0	H	1	0	0	1	H	1	H	1	0	

3. Express each bit position containing a 1 as a 4-bit binary number, and exclusive-OR each of these numbers together. Starting from the left, bit positions 14, 12, 9, 6, 4, and 2 are exclusive-ORed together. This will result in the value of the Hamming bits.

$$
\begin{array}{rl}
 & 1110 = 14 \\
\oplus & \underline{1100} = 12 \\
 & 0010 \\
\oplus & \underline{1001} = 9 \\
 & 1011 \\
\oplus & \underline{0110} = 6 \\
 & 1101 \\
\oplus & \underline{0100} = 4 \\
 & 1001 \\
\oplus & \underline{0010} = 2 \\
 & 1011 \leftarrow \text{Hamming bits}
\end{array}
$$

4. Place the value of the Hamming bits into the transmitted message stream shown in step 2.

14	13	12	11	10	9	8	7	6	5	4	3	2	1	← bit position
1	1	1	0	0	1	0	0	1	1	1	1	1	0	← transmitted bit stream
1	1	1	0	0	1	0	0	0	1	1	1	1	0	← received bit stream

↑
error in bit position 6

Let us now assume that bit position 6 was received in error.

5. The Hamming bits are extracted from the received message stream and exclusive-ORed with the binary representation of the bit positions containing a 1. This will detect the bit position in error, or the syndrome.

14	13	12	11	10	9	8	7	6	5	4	3	2	1	
1		1	0		1	0	0	0		1		1	0	
	1			0					1		1			← extracted Hamming bits

$$1011 = \text{Hamming bits}$$
$$\oplus \underline{1110} = 14$$
$$0101$$
$$\oplus \underline{1100} = 12$$
$$1001$$
$$\oplus \underline{1001} = 9$$
$$0000$$
$$\oplus \underline{0100} = 4$$
$$0100$$
$$\oplus \underline{0010} = 2$$
$$0110 \leftarrow \text{syndrome equals bit position 6}$$

To detect multiple bit errors, more elaborate FEC techniques are necessary. Additional redundancy must be built into the message stream. This further reduces the efficiency of the channel and lowers the transmission system's throughput. Unlike ARQ, which is extremely reliable, the best FEC techniques are not, particularly when multiple bits are destroyed due to noise bursts. Generally, FEC is employed only in applications when ARQ is not feasible. The detection of multiple-bit errors is beyond the scope of this book.

PROBLEMS

1. Draw two circuit diagrams that can be used for odd parity generation for an 8-bit word.
2. Draw two circuit diagrams that can be used for even parity checking.
3. Explain why an even number of bit errors in a character will go undetected using parity for error detection. Show an example to support your explanation.
4. Using 7-bit ASCII and parity, determine the block check character using LRC for the message "Just do it!" Use even parity.
5. In problem 4, show how a combination of LRC and VRC can detect an error if bit D2 were to change in the letter o during the course of transmission.
6. Given the generator polynomial $G(x) = X^5 + X^3 + X + 1$ and the message polynomial $M(x) = X^9 + X^7 + X^6 + X^2 + 1$, compute the following:
   a. Number of bits in the BCC
   b. Product of $X^{n-k}[M(x)]$
   c. Discarded quotient
   d. BCC, $B(x)$
   e. Total transmitted message block, $T(x) = X^{n-k}[M(x)] + B(x)$
7. Repeat problem 6 using CRC-CCITT for the message polynomial $M(x) = X^{15} + X^{14} + X^{12} + X^8 + X^6 + X^5 + X^3 + 1$.
8. For problem 7, show how the receiver performs a CRC-16 check on the received message stream to verify that the message was received without errors.
9. Name four types of checksums.
10. What happens to any carry bit in single-precision checksums?
11. Compute the single-precision checksum for a 4-byte block with hex characters 4E, 3D, 92, and EA.
12. Compute the single-precision checksum for a 5-byte block with hex characters 7B, 2F, 37, 6A, and 4C.
13. Repeat problem 12, but use the double-precision checksum technique.
14. What is the advantage of the double-precision checksum over the single-precision checksum?

15. Compute the Honeywell checksum for a 6-byte message block with hex characters 12, BC, F4, 8C, CA, and 68.
16. What is the advantage of the Honeywell checksum over single- or double-precision checksums?
17. Compute the residue checksum for the six-byte message block in Problem 15.
18. Define *SA1 error* and *SA0 error*.
19. Explain the difference between ARQ and FEC.
20. Are Hamming codes used in ARQ or FEC?
21. Using the Hamming code developed in Section 17.7.1.1, compute the following:
    a. Even parity check bits C_0 through C_3, for the 10-bit message 1011101011
    b. Total message stream with the check bits included
    c. Syndrome, through parity checks, if bit position 4 is corrupted
    d. Syndrome, through parity checks, if bit position 13 is corrupted
22. Using the alternative method described in this chapter for Hamming codes and given the 12-bit message 101110101011, determine the following:
    a. Number of Hamming bits, m, required
    b. Total number of transmitted bits, n
    c. Values of the Hamming bits if they are placed in odd *bit positions* starting from the MSB of the total transmitted bit stream and proceeding to the LSB until all Hamming bits are used
    d. Syndrome if bit position 10 is corrupted. (Be sure to show this through the exclusive-OR process outlined in the chapter.)

18

FIBER OPTICS

Fiber optics is one of the most explosive technologies in today's informational age. In the past few decades alone, technical advances in this field have grown from mere laboratory experiments to major industries involved with the development and production of advanced optical communication systems. Fiber optics is finding use in virtually every application involving transmission of information. Computers can now be linked together with fiber-optic cables capable of transferring data several orders of magnitude faster than copper circuits. In the medical industry, fiber-optic technology is being used to monitor and perform complex surgical operations. Throughout the world, telephone and cable TV companies are laying thousands of miles of fiber underground, below oceanic floors and rivers and through manholes and existing conduit facilities. Thousands of simultaneous voice conversations are now being transmitted over these tiny strands of fiber less than the diameter of a human hair.

Fiber optics is defined as that branch of optics that deals with the transmission of light through ultrapure fibers of glass, plastic, or some other form of transparent media. From a decorative standpoint, most of us are familiar with the fiber-optic lamp, which uses bundles of thin optical fibers illuminated from the base end of the lamp by a light source. The light source is made to vary in color, which can be seen at the opposite ends of the fiber as a tree of illuminating points radiating various colors of the transmitted light. Although the lamp is used for decorative purposes only, it serves as an excellent model of how light can be transmitted through fiber.

Fiber Optics
A communications technology using transmission of light over glass or plastic fibers.

18.1 HISTORY OF FIBER OPTICS

The use of light as a mechanized means of communicating has long been a part of our history. Paul Revere, as we know, used light back in 1775 to give warning of the approach of British troops from Boston. In 1880, Alexander Graham Bell invented a device called the *photophone*. The photophone used sunlight reflected off a moving diaphragm to communicate voice information to a receiver. Although the device worked, it was slightly ahead of its time.

One of the first noted experiments that demonstrated the transmission of light through a dielectric medium has been credited to a British natural philosopher and scientist named John Tyndall. In 1854, Tyndall demonstrated before the British Royal Society that light could be guided through a stream of water based on the principle of *total internal reflection*: rays of light can propagate through a transparent medium

Photophone
A device that uses sunlight reflected off a moving diaphragm to communicate voice information.

Total Internal Reflection
The principle, used in fiber optics, governing how light rays propagate through a transparent medium by reflecting off its boundaries.

539

by reflecting off its boundaries. (This vital principle is discussed in detail later in this chapter.) Tyndall's apparatus is shown in Figure 18-1. It included a bucket of water illuminated at its surface by a bright light source. A hole was punched and corked off near its bottom. When Tyndall released the cork, gravitational force caused the water to jet out of the hole and arc its way down to a lower glass container. Light could be seen arcing its way down to the lower container, which in turn was illuminated by the dispersion of the propagating medium. Much to the dismay of his audience, his experiment was successful and dispelled earlier theory that light travels in a straight line.

18.1.1   Milestones in Fiber Optics

Tyndall's experiment marked one of the first major milestones in the development of fiber-optic technology as it stands today. The progressive sequence of milestones to follow were few and generally regarded as interesting concepts only to the scientific

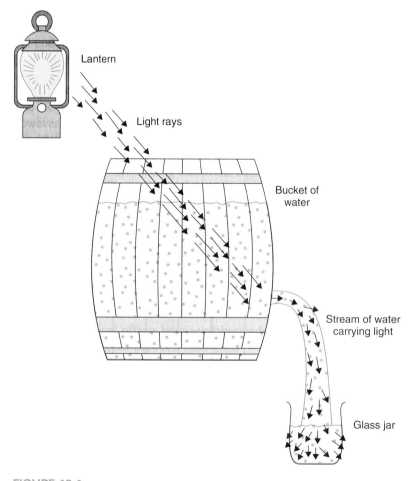

FIGURE 18-1
John Tyndall's demonstration before the British Royal Society proved that light could be guided through a transparent medium based on the principle of total internal reflection.

elite. Not until the last few decades has fiber optics become a revolutionary trend in industry. Consider the major milestones to this date:

1854   John Tyndall demonstrated before the British Royal Society that light could be guided by its boundaries through a transparent medium based on the principle of *total internal reflection.*

1880   Alexander Graham Bell invented the *photophone,* a device that transmits voice signals over a beam of light.

1950s   Brian O'Brien, Sr., Harry Hopkins, and Naringer Kapany developed the two-layer fiber consisting of an inner *core,* in which light propagates, and an outer layer surrounding the core called the *cladding,* which is used to confine the light. The fiber was later used by the same scientists to develop the flexible *fiberscope,* a device capable of transmitting an image from one end of the fiber to its opposite end. Its flexibility allows peering into areas that are normally not accessible. The fiberscope, to this day, is still widely used, particularly in the medical profession to peer into the human body.

1958   Invention of the *laser* (light amplification by stimulated emissions of radiation) by Charles H. Townes allowed intense and concentrated light sources to be coupled into fiber.

1966   Charles K. Kao and George Hockham of Standard Telecommunications Laboratories of England performed several experiments to prove that if glass could be made more transparent by reducing its impurities, light loss could be minimized. Their research led to a publication in which they predicted that optical fiber could be made pure enough to transmit light several kilometers. The global race to produce the optimum fiber began.

1967   Losses in optical fiber were reported at 1000 dB/km.

1970   Losses in optical fiber were reported at 20 dB/km.

1976   Losses in optical fiber were reported at 0.5 dB/km.

1979   Losses in optical fiber were reported at 0.2 dB/km.

1987   Losses in optical fiber were reported at 0.16 dB/km.

1988   NEC Corporation sets a new long-haul record of 10 Gbits/s over 80.1 km of dispersion-shifted fiber using a distributed feedback laser.

1988   The *Synchronous Optical Network (SONET)* was published by the *American National Standards Institute (ANSI).*

1993   The emergence of wavelength-division multiplexing (WDM).

1998   Dense wavelength-division multiplexing (DWDM) emerges, with 80-color-band systems operating at 400-Gbps speeds.

2000   Lucent Technologies' Bell Labs envisions lasers pulsing at 40 Gbps, with hundreds of DWDM beams operating at terabit (trillion) speeds—and beyond.

18.2 ADVANTAGES OF FIBER-OPTIC SYSTEMS

The advantages of fiber-optic systems warrant considerable attention. This new technology has clearly affected the telecommunications industry and will continue to thrive due to the numerous advantages it has over its copper counterpart. The major advantages include:

Bandwidth   One of the most significant advantages of fiber over copper or other transmission media is bandwidth. Bandwidth is directly related to the amount of information that can be transmitted per unit time. Today's advanced fiber-optic systems transmit several *gigabits* per second over hundreds of kilometers. Thousands of voice channels can now be multiplexed together and sent over a single fiber strand.

Less Loss   Currently, fiber is being manufactured to exhibit less than a few tenths of a decibel of loss per kilometer. Imagine glass so pure that you could see through a window over 75 miles (120 km) thick! Repeaters can now be spaced 50 to 75 miles apart from each other.

Noise Immunity and Safety   Because fiber is constructed of dielectric material, it is immune to inductive coupling or crosstalk from adjacent copper or fiber channels. In other words, it is not affected by electromagnetic interference (EMI) or electrostatic interference. This includes environments where there are electric motors, relays, and even lightning. Likewise, because fiber-optic cables transmit light instead of current, they do not emit electrical noise, nor do they arc when there is an intermittent in the link. Thus, they are useful in areas where EMI must be kept to a minimum. With the telecommunications highways of the air as congested as they are, the use of fiber is an attractive alternative.

Less Weight and Volume   Fiber-optic cables are substantially lighter in weight and occupy much less volume than copper cables with the same information capacity. Fiber-optic cables are being used to relieve congested underground ducts in metropolitan and suburban areas. For example, a 3-in. diameter telephone cable consisting of 900 twisted-pair wires can be replaced with a single fiber strand 0.005 in. in diameter (approximately the diameter of a hair strand) and retain the same information-carrying capacity. Even with a rugged protective jacket surrounding the fiber, it occupies enormously less space and weighs considerably less.

Security   Because light does not radiate from a fiber-optic cable, it is nearly impossible to secretly tap into it without detection. For this reason, several applications requiring communications security employ fiber-optic systems. Military information, for example, can be transmitted over fiber to prevent eavesdropping. In addition, fiber-optic cables cannot be detected by metal detectors unless they are manufactured with steel reinforcement for strength.

Flexibility   We normally think of glass as being extremely brittle. If one were to attempt to bend a 1/8-in. thick glass window, it would certainly break at some point. One reason is that the glass we are familiar with has a considerable amount of surface flaws, although it appears polished. The outer surface of the glass would bend considerably more than the inside. The surface flaws would initiate the crack in the same manner that long scratches are intentionally used to crack and form glass windows. The surface of glass fiber is much more refined than ordinary glass. This, coupled with its small diameter, allows it to be flexible enough to wrap around a pencil. In terms of strength, if enough pressure is applied against it, a 0.005-in. strand of fiber is strong enough to cut one's finger before it breaks.

Economics   Presently, the cost of fiber is comparable to copper, at approximately $0.20 to $0.50 per yard, and is expected to drop as it becomes more widely used.

Because transmission losses are considerably less than for coaxial cable, expensive repeaters can be spaced farther apart. Fewer repeaters means a reduction in overall system costs and enhanced reliability.

Reliability   Once installed, a longer life span is expected with fiber over its metallic counterparts, because it is more resistant to corrosion caused by environmental extremes such as temperature, corrosive gases, and liquids. Many coating systems made of lacquer, silicons, and ultraviolet-cured acrylates have been developed to maintain fiber strength and longevity.

18.3   DISADVANTAGES OF FIBER-OPTIC SYSTEMS

In spite of the numerous advantages that fiber-optic systems have over conventional methods of transmission, there are some disadvantages, particularly because of its newness. Many of these disadvantages are being overcome with new and competitive technology. Disadvantages include:

Interfacing Costs   Electronic facilities must be converted to optics to interface to fiber. Often these costs are initially overlooked. Fiber-optic transmitters, receivers, couplers, and connectors, for example, must be employed as part of the communication system. Test and repair equipment is costly. If the fiber-optic cable breaks, splicing can be a costly and tedious task. Manufacturers, however, are continuously introducing new and improved field repair kits.

Strength   Fiber, by itself, has a tensile strength of approximately 1 lb, compared with coaxial cable at 180 lb (RG59U). Surrounding the fiber with stranded *Kevlar** and a protective PVC jacket can increase the pulling strength to 500 lb. Installations requiring greater tensile strengths can be achieved with steel reinforcement.

> **Kevlar**
> A nonmetallic, difficult-to-stretch, strengthening material.

Remote Powering of Devices   Occasionally, it is necessary to provide electrical power to a remote device. Because this cannot be achieved through the fiber, metallic conductors are often included in the cable assembly. Several manufacturers now offer a complete line of cable types, including cables manufactured with both copper wire and fiber.

18.4   A TYPICAL FIBER-OPTIC TELECOMMUNICATIONS SYSTEM

Before we begin a detailed discussion of fiber optics, a simplified optical telecommunications system is now considered. Figure 18-2 illustrates such a system. The analog signal generated by the telephone set is input to the coder section. Here, it is digitized and encoded into a 64-kbps binary serial bit stream. The bit stream is used to modulate the light source, which in turn transmits the series of light pulses into the optical fiber. At the receiving end, the impulses of light are converted back to an electrical signal by the light detector. The decoder section of the system converts the

---

*Kevlar is a registered trademark of E.I. du Pont de Nemours Corporation. It is a nonmetallic material that is difficult to stretch.

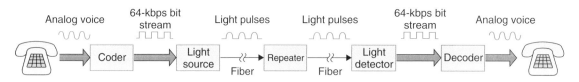

FIGURE 18-2
Simplified optical telecommunications system.

binary serial bit stream back to the original analog signal. This signal can now be used by the telephone set to reproduce the original sound energy.

There is nothing new about the analog-to-digital conversion process. Telephone companies have been digitizing voice signals since the early 1960s. It is the conversion from electrical impulses to light impulses, and vice versa, that the more modern technology employs.

The light source, acting as the transmitting element, must be turned on and off in accordance with the binary serial bit stream. Infrared *light-emitting diodes (LEDs)* and *injection laser diodes (ILDs)* are used for this purpose. These devices are specially designed to turn on and off several millions and, in some cases, billions of times per second.

The light detector, acting as the receiving element, converts the received light pulses back to pulses of electrical current. Two devices commonly used for this purpose are the *photodiode* and *phototransistor.* Both behave in their normal manner, except that they are activated by light instead of bias current.

If two stations are separated far enough from each other, at some point in the fiber-optic link the light pulses become so weak and distorted that the underlying signal is not recoverable. Fiber-optic repeaters are necessary in this case. From a scientific standpoint, optical amplifiers could be used to amplify the weak light pulses. However, from a practical standpoint, this is not what is done. Instead, an optical receiving element is used to convert the signal back to electrical form. The reproduced weak and distorted electrical signal is then processed in the same manner as a repeater would in a metallic cable or microwave radio link. The reconstructed signal is then converted back to light by a transmitting element and sent back into the fiber-optic cable.

18.5 THEORY OF LIGHT

The subject of *light* remains an extraordinary phenomenon. Since the earliest known existence of people, philosophers, mathematicians, and physicists have theorized and refuted each other in an attempt to explain the nature of light. Few subjects in the scientific realm have been studied to such an extreme as light, yet to this date, there is no simple explanation.

In the seventeenth and eighteenth centuries, there were two schools of thought regarding the nature of light. Sir Isaac Newton and his followers believed that light consisted of rapidly moving *particles* (or *corpuscles*), whereas Dutch physicist Christian Huygens regarded light as being a series of *waves.*

The wave theory was strongly supported by an English doctor named Thomas Young. As a student at Cambridge University, Young's interests included the study of sound waves and their effects on the human ear. Noting the similarities between the interaction of sound waves and waves produced by water, Young was inspired to in-

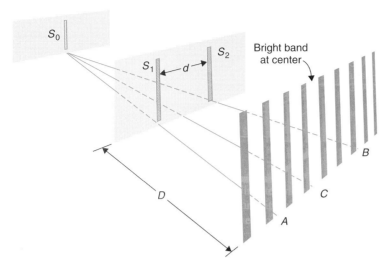

FIGURE 18-3
A light from a distant line source, S_0, is incident (near normal) on a screen having two closely spaced parallel slits, S_1 and S_2. The light from the two parallel slits is observed to form alternating bright and dark bands (fringes) on a distant screen, with a bright fringe at the center, *C*, of the screen. According to the particle theory, there should be bright light *only* at positions *A* and *B*, not at *C*. (From H.Y. Carr and R. Weidner, *Physics from the Ground Up* [New York: McGraw-Hill, 1971].)

vestigate the hypothesis that light was also a series of waves. This lead to Young's famous *double-slit experiment*, shown in Figure 18-3. His experiment clearly proved that the particle theory was seemingly absurd. In addition, if two beams of light were viewed crossing each other, the particle theory would support the occurrence of collisions at the intersection. Crossing two beams, however, does not seem to influence each other.

By the twentieth century, light was fundamentally accepted as having many of the properties established by James Clerk Maxwell. In 1860, Maxwell theorized that *electromagnetic radiation* consists of a series of oscillating waves made up of an electric field and a magnetic field propagating at right angles to each other. By 1905, however, quantum theory, introduced by Albert Einstein and Max Planck, showed that when light is emitted or absorbed it behaves not only as a wave but also as an electromagnetic *particle* called a *photon*. A photon is said to possess energy that is proportional to its frequency (or inversely proportional to its wavelength). This is known as *Planck's Law*, which states that

> **Photon**
> An electromagnetic particle, regarded as a particle of light, possessing energy in proportion to its frequency.

$$E = h \times v \qquad \textbf{(18-1)}$$

where E = photon's energy (J)
h = Planck's constant, 6.63×10^{-34} J-s
v = frequency of the photon (Hz)

Compute the energy of a single photon radiating from a standard light bulb. Assume that the average frequency of the emitted light is 10^{14} Hz (which has a wavelength equal to 300 nm).

**EXAMPLE
18.1**

Solution:

$$E = h \times v$$
$$= 6.63 \times 10^{-34} \text{ J-s} \times 10^{14} \text{ Hz}$$
$$= 6.63 \times 10^{-20} \text{ J}$$

Using the particle theory, Einstein and Planck were able to explain the *photo-electric effect:* when visible light or electromagnetic radiation of a higher frequency shines on a metallic surface, electrons are emitted, which in turn produce an electric current. The photoelectric effect is used in burglar alarms, door openers, and the like. And so it stands; the nature of light can be described as a particle or as a wave, depending on the circumstances.

18.5.1 Electromagnetic Spectrum

Maxwell's extensive research on electromagnetic wave theory has enabled other scientists to establish frequencies and wavelengths associated with various forms of light. Fundamentally, light has been accepted as a form of electromagnetic radiation that can be categorized into a portion of the entire *electromagnetic spectrum,* as shown in Figure 18-4. The spectrum, as it stands today, covers DC to cosmic rays. Each frequency has its own characteristic in terms of behavior and physical response to a given transmission medium. In addition, each frequency can be specified in terms of its equivalent *wavelength.* Frequency and wavelength are directly related to the speed of light. For most practical purposes, they are governed by the equation

> **Electromagnetic Spectrum**
> The range of electromagnetic radiation, from DC to cosmic rays.

$$c = f \times \lambda \tag{18-2}$$

where c = speed of light, 3×10^8 m/s
f = frequency (Hz)
λ = wavelength (m)

EXAMPLE 18.2

Compute the wavelength for a frequency of 7.20 MHz.

Solution:

$$c = f \times \lambda$$

Therefore,

$$\lambda = \frac{c}{f}$$

$$= \frac{3 \times 10^8 \text{ m/s}}{7.2 \times 10^6 \text{ Hz}} = 41.7 \text{ m}$$

That portion of the electromagnetic spectrum regarded as light has been expanded in Figure 18-4 to illustrate the three basic categories of light:

1. *Infrared:* That portion of the electromagnetic spectrum having a wavelength ranging from 770 to 10^6 nm. Fiber-optic systems operate in this range.
2. *Visible:* That portion of the electromagnetic spectrum having a wavelength ranging from 390 to 770 nm. The human eye, responding to these wavelengths, allows us to see the colors ranging from violet to red, respectively.

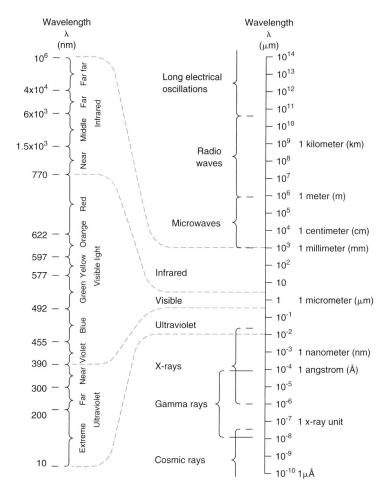

FIGURE 18-4
Electromagnetic spectrum showing the approximate boundaries between spectral regions. (Courtesy of RCA.)

3. *Ultraviolet:* That portion of the electromagnetic spectrum having a wavelength ranging from 10 to 390 nm.

Light waves are commonly specified in terms of wavelength instead of frequency. Units typically used are the *nanometer, micrometer,* and *angstrom*. Table 18-1 lists their relationship to the meter and the inch.

TABLE 18-1
Units Typically Used to Designate the Wavelength of Light

Unit	Meters	Inches
Nanometer	10^{-9}	39.4×10^{-9}
Micrometer	10^{-6}	39.4×10^{-6}
Angstrom	10^{-10}	3.94×10^{-9}

The light that we use for most fiber-optic systems occupies a wavelength range from 800 to 1600 nm (for reasons explained later). This is slightly larger than visible red light in terms of wavelength and falls within the infrared portion of the spectrum.

18.5.2   Speed of Light

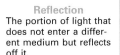

Speed of Light
Approximately 3×10^8 meters per second, or 186 thousand miles per second, in a vacuum.

The *speed of light* is at its maximum velocity when traveling in a vacuum or free space. It is equal to

$$(2.997925 \pm 0.000001) \times 10^8 \text{ m/s} \approx 3 \times 10^8 \text{ m/s}$$

(300 million meters per second or 186,000 miles per second). This figure has been universally established as a fact of nature despite numerous attempts to exceed it by changing parameters such as wavelength, intensity, transmission medium, and point of reference. In mediums other than free space, the speed of light is noticeably *reduced* and no longer independent of wavelength. Its direction and reduced speed, however, will remain the same, just as in a vacuum, as long as the composition of the medium in which it propagates is uniform throughout. If the medium changes, both speed and direction will change.

18.5.3   Snell's Law

For light to propagate in any medium, the medium must be *transparent* to some degree. The degree of transparency determines how far light will propagate. Transparent materials can be in the form of a liquid, gas, or a solid. Some examples are glass, plastic, air, and water.

Reflection
The portion of light that does not enter a different medium but reflects off it.

One of the most fundamental principles of light is that when it strikes the interface between two transparent mediums, such as air and water, a portion of the light energy is reflected back into the first medium and a portion is transmitted into the second medium. The path in which light travels from one point to another is commonly referred to as the *ray*. Figure 18-5 illustrates the classic example of a ray of light incident on the surface of water. Note that part of the light is *reflected* off the

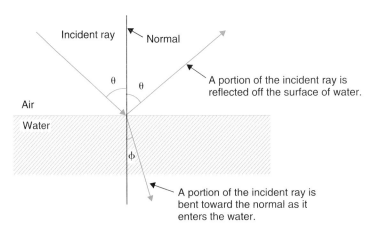

FIGURE 18-5
A light ray incident on the surface of water is bent toward the normal.

surface of the water and part of it penetrates the water. The ray penetrating the water is said to be *refracted* or *bent* toward the *normal*. The normal is a line drawn perpendicular to the surface. The angle of incidence is equal to the angle of reflection, whereas the angle of refraction is bent toward the normal. This bending occurs at the surface of the water because of a change in the speed of light. Light actually travels slower in a more dense medium, which in this case is the water. If the direction of the light ray were reversed, the opposite effect would occur: the speed of the light ray would increase as it exits the more dense medium of water into the less dense medium of air. The light ray would bend *away* from the normal. Figure 18-6 illustrates how light interacts through a glass plate and through a lens.

The amount of bending that light undergoes when entering a different medium is determined by the medium's *index of refraction*, generally denoted by the letter n. Index of refraction is the ratio of the speed of light in a vacuum, c, to the speed of light in the given medium, v. This relationship is given by the equation

$$n = \frac{c}{v} \tag{18-3}$$

Because the speed of light is lower in mediums other than a vacuum, the index of refraction in such mediums is always *greater* than 1. Table 18-2 lists the index of refraction for several common materials.

> **Refraction**
> Bending of light, either toward or away from normal, when it enters a different medium.

> **Normal**
> A perpendicular line drawn to the surface of an object or medium.

> **Index of Refraction**
> Determines the amount of bending that light undergoes when entering a different medium.

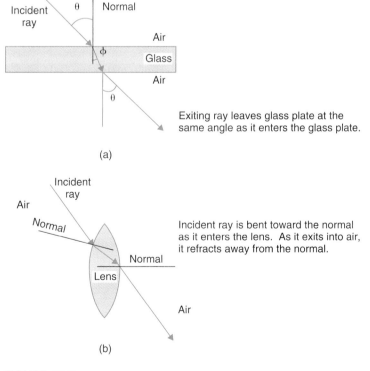

(a)

(b)

FIGURE 18-6
(a) A light ray enters a glass plate and is bent toward the normal. Its speed is reduced. As it emerges from the glass plate, it is bent away from the normal and returns to its original speed. (b) A light ray is bent toward the normal as it enters a lens. As it exits the lens, it is bent away from the normal.

TABLE 18-2
Index of Refraction for Various Mediums

Medium	Index of Refraction
Vacuum	1.0
Air	1.0003
Water	1.33
Ethyl alcohol	1.36
Fused quartz	1.46
Optical fiber	1.6 (nominal)
Diamond	2.2 (nominal)

In 1621, the Dutch mathematician Willebrord Snell established that rays of light can be traced as they propagate from one medium to another based on their indices of refraction. *Snell's Law* is stated by the equation

> **Snell's Law**
> A fundamental law in optics that predicts the path of light rays as they travel between media.

$$\textbf{\textit{Snell's Law:}} \qquad n_1 \sin \theta_1 = n_2 \sin \theta_2 \tag{18-4}$$

where
n_1 = refractive index of material 1
θ_1 = angle of incidence
n_2 = refractive index of material 2
θ_2 = angle of refraction

EXAMPLE 18.3

Refer to Figure 18-7. Using Snell's Law (equation 18-4), compute the angle of refraction for a light ray traveling in air and incident on the surface of water at an angle of 52° with respect to the normal.

Solution:
Because water is more dense than air, the light ray will bend toward the normal. From Table 18-2, the index of refraction for air is approximately 1 and for water 1.33.

$$n_1 \sin \theta_1 = n_2 \sin \theta_2$$
$$\sin \theta_2 = \frac{n_1 \sin \theta_1}{n_2}$$
$$\theta_2 = \sin^{-1}\left(\frac{n_1 \sin \theta_1}{n_2}\right) = \sin^{-1}\left(\frac{1.00 \sin 52°}{1.33}\right)$$
$$= 36.3°$$

18.5.4 Total Internal Reflection

The importance of Snell's Law with regard to fiber optics cannot be overstated. We can now consider how light is guided and contained within an optical fiber strand. In Example 18-3, if we reverse the direction of the light ray from water to air, as shown in Figure 18-8, according to Snell's Law, we would expect the light ray to bend *away* from the normal, because it travels from a more dense medium to a less dense medium.

In Example 18.4, Snell's Law is used to compute the refracted angle of the light ray as it exits the water and enters the air. In our solution, we can see that it is im-

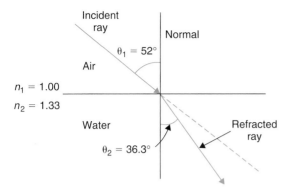

FIGURE 18-7
A light ray is incident on the surface of water at an angle of 52° with respect to the normal. The light ray refracts toward the normal as it enters the more dense medium of water.

possible to have an angle whose sine is greater than 1. When this happens, a phenomenon known as *total internal reflection* occurs. Instead of the light ray refracting away from the normal as it enters the air, the ray is *reflected off the interface and bounces back into the water.*

Refer to Figure 18-8. The direction of the light ray in Example 18.3 is reversed so that the light ray emerges from the water into air. Compute the angle of refraction in air for a ray with the same incident angle of 52°.

EXAMPLE
18.4

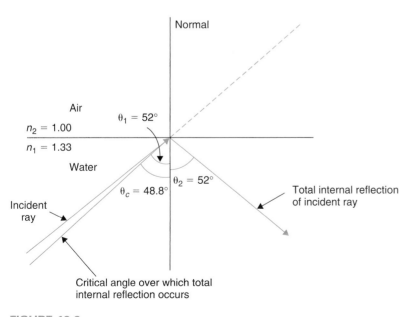

FIGURE 18-8
Light entering a medium whose index of refraction is less than the medium from which it exits will refract away from the normal unless the angle of incidence exceeds the critical angle. When this occurs, as in Example 18.4, total internal reflection occurs.

Solution:

Because air is less dense than water, we would expect the emerging ray to refract away from the normal as shown. From Snell's Law, however, the sine of the refracted angle is greater than 1; therefore, there is no mathematical solution to this problem using Snell's Law.

$$n_1 \sin \theta_1 = n_2 \sin \theta_2$$

$$\sin \theta_2 = \frac{n_1 \sin \theta_1}{n_2}$$

$$\theta_2 = \sin^{-1}\left(\frac{n_1 \sin \theta_1}{n_2}\right) = \sin^{-1}\left(\frac{1.33 \sin 52°}{1.00}\right)$$

$$= \sin^{-1}\left(\frac{1.05}{1}\right) \text{ no such angle!}$$

When the angle of incidence, θ_1, becomes large enough to cause the sine of the refracted angle, θ_2, to exceed the value of 1, total internal reflection occurs. This angle is called the *critical angle, θ_c.* The critical angle, θ_c, can be derived from Snell's Law as follows:

$$n_1 \sin \theta_1 = n_2 \sin \theta_2$$

$$\sin \theta_1 = \frac{n_2 \sin \theta_2}{n_1}$$

When $\sin \theta_2 = 1$, then $\sin \theta_1 = n_2/n_1$. Therefore,

$$\text{\emph{Critical Angle: } } \theta_c = \sin^{-1}\left(\frac{n_2}{n_1}\right) \tag{18-5}$$

EXAMPLE 18.5

Refer to Figure 18-8. Using equation (18-5), compute the critical angle above which total internal reflection occurs.

Solution:

$$\theta_c = \sin^{-1}\left(\frac{n_2}{n_1}\right) = \sin^{-1}\left(\frac{1.00}{1.33}\right) = 48.8°$$

EXAMPLE 18.6

Refer to Figure 18-9. Using equation (18-5), compute the critical angle above which total internal reflection will occur for light traveling in a glass slab surrounded by air. The glass slab has an index of refraction equal to 1.5; for air, it is equal to 1.

Solution:

$$\theta_c = \sin^{-1}\left(\frac{n_2}{n_1}\right) = \sin^{-1}\left(\frac{1.00}{1.5}\right) = 41.8°$$

By surrounding glass with material whose refractive index is less than that of the glass, total internal reflection can be achieved. This is illustrated in Figure 18-9. Ray A penetrates the glass–air interface at an angle exceeding the critical angle, θ_c,

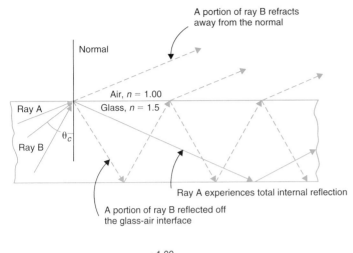

$$\theta_c = \sin^{-1} \frac{1.00}{1.5} = 41.8°$$

FIGURE 18-9
Light rays are transmitted into a glass slab surrounded by air, Ray A exceeds the critical angle and experiences total internal reflection. Ray B is less than the critical angle. Total internal reflection does not occur. A portion is reflected back into the glass, and a portion exits the glass into air and refracts away from the normal.

and experiences total internal reflection. On the other hand, ray B penetrates the glass–air interface at an angle less than the critical angle, and total internal reflection does not occur. Instead, a portion of ray B escapes the glass and is refracted away from the normal as it enters the less dense medium of air. A portion is also reflected back into the glass. Ray B diminishes in magnitude as it bounces back and forth between the glass–air interface. The foregoing principle is the basis for guiding light through optical fibers.

Two key elements that permit light guiding through optical fibers are its *core* and its *cladding*. The fiber's core is manufactured of ultrapure glass (silicon dioxide) or plastic. Surrounding the core is a material called cladding. A fiber's cladding is also made of glass or plastic. Its index of refraction, however, is typically 1% less than that of its core. This permits total internal reflection of rays entering the fiber and striking the core–cladding interface above the critical angle of approximately 82° [$\sin^{-1}(1/1.01)$]. The core of the fiber, therefore, *guides* the light, and the cladding *contains* the light. The cladding material is much less transparent than the glass making up the core of the fiber. This causes light rays to be absorbed if they strike the core–cladding interface at an angle less than the critical angle.

In Figure 18-10, a light ray is transmitted into the core of an optical fiber. Total internal reflection occurs as it strikes the lower-index cladding material. Note that the ray is totally contained within the core and behaves in accordance with the property: the angle of incidence is equal to the angle of reflection. The ray continues to propagate down the fiber by bouncing back and forth against the core–cladding interface.

18.5.5   Propagation Modes and Classifications of Fiber

In fiber optics, it is important to consider the term *mode*. A fiber's mode describes the propagation characteristics of an electromagnetic wave as it travels through a

> **Core**
> The center of an optical fiber, consisting of ultra-pure glass or plastic.

> **Cladding**
> The portion of an optical fiber surrounding the core also consisting of glass or plastic but with a slightly lower index of refraction.

> **Mode**
> Describes an electromagnetic wave's propagation characteristics when traveling through a particular type of optical fiber.

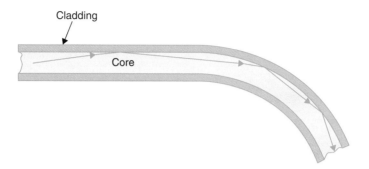

FIGURE 18-10

A light ray is transmitted into the core of an optical fiber strand. The critical angle between the glass core and its cladding is exceeded; therefore, total internal reflection occurs.

---

particular type of fiber. There are basically two modes of transmission in a fiber. When a ray of light is made to propagate in one direction only, that is, along the center axis of the fiber, the fiber is classified as *single-mode fiber.* If there are a number of paths in which the light ray may travel, the fiber is classified as *multimode fiber.*

Several mathematical equations are used to represent the various modes of propagation in multimode fiber. From equation (18-6), it can be seen that the number of modes is a function of core diameter, index of refraction, and the wavelength of the light:

> **Single-Mode Fiber**
> An optical fiber that allows light to propagate in one mode only.

> **Multimode Fiber**
> An optical fiber that allows light to propagate in several modes.

$$f = \left[\frac{\pi d}{\lambda} \sqrt{(n_1)^2 - (n_2)^2} \right]^2 \tag{18-6}$$

where n_1 = index of refraction of the core
   n_2 = index of refraction of the cladding
   d = core diameter (m)
   λ = wavelength (m)
   f = number of propagating modes

EXAMPLE 18.7

Using equation (18-6), compute the number of transmission modes for a light ray transmitted into a multimode step-index fiber having a core diameter of 50 μm, a core index of 1.60, and a cladding index of 1.584. The wavelength of the light ray is 1300 nm.

Solution:

$$f = \left[\frac{\pi d}{\lambda} \sqrt{(n_1)^2 - (n_2)^2} \right]^2 = \left[\frac{\pi(50 \times 10^{-6})}{1300 \times 10^{-9}} \sqrt{(1.6)^2 - (1.584)^2} \right]^2 = 372$$

Now consider the light source shown in Figure 18-11. Rays of light corresponding to electromagnetic waves are incident on the surface end of a multimode step-index fiber. There are several modes in which the rays travel through the fiber. Ray A does not penetrate the core or the cladding and is lost in the surrounding air. Ray

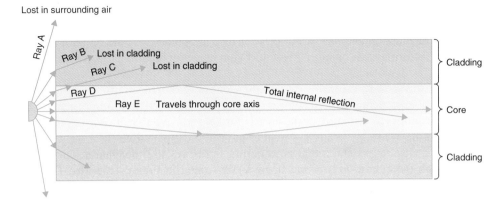

FIGURE 18-11
Transmission modes shown for various rays of light.

B is incident on the cladding. Note the refraction of the ray is toward the normal due to the higher index of refraction of the cladding material over air. These rays are lost in the cladding through absorption, which is discussed later. Ray C penetrates the core of the fiber and immediately bends toward the normal. As it strikes the core–cladding interface, however, its angle of incidence does not exceed the critical angle. Consequently, ray C is lost in the cladding. Ray D strikes the interface at an angle exceeding the critical angle and, therefore, experiences total internal reflection. Ray E propagates directly through the center of the core.

 Fibers are further classified by the refractive index profile of their core, which can be either *step index* or *graded index*. Figure 18-12 illustrates these profiles for the three main types of fibers: *multimode step-index fiber, single-mode step-index fiber,* and *multimode graded-index fiber.*

18.5.5.1 Multimode Step-Index Fiber

Multimode step-index fiber is useful in local applications that do not require enormous transmission speed. Core diameters range from 50 to 1000 μm. This relatively large core size, as shown in Figure 18-12(a), supports many propagation modes and permits the use of simple and inexpensive LED transmitters and PIN diode receivers.

 The index of refraction is manufactured uniformly throughout the core of multimode step-index fiber, as shown by its index profile in Figure 18-12(a). Light rays entering the fiber and exceeding the critical angle will bounce back and forth to the end of the fiber. This abrupt change in index of refraction between the core and the cladding has resulted in the name *step-index* or *multimode step-index fiber.* Each ray will obey the law stating that the angle of incidence is equal to the angle of reflection. Note that light rays exhibiting the steepest angles relative to the central axis of the core have a longer distance to travel as they propagate to the end of the fiber and, consequently, take more time to reach the receiving element. These rays may be reflected or bounced back and forth against the cladding several thousand times before they reach the end of the fiber. Rays that have a shallower angle have less distance to travel and, therefore, arrive at the receiver much sooner. The effect of this on a light pulse is distortion. Transmitted light pulses will broaden as they reach their destination. This is referred to as *pulse spreading* or *modal dispersion* due to the various propagation modes that the light rays take. The greater the pulse spreading, the far-

> **Multimode Step-Index Fiber**
> The index of refraction steps from the core down to the cladding.

> **Multimode Graded-Index Fiber**
> Optical fibers whose index of refraction of the core is manufactured to be graded from the center out to the cladding interface.

> **Modal Dispersion**
> Results from the different transit lengths for different propagating modes through the multimode optical fiber. Also referred to as *pulse spreading.*

ther the transmitted pulses must be separated from each other and, therefore, the less information that can be transmitted per unit time.

Good attenuation and bandwidth performance are obtained in the 820-nm region. Even better performance is obtained in the 1300-nm range for multimode step-index fiber.

18.5.5.2 Single-Mode Step-Index Fiber For single-mode step-index fiber, the core of the fiber is manufactured substantially smaller relative to multimode fiber. In addition, the index of refraction of the core is further reduced, thus increasing the critical angle or decreasing the angle at which the ray must penetrate the core with respect to its central axis. The intent is to permit light rays to propagate in one mode only: through the central axis of the fiber, as illustrated in Figure 18-12(b). The advantage to this is that all light rays travel the same path and, therefore, take the same length of time to propagate to the end of the fiber. Modal dispersion is minimized, and higher transmission speeds are attained.

Today's single-mode fiber dominates the telecommunications industry. Although it is costly, it offers the best performance in terms of information capacity (bandwidth) and transmission distance. The disadvantage, however, is that the small core diameter tightens the requirements for coupling light energy into the fiber. A laser is typically used as the light source. Another disadvantage with single-mode fiber is the task of splicing and terminating the fiber. Alignment of the fiber requires precise control.

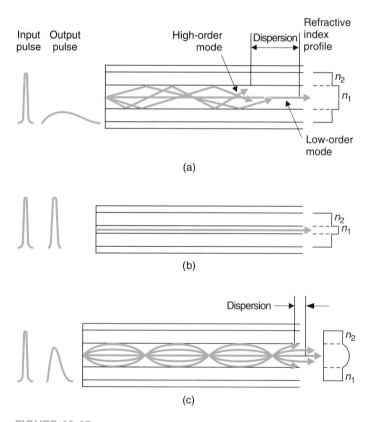

FIGURE 18-12
Three major classifications of optical fibers and their index profiles: (a) multimode step index; (b) single-mode step index; (c) multimode graded index. (Courtesy of AMP Incorporated.)

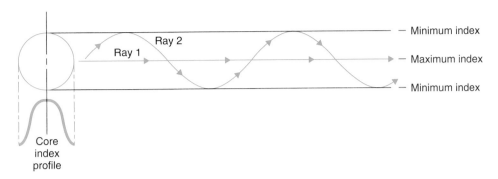

FIGURE 18-13
Multimode graded-index fiber. Ray 1 travels much less distance than ray 2; however, ray 2 increases in velocity as it propagates farther away from the core. This is caused by the graded index of the fiber. Ray 2 makes up in distance by its increase in velocity. Pulse spreading is minimized.

18.5.5.3 Multimode Graded-Index Fiber

To reduce the amount of pulse spreading or modal dispersion arising from various propagation delay times associated with multimode step-index fiber, *multimode graded-index fiber* is used. This type of fiber serves as an intermediary between single-mode and multimode step-index fiber in terms of cost and performance. Multimode graded-index fiber is characterized by its core having an index of refraction that is *graded* from its center out to the cladding interface; that is, the index of refraction is highest at the center and gradually tapers off toward the perimeter of the core. A bending effect is produced on light rays as they deviate from the central axis of the fiber, as illustrated in Figure 18-12(c).

For simplicity, consider the two rays shown in Figure 18-13. Ray 1 propagates directly through the central axis of the core, whereas ray 2 travels in a sinusoidal manner. Clearly, ray 2 has a greater distance to travel to the end of the core than ray 1. However, because the index of refraction is constantly reduced (roughly parabolically) from the center of the core out, ray 2 makes up for distance by its increase in velocity as it deviates from the central axis. The net effect is that light rays take the same amount of time to propagate to the end of the fiber regardless of the path they take. Modal dispersion is considerably reduced.

Unfortunately, graded-index fiber is not without its trade-offs. Optical sources of light, such as lasers and especially LEDs, emit a range of frequencies and, consequently, a range of wavelengths. Different wavelengths travel at different velocities. The differences in refractive indices at different wavelengths cause the spreading of a light pulse as it travels to its destination. This is called *chromatic dispersion*. Chromatic dispersion can be reduced by using lasers with very narrow spectral widths or by using step-index fiber.

18.6 WAVELENGTH-DIVISION MULTIPLEXING (WDM)

The optical technology used in today's high-speed, high-volume fiber optic backbones is called *wavelength-division multiplexing (WDM)*. In WDM, multiple optical signals are simultaneously combined, amplified as a group, and transported over a single fiber similar to the manner in which FDM signals are simultaneously transported over a coaxial cable or microwave link. This dramatically increases the capacity of the embedded fiber. Figure 18-14 illustrates this principle.

Wavelength-Division Multiplexing (WDM) A technology in which multiple optical signals are combined at different wavelengths, amplified, and transported over a single optical fiber.

FIGURE 18-14

Wavelength-Division Multiplexing (WDM) combines multiple optical signals at different wavelengths and transports them over a single fiber.

Despite the tiny core of the fiber, optical engineers have developed complex prisms that split infrared light into many wavelengths, colors, or hues. Independent wavelengths (λ_1, λ_2, λ_3 . . . , λ_n) are assigned to different incoming signals and combined together by the WDM multiplexer. Each signal is separated by enough wavelength so they do not interfere with each other. Because they are on separate, noninterfering wavelengths, each signal is bit-rate independent was well as protocol independent. For example, multiple SONET and ATM formatted signals operating at OC-48 (2.488 Gbps) and OC-98 (4.98 Gbps) rates can be multiplexed together and transmitted over a single fiber. WDM systems referred to as *dense WDM (DWDM)* are currently being developed and carry as many as 80 wavelengths of OC-48, for a total of 200 Gbps, and as many as 40 wavelengths of OC-192, for a total of 400 Gbps. This is enough capacity to transmit 90,000 volumes of an encyclopedia in one second.* Optical engineers know that this is only the beginning, however, and they envision 200 terabit (trillion bits) speeds in optical fibers. This is the equivalent of entire Library of Congress being delivered to a remote location over a single fiber strand in one second.

> **Dense Wavelength-Division Multiplexing (DWDM)**
> A very dense form of WDM.

18.7 FIBER-OPTIC CABLE CONSTRUCTION

Figure 18-15 illustrates the basic construction of a typical fiber-optic cable. The fiber itself is generally regarded as the core and its cladding. The material composition of these two layers can be any of the following:

- Glass cladding and glass core
- Plastic cladding and glass core
- Plastic cladding and plastic core

Surrounding the fiber's cladding is a *coating* that is typically applied to seal and preserve the fiber's strength and attenuation characteristics. Coating materials include lacquer, silicones, and acrylates. Some fibers have more than one protective coating system to ensure that no changes in characteristics occur if the fiber is exposed to extreme temperature variations.

> **Stress Corrosion**
> A defect in an optical fiber caused by exposure to humidity that may produce spontaneous fractures. Also referred to as *static fatigue*.

Sealing the fiber with a coating system also protects the fiber from moisture. A phenomenon called *stress corrosion* or *static fatigue* may occur if the glass fiber is exposed to humidity. Silicon dioxide crystals will interact with the moisture and cause

*Lucent Technologies, *Dense Wavelength Division Multiplexing (DWDM)*, The International Engineering Consortium, http://www.webproforum.com/dwdm/topic03.html

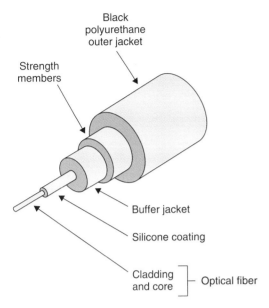

FIGURE 18-15
Basic construction of a fiber-optic cable. (Courtesy of Hewlett-Packard Optical Communication Division.)

bonds to break down. Spontaneous fractures can occur over a prolonged period of time.

The coating is further surrounded by a *buffer jacket,* which provides additional protection from abrasion and shock. Some fibers have *tightly buffered jackets,* and some have *loosely buffered jackets.*

Surrounding the buffer jacket is the *strength member.* As its name implies, it gives the fiber strength in terms of pulling. Various methods used to strengthen a fiber-optic cable are considered next.

Finally, the *outer jacket* is used to contain the fiber and its surrounding layers. The outer jacket is usually made of polyurethane material.

> **Buffer Jacket**
> The coating around an optical fiber to provide additional protection.

18.7.1 Strength and Protection

One disadvantage of fiber is its lack of pulling strength, which may be on the order of 1 lb. (This is much larger than that of copper and comparable to that of steel, having the same diameter.) Although this may seem relatively large for a strand of material having a diameter the thickness of a human hair, it is not sufficient for most installation requirements. Therefore, the fiber must be reinforced with strengthening material so that it can withstand the mechanical stresses from being pulled through ducts, hung on telephone poles, and buried underground.

Several materials are used by manufacturers to strengthen and protect the fiber from abrasion and environmental stress. The extent to which the fiber is protected depends on the application. Commonly used materials are:

- Steel
- Fiberglass
- Plastic

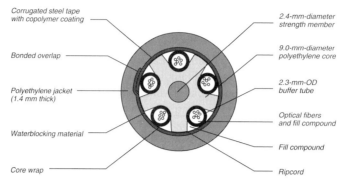

Corrugated steel tape with copolymer coating

Bonded overlap

Polyethylene jacket (1.4 mm thick)

Waterblocking material

Core wrap

2.4-mm-diameter strength member

9.0-mm-diameter polyethylene core

2.3-mm-OD buffer tube

Optical fibers and fill compound

Fill compound

Ripcord

Maximum number of fibers per tube 6
Maximum number of fibers per cable 30
Maximum number of PIC pairs per slot . . . . 1 (22 AWG) or 2 (24 AWG)
Maximum recommended pulling tension . . . . 2700 N (600 lb)
Cable outside diameter . . . . 14.0 ± 0.5 mm (0.55 in.)
Minimum bend radius static . . . . 140 mm (5.5 in.)
               dynamic . . . . 224 mm (8.8 in.)
Approximate unit weight. . . . . 206 kg/km (0.14 lb/ft)
Maximum length (78 in. flange × 43 in. width) . . . . . 6000 m (19,700 ft)
Recommended temperature range   installation . . . −30 to +70°C (−22 to +158°F)
                               operating . . . . −40 to +70°C (−40 to +158°F)

TubeStar Design

Northern Telecom TubeStar Optical Fiber Cable combines the strength, durability and ruggedness of Northern Telecom's proven slotted core design with the convenience of a buffer tube cable. It features a proprietary core design with a central strength member surrounded by an oscillating slotted polyethylene core. The central strength member of steel or fiberglass rod provides for maximum pulling tensions, equal or superior to industry standards. The oscillating slots surrounding the central axis eliminate bending effects on fibers, and minimize the effects of temperature variations and mechanical loads. Attenuation remains constant regardless of temperature.

Features

- Enhanced tube cable design with improved fiber protection provided by a star core.
- Fibers are isolated from cable bending, twisting and temperature variations resulting in reliable consistent performance.
- Superior crush and impact resistant cable suitable for all applications.
- High grade flexible buffer tubes prevent crimping and fiber damage during cable preparation and splicing.
- Decisive PIC color coding for both tubes and fibers provide for easy identification and segregation of working and protection fibers.
- Popular steelpeth and polysteelpeth cable jackets of composite heat bonded steel and polyethylene are both rugged and flexible.
- Medium density outer jacket provides maximum resistance to external forces encountered in harsh environmental terrains and underground duct structures.
- Designed to meet BellCore TR-TSY-000020, EIA mechanical tests and REA requirements.

(a)

FIGURE 18-16

Various optical fiber cable configurations: (a) Northern Telecom's TubeStar design can be used for underground ducts, aerial, direct burial, and submarine applications (courtesy of Northern Telecom Inc.); (b) Remfo's series 10 light-duty construction indoor simplex cable (courtesy of Remfo Fiber Optic Division); (c) Remfo's series 12 indoor/outdoor multi-fiber cable. (Courtesy of Remfo Fiber Optic Division.)

- FR-PVC (flame-retardant polyvinyl chloride)
- Kevlar yarn
- Paper

Figure 18-16 depicts how some of these materials are used in relationship to the fiber. Note that tensile strengths in excess of several hundred pounds can be achieved by reinforcing the fiber with strengthening materials.

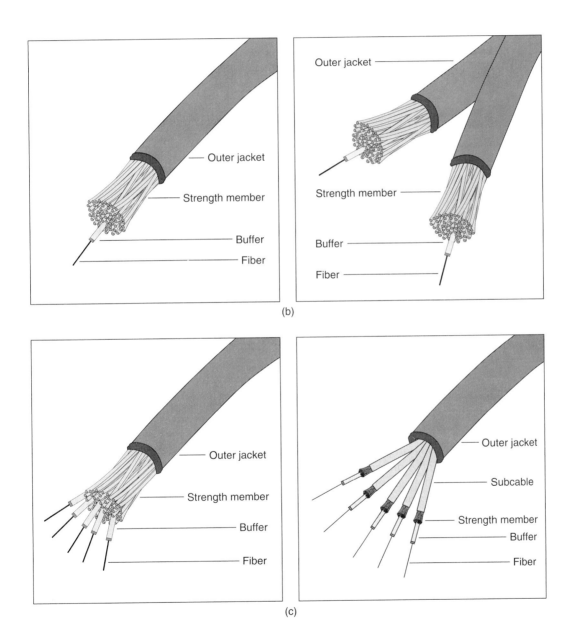

FIGURE 18-16
(continued)

18.8 ATTENUATION LOSSES IN OPTICAL FIBERS

> **Attenuation**
> Used by manufacturers to denote the decrease in optical power in a fiber from one point to another.

One of the most important performance specifications for an optical fiber is its attenuation rating. *Attenuation* is the term used by fiber manufacturers to denote the decrease in optical power from one point to another. This loss per unit length is expressed logarithmically in decibels per kilometer at a given wavelength and is given by the standard power equation:

$$\text{loss} = 10 \log \frac{P_{\text{out}}}{P_{\text{in}}} \quad \text{dB} \tag{18-7}$$

A 10-dB/km loss, for example, corresponds to 10% of the light making it to the end of a 1-km length of fiber. If the same fiber were doubled in length, 1% of the transmitted light (20 dB) would emerge from the end of the fiber. By today's standards, this amount of attenuation is enormous. It is not uncommon for optical fibers used for telecommunication systems to have an attenuation specification of less than 0.5 dB/km.

Attenuation losses in a fiber are wavelength dependent as shown in Figure 18-17. Note that there are peaks and troughs in the curve, meaning that there are optimum wavelengths to which transmitters and receivers must be tailored to minimize attenuation losses. For example, there is significantly less attenuation for glass fibers at 820 nm than at 1000 nm, and even less at 1300 and 1550 nm. Most fiber-optic components are, therefore, designed to operate in these regions. Table 18-3 lists the attenuation characteristics for various classifications of fiber.

18.8.1 Absorption Loss

The intrinsic impurities of fiber only amount to a few parts per billion. These impurities, however, *absorb* photons of light at specific wavelengths, depending on the type of impurity. Molecular agitation resulting from absorption produces heat that is lost in its surroundings.

Figure 18-18 depicts how absorption losses in fiber are wavelength dependent. At approximately 1.4 μm, a very minute residual of water (OH) in the fiber absorbs a significant portion of the light. Above 1.6 μm, glass is no longer transparent to infrared light. Instead, the light is absorbed by the glass and converted to heat.

18.8.2 Rayleigh Scattering

> **Rayleigh Scattering**
> A type of loss, caused by microirregularities in an optical fiber, in which light becomes scattered throughout the fiber.

By 1970, the transparency of optical fibers was so pure (99.9999%) that the presence of impurities no longer set the lower limits of attenuation. At that time, this loss was approximately 1.5 dB/km for light transmitted in the 800-nm region. A mechanism called *Rayleigh scattering* prevents any further improvement in attenuation loss. Rayleigh scattering is caused by microirregularities in the random molecular structure of glass. These irregularities are formed as the fiber cools from a molten state. Normally, electrons in glass molecules interact with transmitted light by absorbing and reradiating light at the same wavelength. A portion of the light, however, strikes these microirregularities and becomes scattered in all directions of the fiber, some of which is lost in the cladding. Consequently, the intensity of the beam is diminished.

Rayleigh scattering is wavelength dependent and decreases as the fourth power of increasing wavelength. This is illustrated in Figure 18-18. At approximately 800 nm, Rayleigh scattering sets the lower limits of attenuation to approximately 1.6 dB/km.

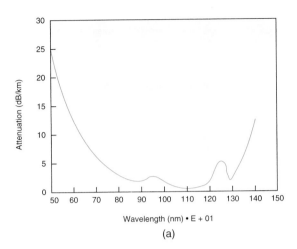

(a)

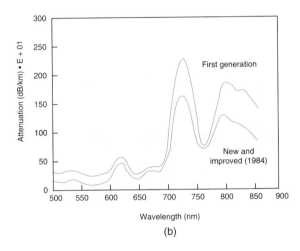

(b)

FIGURE 18-17
Attenuation loss as a function of wavelength for: (a) glass fibers and (b) plastic fibers. (Courtesy of Hewlett-Packard Optical Communication Division.)

By doubling the wavelength of light from 800 to 1600 nm, one-sixteenth $\left(\frac{1}{2}\right)^4$ the amount of Rayleigh scattering loss occurs. Attenuation loss can be reduced to less than a few tenths of a decibel per kilometer.

18.8.3   Radiation Losses

A phenomenon called *microbending* can cause radiation losses in optical fibers in excess of its intrinsic losses. Microbends are miniature bends and geometric imperfections along the axis of the fiber that occur during the manufacturing or installation of the fiber. Mechanical stress such as pressure, tension, and twist can cause microbending (Figure 18-19[a]). This geometric imperfection causes light to get coupled to various unguided electromagnetic modes that radiate and escape the fiber. With a good coating system and jacketing around the fiber, microbending losses normally

> **Microbending**
> A type of loss caused by miniature curvatures along the axis of an optical fiber.

TABLE 18-3
Attenuation Characteristics for Various Classifications of Fiber

Type	Core Diameter, μm	Cladding Diameter, μm	Buffer Diameter, μm	Numerical Aperture	Bandwidth, MHz-km	Attenuation, dB/km
Single mode	8	125	250		6 ps/km[a]	.5 @ 1300 nm
	5	125	250		4 ps/km[a]	.4 @ 1300 nm
Graded index	50	125	250	.20	400	4 @ 850 nm
	63	125	130	.29	250	7 @ 850 nm
	85	125	250	.26	200	6 @ 850 nm
	100	140	250	.30	20	5 @ 850 nm
Step index	200	380	600	.27	25	6 @ 850 nm
	300	440	650	.27	20	6 @ 850 nm
PCS	200	350	—	.30	20	10 @ 790 nm
	400	550	—	.30	15	10 @ 790 nm
	600	900	—	.40	20	6 @ 790 nm
Plastic		750	—	.50	20	400 @ 650 nm
		1000	—	.50	20	400 @ 650 nm

[a]Dispersion per nanometer of source width.

contribute less than 20% to the overall attenuation. For a fiber-optic cable having an attenuation rating of 0.5 dB/km, microbending losses typically contribute less than 0.1 dB/km.

Fiber curvatures on a larger scale can also cause radiation losses. This is referred to as *macrobending.* Macrobending occurs when a fiber is bent to a radius less than the fiber's *minimum bend radius* specification, as shown in Figure 18-19(b). This may be on the order of 10 to 20 cm.

> **Macrobending**
> A type of loss caused by large curvatures along the axis of an optical fiber.

> **Minimum Bend Radius**
> The radius of an optical fiber less than which macrobending occurs.

18.9 NUMERICAL APERTURE

An important characteristic of a fiber is its *numerical aperture (NA).* NA characterizes a fiber's light-gathering capability. Mathematically, it is defined as the sine of half the angle of a fiber's light *acceptance cone,* which is shown in Figure 18-20. Equations (18-8) and (18-9) are used to compute NA.

> **Numerical Aperture (NA)**
> A measure of an optical fiber's light-gathering capability.

$$NA = \sin \theta_A \qquad \textbf{(18-8)}$$

Also,

> **Acceptance Cone**
> The area in which an optical fiber gathers light.

$$NA = \sqrt{n_1^2 - n_2^2} \qquad \textbf{(18-9)}$$

where n_1 is the refractive index of the core and n_2 is the refractive index of the cladding.

Equations (18-8) and (18-9) are straightforward for multimode step-index fiber. For graded-index fiber, however, n_1 depends on the core profile. The largest acceptance angle is measured at the core center. Therefore, the index of refraction at the core center must be used to compute NA. Typical values for NA are 0.25 to 0.4 for multimode step-index fiber and 0.2 to 0.3 for multimode graded-index fiber (see Table 18-3).

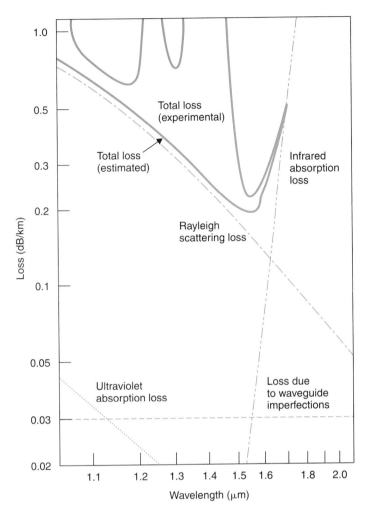

FIGURE 18-18

Factors contributing to fiber attenuation in the 1500-nm region. (Courtesy of Corning Glass Works.)

Although a fiber having a large NA gathers more light, a greater amount of modal dispersion occurs due to the large number of propagation modes. Conversely, a fiber having a low NA makes it more difficult to couple light into the fiber but offers greater propagation efficiency, because there are fewer modes.

18.10 FIBER-OPTIC CONNECTIONS

Once a fiber-optic cable has been manufactured, a connection must be made. This connection may involve a splice to lengthen or repair the cable or to mount a connector for mating purposes. A splice is used when the connection is permanent, whereas a connector is used for temporary connections. This may involve another fiber's connector, a transmitter, or a receiver. Whether the connection is made by a splice or a connector, the two ends must be physically aligned with enough precision that an appreciable amount of light energy is coupled from one fiber end to the other. Unlike

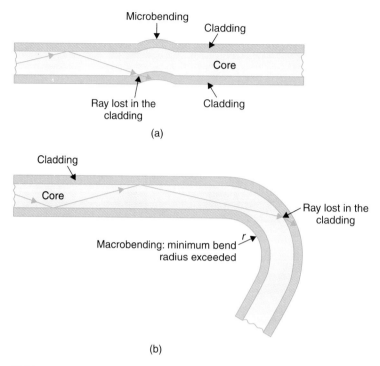

FIGURE 18-19

Radiation losses occur in microbends or macrobends: (a) microbending occurs when there are miniature bends and geometric imperfections along the axis of the fiber; (b) macrobending occurs when a fiber is bent to a radius that is less than the fiber's minimum bend radius (typically 10 to 20 cm).

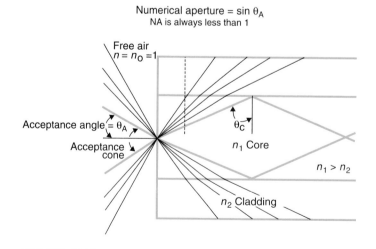

FIGURE 18-20

Acceptance cone for measuring NA. (Courtesy of Hewlett-Packard Optical Communication Division.)

copper, fiber is so fine in diameter that several complexities arise in making the connection. Special tools, training, manual dexterity, and practice are essential requirements for the technician to make good connections.

18.10.1 Splice Connection

Two methods are used for splicing fiber ends together: the *mechanical splice,* and the *fusion splice.* In a mechanical splice, two ends of fibers are brought together, aligned with a mechanical fixture, and glued or crimped together. In a fusion splice, alignment is performed under a microscope. An electric arc is drawn that melts the two glass ends together and forms a strong bond. In general, the fusion splice offers better performance specifications in terms of splice loss. Both methods are commonly used in the field, but one method may not necessarily be better than the other. That is, some technicians feel more comfortable with one method than with the other. The more sophisticated mechanical and fusion splices often include prealignment under a microscope and final precision alignment performed automatically.

> **Mechanical Splice**
> Aligning two optical fiber ends with a mechanical fixture and then gluing or crimping them together.

> **Fusion Splice**
> Splicing two optical fiber ends together with an electric arc.

18.10.1.1 Fiber Preparation
Cable preparation is necessary before splicing. The cable manufacturer's procedures should be carefully followed for each cable design. Fiber ends are typically stripped of their plastic jacket and strength member and *cleaved* to a 90° angle. It may be necessary to remove any coating material. A number of methods are used to do this, such as mechanical stripping tools, thermal stripping equipment, and chemical strippers.

The goal of cleaving is to produce a flat, smooth, perpendicular fiber end face.* The scribe-and-break method is generally used to cleave fibers. Both manual and automated tools are available. The quality of the cleave is one of the most important factors in producing high-quality, low-loss fusion or mechanical splices. Whatever the method used, the cleave must be a clean break with no burrs or chips. The fiber end angle should be less than 1°. The ends are then polished and cleaned with a cleaning agent such as isopropyl alcohol or freon.

18.10.1.2 Mechanical Splice
Dozens of mechanical splicing techniques are used to join both single-mode and multimode fiber ends. Each has its advantages and disadvantages. To achieve performances comparable to fusion splicing, large, bulky, and expensive equipment is often used. This may include fixtures with built-in microscopes, micrometers, digital alignment test circuitry, and ultraviolet curing lamps. A considerable amount of operator training and judgment is required. The current trend by many manufacturers is to produce inexpensive mechanical splicing kits that make splicing efficient and easy to perform with little training. Two of the more popular types of mechanical splices are the *V-groove splice* and the *tube splice.*

18.10.1.3 V-Groove Splice
The V-groove splice shown in Figure 18-21, uses a block or substrate with a precisely cut groove through its center. For multiple splices, in the case of ribbon cables several V-grooves are manufactured into the substrate for alignment. The fibers are placed in the grooves and butted up against each other. Index matching glue is often used to bond the ends together and reduce reflection losses. Assuming the core and cladding of the fibers are the same diameter, the groove will

---

*Corning Glass Works, *Application Note 113.*

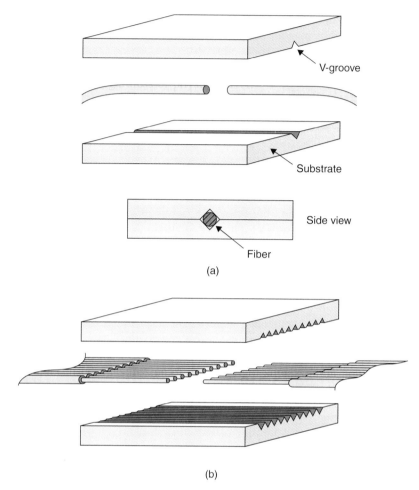

FIGURE 18-21
(a) V-groove splice; (b) multiple V-groove splice for ribbon cable.

cause them to align with each other on the same axis. A top matching plate is placed over the spliced fiber and secured. The entire splice is placed into a box called a *splice enclosure,* which is used for environmental protection and strain relief.

18.10.1.4 Tube Splice Fibers can also be aligned and spliced together through the use of capillary tubes. The tubes are machined to the diameter of the fiber and funneled at each end to allow the fibers to be easily inserted. For single-mode fiber, the capillary is typically round-holed, whereas for multimode fiber, the capillary is triangular-holed. Figure 18-22 illustrates various types of tube splices.

Fiber ends are initially prepared in the manner described earlier. Index matching fluid is then inserted into the tube, and the fibers are pushed to the center of the tube against each other. The splice is exposed to ultraviolet light, which is used to polymerize or cure the epoxy or index matching fluid, thus forming a strong bond.

Some of the latest tube splice designs have become extremely popular due to their simplicity. Many do not require epoxy, thus eliminating the need for ultraviolet curing equipment. Instead, the fibers are held in place by a mechanical fixture or a crimp, as

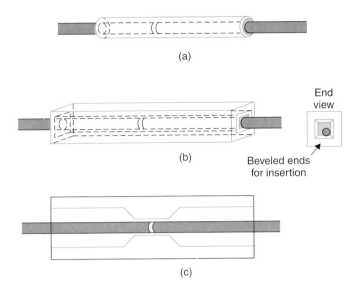

FIGURE 18-22
Various tube splices: (a) snug tube splice; (b) loose tube splice; (c) transparent capillary tube.

shown in Figure 18-23. Losses tend to be slightly higher for these types of designs (0.1 to 0.2 dB); however, they are extremely reliable, economical, and easy to install.

18.10.2   Fusion Splice

The fusion splice uses an electric arc to fuse or weld two fiber ends together. The resulting splice is usually stronger than that of unspliced fiber. Losses under 0.01 dB can be achieved with a fusion splice. The trade-off, however, is that operator training and judgment are relatively high compared to that required for the mechanical splice. In addition, equipment is bulky and often very expensive. Sophisticated microprocessor controllers are used to eliminate operator judgment by automating most of the process. Figure 18-24 illustrates Siecor's popular X75 microprocessor-controlled fusion splicer and FBC006 cleaver.

18.10.3   Connectors

Connectors are necessary in fiber optics to interface the fiber to transmitting and receiving components. They are also used for interfacing to other optical fibers. There are a myriad of connectors on the market, thus making it difficult to discuss any one type. Unfortunately, connector standards for the fiber-optic community have been slow in the making. For the most part, manufacturers have tailored their designs toward existing mechanical standards. Among the most popular connector types* are:

- *USA:* BICONIC, ST, SMA
- *Japan:* FC, D4, PC
- *Europe:* DIN/IEC, RADIALL, STRATOS

Fiber Optics Handbook, Hewlett-Packard, ©1988.

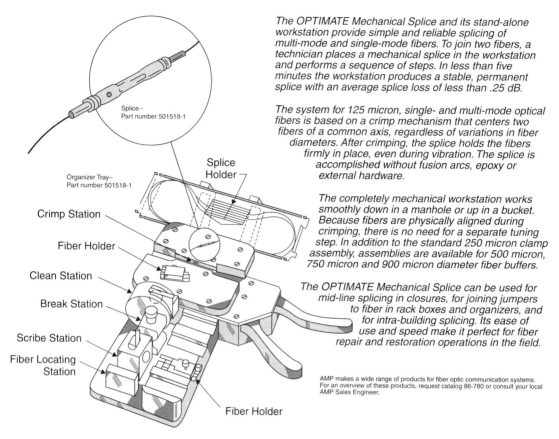

The OPTIMATE Mechanical Splice and its stand-alone workstation provide simple and reliable splicing of multi-mode and single-mode fibers. To join two fibers, a technician places a mechanical splice in the workstation and performs a sequence of steps. In less than five minutes the workstation produces a stable, permanent splice with an average splice loss of less than .25 dB.

The system for 125 micron, single- and multi-mode optical fibers is based on a crimp mechanism that centers two fibers of a common axis, regardless of variations in fiber diameters. After crimping, the splice holds the fibers firmly in place, even during vibration. The splice is accomplished without fusion arcs, epoxy or external hardware.

The completely mechanical workstation works smoothly down in a manhole or up in a bucket. Because fibers are physically aligned during crimping, there is no need for a separate tuning step. In addition to the standard 250 micron clamp assembly, assemblies are available for 500 micron, 750 micron and 900 micron diameter fiber buffers.

The OPTIMATE Mechanical Splice can be used for mid-line splicing in closures, for joining jumpers to fiber in rack boxes and organizers, and for intra-building splicing. Its ease of use and speed make it perfect for fiber repair and restoration operations in the field.

AMP makes a wide range of products for fiber optic communication systems. For an overview of these products, request catalog 86-780 or consult your local AMP Sales Engineer.

FIGURE 18-23
Tube splice held together by a crimp. (Courtesy of AMP Incorporated.)

Today, most connectors are based on the physical contact of two well-cleaved fibers to allow the direct transition of optical power between each other. Figure 18-25 illustrates a popular SMA-type connector assembly. The following set of procedures are typically used to install a connector assembly to a fiber end:

1. Strip the jacket and coating until only core and cladding are left.
2. Center and fix the uncoated fiber in the ferrule.
3. Grind and polish the ends of the fiber and ferrule.
4. Clean the fiber ends with a cleaning agent such as freon or isopropyl alcohol.
5. Assemble the connector housing.

18.10.4 Insertion Losses for Connectors and Splices

Connecting losses fall into two categories: *intrinsic*, and *extrinsic*. The two combined make up the total insertion loss of a connection.

Intrinsic Losses   These types of losses are due to factors beyond the control of the user. They include variations in:

(a)

(b)

FIGURE 18-24
(a) Siecor's popular X75 microprocessor-controlled fusion splicer; (b) Siecor's FBC006 fiber-optic splicer. (Courtesy of Siecor.)

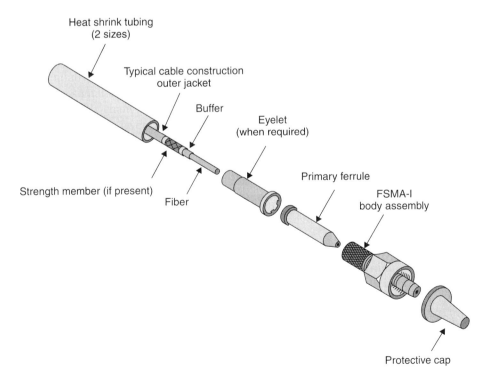

FIGURE 18-25
SMA-style connector. (Courtesy of AMP Incorporated.)

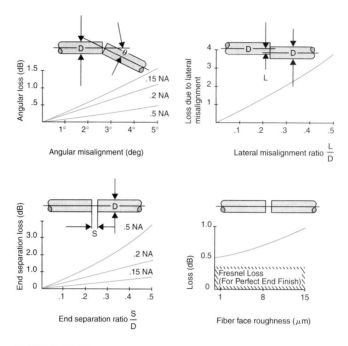

FIGURE 18-26

Four major extrinsic losses that can occur in a fiber connection. (Courtesy of AMP Incorporated.)

- Core diameter
- Numerical aperture
- Index profile
- Core/cladding eccentricity
- Core concentricity

These factors can be expected to vary at random, even between fibers with the same specifications or from the same cable spool. They are influenced by the manufacturing process and quality control rather than by the nature of the connection.

Extrinsic Losses   Extrinsic losses are those resulting from the splicing and connector assembly process. They include the following errors:

- Mechanical offsets between fiber ends
- Contaminants between fiber ends
- Improper fusion, bonding, and crimping methods
- End finishes

Most connection losses can be attributed to extrinsic losses caused by the user and the equipment being used to perform the splice. They can be reduced or eliminated by ensuring that equipment is maintained and manufacturing procedures are followed.

18.10.4.1   Mechanical Offsets   Regardless of the method used to splice or connect fibers, in most cases major extrinsic losses can be attributed to mechanical offsets, which are classified as follows:

- Angular misalignment
- Lateral misalignment
- End separation
- End face roughness

Figure 18-26 illustrates these types of losses. In each case, a portion of the light escapes from its normal path and contributes to the total insertion loss.

18.10.4.2 Losses Due to Reflections Whenever light enters glass from air, it can be shown mathematically that approximately 4% of the light is reflected back into the air. The same effect occurs in the reverse direction: when light exits glass into air, 4% of it is reflected back into the glass. We will not dwell on the mathematics behind this but, rather, on the importance of correcting for some of this loss. Because light must exit and reenter the surface of the fiber ends in a connection, there is an 8% overall reduction, which amounts to approximately a 0.4-dB loss. For splices, this reflective loss can be reduced by applying an index matching material between the fiber ends. This material is usually a transparent glue or epoxy with an index of refraction of approximately 1.5, which is equivalent to that of the fiber. The glue also serves the purpose of bonding the fiber ends together. We do not do this between connectors, because periodic disconnection is required.

18.11 LIGHT-EMITTING DEVICES

Several devices are emitters of light, both natural and artificial. Few of these devices, however, are suitable for fiber-optic transmitters. What we are interested in is a light source that meets the following requirements:

- The light source must be able to turn on and off several tens of millions, and even billions, of times per second.
- The light source must be able to emit a wavelength that is transparent to the fiber.
- The light source must be efficient in terms of coupling light energy into the fiber.
- The optical power emitted must be sufficient enough to transmit through optical fibers.
- Temperature variations should not affect the performance of the light source.
- The cost of manufacturing the light source must be relatively inexpensive.

Two commonly used devices that satisfy the above requirements are: the *LED (light-emitting diode),* and the *ILD (injection laser diode).* Both are semiconductor devices, and each has advantages over the other depending on the application.

> **Light-Emitting Diode (LED)**
> A semiconductor that converts electrical energy to light energy.

18.11.1 LED Versus ILD

The major difference between the LED and the ILD is the manner in which light is emitted from each source. The LED is an *incoherent* light source that emits light in a *disorderly* way as compared to the ILD, which is a *coherent* light source that emits light in a very *orderly* way. The ILD can, therefore, launch a much greater percentage of its light into a fiber than an LED. Figure 18-27 illustrates the differences in radiation patterns. Both devices are extremely rugged, reliable, and small in size.

In terms of spectral purity, the LED's half-power spectral width is approximately 50 nm, whereas the ILD's spectral width is only a few nanometers. This is shown in

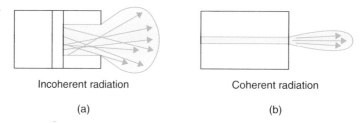

Incoherent radiation

(a)

Coherent radiation

(b)

FIGURE 18-27
Radiation patterns for: (a) LED; (b) ILD.

Figure 18-28. Ideally, a single spectral line is desirable. As the spectral width of the emitter increases, attenuation and pulse dispersion increase. The spectral purity for the ILD and its ability to couple much more power into a fiber make it better suited for long-distance telecommunications links. In addition, the injection laser can be turned on and off at much higher rates than an LED. The drawback, however, is its cost, which may approach several hundred dollars as compared to a few dollars for LEDs in large quantities. Table 18-4 lists the differences in operating characteristics between the LED and the ILD.

18.11.2 Light-Emitting Diode

Because of its simplicity and cost, the LED is by far the most widely used light-emitting device in the fiber-optic industry. Most of us are familiar with LEDs capable of emitting visible light. They are used in calculators, watches, and a multitude of other visible displays. The LEDs used in fiber optics operate on the same principle. By passing current through the LED's PN junction, recombination occurs between holes and electrons. This causes particles of light energy called *photons* to be released or

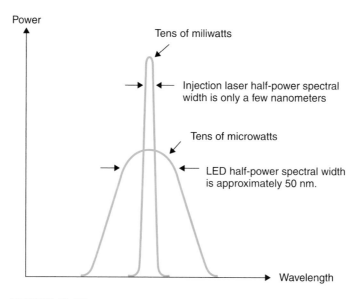

FIGURE 18-28
Comparison of special widths between the fiber-optic LED and ILD.

TABLE 18-4
Typical Source Characteristics for LEDs and ILDs

Type	Output Power, μW	Peak Wavelength, nm	Spectral Width, nm	Rise Time, ns
LED	250	820	35	12
	700	820	35	6
	1500	820	35	6
Laser	4000	820	4	1
	6000	1300	2	1

emitted. The wavelength of these photons is a function of the crystal structure and composition of the material.

Extensive research in material science, physics, and chemistry has made it possible to grow highly reliable crystals used in the manufacturing of fiber-optic LEDs. These LEDs are designed to emit light in the infrared region for reasons explained earlier. Various semiconductor materials are used to achieve this. Pure *gallium-arsenide (GaAs)* emits light at a wavelength of approximately 900 nm. By adding a mixture of 10% aluminum (Al) to 90% GaAs, *gallium-aluminum-arsenide (GaAlAs)* is formed, which emits light at a wavelength of 820 nm. Recall that this is one of the optimum wavelengths for fiber-optic transmission. By tailoring the amount of aluminum mixed with GaAs, wavelengths ranging from 800 to 900 nm can be obtained.

To take advantage of the reduced attenuation losses at longer wavelengths, it is necessary to include even more exotic materials. For wavelengths in the range 1000 to 1550 nm, a combination of four elements is typically used: *indium, gallium, arsenic,* and *phosphorus.* These devices are commonly referred to as *quaternary devices.* Combining these four elements produces the compound *indium-gallium-arsenide-phosphide (InGaAsP).* By tailoring the mixture of these elements, 1300- and 1550-nm emissions are possible. Figure 18-29 illustrates the construction of various fiber-optic LEDs. Table 18-5 lists their differences.

18.11.3 Injection Laser Diode

The term *laser* is an acronym for *light amplification by stimulated emissions of radiation.* There are many types of lasers on the market. They are constructed of gases, liquids, and solids. For many of us, when we think of a laser what comes to mind is a relatively large and sophisticated device that outputs a highly intense beam of visible light. Although this is in part true, the laser industry is currently devoting a great deal of effort toward the manufacture of miniature semiconductor laser diodes. Laser diodes are also called *injection laser diodes (ILDs),* because when current is injected across the PN junction, light is emitted. Figure 18-30 illustrates the construction of an ILD. ILDs are ideally suited for use within the fiber-optic industry due to their small size, reliability, and ruggedness. Various ILD package designs are shown in Figure 18-31.

The ILD is basically an oscillator. A cavity built into its layered semiconductor structure serves as a feedback mechanism to sustain oscillation. The amplification necessary for oscillation is produced by creating a condition in the cavity called a *population inversion.* A large density of holes and electrons in the cavity of the ILD

Laser
A coherent light source used as a transmitter in fiber-optic systems.

Injection Laser Diode (ILD)
A semiconductor diode used as a transmitter for fiber-optic communications.

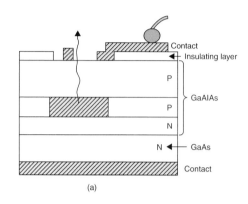

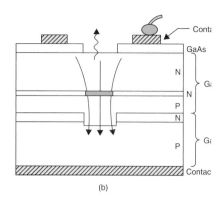

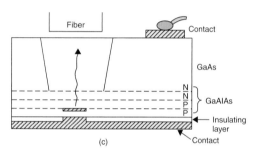

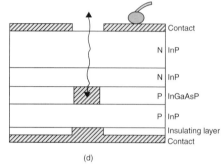

FIGURE 18-29

Construction of various LEDs: (a) S-PUP (Silox P side up) emitter, 820 nm (surface LED); (b) enhanced emitter design, 820 nm; (c) etched-well emitter, 820 nm; (d) 1300-nm emitter. (Courtesy of Hewlett-Packard Optical Communication Division.)

TABLE 18-5
LED as a Fiber-Optic Source

Device	GaAsP	GaAlAs		InGaAsP
	Surface LED	Surface LED	Etched-Well LED	Transparent Substrate LED
1. Wavelength, nm	665	820	820	1300
2. Spectral line width, nm	30	40	40	120
3. Ext. quantum efficiency, $\eta(\%)$	0.1–0.2	1.5–2.0	4	4
4. Response time, nsec	<40	5–15	<15	<10
5. Relative cost	Low	Medium	Higher	Highest

Source: Hewlett-Packard Optical Communication Division.

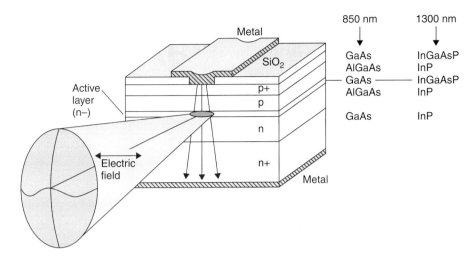

FIGURE 18-30
Construction of the injection laser diode. (Reprinted with permission from Hewlett-Packard.)

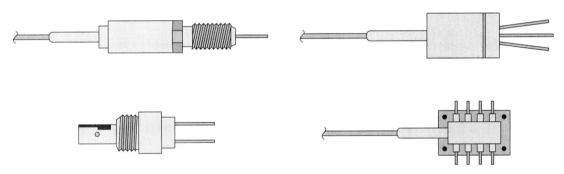

FIGURE 18-31
Typical injection laser diodes.

is waiting to recombine. By injecting a large density of current (holes and electrons) into the cavity, some holes and electrons in the cavity recombine and release photons of light. A population inversion occurs when a greater percentage of these holes and electrons combine to release photons of light instead of creating additional holes and electrons. The released photons stimulate other holes and electrons to recombine and release even more photons, thus producing gain or amplification. To achieve oscillation, the ends of the crystal structure are polished to a mirror finish. This provides a feedback mechanism that causes light to reflect back and forth in the cavity, stimulating other electrons and holes to recombine and release more photons. *Lasing* is said to occur.

18.12 LIGHT-RECEIVING DEVICES

The function of the fiber-optic receiving device is to convert light energy into electrical energy so that it may be amplified and processed back to its original state. A device commonly used for this purpose is the *photodiode* or *photodetector.* Photodetectors are made of semiconductor materials. Here, again, the composition of the structure determines the wavelengths to which it is sensitive.

Photodetectors use the reverse mechanism of transmitting devices. Instead of stimulated emissions of radiation, *absorption* of photons occur. When photons are absorbed, holes and electrons are created, thus producing current. This is known as the *photoelectric effect.*

18.12.1 Receiver Sensitivity

Receiver sensitivity can be characterized by one of two parameters: *quantum efficiency,* or *responsivity.* Both parameters are essentially the same. Both are a measure of an optical receiver's sensitivity to a particular wavelength.

If each particle of light (photon) illuminating the surface of a photodetector were converted to a useful electron-hole pair, the quantum efficiency would be equal to 1, or unity. If 10% of the light were reflected off of its surface, the quantum efficiency would be equal to 90%, and so forth.

From a system designer's point of view, a more practical way of interpreting a receiver's sensitivity is to consider the amount of optical power that is directly converted to current at a specific wavelength. Most manufacturers specify their receivers in this manner, which is called *responsivity.* Responsivity has the units of amperes per watt (A/W) or microamperes per microwatt (μA/μW). Typical values may range from 0.2 A/W to as high as 100 A/W.

18.12.2 PIN Photodiode

The most common photodetector used in fiber optics is the *PIN photodiode.* PIN is an acronym for P-type, intrinsic (I), N-type semiconductor material. The P and N regions shown in Figure 18-32 are heavily doped. The I region (shown as the depletion region) is a lightly doped (near intrinsic) N-type material. Its purpose is to increase the depletion and absorption regions when a reverse-biased potential is applied to the diode. In comparison to the LED, which emits light in the forward-biased condition, the PIN photodiode is used in the reverse-biased condition. Current does not flow unless light (photons) penetrates the depletion region. When this occurs, electrons are raised from their valence band to the conduction band, thus leaving excess holes. These current carriers will begin to flow due to the attractive force of the applied po-

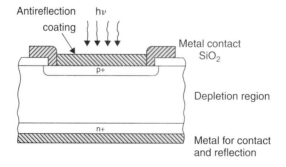

FIGURE 18-32
Structure of the PIN photodiode. (Reprinted with permission from Hewlett-Packard.)

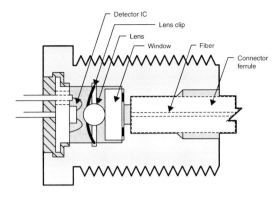

HFBR-2208 SMA Style Compatible

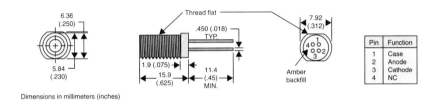

Dimensions in millimeters (inches)

FIGURE 18-33

Hewlett-Packard's HFBR-2208 PIN photodiode receiver. (From *Hewlett-Packard Optoelectronics Designer's Catalog*, 1988–1989, pp. 8–98.)

tential. The magnitude of the current is proportional to the intensity of the light. Typical values for responsivity are in the order of 0.5 A/W. Bias voltages may range from 5 to 20 V.

The degree of absorption in a PIN photodiode depends on the wavelength and material of which the device is made. For example, if the diode is made of silicon, wavelengths of light in the range 800 to 900 nm will penetrate. PIN diodes made of indium-gallium-arsenide absorb light in the 1300-nm range. Sensitivity to longer wavelengths is achieved with indium-gallium-arsenide-phosphide. Figure 18-33 gives the dimensions and a cross-sectional view of a typical silicon PIN photodiode sensitive to light in the 800 nm range.

18.12.3 Avalanche Photodiode

Although the PIN photodiode is extremely well suited for most fiber-optic applications, its sensitivity to light (responsivity) is not as great as the *avalanche photodiode (APD)*. Due to their inherent gain, typical values of responsivity for APDs may range from 5 A/W to as high as 100 A/W. This is considerably higher than the PIN photodiode, which makes it extremely attractive for fiber-optic communications receivers.

The APD functions in the same manner as the PIN photodiode, except that a larger reverse-biased potential is necessary. This is usually on the order of more than 100 V. The APD is constructed in a manner that causes an avalanche condition to occur if a sufficiently large reverse-biased potential is applied to it. As the reverse bias increases, electron-hole pairs gain sufficient energy to create additional electron-hole

> **Avalanche Photodiode (APD)**
> A photodetector used as a receiver for fiber-optic communications and having a higher responsivity compared with the PIN photodiode.

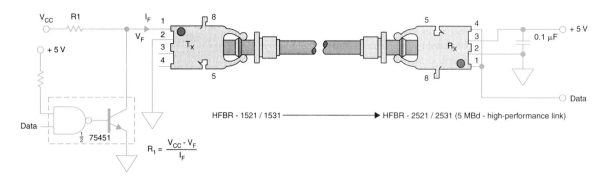

$$R_1 = \frac{V_{CC} - V_F}{I_F}$$

FIGURE 18-34

Hewlett-Packard's Versatile Link. (Courtesy of Hewlett-Packard Optical Communication Division.)

pairs, thus creating additional ions (positive- and negative-charged particles). A multiplication or avalanche of carriers occurs. This effect is called *impact ionization,* which is considered to be an internal gain advantage over the PIN photodiode.

Although the APD is extremely responsive to light, it is not without its drawbacks. Unfortunately, temperature and bias stabilization are necessary with the APD, as both of these parameters influence its performance. Also, costs are considerably higher than for PIN photodiodes. In terms of size, the APD is similar to the PIN photodiode.

18.13 A LOW-COST FIBER-OPTIC LINK

There are several applications that do not require high-speed transmission over long distances. For many of these, a low-cost fiber-optic link would be a solution. Figure 18-34 depicts Hewlett-Packard's low-cost *Versatile Link.* This link* will function at speeds ranging from DC to 5 Mbps. Extended distance links can be up to 82 m. This low-cost fiber-optic link is TTL and CMOS compatible.

PROBLEMS

1. Name at least six advantages of using fiber.
2. Name at least two disadvantages of using fiber.
3. What are the two classic theories of light?
4. Using equation (18-1), compute the energy of a single photon having a frequency of 3.65×10^{14} Hz.
5. Refer to Figure 18-4. In problem 4, what portion of the electromagnetic spectrum does the light emitted by this photon fall under?
6. Using equation (18-2), compute the wavelength of the photon in problem 4.

Hewlett-Packard Optoelectronics Designer's Catalog, 1988–1989, p. 8–13.

7. Compute the wavelength for the following frequencies:
   a. 1.6 MHz
   b. 88 MHz
   c. 4 GHz
   d. 6 GHz
   e. 1.94×10^{14} Hz
8. Refer to Figure 18-4. What are the wavelengths associated with:
   a. Infrared light?
   b. Visible light?
   c. Ultraviolet light?
9. Convert 1300 nanometers to inches.
10. What is the velocity of light in free space?
11. The speed of light in a given medium is measured at 2.00×10^8 m/s. Compute the index of refraction using equation (18-3).
12. Refer to Table 18-2. Compute the speed of light:
    a. In water
    b. In an optical fiber
    c. In fused quartz
13. Refer to Figure 18-5. Using Snell's Law, compute the angle of refraction in water for a light ray traveling in air and incident on the surface of water at an angle of 60°.
14. Refer to Figure 18-5. A ray of light is refracted in water at an angle of 45°. Compute the angle of the incident ray in air, θ.
15. In problem 14, the direction of the ray of light is reversed so that the light ray emerges from water into air. Compute the angle of refraction in air, θ, for a light ray striking the interface at 45°.
16. Define *total internal reflection.*
17. Define *critical angle.*
18. A glass slab having an index of refraction of 1.55 is surrounded by water whose index of refraction is 1.33. Compute the *critical angle, θ_c,* above which total internal reflection occurs in the glass slab.
19. A glass fiber has an index of refraction of 1.62. It is surrounded by cladding material having an index of refraction of 1.604. Compute the critical angle, θ_c.
20. Explain the difference between single-mode fiber and multimode fiber.
21. Using equation (18-6), compute the number of transmission modes for a multimode step-index fiber having a core diameter of 62 μm, a core index of 1.60, and a cladding index of 1.584. Light having a wavelength of 1300 nm is used.
22. Repeat problem 21 for light having a wavelength of 820 nm.
23. Explain *graded-index fiber.*
24. What does *WDM* stand for?
25. What does *DWDM* stand for?
26. Name two strengthening materials used with fiber-optic cables.
27. An LED launches 180 μW of power into the end of a fiber.
    a. How much power would emerge at the end of the fiber at a distance of 500 m if the fiber were specified as having a loss of 0.2 dB/km?
    b. What would the loss of the fiber be in decibels per kilometer if 172 μW were measured at the output of the fiber 500 m away?
28. Explain what causes the following losses:
    a. Absorption loss
    b. Rayleigh scattering
    c. Radiation loss
29. Compute the NA for the fiber in problem 19.
30. Refer to Figure 18-20. A multimode fiber has a NA of 0.25. Compute the angle of the fiber's acceptance cone.
31. What are the two commonly used methods for splicing fiber ends?

32. Explain the difference between *intrinsic* and *extrinsic* losses in connectors and splices.
33. What semiconductor materials are used in LEDs to emit light at 820 nm?
34. To take advantage of the reduced attenuation losses at wavelengths above 1000 nm, what four elements are typically used?
35. What does *laser* stand for?
36. Explain a *population inversion.*
37. What specification is used to characterize the sensitivity of photodiodes?
38. Explain the difference between a PIN diode and an APD.

19

WIRELESS COMMUNICATIONS

The public interest in *wireless communications* has soared due to the ever-increasing technological advances in the communications industry coupled with the demands for personal mobility. What is wireless communications? Virtually any electronic communications device imaginable has become a part of the new wireless frontier. Cellular telephones and pagers are a ubiquitous sight; this will only increase with the unleashing of *personal communication services (PCS),* a multibillion dollar industry representing the latest advancements in digital wireless telecommunications.

Wireless communications is a technology that includes more than just pagers and cell phones. It also includes wireless speakers and intercoms, cordless telephones (including those capable of being used up to a mile away from their base stations), two-way radio systems, mobile communications, palmtop computers and fax machines linked to wireless modems, wireless medical instruments, the *global positioning system (GPS),* and more. The proliferation of wireless local area network (LAN) and wide area network components has permitted workstations to be linked without use of cabling media. These technologies are all evidence of the rising popularity of wireless communications.

This final chapter discusses the "wireless" the cordless telephone, cellular telephony and paging technology and their emergence into the wireless PCS industry, and the wireless LAN. It addresses some of the modulation techniques and frequency bands associated with each technology, and it gives examples and illustrations to reinforce the student's basic understanding of the topics covered.

> **Wireless Communications**
> A radio frequency (rf) or infrared (IR)-based communications technology that eliminates use of cabling.

> **Global Positioning System (GPS)**
> A satellite-based communications network that provides a user his or her exact longitude and latitude.

19.1 PERSONAL COMMUNICATIONS SERVICES

The most recent multibillion dollar wireless technology to explode is *personal communications services,* or simply *PCS.* The latest advances in digital wireless telecommunications are now available through long-distance and local-exchange PCS carriers. The broad range of PCS services include digital cellular telephony with voice mail, e-mail, caller ID, and alphanumeric two-way paging systems, all available on a handheld, wireless PCS telephone or two-way alphanumeric pager.

Intense competition among service providers, semiconductor and equipment manufacturers, and the like will continue as each attempts to capture and enlarge their

> **Personal Communications Services (PCS)**
> A digital wireless telecommunications technology.

portions of the business and consumer markets. This competition will fuel the demand for PCS services throughout the world and help to promote the next generation of the wireless communications revolution, called *PCSS,* which stands for *personal communications satellite services.* Advances in satellite systems and wireless technology will soon put the cellular phone system in the sky.

The FCC has allocated frequency bands for nationwide PCS coverage in the 902 to 928 MHz and 1.8 to 2.2 GHz frequency bands. Narrowband FM is used in the 902 to 928 MHz band. Broad-band PCS services operating in the 1.8 to 2.2 GHz band employ 100% digital technology, which is much more efficient in terms of bandwidth than conventional narrowband FM. Modulation techniques such as *time-division multiple access (TDMA), code-division multiple access (CDMA), frequency-division multiple access (FDMA),* and *frequency-division duplex (FDD)* are employed. Each technique has its advantages and disadvantages. Many experts believe that CDMA technology, a spread-spectrum technique discussed in section 19.6.2, will prevail in the years to come, because it utilizes the bandwidth more efficiently than its counterparts.

In the United States, PCS is governed by *Common Air Interface Standards* developed by seven PCS *Technical Advisory Groups (TAGs).* They provide a number of alternatives for different end-user requirements. Table 19-1 lists the TAGs and their technology bases.

TABLE 19.1

U.S. PCS Technical Advisory Groups and Their Technology Bases

TAG	Name	Technology[a]	Based On	Proponent	Supporters
1	PCS2000	TDMA/TDD CDMA/FDMA	New proposal	Omnipoint	
2	IS-95	CDMA/FDD	US CDMA	Motorola, Qualcomm	
3	PACS U-PACs	TDMA/FDD TDMA/TDD	Bellcore TR 1313 PHS	Motorola, Hughes, PCSI Japan, Inc.	PTAG
4	IS-136	TDMA/FDD	US TDMA	AT&T Ericsson/GE	McCaw BellSouth
5	PCS-1900 DCS-1800	TDMA/FDD	European GSM	NT, Ericsson GE, Siemens	MCI
6	DCTU	TDMA/FDD	European DECT	Ericsson	
7	W-CDMA	CDMA/FDD	New Proposal	OKI, AT&T Interdigital	

[a]Explanation of terms:
Multiple access: Multiple users share same channel
Duplex: Both parties can talk at the same time
CDMA: Code-Division Multiple Access
FDD: Frequency-Division Duplex
TDMA: Time-Division Multiple Access
TDD: Time-Division Duplex
FDMA: Frequency-Division Multiple Access

(*Source: Wireless Design & Development,* September 1996, Volume 4, Number 10, p. 40.)

19.2 CELLULAR TELEPHONY

Congested frequency bands coupled with increased demands for mobile communications have given rise to a technology called AMPS (advanced mobile phone service). AMPS was developed by AMPS, Inc., a subsidiary of AT&T. AMPS has also become known as *cellular telephone*. As of 1983, the FCC has been granting approval to implement cellular telephone service throughout the United States. The basic concept behind this wireless technology is to divide heavily populated areas into many small regions called *cells*. As depicted in Figure 19-1, each cell is linked to a central location called the *mobile telephone switching office (MTSO)*. The MTSO coordinates all mobile calls between an area comprised of several cell sites and the central office. Time and billing information for each mobile unit is accounted for by the MTSO.

At the cell site, a base station is equipped to transmit, receive, and switch calls to and from any mobile unit within the cell to the MTSO. The cell itself encompasses only a few square miles, thus reducing the power requirements necessary to communicate with cellular telephones. This permits the same frequencies to be used by other cells, because the power levels emitted diminish to a level that does not interfere with other cells. In this manner, heavily populated areas can be serviced by several transmission stations, rather than one, as used by conventional mobile techniques.

> **Cellular Telephone**
> A telephone technology employing low-power mobile radio transmission rather than a subscriber loop connection to the central office.

> **Mobile Telephone Switching Office (MTSO)**
> Coordinates all mobile calls between cell sites and the central office.

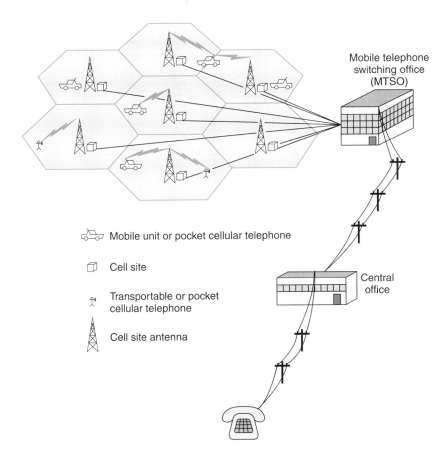

Mobile telephone switching office (MTSO)

Central office

Mobile unit or pocket cellular telephone

Cell site

Transportable or pocket cellular telephone

Cell site antenna

FIGURE 19-1
Cellular network.

19.2.1 Theory of Operation

For cellular communications, the FCC has apportioned 40 MHz of the frequency spectrum, ranging from 825 to 845 MHz and 870 to 890 MHz. Full-duplex operation is possible by separating transmit and receive signals into separate frequency bands. Cellular phone units transmit in the lower band of frequencies, 825 to 845 MHz, and receive in the higher band, 870 to 890 MHz. The opposite frequency bands are used by the base units at the cell sites. Within these two bands, 666 separate channels (333 channels per band) have been assigned for voice and control. Each channel occupies a bandwidth of 30 kHz.

When a cellular phone is turned on, its microprocessor samples dedicated *setup* channels and tunes to the channel with the strongest signal. A closed loop is effectively established between the mobile unit and cell site at all times.

To place a call from the cellular phone to the MTSO, a local seven-digit number or a 10-digit long-distance telephone number is entered via the keypad. A quick glance at the numerical display confirms that the numbers have been entered correctly. The send button is now depressed, causing a burst of data to be transmitted onto a setup channel. These data include the cellular phone's identification number and the subscriber number being called. From the cell site, the data are forwarded to the MTSO along with the cell site's identification number. An unused voice channel is established by the MTSO's controller. This information, along with the cellular phone's identification number, is sent back through the cell site to the mobile unit for processing. The microprocessor within the cellular phone adjusts its frequency synthesizer for transmitting and receiving on the designated voice channel. Once the MTSO detects that the cellular phone's carrier frequency is on the designated channel, the call is placed to the central office for processing. Ringing can now be heard at the cellular phone's receiver.

If the cellular phone's signal strength significantly diminishes as a result of traveling outside one cell and entering another, the MTSO polls through all of its cell sites to determine the new cell that it is located in. This will be the cell in which the maximum signal strength is received. A new voice channel is automatically assigned to the cellular phone by the MTSO. This is called a *handoff*. Handoffs are transparent to the user. Conversation can go uninterrupted as the mobile unit travels from cell to cell.

> **Handoff**
> When the MTSO assigns a new channel to an active cellular telephone that enters a new cell.

In addition to controlling handoffs, the MTSO also regulates the amount of power transmitted by the cellular phone. Cellular phones transmitting in close proximity to the cell site are commanded by the MTSO to reduce power to prevent interference with other channels.* Power is reduced or increased (as need be) in steps of 4 dB with a maximum permitted power of 7 watts, or 8.45 dBW.

When a call is placed from a land line to a cellular phone, a connection is made between the central office and the MTSO. After determining if the subscriber number is valid, the MTSO begins a regional search through each cell to establish the location of the cellular phone. This process is referred to as *paging*. The MTSO pages a cellular phone by sending its identification number to every cell site in a given service area over every setup channel, one of which the cellular phone is constantly lis-

---

*Stan Prentiss, *Introducing Cellular Communications: The New Mobile Telephone System* (Blue Ridge Summit, Pa.: TAB Books, 1984).

tening to. If there is no response from the system-wide page, a recorded message is sent back to the caller indicating that the cellular phone is not available. If the mobile unit responds to the page, an idle trunk between the serving cell site and MTSO is seized. An unoccupied voice channel is set up by the cell site as instructed by the MTSO. The cellular phone tunes its transmitter and receiver accordingly, and communication begins. Signal strength is monitored by the MTSO, and handoffs are made as required.

Normally, the cellular phone is used only within the metropolitan area in which the cellular phone is registered. This may include several cities or counties. Frequently, there is a need to operate a cellular phone outside the home area. This is called *roaming*. Roaming is possible anywhere throughout the country provided that cellular services are available and a prearranged agreement has been made between telephone companies and their users. A roam LED indicator on the cellular phone will light when the cellular phone travels outside the home area. With new cell coverage being implemented every day, a cellular phone can be used in virtually every major city throughout the United States and Canada. Calls can be placed to anywhere in the world.

> **Roaming**
> When a cellular telephone operates outside a registered metropolitan area.

Most of today's cellular phones offer dozens of microprocessor-controlled features, such as alphanumeric directories with scrolling displays, LCD and LED displays, programmable security codes, horn alert, scratch pad dialing, recall dialing, hands-free operation in automobiles, 32-digit dialing, paging, and even vibrators for pocket phones. Some models even include voice-recognition circuits capable of automatically dialing a number through voice-activated commands. Many mobile telephone units can also be used as a *transportable unit*. Transportable cellular phones offer the convenience of operation outside the automobile with up to 3 W of output power. A battery pack permits several hours of operation in the field. Figure 19-2(a) illustrates Motorola's *Star TAC™* wearable cellular telephone. Introduced in 1996, the StarTAC is one of the smallest and lightest cellular telephones in the world, weighing only 3.1 ounces. Figure 19-2(b) illustrates Motorola's *Micro TAC Select 6000™*. Weighing only 5.1 ounces, the Select 6000 has a display capable of four full lines of text plus two additional rows of icon graphics. A discreet vibrating feature is included with this new PCS cellular phone.

19.3 MOBILE TELEPHONY

Mobile telephony has been around for many decades, providing the luxury and convenience of placing calls through the telephone company directly from one's automobile. The conventional mobile setup illustrated in Figure 19-3 includes a single base station connected to the central office and the mobile unit in which the mobile telephone set is installed. The base station is capable of transmitting and receiving on several UHF channels in succession. A high-power transmitter delivers 200 to 250 W to the base station's antenna, which typically is elevated on a tower or a building. The mobile unit can travel within a 30-mile radius of the base station and reliably communicate with a transmission power output of up to 25 W. Unfortunately, such extreme amounts of power have caused interference between adjacent channels when mobile units are in proximity to each other or the base. In addition, only one conversation can be held at a time on the limited number of frequency channels available within a given service area. Under these circumstances, the use of the mobile

(a)

(b)

FIGURE 19-2
(a) Motorola's StarTAC™ wearable cellular telephone. (b) Motorola's *MicroTAC Select 6000*™ PCS cellular telephone. (Courtesy of Motorola.)

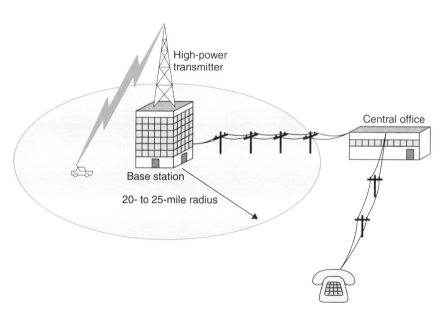

FIGURE 19-3
Conventional mobile telephone setup.

telephone has been limited to public safety services such as fire and police, forestry services, the construction industry, and other private organizations.

19.4 THE CORDLESS TELEPHONE

The *cordless telephone* has become a common household item. Its declining cost as well as convenience of operating without the restrictions of an attached cord have made it more useful than the standard telephone set. Figure 19-4 illustrates the cordless telephone.

Cordless Telephone
A telephone that operates, typically within the home, without an attached cord.

As its name implies, the cordless telephone operates without an attached cord. There are two units that make this possible: a *base unit*, and a *portable unit*. The base unit is powered by the 117-V AC household line, whereas power for the portable unit comes from an internal, rechargeable battery. Each unit contains an FM transmitter and receiver connected to a whip antenna. The base unit is directly connected to the subscriber loop through a standard telephone jack, and it transmits and receives all signals between the portable unit and the central office, including both voice and control, such as ringing and dial tone.

19.4.1 Cordless Telephone Frequencies

Earlier cordless telephones used the 117-V AC, 60-Hz household electrical wiring as a transmitting antenna for the base unit. This permitted the portable unit to receive signals uniformly throughout the house and around its perimeter. A carrier frequency in the range 1.6 to 1.8 MHz was frequency modulated by the base unit and transmitted onto the AC line. Signals transmitted from the portable unit to the base unit had a carrier frequency in the range of 49.8 to 49.9 MHz. Transmission over the 117-V household line proved to be inconsistent, however, particularly where electrical conduit was used. Therefore, this technique was abandoned by cordless telephone manufacturers. Virtually all of today's cordless telephones transmit and receive signals using a whip antenna.

In January 1984, the FCC extended the allowable cordless telephone frequencies from the previous 49.8 to 49.9 MHz down to the 46-MHz region. Ten pairs of carrier frequencies were assigned for use between the base unit and the portable handset. In June 1995, the band of cordless frequencies was further extended, down to the 43-MHz region, and 15 additional channels were added. A total of 25 channels now occupy frequencies from 43 MHz to the upper 49-MHz region; these are listed in Table 19-2. Channels 16 through 25 are the 10 original channels. The *base unit* frequencies are transmitted by the base unit and received by the portable unit, whereas the *portable unit* frequencies are transmitted by the handset and received by the base unit.

More recent cordless phones are called *900-MHz cordless phones*. These phones offer far superior SNR performance operating in the *industrial* portion of the industrial, scientific, and medical (ISM) band. The FCC has designated this portion of the band to occupy the range of frequencies from 902 to 928 MHz. Base stations and portable handsets transmit and receive on narrowband FM channels typically spaced 30 to 100 kHz apart from each other. Most 900-MHz phones offer multiple channel switching features in case of excessive noise on one channel or another cordless phone in the home or workplace operating on the same channel.

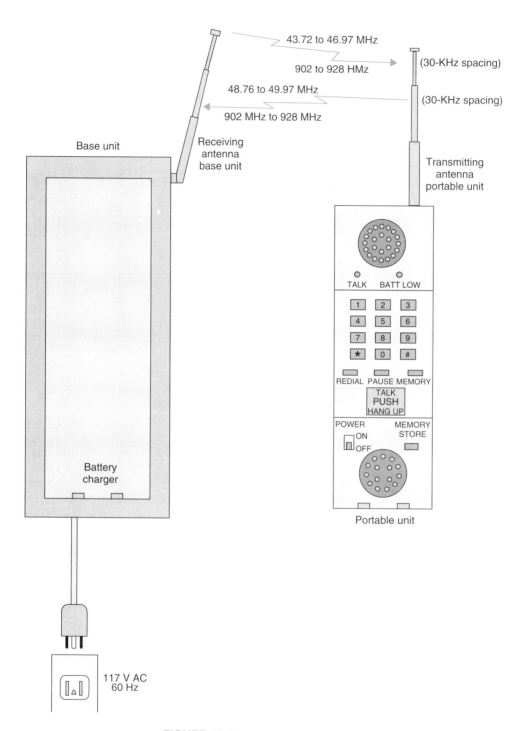

FIGURE 19-4
The cordless telephone. Most models use the 43.72-to 49.97-MHz band. The more recent 900-MHz cordless phones use the 902-to 928-MHz portion of the industrial, scientific, and medical (ISM) band.

TABLE 19-2
Cordless Telephone Frequencies in the 43- to 49-MHz Band

Channel	Base Unit, MHz	Portable Unit, MHz
1	43.72	48.76
2	43.76	48.84
3	43.82	48.86
4	43.84	48.92
5	43.92	49.00
6	43.96	49.08
7	44.12	49.10
8	44.16	49.16
9	44.18	49.20
10	44.20	49.24
11	44.32	49.28
12	44.36	49.36
13	44.40	49.40
14	44.46	49.46
15	44.48	49.50
16	46.61	49.67
17	46.63	49.845[a]
18	46.67	49.86[a]
19	46.71	49.77
20	46.73	49.875[a]
21	46.77	49.83[a]
22	46.83	49.89[a]
23	46.87	49.93
24	46.93	49.99
25	46.97	49.97

[a]Frequencies also used for baby monitors.

19.4.2 Cordless Telephone Operation

FM is the modulation technique employed by cordless phones operating in the 43- to 49-MHz and the 900-MHz bands. A telescoping whip antenna is used by both the portable and base units for transmitting and receiving these signals. To operate from a remote location, the portable unit is normally placed in the stand-by mode. In this mode, the portable unit's receiver is ON and its transmitter is OFF. The base unit maintains the on-hook condition to the subscriber loop. For incoming calls, the low-power receiver section of the portable unit actively awaits ring signals from the base unit. When ringing is detected from the central office, the base unit transmits its own ring signals to the portable unit, which are detected and used to drive a speaker built into the portable unit. Ringing prompts the called party to answer the telephone. The whip antenna is pulled out at this time, and the transmitter is activated by depressing the TALK/HANG-UP switch located on the portable unit. A signal is sent back to the base unit, which answers the phone call by going off-hook. Simultaneous conversations can now take place on the high-and low-frequency channels.

The portable unit can also be used to place calls from a remote location. With the whip antenna pulled out, the TALK/HANG-UP switch is depressed, which sends a signal to the base unit causing it to go into the off-hook condition. The dial tone received from the central office is transmitted from the base unit back to the portable unit. Dialing is accomplished through the use of the keypad on the portable handset. Its carrier frequency is modulated with dual-tone multifrequency (DTMF) tones or dial pulses representing the key depressed on the handset. The base unit demodulates these tones, and it places them onto the subscriber loop where they are sent to the central office for processing. Return signals generated from the central office, including call progress tones and voice, are frequency modulated onto the carrier signal and sent back to the portable unit for the caller to hear. When the portable unit is not in use, it should be placed back on the base unit to recharge its batteries.

19.5 PAGERS

Pager
A wireless messaging device designed to be worn by the user.

The wireless messaging revolution is best represented by the ever-conspicuous *pager*. A lowly "beeper" device once worn only by doctors, the pager has grown into one of the most visible and widely used message retrieval systems of this decade. Today's pagers are available with numerous display and alert features as well as PCS options. Consider the following:

- Numeric display
- Alphanumeric display
- Graphics display
- Data/time display
- Message time/data stamp
- Alarm clock
- Tone/music/vibrate alert
- E-mail/voice mail notification
- E-mail/voice mail retrieval
- Two-way alphanumeric paging
- 50,000+ character memory storage
- Message security

19.5.1 Pager History

Paging technology dates back to the 1920s, when pagers were limited to government agencies, police departments, and military officials. Powerful transmitters were used to broadcast one-way voice messages to a mobile paging unit, called a *base station.* No addressing system was used. Therefore, all pagers received the same message.

In 1977, Motorola introduced the *Motorola Pageboy.* Although each Pageboy had its own unique address with an audio tone used to "beep" its user, it had no display or message buffering. In the early 1980s, new standards evolved to include digital encoding and error-control algorithms to advance paging services to include tone, numeric, and alphanumeric displays. Some of these early standards include *2-tone, 5/6- tone,* and *Golay Sequential Code (GSC),* all of which are slowly being replaced today by more efficient standards.

Post Office Code Standardization Advisory Group (POCSAG)
The first-high-speed paging protocol, which can support as many as 221 million pager addresses.

In 1981, an internationally recognized standard called *POCSAG (Post Office Code Standardization Advisory Group)* was introduced as the first high-speed paging protocol. Developed by a consortium of engineers throughout the world, the POCSAG protocol is still widely used today, and it has been adopted by most pager service providers worldwide. The POGSAG protocol supports three baud rates: 512, 1200, and 2400 bps. As many as 221 million pager addresses can be supported.

The most recent pager standard, which was developed by Motorola in 1993, is called *FLEX*. Many pager experts believe that FLEX is the standard that will allow major PCS growth into the next millennium. It can support more than 1 billion pager addresses (five times the capacity of POCSAG 1200). The FLEX standard has been adopted by most pager service providers around the world, including those in Northern America, Europe, Asia, and the Middle East. Two other FLEX spin-off standards are *ReFLEX* and *InFLEXion*. ReFLEX adds two-way messaging capabilities to the FLEX protocol, and InFLEXion builds on the ReFLEX protocol to permit voice paging service.

In summary, the following paging standards used today are:

> FLEX
> A paging standard that can support more than 1 billion pager addresses and is used by most service providers.

2-Tone (limited use)
5/6-Tone (limited use)
POCSAG (Post Office Code Standardization Advisory Group, 1981)
GSC (Golay Sequential Code, Motorola 1983)
ERMES (European Radio Messaging System, European community 1990)
FLEX (Motorola, 1993)
ReFLEX (Motorola, 1994)
InFLEXion (Motorola, 1997)

Today, there are millions of pagers in operation throughout the world. *Paging Network, INC.,* better known as *Page Net,* is the world's largest and fastest-growing wireless messaging company, with 8.4 million subscribers across the United States and Canada. PageNet offers numeric and alphanumeric paging as well as a progressive line of value-added services, including exclusive CNN news updates, Internet messaging, and voice mail. PageNet owns and operates the nation's most extensive wireless network, a satellite-controlled system distributing digital information through 5000 transmission stations from coast to coast. Figure 19-5 illustrates PageNet's nationwide regional service coverage area throughout the United States.

19.5.2   Types of Pagers

Pagers come in a variety of shapes, colors, features, and sizes. Most of the palm-sized devices are approximately 2-in. wide by 3-in. long and are designed to be strapped to a belt or a purse. The microprocessor-controlled pager derives its power from an AA or AAA battery. Colors range from the traditional black or gray matte to a rainbow of designer shades and hues. Despite the numerous variations in appearance, however, the pager's primary function is the same: to alert its user of an incoming message. Figure 19-6 illustrates Motorola's most popular pagers. Pagers can be classified into several categories:

Tone-Only Pagers   Tone-only pagers receive tone messages only. They alert the user of a prearranged caller attempting to make contact. Different tones mean different people who want the user to call them. Air time to send the tone-only message is minimized, thus minimizing frequency congestion.

Numeric Pagers   The most popular paging service is for numeric pagers, which receive and decode an alert-tone message followed by the telephone number that the user is prompted to call back. A numeric display is used to display the caller's telephone number.

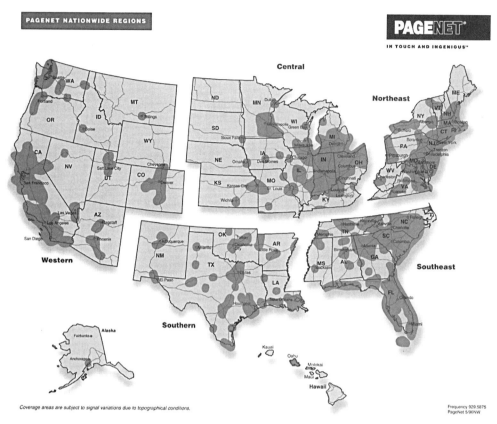

FIGURE 19-5

PageNet's regional service coverage area. (Courtesy of PageNet.)

Alphanumeric Pagers Alphanumeric pagers receive alphabetical and numeric full-text messages, with or without a telephone number. More memory and a larger display are necessary to receive and display the alphanumeric message. With PCS service, the added feature of receiving e-mail, fax news, and other information services can now be received by the alphanumeric pager.

Two-Way Pagers Two-way pagers represent the latest paging technology on the market. Two-way pagers make use of the growing narrowband PCS market by permitting a user to respond to his or her paged alphanumeric message. The 900-MHz band auctioned off by the FCC in 1995 is used. Motorola's *Page Writer* is an example of a two-way pager and is approximately the size of a deck of cards. The PageWriter includes a fold-open miniature alphanumeric keyboard and a display that can be used either to respond to a page or to originate a message. The message is simply typed and sent to the service provider, where it can be stored for retrieval.

19.5.3 Pager Operation

As stated, the most basic function of a pager is to alert its user of an incoming message. To do this, the pager must receive the transmitted message from the calling source. Figure 19-7 illustrates the paging system. Transmitters throughout the service area are linked to a device called a *paging terminal,* which is also linked to the public switched telephone network (PSTN). Its function is to encode the caller's message into a unique paging code that in turn is sent to the various transmitters throughout the coverage area.

Paging a person is quite simple. First, you must know the pager number of the person you are paging. To page a person with a numeric pager:

1. The pager number is dialed through the telephone system just as a touch-tone telephone number is dialed. The pager number is routed to the *paging terminal,* which automatically validates the pager number and sends a unique paging tone back to the caller.

> **Paging Terminal**
> A device that encodes the caller's message into a unique paging code.

(a)

(b)

(c)

FIGURE 19-6

Motorola pagers: (a) Bravo FLX numeric pager; (b) AdvisorGold FLX alphanumeric pager; (c) WordSender telephone and message delivery system sends complete messages to alphanumeric-capable pagers.

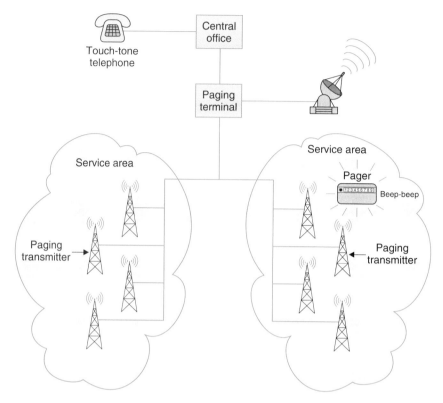

FIGURE 19-7
One-way paging system for numeric pagers.

2. The caller hears the paging tone, which is a prompt indicating that the paging system is awaiting his or her telephone number. The caller's telephone number (or some coded message) is entered via the touch-tone keypad and is followed by a pound sign (#) to signify the end of the message. If the pound sign is not pressed, the message will still be sent; however, it may take a little longer.

3. The paging terminal automatically hangs up on receiving the pound sign.

4. The paging terminal encodes the message into a special pager code and sends it to the various transmitters linked to the paging terminal. The transmitters send the pager code as a radio frequency (RF) signal throughout the entire coverage area.

5. When the pager receives its own paging code from a transmitting station, it decodes the incoming message for display, generates a beep tone, and causes an LED to flash. This notifies the user that he or she is being paged. Most pagers are equipped with silent, vibrating motors that can override the alerting beeper tone.

6. The user responds to the message by dialing the telephone number displayed on the pager through use of a regular or cellular telephone.

Figure 19-8 illustrates an alphanumeric paging system. To page a person with an alphanumeric pager, the procedure is the same as described for a numeric pager, except that alphanumeric messages can be sent. There are three ways a caller can send a message to someone with an alphanumeric pager:

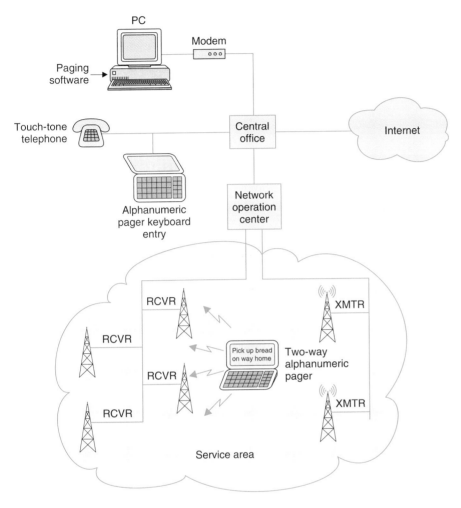

FIGURE 19-8
Two-way alphanumeric paging system.

1. The caller can speak with a paging service representative, who in turn transcribes the message and transmits it to the user's pager. As with numeric and tone-only pagers, only the pager with the appropriate address code will decode the message.
2. A special software program designed for alphanumeric pagers can be used by the caller to type a message and send it through a modem to the paging service provider, which in turn transmits it to the user's pager.
3. An alphanumeric entry device designed to be interfaced with the telephone line can be used to type a caller's message. The message is sent over the phone lines to the paging terminal, which in turn transmits it to the user's pager.

19.5.4   Pager Service Providers

Service providers that operate paging systems for the general public are called *Radio Common Carriers (RCCs)*. An RCC must be licensed by the FCC to provide radio

> **Radio Common Carriers (RCC)**
> FCC-licensed service providers that operate paging systems for the general public.

FIGURE 19-9
Frequency bands used by pagers.

paging services throughout its service area. Companies like Motorola often manufacture and sell their pagers to RCCs, who in turn place their own names on the product and sell or lease their pager services through various retailers, such as Target and Service Merchandise.* Examples of RCCs include:

> AirTouch
> AT&T
> MobileComm
> Nevada Bell
> PageNet
> SkyTel
> U.S. West

It is also possible for paging systems to be privately owned. Government organizations, hospitals, hotels, restaurants, and manufacturing and construction companies often prefer to be independent of RCCs. Like RCCs, these organizations must comply with FCC rules and regulations.

19.5.5   Pager Frequencies

Numerous frequency bands are used by pagers. Some of the variables that determine the operating frequency band are the paging protocol, pager manufacturer and model type, service area, and country of use. Figure 19-9 lists the frequency bands used by pagers. Those designed for PCS will continue to be developed as pager technology advances.

19.6   THE WIRELESS LAN

Until recently, PCs, modems, and printers were tethered to expensive telecommunications cabling systems to form a LAN. With the availability of relatively inexpensive wireless LAN products, more and more corporate LAN managers are shifting to the wireless alternative and omitting the use of cables. The wireless LAN can provide a portable computer interface that can be rapidly set up, torn down, and moved throughout a building. When users need a workstation or group of workstations in another office or floor in which a backbone or link does not exist, they can quickly establish an RF or infrared (IR) link to extend an existing LAN. Wireless hubs, network interface cards, bridges and routers, and even wireless modems and printers are all available today to provide LAN mobility and ease of connection. Figure 19-10 illustrates the wireless LAN connection.

---

*An Explanation of Subscriber vs. Customer-Owned Paging, Motorola, http://www.mot.com/MIMS/M

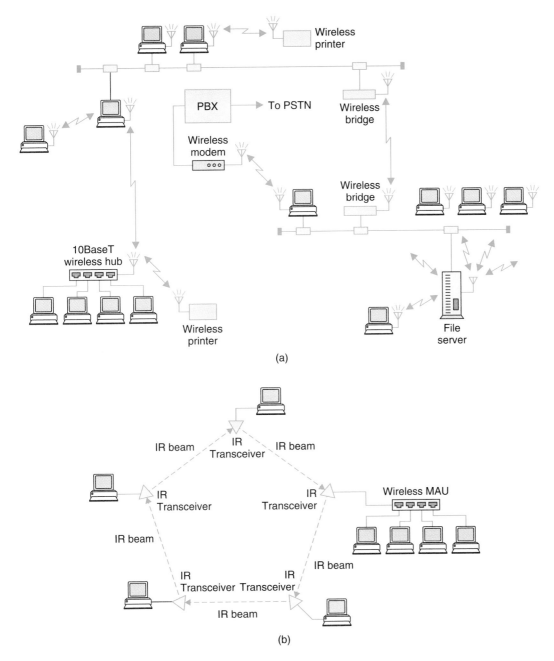

FIGURE 19-10

The wireless LAN connection: (a) Ethernet wireless RF-based LAN; (b) Token Ring wireless IR-based LAN.

Since 1991, the IEEE 802.11 committee has been responsible for establishing the wireless LAN standard, which recommends the basic transmission media, procedures, throughput requirements, and range characteristics. Having this standard in place will help network managers to please an increasingly restless workforce. Some of the most vital definitions included in the standard are:

Common Frame Format Frames formats shall remain the same for IEEE 802.3 (Ethernet) or IEEE 802.5 (Token Ring).

Common MAC Layer All IEEE 802.11-compliant wireless LANs use the CSMA/CA algorithm regardless of physical layer.

Multiple Physical Media Frequency hopping and direct sequencing spread-spectrum radio as well as IR light shall be used unless additional media is approved in the future.

Multiple On-Air Data Rates One or 2 Mbps data rate, with the possibility of higher rates in the future.

Power Limit A maximum power of 1 W or 30 dBm as mandated by the FCC. There is no minimum power requirement, which opens the possibility of low-power implementations.

19.6.1 RF-Based LANs

Today, most wireless LANs employ RF technology. The major advantage of RF over IR technology is that RF signals can propagate through walls, ceilings, people, and other obstructions without adversely affecting reception of the signal.

In 1985, the FCC and its foreign counterparts set aside a band of frequencies for unlicensed transmission of up to 1 W of signal output power, with up to 6 dB of antenna gain, provided that the signal was sent using *spread-spectrum modulation.* This band of frequencies is called the *ISM band (industrial, scientific, and medical band).* The FCC's objective was to stimulate the wireless RF LAN industry. The ISM band of frequencies is shown in Figure 19-11.

> **Industrial, Scientific, and Medical (ISM) Band**
> The range of frequencies from 902 to 928 MHz.

19.6.2 Spread-Spectrum Technology

Much of the wireless communications revolution has been based on a digital modulation technique called *spread spectrum.* Not only is spread-spectrum technology widely used in wireless RF LAN products, it is also the modulation technology employed in PCS cellular phones and pagers.

Spread spectrum has been around since World War II, and it has become one of the most important technologies of our time. It was invented by Austrian actress Hedy Lamarr and her composer, George Antheil. Lamarr and Antheil received the patent in 1942. With no technical training in electronics, the two outlined a procedure for shielding radio-controlled torpedoes from German signal jamming during World War II.

> **Spread Spectrum**
> A digital wireless communications technology that modulates a signal over a wide range of frequencies.

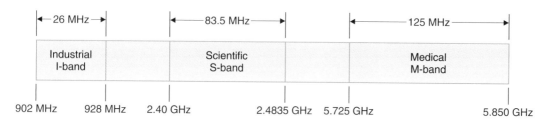

FIGURE 19-11
FCC frequency allocation for the ISM (Industrial, Scientific, and Medical) band.

Their patented technique was based on the principle of spreading a signal among many frequencies to prevent interference and eavesdropping, similar to the random manner in which a pianist skips from one note or key to the next. Thus, spread-spectrum technology is so named because the technique spreads the transmitted spectrum over a wide range of frequencies. It has since been employed in military applications because of its low probability for detection and interference from enemy jamming.

Figure 19-12 illustrates the concept of spread spectrum. In contrast to a narrowband signal, spread spectrum "spreads" a signal's power over a wide bandwidth. The spectral power density (Watts per Hertz) is minimal. At first glance, one may think that SNR performance is degraded. On the contrary, overall SNR is improved. Because noise tends to be bursty and narrowband in nature, only a small portion of the spread spectrum's signal will be affected by the interference. The spread of signal energy over a wide band makes the spread-spectrum signal less likely to interfere with narrowband communication systems. Conversely, narrowband signals have little effect on the spread-spectrum system.

Several techniques can generate the spread-spectrum signal. The two main techniques used in the telecommunications industry are *direct sequence* and *frequency hopping*. In both cases, the carrier frequency is modulated by the intelligence using some pseudo-random spreading code or pattern (other than the data), thus causing it to spread over a large bandwidth. This bandwidth can range from 10 to several hundred times the bandwidth of the intelligence. The spread-spectrum signal becomes inconspicuous and has the appearance of random noise. It even is unlikely to interfere with other signals transmitted over the same band. Therefore, many spread-spectrum signals can share the same frequency band, and bandwidth efficiency is greatly increased.

> **Frequency Hopping**
> A technique for generating the spread-spectrum signal by "hopping" the carrier frequency.

> **Pseudo-Random Noise (PN)**
> A pseudo-random code used for "hopping" the carrier frequency.

19.6.2.1 Frequency Hopping Spread Spectrum In *frequency hopping,* the spread-spectrum signal is generated by "hopping" the carrier frequency in accordance with some *pseudo-random noise (PN)* code. The same PN code used by the transmitter must be used by the intended receiver. Figure 19-13 illustrates a simplified

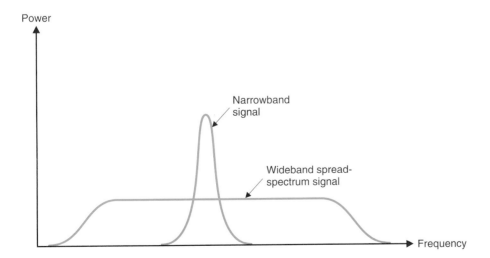

FIGURE 19-12
The spread-spectrum signal requires a wider bandwidth than a narrowband signal but is less prone to noise interference.

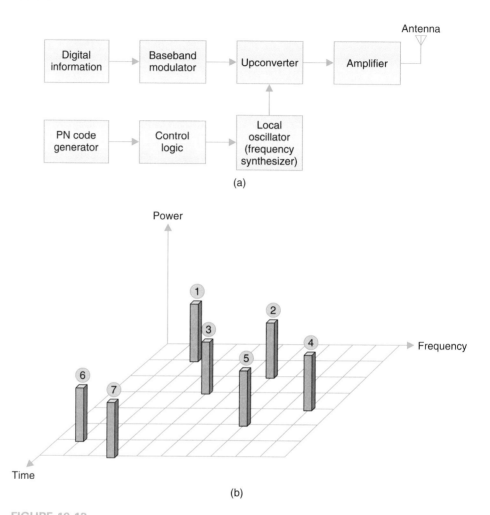

FIGURE 19-13

(a) Block diagram of a frequency hopping spread-spectrum transmitter; (b) the frequency hopping concept.

block diagram of a frequency hopping spread-spectrum transmitter and the spread-spectrum signal it generates.

The digital information signal is applied to a conventional modulator, which generates an intermediate frequency (IF) signal.* The PN code is applied to a logic circuit that controls the fast-switching frequency synthesizer used as a local oscillator (LO). The LO upconverts the IF signal to the RF frequency band, where the spread-spectrum signal is transmitted out the antenna. Note that the amplitudes of each frequency component hopped across the given band are equal, and the bandwidth of the frequency hopping signal is the product of the number of frequency hops available multiplied by the bandwidth of each hop channel. If the information signal's band-

---

*Gary A. Breed, "A First Introduction to Frequency Hopping Spread Spectrum," *RF Design*, May 1994, pp. 64–69.

width is 100 kHz and a spread-spectrum bandwidth of 100 MHz is available, then it is possible to have up to 1000 frequency hops.

$$BW_{SS} = n \cdot BW_H \qquad \textbf{(19-1)}$$

where BW_{SS} = spread-spectrum bandwidth of the frequency hopped signal
$\qquad n$ = total number of frequency hops
$\qquad BW_H$ = bandwidth of hop channel

EXAMPLE
19.1

The spread-spectrum signal shown in Figure 19-13 has a hop channel bandwidth of 200 kHz. Compute the bandwidth of the signal.

Solution:

The bandwidth can be computed by noting there are a total of seven hop frequencies, n; therefore,

$$BW_{SS} = n \cdot BW_H$$
$$= 7 \times 200 \text{ kHz}$$
$$= 1.4 \text{ MHz}$$

To further disguise the frequency hopping pattern generated by the PN code, the code itself is frequently updated. Furthermore, the amount of time that the synthesizer stays on any one hop channel is typically less than 10 ms.* Clearly, the key element in a frequency hopping system is the frequency synthesizer, because it must rapidly switch across the entire spread-spectrum band with minimal settling time and distortion. This can be a difficult and costly engineering task.

19.6.2.2 Direct Sequence Spread Spectrum   In frequency hopping, the signal is essentially FM based, whereas the *direct sequence* method of generating the spread-spectrum signal is AM based. Unlike frequency hopping, in which the signal is spread by periodically changing the frequency, direct sequencing modulates the original base-band signal with a very wide band digital signal. The name *direct sequence* stems from employing a high-speed PN code directly to the digital information being sent. Figure 19-14 shows a simplified block diagram of a direct sequence spread-spectrum transmitter.

> **Direct Sequence**
> A technique for generating the spread-spectrum signal by modulating the original baseband signal with a very wide-band digital signal.

To generate the direct sequence spread-spectrum signal, the digital information is *multiplied* with a PN code that runs at a much higher rate than the digital information rate. The digital multiplication process is essentially an exclusive-NOR function. The PN code is a high-speed sequence of binary 1s and 0s called *chips*. Each chip has a value of -1 or $+1$ for a bipolar signal, or 0 or 1, respectively, for a unipolar signal. Chip values are random. That is, there are an equal number of 1s and 0s over time, thereby producing a pseudo-white-noise-like effect. Figure 19-15 shows the multiplication process used to spread the information data stream. The PN code here uses five chips per data bit time. For direct sequence spread-spectrum systems, this is referred to as a *spreading factor* of 5. The bandwidth of the signal is spread by a factor of 5.

Why Spread Spectrum, Cylinks Corporation, 1997, p. 4 of 7 http://www.cylink.com

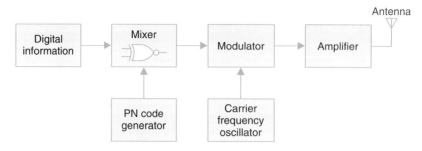

FIGURE 19-14
Block diagram of a direct sequence spread-spectrum transmitter.

The composite PN-coded signal is then fed to a modulator to produce a double-sideband suppressed carrier signal that is transmitted out the antenna. This signal can also be thought of as a BPSK signal (binary phase shift keying). The transmitted RF signal is centered about the carrier frequency and produces the $2(\sin x/x)$ function shown in Figure 19-16. A comparison is also made between the direct sequence and frequency hopped spread-spectrum signals. The receiving device must use the same PN code to detect the original message.

19.6.3   IR Wireless LANs

The IR wireless LAN is not nearly as established and popular as RF-based LANS; however, IR offers an attractive alternative to RF for some LAN managers. For example, it cannot penetrate walls and ceilings like RF and, therefore, offers the security needed by some organizations. Another advantage is that IR transmission does not interfere with surrounding electronic equipment that might be susceptible to noise. Conversely, electromagnetic noise sources do not interfere with the light signal, and for this reason, no government licensing is required.

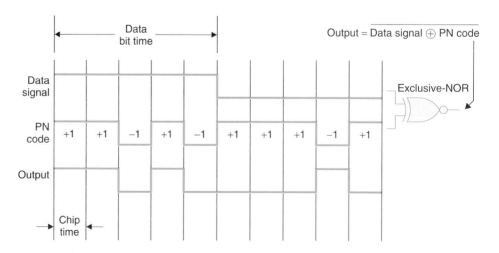

FIGURE 19-15
PN code used to spread the data signal for direct sequence spread spectrum.

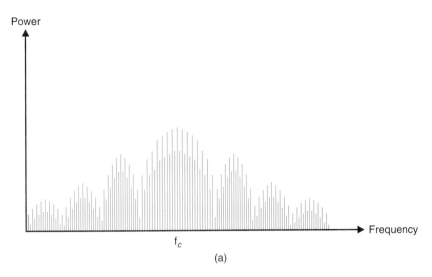

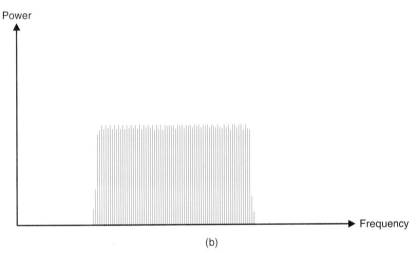

FIGURE 19-16
Spread spectrum for: (a) direct sequence; (b) frequency hopping.

IR networking equipment is limited to line-of-sight transmission or to transmission within an enclosed area capable of reflecting the light off walls or ceilings. Any obstruction to the path of the light, including people, objects, dust, smoke, smog, and moisture in the air, will hinder the performance of an IR-based LAN.

Light sources used for IR-based LANs are lasers or LEDs that transmit at a wavelength of approximately 820 nm. This wavelength occupies that part of the electromagnetic spectrum with a frequency less than that of visible red light and higher than that of microwaves. Therefore, the light is invisible. Because IR allows data signals to be modulated over light waves, it is one of the fastest transmission technologies currently available. Both 4- and 16-Mbps Token Ring and 10-Mbps Ethernet-compliant LAN products are available to set up all, or a portion of, an IR-based LAN. Two types of IR-based LANs are discussed here: *diffused IR,* and *point-to-point IR.*

Diffused IR
An infrared-based LAN that uses a room's walls, floors, and ceiling to bounce signals between the transmitter and receiver.

Point-to-Point IR
An infrared-based LAN that uses line-of-sight transmission.

19.6.3.1 The Diffused IR LAN

The *diffused IR-based LAN* uses a room's walls, floors, and ceiling surfaces to bounce data signals between the transmitter and receiver in the same way that visible light illuminates a room. Optical IR transceivers can be mounted on or near the workstation or peripheral. Figure 19-17 illustrates the principle of the diffused IR-based LAN, and two types of diffused optical transceivers are shown. One is based on the *scattering* of IR light in all directions; the other is based on *reflection* off a common spot on the ceiling or wall. Reflective IR systems are more reliable than scatter IR systems due to their directional capabilities. An analogy would be several flashlights shining on a common spot. Reflective IR systems also tend to work best in facilities with high ceilings.

19.6.3.2 The Point-to-Point IR LAN

An inherent problem with diffused IR systems is that the throughput speed or transmission rate of the data is limited due to a phenomenon called *multipath*. Multipath is a form of phase distortion resulting from a signal taking several paths to reach its destination. The digital binary bit stream of the diffused IR signal bounces off walls, ceilings, and other objects, consequently taking multiple paths to reach the IR receiver. The received digital binary bit stream does not maintain the best phase relationship between pulses. Multipath distortion is similar to the modal dispersion that occurs with light that is guided through fiber-optic media, and it becomes more pronounced at higher transmission rates.

> **Multipath**
> Phase distortion resulting from a signal taking several paths to its destination.

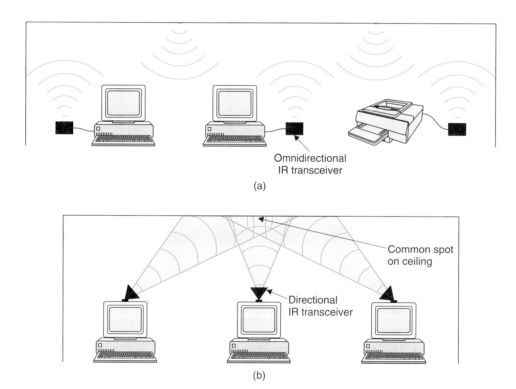

Omnidirectional
IR transceiver

(a)

Common spot
on ceiling

Directional
IR transceiver

(b)

FIGURE 19-17
Two types of diffused IR-based LANs: (a) a scatter system bounces IR light off walls, ceilings, and other objects; (b) a reflective system bounces IR light off a common spot on the ceiling or wall.

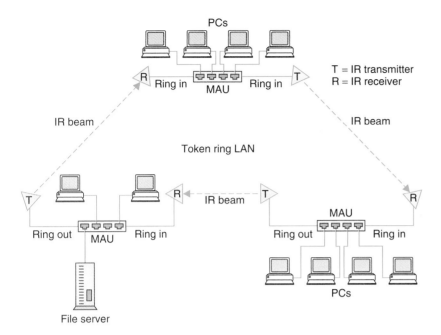

FIGURE 19-18
The point-to-point IR-based LAN uses line-of-sight transmission. The Token Ring system shown here uses wireless IR transmitters and receivers to form a MAU-to-MAU, star-wired ring connection.

The *point-to-point IR-based LAN* employs line-of-sight transmission. Multipath distortion is minimized by using a highly concentrated light source, such as a laser. A point-to-point IR-based LAN is shown in Figure 19-18, which illustrates a Token Ring system that uses wireless IR transmitters and receivers to form a multistation access unit (MAU)-to-MAU, star-wired ring connection. The transmitters and receivers must be focused and aligned beforehand. It is important to remember that the point-to-point IR connection cannot be obstructed by people walking through the signal path. Transmitters and receivers, therefore, must be installed in places where the signal path cannot be interrupted.

In an industrial setting, a speedy, reliable connection between buildings up to 1 mile apart can be made using IR laser beams. Although severe weather conditions can hinder the performance of such an outdoor point-to-point link, a company can still avoid the time-consuming and costly task of setting up a microwave link or private-line connection.

PROBLEMS

1. Define *PCS*.
2. What does *MTSO* stand for, and what function does it serve?
3. Explain what a *handoff* is.
4. Define *roaming*.
5. What are the frequency bands used by cordless telephones for the base unit versus the portable unit operating in the 40-MHz region?
6. What is the frequency band used by 900-MHz cordless phones?

7. What modulation technique is used by 900-MHz cordless telephones?
8. Name at least four features of a pager.
9. Name at least four paging standards.
10. What is the difference between numeric and alphanumeric pagers?
11. List the three ways that one can send a message to an alphanumeric pager.
12. What is an *RCC*? Name one.
13. What are the *ISM bands*, and what are their frequencies?
14. Who invented *spread spectrum*?
15. List the two types of spread-spectrum techniques discussed.
16. Draw the block diagram of a direct sequence spread-spectrum system.
17. Draw the block diagram of a frequency hopping spread-spectrum system.
18. Compute the spread-spectrum bandwidth for a frequency hopping system that has a hop channel bandwidth of 200 kHz and a total of 1000 frequency hops.
19. Compute the spread-spectrum bandwidth for a frequency hopping system that has a hop channel bandwidth of 250 kHz and a total of 1500 frequency hops.
20. What are the two types of *IR LANs* discussed?
21. What are the two types of *diffused IR transceivers* discussed?
22. Explain *multipath*.
23. What type of IR-based LAN system minimizes multipath distortion?

GLOSSARY

2B1Q *2-Binary, 1-Quaternary* The line coding technique used by the ISDN protocol. Two levels of amplitudes are used: ± 2.5 V, and ± 0.8 V. This permits the encoding of 2 bits per baud.

A-Law Companding law used in Europe.

Absorption Loss The loss of signal energy caused by a medium's impurities.

Acoustically Coupled Modem A low-speed modem (1200 baud or less) that connects indirectly to the telephone lines through the use of an *acoustic coupler*. Two rubber cup-size sockets on the modem are used to mount a telephone set's handpiece to the coupler.

Acoustic Coupler A transducer that converts sound energy to electrical energy, and vice versa. Used with *indirect connect modems*.

A/D Converter *Analog-to-Digital Converter* Used to convert an analog signal into digital format.

Adaptive Equalizer A line-conditioning circuit used in a receiver to provide postequalization of a signal. It is implemented in the receiver section of a high-speed modem.

ADSL *Asymmetric Digital Subscriber Line* A digital subscriber line (DSL) technology that offers a high-speed digital connection over POTS (Plain Old Telephone Service) lines. Downstream transmission, which can be as much as 1.1 Mbps, is faster than upstream transmission; therefore, transmission is referred to as asymmetric.

ALB *Analog Loop Back Test* A test used by a transmitting and receiving device (e.g., a modem) that verifies the operation of its transmitter and receiver sections by internally looping back the transmitter's analog signal back to its own receiver section.

Aloha A *LAN* protocol that uses a contention scheme to gain access to the channel.

AM *Amplitude Modulation* A fundamental modulation technique in which a carrier frequency's amplitude is varied in proportion to the instantaneous amplitude of a modulating voltage.

AMI *Alternate Mark Inversion* See *B8ZS*.

Analog Any continuous and variable quantity of information.

Angle Modulation A modulation technique in which the intelligence of the modulating signal is conveyed by means of varying the frequency (FM, *frequency modulation*) or phase (PM, *phase modulation*) of the carrier signal.

Anonymous FTP An Internet search tool allowing its user to access public databases and archives without an account. When Anonymous FTP is enabled at an FIP site, *anonymous* is given as the login name, and FTP will generally accept any string, usually an e-mail address, as a password.

ANSI *American National Standards Institute* The official U.S. agency and voting representative for ISO. ANSI develops information exchange standards above 50 Mbps.

Answer Modem The modem that has been designated to answer a call initiated by an *originate modem*.

Antitinkle Circuit That portion of a telephone circuit used to suppress transients and prevent sparking across the dial contacts. Without it, a tinkling noise produced by the high-voltage spikes across the ringer can be heard when dialing.

APD *Avalanche Photodiode* A photodetector used as a fiber-optic receiver. The APD exhibits high *responsivity* in comparison to the PIN photodiode. When reverse-biased, current carriers flow when light penetrates the depletion region.

Archie A file and directory search program developed at McGill University in Canada that automatically interrogates host servers across the Internet on a regular basis and updates its own database directory with files available on other Archie servers.

ARPANET *Advanced Research Projects Agency Network* A four-node packet-switched network developed in 1969 by DARPA (Defense Advanced Research Projects Agency), a U.S. Department of Defense organization, where the origin of the Internet can be traced.

ARQ *Automatic Repeat Request* Any error correction technique used whereby a receiver requests the retransmission of a block received in error.

ASCII *American Standard Code for Informational Interchange* A 7-bit alphanumeric code used extensively in data communications. A parity bit is often added to the 7-bit code for error detection.

ASK *Amplitude Shift Keying* A form of amplitude modulation whereby a carrier's amplitude is shifted in accordance with a serial binary bit stream.

ASL *Adaptive Speed Leveling* A U.S. Robotics' proprietary technology that boosts modem speeds from 19,200 to 21,600 bps.

Asynchronous Transmission The transmission of characters separated by time intervals that vary in length, usually in accordance with the key entries of a terminal operator. Start and stop bits are used to identify the beginning and end of the asynchronously transmitted character.

ATM *Asynchronous Transfer Mode* A high-speed form of packet switching developed as part of *BISDN*. ATM uses short, fixed-length packets called *cells* that find their way through the network.

Attenuation Distortion A parameter used by the PSTN to specify the limits of amplitude variations in the passband of the telephone lines. Ideally, a flat frequency response is desired.

AUI *Attachment Unit Interface* A connector used to attach the transceiver cable from the controller card to the Ethernet transceiver. The AUI connector is a standard DB-15 connector.

B8ZS *Bipolar with 8 Zero Substitution* A self-clocking RZ encoding technique used for ensuring compliance with pulse density requirements for synchronization. B8ZS coding ensures adequate signal energy by substituting any string of eight consecutive zeros within the serial bit stream with a specific 8-bit code. Also known as *Alternate Mark Inversion.*

Balanced Electrical Circuit A circuit that has two signal paths on which the transmitted signal propagates. Each signal path has the same impedance with respect to signal ground.

Balanced Modulator A device used to eliminate or suppress the carrier frequency to produce the *DSBSC* signal. Multiplication of two inputs, the carrier frequency input and the modulation frequency input, is performed, resulting in the sum and difference products.

Bar Code A series of consistently sized white and black bars that are pasted, painted, or burned onto items for purposes of identification. The wide and narrow bars, representing 1s and 0s, are read by an optical scanner and sent to a computer for processing.

Baseband An encoded analog or digital signal transmitted directly onto a channel without modulating a carrier frequency beforehand.

Baudot A 5-bit code used in the field of telegraphy and Radio Teletype (RTTY).

Baud Rate The rate at which a signal is changed or modulated. Baud rate is directly related to the number of bits transmitted per second.

BBS *Bulletin Board System* An online service or computer data bank into which users with accounts can dial through a modem.

BCC *Block Check Character* A redundant character sent at the end of a message block for error detection. Its value is computed based on the bit pattern of the message stream.

BCD *Binary Coded Decimal* A code used to express a decimal number with four binary bits. It is also referred to as 8421 code due to the binary weighting of each bit.

Bel A unit of sound named in honor of Alexander Graham Bell.

BER *Bit Error Rate* Specifies the number of bits that are corrupted or destroyed as data are transmitted from source to destination. BER is typically expressed as a power of ten (e.g., 10^{-5} means that one bit out of 100,000 was destroyed during transmission).

Bessel Function A complex mathematical integral used in analyzing frequency components and their respective amplitudes in the FM wave. Bessel functions are represented by each set of upper and lower sidebands displaced from the carrier frequency by an integral multiple of the modulation frequency.

Binary A base 2 numbering system that uses the binary digits 1 and 0.

Binder Unit In telephone feeder network cables, binder units are used to identify groups of 25-pair lines. Color-coded Mylar wrapping is used to group each binder unit.

Bipolar A transmission code in which the polarity of the bit stream takes on positive and negative values.

Bipolar RZ *Bipolar Return-to-Zero* A *self-clocking code* in which two non-zero voltages are used. A logic 1 and 0 alternate in polarities, each taking half the bit time before returning to zero.

Bipolar Violation Occurs in a T1 signal whenever two consecutive pulses occur with the same polarity regardless of the number of zero bit times that separate the two pulses.

bis French for "second revision."

BISDN *Broadband Integrated Digital Services Network* A broadband PSTN service intended to support transmission speeds from 150 Mbps to 2.5 Gbps.

BISYNC *Binary Synchronous Communications* A byte-oriented synchronous serial communications protocol developed by IBM. Also referred to as BSC protocol.

Bit-Oriented Protocol Any protocol that uses special groups of uniquely defined bit patterns to control the framing, error checking, and flow between devices.

Bit Rate The number of bits transmitted per second.

Bit Stuffing The technique used in bit-oriented protocols to achieve *transparency* in the data field of a transmitted block. A 1 bit is "stuffed" by the transmitter after any succession of five consecutive 1 bits that are sent. This ensures that no pattern of the opening or closing flag is sent within the data field of the block. Also referred to as *zero bit insertion.*

Bit Time The length of time required to transmit 1 bit.

Blocking An event that occurs when a central office is overburdened with more calls than it can accommodate. A blocked call is identified by a fast *busy tone* that is sent to the caller.

Block Mode of Transmission For ASCII terminals, a high-speed mode of synchronously transmitting groups of contiguous characters. The characters typed at the terminal are stored in the terminal's buffer and transmitted all at once rather than asynchronously.

BOC *Bell-Operating Companies* The local telephone companies spun off from AT&T as a result of divestiture. BOCs are organized into seven regions within the United States. Also known as *RBOC* (*Regional BOC*).

BPSK *Binary Phase Shift Keying* PSK modulation technique when only two phases are used.

BRI *Basic Rate Interface* Delivers *ISDN* services to the subscriber over a standard twisted-pair telephone wire. The BRI carries two 64-kbps B-channels and one 16-kbps D-channel.

Bridge An internetworking device that is used to link two *LAN* segments together. The bridge operates at the data link layer of the *OSI seven-layer model*.

Broadband In contrast to baseband, broadband transmissions use one or more carrier frequencies to convey the intelligence. Frequency-division multiplexing (FDM) is employed.

Bus LAN A network topology that uses a multipoint or multidrop configuration of interconnecting nodes on a shared channel.

Busy Bit In Token Ring, the *T-bit* that is set within the access control byte when a station needs to modify the free token into a *dataframe.*

Byte-Oriented Protocol Any protocol in which the transmission of data blocks are controlled by special characters (e.g., ASCII or EBCDIC control characters such as SYN, SOH, ETX, etc.).

Cable Modem A modem designed to provide high-speed Internet access and video services, including picture phone, to the millions of subscribers already connected to the cable TV (CATV) network.

CAM *Content Addressable Memory* That portion of a LAN switch's memory that stores and timestamps frame addresses.

CAP *Carrierless Amplitude Phase* A QAM (Quadrature Amplitude Modulation) modulation or line coding technique used with *DSL* modems.

Carson's Rule A rule stating that for transmission of an angle-modulated wave, the minimum bandwidth required is equal to two times the sum of the peak frequency deviation, δ, plus the highest modulation frequency, f_m: $BW = 2(\delta + f_m)$.

Cathode Ray Tube A vacuum tube designed to direct an intense electron beam to a fluorescent screen for displaying electrical signals.

CATV *Community Antenna Television or Cable TV* Broadband television transmission over 75-Ω (typ.) coaxial cable.

CCITT *Consultative Committee for International Telephony and Telegraphy* An agency of the United Nations that develops recommended worldwide standards and protocols for the telecommunications industry. CCITT is now known as *ITU-TS.*

CDMA *Code-Division Multiple Access* A direct sequencing spread-spectrum technology used to increase channel capacity in digital cellular telephony.

Cell A geographical area that services cellular mobile telephones.

Cell Site A base station used in cellular telephony that is equipped to transmit and receive calls from any mobile unit within the cell.

Cellular Telephone A telephone technology that employs low-power mobile radio transmission as an alternative to a subscriber loop connection to the central office.

Central Office The local telephone switching exchange.

CERN *European Laboratory for Particle Physics* In Geneva, Switzerland, where the World Wide Web was invented by Tim Berners-Lee in 1989.

Channel Any communications link over which information is transmitted.

Channel Capacity The maximum theoretical data transfer rate over a channel based on the channel's bandwidth and SNR. Channel rate is expressed in bits per second (bps).

Character Mode of Transmission An asynchronous mode of transmission featured by a terminal. Characters are transmitted to a host computer only when a key is depressed by an operator.

Cheapernet A scaled-down version of *Ethernet* that utilizes RG58 50-Ω coaxial cable. Cheapernet is also known as *Thin-net* or *Thin Ethernet.*

Check Bit A redundant parity bit inserted into a message stream for the purpose of *forward error correction* (*FEC*).

Checksum An error-detection technique that basically computes the sum of data and appends this value to the end of a transmitted block of data.

Chromatic Dispersion The spreading of a light pulse caused by the difference infractive indices at different wavelengths.

Circuit Switching A switching technology utilized by the PSTN that permits DTE to establish an immediate full-duplex connection to another station on a temporary basis. Exclusive use of the channel is available until the channel is relinquished by one of the stations.

Cladding The surrounding layer of a fiber-optic core that is used to confine light. Its index of refraction is less than that of the core, thus permitting *total internal reflection* of the transmitted light within the fiber's core.

CLEC *Competitive Local Exchange Carrier* Smaller telephone companies that compete with *LECs.*

Client   A station on the network that permits its user to request the shared services provided by the network server.

Client/Server Network   A network in which the server is dedicated to serving the network and cannot be used as a workstation.

CMRR   *Common-Mode Rejection Ratio*   A measure of a differential amplifier's ability to reject signals common to its input pair of lines.

Coaxial Cable   Wire consisting of an inner conductor, typically copper wire, surrounded by a dielectric insulator. A wire mesh or copper tube, acting as an electrical shield, encases the dielectric. A protective insulating material, such as PVC, often surrounds the entire construction for protection.

Code 39   An alphanumeric *bar code* consisting of 36 characters and 7 special characters.

Codec   A contraction of the words *co*der and *dec*oder. It is a device that takes an analog signal, such as voice, and converts it to a binary serial bit stream (PCM signal) through use of an internal analog-to-digital (A/D) converter. It also performs the reverse process of converting a binary serial bit stream back into its original analog form through use of an internal digital-to-analog (D/A) converter. The codec also performs the function of *companding*.

Collision   The event that occurs when two transmitters are transmitting at the same time over the same channel. Data are destroyed.

Collision Domain   In a LAN, a collision domain represents an area where collisions can occur (e.g., an Ethernet segment represents a collision domain).

Colpitts Oscillator   A tuned oscillator circuit that uses capacitive feedback to sustain oscillations.

Common Battery   A system in which telephone sets receive power from the central office for signaling and switching is performed automatically.

Companding   The process of COMpressing a signal's dynamic range before it is transmitted and exPANDING it back to its original range at the receiver. SNR is greatly improved at the receiver.

Compromise Equalizer   Provides pre-equalization of a signal. It is implemented in the transmitter section of a high-speed modem.

Concentrator   A device allowing a bus or ring topology to be collapsed into the hub to form a star topology. Various cabling media can be interfaced to the concentrator. A concentrator is often referred to as a *hub*.

Contention   The process whereby multiple stations vie for the use of the communications channel.

Continuous Code   A bar code without intercharacter spaces as part of its structure.

CPE   *Customer Premises Equipment*   Equipment on the customer premises, such as PBXs, LAN gateways, and host computers.

CRC   *Cyclic Redundancy Check*   The most commonly used method for error detection in block transmission. The transmitted message block is divided by a polynomial. The quotient is discarded and the remainder is transmitted at the end of the message block as the *block check character* (BCC).

Critical Angle   In fiber optics, the angle above which *total internal reflection* occurs for light rays.

Critical Resource   Any part of a LAN system that fails and consequently disables the entire system.

Crossbar Switch   An electromechanical switch used in older central office switching systems. The crossbar switch consists of a lattice of horizontal and vertical crossbars with contact points that make and break contact for telephone calls.

Crosstalk   Electrical noise or interference caused by inductive and capacitive coupling of signals from adjacent channels.

CSMA/CD   *Carrier Sense Multiple Access with Collision Detection*   One of the most widely used protocols for bus LAN systems. Used in Ethernet LAN systems.

Current Loop   A serial interface standard that has evolved from the old electromechanical Teletype, which used current to activate its relays. Typically 20 or 60 mA is turned on and off in accordance with the binary serial data.

Cut-Through Switching   A mode of switching whereby only the initial portion of an Ethernet frame is tested before forwarding it to the outgoing ports of the switch.

Data Communications   The transmission and reception of digital signals from one location to another.

Data Compression   The mechanism used to reduce the number of data bits that is normally used to carry a given amount of information.

Data Encapsulation/Decapsulation   The process of assembling and disassembling the Ethernet frame structure.

Data Set   The name given to a modem by telephone companies.

Data Transparency   The condition when data are not mistaken for control characters. It is achieved when raw data incorporate special encoding techniques into the code.

dBm   A unit of gain or loss expressed as an absolute value, because it is referenced to 1 mW or some known standard value.

DCE   *Data Communications Equipment*   Typically a modem or data set used to interface a terminal or computer to the telephone lines.

Decibel (dB)   One tenth of a *bel*. Originally a unit of sound, the decibel is now commonly used as a unit representing relative voltage or power gain.

De-emphasis   The process through which an FM receiver brings back pre-emphasized signals to their original amplitudes by the same extent during pre-emphasis. De-emphasis takes place after the FM signal has been demodulated.

Delivery Point Bar Code (DPBC) An extension of the *POSTNET* bar code. The DPBC adds two more digits to the nine-digit ZIP + four to represent the last two digits of a street address or P.O. box number.

Dial Tone An audible tone acknowledging connection to the central office when a caller goes off-hook.

Dial-Up Line The standard unconditioned two-wire switched voice-grade line.

Dibit Two bits encoded into one of four possible phase changes.

Differential Manchester Encoding An encoding technique for binary serial bit streams in which a transition from high to low or from low to high occurs at the center of each cell, thus providing the self-clocking mechanism.

Diffused IR LAN An IR (infrared)-based LAN that uses a room's walls, floors, and ceiling surfaces to bounce data signals between the transmitter and receiver in the same way that visible light illuminates a room.

Digital Information that is encoded into two discrete binary levels: a "1" or a "0."

Digital Channel Bank Equipment used by the central office to digitize and time-division multiplex several voice channels together.

Digital Signal A digital signal is characterized as having two discrete values, a logic 1 and logic 0, as a function of time. A digital pulse steam is an example. A digital signal can also be an analog waveform with two discrete values. Two frequencies shifting between each other is an example.

Direct Connect Modem A modem that is capable of electrically connecting directly to telephone lines.

Direct Sequence A technique used to generate the spread-spectrum signal by modulating the original baseband signal with a very wide band digital signal. It also employs a high-speed pseudo random noise (PN) code directly to the digital information being sent.

Discrete Code A bar code with intercharacter spaces or gaps between characters. Each character within the bar code symbol is independent of every other character.

DLB *Digital Loop Back Test* A test used to verify the transmitter and receiver sections of a local and remote station. A command, issued by the local station, is sent to the remote station to *loop back* the detected digital data. The communications channel, modem interface, and I/O device used to issue the command are also tested.

DLE *Data Link Escape* An ASCII and EBCDIC control character used to control the flow of data between two stations.

DM *Delta Modulation* A special form of pulse code modulation (PCM) in which the analog input signal is converted to a 1 bit continuous serial data stream of 1s and 0s at a rate determined by a sampling clock.

DMT *Discrete Multitone* A modulation of line coding technique used by *DSL* modems. DMT employs a combination of *QAM* and *FDM*.

DNS *Domain Name System* A method of mapping domain names and Internet Protocol (IP) addresses to computers linked to the Internet.

Domain A node and its descendant nodes on a network.

Domain Name The unique name of a particular node within the domain and made up of subdomains, which are nodes leading to a particular node.

Double Buffering The process of using two registers to store data. One register is used to hold the data and the other is used to process it.

Double-Ended Amplifier An amplifier used to transmit or receive signals on a balanced electrical circuit. Differential amplifiers and receivers fall into this category.

Down-Link Frequencies A 4-GHz band of frequencies, ranging from 3.7 to 4.2 GHz, to which earth station receivers are tuned.

Downstream Transmission A cable TV (CATV) signal's direction of travel from the CATV station antenna to community subscribers.

DPSK *Differential Phase Shift Keying* A modulation technique in which the phase of the carrier frequency is shifted in accordance with the binary serial data. Groups of bits are encoded into a single phase change relative to the phase of the previously encoded interval.

DSBFC *Double-Sideband Full-Carrier* The total composite AM signal comprised of two sidebands and a carrier frequency.

DSBSC *Double-Sideband Suppressed Carrier* Suppression of the carrier component of the AM signal so that the transmitted wave consists only of the upper and lower sidebands.

DSL *Digital Subscriber Line* A family of high-speed digital modem technologies designed to operate over *POTS* lines.

DSLAM *Digital Subscriber Line Access Multiplexer* At the central office, the DSLAM performs the task of multiplexing and demultiplexing *DSL* signals between the customer and *ISP*.

DTE *Data Terminal Equipment* In data communications, an end user or terminating circuit, typically a terminal or computer.

DTMF *Dual-Tone Multifrequency* The technology that utilizes telephone numbers on a pushbutton keypad that are encoded into audible tones when a key is depressed. Each tone is comprised of a pair of sine waves called a DTMF tone. DTMF is also referred to as *Touch Tone*.

Dynamic Range The functional operating range over which a device operates.

DWDM *Dense Wavelength-Division Multiplexing* An optical multiplexing technique that uses multiple wavelengths to transport multiple signals over a single fiber-optic strand.

E-mail *Electronic-mail* The single most widely used application of the Internet, which permits millions of people around the world to converse with each other without having to wait days for messages to be sent and received via the postal system. E-mail allows users to send and receive text, program files, and graphic images.

EBCDIC *Extended Binary-Coded Decimal Interchange Code* An 8-bit alphanumeric code (no parity) developed by IBM and used in many of its mainframe computers and peripherals.

Echo A reflected signal. In long-distance transmission over the PSTN, impedance mismatches can cause a signal to be reflected back to the caller. This echo is especially annoying when the round-trip delay time exceeds about 50 ms. This occurs at distances beyond 1500 miles.

Echo Cancellation A technique used by high-speed modems to achieve true full-duplex operation over switched lines. An inverted replica of the transmitted signal is added to the received signal to eliminate interference.

Echo Canceller A device used in long-haul networks to electrically cancel any returned echo from a long-distance contact.

Echo Suppressor A device used in long-haul networks to suppress or attenuate any returned echo from a long-distance contact.

EIA *Electronic Industries Organization* A U.S. organization of manufacturers that establishes and recommends industrial standards.

End Office Same as *central office.*

Envelope Delay Distortion A parameter used by the PSTN to specify the limits of phase variations that can occur over the passband of the telephone lines. Ideally a constant phase response is desired.

Equalizer A circuit used by the PSTN to equalize any variations in gain or phase across the passband of the telephone lines.

Ergonomics The study of people adjusting to their working environment. Ergonomics seeks ways to improve the working environment.

Escape Sequence Escape sequences are used to perform special command and control functions, such as cursor movement on a terminal, clearing the screen, controlling a printer, and so on. For ASCII terminals, escape sequences begin with the ASCII character ESC and end with a single character or string of characters.

ESS *Electronic Switching System* A solid-state computer-controlled switching system used by the PSTN for routing and processing telephone calls.

Ethernet A baseband LAN system standardized by the IEEE 802.3 Committee. Channel access is established through a contention protocol called *CSMA/CD.*

Ethernet Transceiver A device to which the Ethernet controller card residing in the computer must be interfaced.

Excess 3 Code A BCD code similar to 8421 BCD except that 3 is added to the decimal number before it is encoded into a 4-bit word.

Exclusive-OR A logic function that compares two binary bits and is true when the two bits do not equal each other (1 and 0, or 0 and 1) and is false when they do (0 and 0, or 1 and 1).

Extrinsic Losses In optical fibers, these types of losses are a result of the splicing and connector assembly process. They include mechanical offsets between fiber ends, contaminants, improper fusion, gluing, crimping methods, and so on.

F-Bit A *framing* bit added to the beginning of the 192 bits to make up the T1 carrier frame.

Fast Ethernet The IEEE 802.3μ 100BaseT standard. Ethernet's speed is increased from 10 Mbps to 100 Mbps while maintaining the CSMA/CD access control protocol.

FCS *Frame Check Sequence* A *block check character (BCC)*, typically 16 bits in length, used in bit-oriented protocols for error-detection purposes.

FDDI *Fiber Distributed Data Interface* An ANSI standard designed to enhance LAN technology through the use of fiber optics.

FDM *Frequency-Division Multiplexing* This type of multiplexing utilizes the *frequency domain* to send multiple signals simultaneously over a channel's available bandwidth.

FEC *Forward Error Correction* Any error correction technique used in simplex communications whereby a redundant code, inserted into the message, is extracted and used to predict and correct an error without having to request a retransmission.

Feeder Network The network of subscriber loop cables consisting of multiple pairs of tip and ring lines that feed the community.

Fiber Optics The communications technology that utilizes the transmission of light over glass or plastic fibers.

Fibre Channel An ANSI standard designed to transfer data at speeds up to 1 Gbps using fiber-optic transmission media.

File Server A program that permits users to access disk drives and other mass storage devices for storing and retrieving common databases and applications programs.

Firewall An intranet security system designed to limit Internet access to a company's intranet.

FLEX A paging standard developed by Motorola in 1993 that can support over 1 billion pager addresses and is adopted by most service providers around the world.

Flywheel Effect The oscillatory effect sustained by applying a pulsating DC signal to a resonant tank circuit. Complete sinusoids, whose amplitudes are proportional to each pulse's amplitude, are generated.

FM *Frequency Modulation* An angle modulation technique in which the carrier's frequency is varied in proportion to the instantaneous amplitude of the modulating signal. FM is more immune to noise than AM.

Four-Wire Circuit   Two physically separate pairs of lines designed for full-duplex operation: one for transmit, and one for receive.

Fragment-Free Switching   A form of *cut-through switching* whereby the first 64 bytes of an Ethernet frame are read into the switch's buffers, tested, and forwarded to the output ports of the switch.

Frame   In data communication systems, a group of synchronous serial binary data bits representing information of some form. A preamble and postamble mark the beginning and end of the frame, respectively. A frame is also referred to as a *packet* or *block* by some protocols.

Frame Relay   A fast-packet switching protocol defined by ITU-TS that supports variable-length frame structures transmitted on LAN, MAN, and WAN networks.

Framing   The procedure used to identify the beginning and end of a group of data bits.

Framing Error   This type of error occurs when a receiver loses synchronism to the incoming data.

Frequency Deviation   In an FM signal, frequency deviation, δ, is the maximum frequency deviation of the carrier frequency caused by the amplitude of the modulating signal.

Frequency Hopping   A technique used to generate the spread-spectrum signal by "hopping" the carrier frequency in accordance with some pseudo random noise (PN) code.

FSK   *Frequency Shift Keying*   A modulation technique used with low-speed modems (300 to 1800 bps). The carrier frequency is shifted between two discrete frequencies in accordance with the binary serial data.

FTP   *File Transfer Protocol*   An internet search tool allowing its user to copy or transfer text, graphics, or video files from one computer to another across the Internet. Use of FTP often requires a login name and password for the computer database located at the FTP site.

Full-Duplex   Simultaneous two-way transmission.

Fusion Splice   A method of splicing two optical fiber ends together with an electric arc. The fusion splice is typically performed under a microscope.

Gateway   An internetworking device that functions at all seven layers of the ISO/OSI seven-layer model. The gateway permits the interlinking of LANs together that have completely different architectures.

Gaussian Noise   This type of noise is the accumulative effect of all random noise, averaged over a period of time, generated internal and external to the telecommunication system.

Geosynchronous Orbit   Modern telecommunications satellites are positioned 22,300 miles above the equator. At this altitude (geosynchronous orbit), the satellite travels at a velocity that maintains a fixed position relative to a point above the equator.

Glitch   A noise transient.

Go Back N   An ARQ (automatic repeat request) error-correction protocol that requests the retransmission of *N* blocks from the transmitter.

Gopher   A menu-driven information service program developed at the University of Minnesota, home of the Golden Gophers, that allows its users to access information databases throughout the world (Gopher space) without having to use special names, addresses, or commands.

Gopher Space   Information databases throughout the world.

GPIB   *General-Purpose Interface Bus*   See *IEEE-488.*

Granular Noise   Noise generated from quantization errors and occurring in the form of a square wave for analog input signals that do not change. Granular noise is analogous to *quantization noise* generated by A/D converters.

Gray Code   An unweighted code that provides a single bit change between successive counts. Gray code reduces switching noise and bit errors.

GSC   *Golay Sequential Code*   A paging standard developed by Motorola in 1983.

Guard Band   A frequency band above and below a signaling channel that prevents the sidebands from interfering with adjacent channels.

Half-Duplex   Alternating two-way transmission.

Hamming Code   A redundant set of bits inserted into a message stream for *forward error correction* (*FEC*) purposes. If a receiver detects an error in a message stream, the Hamming code is used to identify the location of the error. This location is referred to as the *syndrome.*

Handoff   When a mobile unit employing an active cellular telephone approaches the perimeter of the cell it is traveling in, its signal strength diminishes. As it enters a new cell, the mobile telephone switching office (MTSO) automatically assigns it a new channel within the new cell. This is called a *handoff.* Handoffs are transparent to the user.

Handshaking   A signaling technique that controls the flow of data between two devices through acknowledgments.

Harmonic   A multiple of the fundamental frequency.

HDLC   *High-Level Data Link Control*   A bit-oriented protocol proposed by *ISO.* HDLC is an internationally recognized standard. It is used to implement the X.25 packet switching network.

Headend   In broadband communication systems, that part of the network serving as the origin and destination of all radio frequency (RF) signals distributed to and from devices connected to the network.

Hexadecimal   The base 16 numbering system that uses the digits 0 through 9 and A through F. Also referred to as *HEX.*

Home Page   A more specific type of Web page that acts as the introductory page, serving as a home base for navigating the Web.

Hot Swappable   A term used to denote that a device can be removed or installed in a computer without powering down or rebooting the system.

HP-IB   *Hewlett-Packard Interface Bus*   An 8-bit, bidirectional, asynchronous parallel bus developed by Hewlett-Packard Corporation on which the IEEE-488 Interface Standard is based.

HTML   *HyperText Markup Language*   The language used for coding Web documents. Residing on the Web server, documents written in HTML are plain-text ASCII files that can be generated with a text editor and identified with an *.html* or *.htm* extension.

HTTP   *HyperText Transport Protocol*   The Web's main protocol for transporting HTML documents between clients and servers across the Web and is the first part of a URL address specifying that protocol.

Hub   An internetworking device used as a multiport repeater. The hub operates at the physical layer of the OSI seven-layer model. Also referred to as a *concentrator.*

Huffman Encoding   One of the oldest data compression techniques. Huffman encoding is used to reduce the number of bits representing those characters that have a high frequency of occurrence.

Hybrid   In telephony, a *hybrid* is a balancing network used to convert a two-wire circuit into a four-wire circuit. Transmitted and received signals are electrically separated by the hybrid and placed onto separate pairs of wires.

Hypertext   Highlighted underlined text or graphical icons embedded into the Web page. Also referred to as *hypermedia.*

IEEE   *Institute of Electrical and Electronic Engineers*   A U.S. professional organization of engineers.

IEEE-488   An asynchronous parallel bus interface standard for interconnecting digital programmable instruments (DPI). The original standard, *HP-IB,* was developed by Hewlett-Packard. The bus is also known as the *General Purpose Interface Bus* (*GPIB*).

ILD   *Injection Laser Diode*   A semiconductor laser diode used as a transmitting device for fiber-optic communications.

Impulse Noise   Any sudden burst of noise induced into a circuit from electromagnetic switching relays, electric motors, lightning, and so on. Impulse noise is the familiar cracking and popping noise heard at the output of a receiver.

Index Matching Fluid   A glue or epoxy used to bond two fiber ends together. To minimize loss, the glue's *index of refraction* is made to match that of the fiber.

Index of Refraction   The ratio of the speed of light in a vacuum to the speed of light in a given medium. As light passes from one medium to another, it is bent at the surface, where the refractive indices change. The amount of bending is directly related to a medium's index of refraction.

Indirect Connect Modem   An acoustically coupled modem.

Information Superhighway   The Internet and the World Wide Web.

Infrared Light   That portion of the electromagnetic spectrum having a wavelength ranging from 770 to 10^6 nm. Fiber-optic systems operate in this range.

Internet   A wide area network (WAN) with a collection of thousands of linked computer networks spanning the globe, thereby making it possible for millions of users throughout the world to communicate with each other.

Intranet   A corporate network infrastructure based on Internet Standards. Its purpose is to link a company's employees and information together to improve productivity and information flow.

Interoffice Trunk   A circuit interconnecting two class 5 central office switching centers.

Intrinsic Losses   In optical fibers, these types of losses are beyond the control of the user. They include variations in core diameter, numerical aperture (NA), core concentricity, and so on.

ISDN   *Integrated Services Digital Network*   An ITU-TS standard developed to provide a standardized interface and signaling protocol for delivering integrated voice and data via the PSTN.

ISDN Modem   See *TA (Terminal Adapter) Modem.*

ISM Band   *Industrial, Scientific, and Medical Band*   902 to 928 MHz.

ISO   *International Standards Organization*   One of the largest and most widely recognized standards organizations in the world.

ISO/OSI Seven-Layer Model   A seven-layer hierarchy of data communication protocols that encourages an *Open Systems Interconnect* (*OSI*) between computers, terminals, and networks for the exchange of information.

ISP   *Internet Service Provider*   The Internet server to which a client is linked. ISPs provide users access to the Internet and World Wide Web for a monthly or hourly fee.

ITU-TS   *International Standards Union–Telecommunication Standardization Sector*   Formerly *CCITT.*

Jamming   The process of completing the transmission of a packet onto the communications channel, even though a collision has occurred with another packet. This ensures that all system nodes detect the collision.

Johnson Noise   See *Thermal Noise.*

Kermit   A data communications protocol developed at Columbia University for file transfers between microcomputers and mainframes.

LAN   *Local Area Network*   A privately owned network of interconnecting data communicating devices that share resources (software included) within a local area. The local area can be a single room, building, or group of buildings, generally within less than a few miles of each other.

LAP B *Link Access Procedure B* A data communications protocol used in the X.25 public data network.

LAP D *Link Access Procedure D* A data communications protocol used in *ISDN*.

LAP M *Link Access Procedure for Modems* A data communications protocol recognized by CCITT's V.42 standard: Error Correction Procedures for DCEs.

Laser *Light Amplification by Stimulated Emission of Radiation* A coherent light source used as a transmitter in fiber-optic communication systems.

LEC *Local Exchange Carrier* The local telephone company that provides *POTS* under federal and state regulation.

LED *Light-Emitting Diode* A semiconductor device that converts electrical energy to light energy.

Limiter A circuit in the FM receiver that removes any variations in signal amplitude before detection or demodulation of the signal.

Limpel-Ziv A data compression technique based on the principle of assigning numbers to strings of characters of varying length.

Line Conditioning Electrical compensation for attenuation and phase delay distortion exhibited by the PSTN. Conditioning is performed through the use of *equalizer* circuits.

Link The communications channel.

Loading Coils Coils used for adding series inductance to the line at various intervals between the subscriber and the central office to improve the transmission characteristic of the phone line.

Lobe The interface cable between the computer station and a MAU in a Token Ring system.

Local Battery System A system in which telephones were individually powered with batteries.

Local Echo When a terminal is configured to route its transmitted character internally around to its receiver section for display, a local echo is said to be generated.

Local Loop See *Subscriber Loop*.

Long-Haul Network This portion of the PSTN includes class 1 through 4 switching exchanges. Long-distance calls beyond the local switching exchange are routed through these higher levels of switching centers and are subject to toll charges.

LRC *Longitudinal Redundancy Check* A parity check performed on an accumulation of the value of individual bit positions in a message stream. The resulting word is used as a *block check character* (BCC) transmitted at the end of the message stream.

LSB *Lower Sideband* In AM, the mathematical difference between the carrier frequency, f_c, and the modulation frequency, f_m: $f_c - f_m$.

LSB *Least Significant Bit* The binary bit with the least significant weighting in a binary number, typically the rightmost bit.

M-ary Derived from the word "bi-nary," M-ary is used to denote the number of encoded bits used to modulate a carrier frequency.

MAC Address *Media Access Control Address* A 48-bit physical address required by every device on a network. The MAC address is permanently stored in ROM (read-only memory) on all *NIC cards.*

Man *Metropolitan Area Network* A network of data communicating devices connected to service a metropolitan area.

Manchester Encoding A method of encoding a binary serial bit stream such that each bit interval exhibits at least one signal-level transition regardless of the data bit pattern. This allows a receiving device to synchronize to the bit stream without the use of a separate clock. The signal is said to be self-clocking.

Mark A logic 1.

MAU *Multistation Access Unit* A central connection point at which computer stations are linked together. The MAU acts as the hub of a Token Ring network and connects up to eight nodes or computers. MAUs can also be linked together to extend the number of nodes on the network.

Mechanical Splice A method of splicing two optical fiber ends together by aligning them with a mechanical fixture and gluing or crimping them together.

Media Filters Low-pass filters designed to reduce noise on the line.

Message Switching A switching technology utilized by the PSTN that permits the transfer of messages between DTE by temporarily "storing" the message at the exchange and "forwarding" it to the next exchange. Message switching is also known as "store and forward."

Microbending Losses In optical fibers, this type of loss is caused by miniature bends and geometric imperfections along the axis of the fiber. These imperfections cause light to get coupled to various unguided electromagnetic modes that radiate and escape the fiber.

Microsegmentation On an Ethernet switch, microsegmentation refers to the dedicated bandwidth offered on each port of the switch. Each port is a separate collision domain.

Miller Encoding A self-clocking technique in which a transition occurs at the center of each cell for logic 1s only. No transition is used for a logic 0 unless it is followed by another 0, in which case the transition is placed at the end of the cell for the first 0.

MNP *Microcom Network Protocol* A data communications protocol for modems designed by Microcom Inc. MNP is recognized by CCITT's V.42 standard: Error Correction Procedures for DCEs.

Modal Dispersion   In multimode fiber, pulse stretching occurs as a result of the different transit lengths for different propagating modes throughout the fiber.

Modem   A contraction of the words *modulator/demodulator*. The modem converts a computer's digital bit stream into an analog signal suitable for the telephone lines, and vice versa.

Modem Turnaround Time   The time that it takes for transmission directions to change between two stations in half-duplex operation.

Modulation Index   A measure of the degree of modulation. In AM, it is the ratio of the peak amplitude of the modulation voltage, V_m, to the peak amplitude of the carrier voltage, V_c. In FM, it is the ratio of the maximum frequency deviation to the modulation signal's frequency. Also referred to as *percent modulation, modulation factor,* and *depth of modulation.*

Morse Code   A digital code made up of a series of dots and dashes representing the alphabet, punctuation, and decimal number system.

MSB   *Most Significant Bit*   The binary bit with the most significant weighting in a binary number, typically the leftmost bit.

MTSO   *Mobile Telephone Switching Office*   In cellular telephony, the MTSO coordinates all mobile calls between cell sites and the central office.

μ-Law   Companding law used in the United States.

Multidrop   A communications link in which a single channel is shared by several stations (e.g., a computer shared by several terminals). Only one station may transmit at a time. Multidrop is also referred to as *multipoint.*

Multimode Fiber   Optical fibers that permit light to travel in many paths (modes) throughout the core of the fiber.

Multimode Graded-Index Fiber   Optical fibers whose cores are manufactured with an index of refraction that is graded from the center of the core, out to the *cladding* interface. This permits light rays to travel faster as they deviate from the central axis of the fiber's core, thus minimizing pulse spreading.

Multimode Step-Index Fiber   Optical fibers that are manufactured with an index of refraction that is uniform throughout the core. The index of refraction is said to "step" from the core value to the cladding value. Light rays bounce back and forth to the end of the fiber.

Multipath   A form of phase distortion resulting from a signal taking several paths to reach its destination.

Multipoint   A communications mode of operation between a host computer and several terminals in which internal and external switch settings, or the terminal's software, are configured for block mode operation.

NA   *Numerical Aperture*   A measure of an optical fiber's light-gathering capability.

Narrowband FM   FM systems with FCC-allocated bandwidths ranging from 10 to 30 kHz.

NC   *Network Computer*   An inexpensive, disk-free computer terminal connected to a server.

NIC   *Network Interface Card*   An Ethernet or Token Ring adapter card designed to plug into a PC or notebook computer's bus expansion slot.

NID   *Network Interface Device*   The demarcation box typically mounted on the outside of the home. The NID includes overvoltage and current protection on the customer's tip and ring lines.

Node   An addressable device on a communications network. Nodes are also referred to as *stations.*

Noise   Any extraneous and undesirable portion of a signal that does not contribute to the original intelligence.

Noise Factor   A measure of how noisy a device is. It is the ratio of a device's input SNR to its output SNR.

Noise Figure   The same as *noise factor* but expressed in decibels.

Noise Immunity   A circuit with a high *noise margin* is said to have a high noise immunity.

Noise Margin   A quantitative measure of a circuit's ability to tolerate noise transients.

Normal   A perpendicular line drawn to the surface of an object or medium.

NRZ   *Nonreturn-to-Zero*   An encoding technique that uses two discrete voltage levels to represent a binary 1 and 0. It can be two positive voltage levels or two discrete negative levels.

NRZI   *Nonreturn-to-Zero Invert*   A variation of NRZ encoding. It is considered a differential encoding technique since its level is a function of the previous signal element.

Null Modem   A cable that replaces the modem interface, thus allowing two DTEs to communicate with each other without the use of DCE. Connector wires are interchanged to achieve this.

Nyquist Sampling Rate   A theorem stating that a signal must be sampled at a rate that is at least twice the highest-frequency component that it contains for it to be fully recovered.

Octal   The base 8 numbering system that uses the digits 0 through 7.

Octet   In HDLC, a byte or 8 bits.

Optocoupler   A sealed infrared emitter and photodetector used to couple an electrical signal by light. The optocoupler or *optoisolator* is used to isolate high voltage and noisy circuits from their respective controlling circuit.

Originate Modem   The modem that initiates the telephone call for data communications.

OSI   *Open Systems Interconnect*   An hierarchy of protocols developed through the combined efforts of ANSI, ITU-TS, EIA, IEEE, ISO, and others. The OSI model encourages an open system by providing a structural guideline for exchanging information between computers, terminals, and networks. See *ISO/OSI.*

Overrun Error   An overrun error occurs when a CPU does not read an available character from a buffer before the next one is available. The previous character is destroyed.

Packet   A block of data designed for independent processing in the *X.25 packet switching network.* See also *Frame.*

Packet Switching   A communications protocol used in networks such as the telephone system. Messages are divided up into discrete units called *packets* and routed independently of each other to their final destination.

Pager   A wireless messaging device, designed to be worn, with numerous display and alert features as well as PCS options.

Paging Terminal   A device to which transmitters placed throughout the service area are linked. The paging terminal, whose function is to encode the caller's message into a unique paging code, is also linked to the Public Switched Telephone Network (PSTN).

PAM   *Pulse Amplitude Modulation*   A modulation technique that produces a series of pulses whose amplitudes are in proportion to the modulating voltage at the time of the sample.

Parity   An error-detection method whereby a single bit is added to a group of bits to make the total number of 1 bits, either even or odd.

Parity Error   Indicates that the total number of 1 bits in a received character does not agree with the even or odd parity bit sent with the character.

Patch Cable or Cord   A cable used to interconnect two parties' subscriber loops or, in Token Ring systems, to interconnect MAUs.

PC Card   See *PCMCIA.*

PCM   *Pulse Code Modulation*   The process of converting an analog signal into an encoded digital value for transmission.

PCMCIA   *Personal Computer Memory Card International*   The international standards body that has defined and standardized the 68-pin, credit card–size peripheral device and PC CARD slot into which it is plugged. Also referred to as the *PC Card standard.*

PCS   *Personal Communication Services*   A multibillion dollar wireless technology using the latest advancements in digital wireless telecommunications and available through long-distance and local-exchange PCS carriers.

PDM   *Pulse Duration Modulation*   See *PWM.*

Peer-to-Peer Network   A network operating system in which any workstation can be configured as a client or a server or both.

Photodetector   A device used to convert light energy to electrical energy. *Photodiodes* and *phototransistors* are commonly used for this purpose.

Photoelectric Effect   The transformation of light, incident on a metallic surface, to an electric current.

Photon   An electromagnetic particle that possesses energy in proportion to its frequency. Photons are regarded as particles of light.

Photophone   A device invented in 1880 by Alexander Graham Bell that uses sunlight reflected off a moving diaphragm to communicate voice information.

PIN Photodiode   *P-type Intrinsic N-type diode*   A *photodetector* used as a fiber-optic receiver. The PIN diode is used in the reverse-bias condition. Current carriers flow when light (photons) penetrate the depletion region.

Ping-Pong   A *pseudo full-duplex* mode of transmission. Full-duplex operation is simulated between two modems by buffering each modem's data and rapidly turning their modulated carriers on and off in a successive fashion using flow control procedures.

Planck's Law   A law stating that the energy of a photon is directly proportional to its frequency in the electromagnetic spectrum.

PLL   *Phase-Locked Loop*   A circuit designed to achieve phase and frequency synchronization to an incoming signal.

Plug and Play (PnP)   A hardware and software specification developed by Intel that permits PnP adapter cards to automatically configure themselves via a computer's PnP BIOS (Basic I/O System) or the PnP software provided by an adapter card's vendor.

PM   *Phase Modulation*   An angle modulation technique in which the carrier's phase is made to vary as a function of the instantaneous amplitude of the modulating signal.

POCSAG   *Post Office Code Standardization Advisory Group*   An internationally recognized paging standard developed in 1981 by a worldwide consortium of engineers and introduced as the first high-speed paging protocol that can support up to 221 million pager addresses. Still widely used, POCSAG supports three baud rates: 512, 1200, and 2400 bps.

Point-to-Point   In contrast to *multidrop or multipoint,* a communications link connecting two stations.

Point-to-Point IR LAN   An IR (infrared)-based LAN that uses line-of-sight transmission, which minimizes multipath distortion.

Polling   A communications control procedure in which a host computer systematically addresses one of several *tributaries* to enquire (ENQ) if it has any data to send. Used in conjunction with *device selecting*: the addressing of a tributary to enquire if it is ready to receive data.

Population Inversion   The condition that occurs in a laser when holes and electrons recombine and release photons of energy (light). The released photons further excite other holes and electrons to recombine, thus releasing more light. Light amplification occurs.

POSTNET *Postal Numeric Encoding Technique* A *bar code* developed by the U.S. Postal Service to increase the sorting speed, delivery, and accuracy of mail based on ZIP codes.

POTS *Plain Old Telephone Service* The standard voice-grade telephone lines.

POTS Splitter A filtering device used to separate low-speed voice signals from high-speed DSL signals.

PPM *Pulse Position Modulation* A modulation technique in which the position of a pulse relative to its unmodulated time of occurrence is made to vary with the modulation voltage. PPM makes it possible to eliminate the PWM signal's variance in power dissipation by preserving only the pulse transitions in the PWM signal.

Pre-emphasis The process through which FM transmitters boost the signal levels of the higher modulating frequencies prior to the modulation process to maintain a uniform SNR for the higher modulation frequencies.

PRI *Primary Rate Interface* An ISDN trunking technology that delivers ISDN services to digital PBXs, host computers, and LANs. The PRI carries 23 64-kbps B-channels and one 64-kbps D-channel.

Private Line A hard-wired leased line that bypasses the normal central office switching facility.

Protected Field When a terminal is configured for *block mode*, certain areas on the terminal's display cannot be written to. These areas are called protected fields.

Protocol A set of rules that govern the manner in which data are transmitted and received.

Protocol Efficiency A measure of how efficient a protocol is in terms of transmitting data from source to destination, without error, in a minimal amount of time.

Protocol Overhead A measure of how much redundancy is added to a message stream for framing, flow control, and error detection.

Pseudo Full-Duplex A transmission mode used by some modems (e.g., the Bell 202 modem) whereby a low-speed reverse channel is used in the lower portion of the available passband. This is also referred to as *statistical duplexing*. See also *Ping-Pong*.

PSK *Phase Shift Keying* A modulation technique in which the carrier frequency remains constant and its phase is shifted in accordance with the binary serial bit stream.

PSTN *Public Switched Telephone Network* The dial-up telephone network.

Pure Aloha A protocol in which stations must contend for the use of the communications channel. A station wishing to transmit a message does so at any time, running the risk of a collision from other stations.

PWM *Pulse Width Modulation* A form of modulation in which the width of pulse carrier is made to vary with the modulation voltage. Also known as *pulse duration modulation* (PDM).

QAM *Quadrature Amplitude Modulation* A modulation technique employed in high-speed modems. A combination of ASK and DPSK is used to encode 4 bits into one of 16 signaling state changes.

QPSK *Quadrature Phase Shift Keying* Four-phase DPSK.

Quadbit Four binary bits encoded into one of 16 possible signaling state changes. The ITU-TS V.22bis standard uses quadbit encoding for its QAM modulation technique.

Quantization The division of a signal's dynamic range into discrete numerically encoded binary values.

Quantization Error The error resulting from quantizing an analog signal. This error can be a maximum of half a quantized level.

Quantization Noise The noise resulting from a reconstructed signal that was quantized before transmission.

Quantum Efficiency A measure of how efficient an optical receiver is in terms of converting particles of light (photons) to current carriers. Quantum efficiency is expressed as a percentage.

Quintbit Five binary bits encoded into one of 32 possible signaling state changes. The ITU-TS V.32 standard uses *trellis encoding* of five bits in its 32-point signal constellation.

Rayleigh Scattering A type of loss in optical fibers caused by microirregularities formed as the fiber cools from its molten state during manufacturing. As light strikes these irregularities, it becomes scattered in all directions of the fiber.

RBOC *Regional Bell-Operating Companies* See *BOC*.

RCC *Radio Common Carriers* FCC-licensed pager service providers that operate paging systems for the general public.

Redundancy In data transmission, any part of a message stream that is not part of the original intelligence being conveyed. This includes framing, error control, addressing, and so on.

Refraction The bending of light, either toward or away from the normal, as it exits one transmission medium and enters another.

Regenerative Repeater A repeater that uses *threshold detection* to recover, reconstruct, and retransmit a PCM signal.

Remote Echo An *echo* generated from a remote terminal as a result of receiving an asynchronous character.

Repeater A device used to extend the transmission distance of a signal by conditioning the signal through amplifiers, filters, and so on, and retransmitting the conditioned signal.

Responsivity A measure of how sensitive to light an optical receiver is in terms of converting optical power to electrical current. Responsivity has the units of amperes per watt (A/W).

RFC *Request for Comments* Publications for the Internet community on which the official TCP/IP standards are based. RFCs originated in the days of the ARPANET when protocols were being developed.

Ring LAN A network *topology* in which nodes are connected *point-to-point* in a closed-loop configuration.

rms *Root mean square* For the sine wave, the rms value is equal to 0.707 times the peak value of the sine wave. This is the equivalent DC value of the sine wave. The rms value is also referred to as the *effective value.*

Roaming Operation of a cellular mobile telephone outside a registered metropolitan area. A roam LED indicator on the cellular telephone unit turns on when roaming. Roaming is possible throughout the country, provided that there is a prearranged agreement between the user and the telephone company beforehand.

Routed Protocol Networking protocols that can direct traffic on a network. Examples include Novell's IPX, Appletalk, DECNET, and IP.

Router An internetworking device that is used to link two or more LANs together that have the same communications protocol. Unlike a repeater or bridge, the router is an addressable device that is not transparent to the end user. Instead, the router acts as a node that is capable of processing information embedded in a packet's control header. A router performs functions at layer three of the ISO/OSI seven-layer model.

Routing Protocol Networking protocols that maintain routing tables between routers. Examples include Routing Information Protocol (RIP), Open Shortest Path First (OSPF), Interior Gateway Routing Protocol (IGRP), and Enhanced IGRP (EIGRP).

RS-232 A serial interface standard that specifies the electrical, functional, and mechanical interface specifications between data communicating devices.

Run-Length Encoding In data compression, for characters that repeat themselves data are encoded into a word indicating the number of repeated characters that follow rather than sending a repeated string of the characters.

RZ *Return-to-Zero* An encoding technique, classified into *unipolar RZ* and *bipolar RZ,* in which a signal level returns to zero.

Screen Capacity The maximum number of characters that can be displayed on a terminal's screen, typically 1920 (24 rows by 80 columns) characters.

SCSI *Small Computer Systems Interface* Pronounced "scuzzy," this parallel I/O interface bus is used to connect as many as eight SCSI peripheral devices to a computer.

SDLC *Synchronous Data Link Control* A *bit-oriented protocol* developed by IBM and used in its *Systems Network Architecture* (*SNA*). SDLC is functionally identical to HDLC. See *HDLC.*

SDM *Space-Division Multiplexing* Signals that are multiplexed together by physically combining conductors into a bundled cable. Space is required for this type of multiplexing.

Search Engine The most common tool for navigating the World Wide Web, used to search for virtually any form of intelligence.

Self-Clocking Codes Encoding techniques, performed by phase-locked loop (PLL) technology, used to ensure that each bit time associated with the binary serial bit stream contains at least one level transition (1 to 0 or 0 to 1).

Segment A coaxial cable link used in *Ethernet* that can span a maximum of 500 m and can include up to 100 *nodes.*

Server A high-powered computer or workstation that shares its resources as a service to network users.

S/H Amplifier *Sample-and-Hold Amplifier* An amplifier that samples an analog signal and holds its value so that it may be processed, typically by an A/D converter.

Shannon's Law A fundamental law used in telecommunications to compute *channel capacity.*

Shot Noise This type of noise results from the random arrival rate of discrete current carriers (holes and electrons) at the output electrodes of semiconductor and vacuum tube devices.

Sidetone The small amount of signal fed back from a telephone set's transmitter to its receiver that allows a person speaking into the handset to hear himself or herself.

Simplex Transmission in one direction only.

Single-Ended Amplifier An amplifier with a single output referenced to a common ground and used to drive an *unbalanced electrical circuit.*

Single-Mode Fiber Optical fiber that is manufactured so that rays of light travel only along the central axis of the fiber.

Skin Effect The tendancy for AC current to flow on the outer portion of a conductor, especially at high frequencies.

Slotted Aloha A refinement of the *Aloha* contention scheme whereby all stations on the network are time synchronized to each other. Transmissions are restricted to predefined intervals of time, called *slots.*

Slotted Ring A variation of token passing in a *ring LAN.* A fixed number of contiguous time slots are circulated around the ring LAN. A *node* wishing to transmit a *packet* simply fills an empty slot. The filled slot circulates around the ring to its destination.

Slot Time The round-trip propagation time for a *packet* to travel between the farthest two *nodes* in a *bus LAN.*

SMDS *Switched Multimegabit Data Service* A PSTN service designed to offer customers efficient and economical connectivity between LAN and WAN systems.

Snell's Law A fundamental law used in optics to predict the path of light rays as they travel from one medium to another based on each medium's *index of refraction.*

SNR *Signal-to-Noise Ratio* The ratio of signal power to noise power. Also referred to as *S/N*.

SONET *Synchronous Optical Network* Published by *ANSI* in 1988, SONET is a fiber-optic communications standard designed to allow the internetworking of optical communications equipment between different vendors.

Space A logic 0.

Speed Governor A device included in the dial assembly of a rotary telephone that maintains a constant angular velocity as the dial returns to its resting position.

Spread Spectrum A digital modulation technique with a low probability of detection and interference. Spread spectrum spreads a signal over a wide range of frequencies.

SSBSC *Single-Sideband Suppressed Carrier* Suppression of the carrier frequency and one of the sidebands to realize an overall power savings of at least 83.33% for 100% modulation. Also referred to as *SSB* or *Single Sideband*.

Star LAN A network *topology* in which several *nodes* are radially linked to a central node through *point-to-point* connections.

Star-Wired Ring IBM's Token Ring LAN topology.

Start Bit The first bit used to frame an asynchronously transmitted character. Its logic level is a 0 (space).

Statistical Duplexing See *Pseudo Full-Duplex*.

Stop Bit The last bit used to frame an asynchronously transmitted character. Its logic level is a logic 1 (mark).

Store and Forward The principle of message switching on which transmission of e-mail over the Internet is based.

Store and Forward Switching A mode of switching whereby the entire Ethernet frame is read by the switch and checked for *CRC* errors before forwarding it to the output ports of the switch.

STP *Shielded Twisted-Pair* Twisted-pair cables with aluminum foil surrounding them that serves as a shield against electromagnetic interference from external sources, including adjacent channel crosstalk.

Stress Corrosion A defect in an optical fiber caused by the exposure of the glass fiber to humidity. Spontaneous fractures can occur as a result of stress corrosion. Also known as *static fatigue*.

Strowger Switch An electromechanical step-by-step switch used in older central office switching systems.

STS *Synchronous Transport Signals* Signals designed to be transported on the SONET network.

Subscriber Loop The set of wires connecting the telephone set to the central office.

Superframe Twelve contiguous *T1 carrier frames*.

Switch An internetworking device that operates at the data link layer of the OSI seven-layer model. A switch is essentially a multiport bridge. It forwards frames based on *MAC addresses*.

Synchronous Transmission High-speed communication whereby data characters are sent in direct succession to each other without the use of *start* and *stop bits*.

Syndrome Identifies the bit location of an error in a message stream in systems that employ *forward error correction* (*FEC*).

System Redundancy A *critical resource's* backup protection in case of a failure of that portion of the communication system. It can be hardware or software built into the system or provided as an equivalent replacement for the failed part.

T1 Carrier A *time division multiplexed* (*TDM*) *PCM* standard developed by Bell Laboratories. The T1 carrier is used in most major telephone circuits today. The transmission rate for the standard T1 carrier is 1.544 Mbps.

T1 Carrier Frame The basic T1 carrier frame consists of 24 channels, 8 bits per channel, making a total of 192 bits. A 193rd framing bit is added to the *frame* for synchronization. Each voice channel is sampled at an 8-kHz rate, making a total of 1.544 Mbps (8 kHz × 193 bits).

TA (Terminal Adapter) Modem A digital modem that permits a user to transmit and receive voice, video, and data over a single ISDN digital connection between the central office and the user.

Tandem Office A class 5 switching center used to interconnect central offices in tandem, thereby minimizing the number of trunk circuits that a local call must be routed through to reach its destination.

Tandem Trunk A circuit used to interconnect two class 5 switching centers in tandem.

TCP/IP *Transmission Control Protocol/Internet Protocol* The communications protocol used for the Internet, implemented in computers throughout the world. The two protocols describe the movement of data between host computers. The protocol in its entirety is a suite consisting of a multitude of protocols that provide for reliable communications across the Internet and the World Wide Web.

TDM *Time Division Multiplexing* This type of multiplexing utilizes the *time domain* to interleave multiple signals together for transmission over a single channel.

Telecommunications Long-distance communications via a conglomeration of information-sharing networks tied together.

Telex An international Teletype exchange that uses *baudot* code.

Telnet A terminal emulation protocol used to remotely log on to other host computers on the Internet. The host computer can be located in another city, state, or country. Once a connection is made, it is as if you are directly connected.

ter French for "third revision."

Terminal An input/output device used by an operator to communicate with a host computer. It consists of a keyboard and a display to monitor alphanumeric characters entered at the keyboard or received from a remote device.

Terminal Adapter   In *ISDN,* a terminal adapter (TA) is a device that converts noncompatible ISDN signals to compatible ISDN signals. The TA is also referred to as an *ISDN modem.*

Thermal Noise   This type of noise is generated by the random motion of free electrons and molecular vibrations in resistive components. Thermal noise power is proportional to both temperature and bandwidth. Also referred to as *Johnson noise* or *white noise.*

Thick Ethernet   Same as *Thicknet.*

Thicknet   Ethernet standard that uses thick RG8 coaxial cable technology. Also referred to as the *IEEE 802.3 (Ethernet) 10Base5 standard.*

Thin-net   Ethernet standard with cabling technology that uses 50-Ω RG58 coax and BNC connector technology. Also referred to as the *IEEE 802.3 (Ethernet) 10Base2 standard.*

Threshold Detection   The process used to compare the voltages of two signals, one of which is used as a threshold. When one exceeds the other (i.e., the threshold), a logic 1 is output; otherwise, a logic 0 is output.

Throughput   A measure of transmission rate based on the time required to transmit and receive successfully a maximum amount of data per unit time. This includes the added time required for acknowledgments, framing, and error control.

Time-out Error   This type of error occurs when a device fails to respond to a message within a given period of time.

Tip and Ring   Contacts of a jack on each end of a cord used to connect two subscriber loop lines.

Token   A special bit pattern or packet that circulates around a *ring LAN* from *node* to node.

Token Passing   The channel access scheme used in *ring LAN*s for sharing the use of the channel. A *token* is circulated around the ring from *node* to node. Possession of the token gives a node exclusive rights to the channel for communications.

Toll Center   A class 4 central office switching center that processes calls outside the local area.

Toll Trunk   A circuit interconnecting a class 5 central office switching center to a class 4 *toll center.*

Topology   The geometric pattern or configuration of intelligent devices in a LAN.

Total Internal Reflection   The principle behind fiber optics that governs how rays of light propagate through a transparent medium by reflecting off its boundaries.

Touch Tone   See *DTMF.*

Transceiver Cable   The cable used to interface with the Ethernet transceiver.

Transparency   In synchronous serial communications, data are said to be *transparent* when any received bit patterns, equivalent to control characters, are disregarded in terms of the normal control procedures.

Transponder   A device used in a satellite to receive the weak microwave signal, amplify and condition it, and retransmit the signal back to another earth station in a different location on Earth.

Transportable   A *cellular telephone* that can be used outside the mobile unit.

Trellis Encoding   A 32-point signal constellation specified by the ITU-TS V.32 recommendation for modems. Five consecutive binary digits, called a *quintbit,* are encoded into one of 32 signaling states represented in the constellation.

TRIB   *Transmission Rate of Information Bits*   A formula used to compute system *throughput.*

Tribit   Three bits encoded into one of eight possible phase changes.

Tributary   A terminal or station, other than the controlling station, that must be *polled* or *selected* by a host computer to transmit or receive data, respectively.

Trunk   A circuit interconnecting two telephone switching centers.

TTY   *Teletype*   Used in the *Telex* exchange. An electromechanical terminal consisting of a keyboard, printer, paper tape reader, and punch. Teletype is a trademark of the former Teletype Corporation.

Turnaround Time   For modems, the time that it takes for transmission direction to change between two stations operating over a *half-duplex* link.

Twisted-Pair Wire   Insulated pairs of wire twisted together to minimize *crosstalk* interference. Twisted-pair wire is widely used in *subscriber loop* and short-haul trunk circuits.

Twistor Memory   Superpermanent memory that stores the control program for *ESS* systems.

Two-Wire Circuit   *Twisted-pair* wire that connects the subscriber's telephone to the central office. Signals are transmitted and received over the same pair.

UART   *Universal Asynchronous Receiver/Transmitter*   A peripheral device that data terminal equipment uses to transmit digital information over a single transmission line. The UART must be programmed by the central processing unit to communicate between two devices.

Ultraviolet Light   That portion of the electromagnetic spectrum having a wavelength of 10 to 390 nm.

Unbalanced Electrical Circuit   A circuit in which the transmitted signal propagates down a single transmission line accompanied by its signal return line or common.

Unipolar   The simplest transmission code, in which the signal has the format of only one polarity.

Unipolar RZ   *Unipolar Return-to-Zero*   An encoding technique in which a binary 1 is represented with a high level for half the bit time and returns to zero for the other half.

Unprotected Field   When a terminal is configured for *block mode,* certain areas of the display can be written to or edited. These areas are called unprotected fields.

Unweighted Code   Any code whose bits do not have any numerical weighting.

Up-Link Frequencies   Satellite carrier frequencies in the 6-GHz band, ranging from 5.92 to 6.43 GHz.

UPC   *Universal Product Code*   A 12-digit numerical bar code adopted by the *National Association of Food Chains.* UPC is most commonly found on grocery items.

Upstream Transmission   A cable TV (CATV) signal's direction of travel from community subscribers to the CATV station antenna. This is the reverse direction of *downstream transmission.*

URL   *Uniform Resource Locator*   A unique address all Web pages and Internet resources have that permits its user to retrieve documents from the Internet server.

USART   *Universal Synchronous Asynchronous Receiver Transmitter*   A programmable device used to convert parallel data from a CPU to a serial data stream for transmission. The USART can also receive serial data and convert it back to parallel format for a CPU to read.

USB   *Upper Sideband*   In AM, the mathematical sum of the carrier frequency, f_c, and the modulation frequency, f_m: $f_c + f_m$.

UTP   *Unshielded Twisted-Pair Wire*   A transmission medium that has gained popularity in LAN systems (e.g., the IEEE 802.3 10BaseT standard).

V.90 Specification   A high-speed, 56-Kbps modem standard.

Varistor   A semiconductor device whose resistance varies inversely with current and is used as a gain-controlling mechanism (in telephones) to maintain constant transmit and receive amplitudes.

VDT   *Video Display Terminal*   Same as a *terminal.*

Veronica   *Very Easy Rodent-Oriented Net-wide Index to Computerized Archives*   A keyword search program designed at the University of Nevada used exclusively as a Gopher aid in searching through Gopher space.

Visible Light   That portion of the electromagnetic spectrum having a wavelength ranging from 390 to 770 nm.

VRC   *Vertical Redundancy Check*   A *parity* check performed on a per-character basis.

VSB   *Vestigial Sideband*   An intermediate AM technique between SSB and DSBFC in which a portion of the lower sideband is transmitted along with the full carrier power and upper-sideband content thus ensuring that the USB, including the video carrier, is transmitted in its entirety. VSB is used in the commercial TV industry for the transmission and reception of television video signals.

WDM   *Wavelength-Division Multiplexing*   An optical multiplexing technique that uses different wavelengths to transport different signals over a single fiber-optic strand.

WAIS   *Wide-Area Information Services*   A text-searching engine (developed jointly by Apple Computer, Thinking Machines Corp., and Dow Jones) that allows its user to search and retrieve text files, called *sources,* from the vast resources of the Internet, including scientific, government, and private databases, as well as Usenet newsgroups.

WAN   *Wide Area Network*   A long-distance network of data-communicating devices designed to service users beyond the local area.

Wavelength   The distance between two successive peaks (or troughs) of a sinusoidal waveform.

Web Browser   A program that permits its users to navigate the Web by accessing Web documents that have been coded in HTML (hypertext markup language).

Web Page   A computer-displayed document designed to be read and used as a cross-reference to other documents on the Web through use of hypertext or hypermedia links.

Wireless Telecommunications   A digital wireless technology that eliminates the use of cabling. Wireless technology in telecommunications includes digital and analog cellular telephony, cordless telephony, wireless LANs, wireless PBXs, and wireless personal communication services (PCSs).

Workstation   An intelligent terminal that features a self-contained operating system, high-resolution graphics, and 32-bit microcomputer architecture.

WWW   *World Wide Web*   A global information system that combines text, graphics, and sound on a series of computer-displayed documents, developed by Tim Berners-Lee in 1989 at the European Laboratory for Particle Physics (CERN) in Geneva, Switzerland. Simply referred to as the *Web,* it is also a user-friendly network in which information from many sources can be accessed from anywhere in the world with one universal program.

X.25   The CCITT recommendation for *packet switching networks.*

Xmodem   A modem protocol used in data communications to ensure the reliable transfer of files between PCs.

XOFF   *Transmit Off*   A device control character (DC3) used to control the flow of data between two devices. XOFF is used as a *handshake* with XON.

XON   *Transmit On*   A device control character (DC1) used to control the flow of data between two devices. XON is used as a *handshake* with *XOFF.*

Ymodem   A modem multiple file transfer protocol developed by Chuck Fosberg of Omen Technology, Inc.

Ymodem/G   Same as Ymodem but supports MNP data compression and error control in the modem's hardware.

Zero-Bit Insertion   See *Bit Stuffing.*

Zmodem   A multiple file transfer protocol developed by Chuck Fosberg of Omen Technology, Inc. Zmodem uses a 32-bit CRC for error checking.

ANSWERS TO ODD-NUMBERED PROBLEMS

CHAPTER 1

1. Telecommunications has affected our lifestyles and will continue to do so for the foreseeable future. Many of our jobs, educational courses, and everyday events require skills necessary to communicate with each other using computers, telephones, radio, and television.

3. *Telecommunications* can be defined as long-distance communications via a conglomeration of information-sharing networks tied together.

5. Voltage

7.

| 1 | 0 | 1 | 1 | 1 | 0 | 1 |

9. LAN stands for *local area network,* MAN stands for *metropolitan area network,* and WAN stands for *wide area network.*

11. On-line computer services or users must restrict minors' access to "indecent" material.

13. LEC stands for *local exchange carrier.*

CHAPTER 2

1. a. $A_p = 20$
   b. $A_{p(dB)} = 26.02$ dB
3. $P_L = 5.50$ mW
5. a. $A_v = 25.12$
   b. $V_o = 377$ μV
   c. $A_{v(dB)} = -9.542$ dB
7. $P = 1$ μW
9. a. $V_{rms} = 56.17$ mV

    b. $V_p = 79.45$ mV

    c. $V_{p-p} = 158.9$ mV

11. SNR = $10 \log (3.58 \text{ mW}/45 \ \mu\text{W}) = 19$ dB

13. a. 20.97 dB

    b. 19.5 dB

    c. 1.4

    d. 1.46 dB

15. 12.5×10^{-6}

17. 30 kbps

19. 15.6 μV

21. 69.3 nA

23. 12 bits

CHAPTER 3

1. The op-amp summing device shown in Figure 3–1 does not produce an AM wave, because it is missing a nonlinear device and a resonant tank circuit.

3. $e_m = V_m \sin 360 \ (1 \text{ kHz}) \ t$

5. $m = 0.3750; M = 37.50\%$

7. $m = 0.8333$

9. a. M = 14.14%

    b. $(+)e_{ENV} = 45.16$ V; $(-)e_{ENV} = -45.16$ V

    c.

$$\theta = \omega t = 2\pi \ (2 \text{ kHz})(810 \ \mu\text{s}) = 583.2°$$

11. $e_{AM} = \underbrace{V_c \sin \omega_c t}_{\substack{\text{Carrier frequency} \\ f_c}} + \underbrace{m \ (V_c/2) \cos (\omega_c - \omega_m) \ t}_{\substack{\text{Lower sideband (LSB)} \\ f_c - f_m}} - \underbrace{m \ (V_c/2) \cos (\omega_c + \omega_m) \ t}_{\substack{\text{Upper sideband (USB)} \\ f_c + f_m}}$

13. a. USB = 1.005 MHz; LSB = 995 kHz

    b. $V_m = 6.96$ V

    c. $V_{USB} = V_{LSB} = 3.48$ V

    d. $V_{max} = 18.96$ V

15. a. $P_T = 2.588$ W

    b. $V_c = 14.561$ V

    c. M = 20.98%

    d. $V_m = 3.055$ V

    e. $V_{USB} = V_{LSB} = 4.062$ V

17. a. $P_T = 25.781$ kW
    b. $P_{USB} = P_{LSB} = 6.25$ kW
19. D2 and D3.
21. 76–82 MHz

CHAPTER 4

1. A modulation technique through which the carrier's instantaneous frequency deviation from its unmodulated value is made to vary in proportion to the instantaneous amplitude of the modulating signal.
3. $e_{FM} = A_c \sin(\omega_c t + m_f \sin \omega_m t)$
5. $m_f = 4$
7. $J_0 = -0.40 \times 5$ V $= -2.00$ V
   $J_1 = -0.07 \times 5$ V $= -0.350$ V
   $J_2 = 0.36 \times 5$ V $= 1.80$ V
   $J_3 = 0.43 \times 5$ V $= 2.15$ V
   $J_4 = 0.28 \times 5$ V $= 1.40$ V
   $J_5 = 0.13 \times 5$ V $= 0.650$ V
   $J_6 = 0.05 \times 5$ V $= 0.25$ V
   $J_7 = 0.02 \times 5$ V $= 0.100$ V
9. An *eigenvalue* is when the J_0 carrier frequency component or various J_n sideband amplitude components go to zero.
11. a. 6
    b.

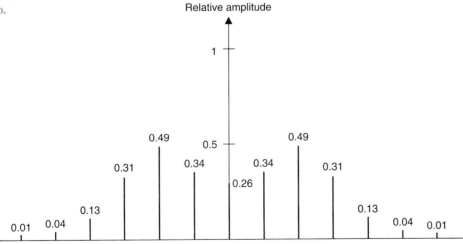

    c. $\delta = 22.5$ kHz
13. a. $m_f = 10$
    b. BW $= 2(14 \times 3$ kHz$) = 84$ kHz
    c. BW $= 2(30$ kHz $+ 3$ kHz$) = 66$ kHz
15. $P_T = (0.707 \times 5$ V$)^2/50 \ \Omega = 250$ mW
17. a. 3.82°
    b. 15:1
19. $m_f = 5$
    $\alpha = 11.5° = 0.201$ radians
    $\delta_N = \alpha f_m = 0.201 \times 15$ kHz $= 3.02$ kHz
    $SNR_{FM} = \delta/\delta_N = 75$ kHz$/3.02$ kHz $= 24.8$ or 24.8:1

21. A varactor diode's *tuning ratio* is the ratio of its junction capacitance, C_T, measured at a reverse-bias potential of 4 V DC divided by its junction capacitance measured at a reverse-bias potential of 60 V DC.

CHAPTER 5

1. Noise immunity, time-division multiplexed, and error detection and correction.
3. 1024
5. 6.80 kHz
7. A *regenerative repeater* is a repeater that filters, amplifies, and reconstructs a digital binary bit stream that has been attenuated and corrupted with noise, thus enabling the signal to be transmitted further distances.
9. A *codec* takes an analog signal and converts it to a binary serial bit stream through the use of an internal A/D converter and performs the reverse operation of converting a binary serial bit stream back to its original analog form.

11.

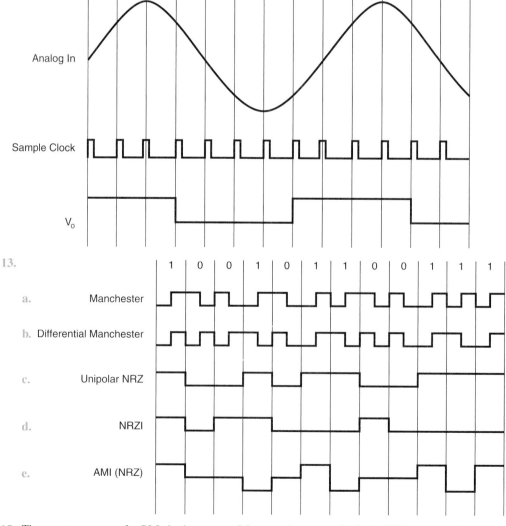

13.

15. The *capture range* of a PLL is the range of frequencies over which the PLL can acquire lock from an unlocked condition.

CHAPTER 6

1. a. $110101101_2 = 655_8 = 429_{10} = 1AD_{16}$
   b. $1111000001010_2 = 17012_8 = 7690_{10} = 1EOA_{16}$
   c. $10101011101000111_2 = 253507_8 = 87879_{10} = 15147_{16}$
3. a. $17_8 = 1111_2 = 15_{10} = F_{16}$
   b. $566_8 = 101110110_2 = 374_{10} = 176_{16}$
   c. $7123_8 = 111001010011_2 = 3667_{10} = E53_{16}$
5. a. 0111
   b. 0001 0010 0011
   c. 1001 0110
7. Decimal   Excess-3
   $\quad$ 9 $\quad$ 1100
   $\underline{+8}$ $\underline{+1011}$
   $\quad$ 17   1 0111

   When adding two decimal numbers whose sum exceeds nine, a valid answer in BCD is produced if the two numbers are added together using excess-3 code, because the addition of two excess-3 characters has an inherent correction factor of six (three plus three), which is necessary for invalid BCD results.
9. a. 1001
   b. 11111110
   c. 11101011
   d. 100010
11.

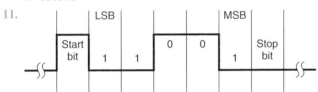

13. Upper- and lower-case letters in EBCDIC have a difference of 40H. Bit 6 is used to distinguish between the two cases. For example, b = 82H, and B = C2H.
15. There are 32_{10} ASCII control characters. In hexadecimal, their codes are distinguished by having values less than 20H.
17. The ASCII character **Nul** is represented by all zeros.
19. ASCII *format effectors* control the position of a terminal's cursor.
21. Two advantages of bar code are low cost and high throughput. Two disadvantages are the extra equipment required and that its use is intended primarily for fixed repetitive data input.
23. A bar code that has intercharacter spaces or gaps between characters; consequently, each character within a bar code symbol is independent of every other.
25. 010101000

27.

R = 100000110

29.

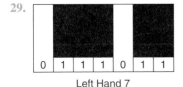

Left Hand 7

31.

check character = 4

$9 + 5 + 1 + 4 + 7 = 26 + 4 = 30$

9 5 1 4 7 4

CHAPTER 7

1. The distinguishing feature of the smart terminal over the dumb terminal is its ability to transmit and receive blocks of data.
3. Computer-aided design, simulation, modeling.
5. 1920 characters (80 columns by 24 rows).
7. Special function keys are software defined. They may be programmed by the manufacturer or user to perform special functions, such as communications control, editing, printing, and so on. They are tremendous time-savers, because they can be programmed to perform several instructions at the touch of a key.
9. $\underline{\text{Odd parity}}$

   1101010<u>1</u>
   0011010<u>0</u>
   1110000<u>0</u>
   1011010<u>1</u>

   $\underline{\text{Even parity}}$

   0011010<u>1</u>
   1010110<u>0</u>
   1111000<u>0</u>
   0011010<u>1</u>
11. A local echo is produced in half-duplex mode.
13. Characters are duplicated on the screen as keys are typed. The first character is produced by the local echo, and the second is the remote echo.
15. An escape sequence is a sequence of characters used to perform special command or control functions. An escape sequence begins with the ASCII character **ESC,** which is followed by one or more characters as defined by the escape sequence.
17. RS-232, IEEE 488, current loop.
19. Type 1: length = 85.6 mm, width = 54.0 mm, thickness = 3.3 mm
    Type 2: length = 85.6 mm, width = 54.0 mm, thickness = 5.0 mm
    Type 3: length = 85.6 mm, width = 54.0 mm, thickness = 10.5 mm
21. A *listener.*

CHAPTER 8

1. A *protocol* is a set of rules governing the manner in which data are transmitted and received.
3. 36.4%
5. The term *modem* is a contraction of the words *modulator–demodulator.*
7. A printer is considered DTE.
9. RS-232 cable lengths should be kept under 50 ft (15 m).

11.

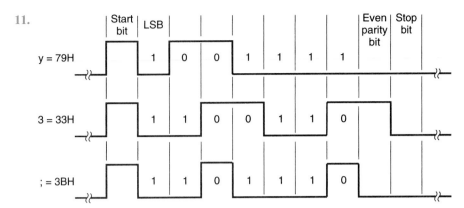

13. The EIA RS-449 nine-pin connector is designed to carry secondary interchange circuits.

15. $V_{ocm} = 678\ \mu V$

17. 10 Mbps

CHAPTER 9

1. *Double buffering* is the mechanism used to provide temporary storage for two data words. While one data word is being processed, the other is being held. This prevents the destruction (writing over) of one of the data words.

3. **a.** 9600 baud
   b. 873 characters per second (cps)

5. Figure 9-6(b), 26 μs; Figure 9-6(c), 13 μs; Figure 9-6(d), 3.26 μs.

7. Transmit Ready (TxRdy).

9. P.E. = 0, PARITY = 0.

CHAPTER 10

1.

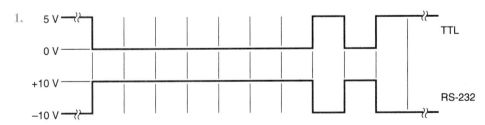

3. **a.** When C/$\overline{D}$ is high, a control command can be issued to the 8251A (command word or a mode word) or its status can be read.
   b. When C/$\overline{D}$ is low, data can be written or read from the 8251A.

5. A mode instruction must be issued to the 8251A to program it for asynchronous operation. The least significant two bits of the mode word determine the asynchronous baud rate factor.

7. DAH

9. Because all control words written after a mode word are interpreted as command words, the 8251A has been designed to provide an internal reset bit in the command word format. This allows the UART to be internally reset through a command word, thus allowing mode word parameters to be reprogrammed without having to perform a power-on reset.

11. *Framing error:* A framing error occurs when the logic state of the asynchronous character's stop bit is tested by the UART and is not a logic 1. This generally implies that the received character's baud rate is different than what the UART has been programmed to receive. *Overrun error:* This type of error occurs when the CPU does not read the available character before the next one is available. The previous character is destroyed. *Parity error:* A parity error occurs when the parity bit level does not correspond to the total number of 1 bits set in the character.

13. 50–256 kbaud

CHAPTER 11

1. Hybrid.

3. The diaphragm of a telephone set's receiver fluctuates in accordance with the electrical current representing sound. This is caused by the varying magnetic field produced by the receiver's coil that is wound around a permanent magnet. The resulting force causes the diaphragm to move, thus reproducing the original sound.

5. The ring potential (90 V_{rms} at 20 Hz) is superimposed on the existing on-hook DC potential (-48 V DC), because the telephone circuit, at this time, is an open circuit for DC. The -48 V DC on-hook potential will remain present until the telephone is answered or goes off-hook.

7. The *ring signal*, 90 V_{rms}, causes the telephone set to ring, whereas the *ring-back* signal is an acknowledgment tone to the party placing the call that the telephone at the destination end is ringing. The two signals occur simultaneously but not necessarily in sync with each other.

9. a. D1 acts as the dial switch.
   b. D2 shunts the receiver off when dialing. This prevents clicking pulses from being heard at the receiver.
   c. Switches S1 and S2 are open when the telephone is in the on-hook position.
   d. Varistors are used to regulate voice amplitude.

11. A dial pulse has a period of 100 ms, a repetition rate of 10 Hz, and a pulse width of 40 ms (60 ms on-hook and 40 ms off-hook).

13. The *interdigit time* is the time interval between the digits dialed.

15. 1225 lines

17. a. pair 9
    b. pair 18
    c. pair 22

19. 258

21. Typically 20 to 80 mA

23. The *receiver off-hook tone* is a very loud tone that alerts the user that the telephone's handset has accidentally gone off-hook and must be placed back on its cradle.

25. The caller ID signal would not be decoded properly and, therefore, would not be displayed.

27. 3400 Hz

29. a. 0.42 dB/mi
    b. 430 Ω
    c. 3440 Hz

31. a. I_{SC} = 48 V/800 Ω = 60 mA
    b. $V_{off-hook}$ = 60 mA × 142 Ω = 8.52 V DC
    c. distance = [(800 Ω − 142 Ω) (1000 ft/8.33 Ω)] × (1 mi/5280 ft) × $\frac{1}{2}$ = 7.48 miles

33. a. 1500 μs
    b. -2 to $+3$ dB

CHAPTER 12

1. a. Interoffice trunk
   b. Tandem trunk
   c. Toll trunk
   d. Intertoll trunk
3. Consistent line characteristics, less prone to noise, less attenuation and delay distortion, higher data transfer rates, available 24 hours a day.
5. For a signal to propagate back and forth between two telephone sets separated by a distance of 2900 miles, it would take 31.2 ms. An echo suppressor or canceller would not be necessary.
7. Signal-to-noise ratio (SNR).
9. When the central office is temporarily overburdened with calls and cannot provide further switching, a call can be *blocked*. A fast busy tone is sent to the caller, indicating that the call must be placed again at a later time when traffic subsides.
11. *Space-division multiplexing (SDM):* The combining of physically separate signals into a bundled cable. Space is shared between the signals. *Frequency-division multiplexing (FDM):* The simultaneous transmission of signals within a designated band of frequencies. Bandwidth is shared between the signals. *Time-division multiplexing (TDM):* The interleaving of two or more signals in the time domain. Time is shared between the signals.
13. a. 648 ns
    b. 8 kHz
    c. 1.5 ms
15. The *extended superframe (ESF)* extends the DS-1 superframe structure from 12 to 24 frames.
17. B8ZS coding stands for *Bipolar with 8 Zero Substitution.*
19.

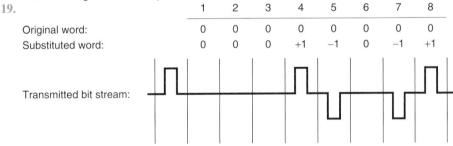

	1	2	3	4	5	6	7	8
Original word:	0	0	0	0	0	0	0	0
Substituted word:	0	0	0	+1	−1	0	−1	+1

Transmitted bit stream:

CHAPTER 13

1. Modulator–demodulator.
3. The acoustically coupled modem suffers a major drawback in terms of transmission speed. The rubber fittings may not always fit the telephone's handpiece snugly. Even if they do, ambient noise levels may still leak through, thus limiting speed and performance.
5. A *dibit* is the encoding of two bits into a single phase or signal change.
7. 2225 Hz
9. *Simplex:* transmission, in one direction only. *Half-duplex:* two-way transmission, one station at a time. *Full-duplex:* simultaneous two-way transmission.
11. 1600
13. 4

15. 12.8 mHz

17. A *POTS (plain old telephone service) splitter* is a DSL device installed in the NID. It separates the low-frequency voice signals from the high-frequency DSL signals.

19. 200 kHz to 1.1 mHz.

21. 128 bytes

23. 99.9999%

25. 4573 bps

27. *Data compression* is the mechanism used to reduce the number of data bits that are normally used to express a given amount of information.

CHAPTER 14

1. A *protocol* is a set of rules and procedures that governs communications.

3. *Applications layer (7):* specifies the application program for the end user. *Presentation layer (6):* addresses any code or syntax conversions necessary to present data to the network in a common format. *Session layer (5):* defines the management of a session. *Transport layer (4):* ensures the reliable and efficient transportation of data on a network. *Network layer (3):* defines how messages are broken down into data packets and sent on a network. *Data link layer (2):* defines the successful transmission of data between devices. *Physical layer (1):* defines the electrical and mechanical specifications of the network.

5. Physical layer.

7. a. DLE STX
   b. DLE ETX or DLE ETB
   c. DLE DLE

9. When a time-out error occurs, an ENQ is issued by the transmitting station to the receiving station. An ACK 0, ACK 1, or NAK in response will allow the transmitting station to determine if the last message was received.

11. a. ENQ
    b. ACK 0 and ACK 1
    c. NAK

13. In BISYNC, a *tributary* is a terminal or station, other than the host computer, that is polled or selected by the host to transmit or receive data, respectively.

15. Circuit switching, message switching, and packet switching.

17. A circuit-switched connection between two stations permits exclusive use of the channel between the two stations until it is relinquished by one of the stations.

19. The *Telex* network is an example of message switching.

21. In packet switching, a PAD assembles a terminal's packet and sends it to the network nodes. It also disassembles received packets from the network nodes for the terminal.

23. HDLC is a bit-oriented protocol.

25. For a two-byte address field in HDLC, the LSB of the first address byte must be a logic 0. This informs the receiver that the address field is more than one byte. The LSB of the second byte must be a logic 1, indicating the final byte of the address field.

27. Zero-bit insertion or "bit stuffing."

29. In HDLC, if a receiving device receives five consecutive 1 bits, after detecting the opening flag, the sixth bit is tested for a 1 or 0. If it is 1, it is assumed to be the closing flag pattern (or an abort pattern). If it is a 0, it is automatically deleted, and the remainder of

the message block continues to be received. The deleted 0 was inserted at the transmitter as part of zero-bit insertion.

31. In HDLC, only the Information Transfer Frame and Unnumbered Frame types can have an information field.

33.

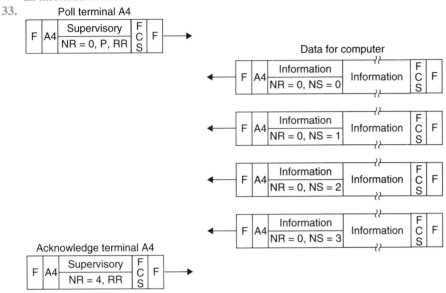

CHAPTER 15

1. LAN stands for *local area network.*

3. LAN *topology* refers to the geometric pattern or configuration of intelligent devices and how they are linked together for communications.

5. a. The critical resource for a bus LAN is the bus cable.

   b. The distinguishing feature of the bus LAN is that control of the bus is distributed among all the nodes on the bus.

   c. A major disadvantage with the bus LAN is that each node must contend for use of the channel. In heavy volumes of traffic on the bus, collisions occur, thus hindering communications.

7. A *collision* is said to occur on a bus LAN when two or more stations assert their packets onto the channel at the same time.

9. CSMA/CD stands for *carrier sense multiple access with collision detection.*

11. The round-trip propagation delay time between the farthest two nodes on a bus LAN is referred to as the *slot time.*

13. In slotted ring, *time slots* are circulated around the ring.

15. A *telecommunications closet* is the transition point between the horizontal cabling and backbone subsystems. It is also referred to as the *intermediate distribution facility (IDF).* An equipment room, in contrast, is referred to as the *main distribution facility (MDF)* and houses the main internetworking equipment.

17. Shielded twisted-pair.
19. IBM Type 1 cable is a two-pair 22-AWG STP data-grade cable with an IBM-style data connector at one end and a DB9 Token Ring controller connector at the opposite end.
21. IBM data connector on one end and a DB9 connector on the opposite end.
23. Radio frequency (RF) and infrared (IR) technology.
25. CATV stands *community antenna television,* or *cable TV.*
27. a. Bus (branching nonrouted tree)
    b. 10 Mbps
    c. 1024 nodes
    d. 500 m
    e. 51.2 μs
    f. 50 m
    g. Repeaters are used to join segments together to extend the area of the network. The repeater is simply tapped into the Ethernet cable in the same manner as a node. A transceiver cable is used.
29.

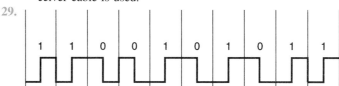

31. Cheapernet uses BNC-type connectors and RG-58 U coaxial cable as a transmission medium.
33. The major advantage of 10BaseT over 10Base5 is that it uses inexpensive UTP and modular wall jacks.
35. Star-wired ring topology.
37. In a client/server network, high-powered computer workstations share their resources to network users, called *clients.* Clients use the server's hardware and software. A peer-to-peer network has no dedicated server on the network. Instead, a workstation can be configured as a client, a server, or both.
39. A *runt packet* is an Ethernet packet that does not meet the minimum Ethernet frame size of 64 bytes.

CHAPTER 16

1. 1969.
3. *FTP* is a file transfer protocol used to copy or transfer files across the Internet. *Anonymous FTP* allows a user to access public archives without an account number as needed in FTP.
5. gopher://[gopher server name]
7. *WAIS* stands for Wide-Area Information Services. It is an Internet text-search engine allowing you to retrieve text files across the Internet.
9. *gov*
11. *ni*
13. warren_hioki@ccsn.nevada.edu
15. *CERN* stands for the European Laboratory for Particle Physics.
17. Mosaic, Netscape Navigator.

19. A *home page* is a Web page that serves as a home base or principal page through which a person, business, educational institute, and so on wants to be represented on the World Wide Web. The home page includes links to other Web pages or sites.

21. http://www.ccsn.nevada.edu

23. bees **and** honey.

25. RFC 1157.

27. A *firewall* is an intranet security system designed to limit Internet access to a company's intranet.

29. In ATM, VP stands for *virtual path* and VC for *virtual channel.* A VC is a connection between communicating entities. A VP is a group of VCs carried between two points.

31. *Header field:* includes address and control information. *Information field:* contains digitized intelligence (e.g., voice, data, image, and video).

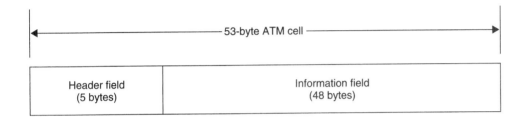

33. *Generic flow control (GFC):* The first four bits of the ATM header control the flow of traffic across the user–network interface (UNI) and into the network. *Virtual path identifier (VPI)/virtual channel identifier (VCI):* The next 24 bits after the GFC make up the VPI and VCI. These bits make up the ATM address field. *Payload type (PT):* This three-bit field specifies one of eight types of message payloads. *Cell loss priority (CLP):* This single-bit field specifies the eligibility of the cell for discard by the network under congested conditions. *Header error control (HEC):* The fifth and final byte of the header field is designed for error control of the header field only.

35. ISDN services provided to residential customers has been slow due primarily to the existing voice-grade lines. These lines have been designed for voice and must be modified for digital signals.

37. An ISDN B (Bearer)-channel is a 64-kbps channel that carries end-user voice, audio, video, or data. An ISDN D (Delta)-channel carries packet-switched user data and call control messaging information at 16 or 64 kbps.

39. R, S, T, and U

41.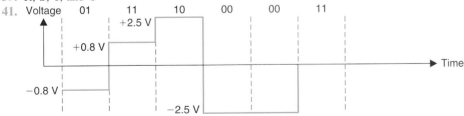

43. 810 bytes/frame $\times$ 8 bits/byte $\times$ 8000 frames/s = 51.84 Mbps

45. 12

47. CAP, DMT, 2B1Q

49. Switched multimegabit data service.

51.

Opening Flag	DLCI	C/R	EA	DLCI	FECN	BECN	DA	CA	Information Field	Frame Check Sequence, FCS	Closing Flag

CHAPTER 17

1.

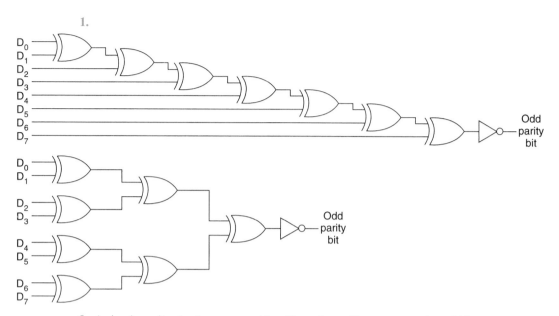

3. A simple parity check, even or odd, will not detect if an even number of bit errors has occurred. For example, if the seven-bit data word below with an odd parity bit were transmitted and bits 3 and 4 were corrupted (changed from 1 to 0), the final parity bit would still agree with the data word received (10001010). The same would be true if four or six bits (an even number) were inverted from the original. The odd parity bit would still indicate that the total number of 1 bits received, including the parity bit, is an odd quantity.

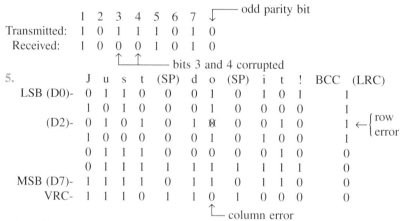

5.

	J	u	s	t	(SP)	d	o	(SP)	i	t	!	BCC (LRC)	
LSB (D0)-	0	1	1	0	0	0	1	0	1	0	1	1	
	1	0	1	0	0	0	1	0	0	0	0	1	
(D2)-	0	1	0	1	0	1	0̸	0	0	1	0	1 ← { row
	1	0	0	0	0	0	1	0	1	0	0	1	error
	0	1	1	1	0	0	0	0	0	1	0	0	
	0	1	1	1	1	1	1	1	1	1	1	0	
MSB (D7)-	1	1	1	1	0	1	1	0	1	1	0	0	
VRC-	1	1	1	0	1	1	0	1	0	0	0	0	

└ column error

7. a. 16
   b. 1101000101101001000000000000000
   c. 1101110010111001
   d. 1101101110011001
   e. 110100010110100111011011100110011001

9. Single-precision, double-precision, Honeywell, Residue.

11. 07H

13. 0197H

15. B1D0

17. 83

19. ARQ (automatic repeat request) is an error-correction technique used in full- and half-duplex communication systems. When a block is received in error, a request for retransmission is made by the receiver to the transmitter. In FEC, this is not possible because communications is simplex. Instead, special error-correcting codes are placed into the message stream so that the receiver can extract the code and predict and correct the error.

21. a. $C_0 = 0$
$C_1 = 1$
$C_2 = 0$
$C_3 = 0$
  b. 10111001010110
  c. 0100
  d. 1101

CHAPTER 18

1. Bandwidth, less weight and volume, less loss, security, flexibility, safety.
3. The two classic theories of light are the *particle theory* and the *wave theory*.
5. Infrared.
7. a. 187.5 m
  b. 3.41 m
  c. 7.5 cm
  d. 5.0 cm
  e. 1546 nm
9. 51.2×10^{-6} in.
11. $n = 1.5$
13. $\phi = 40.6°$
15. $\theta = 70.1°$
17. In transparent mediums, the *critical angle* is the angle above which a ray of light will experience total internal reflection.
19. 81.9°
21. 572 modes
23. *Graded-index fiber* is characterized by having a core whose index of refraction is graded from the center of the core out to its cladding interface.
25. Wavelength division multiplexing.
27. a. 175.9 μW
  b. −0.395 db/km
29. 0.227
31. The two commonly used methods for splicing fiber ends are the *mechanical* splice and the *fusion* splice.
33. Gallium-aluminum-arsenide is used for LEDs that emit light at 820 nm.
35. *Laser* stands for *light amplification by stimulated emission of radiation.*
37. The sensitivity of a photodiode is typically specified by its *responsivity* rating.

CHAPTER 19

1. *PCS* stands for Personal Communication Services.
3. A *handoff* occurs in a cellular telephone when a mobile unit's signal strength diminishes as it exits a cell. The mobile unit is handed a new frequency channel to operate with the new cell site, thus improving signal strength.

5. For cordless telephones operating in the 40-MHz region, the frequency bands are as follows: base unit, 43.72–46.97 MHz; portable unit, 48.76–49.97 MHz.

7. FM.

9. POCSAG, GSC, ERMES, FLEX.

11. **a.** A caller can speak with a paging service representative; **b.** a caller can use a special software program, designed for alphanumeric pagers, to type a message and send it through a modem to the paging service provider; **c.** an alphanumeric entry device designed to be interfaced to the telephone line can be used to type a caller's message.

13. The ISM bands are: Industrial (I-band), 902–928 MHz; Scientific (S-band), 2.40–2.4835 GHz; and Medical (M-band), 5.725–5.850 GHz.

15. *Direct sequence* and *frequency hopping* spread spectrum.

17. Block diagram of a frequency hopping spread spectrum system:

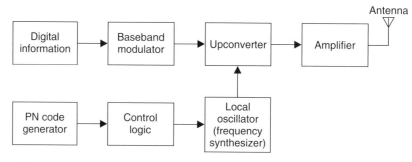

19. 375 MHz

21. *Omnidirectional IR transceiver* and *directional IR transceiver.*

23. *Point-to-Point IR LAN.*

REFERENCES

Abrahams, J. R., *Token Ring Network Design, Implementation and Management*, NCC Blackwell Limited, Oxford, England, 1993.

Anixter, Inc., *1995 Cabling System Catalog*, Skokie, Ill., 1995.

AT&T Technical Reference, Pub. 54075, *56 Kbps Subrate Data Multiplexing*, AT&T Communications, Florham Park, NJ, 1985.

Bell Communications Research, Inc., *The Extended Superframe Format Interface Specification*, Morristown, NJ, 1985.

Bell Laboratories, *Transmission Systems for Communications*, 4th ed., Indianapolis, Ind., 1971.

Bell Laboratories, *A History of Engineering and Science in the Bell-System—Transmission Technology*, AT&T Bell Laboratories, Indianapolis, Ind., 1985.

Bell Laboratories, *A History of Engineering and Science in the Bell System—Communications Science*, AT&T Bell Laboratories, Indianapolis, Ind., 1984.

Bell Laboratories, *A History of Engineering and Science in the Bell System—Switching Technology*, AT&T Bell Laboratories, Indianapolis, Ind., 1982.

Bell System Technical Reference, Pub. 62411, *High Capacity Digital Service Channel Interface Specification*, Basking Ridge, NJ, 1983.

Carr and Weidner, *Physics From the Ground Up*, McGraw-Hill, Inc., New York, NY 1971.

CCITT (ITU-TS) Recommendation V.22bis, *2400 bps Duplex Modem Using the Frequency Division Technique Standardized for Use on the General Switched Telephone Network*.

CCITT (ITU-TS) Recommendation V.32, *A Family of 2-Wire Duplex Modems Operating at Data Signaling Rates of Up to 9600 bps for Use on the General Switched Telephone Network and on Leased Telephone-Type Circuits*, 1984.

CCITT (ITU-TS) Recommendation V.42, *Error Correcting Procedures for DCEs Using Asynchronous-to-Synchronous Conversion*.

Concord Data System's *All About Adaptive Data Compression for Asynchronous Applications*, Concord Data Systems, Inc., Marlborough, Massachussetts.

Concord Data System's *All About Error Protection Protocols for Asynchronous Data Transmission*, Concord Data Systems, Inc., Marlborough, Massachussetts.

Couch, L. W. II, *Digital and Analog Communications Systems*, 2nd ed., Macmillan Publishing Co., New York, NY, 1987.

Digital, *Introduction to Local Area Networks*, Digital Equipment Corp., Santa Clara, California, 1982.

EIA RS-232-C, *Interface Between DTE and DCE Employing Serial Binary Data Interchange*, Washington, D.C., 1969.

EIA RS-422-A, *Electrical Characteristics of Balanced Voltage Digital Interface Circuits*, Washington, D.C., 1978.

EIA RS-423-A, *Electrical Characteristics of Unbalanced Voltage Digital Interface Circuits*, Washington, D.C., 1978.

EIA RS-449, *General Purpose 37-Position and 9-Position Interface for DTE and DCE Employing Serial Binary Data Interchange*, Washington, D.C., 1977.

Fike, J. L. and Friend, G. E., *Understanding Telephone Electronics*, Texas Instruments, Dallas, Texas.

Fink, D. G. and Carrol, J. M., *Standard Handbook for Electrical Engineers*, McGraw-Hill, Inc., New York, NY, 1969.

Gibbs, M. and Smith, R., *Navigating the Internet,* Sams Publishing, Carmel, Indiana, 1993.

Gohring, H. G. and Kauffels, F. J., *Token Ring Principles, Perspectives, and Strategies,* Addison-Wesley Publishing Company, Reading, Massachussetts, 1992.

Hamming, R. W., *Coding and Information Theory,* 2nd ed., Prentice-Hall, Inc., Englewood Cliffs, NJ, 1986.

Hewlett-Packard, *Fiber Optics Handbook,* Hewlett-Packard GmbH, Boeblingen Instruments Division, Federal Republic of Germany, 1988.

Hewlett-Packard, *HP Smart Wand Bar Code Reader User's Manual,* Hewlett-Packard, 1993.

Hewlett-Packard, *Introduction to SONET Networks and Tests,* MCG/Queensferry Telecommunications Division, 1992.

Hewlett-Packard Application Staff, *Optical Communication Application Seminar,* Hewlett-Packard Optical Communication Division, San Jose, California, 1988.

Highhouse, J., *A Guide for Telecommunications Cable Splicing,* Delmar Publishers, Albany, NY, 1997.

Johnson, B., *Analysis of Fault Tolerant Systems,* Addison-Wesley, 1989.

Kennedy, G., *Electronic Communications Systems,* 3rd ed., McGraw-Hill, Inc., New York, NY, 1985.

Lammle, T., Porter J., Chellis, J., *Cisco Certified Network Associate Study Guide,* Sybex Network Press, 1999.

Lane, J., *Asynchronous Transfer Mode: Bandwidth for the Future,* Telco Systems, Inc., Norwood, Massachussetts, 1992.

LaQuey, T. and Ryer, J. C., *The Internet Companion,* Addison-Wesley Publishing Company, Reading, Massachussetts, 1993.

McNamara, J. E., *Local Area Networks; An Introduction to the Technology,* Digital Press, Burlington, Massachussetts, 1985.

McNamara, J. E., *Technical Aspects of Data Communications,* 2nd ed., Digital Equipment Corporation, Bedford, Massachussetts, 1982.

Martin, J., *Telecommunications and the Computer,* 3rd ed., Prentice-Hall, Inc., Englewood Cliffs, New Jersey, 1989.

Moody, D., *ISDN,* Northern Telecom, Issue 2, 1991.

Northern Telecom, *SONET 101: An Introduction to SONET,* Fiber World.

Pearson, G., *MNP Error-Correcting Modems,* Microcom, Norwood, Massachussetts.

Pecar, J., O'Conner, R., Garbin, *Telecommunications Fact Book,* McGraw-Hill, New York, NY, 1993.

Prentiss, S., *Introducing Cellular Communications,* Tab Books, Inc., Blue Ridge Summit, Pennsylvania, 1984.

Racal-Vadic, *Data Communications; A User's Handbook,* Racal-Vadic, Sunnyvale, California.

Rowe, R. I., *Data Compression Algorithm for V.42 Modems,* Adaptive Computer Technologies, Inc., Santa Clara, California. 1988.

Sinnema, W. and McGovern, T., *Digital, Analog, and Data Communications,* 2nd ed., Prentice-Hall, Inc., Englewood Cliffs, NJ, 1986.

Smoot, C. M. and Quarterman, J. S., *Practical Internetworking with TCP/IP and UNIX,* Addison-Wesley Publishing Company, Reading, Massachussetts, 1993.

Sprint Central Telephone, *Nevada First Source Phone Book,* Las Vegas Telephone Directory, Reuben H, Donnelley and Centel Directory Company, July 1993.

Stallings, W., *Data and Computer Communications,* 3rd ed., Macmillan, New York, NY, 1988.

Stallings, W., *Data and Computer Communications,* 4th ed., Macmillan, New York, NY, 1994.

Stein, D. H., *Introduction to Digital Data Communications,* Delmar Publishers Inc., Albany, NY, 1985.

Turlington, S. R., *Walking the World Wide Web,* Ventura Press, Research Triangle Park, NC, 1995.

INDEX